ANTIQUES

SOURCE | 2004
BOOK | 2005

THIS IS A SEVENOAKS BOOK

Copyright © 2004 Martin Miller

This edition published by in 2004 by Sevenoaks
An imprint of the Carlton Publishing Group
20 Mortimer Street
London W1T 3JW

Edited and designed for Carlton Books by PAGE*One*

A CIP catalogue for this book is available from the British Library.

ISBN 1-86200-136-7

ANTIQUES

SOURCE BOOK | 2004–2005

The Definitive Guide to Retail
Prices for Antiques and Collectables

MARTIN MILLER

SEVENOAKS

Contents

Acknowledgements 6
How to Use This Book 7
Introduction 9

Antiquities 11
Architectural & Garden Furniture 27
Arms & Armour 40
Automobilia 47
Books, Maps & Atlases 51
Carpets & Rugs 66
Ceramics
        English 72
        European 103
        Oriental 116
Clocks, Watches & Scientific Instruments
        Clocks 130
        Watches 142
        Scientific Instruments 152
Collector's Items
        Advertising & Packaging 156
        Bottles 160
        Cameras 166
        Chess Sets 172
        Coins & Medals 174
        Commemorative Ware 185
        Fans 191
        Gentlemen's Accessories 192
        Handbags 195
        Kitchenalia 203
        Luggage 213
        Mechanical Music 218
        Photographs 221
        Portrait Miniatures 225
        Posters 227
        Radios 235
        Rock & Pop 237
        Sewing Items 242
        Snuff Boxes & Smoking Equipment 248
        Telephones 252
        Tools 255
        Walking Sticks 259
Decorative Arts
        Figures & Busts 261
        Lighting 268
        Metalware 275
Furniture
        Beds 281
        Bookcases . . . . :.285
        Boxes 289
        Bureaux 300
        Cabinets 303
        Campaign Furniture 310
        Canterburies 312

Chairs 313
Chests of Drawers & Commodes 335
Davenports 345
Desks 347
Dressers 353
Dumb Waiters & Whatnots 355
Mirrors 358
Miscellaneous 366
Screens 370
Settees & Sofas 372
Stools 377
Tables 382
Wardrobes 398
Glass 401
Jewellery 416
Marine Items 436
Musical Instruments 440
Silver & Pewter 446
Sporting Items
General 475
Fishing 479
Shooting 483
Taxidermy 485
Textiles 487
Toys, Games & Dolls 499
Treen 511
Tribal Art 513
Twentieth-Century Design
Ceramics 516
Furniture 525
Glass 534
Lighting 540
Metalware 550
Wine-Related Items 560
Works of Art & Sculpture
Asian/Oriental 571
Islamic 578
Russian 583
Writing Equipment 589

Period Reference .597
Glossary 601
Directory of Dealers 609
Directory of Antiques Centres & Markets 629
Index 635

ACKNOWLEDGEMENTS

GENERAL EDITOR
Martin Miller

CO-ORDINATING EDITOR
Caroline Proctor

EDITORS
Clair Whiteman
Richard Bundy
Marianne Blake

PHOTOGRAPHERS
Abigail Zoe Martin
Julia Morley
James Beam Van Etten

DESIGNERS
Gill Andrews
Jessica Barr
Pauline Hoyle
Alexandra Huchet
Louise Kerby
Robert Law
Michelle Pickering
Tim Stansfield
Mark Tattham

How to Use This Book

by **Martin Miller**

I am delighted to be delivering information on how to use the *Antiques Source Book* for the fifth time, because it shows that the idea of the book has found some favour with its readers. I do hope that our loyal readership will bear with me if I seem a little repetitive – you are welcome to skip this bit and go on to the antiques, while I address the newcomers, who I heartily welcome. The *Source Book* is a retail guide so, at the time of going to press, some of the items included in it will still be available to purchase through antiques dealers. These dealers are identified at the foot of the descriptive passage of every item illustrated in the book and, in the directory at the back of the book, you can find out where they are and how to contact them.

This is not to say that everything appearing in the book will still be in the shop window when you get there. That would show either that we are picking the wrong items, since they are bad examples or badly priced, or the wrong dealers, since they are buying stock that is in scant demand. What we are saying is that these are the best dealers dealing in them. In other words, if these are the antiques in which you are interested, here is the best way for you to source them.

We do not purport to show everything the market has to offer; we carefully select a cross-section that is truly representative of the market place.

The book covers every aspect of antiques collecting, from furniture through to glassware and jewellery through to porcelain. It also covers the area of "collectables" – items that are not technically old enough to qualify as antiques but which are nevertheless ardently accumulated by enthusiasts – comic books, telephones and gardening tools to name but three. There is, in fact, something for every pocket from furniture worth tens of thousands of pounds to items worth no more than a tenner. What they have in common is that we consider them to be good buys, as examples of their genres and as financial investments.

The *Antiques Source Book* is not only useful to collectors, it is also of considerable interest to anyone who likes to be suprised to discover that unconsidered trifles they may possess are actually gathering value at a significant rate, or who might be interested to discover how hopelessly under-insured they are! Every item in the book is illustrated and all illustrations are followed by a brief description, including details of period, size, condition and retail price, as well as the dealer's name. As an additional aid to the potential buyer – or valuer – we include a useful introduction to each section and "expert tip" boxes throughout, giving advice on what to buy and what to avoid and, most particularly, what to look out for.

All in all, the book is designed to help people develop a love for antiques and give them tips on how best to hunt them out.

I have found antiques a lifetime's joy and I am delighted to pass on anything I can to spread the joy around.

Introduction

A contemporary and practical guide to antiques and collectables

Is my antique the real thing, or has it been altered? Is it a reproduction – or even a fake? These are the questions that buyers must most often ask themselves as they commit their hard-earned money into the lottery of collecting. Very often, of course, we can't be sure – and very often this is why we do it. After all, if everything was certain and everyone knew exactly what they were buying, then a lot of the excitement would go out of the business.

There is nothing quite like the buzz that comes from having your suspicions confirmed on a piece that only you have considered to be of merit. Conversely, there are few things worse than finding that you have been duped, albeit unwittingly, and usually by yourself. Your ego often suffers much more than your wallet.

Outright fakes are unusual. After all, they cost about as much to make as an original, plus the cost in time and money of muddying the waters of its past, and the chance of prosecution. However, pieces that are not quite genuine abound. Usually these are honest copies whose provenance has been lost with the passing of the years, or pieces that have been altered for use. Identifying the genuine

– picking the right one – that's the thrill of this particular chase.

The Antiques Source Book is all about buying antiques through dealers rather than at auction. The principal reason for this is that the dealers – or, at least, the accredited dealers who we favour – know their stuff. There is no reason why an owner of a piece should have retained its original provenance – how many of us know where to put our hands on the guarantee for our digital alarm clocks or the instructions for the washing machine? It doesn't make items any less genuine. To the greatest extent we have to rely on experience in identifying antiques, and there is no substitute for the experience of daily handling that only the dealer can boast.

Auction provenance can be less than reliable, particularly the country house sale. A piece bought from the "Palace House Sale" is going to be worth more than a piece bought from an ordinary country auction, but how did it get there? Was it really from a Lord's collection, or was there a friend of the auctioneer who popped the piece into the sale because he'd paid too much for it and hadn't been able to shift it? As we say quite often in our "expert tips" throughout the Antiques Source Book, "Beware!".

The area of antiquities is one in which provenance has always been a vexed question. Attempts have been made for centuries to control the leakage of historical artefacts from their homes in the East to the markets of the West, but there have always been loopholes. A Crusader sword needs a certificate of origin authenticated by a museum and a customs release document before it can be exported. But not if it is identified as a garden implement. The system has always been open to abuse.

It is early to say what, if any, good will come out of the recent war in Iraq but one group of people who, it seems, will probably benefit from it are collectors of antiquities. The armies of the Western allies and the reluctant defenders of dictatorship laid to waste some of the earliest archaeological sites in civilisation and looted museums that Saddam Hussein had considered too sacred to profane, in a manner reminiscent of the English and French armies in Peking 150 years earlier. This has led to a flood of antiquities finding their way into the Western market and, in turn, to much more rigorous regulations governing their sale in British auction

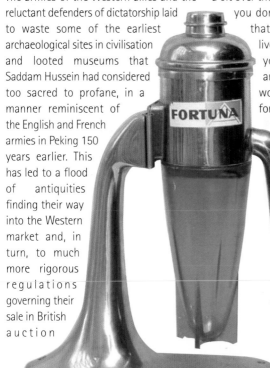

houses, which leads to another "Beware". Take care when buying antiquities in auctions outside the UK.

All of which seems to emphasise the purely financial aspects of antiques collecting, but this is by no means the area that we wish to stress. There is still no better reason for buying anything – an antiquity, a piece of furniture or a bakelite telephone – than your desire to own it. Your appreciation of the design, your admiration of the workmanship and the pleasure you take in the history it evokes should always outweigh any thought of monetary gain. After all, what if you're wrong and the piece isn't quite what you thought it was, or wasn't quite the bargain you had believed? What if you have paid a bit over the top? If you've done that and you don't even like the piece, then that really does make it hard to live with. On the other hand, if you decide you don't like it anyway and it turns out to be worth a lot more than you paid for it, then you could argue that you win both ways; another reason why we try to steer you in the right direction.

Throughout the Source Book we do our best to advise you of the pitfalls of collecting but, in the final analysis, it's up to you. The golden rule really should be, "If you don't like it, don't buy it!"; it's hard to go wrong with this maxim.

Antiquities

Antiquities not only provide the collector with great investment opportunities, just as impressive are the stories they tell.

Antiquities give the lie to the idea that the older an artifact grows, the more valuable it becomes. Many of the ancient items within these pages sell for remarkably reasonable prices, making collecting genuinely affordable.

Often, the objects we now call antiquities – statues and works of art, as well as household goods, glass, funerary artifacts and even items discarded as rubbish, have been collected since they were mere antiques.

For example, Roman nobilityavidly collected articles from earlier civilisations.

The affordability of antiquities can be explained, perhaps, by the abundance of material available as well as by the difficulty of authenticating pieces. Age is usually established by comparison with other items. More precise scientific testing is available, but it is an expensive process. The most practical solution for collectors is to visit a dealer who offers a guarantee of authenticity.

Bronze Luristan Dagger
- *circa 2400 BC*
A bronze dagger from Luristan with a green patina and foliate design on each side.
- *length 36cm*
- £150   • Mazar

Islamic Oil Lamp
- *9th century AD*
Bronze Islamic oil lamp with green patina with an unusual stylised bird handle.
- *height 28cm*
- £1,000   • Mazar

Bactrian Stone Idol
- 2000 BC
Alabaster Bactrian stone idol from Afghanistan.
- *height 37cm*
- £900   • Mazar

Egg-shaped Tent Peg
- *circa 250 BC*
Egg-shaped green-glaze stone with two holes used as a tent peg.
- *height 26cm*
- £600   • Mazar

Harra Pan Vase ▲

- *1800–2200 BC*

Small terracotta vase of ovoid
form with a deep truncated neck
and geometric design applied to
the body, from the Harra Pan
civilisation.
- *height 9cm*
- £250 • Rasoul Gallery

Terracotta Vase ▲

- *1800–2200 BC*

Terracotta vase of ovoid form
with a long inverted neck and a
circular pattern on a black glaze.
- *height 18cm*
- £500 • Rasoul Gallery

Terracotta Wine Strainer ▲

- *1800–2200 BC*

Terracotta wine strainer of
cylindrical form, with uniform
perforations within the body.
- *height 15cm*
- £600 • Rasoul Gallery

Alabaster Cup ▼

- *3000 BC*

Alabaster cup from Afghanistan,
carved from one piece of stone,
with a concave body, and an
extended stem, raised on a
splayed foot.
- *height 24cm*
- £1,500 • Sultani

Amlash Teapot ▼

- *6–8th century*

Amlash teapot made from
terracotta with two ear-shaped
side handles and a large domed
cover.
- *height 12cm*
- £3,500 • Yacobs

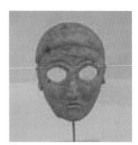

Sumarian Mask ▲

- *2300–2000 BC*

Sumarian mask with an
expressionless composure and
recesses for the eyes.
- *height 7cm*
- £14,000 • Yacobs

Roman Glass ▲

- *2nd century BC*

Roman glass flask of ovoid form
with fluted neck and spiral
decoration with good iridescence.
- *height 10cm*
- £7,500 • Yacobs

Oak Gargoyle

- *Medieval*

English anthropomorphic carved oak gargoyle.
- *20cm x 18cm*
- **£950**
- Boyd-Carpenter

German Lock

- *circa 1600 AD*

Rare and intricate steel door lock from Nuremburg.
- *18cm x 40cm*
- **£1,000**
- Boyd-Carpenter

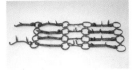

Medieval Comb

- *15th century AD*

Medieval boxwood comb. In extremely good condition.
- *15cm x 9cm*
- **£950**
- Boyd-Carpenter

Steel Dog Collar

- *15th century AD*

Dog collar with restraining spikes.
- *length 41cm*
- **£500**
- Boyd-Carpenter

Carved Buddha

- *500 BC*

A carved stone head of Buddha, Gandhara period.
- *height 18cm*
- **£400**
- Mazar

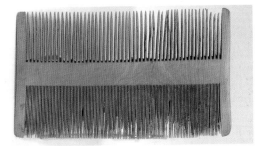

Merman Weather Vane

- *17th century AD*

Early weather vane styled as a merman with original gilding.
- *80cm x 1m*
- **£2,500**
- Boyd-Carpenter

Powder Horn

- *circa 1560 AD*

Ivory powder horn inset with coral and green stones and silver rosettes.
- *16cm x 8cm*
- **£590**
- Boyd-carpenter

Roman Earrings ▼
- *2nd–3rd century AD*
Pair of Roman earrings with circular garnets set in gold-roped banding, with suspended gold strands and beads.
- *length 3cm*
- £2,000   • Pars

Alabaster Drinking Vessel ▼
- *circa 2000 BC*
Bactrian Afghanistan alabaster cylindrical drinking vessel, with engraved circular designs and turned lip.
- *height 10.5cm*
- £650   • Rasoul Gallery

Islamic Pendant ▲
- *circa 9–10th century AD*
Islamic gold pendant in the shape of a bird with beautiful intricate work.
- *height 0.5cm*
- £3,000   • Pars

Roman Gold Earrings ▲
- *circa 1st–3rd century AD*
Pair of late roman gold earrings of teardrop form with beaded circular design.
- *height 3cm*
- £2,000   • Pars

Gold Pendant ▲
- *circa 15th century AD*
Lozenge shaped green stone set within a circular gold pendant with a herringbone design.
- *width 1cm*
- £200   • Pars

Bactrian Vessel ▲
- *circa 2000 BC*
Bactrian alabaster drinking vessel of cylindrical form from Afghanistan.
- *height 12cm*
- £550   • Rasoul Gallery

Roman Gold Pendant ▼
- *7–8th century AD*
Late Roman square gold pendant set with one amethyst lozenge shaped stone and flanked by two circular turquoise stones.
- *width 1.4cm*
- £450   • Pars

Window Weight ▼

- *circa 17th century AD*
Late 17th century window weight with carved figures of William and Mary.
- *20cm x 9cm*
- £320   • Boyd-Carpenter

Bronze Crewell Spur ▲

- *circa 14th century AD*
Spur with revolving stimulator.
- *length 14cm*
- £300   • Boyd-Carpenter

Steel Spur ▲

- *circa 14th century AD*
Early steel spur in original condition.
- *length 14cm*
- £300   • Boyd-Carpenter

Jacob's Ladder ▶

- *Circa 15th century AD*
Fine oak carving of Jacob's Ladder.
- *48cm x 30cm*
- £12,000   • Boyd-Carpenter

Carved Figure ▲

- *circa 1650 AD*
Boxwood carving of a hooded monk with his arms folded, original condition.
- *17cm x 4cm*
- £550   • Boyd-Carpenter

Corpus Christi ▲

- *circa 1420 AD*
Rare early French gothic carving of Corpus Christi.
- *height 35cm*
- £1,500   • Boyd-Carpenter

Expert Tips

Always make sure you have an export license and a museum certificate that confirms the authenticity and origin of the item.

Bronze Sundial ◀

- *circa 17th century AD*
Bronze English sundial with original patina.
- *17cm x 17cm*
- £460   • Boyd-Carpenter

Apothecary Jar ▶
- *circa 1600 AD*

Unusual apothecary jar from Sienna, Italy.
- *height 23cm*
- £2,200   • Boyd-Carpenter

Bronze Leopard ▲
- *circa 2nd century AD*

Bronze figure of a leopard with his paw on the head of Medusa.
- *5cm x 8cm*
- £2,350   • Valeri

Bronze Head of Slave ▲
- *circa 1st century AD*

Small bronze head of a slave.
- *height 2cm*
- £95   • Valeri

Bronze Eagle with Green Patination ▲
- *circa 2nd century AD*

A small bronze eagle with original green patination.
- *height 6cm*
- £750   • Valeri

Chariot Furniture ▲
- *circa 2nd century AD*

Bronze chariot fitting styled as a figure of a man.
- *height 13cm*
- £2,000   • Valeri

Green Man ▲
- *circa 16th century AD*

Fine oak carving of the Green Man.
- *24cm x 14cm*
- £750   • Boyd-Carpenter

Fortuna ▶
- *circa 2nd century AD*

Bronze figure of Fortuna.
- *height 18cm*
- £2,000   • Valeri

Roman Leopard ▲
- *1st century AD*

Roman bronze leopard with raised paw and head slightly turned, standing on a circular base.
- *height 4.5cm*
- £2,500   • Pars

Egyptian Mace Head ▲
- *late 4000 BC*

Egyptian black stone mace head.
- *height 10cm*
- £1,000   • Pars

Bronze Cat ▲
- *635–525BC*

Bronze cat from the Saite period dynasty or late bronze dynasty .
- *height 9.5cm*
- £6,000   • Pars

Venetian Flask ▲
- *5th century BC*

Venetian flask with a pinched lip and strap handle, raised on a pedestal base, with a yellow and green diagonal design on a black ground.
- *height 10cm*
- £2,000   • Pars

Aubergine Glass Flask ▲
- *7th century AD*

Aubergine glass flask with a single handle, a narrow neck and a bulbous body with applied circular raised design.
- *height 9cm*
- £700   • Pars

Transluscent Bowl ▼
- *1st century AD*

Roman translucent, green pillar-moulded glass bowl of shallow form with vertical ribbing, the tondo with three wheel-cut concentric circles.
- *diameter 15cm*
- £2,000   • Pars

Pottery Candleholder ▼
- *circa 8th century*

Byzantine pottery candle holder modelled as a church, with carved arches and openings with a geometric design.
- *height 29cm*
- £2,000   • Pars

Bronze Figure of Aphrodite ▼
- *circa 2nd century AD*

Small bronze figure of Aphrodite, goddess of love.
- *height 9cm*
- £350 • Valeri

Bronze Oil Lamp with Leaf Design ▲
- *3rd century AD*

Bronze oil lamp with stylised foliate thumb rest with original patina.
- *4cm x 16cm*
- £200 • Valeri

Gold Earrings ▼
- *4th century AD*

Gold Roman earrings with large garnet setting.
- *length 6cm*
- £1,100 • Douch

Hellenistic Earring ▶
- *2nd century BC*

Gold Hellenistic earring with a green stone.
- *length 2cm*
- £190 • Douch

Bronze Key Ring ▲
- *2nd century AD*

Bronze ring with key to lock.
- *diameter 2.5cm*
- £100 • Valeri

Gold Hoop Earrings with Beads ▲
- *12th century AD*

Large gold hoop earrings with beaded circular design.
- *diameter 4cm*
- £1,100 • Douch

Medusa Ring ◀
- *4th century AD*

Gold ring with an agate cameo of Medusa.
- *diameter 1cm*
- £1,200 • Douch

Egyptian Hand Earring ▼
- *2nd century BC*
Turquoise Egyptian gold hoop
earring styled as a hand with a
pearl clasp.
- *diameter 1.5cm*
- £45 • Douch

Hellenistic Earring ▲
- *2nd century BC*
Gold hoop Egyptian earring with
a fine head of a bull.
- *diameter 2cm*
- £450 • Douch

Charging Rhinoceros Figure ▼
- *1st century AD*
Rhinoceros in charging position.
Han Dynasty.
- *15cm x 38cm*
- £500 • David Baker

Roman Seal ▲
- *1st century BC*
Roman seal of Mercury in a
modern setting.
- *diameter 1cm*
- £480 • Douch

Roman Oil Lamp ▲
- *2nd–3rd century AD*
Roman pottery oil lamp,
depicting a figure of Mercury.
- *length 10cm*
- £150 • Eastern Satrapy

Terracotta Storage Jar ▼
- *1500 BC*
Painted terraccotta pot with
geometric design.
- *30cm x 30cm*
- £420 • David Baker

Terracotta Han Dynasty ◀
- *1st century AD*
T'ang Dynasty terracotta horse
with original patina.
- *18cm x 36cm*
- £1500 • David Baker

Celtic Warrior ▶
- **100 BC**

A small figure of a bronze Celtic Warrior found in Norfolk.
- *height 7cm*
- **£575**   • Jane Stewart

Claudius Bronze ▲
- **1st century AD**

Small Romano British bronze head of Claudius found in Colchester.
- *height 2.5cm*
- **£225**   • Jane Stewart

Roman Sandal ▲
- **circa 2nd century AD**

A small Romano British brooch in the form of a sandal.
- *length 2cm*
- **£65**   • Jane Stewart

Fibula Brooch ▲
- **2nd century AD**

A Romano British fibula brooch found in Wiltshire.
- *length 2cm*
- **£45**   • Jane Stewart

Votive Altar ▼
- **circa 1st–2nd century AD**

Bronze altar with blue and green enamel decoration, with original patina, dedicated to the god Jupiter.
- *height 2cm*
- **£500**   • Jane Stewart

Romano British Brooch ▶
- **2nd century AD**

A Romano British brooch in the form of a wheel with enameling. Found in Salisbury, Wiltshire.
- *height 2cm*
- **£250**   • Jane Stewart

Bronze Cherub Head Decoration ▼
- **2nd century AD**

Small bronze head of Cupid being part of decoration for a drinking vessel found in Dorset.
- *height 1cm*
- **£75**   • Jane Stewart

Expert Tips

Considering its age, beauty and fragility, Roman glass is a relatively affordable investment for the antiquities collector, and is a good place to start.

Green Glass Flask ▲

- *3rd–4th century AD*
Bottle-shaped green glass flask,
with globular body and
cylindrical neck wound with clear
spiral threads, four applied
handles, flared foot and surface
encrustation.
- *height 11cm*
- £6,500 • Pars

Aubergine Glass Jar ▼

- *7th century AD*
Small ovoid aubergine glass jar,
with moulded rim and extensive
iridescence.
- *height 7cm*
- £800 • Pars

Roman Iridescent Flask ▼

- *4th century AD*
Iridescent green flask with silver
and gold decoration.
- *height 12cm*
- £1,000 • Pars

Roman Cameo Ring ▶

- *circa 1st century AD*
Roman gold cameo ring
decorated with an outstretched
hand squeezing an ear inscribed
"Remember me and always be
mine".
- *width 2cm*
- £5,000 • Pars

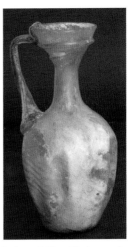

Indented Glass Flask ▲

- *4–6th century AD*
Green glass flask, with applied
handle and six-sided body, with
indented sides.
- *height 15cm*
- £1,000 • Pars

Roman Flask ▲

- *1st century AD*
Roman blue glass flask, the body
encircled with spiral threads.
- *height 9.4cm*
- £1,500 • Pars

Bronze Bull's Head Decoration ▼

- *2nd–3rd century AD*
Fine Romano British bronze bull's head part of decoration to a vessel found in Bath.
- *height 2cm*
- £85
- Jane Stewart

Bronze Fibula Brooch ▲

- *2nd century AD*
Found in Southwark, London a small bronze fibula brooch.
- *length 5cm*
- £40
- Jane Stewart

Roman Bronze Brooch ▲

- *2nd–3rd century AD*
Roman British bronze fibula brooch.
- *height 7cm*
- £75
- Jane Stewart

Gold Cornelian Ring ▼

- *3rd century*
Ibex cornelian and gold ring, European.
- *diameter 1.6cm*
- £595
- Jane Stewart

Cabuchon Garnet Ring ▲

- *1st–2nd century AD*
Romano British gold ring with a cabuchon garnet depicting a figure of a wood nymph found in Bromley, Kent.
- diameter 1.6cm
- £595
- Jane Stewart

Hellenistic Ring ▲

- *4th century BC*
Gold ring with Cabuchon garnet from the Hellenistic period.
- *diameter 2cm*
- £675
- Jane Stewart

Bronze Snake Ring ▶

- *1st century AD*
Bronze Romano British snake ring.
- *diameter 2cm*
- £95
- Jane Stewart

Gold Hoop Earring ◀

- *2nd century AD*
Romano British gold hoop
earring with lozenge shape drop
holding a small Cabuchon garnet.
- *diameter 2cm*
- £135   • Jane Stewart

Romano British Earring ▼

- *2nd century AD*
Small gold-scrolled hoop earring
found by the River Thames,
London.
- *diameter 2cm*
- £195   • Jane Stewart

Roman Bronze Key ▲

- *2nd century AD*
Rare bronze Romano British key.
Found in the River Thames,
London.
- *length 5cm*
- £375   • Jane Stewart

Oyster Spoon ▲

- *2nd century AD*
Romano British bronze oyster
spoon, found in York.
- *length 12cm*
- £275   • Jane Stewart

Blue Glass Melon Beads ▲

- *1st or 2nd century AD*
Three "Blue glass melon beads"
Romano British found in
Gloucester.
- *diameter 1cm*
- £80   • Jane Stewart

Expert Tips

*While ancient locks of iron and
wood are unlikely to survive intact,
bronze keys are sturdier and more
easily collectable today.*

Three Roman
Casket Keys ▲

- *1st–2nd century AD*
Three bronze Romano British
casket keys.
- *diameter 1cm*
- £65 each   • Jane Stewart

Leaf-shaped Bronze
Lamp Base ▶

- *2nd –3rd century AD*
Bronze Romano British lamp
fitting in the form of a leaf found
in Dorset.
- *length 10cm*
- £125   • Jane Stewart

Roman British Weight ▶

- **2nd–3rd century AD**
Romano British bronze weight in
the shape of a heart.
- *length 2cm*
- £85 • Jane Stewart

Mummy Beads ◀

- **300 BC**
Cornelian beads and Mummy
beads necklace.
- *length*
- £250 • Jane Stewart

Oil Vessel ▲

- **1st–2nd century AD**
Terra nigre oil vessel with handle
in good condition.
- *height 13cm*
- £175 • Jane Stewart

Gandhara Vessel ▼

- **500 BC**
Bronze jug in the form of a cow
standing on three feet. Used for
wine.
- *height 20cm*
- £60,000 • Marko Pollo

Celtic Bronze Torque ▲

- **250 BC**
Celtic bronze torque fragment
found in Norfolk.
- *length 2cm*
- £95 • Jane Stewart

Expert Tips

*Interested collectors should go
and have a look at the British
Museum collections of
antiquities, the best in the world*

Buddha Head ▲

- **100 BC**
Carved stone head of Buddha
with gold patina from Hadda.
- *height 23cm*
- £9,000 • Marko Pollo

Gandhara Relief ▶

- *1st century AD*
Black stone carved frieze of
Buddha and figures seated on an
elephant with attendants.
- *30cm x 30cm*
- £14,000   • Marko Pollo

Islamic Drinking Vessel ▶

- *2500 BC*
Islamic terracotta drinking cup
with a geometric pattern of green
and yellow, standing on a circular
container for wine.
- *height 28cm*
- £1,500   • Marko Pollo

Bronze Flower Vessel
from Afghanistan ▲

- *100 BC*
Islamic vessel from Afghanistan
for flowers made from bronze with
cartouches of chickens, rabbits,
and musicians.
- *height 55cm*
- £11,000   • Marko Pollo

Terracotta Wine Vessel ▲

- *1st century AD*
Large bulbous terracotta vessel for
holding wine with six cartouches
of birds and gazelles. Floral design
with three handles.
- *height 32cm*
- £9,000   • Marko Pollo

Marble Eagle ◀

- *500 AD*
Finely carved marble eagle with
extended wings and painted red
eyes.
- *height 12cm*
- £2,000   • Marko Pollo

Egyptian Glass Bangle ▲
- *9th century AD*

Egyptian glass bangle, funerary artifact.
- *diameter 7cm*
- £175 • Jane Stewart

Mother and Child ▲
- *2500 BC*

Mohenjo-Daro, Indus Valley figure of a mother and child from Afghanistan.
- *height 10cm*
- £1,500 • Marko Pollo

Buddhist Temple ▲
- *500 BC*

Crystal Buddhist stupa standing on marble base, used as a portable shrine.
- *height 19cm*
- £10,000 • Marko Pollo

Fertility Goddess ▼
- *2500 BC*

Mohenjo-Daro, Indus Valley figure of fertility goddess from Afghanistan.
- *height 10cm*
- £1,500 • Marko Pollo

Expert Tips

To test that Roman pottery is the genuine article, wet it with your fingers and if it smells very earthy its probably the real thing. Make sure you go to a reputable dealer.

Mohenjo Daro ◄
- *2500 BC*

Terracotta sugar bowl base with fish design surmounted by drinking vessel with hexagonal design.
- *height 17cm*
- £1,000 • Marko Pollo

Architectural &
Garden Furniture

The boom in television gardening programmes has lead to an increase in demand for garden furniture and garden design.

Classic architectural and garden furniture pieces are currently a flourishing market as they can be easily incorporated into a modern home or garden to add historical elegance. Carved mantelpieces and antique glass panels are some of the common indoor pieces available while statues, foutains, steps, friezes and iron garden furniture are some of the more popular items for exterior design.

Many of the wood, stone, metal or marble pieces on the market are usually salvaged from old buildings and vary in condition. Architectural pieces can be

quite large and difficult to move on your own, so check what delivery services (and charges) are offered by the dealer. A tape measure is essential if you are planning to buy an item for an existing space. The results are rewarding as historical pieces can blend in well with modern houses.

Look beyond the large cities when shopping, as dealers often have large warehouses in rural locations. Be warned, though, that prices are rising since makeover programmes have greatly increased the demand.

Five Stone Steps with Balustrades ◀

- *circa 1870*
Fine set of five stone steps flanked by sweeping scrolled balustrades.
- 90cm x 1.52m
- £10,000   • Drummonds

Cast Iron Bull ▼

- *circa 1950*
Impressive cast iron bull with left leg raised in an aggressive manner, mounted on a stylised rocky base.
- 1.55m x 2.5m
- £16,580   • Drummonds

Stone Lion's Head ▲

- *circa 1880*
A circular stone lion's head with a finely carved naturalistic expression.
- 48cm x 38cm
- £825   • Drummonds

Italian Water Fountain ▲

- *early 20th century*

Charming Italian Rosso Verona marble and bronze fountain by Raffaello Romanelli. The marble bowl is supported on the shoulders of a bronze satyr crouching on a marble base. A laughing cherub stands with arms raised in the centre of the bowl, while being squirted by a frog crouching on the rim.
- *height 1.7m*
- *diameter of bowl 92cm*
- £35,000 • Crowther

Stoneware Urns ▲

- *mid 19th century*

One of a pair of stoneware urns, each semi-lobed body with a frieze of stylised foliage beneath a rope twist and lobed rim, on a circular foot and square base stamped, "Pulhams Terra Cotta Boxbourne".
- *height 67cm*
- £9,500 • Crowther

One of a Pair of Urns ▼

- *1910*

Pair of cast iron urns with egg and dart moulded rim above a lobed body, raised on a fluted, splayed foot on a square base.
- *58.5cm diameter*
- £460 • Drummonds

Stone Finials ▼

- *circa 1880*

One of a pair of English sandstone finials, finely carved with scrolled and leaf designs, surmounted with a stylised acorn finial.
- *height 2m*
- £7,500 • Drummonds

Sir Walter Raleigh ▶

- *circa 1880*

Stone statue of Sir Walter Raleigh dressed in a tunic and breeches and holding his cloak.
- *height 1.2m*
- £23,000 • Drummonds

Carved Stone Lions ▲

- *circa 1890*

One of a pair of late 19th-century stone lions in a crouching position, with tail swept onto one side and a finely carved expression.
- *44cm x 1m*
- £14,000 • Drummonds

Cast Iron Fountain ▲

- *19th century*

Cast iron fountain from Ardennes, France, in the form of a young boy holding a staff in one hand and pointing with the other.
- *height 1.22m*
- £3,400 • Drummonds

Stone Frieze with Goats and Cherubs ▶

- *circa 1870*

A stone frieze finely carved with goats and cherubs within a foliate design, this being one of five pairs, each pair being sold separately.

- *60cm x 1.4m*
- £5,700
- Drummonds

Terracotta Garden Bricks with Rose Design ▲

- *circa 1900*

Square terracotta garden bricks with carved rose motif, one of 30 sold separately.

- *22cm x 22cm*
- £22.00
- Drummonds

Ram's Heads ▼

- *circa 1880*

Pair of finely carved stone ram's head mounted on square bases.

- *38cm x 30cm*
- £3,950
- Drummonds

Ceramic Pillars ◀

- *circa 1880*

English stone and ceramic pillars with vertical scrolling acanthus and leaf design. One of six.

- *height 1.8m*
- £1,275
- Drummonds

Gothic Niches ▶

- *circa 1880*

One of a pair of Bathstone Gothic revival niches with foliate carving to the sides and surmounted by a cross with trailing foliage.

- *2.7m x 1.19m*
- £40,500
- Drummonds

Bishop's Head ▲

- *circa 1890*

A finely carved stone head of a bishop.

- *height 34cm*
- £675
- Drummonds

Expert Tips

This may seem an obvious tip but make sure you can get it home, cheaply, and it fits – no guesswork!

Stone Trough ▼

• *circa 1820*
A stone trough with attractive weathering of lichen and moss.
• *40cm x 78cm*
• £260   • Drummonds

Cast Iron Garden Roller ▼

• *circa 1870*
Cast iron garden roller with turned wooden handle and cast iron medallion with maker's logo.
• *height 1.2m*
• £225   • Drummonds

Georgian Columns ▼

• *circa 1730s*
Three early Georgian stone columns with reeded capital, supported by square columns with chamfered corners, raised on stepped, plinth bases.
• *height 1.95m*
• £785 each   • Drummonds

Roll Top Bench ▲

• *20th century*
A two-seater roll top iron bench, with ladder back and seat, and scrolled arms and legs.
• *width 1.2m*
• £425   • Drummonds

Neptune Fountain ▲

• *circa 1890*
Cast iron wall fountain showing Neptune sitting on his throne while wrestling with a carp.
• *height 1.55m*
• £1,775   • Drummonds

Palladian Chimneypiece ▼

• *circa 1730*
An English Palladian statuary marble chimneypiece, after a design by William Kent. The projecting inverted breakfront shelf with moulded edge above a band of lotus moulding and a boldly carved egg and dart moulding, the frieze centred by a rectangular panel carved with a bacchante mask, the hair intertwined with berried vines, and a border of Sienna marble.
• *1.66m x 2.31m*
• £315,000   • Anthony Outred

Stone Trough ▼

• *circa 1820*
A rectangular stone trough with good patination.
• *38cm x 89cm*
• £250   • Drummonds

French Copper Bath ▼

• *circa 1880*
French double skinned bath with copper lining, raised on cast iron claw feet.
• *length 1.67m*
• £7,950   • Drummonds

Brass Lantern ▼
- *1880*

Brass lantern with glass front and sides with pagoda top and small round brass finials.
- *height 45cm*
- £110   • **Myriad**

Chinese Garden Seat ▶
- *1880*

Chinese ceramic garden seat with a cream glaze, pierced lattice panels and lion mask decoration.
- *height 39cm*
- £350   • **Ormonde**

Galvanised Flower Bucket ▲
- *1960*

French flower vendors galvanised display bucket with carrying handles.
- *height 48cm*
- £22   • **Myriad**

Galvanised Tub ▲
- *1880*

One of a pair of galvanised water butts with an inverted linear design.
- *height 54cm*
- £95   • **Myriad**

Ceramic Garden Seat ▶
- *1880*

Chinese ceramic garden seat, in a green glaze, with black floral designs and a repeating pattern of spots.
- *height 39cm*
- £350   • **Ormonde**

Enamel Bucket ▼
- *1920*

French enamelled water bucket with a red rim, pale green body, hand-painted strawberries and original handle.
- *height 29cm*
- £78   • **Myriad**

Expert Tips

Garden furniture, unlike interior furniture, does not need to be perfect in order to create a beautiful garden, as some wear and tear can add mystery and delight to any design. All that is needed is a little imagination.

Green Stucco Pot ◀
- *1950*

Stoneware urn of ovoid form with green glazed lip and neck with rusticated finish to the body.
- *height 44cm*
- £240   • **Myriad**

Oak Doors with Foliate Frieze ▶

- *1860*

An impressive pair of light oak doors with carved pine fruit griffins and mermaids set in a foliate frieze.

- *3.3m x 2.44m*
- £16,000   • Drummonds

Victorian Cloche ▲

- *1880*

A small Victorian cast iron vegetable cloche with original white enamel paint with handle.

- *48cm x 34cm*
- £139   • Drummonds

Victorian Planter ▼

- *circa 1870*

A two-tiered wrought iron Victorian planter with the original green enamel paintwork.

- *86cm x 90cm*
- £750   • Drummonds

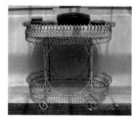

Garden Trolley ◀

- *circa 1920*

A wrought iron garden trolley with a pierced floral design and original white enamel paint.

- *71cm x 48cm*
- £225   • Drummonds

Circular Cast Iron Table with Scrolled Legs ▼

- *circa 1870*

A circular cast iron table base; decorative scrolled legs and feet with a circular marble top.

- *diameter 74cm*
- £850   • Drummonds

Lead Statue of Mercury ▼

- *circa 1900*

A fine lead statue of Mercury with left hand raised on circular base.

- *height 1.1m*
- £2,800   • Drummonds

Balloon Back Chairs ◀

- *circa 1920*

Two wrought iron balloon back chairs being part of a set of six with a circular wrought iron table, original paint.

- *height 83cm*
- £2,500   • Drummonds

Door Lock and Steel Key ▼

- *circa 1870*
A door lock with key made of steel.
- 20cm x20cm
- £395
- Drummonds

Brass Bird-shaped Door Hinge ▶

- *circa 1900*
A brass door hinge in the form of a stylised neck of a bird.
- 20cm x 13cm
- £150
- Drummonds

Sandstone Finials ▲

- *circa 1880*
One of a pair of fine highly decorative sandstone finials, carved with shells and figures from Scotland.
- *height 1.5m*
- £2,500
- Wiseman

Satyr's Head ▼

- *circa 1900*
A French stone-carved head of a satyr.
- *height 50cm*
- £1,600
- Wiseman

Brass Oval Window Locks ◀

- *circa 1890*
A pair of fine oval brass window locks with a circular pierced floral design on the handles.
- 14cm x 9cm
- £400
- Drummonds

Brass Door Handles ▲

- *circa 1880*
Pair of fine brass door handles.
- *diameter 23cm*
- £175
- Drummonds

Cricular Brass Bell ▲

- 1880
Circular brass bell stand with ornate foliate and acorn design.
- 20cm x 14cm
- £225
- Drummonds

Victorian Iron Gates ▲
- *circa 1880*

Pair of Victorian iron gates,
heavily constructed with ball and
spike finial designs.
- *2m x 3m*
- *£5,100*   • Drummonds

Expert Tips

*Decorative fireplaces were
mass-produced from the
1840s, so it is important to
check the grate is complete
with basket and hood, as
perfect replacements are
difficult to find.*

Oak Bar ▲
- *circa 1920*

Circular oak bar with moulded
panelled doors, consisting of a
four door fridge unit, marble
surround and surfaces.
- *length 6.35m*
- *£5,900*   • Drummonds

Architectural Fireplace ▶
- *1800–1900*

Carved wooden fireplace flanked
by two architectural columns
surmounted by a moulded mantle,
with traces of white paint.
- *height 1.28m*
- *£2,350*   • Drummonds

Gothic Window ▼
- *circa 1800*

Carved gothic sandstone window.
- *89cm x 69cm*
- *£675*   • Drummonds

Fire Dogs and Grate ▶
- *circa 1900*

Victorian serpentine-fronted cast-
iron grate and fire back with a
raised design of tulips,
surmounted by two cherubs
holding a wreath.
- *75cm x 80cm*
- *£3,600*   • Drummonds

English Rococo Chimneypiece ▲
- *circa 1840*

An English white marble
chimneypiece signed D Aí.
The serpentine shaped shelf
with moulded edge above an
elaborately carved frieze
decorated with scrolled
acanthus leaves, with a central
scallop carved shell above the
hearth opening and a double
moulded surround with relief
flower heads above three small
acanthus motifs terminating in
scrolled leaves.
- *1.22m x 1.93m*
- *£38,000*   • Outrred

Bronze Angel ▼

- *circa 1900*

Fine bronze head of an angel with pursed lips used as a fountain.
- *44cm x 40cm*
- £1,200   • Wiseman

Victorian Chimneypiece ▶

- *circa 1854*

Belgian black marble shelf above a frieze with fluted column jambs and oak and walnut overmantle with mirror plate. Cornice centred by a portrait of Isaac Newton in full relief.
- *3.76m x 2.44m*
- £68,000   • Lassco

Victorian Marble Chimneypiece ▲

- *late 19th century*

Chimneypiece in Gothic Revival taste having an arched aperture with foliate carvings to the spandrels and a curb fender en-suite.
- *1.44m x 1.83m*
- £5,500   • Lassco

Terracotta Urns ▼

- *circa 1870*

One of a pair of fine terracotta urns by Pulham Broxbourne.
- *height 50cm*
- £1,100   • Wiseman

Expert Tips

Timber copies of marble fire-places are very effective. Add plaster mouldings and a marble paint finish.

Marble Chimneypiece ◀

- *circa 1780*

Georgian chimneypiece with lambrequin carved breakfront shelf above a plain frieze centred by a tablet carved relief of Diana and Cupid.
- *1.56m x 1.79m*
- £36,000   • Lassco

English Brass Andirons ▲

- *circa 1880*

The wrythen standards with lobed ball finials and raised on scrolled hairy paw feet.
- *86cm x 55cm*
- £10,400 for pair   • Lassco

Iron Hob Grate ◀

- *circa 1800*

Grate in the manner of George Bullock with railed basket flanked by pilasters with brass anthemion appliques and paw feet.
- *48.5cm x 1.07m*
- £6,800   • Lassco

Stained Glass Windows

- *circa 1895*
Each Victorian window depicts a
female saint framed by an
architectural border.
- *1.3cm x 40cm*
- **£30,000 for 4**   • Lassco

Florentine Entranceway

- *circa 16th century*
Scalloped demi-lune overdoor
with foliate surmounts above the
frieze panel.
- *3.84m x 1.85m*
- **£17,500**   • Lassco

Stone Winged Lions ▲

- *Late 19th century*
After cast iron originals by
"Societe Anonyme ... du Val
d'Osne", Paris. Each sentinel
beast with displaying wings raised
on a rectangular plinth.
- *height 1.47m*
- **£5,700**   • Lassco

Panelled Room ▲

- *early 18th century*
Raised and fielded panelling with
two ionic order stop-fluted
pilasters, three archways of which
one incorporates a door.
- *height 3.35m*
- **£22,000**   • Lassco

Pine Chimneypiece ▶

- *late 19th–early 20th century*
Constructed from some period
elements, the moulded breakfront
shelf with acanthine and egg and
dart ornaments above an ogee
section acanthine carved eared
aperture.
- *1.33m x 1.32m*
- **£4,300**   • Lassco

Stone Pool Surround ▲

- *20th century*
Eight Italian cornucopia shaped
planters linked by ornate
kerbstones, pleasantly weathered
with adjustable pool diameter.
- *height 36cm*
- **£3,250**   • Lassco

Terracotta Sphinxes ◀

- *Late 19th century*
Each recumbent female figure is
attired in Nemes headwear and
armour al antica on a rectangular
plinth bearing the signature Emil
Muller.
- *92cm x 1.14m*
- **£16,500 the pair**   • Lassco

Mythical Yarli Lions ▼

- *18th century*

One of a pair of Mythical Yarli lions with elephant trunks, standing on top of human heads. Has traces of original paint remaining in excellent condition. Vellore Tamil Naou.
- *height 1.66m*
- £7,800   • Gordon Reece

Pottery Urn ▲

- *circa 1940*

One of a pair of pottery urns with lobed designs around the body and egg and dart motif to the splayed lip, standing on a pedestal base.
- *height 43cm*
- £480   • Myriad

Indian Jarli Window ▼

- *17th century*

Indian Mughal Jarli window carved from red sandstone flanked by four cartouches in the form of Mirabs arches. The central Jarli of interlocking honeycomb is topped by a floral finial with a flower to left and right from Northern Rajastan.
- *83cm x 1.15m*
- £5,800   • Gordon Reece

Wicker Chair ▶

- *circa 1920*

French provincial wicker conservatory chair painted pistachio green with a deep horseshoe back, apron front and splayed legs.
- *height 67cm*
- £240   • Myriad

Wrought Iron Chair ▲

- *circa 1950*

Set of four French wrought iron patio chairs with a heart-shaped back, scrolled arms and original white enamel paint.
- *height 87cm*
- £680 for set of four   • Myriad

Carved Ceiling Panel ▲

- *circa 1850*

Carved rosewood ceiling panel with central flower within a stylised leaf motif, from Southern India.
- *length 56cm*
- £310   • Gordon Reece

French Chair ▲

- *circa 1950*

One of a set of four French wrought iron garden chairs with pierced geometric designs to back splat and seat.
- *height 87cm*
- £680   • Myriad

Brass Urns ▼
• *circa 1910*
One of a pair of brass urns from the modern movement, with unusual angular double handles, the whole on a pedestal foot resting on a square base.
• *height 48cm*
• £880 • Myriad

Zinc Urns ▼
• *1920*
One of a pair of French urns made from zinc with unusual angular designs and a marbled finish.
• *height 31cm*
• £680 • Myriad

Garden Folding Stool ▲
• *1950*
Folding picnic stool with a candy striped linen seat supported by four teak legs.
• *height 41cm*
• £78 • Myriad

Stone Flower Pot ▲
• *1970*
Stone flower pot with a fluted body with carved designs in relief.
• *height 24cm*
• £24 • Myriad

Pink Pottery Bucket ▼
• *1910*
French ceramic pail with salmon pink glaze and white interior with a raffia covered handle.
• *height 24cm*
• £18 • Myriad

Expert Tips

Unglazed period pottery of any value should be covered up and protected if left outside in the winter because ice can destroy it as it expands in the cracks.

Salt Glazed Urn ▼
• *1910*
French salt glazed pottery urn with pinched lip and banding, the body centred with a flower motif in relief on a pedestal base.
• *height 41cm*
• £120 • Myriad

Watering Can ◄
• *1920*
Zinc watering can with an elongated spout.
• *height 26cm*
• £34 • Myriad

Lead Cistern ▲

- *18th century*

Cistern with front panel cast in relief with strapwork centred by a relief cast figure.

- *79cm x 74cm*
- £2,150
- Lassco

Carved Pine Altar ▲

- *Late 19th century*

Victorian altar, the sides pierced with gothic tracery arcades and trefoils – some losses to the carving.

- *95cm x 1.68m*
- £480
- Lassco

Pine-front Entranceway ▼

- *Early 19th century*

Neo-classical painted pine front entranceway in the late Georgian taste with triangular pediment above six panel door and fluted pilasters.

- *282cm x 149cm*
- £5,000
- Lassco

Stained Glass Window ◀

- *19th century*

French stained glass roundel window depicting a praying saint kneeling at an altar.

- *diameter 1.03m*
- £1,750
- Lassco

Victorian Tazza Urns ▲

- *Late 19th century*

Shallow-lobed tazza bowls by the Handyside foundry of Derbyshire raised on a socle foot and stamped to the plinth.

- *49cm x 79cm*
- £1,900 the pair
- Lassco

Bronze Swan Doorstop ▼

- *circa 1890*

Victorian cast-bronze swan doorstop.

- *height 38cm*
- £450
- D. Hume

Mahogany Wheelbarrow ◀

- *circa 1890*

A fine English late 19th century wheelbarrow of finely figured mahogany with brass mounts.

- *45cm x 46cm x 1.07m*
- £18,000
- Mallett

Arms & Armour

There are many avenues to choose from for the collector of militaria including weapons, pictures, prints, postcards and medals.

There are many facets to collecting weapons and war paraphernalia. While full suits of armour are prohibitively expensive, interesting collections can be made from different suits. In particular, military headdress is a popular theme and rare specimens from the eighteenth and nineteenth century hold their value. A variety of military uniforms from the later centuries are widely available, while earlier specimens are much rarer and command a high price.

In terms of weaponry, one of the larger collecting areas is edged weapons. Bayonets and small swords from the nineteenth century can be acquired at fair prices, while the superb quality of many Indian, Persian and Arabic pieces is boosting their value.

Antique firearms must be inspected by a gunsmith before firing. The earliest specimens from the seventeenth century are rare but tend to be of high quality. Those predating the 1870s, when modern firearm design began, are greatly prized.

Colt Navy Revolver ▼
- 1853

Colt navy revolver, most of the original cylinder has seen naval action in the Gulf of Mexico.
- *length 19cm*
- £1,000   • C. Seidler

Double-Action Revolver ▼
- 1860

Coopers double-action revolver with walnut stock 50 per cent original finish 36 calibre.
- *length 10cm*
- £750   • C. Seidler

Single Action Pistol ◄
- *circa 1863*

Single Action pistol, 44 calibre, with Starr original finish.
- *length 20cm*
- £1,400   • C. Seidler

Buffalo Bill Revolver ▼
- *circa 1970*

Percussion Revolver, 31 calibre, as used on frontier mining camps from the "Buffalo Bill" Historical Society Museum, Wyoming. Non-firing replica, with pellets and brass powder containers set in a presentation box.
- *width 30cm*
- £750   • Jessie Western

Belgian Courtier's Sword ▼

- **circa 1860**
Belgian courtier's sword with
mother-of-pearl grip and brass gilt
guard, with foliate designs
together with a black leather
scabbard with gilt mounts.
Inscribed "Docteur Lorthioir" and
the maker's mark 49 Rue des
Fabrique, Brussels.
- *length 85cm*
- **£200**   • C. Seidler

Royal Engineers Busby ▼

- **circa 1910**
Royal engineers officer's bear fur
busby with the gilt flaming bomb
incorporating the Regiments
insignia and patent leather
chinstrap.
- *height 14cm*
- **£375**   • C. Seidler

Fintlock Pistol ▲

- **circa 1790**
English flintlock three barrel tap
action pistol made by Clarke of
London. 62 Cheapside London.
- *length 21cm*
- **£1,900**   • Michael German

Captain's Jacket and Hat ▼

- **1855**
Scarlet tunic of a Captain in
the First Royal Tower Hamlets
Miliita (The King's Own Light
Infantry). Collar insignia of
Crown and Pip with tin case
by Flight Military Tailors,
Winchester, containing belts
and sashes. Plus an Officer's
shako (without plume) with
K.O.L.I plate.
- *large*
- **£1,650**   • Gordon's

General's Aiguilettes ▼

- **1940**
Third Reich General's aiguilettes,
in good condition with only
minor damage to parts of the gilt
wiring.
- *length 42cm*
- **£185**   • Gordon's

Thirty-two Calibre Percussion Revolver ◄

- **1860**
Thirty-two calibre double action
Adams revolver, with hexagonal
barrel, made under licence by
Mass Arms. Co. U.S.A. with
modern bullet mould.
- *length 21.5cm*
- **£550**   • C. Seidler

Double-Trigger Revolver ▶

- *1864*

First mould double-trigger Tranta revolver in 36 bore inscribed "Strand of London", ten per cent original finish.
- *length 20cm*
- £800 ● C. Seidler

Japanese Quiver ▲

- *circa 1800*

A Japanese quiver for carrying arrows, made of wood with black lacquer and a gold floral pattern, with two small circles being the crest of the Satsuma family.
- *height 39cm*
- £2,000 ● Don Bayney

Tsuba Sword Guard ▲

- *circa 1850*

A Japanese sword guard, or Tsuba, depicting an Oni, or demon, made of iron.
- *8cm x 6cm*
- £800 ● Don Bayney

Tachi Sword ◀

- *circa 1750*

A Japanese long sword, or Tachi, used for wearing with armour. The blade is signed "Suke-Sada" the scabbardf is wood with bronze lacquer and bound in leather.
- *length 42cm*
- £4,000 ● Don Bayney

Hoshi Kabuto ▲

- *circa 1750*

An iron plate helmet, or Hoshi Kabuto, with visor and a circular crest, for the Japanese army.
- *height 30cm*
- £2,200 ● Don Bayney

Expert Tips

Always wear cotton gloves when handling weapons to prevent the formation of rust deposits – store in a dry and well-ventilated place

Silver Ho Ho Bird ◀

- *circa 1750*

A Japanese Tachi with a silver Ho Ho bird mounted on the hilt, with two silver hanging loops on the lacquered terracotta scabbard.
- *length 42cm*
- £4,000 ● Don Bayney

Pith Helmet ▶

- *circa 1915*

Turn of the century linen pith helmet for the overseas campaign in India, in fine original condition.

- *size 7*
- £120 • Bentleys

Luftwaffe Belt ▶

- *1940*

Luftwaffe other ranks late pattern standard leather belt, with some wear, but complete.

- *5cm x 3cm*
- £45 • Gordon's

SS Steel Helmet ▼

- *1940*

SS M-44 Steel helmet, a rare early double decal version complete with inner lining and chin strap, stamped "54" on lining and a maker's stamp on inside of helmet, with most of original finish still present.

- *size 8*
- £1,195 • Gordon's

Japanese N.C.O. Sword ▶

- *circa 1939*

Japanese N.C.O. Katena sword with polished folded steel blade and original paintwork to handle. No. 79275, with matching scabbard number.

- *length 59cm*
- £290 • C. Seidler

Officers Belt Pistol ◀

- *circa 1840*

Officers 16 bore percussion pistol, with double back action locks, by Roper of Halifax.

- *length 30cm*
- £875 • C. Seidler

Khula–Khad Helmet ▶

- *circa 1800*

Fine Indo Persian Khula-Khad helmet formed as a face with horns, with chiselled steel designs, gold inlays and chain mail neck guard.

- *height 30cm*
- £3,200 • M. German

Japanese Dagger ▼

- *circa 1870*

A Japanese Tanto dagger with cloisonne hilt and scabbard, the blade is unsigned.

- *length 35cm*
- £1,800 • M. German

Pinfire Revolver ▼

- *circa 1870*

Continental pinfire carbine revolver with "Fabrique de Le Page Freres a Liege, Maison a Paris 12 Rue de Eugieue" etched on barrel.

- *length 66cm*
- £1,200 • M. German

Gentleman's Helmet ▶

- *early 17th century*
Gentleman's steel close helmet,
possibly Flemish.
- *44cm x 36cm*
- **£7,950**   • **Ian Roper**

Hilt Decoration ▼

- *circa 1800*
Sword furniture for the hilt or
Menuki in the form of gilt sea
shells.
- *length 2cm*
- **£150**   • **Don Bayney**

Sword Furniture ▼

- *circa 1800*
A Kodzuka and Kogai sword
furniture made of Shkudo with
gilt dragon.
- *length 20cm*
- **£1,500**   • **Don Bayney**

Dragon Sword Guard ▶

- *circa 1800*
A Tsuba, or sword guard, made of
sentoku, a mixture of bronze and
copper, depicting a dragon
- *7.2cm x 5cm*
- **£500**   • **Don Bayney**

Tanto Blade ▼

- *circa 1800*
A Japanese dagger or Tanto
signed "Suke Sada" with Kodzuka
and Minouki on the hilt.
- *length 22cm*
- **£2,000**   • **Don Bayney**

Japanese Dagger ▼

- *circa 1850*
A European style Japanese
presentation dagger for a Dutch
or Portuguese sea captain
inscribed with the maker's name
"Nabu take" with silver scabbard.
- *length 15cm*
- **£1,800**   • **Don Bayney**

Steel Arrowhead ▲

- *circa 1900*
A Japanese steel arrowhead with
a floral blossom crest.
- *length 20cm*
- **£150**   • **Don Bayney**

Trooper's Sabre ▼

- *circa 1908*
British trooper's sabre, pattern dated and inscribed WWI paint.
- *length 1.1m*
- £275
- C. Seidler

Deane Harding Percussion Pistol ▼

- *circa 1840*
Deane Harding 54 calibre officer's percussion cap and ball pistol, with hexagonal barrel and original grip and varnish. London proof marks.
- *length 30cm*
- £750
- C. Seidler

Luftwaffe Paratrooper Helmet ▶

- **1940**
Luftwaffe paratrooper's helmet. Rare double decal version, with both Luftwaffe eagle and national shield. The chinstrap and liner are complete showing makers mark: Baumuster: Heisler Berlin C2 Hersteller F. W. Muller JR and sizes; Koptwelte GR 61 Stahlhaube Nr. 71, all clearly readable. Helmet stamped on the inside, "ET71", paintwork and overall finish excellent.
- *size 8*
- £3,500
- Gordon's

Schutzenschnur Silver Luftwaffe ▲

- **1940**
Pilot officer's silver braid of the Luftwaffe with an eagle and national insignia.
- *length 14cm*
- £100
- Gordon's

Russian Dagger ▼

- *circa 1880*
Russian Kinjal dagger with ornate silver hilt and scabbard, the blade with long grooves and foliate design in mechanical watering.
- *length 51cm*
- £1,400
- M. German

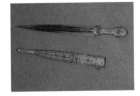

Pocket Flintlock Pistols ▼

- *circa 1720*
Pair of English Queen Anne pocket flintlock pistols, with cannon barrels and silver lion mask butt caps, signed John Segelas. Hammers fitted with dog catches.
- *length 18cm*
- £3,400
- M. German

French Belt Pistol ▼

- **1813**
French cavalryman's belt pistol with flintlock action, brass mounts and walnut furniture.
- *length 21.5cm*
- £1,000
- C. Seidler

Civil War Helmet ▼

- *circa 1640*
English civil war and steel
"Lobster Tail" helmet.
- *20cm x 40cm*
- £2,750 • Ian Roper

Scottish Dirk ▲

- *early 18th century*
Scottish dirk with brass and
leather sheaf, intricate Celtic
carved wooden hilt, and brass
fittings.
- *length 45cm*
- £2,950 • Ian Roper

Fine Tinderlighter ▶

- *circa 1780*
Large brass flintlock tinderlighter
of fine quality with original stand
and candle holder, frame and
tinder container finely engraved.
- *12cm x 19cm*
- £2,800 • M. German

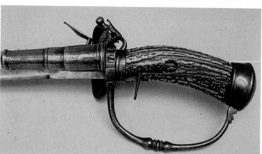

Pikeman's Helmet ▲

- *early 17th century*
English steel pikeman's helmet.
- *44cm x 24cm*
- £2,750 • Ian Roper

Knife Pistol ▲

- *circa 1859*
Unwin & Rogers curiousa knife
pistol featuring nickel barrel with
Birmingham proof marks, horn
side panels, folding trigger, bullet
mould and tweezers.
- *length 17cm*
- £950 • M. German

Sword Pistol ▲

- *circa 1720*
Flintlock sword-pistol with top
serrated blade, two stage cannon-
style barrel on left of hilt, all steel
hilt with the shell guard chiselled
with a lion type animal, and
staghorn grip.
- *length 70cm*
- £3,400 • M. German

Pair of Flintlock Pistols ▶

- *circa 1880*
Pocket flintlock belt pistols by
Sharpe of London fitted with
belthooks, folding triggers,
checkered butts, and top sliding
safeties.
- *length 20cm*
- £2,200 • M. German

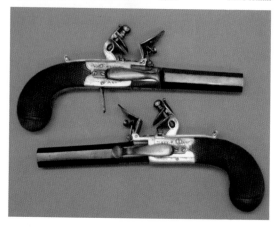

Automobilia

Motor racing and rallies are as popular today as they have ever been along with the collecting of automobile memorabilia.

Since a car is one of the most expensive purchases that people make, there is a great deal of ancillary material, from models, clocks, lights and hub caps, to commemorative badges, posters, paintings and photographs. They all have their collectors and so, they all have a price.

Most automobilia is based around clubs, racetracks and personalities. For example, any memorabilia relating to the Brooklands and Monte Carlo racetracks or the Morgan, Aston Martin and MG car clubs is highly collectable. Collectors are often prepared to pay high prices for a certain badge or mascot to add to their collection.

A huge industry has sprung up around the classic car and for avid colllectors the auto sales held around the country provide an opportunity to acquire prized items such as racing programmes, garage signs, car parts or archival photography. While a vintage car may be too expensive for most people, memorabilia is affordable.

S.A.M.T.C. Lion Badge ▶

- *circa 1960*
S.A.M.T.C. white badge with enamelled crown and badge with rampant lion.
- *14cm x 12cm*
- £65
- Legacy

Eagle Insignia Car Mascot ▼

- *circa 1960*
Square black and white Car Recovery Service Club badge with eagle insignia.
- *height 14cm*
- £8
- Legacy

Chrome Lady Car Mascot ▼

- *circa 1960*
Chrome flying lady mascot for car.
- *height 14cm*
- £120
- Legacy

R.A.C. Key ▼
- *circa 1960*
Metal key, property of the Royal
Automobile Club, London, SW1.
- *height 7cm*
- **£6.50**   Legacy

Lines Bros. Car ▲
- *1930s*
Morris-type open roadster, pressed
steel with folding windscreen,
period running boards and
opening driver's door.
- *40cm x 90cm*
- **£1,750**   • C.A.R.S.

A.A. Badge ▲
- *circa 1960*
Automobile Association metal
badge with yellow ochre
background.
- *11cm x 10cm*
- **£22**   • Legacy

Horn-Playing Satyr Car Mascot ◄
- *1960s*
A rude devil cocking-a-snook car
mascot for rear mounting.
Chromed brass by Desmo.
- *length 12cm*
- **£150**   • C.A.R.S.

A.A. key ▲
- *circa 1970*
Metal A. A. key.
- *height 7cm*
- **£4**   • Legacy

Word Wildlife Fun Panda Car Mascot ►
- *circa 1960*
World Wildlife Fund badge with a
panda on a bottle green
background being held by a pair
of hands.
- *height 14cm*
- **£25**   • Legacy

Bentley Mascot ▼
- **1950s**

Bentley flying winged B radiator mounted mascot, designed by Charles Sykes. This example is post World War II and is shown to be leaning forward. Cast brass, chronuim plated.
- *height 7cm*
- £250   • C.A.R.S

Bentley Mascot ▼
- **1920s**

Bentley flying winged B radiator mounted mascot designed by Charles Sykes. This example is from the 1920s roadster sports model and is a large brass-casting used for a short period.
- *wing span 22cm*
- £400   • C.A.R.S

Bentley Winged B ▶
- **1960–80**

Bentley winged B radiator shell badge, pressed steel, chrome-plated with enamel central black B label.
- *height 14.5cm*
- £100   • C.A.R.S

B.A.R.C. Badge ▲
- **1930s**

Brooklands Automobile Racing Club membership badge issued during the inter-war period up until the closure of the circuit in 1939. Die struck brass, chrome plated and vitreous coloured enamels. Produced by Spencer, London. Usually with members issue No. stamped on the reverse.
- *height 14cm*
- £400   • C.A.R.S

Brighton & Hove Motor Club Badge ▲
- **2001**

Brighton & Hove Motor Club badge of the present day, cut brass, chrome and plastic-based enamel colours.
- *diameter 6cm*
- £20   • C.A.R.S

Bentley B ▼
- **1940s**

Bentley flying winged B radiator mounted mascot, designed by Charles Sykes. This example is shown to be leaning backward. Cast brass, chronuim-plated.
- *wing span 17cm*
- £300   • C.A.R.S

Bentley Flying B ▼
- **1920**

Bentley flying winged B radiator mounted mascot designed by Charles Sykes.
- *height 17cm*
- £300   • C.A.R.S

J.C.C. Badge ▼
- **1960–70**

The Junior Car Club existed to cater for light cars and motorcycles including Morgan type three wheelers. Membership badge in die struck brass, nickel or chrome-plated with vitreous enamel colours.
- *height 14cm*
- £200   • C.A.R.S

Morgan Pedal Car ▼
- *1980s*

Morgan Roadster made by The Morgan Model Co. in moulded fibreglass with vinyl seat and dropdown windscreen.
- *35cm x 95cm*
- £950   • C.A.R.S.

Brookland's Junior Racing Drivers' Club Badge ▼
- *1930s*

Brookland's Junior Car Club badge for the Junior Racing Drivers' Club. Multi-coloured vitreous enamels on chromed shield.
- *height 12cm*
- £1,500   • C.A.R.S.

Bugatti Racing Car ▲
- *1990s*

Bugatti type 35 Grand Prix racing car replica produced by Elantec-Eureka. Aluminium body, working gearshift and handbrake levers and authentic dashboard.
- *50cm x 125cm*
- £2,750   • C.A.R.S.

Brookland's Entry Pass Badges ▲
- *1912*

Brass and enamel Brookland's annual entry pass badges for members (large central badge) and guests pair of brooches in original box of issue.
- *10cm x 4cm*
- £250   • C.A.R.S.

Pressed Steel Pedal Car ▼
- *1960s*

A Ford style saloon, made by Tri-Ang Toys Ltd, marketed as a "Lightning".
- *30cm x 90cm*
- £125   • C.A.R.S.

Austin Pathfinder Pedal Car ▼
- *circa 1949*

Pressed steel monocoque body with vinyl upholstered seat. Has dummy engine under removable bonnet and perspex windscreen.
- *40cm x 1.1m*
- £2,500   • C.A.R.S.

Brookland's Automobile Racing Club Badge ▼
- *1921*

Brookland's Automobile Racing Club Badge in original box, membership number stamped on reverse, brass and red enamel.
- *10cm x 4cm*
- £250   • C.A.R.S.

Books, Maps & Atlases

The binding of a book can considerably add to its appeal and in some cases can be more fascinating than the words contained within.

Books have long been regarded as collectable items, as well as tools for education and entertainment. Although the printing press was introduced just 500 years ago, the first real books appeared shortly after the fall of the Roman empire.

In the 1600s, booksellers at St Paul's Churchyard expected clients to read the latest books unbound before they ordered a copy bound to their taste. Once bound, these books were rarely read, so pristine condition tends to be the norm for that period.

The binding leathers used on a volume give you some idea of its age. Medieval deer or sheepskin editions are very rare; calf with blocked and tooled binding predominated in the sixteenth century when vellum became popular for undecorated books; and goatskin enjoyed a brief popularity in the 1650s.

Today's collector on a budget should try to predict the next bestseller. Failing that, always buy first editions, keep them in mint condition and, if possible, secure the author's signature.

Prisoner of Azkaban ▶

- 1998

Harry Potter and The Prisoner of Azkaban signed by the author J.K. Rowling. First issue published by Bloomsbury.
- *19cm x 13cm*
- **£7,500**   • A. Harrington

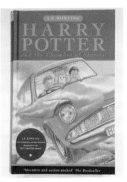

Chamber of Secrets ▲

- 1998

Harry Potter and The Chamber of Secrets signed by the author J.K. Rowling. First published in Great Britain in 1998 by Bloomsbury, London.
- *19cm x 13cm*
- **£2,100**   • A. Harrington

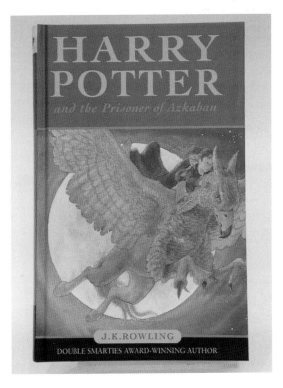

Rebellion and Civil Wars ▼
● *1712*
The History of the Rebellion and Civil Wars in England, begun in the year 1641. Oxford: printed at the Theatre. A very good early edition of Clarendon. Clarendon was Chancellor to both Charles I and Charles II. Panelled calf, banded and ruled in gilt.
● £495   ● Ash Books

Dream Days ▼
● *1899*
Dream Days by Kenneth Graham, New York & London.
● £100   ● Ash Books

The Noh Plays of Japan ▼
● *1922*
The Noh Plays of Japan by Arthur Waley. New York: Alfred A. Knopf. First American edition. Translations of the most celebrated Noh plays. Eight plates of masks. Original linen-backed boards.
● £125   ● Ash Books

Complete English Traveller ▲
● *1771–1773*
The Complete English Traveller by Robert Sanders and Nathaniel Spencer. London: J. Cooke. First edition. A handsome and well illustrated folio containing sixty plates that offer a general survey of the whole of Great Britain.
● £950   ● Ash Books

A Treatise on Money ▲
● *1930*
A Treatise on Money by John Maynard. New York: Harcourt, Brace & Co. First edition: the American issue of the London sheets. Two volumes. Demy 8vo.
● £350   ● Ash Books

The Fortune of War ▼
● *1979*
The Fortune of War, Patrick O'Brian. London: William Collins Sons & Co. First edition. The sixth of the Jack Aubrey and Stephen Maturin novels.
● £400   ● Ash Books

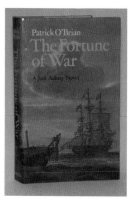

Maitland's History of London ▼
● *1756*
Maitland's History of London, Vol I & II. London: for T. Osborn & J. Shipton and J. Hodges. Second edition. Originally published in one volume in 1739. Five general maps (two folding), 19 maps of wards and parishes (five folding); views of over 60 principal buildings on 42 plates (three folding), and over 80 churches.
● £2,950   ● Ash Books

The Life of Count de Grammont ▲

• *18th century*
Memoirs of the Life of Count de Grammont, containing, in particular, the amorous intrigues of the court of England in the reign of King Charles II. Printed: London and sold by J. Round, W. Taylor and J. Brown, 1714.
• £350 • Ash Books

Malay Sketches ▲

• *1896*
Malay Sketches by Sir Frank Athelstane Swettenham, the distinguished colonial administrator and linguist. London: John Lane. Second edition (i.e. impression) of the original 1895 publication.
• £50 • Ash Books

Orange Fairy Book ▶

• *1906*
First edition of the *Orange Fairy Book* by Andrew Lang. Published in 1906.
• £300 • Ash Books

Prehistoric Man ▼

• *1862*
Prehistoric Man by Sir Daniel Wilston. Cambridge: Macmillan & Co. First edition. Extensive researches into the origin of civilisation in the old and the new world. Colour frontispiece. Map bound without half-titles, in a handsome half roan.
• £250 • Ash Books

Antiquities of Surrey ▼

• *1736*
Antiquities of Surrey by Nathanael Salmon. London: for the Author. First edition; mottled calf expertly re-backed and refurnished, banded and gilt.
• £300 • Ash Books

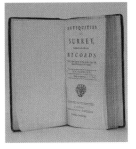

Grimm's Household Tales ▲

• *1946*
Grimm's Household Tales by Brothers Grimm (Jacob Ludwig & Wilhelm Carl). London: Eyre & Spottiswode. Bound in a later full morocco, banded and gilt; all edges gilt.
• £250 • Ash Books

Shakespeare ▲

• *1925–32*
The Tragedies, Comedies and Histories of Shakespeare. London. Oxford University Press. A prettily bound set of the three separately published volumes of the Oxford India-paper edition. Edited by W. J. Craig with a full glossary.
• £250 • Ash Books

Casino Royale ▶

- **1953**

Casino Royale, author Ian Fleming published by Jonathon Cape, Bedford Square, London. First edition, second issue.
- *19cm x 13cm*
- **£2,950**   • A. Harrington

Thunderball ▲

- **1961**

Thunderball by Ian Fleming. First published by Glidrose Publications.
- *19cm x 13cm*
- **£550**   • A. Harrington

A Christmas Carol ▶

- **1915**

A Christmas Carol by Charles Dickens, illustrated by Arthur Rackam and published by William Henemahn, London.
- *19cm x 12cm*
- **£1,450**   • A. Harrington

The Saint ◀

- **1961**

The Saint to the Rescue by Leslie Charters, published by Hodder and Stoughton London and printed by G. Bertram.
- *19cm x 13cm*
- **£220**   • A. Harrington

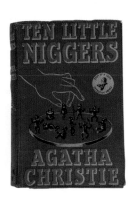

Ten Little Niggers ▲

- **1939**

Ten Little Niggers by Agatha Christie. First edition, published for the Crime Club by Collins, Pall Mall, London.
- *19cm x 13cm*
- **£6,500**   • A. Harrington

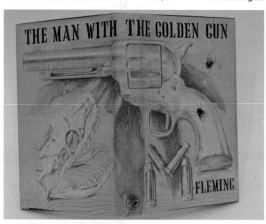

The Man with the Golden Gun ▲

- **1965**

The Man with the Golden Gun by Ian Fleming, "The new James Bond". Printed in Great Britain by Richard Cay. The Chaucer Press, Jonathon Cape.
- *19cm x 13cm*
- **£150**   • A. Harrington

Expert Tips

With old books and maps look out for foxing, or orange stains, because these types of blemishes can be expensive to remove.

Peer Gynt ▶

- **1920**

Peer Gynt, first Rackam edition, published by George G. Harrap & Co. Ltd., illustrated by Arthur Rackam.
- 27cm x 20cm
- **£245**   • A. Harrington

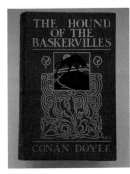

The Hound of the Baskervilles ▲

- **1902**

The Hound of the Baskervilles, a Sherlock Holmes adventure by A. Conan Doyle, published George Newnes London.
- 19cm x 14cm
- **£2,500**   • A. Harrington

Tour of the Seine ▲

- **1829**

Picturesque Tour of the Seine by Jean Baptiste Balthazar. Illustrated with 24 highly finished and coloured engravings and drawings by A. Pugin and J. Gendall. With a map by R. Ackerman, London 1821. Fine contemporary binding of Blake straight grained Morocco gilt titles and in-filled box design to spine. Raised bands and elaborate gilt border.
- 34cm x 28cm
- **£4,250**   • A. Harrington

Charles Dickens ▼

- **1906**

The Works, Letters, and Life of Charles Dickens with plates by illustrators Cruickshank Leech & co., London. The National Edition in 40 vol. Chapman and Hall Ltd., 1906-8 with a signed manuscript and letter addressed to Dr. Hudson in superb contemporary binding by Birsall Morocco with raised bands, gilt titles to spines top edged gilt. The Dr. Hudson to whom Dickens' letter is addressed is presumably Fredrick Hudson, surgeon of Manchester. With regard to the arrangement for the performance of *The Frozen Deep*, the play he wrote with Wilke Collins.
- 18cm x 13cm
- **£8,500**   • A. Harrington

Marine Dictionary ▶

- **1815**

A set of five volumes of a marine dictionary explaining the technical terms and phrases with astronomy, navigation, French sea-phrases and terms. Compiled by William Falconer, this volume had been modernised by William Burnery. Printed for T. Cadell & W. Davies in the Strand.
- 20cm x 28cm
- **£1,450**   • A. Harrington

Treasure Island ▼

- **1890**

Second illustrated edition of *Treasure Island* by Robert Louis Stevenson with original illustration by W.A. Page. Published by Cassell and Co. Ltd., London, Paris, New York, and Melbourne.
- 19cm x 14cm
- **£475**   • A. Harrington

Harry Potter Set ▼
- 1997–2000

An extremely scarce set of first editions of the *Harry Potter* series by J.K. Rowling, which includes: *The Philosopher's Stone*, *The Chamber of Secrets*, *The Prisoner of Azkaban* and *The Goblet of Fire*. Published by Bloomsbury, London. All signed.
- *20cm x 13cm*
- £27,500   • Peter Harrington

The Cat in the Hat ▼
- 1957

First edition of *The Cat in the Hat* by Dr. Seuss. Original pictorial paper covered boards complete with dust wrapper. Illustrated throughout by the author.
- *29cm x 21cm*
- £8,500   • Peter Harrington

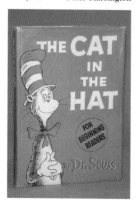

Peter Rabbit ▶
- 1902

The Tale of Peter Rabbit by Beatrix Potter. First edition, and first issue of the flat spine.
- *14cm x 10cm*
- £50,000   • Peter Harrington

Three Guineas ▲
- 1938

First edition of *Three Guineas* by Virginia Woolf. Published by The Hogarth Press, London. Pale yellow cloth, gilt titles to spine, complete with dust wrapper. Illustrated with photographic plates.
- *18cm x 12cm*
- £500   • Peter Harrington

Lady Chatterley's Lover ▲
- 1932

First authorised UK edition of *Lady Chatterley's Lover* by D.H. Lawrence. Publisher's brown cloth with gilt title to spine. Complete with dust wrapper. Published by Martin Secker, London.
- *19cm x 12.4cm*
- £450   • Peter Harrington

Little Lord Fauntleroy ▼
- 1886

First UK edition of *Little Lord Fauntleroy* by Francis Hodgson Burnett. London: Frederick, Warne and Co. With 26 illustrations after Reginald B. Birch.
- *22cm x 14.5cm*
- £210   • Peter Harrington

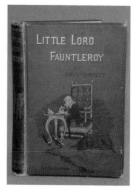

The Hound of Death and Other Stories ▼
- 1933

The Hound of Death and Other Stories by Agatha Christie. First edition. Published by Odhams Press Limited, London.
- *18.5cm x 13cm*
- £350   • Peter Harrington

Expert Tips

Most paper items are susceptible to damage from ultraviolet (UV) and visible light. If UV is present it should be eliminated using filters over windows and bulbs.

Map of Huntingdonshire ▲

- **1645**

Map of Huntingdonshire by J. Willem Blaeu with the inscription, "Hvntingdo-Nensis Comitatvs, Huntington-shire". Published in Amsterdam. Decorated with a ribanded display of coats or arms, the Stuart Royal Arms, and a hunters and hounds title-piece, with stags, falcon, boar, hare and rabbit. Originally produced by Blaeu in 1645.

- **£350**   • **Ash Books**

City of London, Westminster and Southwark ▼

- **1720**

A New Plan Of The City Of London, Westminster And Southwark. Published in London: in 1720. Originally produced to accompany John Strype's revised edition of John Stow's 'Survey of London'. The map is dedicated to Sir George Thorold, Lord Mayor in 1719-1720.

- 48.5cm x 66cm
- **£950**   • **Ash Books**

Map of Northumberland ▼

- **1645**

Map Of Northumberland by J. Willem Blaeu, entitled, "Comitatvs Northvmbria; Vernacule Northumberland" and produced in Amsterdam in1645. Decorated with shields, the Royal Arms, a draped title-piece, ships, cherubs, and a scale-bar showing a 17th-century surveyor at work. Copper line engraving on paper. Full contemporary hand colour.

- 41cm x 49cm
- **£350**   • **Ash Books**

Map of Lothian ◄

- **circa 1500s**

A map depicting the area of Lothian in Scotland, by the Dutch cartographer Joannes Janssonius, 1646, Amsterdam. A fine example of this well-known map of the Edinburgh region.

- 36.5 cm 54cm
- **£400**   • **Ash Books**

Binding Fit for a King ▼

- **1620–1630**

Extremely rare Renaissance gold binding, jewelled and enamelled. Possibly made for King Christian IV of Denmark. Enamelled with a design of different flowers, and a central plaque with the nativity, and decorated with 52 diamonds.

- 9.1cm x 6.4cm
- **£85,000**   • **Bernard Shapero**

Map of the Orkney & Shetland Isles ▲

- **1654**

Map of the Orkney and Shetland Isles by Willem Janszoon Blaeu, Amsterdam, 1645. With the inscription, "Oradvm Et SchetandiE Insvlarvm Accuatissima Descriptio". The maps are finely decorated.

- 40.5cm x 53cm
- **£350**   • **Ash Books**

London ▲

- **1673**

An early map of London by Wenceslas Hollar, with the coat of arms of the City of London, 15 of the great Livery and Merchant Companies and those of Sir Robert Vyner of Viner.

- **£400**   • **Ash Books**

Expert Tips

Ensure your hands are clean and dry before handling paper items, as oily skin can cause staining on paper.

Map of Essex ▲

- **1636**

The rare first issue of the
Janssonius map showing Essex,
entitled,"Essexi Descriptio. The
Description Of Essex". First
published in Amsterdam,
Holland, by the Dutch master
Janssonius (1588–1664) in the
"Atlas Appendix" of 1636. With
copper line engravings on paper.
In full contemporary hand colour.

- *38cm x 49cm*
- **£550** • Ash Books

Map of Norfolk ▼

- *circa 1646*

A fine seventeenth century map
of the county of Norfolk,
England, from the Dutch master
Joannes Janssonius (1588–1664).
The map is highly decorated with
a pastoral cartouche, shields,
putti, sailing ships and a sea
monster. This was originally
produced for the "inovus atlas..."
(Amsterdam 1646).

- *38cm x 49cm*
- **£395** • Ash Books

Map of Scotland ▼

- **1630s**

A decorative map of Scotland by
the Dutch cartographer
Janssonius entitled, "Scotia
Regnvm, Amsterdam" and dated
1636. This map was originally
produced for the "Janssonius
Atlas Appendix" of 1636. It is
decorated with the royal arms,
sailing ships, and a cartouche
featuring unicorns, sheep and
thistles.

- *38cm x 49.5cm*
- **£495** • Ash Books

Seutter British Isles ◀

- *18th century*

Original hand-coloured map of
the British Isles by Matthaeus
Seutter. A scarce antique map of
the British Isles, with an elegant
military lion and unicorn
cartouche. In another corner an
angel with a trumpet bears aloft
the arms of the four nations, and
sailing ships off the coast.
Originally engraved by Tobias
Conrad Lotter (1717–1777) for
Seutter's Atlas Minor in the
1740s.

- **£250** • Ash Books

Map of Somerset ▲

- **1630s**

An amorial map of the county of
Somerset, in England by
Janssonius entitled "Somerset-
Tensis Comitatvs Somerset
Shire". Amsterdam: G.Valk & P.
Schenk, 1636. This was first
published by Janssonius (1588-
1664).The map appears here in
its final form, with the addition of
grid lines to the original
Janssonius image.

- *37.5cm x 49cm*
- **£395** • Ash Books

Merian Map of the British Isles ▼

- *mid 17th century*

Map of the British Isles from
Mathaus Merian the Elder
(1593–1650). With a baroque
title piece draped in cornucopia,
the Royal Arms and sailing ships.
Originally produced for the
"Neuwe Archontolgia Cosmica"
(Frankfurt 1638) and here in a
later issue, with Merian's name
removed.

- **£400** • Ash Books

Our Mutual Friend ▼

- *1860*

Our Mutual Friend by Charles Dickens with illustrations by Marcus Stone, published by Chapman & Hall, Piccadilly. Eighteen copies in original condition in two boxes, a further two boxes available.
- *22cm x 19cm*
- **£1,250** • A. Harrington

Second Edition Cook's Voyage ▼

- *1823*

Atlas Volume of *Cooks Voyage*, part of the Earl of Harewoods volume of *Discoveries of the Southern Hemisphere*, illustrating a Lady from Otahiete.
- *57cm x 43cm*
- **£6,000** • A. Harrington

Führer fur Pilzfreunde ▶

- *1897*

Führer fur Pilzfreunde by Edmund Michael, a book on mushrooms with 68 coloured illustrations.
- *20cm x 12cm*
- **£275** • A. Harrington

Polar Seas ▲

- *1823*

Franklin's *Journey to the Polar Seas* by John Franklin Captain R.N. FRS. and Commander of the expedition, including an account of the progress of a detachment to the eastward by John Richardson. MD. FRS. FCS. and surgeon and naturalist to the expedition illustrated with plates and maps. Published by authority of the Right Honourable secretary of State for Colonial Affairs John Murray, London, printed by William Clowes.
- *29cm x 23cm*
- **£6,250** • A. Harrington

Journey through Bootan ▲

- *1806*

A very rare second edition of *A Narrative of a Journey through Bootan, and part of Tibet*, by Samuel Turner with added views by Lieutenant Samuel Davis consisting of 13 folded plates, and one folding map.
- *30cm x 24cm*
- **£1,450** • A. Harrington

African Game Trails ▲

- *1910*

African Game Trails an account of the African wandering of an American hunter-naturalist by Theodore Roosevelt, published by Charles Scribner & Sons, New York. With photographs and foreword by T. Roosevelt, Kartoum, March 15th, 1910.
- *28cm x 20cm*
- **£425** • A. Harrington

First Edition Cook's Voyage ▲

- *1823*

First edition of *Cook's Voyage*, from the *Discoveries in the Southern Hemisphere*, compiled from the journal which was kept by the Commander and from the papers of Joshua Banks ESQ. Printed by W. Stahan and T. Cadell, London.
- *30cm x 23cm*
- **£6,000** • A. Harrington

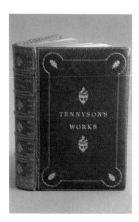

Tennyson's Works ▲

- *1882*

Tennyson's Works published in London by Kegan Paul. Finely bound by Sangorski & Sutcliffe in full-green morocco, spine faded to antique brown, gilt title and decoration to spine. With a fore-edge painting showing "The Lady of Shalott" after William Holman Hunt, and a portrait of Tennyson.
- *18cm x 13cm*
- £350   • Peter Harrington

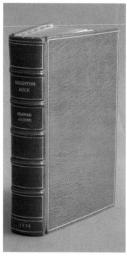

Brighton Rock ▲

- *1938*

First edition of *Brighton Rock* by Graham Greene, published by William Heinemann Ltd London, bound by the Chelsea Bindery.
- *18.5cm x 13cm*
- £950   • Peter Harrington

The Poetical Works of Percy Bysshe Shelley ▼

- *1908*

The Poetical Works of Percy Bysshe Shelley. Macmillan and Co., Limited London. Bound by Riviere in full tree calf, and gilt lettered green morocco label and gilt decoration to spine with marbled end papers, all edges gilded.
- *18cm x 12cm*
- £475   • Peter Harrington

La Reine des Neiges ▼

- *1911*

Hans Christian Andersen, *La Reine des Neiges et Quelques Autres Contes.* Illustration by Edmund Dulac. Publishers decorated vellum, with 29 full colour illustrations by Edmund Dulac. Published by H. Piazza. Paris.
- *20.5cm x 24cm*
- £850   • Peter Harrington

Kew Gardens ▶

- *1919*

Kew Gardens by Virginia Woolf with woodcuts by Vanessa Bell. There were only 150 copies made and Virginia Woolf set the type.
- *23cm x 14cm*
- £18,000   • Peter Harrington

The Tempest ▲

- *1926*

Deluxe edition of Shakespeare's *The Tempest*, illustrated by Arthur Rackham. Published by William Heinemann Ltd. London. Limited to 520 copies of which this is No. 128. Signed by Rackham.
- *32cm x 26cm*
- £3,250   • Peter Harrington

The Kingdom of the Pearl ▲

- *1920*

The Kingdom of the Pearl by Leonard Rosenthal, illustrated by Edmund Dulac. Limited edition of 675 copies of which this is No. 67. Published by Nisbet & Co. London, with ten captioned tissue-pasted colour illustrations.
- *30cm x 24cm*
- £600   • Peter Harrington

Arabian Horse ▶

- **1914**
*The Arabian Horse His Country
and People* by Major General W.
Tweedies. C.S.I. with fine
coloured illustrations published
by William Blakwood and sons,
Edinburgh and London bound in
green leather.
- *31cm x 25cm*
- **£1,800** • **A. Harrington**

Hunting with Eskimos ▲

- **1911**
Hunting with the Eskimos by Harry
Whitney, a unique record of a
sportsman's year among the
northernmost tribe. Illustrated
with photographs, published by
The Century Co., New York.
- *19cm x 15cm*
- **£75** • **A. Harrington**

The Compleat Angler ▼

- **1866**
*The Compleat Angler or The
Contemplative Man's Recreation* by
Charles Cotton and Isaac
Walton, published by Henry G.
Bolton, Covent Garden, London.
Bound in green leather.
- *11cm x 19cm*
- **£175** • **A. Harrington**

Fishing Stories ◀

- **1913**
First edition of *A Book of Fishing
Stories* by F .G. Aflaco. Published
by JM Dent and Sons Ltd.,
Aldine House, Covent Garden
and E.P. Dutton & Co., New York
- *30cm x 23cm*
- **£375** • **A. Harrington**

Our Native Songsters ▼

- **1804**
Our Native Songsters by Anne
Pratt, author of *Wild Flowers*,
published in Brighton, New York
by E. and JB Young and Co.
- *6cm x 12cm*
- **£95** • **A. Harrington**

Mr. Punch on the Links ▼

- **1929**
Mr. Punch on the Links by
E.V. Knox consisting of 8
volumes with 32 illustrations,
numerous golf anecdotes, and
green cloth cover. Published
in New York, Rue D Hendle
Co. Inc.
- *23cm x 17cm*
- **£245** • **A. Harrington**

Fruits from the Garden ◀

- **1850**
Fruits from the Garden and Field
beautifully illustrated and bound
in original tan leather with
embossed foliate design.
- *18cm x 14cm*
- **£225** • **A. Harrington**

Uncle Tom's Cabin ▼

- 1852

Uncle Tom's Cabin or *Life Among the Lowly* by Harriet Beecher Stowe. Boston, John P. Jewett & Company. First edition. Two volumes finely bound by Bayntun-Riviere.

- *height 18cm*
- £3,500   • Peter Harrington

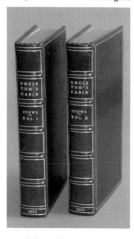

Letters by Mary Wollstonecraft ▼

- 1796

The first account of a business trip made by a woman, Mary Wollstonecraft, written during her short residence in Sweden, Norway and Denmark. Published by J.J. Johnston, St. Paul's Churchyard, London. First edition bound in full tan calf, with gilt lettered and a burgundy label.

- *height 21.5cm*
- £1,250   • Peter Harrington

Gerard Mercator Atlas ▲

- 1632

Gerardi Mercatoris Atlas sive Cosmographicae Meditatones. Amsterdam, Johann Cloppenburg, with fine hand-coloured copperplate "architectural" title and 179 fine recent hand-coloured copperplate maps.

- *22cm x 28cm*
- £27,500   • Peter Harrington

Decline and Fall of the Roman Empire ▲

- 1777

Six volumes of *The History of the Decline and Fall of the Roman Empire*, by Edward Gibbon published London, printed for W. Strahan and T. Cadell. Six volumes four, five and six are first editions. With author's frontis portrait in volume one.

- *height 29cm*
- £3,500   • Peter Harrington

Blackstone Commentaries ▼

- 1765–1769

Blackstone Commentaries by Sir William Blackstone. A rare first edition. With the engraved "Table of Consanguinity" and the "Table of Descents" in Vol II. The date is stamped in black at the base of each spine.

- *28cm x 22cm*
- £9,750   • Peter Harrington

Gone with the Wind ▼

- 1936

Gone with the Wind by Margaret Mitchell. First edition. Macmillan Company, New York. Original publisher's grey cloth, complete with dust wrapper.

- *height 22cm*
- £3,950   • Peter Harrington

Winnie the Pooh ◀

- 1926

Limited to 1/350 *Winnie the Pooh* by A.A. Milne, with wonderful onlaid binding, and decorations by Ernest H. Shephard. Methuen & Co. London, numbered copies, signed by Milne and Shephard.

- *23cm x 17cm*
- £8,500   • Peter Harrington

Natural Order of Plants ▶
- **1868**
One of two volumes of *The Illustrations of the Natural Order of Plants* by E. Twinning with 160 colour plates, published by Sampson Low & Son, Maston.
- *25cm x 17cm*
- **£850** • A. Harrington

Rubaiyat ▲
- **1922**
First edition of the *Rubaiyat of Omar Khayyam*. English verse by Edward Fitzgerald with illustrations by Fish. Published by John Lane, London. Plates by Geo. Givvons & Co., Leicester.
- *29cm x 23cm*
- **£60** • A. Harrington

Fragonard ▲
- **1906**
Fragonard, a limited edition of 500 copies with good quality sepia illustrations by Pierre de Nothac Groupil & Co. Editors Manz Joyant & Co. Bound with original red leather.
- *33cm x 28cm*
- **£550** • A. Harrington

Archery ▼
- **1926**
Archery by Robert P. Elms former champion archer of the United States. Published by The Penn Publishing Co., Philadelphia.
- *18cm x 14cm*
- **£95** • A. Harrington

Brazilian Wilderness ▼
- **1914**
Through the Brazilian Wilderness by Theodore Roosevelt, published by Charles Scribner's and Sons, 332 illustrations and map of the entire South American journey and River of Doubt.
- *28cm x 10cm*
- **£495** • A. Harrington

Tess of the D'urbervilles ▼
- **1890**
First edition of *Tess of the D'urbervilles: A Pure Woman* by Thomas Hardy in three volumes. By James R. Oswool McIlvaine & Co., London.
- *18cm x 12cm*
- **£3,700** • A. Harrington

Constant Gardener ◀
- **2001**
The Constant Gardener signed first edition by John Le Carre. Published by Hodder and Stoughton, London.
- *25cm x 18cm*
- **£85** • A. Harrington

Don Quixote ▼
- **1920**

Don Quixote de le Mancha by Cervantes with 206 illustrations by Sir John Gilbert R.A. in original hand back cover. Published by G. Routledge & Sons Ltd., New York, E. P. Dutton & Co.
- *21cm x 18cm*
- **£45**   • A. Harrington

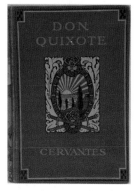

The Hobbit ▶
- **1951**

First edition of *The Hobbit or There and Back Again* by J.R.R. Tolkien illustrated by Aland Lee, published by Harper Collins.
- *26cm x 20cm*
- **£150**   • A. Harrington

Spaniard in the Works ▲
- **1965**

A Spaniard in the Works, First edition by the singer songwriter John Lennon, published by Jonathan Cape, London.
- *14cm x 10cm*
- **£140**   • A. Harrington

Tarantula ▶
- **1966**

First edition of *Tarantula* by the singer and songwriter Bob Dylan.
- *18cm x 12cm*
- **£75**   • A. Harrington

Jane Eyre ▼
- **1847**

First edition of a set of three leather-bound volumes of *Jane Eyre: An Autobiography*, published by Smith Eder & co. Cornhill London.
- *20cm x 12cm*
- **£2,500**   • A. Harrington

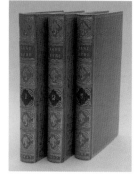

Old French Fairy Tales ◀
- **1920**

Old French Fairy Tales by Comtesse de Segar illustrated by Virginia Frances Sterrett, published in Philadelphia by Penn Publishing Co.
- *30cm x 26cm*
- **£650**   • A. Harrington

George and the Dragon ▲
- **1951**

Manifeste Mystique a pen and ink drawing within a book of *George and the Dragon*, together with original etching from a drawing of the famous Christ of St. John on the Cross, signed and dated by Salvador Dali.
- *40cm x 27cm*
- **£15,000**   • A. Harrington

The Lion, the Witch and the Wardrobe ▲

● *1950*
The Lion, the Witch and the Wardrobe by C.S. Lewis. First edition. Illustrations and colour frontispiece by Pauline Baynes. The first and best known of the Narnia chronicles. Post 8vo. Bound in an elegant recent green quarter-morocco, banded and gilt. Published by Geoffrey Bles.
● £850　　　● Ash Books

Cooke's View of the Thames ▲

● *circa 1811*
Views of the Thames, from the Source to the Sea by Samuel Owen and William Bernard Cooke. London: by W. B. Cooke. Eighty-four tissue guarded etched plates. Contemporary full morocco, all edges gilt.
● £750　　　● Ash Books

Expert Tips

When purchasing an illustrated book, make sure that you check that it still contains all the original plates, because if one is missing it could seriously devalue the item.

The Greater London ▼

● *circa 1884*
The Greater London: A Narrative of its History, its People, and its Places by Edward Walford. London: Cassell & Co. Heavily illustrated with 400 wood engravings. Two volumes Crown 4to. Original decorative cloth. gilt.
● £195　　　● Ash Books

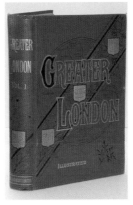

History of Lace ▼

● *1900*
A History of Hand-Made Lace by Emily Jackson. Dealing with the origin of lace, the growth of the great lace centres. Published by Upcott Gill. First edition. Plates and numerous illustrations. Original decorative cloth gilt in an eye-catching lace and cobweb design.
● £185　　　● Ash Books

Sea Kings of Crete ▶

● *1910*
The Sea Kings of Crete by James Baikie. Publishers: Adam & Charles Black, London. First edition. Plates. Maps. Original decorative cloth, top edge gilt.
● £75　　　● Ash Books

Alone ▲

● *1938*
Alone by Richard E. Byrd. Published by Putnam, London. First British edition. Admiral Byrd's harrowing account of his Antarctic sojourn. Decorations by Richard E. Harrison. Demy 8vo.
● £60　　　● Ash Books

Brighton Rock ▲

● *1938*
Brighton Rock by Graham Greene. First edition. Crown 8vo. Bound in a striking full crimson morocco, banded and extra gilt by Bayntun-Riviere. All edges in gilt. Published by William Heinemann.
● £850　　　● Ash Books

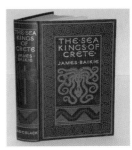

Carpets & Rugs

European needlework carpets of the nineteenth century have become an interesting area for the collector.

Carpets and rugs have a long history, with the oldest surviving pile-knotted rug dating back two-and-half thousand years ago in Siberia. By the Dark Ages, rug-weaving industries had flourished in Egypt, Baghdad, Damascus, Aleppo, and China, but it was not until the seventeenth century that Oriental rugs became

popular in European households and were collected and imported. There are few reliable guidelines in this area and success depends greatly on experience and a good eye. However, collectable carpets and rugs are not as expensive as most expect and there are many opportunities to attain woven masterpieces at very reasonable prices.

Persian Jozan Rug ▼
- *circa 1890*
A rare Persian Jozan rug in perfect condition decorated with deer and an angular floral design in ochre, red, blue, green and black.
- *137cm x 204cm*
- £4,500　　　　• Oriental

Expert Tips

Carpets are a great way to fill large expanses of wall space. Remember, moths love a good carpet so keep them well sprayed with anti-moth repellant.

Baluchi Carpet ▲
- *1860*
Section of a Baluchi carpet from Baluchistan.
- *length 280cm*
- £2,800　　　　• David Black

Bakhtiari Rug ▼
- *circa 1940*
Bakhtiari rugs woven by nomads and villagers of Luri, Kurdish and other ethnic origins from the Chahar Mahal region of Iran. Featuring a medallion design.
- *140cm x 228cm*
- £2,300　　　　• Oriental

French Panel ◄
- *circa 1760–1780*
French needlepoint panel with central figured cartouche in petit point.
- *51cm square*
- £1,950　　　　• Classic Fabrics

Indian Durrie

- *circa 1880*

Indian cotton durrie made by prisoners in the North Indian gaols. Dyed with indigo and turmeric.
- *length 203cm*
- £740   • Gordon Reece

Melas Rug ▶

- *1880*

Melas prayer mat from Turkey, with a central design of a red mosque bordered with rosettes and stars.
- *length 125cm*
- £1,250   • David Black

Tekke Rug ▲

- *circa 1920*

Acha-Tekke are woven by the famous tribesmen from the Tekke tribe who are noted for their fine work. A geometric design in reds, cream and black.
- *20cm x 200cm*
- £1,400   • Oriental

Kashan Rug ◀

- *circa 1920*

Kashan pictorial rug with peacocks in red, blue and green design surrounding a central vase.
- *137cm x 207cm*
- £4,500   • Oriental

Kashan Medallion Rug ▲

- *circa 1920*

Kashan rug with classical elongated medallion designs in coral and dark blue and corner decorations. Extremely good example of a curvilinear Persian floral rug.
- *137cm x 207cm*
- £4,500   • Oriental

Anotonian Kilim ▲
- *1920*
Western Anotonian kilim
covering a beechwood chest.
- *50cm x 90cm*
- *£750* • Oriental

North Persian Runner ▶
- *circa 1890*
Runner from northern Persia.
- *2.5cm x 91cm*
- *£2,500* • David Black

Western Anotonian Kilim Cushion ▲
- *1920*
Western Anotonian kilim
converted into a cushion cover.
- *35cm square*
- *£45* • Oriental

Luri Gabbeh Rug ▲
- *circa 1880*
Exceptional Luri Gabbeh banded
design rug from south west Persia
with incredible use of natural
dyes contrasted by woven bands
of cotton pile.
- *length 148cm*
- *£3,250* • Gordon Reece

Sharshavan Cushion ▶
- *1920*
Cushion made from a Sharshavan
rug, which was originally part of a
cradle.
- *35cm square*
- *£65* • Oriental

Bibibaff Quajquoli ▲
- *circa 1940*
An unusual and fine example of a
Bibibaff Quajquoli.
- *80cm x 118cm*
- *£1,100* • Oriental

Karabagh Cushion ▲
- *1920*
Karabagh kilim converted into a cushion cover.
- *35cm square*
- £50 • Oriental

Luri Gabbeth Rug ▲
- *mid 20th century*
A Luri Gabbeth rug from the Zagros mountains of southern Persia. With bold design of red, blue, brown and cream, the borders with red squares and cream centres.
- *length 180cm*
- £1,450 • Gordon Reece

Turkaman Cushion ▲
- *1860*
Fragment of a Turkaman used as a cushion cover.
- *47cm square*
- £150 • David Black

Kilim Stool ▲
- *1930*
Anotonian kilim upholstered stool.
- *30cm x 40cm*
- £125 • Oriental

Turkish Yurik Runner ▲
- *1870*
A section of a Turkish Yurik runner with four hexagonal designs of blue, red, green, and gold in the centre panel, surrounded by a pink border with blue flowers.
- *length 300cm*
- £1,800 • David Black

Bakhtiari Rug ▶
- *circa 1940*
Bakhtiari rug with a glorious central medallion design in blue, green, coral and cream. The reverse of the carpet shows a very open weaving technique with wefts which may have a bluish hue.
- *127cm x 207cm*
- £490 • Oriental

Bownat Marriage Rug ▲
- *circa 1920*
Bownat marriage rug, produced by a small tribe in Southern Iran. The rug shows courting birds and the name and date in Arabic of the couple to be married. These rugs are some of the most beautiful tribal weaving produced today.
- *210cm x 293cm*
- £1,650 • Oriental

Shuli Gabbeth Rug ◀

- *early 20th century*
Shuli Gabbeh wool rug.
- *length 163cm*
- **£620**   ● Gordon Reece

Anotonian Kilim Stool ▲

- *1930*
Western Anotonian kilim
covering a stool.
- *width 65cm*
- **£240**   ● Oriental

Thracean Rug ▲

- *circa 1870*
Thracean kilim from Turkey with
geometric pattern.
- *119cm x 107cm*
- **£1,500**   ● David Black

Malayer Runner ▲

- *circa 1880*
Malayer runner made by the
Malayers who live 60 miles south
of Hamadan in West Central
Persia. The rug is decorated with
blue, red, ochre and burnt orange
vegetable dyes.
- *100cm x 490cm*
- **£2,950**   ● Oriental

Luri Jijim Rug ▲

- *20th century*
Luri Jijim rug with brown, navy,
blue and cream, woven striped
design, and navy, blue and red
binding on the edge.
- *length 283cm*
- **£990**   ● Gordon Reece

Kilim Cushion ▶

- *1870*
Fragment of a kilim from Turkey
used as a cushion cover.
- *47cm x 38cm*
- **£150**   ● David Black

Tent Trappings ▲

- *1920*
Tent trappings in red, purple,
orange and cream with red,
yellow and brown tassels.
- *height 50cm*
- **£65**   ● Oriental

Tent Trappings ▲
- *1940*

Tent trappings in red, purple, orange and cream with beaded tassels.
- *55cm x 13cm*
- £65 • Oriental

Tibetan Wool Rug ▲
- *circa 1890*

Tibetan rug of natural dyes with a red background with three circles in the centre. Wool on warp and weft.
- *length 145cm*
- £950 • Gordon Reece

Sarouk Rug ▲
- *circa 1940*

Typical Harati design with a large medallion in the centre, the ground colour is coral with blue, pink and cream. Sarouk is a small village of approximately 1,000 houses, west of Iran.
- *89cm x 118cm*
- £1,100 • Oriental

Hammadan Runner ▲
- *1870*

Section of a Hammadan runner.
- *length 300cm*
- £1,500 • David Black

Western Anotonian Kilim ◄
- *circa 1900*

Western Anotonian kilim converted into a cushion cover.
- *width 65cm*
- £125 • Oriental

Indian Dhurrie ▲
- *circa 1860*

Indian cotton dhurrie with a blue background with pink and yellow geometric designs and a pink key pattern design, on a yellow background with a yellow border.
- *269cm x 251cm*
- £2,800 • David Black

Indian Dhurrie ▲
- *1850*

Indian dhurrie, a blue foliate design and gold torchieries, on a pink background.
- *156cm x 230cm*
- £950 • David Black

Ceramics

Condition is a major factor when estimating the value of a ceramic as it is very easy for a piece to become damaged.

Ceramics incorporates porcelain, which is translucent, and pottery, which is opaque. Porcelain tends to be more highly valued than pottery, which was often made for practical use, although some highly decorated pottery pieces can be found. Sought-after English pieces include items from the Chelsea factory, Empire-style cabinet wares made by Worcester and Victorian Staffordshire figures. Interest in minor English factories is growing, but collectors need to be familiar with the confusing system of factory markings used.

The eighteenth century was the golden age for European ceramics, when factories in Germany, France and Italy produced a beautiful array of decorative and domestic wares. Oriental porcelain has continued to be very desirable since the seventeenth century, and includes Japanese Imari porcelain, which is noted for its distinctive blue colouring and red gilding, and the traditional Chinese blue-and-white pattern pieces as well as the more colourful pieces they produced for export to the West.

English Ceramics

Pineapple Creamware ▼
- *circa 1765*
A Creamware vase with pineapple and leaf pattern.
- *13cm x 9cm*
- £2,450   • J. Horne

Staffordshire Teapot ▲
- *circa 1755*
A small moulded Staffordshire blue and brown agate ware teapot standing on three lion's feet with a reclining lion on the lid.
- *16cm x 20cm*
- £4,400   • J. Horne

Green Glazed Jug ◄
- *circa 1670*
Small green jug "Border ware".
- *12cm x 8cm*
- £1,250   • J. Horne

Expert Tips

English and European porcelain is increasing in value and is an international commodity. Condition is critical and perfection is the order of the day.

Worcester Mug ▲

- **1780**

Cylindrical Worcester porcelain tankard decorated with a painted urn in purple enamel, with garlands and sprays of polychrome flowers between underglaze blue and gilt bands. Crescent mark.
- *height 13.5cm*
- **£1,050**   • Dando

Painted Cup and Saucer ▲

- *circa 1850*

English cup and saucer centred with a landscape showing a classical ruin, within a gilded floral border.
- *height 6cm*
- **£1,250**   • Dando

Wileman & Co. Trio ▲

- *circa 1895*

Wileman & Co. The Foley china, English white cup, saucer and plate with gilt borders, hand painted with swallows and flowers.
- *height 6cm*
- **trio £85**   • A. Piotrowski

Wedgwood Figure ▼

- *circa 1810*

Unusual English Wedgwood figure of a young boy feeding a biscuit to a spaniel on a plinth base.
- *height 18.5cm*
- **£750**   • Dando

Worcester Sauce Boat ▼

- **1756**

Worcester cos lettuce moulded sauceboat, painted with scattered floral sprays, and a twig moulded handle. Unmarked.
- *length 8.75cm*
- **£1,250**   • Dando

Coalport Cream Jug ▲

- *circa 1835*

Coalport cream jug with gilded floral designs on a blue ground with small hand painted panels of birds.
- *height 12.5cm*
- **£165**   • Dando

Caughley Plates ▲

- *circa 1785–90*

One of a pair of Caughley plates with scalloped edges and underglaze blue border, probably painted and gilded at Worcester. "S" mark in underglaze blue.
- *diameter 23cm*
- **£650**   • Dando

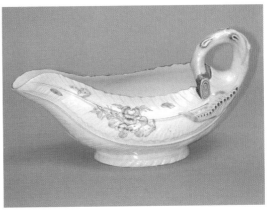

Posset Pot ▼
- *circa 1690*

Staffordshire slipware posset pot, inscribed with the initials M.S. and decorated with a jewel-like glaze.
- *13cm x 17cm*
- **£38,500**
- **J. Horne**

Cauliflower Teapot ▲
- *circa 1765*

Small Staffordshire teapot styled as a cauliflower, with rustic handle.
- *height 12cm*
- **£1,650**
- **J. Horne**

Fulham Pottery ▲
- *circa 1695*

Dwight period tankard with silver rim from Fulham Pottery.
- *height 15cm*
- **£2,950**
- **J. Horne**

Handwarmer ▼
- *circa 1685*

London or Brislington white tin glazed handwarmer in the shape of a book.
- *height 15.2cm*
- **£19,500**
- **J. Horne**

Wedgwood Cup ▲
- *1910*

Wedgwood cup and saucer with separate silver gilt holder.
- *height 7cm*
- **£125**
- **Beverley**

Goat Jug ▲
- *circa 1750*

Very rare small saltglaze Staffordshire milk jug styled as two goats and a bee.
- *height 9cm*
- **£2,600**
- **J. Horne**

Crown Ducal Cup and Saucer ◄
- *1930*

Crown Ducal yellow glaze cup and saucer with a gilded interior.
- *height 5cm*
- **£75**
- **Beverley**

Expert Tips

Staffordshire figures often took their inspiration from popular paintings or prints and were based on actual events such as the theatre.

Miniature Ewer and Stand ▼

- *circa 1835*

English ceramics miniature ewer and stand with original porcelain stopper and a painted floral panel set within gilded borders.

- *height 11cm*
- £420
- Dando

Staffordshire Violinist ▼

- *circa 1840–45*

Staffordshire figure of a violinist in theatrical costume wearing a pink plumed hat.

- *height 21cm*
- £260
- Dando

Staffordshire Boy Piper ▶

- *1820*

Staffordshire spill holder showing a group with a seated piper playing to a pig and a duck.

- *height 17.2cm*
- £655
- Dando

Chimney Sweep ▲

- *circa 1810*

Early Staffordshire pottery figure of a chimney sweep decorated in overglaze colours.

- *height 18cm*
- £445
- Dando

Staffordshire Cats ▲

- *circa 1870*

Pair of Staffordshire cats, painted black and white, with yellow collars.

- *height 8cm*
- £475
- Dando

Staffordshire Spill Vase ▼

- *1815*

Staffordshire pottery "Game Spill" vase of unusual and fine quality in the form of a hollow tree, hung with various game and a hunter's satchel. Pearlware with overglaze enamel colours.

- *height 22cm*
- £400
- Dando

Staffordshire Country Gentleman ▼

- *1870*

Staffordshire figure of a country gentleman, presenting a basket of trout, whilst standing on a naturalistically styled base.

- *height 25.5cm*
- £295
- Dando

Staffordshire Figure ▼

- *1890*

Staffordshire model of a lady
seated on a wall, with a swan at
her feet.
- *height 18cm*
- £150   • Bellum

Elephant Spill Vases ▲

- *1830*

Pair of grey elephant spill vases
with pink saddles.
- *15cm x 10cm*
- £2,700   • J.Oosthuizen

Dinner Plate ▼

- *circa 1880*

Blue and white dinner plate
decorated with classical ruins
with a scrolled floral border.
- *diameter 25cm*
- £145   • Barrett & Towning

Staffordshire Pheasants ▼

- *1860*

Pair of Staffordshire pheasants
with unusual orange and blue
markings on the wings standing
on a rusticated base.
- *26cm x 12cm*
- £1,500   • J.Oosthuizen

Sailor with Parrot ▲

- *1880*

Staffordshire figure of a man in
theatrical dress with a plumed
hat, holding a parrot.
- *height 20cm*
- £175   • Bellum

Leopard Spill Vases ▶

- *1845*

Pair of Staffordshire spill vases
showing two leopards with
bocage, standing on a
naturalistically formed base.
- *16cm x 11cm*
- £3,600   • J.Oosthuizen

Theatrical Dancers ▼

- **1850**

Staffordshire group of theatrical dancers depicting Miss Glover and Mrs Vining as Yourawkee and Peter Wilkins.

- *height 20cm*
- **£295**　　　　• Dando

Staffordshire Figure ▲

- **1880**

Staffordshire figure of a girl wearing a blue dress seated on a large, horned goat.

- *height 12cm*
- **£240**　　　　• Bellum

Staffordshire Gardeners ▲

- *circa 1860–70*

Staffordshire spill vase group of two figures, probably gardeners, the man is holding a basket of flowers and there is a potted plant behind the seated girl.

- *height 21cm*
- **£185**　　　　• Dando

Staffordshire Group ▼

- **1880**

Staffordshire group showing a gentleman with a dog under his arm and a lady wearing tartan.

- *height 17cm*
- **£225**　　　　• Bellum

Staffordshire Children ▲

- **1880**

Staffordshire spill vase with two children seated by the trunk of a tree with a bird resting on a garland of orange flowers.

- *height 14cm*
- **£225**　　　　• Bellum

Staffordshire Soldier ▲

- **1880**

Staffordshire figure of an officer in a blue uniform with gilt buttons and a floral sash, within a bocage.

- *height 15cm*
- **£175**　　　　• Bellum

Staffordshire Inkwell ▶

- **1880**

Staffordshire inkwell showing a boy and his sister seated on an orange base.

- *height 11.5cm*
- **£175**　　　　• Bellum

Carlton Ware Cup and Saucer ▲

- *circa 1900*
Carlton Ware orange lustre cup and saucer with stylised birds and gilding.
- *height 6cm*
- £165   • Beverley

Hammersely Floral Cup and Saucer ▲

- *circa 1930*
Pink floral Hammersely cup and saucer with floral decoration.
- *height 4cm*
- £65   • Beverley

Green Crown Devon Cup and Saucer ▲

- *circa 1930*
Crown Devon cup and saucer with a green pearlised interior.
- *height 6cm*
- £95   • Beverley

Butterfly Handle Cup ▲

- *1930*
Unusual primrose yellow Ainsley cup with gilt rim on cup and saucer with unusual butterfly handle.
- *height 6cm*
- £125   • Beverley

Royal Worcester ▼

- *circa 1930*
Royal Worcester cup and saucer with a trailing foliate decoration with clusters of berries.
- *height 5.5cm*
- £75   • Beverley

Expert Tips

When washing china or pottery look carefully for old restoration work as immersion in warm water can soften old glues and lead to the undoing of repair work. Ultraviolet light can be used to pick out such defects.

Spode Copeland Cup and Saucer ▼

- *circa 1930*
Spode Copeland cup and saucer with floral sprays.
- *height 4cm*
- £69   • Beverley

Royal Winton ◄

- *circa 1920*
Blue Royal Winton with sprays of apple blossom on a royal blue background.
- *height 6cm*
- £95   • Beverley

St Mark ▲

- 1850

Staffordshire figure of St Mark with a lion recumbent at his side, on a rock moulded base.
- height 24cm
- £450 ● J.Oosthuizen

Queen Victoria's Children ▲

- 1880

Staffordshire group depicting Queen Victoria's children.
- height 41cm
- £275 ● J.Oosthuizen

Expert Tips

Some Staffordshire figures were inspired by the famous Newfoundland dog rescuing a child from a river – one of the many faithful and heroic hounds who abound in Victorian literature and art.

Spill Vases ▼

- 1860

Pair of Staffordshire spill vases modelled as foxes with chickens in there mouths, standing on a foliate base.
- height 25cm
- £1,600 ● J.Oosthuizen

Little Red Riding Hood ▼

- 1860

Staffordshire figure of Little Red Riding Hood seated with a fox.
- height 26cm
- £185 ● J.Oosthuizen

Staffordshire Zebras ▲

- 1865

Pair of prancing Staffordshire zebras on a foliate oval base with gilding.
- height 16cm
- £725 ● J.Oosthuizen

Staffordshire Actor ▲

- 1855

Man in theatrical dress sitting on a branch, with a parrot on his shoulder and a spaniel at his side, with gilding on a green foliate base.
- height 37cm
- £450 ● J.Oosthuizen

Staffordshire Children ▲

- 1850

Pair of Staffordshire figures modelled as children playing with rats, raised on oval moulded bases with gilding.
- height 15cm
- £800 ● J.Oosthuizen

Staffordshire Group ▲

- 1880

Ivory Staffordshire group modelled as a cow with her calf, standing on an oval moulded base with gilding.
- 16cm x 21cm
- £350 ● J.Oosthuizen

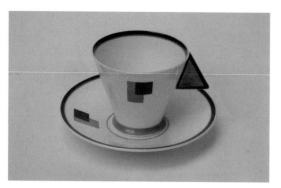

Shelley Ceramic ◄
- *1920*

Shelley made cup and saucer with green and black geometric design Art Deco.
- *height 9cm*
- **£195**
- ● Beverley

Green Jug ▼
- *circa 1775*

Finely rouletted creamware jug with a green glaze fitted with a double strap handle attributed to the Yorkshire Potteries.
- *height 18cm*
- **£4,480**
- ● J. Horne

Shield Toby Jug ▼
- *circa 1775*

Very rare Shield Toby Jug. Derives its name from the applied plaque on the side, which reads "It is all out then fill him again".
- *23cm x 18cm*
- **£14,500**
- ● J. Horne

Shelley Cup and Saucer ▲
- *1930*

Hand-painted Shelley dainty shape cup and saucer with orange and yellow floral spray of flowers.
- *height 10cm*
- **£185**
- ● Beverley

Wedgwood Teapot ▲
- *circa 1765*

Liverpool Wedgwood creamware teapot with a cartouche of a gentleman giving a gift to a lady and child seated beneath a tree.
- *13cm x 19cm*
- **£660**
- ● J. Horne

The Tea Party ▼
- *circa 1770*

Wedgwood jug with Liverpool printed cartouche of a tea party on one side and a pastoral scene on the other.
- *14cm x 10cm*
- **£185**
- ● J. Horne

Staffordshire Lions ▼
- *circa 1820*

Staffordshire lion and lioness, standing on an oval base.
- *8cm x 12cm*
- **£2,850**
- ● J. Horne

Blackware Teapot ▼
- *circa 1765*
Small blackware teapot, with ear shaped handle and a raised floral design, on pad feet, with a bird finial lid.
- *height 8cm*
- £475 • J. Horne

Saltglazed Jug ▼
- *13th century*
Saltglazed jug of bulbous form, with strap handle and turned decoration to the neck.
- *height 22cm*
- £1,300 • J. Horne

Blackware Bowl ▲
- *circa 1765*
Blackware bowl decorated with a raised design of gilt fruit and trailing foliage.
- *diameter 14cm*
- £660 • J. Horne

Blackware Coffee Pot ▲
- *circa 1765*
Blackware coffee pot, raised on three feet with a pinched lip, moulded handle and a bird finial cover.
- *height 15cm*
- £550 • J. Horne

English Sauce Tureen ◄
- *circa 1820*
English blue and white sauce tureen and cover on fitted base with a landscape depicting grazing rabbits within a country setting.
- *height 17cm*
- £375 • Libra

Earthenware Jug ▼
- *12th century*
English earthenware vessel with a dark green glaze and circular design around the neck found at Sible Headingham, Essex.
- *height 29cm*
- £5,500 • J. Horne

Sauce Tureen ▼
- *circa 1820*
India flowers sauce tureen and cover, with floral sprays on a red ground with gilding and acanthus leaf decoration (known as clobbered).
- *height 17.5cm*
- £520 • Libra

Creamware Teapot ▼
- *circa 1795*
Creamware teapot with a foliate pattern in green and a central cartouche painted with a basket of wild flowers.
- *height 17cm*
- £470 • Libra

Creamware Teapot ▶

- *circa 1775*

Small creamware teapot with a red and black mottled design, twig spout and handle and a red finial cover.
- *14cm*
- £750   • Libra

Davenport Tureen and Cover ▲

- *circa 1820*

Davenport polychrome sauce tureen and cover, on fixed stand with chinoiserie designs within a key pattern border, with gilt-banding and a leaf-shaped finial.
- *height 17cm*
- £228   • Libra

Wedgwood Teapot ▲

- *circa 1790*

Small Wedgwood teapot decorated with a tulip pattern in magenta, with designs on spout and handle with a flower finial cover.
- *height 12.5cm*
- £420   • Libra

Swansea Pinwheel Pepperpot ▲

- *1870*

Swansea blue and white "Pinwheel" pepperpot of bulbous form raised on a splayed foot.
- *height 11cm*
- £270   • Libra

Stone China Vase ◀

- *circa 1825*

One of a set of four stone china vases decorated with an apple blossom design with gilt-banded decoration.
- *height 11cm*
- £360   • Libra

Swansea Moulded Jug ▼

- *circa 1825*

Swansea daisy pattern, moulded jug, with "C" scroll handle and shaped lip with red, blue, green and white stripes and a black diagonal stripe across the body.
- *height 22cm*
- £150   • Libra

Pearlware Jug ▼

- *circa 1815*

Pearlware moulded jug decorated with pink roses, cornflowers and leaves, with black-banded decoration.
- *height 12cm*
- £125   • Libra

Pearlware Mug ▼
- *circa 1780*
Baddeley-Litter Staffordshire
Pearlware mug.
- *height 13cm*
- £1,550 • J. Horne

Red Barn ►
- *circa 1828*
A Staffordshire table group of the
"Red Barn".
- *height 23.5cm*
- £14,500 • J. Horne

Royal Doulton Cup and Saucer ◄
- *circa 1930*
Cream Royal Doulton cup and
saucer with sprays of violets and
gilding to rim of cup and handle.
- *height 9cm*
- £55 • Beverley

Dr. Syntax ◄
- *circa 1820*
Staffordshire figure of Dr. Syntax
modelled as a seated figure
holding a book and pen.
- *height 14cm*
- £990 • J. Horne

Dr. Syntax ▲
- *circa 1820*
Staffordshire figure of Dr. Syntax
modelled with his hands tied to
a tree.
- *height 15cm*
- £850 • J. Horne

Paragon Art Deco Cup and Saucer ▲
- *circa 1920*
Fine Paragon pink floral Art
Deco cup and saucer.
- *height 10cm*
- £45 • Beverley

Queen Anne Shelly Cup and Saucer ◄
- *circa 1927*
White hand-painted Shelley cup
with saucer with black trailing
vine and yellow pink and blue
stylised flowers.
- *height 8cm*
- £85 • Beverley

Derby Squab Tureen

- *circa 1760*
Finely painted Derby Squab
tureen, naturalistically styled as a
bird, with floral encrustation.
- *height 10cm*
- £3,400 • Stockspring

Charles Bourne Vase

- *circa 1820*
Charles Bourne vase with a band
of finely painted flowers, between
gilded floral borders on a blue
ground.
- *height 15cm*
- £480 • Stockspring

Yates Egg Cups

- *circa 1820*
An early and rare set of six egg
cups with stand by Yates, with
finely painted flowers between
scrolled cartouches, centred with
birds.
- *height 5cm*
- £750 • Stockspring

Chelsea Dish

- *circa 1750*
Chelsea lozenge-shaped dish
decorated with floral sprays of
pink roses, with a scalloped edge
with gilt trim and scrolling.
- *diameter 25cm*
- £1,450 • Stockspring

Worcester Dish

- *circa 1750*
Worcester dish in the form of a
leaf, centred with a floral spray of
roses and wild flowers, with a soft
green border.
- *diameter 18cm*
- £1,980 • Stockspring

Chelsea Derby Mug

- *1770*
Chelsea Derby white mug
delicately painted in a soft palette
with a spray of pink roses, with
scrolled handle and gilt rim.
- *height 10cm*
- £1,100 • Stockspring

Derby Figures ▼

- *1765*

Pair of Derby figures of a young girl holding a basket and her companion holding a lamb under his arm, standing on a scrolled base scattered with flowers.
- *height 24cm*
- **£3,600 the pair** • Stockspring

Worcester Creamer ▼

- *circa 1765*

Worcester cream jug with a central cartouche of two Chinese men in a landscape carrying a lantern, and a blue floral design on the inside of the moulded rim.
- *height 7cm*
- **£760** • Stockspring

Derby Figure ▲

- *circa 1770*

Derby figure of a young maiden wearing a white dress and bonnet holding a basket of green and red grapes under her arm, on a circular base with gilt banding.
- *height 14cm*
- **£1,180** • Stockspring

Bow Candleholder ◄

- *circa 1760*

Bow candleholder encrusted with yellow and pink flowers around the trunk of a tree with two pheasants perched on the top and a central flower candleholder.
- *height 23cm*
- **£1,850** • Stockspring

Bow Plates ▼

- *circa 1760*

One of a pair of octagonal Bow plates decorated with the Quail pattern, showing a chinoiserie tree with terracotta and gold flowers and a terracotta trim linked with gold.
- *diameter 22cm*
- **£1,680** • Stockspring

Bow Grape Sellers ▲

- *circa 1760*

Pair of Bow figures, of a young girl wearing a pink hat with finely painted dress of pink flowers and boy seated with matching breeches, and outstretched arm holding grapes.
- *height 16.5cm*
- **£3,800 pair** • Stockspring

English Danielle Cups with Saucer ◀

- *circa* 1830

Trio of two cups and one saucer early English Danielle, hand painted blue with cartouches of pink and yellow flowers with sprays of gilt folia with gilt rim and handle.

- *height 7cm*
- £135
- Beverley

Coalport Trio ◀

- *circa* 1900

Coalport cup, saucer, and plate with sprays of roses and blossom with gilding to rim of cup and handle.

- *height 7cm*
- £125
- Beverley

Royal Paragon Trio ▲

- *circa* 1930

Royal Paragon cup, saucer and plate painted with yellow blue and pink flowers and three green circular green bands and stylised handle.

- *height 9cm*
- £85
- Beverley

Paragon Trio ▲

- *circa* 1920

Paragon trio with octagonal plate with orange floral sprays, dramatic black and orange handle.

- *height 7.5cm*
- £115
- Beverley

Foley Trio ▲

- *circa* 1920

Trio of cup saucer and plate with orange flowers and banding with an unusual geometric handle.

- *height 8cm*
- £75
- Beverley

Expert Tips

Doulton was made from about 1820 to 1854 – go for named artists like George Tinworth, Hannah Barlow and Frank Butler.

Burleigh Ware Cup and Saucer ▲

- *circa* 1930

Burleigh Ware cup and saucer with painted daffodils and leaves and rusticated leaf handle.

- *height 7cm*
- £46
- Beverley

Bell-shaped cup ▲

- *circa* 1920

Ainsley bell-shaped cup saucer and plate with a profusion of yellow and white flowers.

- *height 7cm*
- £75
- Beverley

Royal Doulton Pepper Pot ▲
- *1884*

Royal Doulton pepper pot with blue glazed neck decorated with a raised, repetitive design, above a turned body, raised on a moulded foot.
- *height 8cm*
- £65　　　　● Lynda Brine

Doulton Jug ▲
- *1876*

Royal Doulton Lambeth jug designed by Frank Butler with a silver lid and thumb piece, the body decorated with a stylised leaf pattern, with jewelling.
- *height 17cm*
- £235　　　　● Lynda Brine

Fruit Bowl ▲
- *1920*

Blue and white fruit bowl with a rural scene with cows in the foreground, within a bold floral border.
- *diameter 19cm*
- £140　　　　● Libra

Staffordshire Figure of Neptune ▼
- *1830*

Figure of Neptune with trident, standing on a rock encrusted with seashells with a sea monster at his feet.
- *height 18cm*
- £495　　　● Pieter Oosthuizen

Davenport Stilton Dish and Cover ▼
- *1860*

Davenport blue and white stilton dish and cover decorated with a Chinoiserie harbour scene.
- *height 35cm*
- £2,600　　　　● Libra

Staffordshire Group ▶
- *1850*

Staffordshire figure of a lady wearing a pink top with a floral skirt holding a baby, with a child at her side.
- *height 23cm*
- £395　　● Pieter Oosthuizen

Staffordshire Group ▲
- *1850*

Staffordshire group seated on a mossy bank with a tree in the background.
- *height 25cm*
- £595　　● Pieter Oosthuizen

Staffordshire Musician ▲
- *1840*

Staffordshire figure of a musician wearing a yellow hat with blue plumes, holding a mandolin with a lamb and flowers at his feet.
- *height 24cm*
- £425　　● Pieter Oosthuizen

Newhall Jug ▲
• *1814*
Newhall cream jug with pinched lip, decorated with a floral ribbon design and raised on a moulded foot.
• *height 9.5cm*
• **£280**   • Stockspring

Newhalls Walberton Teapot ▲
• *1810*
Newhalls Walberton patent teapot and cover, with a gilt finial lid and foliate designs. The body is profusely gilded and decorated with a painted landscape, with a blue enamelled band at the base of the spout.
• *height 16cm*
• **£1,290**   • Stockspring

Pepper Pot ▼
• *1884*
Royal Doulton pepper caster of bulbous form, with pewter cover and finial top, the neck and body decorated with a stylised leaf design, with jewelling.
• *height 10cm*
• **£95**   • Lynda Brine

Mason's Jug ▲
• *1812*
Small Mason's jug with scrolled handle and pink Imari design around the body, with gilt trailing foliage and banding.
• *height 7cm*
• **£170**   • Stockspring

Derbyshire Bowl ▼
• *1810*
Derbyshire double-handled sugar bowl, decorated with a pink heart shaped pattern and gilt foliate designs and banding.
• *height 9cm*
• **£360**   • Stockspring

Staffordshire Archer ▲
• *1840*
Staffordshire figure of a lady archer wearing a plumed hat and green coat, holding a bow and arrow, standing on a plinth base.
• *height 17cm*
• **£295**   • Pieter Oosthuizen

Worcester Sauce Tureen ▲
• *1820*
Worcester double-handled sauce tureen, finely painted with a floral design on a yellow, white and grey enamel, with gilt acorn finial.
• *height 14cm*
• **£480**   • Stockspring

Coral Firs Cup and Saucer ▼

- *circa 1930*
A Clarice Cliff "Coral Firs" design from the Bizarre range with stylised terracotta trees.
- *height 9cm*
- £335 • Beverley

Clarice Cliff Trio ▲

- *circa 1930*
Clarice Cliff orange green and cream star decoration cup, saucer and plate.
- *height 7cm*
- £395 • Beverley

Susie Cooper Trio ◄

- *1950*
"Green Dresden Spray" two tone green cup, saucer and matching plate trio with floral entwined sprays by Susie Cooper.
- *height 5cm*
- £48 • Beverley

Burleigh Ware Cup and Saucer ◄

- *circa 1930*
Burleigh Ware cup and saucer with painted daffodils and leaves and rusticated leaf handle.
- *height 7cm*
- £46 • Beverley

Pink Floral Trio ▲

- *circa 1930*
Royal Doulton trio with pink floral design and a blue and cream gilded background.
- *height 8cm*
- £75 • Beverley

Expert Tips

Minton was founded in 1793 and is one of the finest potteries. Early Minton has the letter "L" painted sometimes with a number under it. Tea and dessert services were beautifully decorated – names to look for are Joseph Bancroft, George Hancock, and Thomas Steel.

Pink Azalea Trio ◄

- *1950*
Pink Azalea cup, saucer and plate trio, by Susie Cooper.
- *height 8cm*
- £55 • Beverley

Crown Devon Trio ▲

- *1950*
Crown Devon cup saucer and plate, with exotic birds their wings outstretched on a red glazed background.
- *height 8cm*
- £165 • Beverley

Worcester Dish ▶

- *circa 1768*

Worcester oval Imari pattern dish with a central cartouche of a pagoda and a orange blossom tree with clouds to the side, and twig orange handles.
- *length 28cm*
- £11,500　　● Stockspring

Worcester Tea Bowl ▼

- *1760*

Small Worcester tea bowl decorated with a courting couple in a classical setting, a small dog and garden roller in the foreground.
- *height of bowl 5cm*
- £560　　● Stockspring

Worcester Jug ▼

- *circa 1765*

Small Worcester jug decorated with a spray of pink flowers, an orange line and scalloping on the inside of the rim.
- *height 8.5cm*
- £980　　● Stockspring

Chelsea Dish ▼

- *circa 1760*

Chelsea dish in the shape of a peony encircled by a green leaf, with a turquoise handle in the shape of a branch with a bud.
- *diameter 19cm*
- £2,700　　● Stockspring

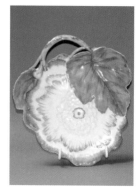

Longton Hall Plate ▼

- *circa 1755*

Longhton Hall plate decorated with a raised design of strawberries and flowers, with a central panel of birds and a parrot in a tree.
- *diameter 24cm*
- £1,890　　● Stockspring

Worcester Jug ▲

- *1805*

Worcester jug with terracotta, dark blue and white floral and scroll design, with gold trim on rim and handle.
- *height 18cm*
- £1,280　　● Stockspring

Crown Ducal Breakfast Set ◀

- **1930**

Crown Ducal breakfast set, in the Wild Rose design.
- *height 7cm*
- £45 • Beverley

Chrysanthemum Trio ▲

- **1895**

Charles Wileman chrysanthemum pattern cup and saucers
- *height 6cm*
- £65 • Beverley

Purple Iris Trio ◀

- **1920**

Royal Doulton trio decorated with purple irises, having unusual rusticated leaf design handle.
- *height 8cm*
- £145 • Beverley

Daisy-shaped Trio ▲

- **1897**

Daisy shape with Snowdrop design by Charles Wileman.
- *height 6cm*
- £95 • Beverley

Coalport Trio ▲

- **1920**

Coalport matching trio with blue floral design and gilding to rim cup and handle.
- *height 7cm*
- £95 • Beverley

Blue Floral Trio ◀

- **1920**

Matching cup, saucer, and plate by Royal Doulton with unusual blue floral design and bronze and gold sponge underglaze.
- *height 6.5cm*
- £75 • Beverley

Worcester Cornucopias ◀

- *circa 1756–1758*

Pair of blue and white moulded
Worcester cornocupias decorated
with small blue flowers.
Workman's mark.
- *height 22cm*
- £4,500   • Stockspring

Large Worcester Mug ▲

- *circa 1805*

Large Worcester mug, with two
yellow enamel bands between gilt
banding and a central repetitive
design of stylised feathers.
- *height 12cm*
- £680   • Stockspring

Minton Cup ▼

- *circa 1805*

Minton cup decorated with three
cartouches and a foliate design in
terracotta, set amongst profuse
gilding. With mark on base:
M.205.
- *height 6.5cm*
- £139   • Stockspring

Lowestoft Tea Bowl ▲

- *circa 1760*

Lowestoft tea bowl decorated
with a blue and white chinsoserie
scene depicting a house behind a
wall with a tree and birds.
- *height of bowl 5cm*
- £690   • Stockspring

Worcester Tea Bowl ▲

- *circa 1740*

Worcester octagonal tea bowl
with finely painted sprays of
flowers and insects with gilding,
from the studio of James Giles.
- *height 5cm*
- £420   • Stockspring

Pinxton Jug ▶

- *circa 1805*

Small Pinxton cream jug with a
scrolled handle and shaped rim
with blue banding. Delicately
painted body with three fuchsia
sprigs.
- *height 10cm*
- £690   • Stockspring

Grindly Floral Trio

- **1920**

Hand-painted Grindley cup, saucer and plate with yellow floral decoration and a pale pink raised background.
- *height 9cm*
- **£55**   • Beverley

Limoges Cup and Saucer

- *circa 1875*

Limoges cup, saucer and plate, gilded, with clusters of roses.
- *height 7cm*
- **£45**   • Beverley

Melba Nasturtium Trio

- **1931**

Unusual octagonal Melba trio with yellow and orange nasturtiums and floral handle.
- *height 8cm*
- **£55**   • Beverley

Shelley Vogue Trio

- **1930**

Shelley Vogue trio with various shades of green with a triangular shape handle.
- *height 7cm*
- **£275**   • Beverley

Spode Copeland Trio

- **1910**

Spode Copeland trio with pale pink roses, gilding on a dark blue background.
- *height 6.5cm*
- **£65**   • Beverley

Charles Wileman
Snowdrop Trio

- *circa 1895*

Charles Wileman trio shaped as snowdrops.
- *height 8cm*
- **£115**   • Beverley

Crescent Trio
- *circa 1900*
English Crescent china trio with garlands of pink roses, gilding to cup and handle.
- *height 7cm*
- £55   • Beverley

Ainsley Trio
- *circa 1900*
Ainsley royal blue trio with gilding.
- *height 7cm*
- £45   • Beverley

Ainsley Floral Trio
- *circa 1895*
A Victorian Ainsley ceramic trio with a cluster of roses and foliage.
- *height 7.5cm*
- £40   • Beverley

Wedding Band Cup and Saucer
- *circa 1930*
Susie Cooper coffee cup with a wedding band pattern.
- *height 7cm*
- £45   • Beverley

Staffordshire Jug
- *1830*
A transfer printed rare Staffordshire jug with a verse for each month of the year and pictures of a mother and her children.
- *20cm x 17cm*
- £1,100   • Vanbrugh

Drabware Urns
- *1828*
A pair of Drabware urns with blue and white flowers on a green underglaze pattern.
- *20cm x 15cm*
- £850   • Vanbrugh

Expert Tips

Spode was started in 1770 by Josiah Spode, whose son invented bone china (made with bone ash). The most collected are enamel, painted items by Henry Daniel.

Soup Tureen

• 1827
Soup tureen manufactured by Jones to celebrate the Coronation of George IV.
• height 31cm
• £1,273　　　　　• Libra

Leeds Egg Cup

• 1820
Leeds blue and white egg cup decorated with two boys fishing beside a river within a parkland setting.
• height 7cm
• £195　　　　　• Libra

Dresden Sauceboat

• 1225
Dresden sauceboat with scrolled handle, shaped lip, vase and floral decoration, raised on a moulded, splayed foot.
• height 8cm
• £120　　　　　• Libra

Platter

• 1820
Blue and white platter with a moonlit naval battle scene surrounded by tropical shells and fauna.
• width 53cm
• £1,350　　　　　• Libra

Tea Bowl and Saucer

• 1790
Pearlware tea bowl and saucer, with finely fluted decoration, painted with a dark blue trailing band with stylised flowers.
• diameter 8.5cm
• £195　　　　　• Libra

Ewer and Bowl

• 1820
Blue and white ewer and bowl decorated with a view of Worcester, and the word "Worcester" inscribed on the base.
• height of jug 20cm
• £490　　　　　• Libra

King of Prussia Teapot ▶

- **1765**

Staffordshire salt glaze teapot
with black arrow pattern, and a
cartouche of the King of Prussia
with stylised twig handle, spout
and finial top.
- *height 9cm*
- **£3,850**
  - J. Horne

Creamware Teapot ▲

- **1765**

English creamware teapot with
farm hands resting in a pastoral
setting, and a cottage on the
reverse, with leaf designs to the
handle and spout.
- *height 10cm*
- **£1,100**
  - J. Horne

Saltglaze Teapot ▲

- *circa 1765*

Staffordshire salt glaze teapot
decorated with pink wild flowers
on a crimson ground, with twig
handle and spout.
- *height 10cm*
- **£2,100**
  - J. Horne

Staffordshire Teapot ▲

- *circa 1765*

Staffordshire salt glazed teapot
with a musician wearing a pink
jacket and a black hat, in
chinioserie style, playing a flute,
whilst seated on a riverbank.
- *height 9.4cm*
- **£3,650**
  - J. Horne

Staffordshire Creamer ▼

- *circa 1765*

Early Staffordshire creamer with
the inscription "William Dixson"
within a cartouche of flowers.
The side of the jug is a painted
figure of a musician wearing a red
jacket and black tri-cornered hat.
- *height 18.4cm*
- **£6,850**
  - J. Horne

Staffordshire Sauceboat ▼

- *circa 1745*

Staffordshire sauce boat with a
scrolled handle, decorated with a
pink house and clouds, with
shaped rim and foot.
- *height 8cm*
- **£1,850**
  - J. Horne

Saltglazed Stand with Teapot ▼

- *circa 1755*

Staffordshire teapot decorated
with green and yellow vases and
foliate design around the handle
and spout, and standing on three
raised feet.
- *height 8cm*
- **£3,950**
  - J. Horne

Staffordshire Greyhounds ▼
- 1860
Pair of terracotta greyhounds recumbent on a cobalt blue base.
- *height 9cm*
- £300 • J.Oosthuizen

Terracotta Greyhounds ▼
- 1890
Pair of Staffordshire terracotta greyhounds sitting attentively on a circular moulded base.
- *height 10cm*
- £300 • J.Oosthuizen

Staffordshire Group ▼
- 1830
Unusual Staffordshire group depicting a dog with puppies and a cat with kittens.
- *height 11cm*
- £2,500 • J.Oosthuizen

Staffordshire Giraffes ▼
- 1900
Pair of Staffordshire giraffes reclining by a palm tree, on an oval moulded base.
- *height 14cm*
- £2,700 • J.Oosthuizen

Staffordshire Lions ▲
- 1860
Pair of Staffordshire lions with a lamb resting at their side, reclining on an oval moulded base, with gilding.
- *27cm x 17cm*
- £6,500 • J.Oosthuizen

Spill Vases ▲
- 1845
Staffordshire spill vases modelled as a pair of lions with bocage, standing on an oval base with gilding.
- *height 14cm*
- £2,400 • J.Oosthuizen

Expert Tips

Functional redwares made from alluvial clay, were first made in America from around 1625 and continued well into the nineteenth century. New England pieces tend to be plain, though often with richly coloured glazes.

Creamware Baskets ◀

- *circa 1820*
One of a pair of Spode creamware
baskets with oval stands.
- *8cm x 26cm*
- £650 • Vanbrugh

Vegetable Tureen ▲

- *circa 1830*
A Masons ironstone vegetable
tureen with lid, orange
chrysanthemums and pink roses
and gilding to handle.
- *21cm x 35cm*
- £350 • Vanbrugh

Blue and White Footbath ◀

- *circa 1820*
English footbath with a figure of a
seated shepherd playing a musical
instrument to his sheep.
- *24cm x 51cm*
- £2,500 • Vanbrugh

Wedgwood Plaque ▶

- *circa 1800*
A black and white Wedgwood
plaque depicting Domestic
Employment by Lady Templeton.
Unrecorded.
- *16cm x 47cm*
- £3,500 • Vanbrugh

Ironstone Vases ▼

- *circa 1830*
One of a pair of Ironstone Vases
with lids, terracotta and royal
blue flowers and gilding.
- *41cm x 23cm*
- £1,850
  • Vanbrugh

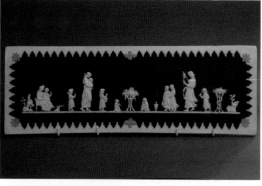

Blue and White Platter ▶

- *circa 1830*
English blue and white platter.
- *45cm x 53cm*
- £550 • Vanbrugh

Staffordshire Group ▼

- *circa 1850*

Early Staffordshire brown and white spaniel with puppy, resting on an oval white base with gilding.

- *height 8.5cm*
- £460   • Dando

Copper Lustre Jug ▼

- *circa 1840*

Large copper lustre jug with moulded band of shamrocks and thistles in pale blue relief.

- *height 19cm*
- £210   • Dando

Staffordshire Figure ▲

- *circa 1810*

Staffordshire pottery figure of Iphegenia shown gathering her skirts with her head to one side.

- *height 18.5cm*
- £850   • Dando

Ralph Wood Group ▲

- *1785*

Fine quality Ralph Wood group of the "Vicar and Moses" showing two seated figures, painted in brown and grey hues.

- *height 23.5cm*
- £1,650   • Dando

Staffordshire Stag ▼

- *1810*

Fine quality Staffordshire pottery stag shown recumbent on a naturally formed oval base.

- *height 19cm*
- £740   • Dando

Samuel Alcock Spaniel ▲

- *circa 1835*

Samuel Alcock model of a brown and white spaniel sitting attentively on a yellow base.

- *height 14cm*
- £440   • Dando

Musician ▲

- *circa 1840*

Small figure of a boy musician, playing a penny whistle with a poodle at his side.

- *height 16cm*
- £215   • Dando

Waterloo Jug ▲

- *circa 1830*

English water jug with floral pattern with the words "Waterloo Band".
- *25cm x 22cm*
- £1,250   • Vanbrugh

Fruit Dish ▲

- *circa 1805*

Fruit dish with blue flowers and gilding.
- *11cm x 38cm*
- £950   • Vanbrugh

Calypso Pot ◀

- *circa 1980*

Black and turquoise lustreware Poole Calypso range pottery. Owned by Lord Queensbury.
- *height 25cm*
- £600   • Brian Moore

Festival of Britain ▲

- **1952**

Tulip-shaped vase designed by Alfred Reed for the Festival of Britain with cream stripes and oblong design circling the vase.
- *height 20cm*
- £230   • Brian Moore

Honiton Pottery Water Jug ▲

- *circa 1930*

Bulbous-shaped water jug by Honiton pottery with a foliate and a floral design.
- *height 55cm*
- £110   • Brian Moore

Cruet Set ◀

- *circa 1950*

Festival of Britain cruet set designed by Alfred Reed with a lattice pattern.
- *height 8cm*
- £60   • Brian Moore

Blue and White Jug ▲
- *1817*

Large blue and white jug decorated with an Indian hunting scene with elephants and hounds giving chase to a tiger.
- *height 28cm*
- £1,700   • Libra

Winchester Measure Jug ▲
- *1815*

Winchester measure jug with scrolled handle and pinched lip, with moulded leaf design around the neck and blue banded decoration.
- *height 14cm*
- £290   • Libra

Lustreware Jug ▼
- *1826*

Pink lustreware jug inscribed "John Evendon aged 17, 1826" with a view of the River Wear in Sunderland.
- *height 12.5cm*
- £140   • Libra

Wine Jug ◄
- *circa 1820*

Large blue and white wine jug, with a scene depicting wine makers at the press, with vine and fruit decoration.
- *height 24cm*
- £1,150   • Libra

Pink Lustre Jug ▼
- *1825*

Pink lustre jug which is part of a set of ten cups and saucers with cream jug and two small bowls.
- *height 7cm*
- £280   • Libra

Swansea Mug ▼
- *1870*

Blue and white Swansea mug with chinoiserie decoration and a bamboo moulded handle.
- *height 18cm*
- £340   • Libra

Sugar Bowl ▼
- *1825*

Dawson Squire and Lackey blue and white sugar bowl, with cover and finial lid, decorated with a scene depicting a castle in a parkland setting.
- *height 10cm*
- £245   • Libra

Reed Bowl ◄

- *1950*

Alfred Reed design bowl with grey glaze and a lattice design in red and white.
- *diameter 20cm*
- £210 • Brian Moore

Butter Dish ◄

- *circa 1930*

Cream Poole Pottery butter dish designed by Truda Carter with yellow and red flowers.
- *height 9cm*
- £72 • Brian Moore

Biscuit Jar ▲

- *1930*

Poole pottery biscuit jar painted by Claire Heath with lid and wicker handle in original condition.
- *height 18cm*
- £190 • Brian Moore

Rye Pottery ▶

- *circa 1950*

A Rye pottery jug with light grey glaze decorated with a trailing stylized foliate design.
- *height 20cm*
- £125 • Brian Moore

Expert Tips

Staffordshite figures are the most inexpensive of factory ware – pure Victoriana. Mat-backed and early figures are modelled completely – no flat backs. Very rare are examples of figures of Jenny Lind and Mrs Bloomer.

Poole Pottery ▼

- *circa 1930*

A Truda Carter design vase from Poole Pottery by Rene Hayes.
- *height 18cm*
- £330 • Brian Moore

Ironstone Bowl ▼

- *circa 1820*

Nineteenth century ironstone "Japan" pattern bowl.
- *5cm x 30cm*
- £300 • D. Hume

Floral Vase ▲

- *1930*

Fine Poole Pottery vase painted by Ruth Paverley with stylized tulips and roses.
- *height 20cm*
- £420 • Brian Moore

European Ceramics

Frechen Earthenware Jug ▶
- *circa 1650*
Brown German earthenware jug
modelled by Frechen.
- *height 22cms*
- £1,350   • J. Horne

German Tankard
with Pewter Lid   ◀
- *circa 1697*
Small German tankard with E.R.
1697 inscribed on the pewter lid.
- *height 19cms*
- £4,850   • J. Horne

Blue and White
Bottle Vase   ▶
- *circa 1700*
Dutch Delft blue and white bottle
vase, decorated in the Chinese
Transitional style, the body with
flowers and birds, the neck with
stiff pendant leaves.
- *height 28cm*
- £580   • Guest & Gray

Bloor Derby Figures   ◀
- *circa 1830*
Pair of Bloor Derby figures of a
rural couple – the man holds a
basket of fruit and the woman, a
basket of flowers.
- *height 15cm*
- £350   • Guest & Gray

Dresden Cup   ▲
- *circa 1900*
Dresden cup and saucer enameled
and gilded with cartouches of a
romantic scene.
- *height 9cm*
- £115   • Beverley

Blue and White Plate   ◀
- *1728*
Blue and white Delftware plate
with the inscription "TDM" and
"1778" surrounded by a foliate
design.
- *diameter 12cms*
- £2,750   • J. Horne

Expert Tips

*Crazing, a network of patterns
appearing when a lead glaze warps,
can be faked but is easy to spot
once compared to genuine items.*

Meissen Shell Salt ▲
- *circa 1755*

Meissen shell salt in the form of an upturned shell the interior painted with a spray of puce, iron-red and yellow flowers with scattered sprigs, on scroll moulded feet, blue crossed swords mark.
- *diameter 10.2cm*
- £1,200 • London Antique

French Cup and Saucer ▲
- *circa 1860*

French cup, saucer and plate, centred with a cartouche of a chateau with gilt-banding.
- *plate diameter 18.5cm*
- £140 • A. Piotrowski

Nudenmiller Sauce Boat ▲
- *1780*

Nudenmiller sauce boat with scrolled handle and shaped rim, with floral sprays and gilding.
- *width 15cm*
- £400 • Stockspring

Dutch Delft Kylins ▼
- *1860*

One of a pair of Dutch Delft Kylins decorated with a blue and white floral design, seated with their mouths open.
- *height 32cm*
- £795 • Gloria Sinclair

Limoges Plate ▲
- *1895*

Limoges plate enamelled with a floral spray of crimson and pink flowers with green and gold leaves, within a heavily gilded border.
- *diameter 23cm*
- £115 • A.Piotrowski

Irish Belleek Basket ▲
- *circa 1880*

Irish Belleek moulded cream latticework basket with three bunches of roses and daisies.
- *height 5cm*
- £155 • London Antique

Sèvres Dinner Plate ▲
- *circa 1814*

Sèvres dinner plate decorated with cherubs holding roses, on the side is the royal crest of M Imple de Sèvres, lst Empire.
- *diameter 24cm*
- £225 • London Antique

Faenza Maiolica Albarello ▼

- *circa 1530*
Painted with label inscribed in blue with "u.agrippa" against a background of scrolling foliage in green, blue, yellow and ochre.
- *height 16.5cm*
- £1,850   • Guest & Gray

Apothecary Jar ◀

- *18th century*
Dutch Delft apothecary jar with moulded spout above scrolled Peacock and fruit cartouche marked "Rosarum".
- *height 20.3cm*
- £1,350   • Guest & Gray

Faience Tankard ▲

- *1805*
Frankfurt pewter-mounted faience tankard decorated with figures in a garden above a band of stiff stylised leaves, with pewter lid.
- *height 27cm*
- £900   • Guest & Gray

Neptune Plate ▲

- *circa 1815–30*
Blue-printed plate decorated with Neptune riding an eagle.
- *diameter 25cm*
- £120   • Guest & Gray

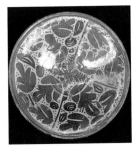

Dish with Leaves ▲

- *17th century*
Hispano Moresque dish, 17th century, divided into four compartments and decorated with leaves.
- *diameter 28cm*
- £880   • Guest & Gray

Expert Tips

Restoration reduces the value of an object. Repairs are acceptable but only when they are done well. Some repairs are obvious; staples are the best kind of honest repair, while modern glues can destroy a piece. When an antique ceramic is damaged, the current orthodoxy is to leave the damage showing. Certainly do not try to overpaint and never file away original surfaces to make repair work easier.

Russian Palace Plate ◀

- *circa 1815–30*
Blue-printed plate decorated with Russian Palace pattern.
- *diameter 25cm*
- £130   • Guest & Gray

Miniature Flower Pot ▼

• *circa 1900*
Miniature flower pot decorated
with flowers, a bird, insects and a
butterfly. Made in Paris, France.
• *height 11cm*
• £48   • London Antique

Continental Figurative Group ▼

• *circa 1880*
Continental romantic figurative
group modelled as a gentleman
seated beside a small round table,
wearing a finely painted floral
brocade jacket, accompanied by a
lady and her mother, on a
serpentine base with a central
Royal Crest and a gold "D".
• *22cm x 25cm*
• £255   • London Antique

Expert Tips

*Imari refers to a type of
Japanese porcelain made from
the beginning of the 17th
century, which featured
decoration based on native
textiles and brocade.*

Westerwald Ewer ▲

• 1630
Westerwald blue and white ewer
with pewter cover, a central
cartouche of Jesus on the cross
with two figures to either side,
ten angels each side of the handle
and lion mask decoration on lip.
• *height 23cm*
• £3,300   • J. Horne

Meissen Figurative Group ◄

• *circa 1880*
Meissen figurative group with two
children seated around a central
column encrusted with flowers, a
central cartouche of gilt scrolling,
and blue and pink flowers on a
circular moulded base with a
conversion for an electric light.
• *height 26cm*
• £485   • London Antique

Meissen Teapot ▶

- *circa 1735*

Meissen billet-shaped teapot and cover with a painted cartouche on each side, within a purple lustre and gilt scrollwork, encircling a Kauffahoftei scene of merchants and their wares.

- *height 10cm*
- £6,500 • London Antique

Royal Vienna Huntsman ▲

- *circa 1890*

Royal Vienna prancing white horse with a huntsman and hounds on a white base.

- *height 20cm*
- £320 • Gloria Sinclair

Dresden Coffee Pot ▲

- *circa 1800*

Dresden white coffee pot decorated with yellow and lilac floral swags and gilt-scrolling around the base, handle and spout. With Crown and Dresden on the base.

- *height 19cm*
- £180 • London Antique

Saltglazed Jug and Cover ▲

- *17th century*

Westerwald blue and cream saltglazed stainwear jug of bulbous form with a pewter handle with cartouches of cherubs with wings and a gentleman with a wig, wearing a hat.

- *height 23cm*
- £2,800 • J. Horne

Royal Vienna Plate ▲

- *circa 1870*

Royal Vienna plate hand-painted with a scene of lovers in a boat, with one cherub holding a basket and the other has his arm around the lady, to the side is a man pulling up the anchor.

- *diameter 24cm*
- £375 • Gloria Sinclair

Dresden Cup and Saucer ▼

- *circa 1880*

Dresden tall moulded cup and saucer decorated with lilac and orange flowers, with gilt-scrolling to the rim and handle, and saucer.

- *height 9cm*
- £1,125 • London Antique

Meissen Tea Bowl and Saucer ▲

- *circa 1735*

Meissen tea bowl and saucer painted with a continuous scene of a merchant's encampment beside an estuary and the interior with a quayside scene.

- *height 5cm*
- **£2,450** • **London Antique**

Dresden Teapot ▲

- *circa 1843*

Dresden blue miniature square teapot of bulbous form, with a central cartouche of a courting couple in a pastoral setting on a white background, marked A.R. Helena Wolfsohn Dresden.

- *height 9cm*
- **£145** • **London Antique**

Expert Tips

Sèvres porcelain has been extensively faked. Many minor French factories used the interlaced "Ls" mark on their wares. They are identifiable through their inferior quality.

Meissen Salts ▶

- *circa 1750*

Pair of Meissen salts of a lady and gentleman with tri-cornered hats seated on a pair of baskets.

- *height 15.5cm*
- **£780** • **London Antique**

Gilded Plate ▲

- *circa 1814–60*

Meissen plate with heavily gilded water serpents with shells, and a central flower, within a gilt rope border. Blue cross swords.

- *diameter 22cm*
- **£165** • **London Antique**

Westerwald Tankard ▶

- *circa 1600*

Blue and cream saltglazed stainwear tankard with three cartouches depicting scenes of Frankfurt, with turned decoration, pewter lid and thumb piece.

- *height 17cm*
- **£2,500** • **J. Horne**

Dresden Trembleuse ▲

- *circa 1880*

Dresden "trembleuse" cup and saucer decorated with pink, yellow and orange flowers. The saucer has a lattice container to hold the cup in place for trembling hands. Blue crown and "D" on the base, by Helena Wolfsohn.

- *height 11.5cm*
- **£2,325** • **London Antique**

Polychrome Plate with Birds ▶

- *circa 1740*
Dutch Delft polychrome plate decorated with birds in a fenced garden, has mark of Jan Jansz Van der Laen.
- *diameter 22.4cm*
- £280 • Guest & Gray

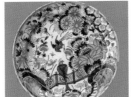

Venice Drug Jar ▲

- *circa 1550*
Venice drug jar with portrait of figure with orange hair.
- *height 16cm*
- £2,200 • Guest & Gray

Hispano Moresque Dish with Bird ▼

- *17th century*
Hispano Moresque dish decorated with a bird in the centre.
- *diameter 20cm*
- £180 • Guest & Gray

Pair of Italian Maiolica Wet Syrup Jars ▼

- *early 17th century*
Jars with ovoid bodies surmounted with a slightly flared rim, the handles in the form of stylised snakes, decorated in the beritinno style with blue scrolling foliage on a light blue ground.
- *height 19.8cm*
- £3,300 • Guest & Gray

Italian Maiolica Deruta Tazza ◀

- *circa 1710*
Painted by the Maestro Del Reggimento with a biblical scene of Virgin Mary with other figures including a saint kissing the Christ child.
- *diameter 32.2cm*
- £3,000 • Guest & Gray

Italian Maiolica Savona Flask ▲

- *late 17th century*
Rare flask with sides painted with ships or houses or plants; the base with the Savona shield in underglaze blue.
- *height 19cm*
- £1,800 • Guest & Gray

Meissen Salts ◄
- *circa 1736–40*

Meissen salts modelled by J.F. Eberlein, basket shaped bowl with rope twist handles painted with a bird, supported by three male caryatid figures terminating in gilt-edged double scroll feet. Completed by Eberlein for the Sulkowsky service. Listed in the factory records of June 1736.
- *height 10cm*
- **£1,950**   • London Antique

Dresden Goblet ►
- *circa 1880*

Dresden goblet with saucer decorated with cherubs and children playing, with a blue iridescent interior and gilt leaves circling the base and saucer marked with a Crown and Dresden.
- *height 9cm*
- **£465**   • London Antique

Saltglazed Stainwear Tankard ▲
- *1690*

Westerwald saltglazed stainwear tankard with a pewter cover and cartouches of royalty.
- *height 17cm*
- **£1,650**   • J. Horne

Russian Bear ▲
- *circa 1890*

Russian mother bear with two baby bears in a cradle covered with an orange cover with white spots, set on a circular floral and green base.
- *height 20cm*
- **£250**   • Gloria Sinclair

Parisian Porcelain Plates ▲
- *1830*

Part of a set of six Parisian porcelain plates with a green border and gilt foliate designs with dragonflies and central cartouche of flowers.
- *diameter 16cm*
- **£980** • Stockspring Antiques

Dresden Group ▲
- *circa 1870*

Dresden group of young girl and two men around a pillar with a cherub holding a rose, on the base is a basket overflowing with pink roses and garlands.
- *height 30cm*
- **£675**   • Gloria Sinclair

Sicilian Maiolica Albarello ▲

- *Early 18th century*
Sicilian maiolica albarello of
waisted cylindrical form, painted
in green, yellow, and manganese
with gothic foliage.
- *height 24cm*
- £880   • Guest & Gray

Multiple Tulip Vase ◀

- *early 18th century*
Blue and white Dutch Delft
multiple tulip vase, heart-shaped
on a stepped rectangular pedestal
foot with eight flower holders
arranged symmetrically at the
top.
- *height 20.5cm*
- £7,000   • Guest & Gray

Dutch Polychrome Tile ▲

- *17th century*
Dutch Delft polychrome tile
decorated with central diamond
surrounding a vase of flowers.
- *12cm x 12cm*
- £75   • Guest & Gray

Hispano Moresque Dish with Stylized Bird ▼

- *17th century*
Hispano Moresque dish decorated
with stylized image of a bird.
- *diameter 28cm*
- £800   • Guest & Gray

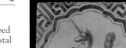

Kraak Tile with Unicorn ▲

- *17th century*
Dutch Delft blue and white Kraak
tile with a unicorn in the centre.
- *12cm x 12cm*
- £65   • Guest & Gray

Kraak Tile with Flowers ▲

- *17th century*
Dutch blue and white Delft Kraak
tile featuring a vase of flowers in
the centre.
- *12cm x 12cm*
- £65   • Guest & Gray

Expert Tips

*Most tiles of value will probably
be Dutch delft. The pattern was
set up in Antwerp in 1512 and
the factory was destroyed by a
gunpowder explosion in 1654.
It produced a massive output
of tiles, wall panels, shop signs
and the most collected are the
composite tile pictures. From
the early 17th century the
potttery had an eastern
influence and emulated
Chinese porcelain.*

Coffee Pot and Teapot ▲

• *circa 1800*
Meissen coffee and teapot, part of
a set including milk jug, sugar
bowl, cups and saucers, cake
plates and one large plate.
• *height 27cm*
• £2,550 • London Antique

Meissen Figurative Group ▲

• *circa 1880*
Meissen figurative group of Diana
the Huntress seated on a lion
holding a cornucopia of flowers,
with cherubs holding a key and
garlands.
• *26cm x 24cm*
• £1,580 • London Antique

Westerwald Storage Jar ▶

• *17th century*
Rhineland blue salt glazed
stainwear jar, with pewter cover
and handle, with a cartouche on
each side depicting William III,
within a raised floral design.
• *height 27cm*
• £4,850 • J. Horne

Dresden Europa and the Bull ▲

• *circa 1860*
Dresden group of Europa and the
Bull, the lady wearing a lilac
tunic, and the bull with a garland
of flowers around its neck.
• *height 22cm*
• £350 • Gloria Sinclair

Neptune ▲

• *1760*
Meissen figure of Neptune astride
a sea horse with trident.
• *height 15cm*
• £980 • Stockspring

Dresden Cup and Saucer ▲

• *circa 1880*
Dresden cup standing on three
paw feet and saucer decorated
with orange borders and a central
cartouche of boats in a harbour.
• *height 10cm*
• £285 • London Antique

Expert Tips

*Originating in the Kangxi period,
famille vert is a palette of
enamels in which a strong green
predominates. It influenced the
decoration of English soft paste
porcelain in the 18th century,
before being overtaken by
famille rose colours.*

Italian Castelli Dish

- *circa 1720*
Fine Italian Castelli dish
romantically painted by Grue
with figures by classical ruins in a
wooded landscape.
- *diameter 17.5cm*
- £1,800　　• Guest & Gray

Sicilian Tall
Waisted Albarello

- *circa 1700*
Decorated with scrolling foliage
and flower heads in yellow and
blue against a blue background
- *height 13.7cm*
- £1,350　　• Guest & Gray

Italian Abruzzi, Waisted
Albarello

- *circa 1700*
Small albarello decorated with a
cartouche containing a label
below cross keys inscribed
"TROCIRCADIA.RODM".
- *height 11.4cm*
- £900　　• Guest & Gray

Sicilian Albarello

- *16th century*
Sicilian albarello decorated with
yellow flower heads against a blue
background.
- *height 11.5cm*
- £880　　• Guest & Gray

Delft Punch Bowl

- *circa 1750*
Dutch Delft blue and white
punch bowl featuring exterior
decorated with swirling panels of
flowers and interior with a
stylised foliate motive.
- *diameter 26.2cm*
- £880　　• Guest & Gray

Hispano Moresque Dish
with Three Lines

- *17th century*
Hispano Moresque dish decorated
with scrolling foliage divided in
the centre by three lines.
- *diameter 18cm*
- £350　　• Guest & Gray

Meissen Tea Bowl and Saucer ◄

- *circa 1750*

Meissen tea bowl and saucer painted with a central cartouche of merchants' boats, with a yellow background and purple flowers.

- *height 5cm*
- £1,950   • London Antique

Saltglazed Vessel ▼

- 1670

Westerwald saltglazed stainwear vessel of bulbous form, with turned decoration and floral designs between courtly figures.

- *height 20cm*
- £650   • J. Horne

Limoges Plate ▲

- 1895

Limoges plate enamelled with a floral spray of chrysanthemums on a cream ground within a heavily gilded border.

- *diameter 23cm*
- £115   • A. Piotrowski

Lion and the Hare ▲

- *circa 1890*

A Russian lion seated and holding a white hare by the scruff of its neck.

- *height 15cm*
- £240   • Gloria Sinclair

Dresden Cup and Saucer ◄

- *circa 1900*

Dresden cup and saucer standing on three paw feet decorated with pink panels of courting couples and flowers divided by gilt-scrolling design.

- *height 4cm*
- £235   • London Antique

Dresden Groups ▶

- *circa 1870*

A pair of Dresden groups showing amorous courting couples.

- *height 22cm*
- £500   • Gloria Sinclair

Expert Tips

English slipwares and German stonewares have been honestly copied as well as faked. Copies of Raeren Brown stoneware are often very close to the style of the originals but are marked by the maker, for example, H.S. for the pottery-maker Hubert Schiffer.

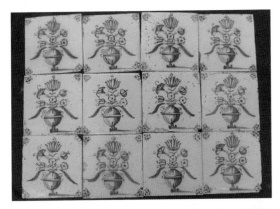

Delft Blue and White Tiles

- **18th century**

Dutch Delft blue and white tiles featuring vase with flowers in the centre.

- *12cm x 12cm*
- **£450**   • **Guest & Gray**

Stoneware Tankard

- **18th century**

German stoneware tankard with pouring lip and flat pewter cover, decorated with applied blossoms and flowers connected by engraved stems with embossed diamond pattern above and below.

- *height 23cm*
- **£650**   • **Guest & Gray**

Castelli Beaker

- **18th century**

Castelli beaker decorated with a putto resting in woodland.

- *height 7.7cm*
- **£650**   • **Guest & Gray**

Majolica Chestnut Dish

- **1863**

Victorian Minton majolica chestnut dish and ladle.

- *length 26cm*
- **£1,250**   • **D. Hume**

Faïence Sconces

- *circa 1860*

Very attractive pair of Italian 19th century Faïence wall brackets molded with bust heads and swags.

- *43cm x 28cm*
- **2,500**   • **Rankin & Conn**

Oriental Ceramics

Famille Rose Charger

- *circa 1760*

Chinese export *famille rose* charger in the silver form. Qianlong period.
- *width 39cm*
- £850   • Rankin & Conn

Kutani Cup

- 1890

Rare Japanese Kutani opaque cup and saucer with hand-painted face of geisha girl on the saucer.
- *height 6cm*
- £55   • Beverley

Hexagonal Tea Jars ▶

- *circa 1849*

Chinese export blue and white hexagonal tea jars decorated with dragons chasing flaming pearls, in good condition.
- *height 36cm*
- £4,508   • Rankin & Conn

Gros de Bleu Temple Jars ▼

- *circa 1830*

Fine massive pair of Chinese export *gros de bleu* temple jars and covers in the Qianlong style. Exceptional gilding bright and unrubbed.
- *height 65cm*
- £9,500   • Rankin & Conn

Late Ming Punchbowl ▶

- *1573–1620*

Extremely rare late Ming (Wanli period) punchbowl in the Kraak style with European inspired decorations of figures amid landscapes.
- *16cm x 36cm*
- £3,200   • Rankin & Conn

Cylindrical Hat Stand ▲

- *circa 19th century*

Cylindrical shape porcelain hat stand painted with a pink cherry blossom tree with a song bird, sitting above a pond, with a poem dedicated to the owner with leaf shape openings for airing. Seal of manufacturer on the base. Ex-Guonxi period.
- *height 29cm*
- £385   • Iren Rakosa

Chinese Sauce Tureen ▶

- *circa 1760*

Very rare Chinese export sauce tureen and cover, modelled as a sitting quail on its nest and painted in iron red, black and green. From the Qianlong period.
- *height 9cm*
- £6,700   • Cohen & Cohen

Expert Tips

To authenticate a piece of Ming blue and white ware, it is necessary to study the following aspects of the piece: painting techniques, wash methods, lines, brush strokes, form and shape, clay and glazes used and the evolution of motifs.

Chinese Vase ▼

- *circa 1770*

A fine quality Chinese export porcelain two-handled vase, decorated with a turquoise chicken skin ground and bright "Mandarin" panels. Quianlong Period.
- *height 24cm*
- £420   • Dando

Famille Rose Teapot ◀

- *circa 1790*

Famille rose teapot with a scene after Watteau of Europe, in a garden watched by Pierot. Qianlong Period.
- *height 12cm*
- £1,000   • Cohen & Cohen

Chinese Spoon Dish ▲

- *circa 1760*

Miniature Chinese export spoon dish with shaped rim and a central panel of fruit and flowers in a bowl.
- *length 13cm*
- £240   • Andrew Dando

Annamese Dish ▲

- *12th century*

Annamese dish with scalloped edge with a bold chrysanthemum in the centre, under an olive-green glaze.
- *diameter 15cm*
- £250   • Ormonde Gallery

Meiping Vase ▶

- *circa 1745*
Famille rose "Meiping" vase of globular form, boldly painted with a phoenix among branches of prunus blossom. From the Qianlong period.
- *height 34cm*
- £9,100   • Cohen & Cohen

Lemonade Jug ▲

- *circa 1780–1820*
Extremely rare (so far only one known) Canton enamel lemonade jug decorated with a pastoral scene and figures. The yellow background is decorated with foliate designs and pink blossom, with a lip incorporating a blue foliate design, with a chrysanthemum to the centre.
- *height 18cm*
- £1,200   • Ormonde Gallery

Octagonal Meat Dish ▼

- *circa 1760*
Famille rose octagonal meat dish, brightly enamelled with butterflies feeding from fruit and flowers within a motttled border of pale green and brown. From the Qianlong period.
- *length 33cm*
- £1,300   • Cohen & Cohen

Glazed Jug ▲

- *11th century*
Globular-shaped jug with strap handle, wide splayed neck, lobbed body and spout, raised on a circular foot with stops to the base.
- *height 24cm*
- £950   • Ormonde Gallery

Famille Rose Plate ◀

- *circa 1760*
Chinese export porcelain *famille rose* pattern plate.
- *diameter 32cm*
- £340   • Dando

Chinese Coffee Cup ▲

- *circa 1760*
Chinese export coffee cup of unusual size with ear-shaped handle and a *famille rose* pattern.
- *height 8cm*
- £95   • Dando

Chinese Export Vases ▲
- *circa 1780*

A pair of Chinese export vases
and stands in Mandarin palette
on turquoise ground, each with a
tapering square section and
butterfly handles. Qianlong
period.
- *height 24cm*
- £24,000   • Cohen & Cohen

Sawankalok Bowl ▲
- *15th century*

Tia Sawankalok green bowl with
a wide lip with a moulded rim,
above a stylised lotus flower
design, centred with a
chrysanthemum.
- *diameter 26cm*
- £280   • Ormonde Gallery

Expert Tips

*Early Ming potters used
calligraphic strokes to draw the
motifs. The pieces are thicker
and more translucent than late
Ming pieces which have a
thinner, transparent glaze.*

Chinese Teapoy ▲
- *circa 1790*

Chinese export polychrome
teapoy and cover with a scene
after Watteau of Europeans in a
garden, watched by a Pierrot.
From the Qianlong period.
- *height 16cm*
- £1,750   • Cohen & Cohen

Incense Burner ▼
- *5th century*

Green circular incense burner of
two tiers with a dog on the upper
section, the whole resting on
three feet.
- *height 7cm*
- £150   • Ormonde Gallery

Chinese Bowl ▼
- *circa 18th century*

Elegant blue bulbous bowl
supported on three button feet.
- *diameter 24cm*
- £480   • Iren Rakosa

Quianlong Plates ▼
- *1760*

One of a pair of Chinese export
porcelain plates, painted with
elaborate scenes within border in
famille rose enamels.
- *diameter 21.5cm*
- £750   • Dando

Sung Dynasty Bowl ◄
- *11–12th century*

Sung Dynasty bowl with an
incised repetitive design of
stylised flowers, under a
green glaze.
- *diameter 20.4cm*
- £400   • Ormonde Gallery

- *circa 1760*
Pair of Chinese export *famille rose* meat dishes.
- *21cm x 29cm*
- **£1,650**   • Rankin & Conn

Japanese Imari Jars ▶

- *circa 1850*
Good pair of Japanese Imari jars with moulded bodies and unusual decoration of braid on the necks.
- *height 30cm*
- **£950**   • Rankin & Conn

Tureen and Stand ▲

- *circa 1770*
Excellent Chinese export *famille rose* tureen and stand from the Qianlong period. Decorated with a pretty floral motif.
- *20cm x 28cm*
- **£5,800**   • Rankin & Conn

Samson Armorial
Wine Cooler ▶

- *circa 1850*
Samson Armorial wine cooler decorated in the Imari colours
- *height 19cm*
- **£850**   • Rankin & Conn

Imari Fish Dishes ◀

- *circa 1850*
Pair of 19th century Japanese Imari fish dishes.
- *height 29cm*
- **£950**   • Rankin & Conn

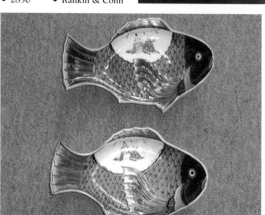

Expert Tips

On of the most famous copiers was Edme Samson, who worked in France from 1845. Samson copied Bow, Worcester, Meissen and Chinese and Japanese ware. His wares are often marked with an "S", which can appear with the factory mark – sometimes the "S" is tampered with and removed. His pieces are collectable in their own right.

Chinese Tankard ▼
- *circa 1770*

Export Chinese porcelain tankard with "Mandri"-style panel depicting a courtly scene.
- *height 24cm*
- £235 ● Dando

Oriental Cup ▼
- *16th century*

Blue and white cup with a wide splayed rim, with a blue lattice design running around the exterior, above a song bird with prunus blossom.
- *height 5cm*
- £450 ● Ormonde Gallery

Sauce Tureen and Cover ▶
- *circa 1765*

Rare Chinese export sauce tureen, cover and stand of English creamware form. Painted with the arms of Parker imp. Nesbitt, within a diaper border. Qianlong period. Made for the widow of the second Earl of Macclesfield (Parker), she was a Nesbitt.
- *height of tureen 13cm*
- £16,000 ● Cohen & Cohen

Desk Set ▲
- *circa 1760*

Rare and unusual *famille rose* desk set from the Qianlong period. Comprising five quill holders, two inkwells with pewter liners and a covered box.
- *height 6cm*
- £4,800 ● Cohen & Cohen

Chinese Marriage Plate ▲
- *circa 1750*

Exceptionally rare Chinese export marriage plate made for the Dutch market, with a polychrome depiction of the ship Slooten, from the Qianlong period.
- *diameter 36cm*
- £12,500 ● Cohen & Cohen

Tea Bowl and Saucer ▲
- *circa 1735*

Chinese export porcelain tea bowl and saucer, profusely gilded with floral sprays and cartouches of prunus with a central panel of a Chinese gentleman.
- *diameter of cup 6cm*
- £225 ● Dando

Nanking Bowl and Saucer ▲
- *1790*

Nanking blue and white bowl and saucer with pagoda scenes and later English gilding.
- *diameter of saucer 13cm*
- £125 ● Dando

Chinese Dinner Plate ◄

- *circa 1740*

Fine Chinese export *famille rose* dinner plate from the Qianlong period, painted with the "Arbour Pattern" after Cornelis Pronk.
- *diameter 23cm*
- £5,200 • Cohen & Cohen

Chinese Candlesticks ▼

- *circa 1770*

Pair of *famille rose* candlesticks of European silver form, on octagonal bases, painted with Chinese domestic scenes on a gilt ground. Qianlong period.
- *height 18cm*
- £10,700 • Cohen & Cohen

Storage Jar ▼

- 1640

Blue and white storage jar of bulbous proportions decorated with a repetitive pattern of blue flowers on a white ground.
- *height 35cm*
- £550 • Ormonde Gallery

Stoneware Jar ▲

- *Tang 618–906 AD*

Stoneware jar of globular form, with a flared neck and an uneven straw coloured glaze around the middle from the Tang Dynasty, raised on a circular foot.
- *height 12cm*
- £352 • Ormonde Gallery

Famille Rose Ewer ▼

- *circa 1760*

Famille rose ewer and cover with "C" shape handle and matching basin all painted with flowering chrysanthemum growing from rockwork. Qianlong period.
- *height of ewer 22cm*
- £5,000 • Cohen & Cohen

Expert Tips

The early Ming period is marked by a strict control of political and cultural development, for example, a decree was issued in 1371 during the reign of Hong Wu forbidding certain subjects such as previous emperors, queens, lions or saints on porcelains.

Fo Dogs on Bases ▼
- *circa 1850*
Large pair of *famille verte* figures
of Fo dogs and puppies with
detachable square bases in the
Chinese Kangxi period style, by
Samson de Paris.
- *height 48.5cm*
- £2,900 • Rankin & Conn

Kangxi Bowl ▶
- **18th Century**
Beautiful Chinese export Kangxi
period moulded bowl. Finely
moulded and decorated with a
swirling design of flowers.
- *11cm x 22cm*
- £2,500 • Rankin & Conn

Kangxi Ewer ◀
- *circa 1675*
Exceptionally rare Chinese
export Kangxi period ewer.
Originally made for the Islamic
market copying earlier metal
forms. There are similar examples
in the Topkapi museum in
Istanbul.
- *28cm x 23cm*
- £7,500 • Rankin & Conn

Kangxi Temple Jar ◀
- *circa 1670*
Superb Kangxi temple jar.
Cover decorated with a scrolling
peony motif and a biscuit Fo dog
finial.
- *height 60cm*
- £5,500 • Rankin & Conn

Expert Tips

*Eighty per cent of all reign
marks on Chinese porcelain are
retrospective, this is intended as
a tribute to imperial ancestors.*

Famille Verte Vase ▼
- *circa 1850*
19th century *famille verte* vase
decorated on the biscuit.
- *height 18.5cm*
- £2,250 • Rankin & Conn

Blanc de Chiné Fo Dogs ◀
- *circa 1710*
Pair of Kangxi period *blanc de
chiné* taper stick holders of Fo
dogs standing on square bases.
- *28cm*
- £1,600 • Rankin & Conn

Chinese Chocolate Pot ◀

- *circa 1775*
Unusual Chinese export bulbous chocolate pot.
- *height 19.5cm*
- £9,000 • Cohen & Cohen

Tea Bowl and Saucer ▲

- *circa 1770*
Famille rose tea bowl and saucer, decorated with a group of European figures in a garden within a gilt, pink and grisaille border. Qianlong period.
- *height of cup 4.5cm*
diameter of saucer 13cm
- £950 • Cohen & Cohen

Famille Rose Plate ▼

- *circa 1740*
One of a pair of fine and rare *famille rose* botanical plates, each vividly painted with a cornucopia of European flowers, made in the Qianlong period.
- *diameter 23cm*
- £10,700 • Cohen & Cohen

Chinese Export Plate ▲

- *circa 1760*
Chinese export *famille rose* porcelain plate with floral sprays and gilding.
- *diameter 15cm*
- £375 • Dando

Chinese Hat Stand ▶

- *circa 19th century*
Porcelain hat stand of cylindrical form with a polychrome glaze of scholarly objects, flora and Buddhist symbols. The stand has a six-leaf shape opening for airing. Seal at the base. Ex-Guonxi period.
- *height 29cm*
- £350 • Iren Rakosa

Expert Tips

During the early Ming period the majority of the wares produced tended to be of a functional nature such as bowls, plates, covered jars and incense burners, with only a narrow range of motifs.

Lobed Imari Dish ◄

- *circa 1870*
Koransha Imari lobed dish
showing Kintaro on his carp in
the centre.
- *width 29cm*
- £950 • Rankin & Conn

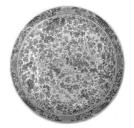

Kangxi Charger ▲

- *1662–1722*
Chinese *famille verte* charger,
decorated with flowers and leafy
tendrils within a conforming
border.
- *diameter 38cm*
- £450 • Guest & Gray

Rouge de Fer Plates ▶

- *1736–95*
Chinese *rouge de fer* plates
decorated with prunus blossoms
issuing from a branch and
chrysanthemums in a vase.
- *diameter 21.5*
- £220 • Guest & Gray

Famille Verte Ginger Jar ▼

- *1662–1722*
Chinese *famille verte* ginger jar
decorated with birds peonies and
flowers on rockwork.
- *height 22cm*
- £1,800 • Guest & Gray

Famille Verte Plate ▶

- *1662–1722*
Chinese *famille verte* plate
decorated with eight horses.
- *diameter 21.5cm*
- £750 • Guest & Gray

Famille Rose Plate ▲
- *circa 1760*
One of a pair of Chinese export plates, painted with elaborate scenes within borders in *famille rose* enamel.
- *diameter 22cm*
- £750 pair • Dando

Chinese Soup Plate ▲
- *1775*
Octagonal Chinese export soft paste porcelain soup plate.
- *diameter 23cm*
- £150 • Dando

Oriental Jar ▲
- *circa 16th century*
Small blue and white jar with an inverted rim and tapered body, decorated with a repeated design of fir trees.
- *height 5cm*
- £240 • Ormonde Gallery

Inkwell ▲
- *11–12th century*
Inkwell from the Sung Dynasty. Designed in a compressed globular form with a stylised flower pattern in relief, under a green glaze.
- *height 10cm*
- £350 • Ormonde Gallery

Chinese Export Basin ▲
- *circa 1725*
Yongzheng period Chinese export basin, richly decorated in rouge de fer and gilt, with the arms of Mertins imp. Peck. The border is decorated with *famille rose* flower heads.
- *diameter 39.5cm*
- £8,500 • Cohen & Cohen

Grisaille Chinese Plate ▶
- *circa 1750*
Important Chinese export plate decorated en grisaille with a portrait of Martin Luther above a panel of Christ and his disciples all within a gilt scroll border. Qianlong Period.
- *diameter 24cm*
- £2,250 • Cohen & Cohen

Blue and White Teacaddy ▲

- **1736–95**

Chinese blue and white teacaddy of shouldered rectangular form and decorated with willow pattern.
- *height 11cm*
- **£280** • Guest & Gray

Blue and White Chinese Dish ▲

- **circa 1600**

Chinese blue and white dish with two hairline cracks.
- *diameter 27.2cm*
- **£380** • Guest & Gray

Qianlong Teacaddy ◄

- **1736–95**

Chinese blue and white teacaddy of shouldered rectangular form decorated with flowers and without cover.
- *height 11cm*
- **£250** • Guest & Gray

Expert Tips

Teacaddies should have orginal locks, screws and hinges and, if appropriate, glass bowls or lining.

Famille Verte Dish with Gardens ▼

- **1662–1722**

Chinese *famille verte* dish decorated with a central basket of peonies and daisies within shaped panels of flowering gardens, mythical beasts, vases of flowers and precious objects.
- *diameter 35cm*
- **£4,500** • Guest & Gray

Famille Verte Charger with Battle Scene ◄

- **1662–1722**

Chinese *famille verte* charger decorated with a battle scene showing soldiers charging each other on horseback with spears and swords. The scalloped rim has landscape cartouches.
- *diameter 37cm*
- **£2,800** • Guest & Gray

Famille Rose Teapot with Flowers

- *1736–95*

Chinese *famille rose* teapot decorated with scattered flowers.

- *height 12.5cm*
- £150 • Guest & Gray

Famille Verte Bowl and Cover

- *1662–1722*

Chinese *famille verte* bowl decorated with floral patterns and matching lid with raised knob topped by red flower.

- *diameter 35cm*
- £850 • Guest & Gray

Blue and White Tea Bowl and Saucer

- *1662–1722*

Chinese blue and white tea bowl and saucer with small hairline crack to tea bowl.

- *diameter 15cm*
- £140 • Guest & Gray

Famille Rose Punch Bowl

- *1736–95*

Large magnificent Chinese *famille rose* punch bowl, finely painted with large Mandarin figures.

- *diameter 38cm*
- £2,200 • Guest & Gray

Pair of Famille Rose Scalloped Bowls

- *1736–95*

Pair of *famille rose* scalloped bowls decorated with floral sprays.

- *diameter 27cm*
- £750 • Guest & Gray

Mandarin Vases ▲

- *circa 1780*

Pair of Mandarin vases and covers
with figurative scenes reserved on
a gilt ground with *rouge de vert*
with diaper covers showing small
landscape scenes and dogs. With
Fo. Qianlong period finials.
- *height 37cm*
- **£20,000** • **Cohen & Cohen**

Satsuma Vases ▲

- *circa 1870*

A pair of gold Satsuma vases of
baluster form, painted with holy
men and a dragon who keeps
away the evil spirits and brings
prosperity to the family.
- *height 23cm*
- **£450** • **Barrett/Towning**

Swato Dish ▼

- *15th century*

A slip decorated Swato dish,
raised from a shipwreck off the
coast of East Timor, from the late
Ming Dynasty. The centre is
decorated with a spray of
chrysanthemums, in a stippled
and feather technique, the simple
scroll border with stippled
blooms, all on an even cobalt-
blue ground. The underside is
plain, with a grit base.
- *diameter 38cm*
- **£650** • **Ormonde Gallery**

Ming Dish ▲

- *16–17th century*

Ming dish with scalloped rim and
a raised floral design under a
green glaze.
- *diameter 15cm*
- **£3,800** • **Ormonde Gallery**

Transitional Food Jar ▼

- *1640*

Blue and white transitional food
jar of ovoid form, with a floral
design running around the
shoulders and figures in a pastoral
setting running around the body.
- *height 16cm*
- **£550** • **Ormonde Gallery**
Dscn5675

Chinese Bowl ◀

- *circa 1736–1795*

Rare salesman's bowl showing
different patterns available to
customers ordering from China.
Qianlong Period.
- *diameter 11cm*
- **£3,000** • **Cohen & Cohen**

Clocks, Watches & Scientific Instruments

The world of the scientific instrument is fascinating and the subject is still in its infancy as far as collectors are concerned.

Clocks and other timepieces are some of the most personal antiques, often passing down through families for generations. This, and the fact that most English and some European clocks bear maker's marks, is very helpful for collectors wanting to know the history of their pieces. However, clocks and other scientific instruments are mechanical objects that require periodic attention and maintenance in order to function. Neglected clocks can be extremely expensive to repair and though removing worn wheels or pinions is acceptable, replacement of other original parts such as a dial can greatly reduce the overall value. Whenever possible, request a condition report on the case, movement and dials of an item that you are considering purchasing.

On a brighter note, even non-working clocks are beautiful pieces that can be used to adorn a home. Fine mahogany longcase clocks with painted faces, complex skeleton clocks and decorative carriage clocks are currently much sought-after items that are likely to increase in value.

Clocks

French Louis XV Clock ▶

- *circa 1765*

A magnificent French Louis XV transitional, ormolu mantel clock on ormolu-mounted ebonised base. Finely chased bronzework. Swan's head handles, rosettes and guilloche decoration to the base. English purpose-made chain fusee movement signed on dial and backplate, "Barwise, London".
- *height 40cm*
- £19,875 • Gavin Douglas

Lyre Clock ◀

- *circa 1890*

Fine Louis XV style *bleu du roi* porcelain and ormolu Apollo lyre clock with moving gridiron bezel pendulum with brilliants. Eight-day bell strike. Floral sprays painted on dial and bronze hands.
- *height 48cm*
- £9,750 • Gavin Douglas

Boy Riding a Dolphin Clock ▼

- *circa 1880*

Outstanding French ormolu and blue porcelain mantel clock, surmounted by a boy riding a dolphin. Depictecd on each panel are a merman, a woman, the dial and Venus in her chariot. Silver highlights to the original ormolu, eight-day bell striking movement.
- *height 35cm*
- £3,950 • Gavin Douglas

Cupid Clock ▼

- *circa 1860*

Fine and unusual glove clock with ormolu cupid resting on a white marble circular base. Eight-day bell strike lever movement.
- *35cmx 18cm*
- **£2,750**   **Gavin Douglas**

Brass Clock ▲

- *circa 1880*

Unusual brass clock in the style of Cole signed Hancock. Fine English lever escapement.
- *height 41cm*
- **£6,250**   • **Gavin Douglas**

Louis XV Style Clock ▲

- *circa 1820*

Outstanding English double-fusee mantel clock in the style of Louis XV by the eminent maker James McCabe, with a fine rococo case, standing upon original base. Superbly cast, chased and gilded. Double fusee movement with original chains and pendulum strikes the hours on a bell.
- *height 14.5.cm*
- **£7,750**   • **Gavin Douglas**

Desk Compendium ▼

- *circa 1880*

Fine quality English gilt bronze and enamel desk compendium in the form of a satchel with deep blue enamel buckles to the straps. Inside a watch in the manner of Cole, together with an inkwell stamp box, pin holder and pen rest.
- *9.5cm x 17.5cm*
- **£2,450**   • **Gavin Douglas**

Cloisonné Clock Set ▲

- *circa 1900*

A very attractive three piece gilt bronze cloisonné clock set. The side pieces in the form of urns each with handles and a cupid. Eight-day lever escapement movement.
- *height 27cm*
- **£4,600**   • **Gavin Douglas**

Expert Tips

A specialist should carry out the cleaning and oiling of a clock's mechanism. Wheels and pinions should never be oiled.

Mahogany Longcase Clock ▼

- *circa 1770*

A George III mahogany five pillar brass dial longcase clock with eight-day brass dial movement with silver chapter ring. Subsidiary seconds and date with separate engraved makers name plaque. Chimes hourly on a bell.
- *2.24m x 56cm*
- £9,500   • Gütlin Clocks

English Bracket Clock ▼

- *circa 1840*

Mahogany English bracket clock by Taylor of Bristol. The twin gut fusee movement with shoulder plates and hour strike on a bell. White painted convex dial signed Taylor of Bristol with black spade hands.
- *53.5cm x 30cm x 18cm*
- £3,500   • Gütlin Clocks

Victorian Bracket Clock ▲

- *circa 1870*

An English triple-fusee, black ebonised, quarter-chiming Victorian bracket clock. The three train movement striking the quarters on eight bells with hour strike on a gong. The brass dial with silvered and engraved chapter ring, silvered strike/silent ring and finely chiselled brass spandrels.
- *38cm x 30.5cm*
- £5,500   • Gütlin Clocks

Bracket Clock ▲

- *circa 1850*

Burr walnut double fusee English bracket clock by Payne & Co, 163 New Bond Street, London. Numbered clock No.3234. The double chain fusee eight-day numbered and signed English movement.
- *43.5cm x 30.5cm*
- £6,500   • Gütlin Clocks

Grand Sonnerie Bracket Clock ▼

- *circa 1750*

Oak cased original verge escapement Austrian Grand Sonnerie bracket clock. The triple fusee Austrian movement of short duration (30-hour) with original verge escapement. Makers name plague signed "Augustin Heckel".
- *53.5cm x 25.5cm*
- £3,90   • Gütlin Clocks

Timepiece Clock ▼

- *circa 1830-35*

Victorian flame mahogany, unnamed, single-fusee timepiece clock, the single gut fusee eight-day English movement with original pendulum holdfast.
- *29cm x 17.5cm*
- £1,800   • Gütlin Clocks

Queen Anne Clock ▼

- *circa 1860-1890*

Fine bracket clock in the Queen Anne style in blonde tortoiseshell and lacquered bronze. Eight-day movement having steel suspended pendulum and striking the hours and halves on a gong.
- *height 33cm*
- **£7,750** • Gavin Douglas

Apollo's Lyre Clock ▼

- *circa 1817*

Fine French Empire clock in the form of Apollo's lyre, the case resting on four bun feet and with a trumpet mount to a rectangular base. Eight-day striking movement with silk suspension. Attributed to André Galle. Superb dial.
- *height 48cm*
- **£6,750** • Gavin Douglas

Ormolu Clock ▶

- *circa 1860*

Cut and engraved ormolu English strut clock in the manner of Cole silvered dial with blue steel hands. Eight-day lever movement.
- *height 28cm*
- **£2,450** • Gavin Douglas

Ormolu Clock ▲

- *circa 1870*

French original ormolu and blue celeste porcelain clock. Surmounted by an ormolu mounted porcelain urn, eight-day bell striking movement.
- *height 43cm*
- **£3,450** • Gavin Douglas

White Marble Clock ▼

- *circa 1780*

French white marble and ormolu Directoire mantle clock in Gout d'Egypte. Sphynx figures to the sides of the clock. Brickwork column holding an ormolu fountain eight-day bell strike with silk suspension.
- *height 39cm*
- **£4,250** • Gavin Douglas

French Lyre Clock ▲
- *1880*
French Ormolu mounted birds-eye maple, lyre clock with foliate ormolu mounts.
- *height 44cm*
- £2,000   • Vincent Freeman

Skeleton Clock ▲
- *circa 1860*
English cathedral two-train skeleton clock modelled as a cathedral encased in dome-shaped glass case on a moulded marble base.
- *height 65cm*
- £4,000   • Vincent Freeman

French Zodiac Clock ▼
- *1885*
French clock made for the Spanish market with barometer, thermometers and revolving signs of the zodiac. The clock is encased within a globe of the world with a silver cloud formation running through the centre of the piece.
- *height 43cm*
- £3,000   • Vincent Freeman

German Porcelain Clock ▼
- *circa 1880*
German porcelain clock modelled as a cherub sitting in a chariot drawn by two lions, raised on a painted rectangular base with a painted panel of a landscape.
- *51cm x 46cm*
- £3,500   • Vincent Freeman

French Clock Set ▲
- *1800*
French slate mantle clock set, with eight-day movement and inlaid with brass. With two side urns, the base of each urn decorated in brass with a scene of children playing within a forest setting with animals.
- *height 46cm*
- £375   • Julian Smith

Viennese Clock ▲
- *1880*
Vienna clock with porcelain cartouches of celestial scenes with blue enamelled architectural pillars and gilding, raised on gilt ball feet.
- *height 40cm*
- £4,000   • Vincent Freeman

Folding Clock ▶

- *circa 1927*

English silver and enamel folding travelling clock Birmingham.
- *height 4cm*
- £675 • Gavin Douglas

Knight Mantel Clock ▲

- *circa 1880*

A French mantel clock in the style of a knight's helmet with white porcelain dial.
- *23cm x 18cm*
- £1,250 • Chelsea

Silver and Blue Clock ▲

- *circa 1930*

Silver and blue enamel Art Deco strut clock with Swiss dial.
- *height 11cm*
- £765 • Gavin Douglas

Chinoiserie Clock ▼

- *circa 1930*

Art Deco chinoiserie-decorated clock with mother-of-pearl dial with geometric blue enamelling.
- *height 10cm*
- £1,475 • Gavin Douglas

Blue Enamel Clock ◀

- *circa 1930*

Art Deco blue enamel guilloche clock.
- *height 11cm*
- £675 • Gavin Douglas

French Lyre Clock ▼

• *circa 1900*

A satinwood and gilt ormolu mounted French timepiece lyre clock retailed by "Howell and James", Paris. eight-day French movement with original English lever escapement, convex cream enamel dial with hand painted swags of roses boarding black arabic numerals.

• *25.5cm x 12.5cm*
• £1,600   • Gütlin Clocks

Three-Piece Clock Garniture ▼

• *circa 1870*

French gilt bronze and cloisonne-enamelled three-piece clock garniture. Eight-day movement, chiming hours and half hours on a bell. Urn-shaped side pieces in gilt bronze and blue porcelain with fine cloisonne-enamelling to match.

• *40.5cm x 22.5cm*
• £3,700   • Gütlin Clocks

Three-Piece Clock Garniture ▲

• *circa 1860*

A gilt bronze and jewelled pink porcelain three-piece clock garniture with porcelain panels surmounted by an urn. Eight-day French movement, chiming hours and half hours.

• *43cm x 30.5cm*
• £5,500   • Gütlin Clocks

Mantle Clock ▲

• *circa 1890*

A white Paris Bisque French timepiece mantle clock with small French eight-day timepiece movement, white convex enamel dial with roman numerals and counter poised moon hands.

• *25.5cm x 15.5cm*
• £750   • Gütlin Clocks

Black Marble Clock ▼

• *circa 1860*

French black marble mantle clock with a gilt bronze figure of a maiden reading a book resting on a column with a lyre beside her, eight-day French movement. Half hour strike on a bell.

• *61cm x 56cm*
• £3,500   • Gütlin Clocks

French Four Glass Clock ▼

• *circa 1870*

A polished brass French four glass clock with diamonte bezel. Eight-day movement with hour and half hour strike on a gong and mercury pendulum, the white enamelled dial is painted with pink music sheets.

• *25.5cm x 5cm*
• £1,600   • Gütlin Clocks

Mantle Clock ◀

• *circa 1880*

French gilt metal and porcelain mantle clock, the gilt ormolu case swags to the sides, acanthus cast gallery to the base raised on toupie feet. The pink porcelain panels with gilt-bordered white reserves painted with flowers.

• *51cm x 25.5cm*
• £2,300   • Gütlin Clocks

Chinoiserie Clock

- *circa 1930*
A brass dial with a blue
chinoiserie figurative frame
resting on a brass stand.
- *20cm x 20cm*
- £420   • Chelsea

Travelling Timepiece

- *circa 1930*
Art Deco silver with enamel
travelling clock stamped Levi
Nande.
- *2.5cm x 2cm*
- £825   • Gavin Douglas

Boudoir Clock

- *circa 1930*
A rare silver and enamel clock
with watch inset.
- *6cm x 8cm*
- £2,450   • Gavin Douglas

Eight-Day French Clock

- *circa 1930*
Unusual boulle mantel clock with
French eight-day movement
regulated by a cylinder
escapement.
- *height 15cm*
- £1,275   • Gavin Douglas

Art Deco Timepiece

- *circa 1930*
Art Deco silver clock with
enamel flying birds in the
chinoiserie style.
- *11cm x 8cm*
- £1,275   • Gavin Douglas

French Carriage Clock ▼

- *circa 1880–90*
Carriage clock with eight-day
French timepiece movement and
original silvered cylinder platform
escapement, the polished brass
corniche style case with solid cast
scroll shaped carrying handle.
- *10.4cm x 10cm*
- £550   • Gütlin Clocks

Carriage Clock ▲

- *circa 1880–90*
French polished brass corniche
cased timepiece with alarm, the
eight-day movement with alarm
sounding on a bell.
- *11cm x 7.5cm*
- £550   • Gütlin Clocks

English Bracket Clock ▲

- *circa 1860*
A solid mahogany and brass
inlaid English bracket clock with
quarter striking triple fusee.
Retailed by Dixon of Norwich
chiming every quarter on four
bells. With eight day triple-fusee
movement.
- *68.5cm x 41cm*
- £5,500   • Gütlin Clocks

Brass Carriage Clock ▼

- *circa 1880–90*
French polished brass Anglaise
Riche case chiming carriage
clock. The eight-day French
chiming movement striking the
hours and half hours on a gong
with original silvered English
lever platform escapement.
- *12.5cm x 8.2cm*
- £1,800   • Gütlin Clocks

French Carriage Clock ▲

- *circa 1890–1900*
French miniature polished brass
Corniche cased eight-day carriage
clock timepiece with eight-day
movement and silvered English
lever platform escapement.
- *7.5cm x 5cm*
- £950   • Gütlin Clocks

Gothic Bracket Clock ▲

- *circa 1839*
An early English flame mahogany
silvered dial gothic bracket clock.
The eight-day two-train gut fusee
movement with hour and half
hour strike on a large nickel bell.
Signed and dated D. Shaw,
Leicester, 1839.
- *71cm x 46cm*
- £3,900   • Gütlin Clocks

Rosewood Clock ◀

- *circa 1860*
Fine balloon-shaped rosewood
mantel clock inlaid with brass
and copper with a porcelain dial
with blued steel moon hands.
Eight-day striking movement.
- *height 25cm*
- £2,950   • Gavin Douglas

Black Forest Clock ▼

- *circa 1860*
German Black Forest clock in the
style of a church with bell tower,
monk chime on the half hour and
hour standing on a rusticated base
- *70cm x 37cm*
- £3,500   • Chelsea

French Clock ▲

- *circa 1890*
Mahogany French Art Nouveau
clock with floral fruitwood inlay
standing on four brass-turned
feet.
- *31cm x 9cm*
- £600   • Chelsea

Asprey Dial Clock ▲

- *circa 1920*
Rosewood with satinwood inlays
and the dial signed by Asprey.
French eight-day cylinder
escapement.
- *height 45cm*
- £1,700   • Gavin Douglas

Regency Clock ▶

- *circa 1800*
A Regency ebonised Bracket
clock by Thos. Moss with brass
geometrical inlay and lion head
handles, standing on four brass
ball feet.
- *84cm x 24cm*
- £4,750   • Chelsea

Revolving Lighthouse Clock ▶

- *circa 1880*

An unusual brass clock representing a lighthouse with a thermometer and revolving movement.
- *height 39cm*
- £3,200
  - Chelsea

Skeleton Clock ▲

- *circa 1880*

A brass skeleton clock in the style of a Cathedral with silvereddial standing on a marble base with original glass dome.
- *48cm x 33cm*
- £1,850
  - Chelsea

French Timepiece ▼

- *circa 1900*

French mahogany clock with fruitwood inlay and surmounted by a brass finial.
- *26cm x 13cm*
- £595
  - Chelsea

Ebonised Mantel Clock ▼

- *circa 1880*

Fine ebonised French clock, standing on four pillars with brass trailing encrusted vines and a young girl on a swing.
- *53cm x 33cm*
- £1,550
  - Chelsea

Expert Tips

The springs from which pendulums are suspended are easily broken in transit. Secure or remove them for journeys.

French Mantel Clock ▼

- *circa 1860*

A fine French ebonised mantel clock with four pillars and brass trailing foliage. White porcelain dial flanked by cherubs and scrolling gilt foliate design.
- *49cm x 23cm*
- £1,350
  - Chelsea

Green Enamel Clock

- *circa 1931*
Silver and green Art Deco
guilloche enamel clock.
- *10cm x 11cm*
- **£875** • **Gavin Douglas**

Brass Travel Clock

- *circa 1870*
Brass travelling carriage clock
with compass and thermometer
on the top with brass handle for
carrying.
- *25cm x 15cm*
- **£1,350** • **Chelsea**

Gray of Paris Mantel Clock

- *circa 1870*
Gilt mantel clock with foliate
scrolling and grapes by Gray of
Paris, signed on the VI, of the
white porcelain and navy blue
numerals.
- *30cm x 20cm*
- **£1,350** • **Chelsea**

Globe Clock

- *circa 1920*
Unusual globe converted to a
clock with circular timepiece on a
mahogany stand with attached
movement, made in Leipseig.
- *61cm x 30cm*
- **£2,200** • **Chelsea**

Elephant Clock

- *circa 1880*
Fine French patinated bronze and
original ormolu elephant clock.
Surmounted by a China-man
holding a parasol. Eight-day bell-
striking movement with a steel
suspended pendulum.
- *height 30cm*
- **£5,750** • **Gavin Douglas**

Watches

Rare Agate and Gold Watch with Chatelaine ◀

- *circa 1740*

A rare English agate watch in gold settings with matching chatelaine. Full plate fire gilt movement with square baluster pillars.
- *diameter 51mm x 17mm*
- £7,500   • Pieces of Time

Iron Fusee Drum Timepiece ▼

- *1540*

A rare German verge fusee timepiece in a gilt metal drum case. Deep circular movement constructed of iron with three pillars.
- *54mm x 39mm*
- £25,000   • Pieces of Time

Gold Skeletonised Swiss Verge ▼

- *1780*

Swiss verge in a gold and stone set double sided consular case. The plate and barrel cover pierced and engraved to reveal the train and blue steel mainspring.
- *diameter 40mm*
- £1,900   •Pieces of Time

Skull Watch ▼

- *mid 19th Century*

Swiss verge in a silver case in the form of a skull with matching silver chain. Small full plate gilt fusee movement with pierced and engraved bridge cock.
- *diameter 6cm*
- £5,000   • Pieces of Time

Mandolin Watch ▶

- *circa 1820*

Austrian verge form watch in a gold and enamel case in the form of a mandolin.
- *length 5cm*
- £1,600   • Pieces of Time

Ladies Swiss Watch ▼
- *1920s*

Ladies Swiss made 18ct gold with
a white enamelled dial with
Roman numerals.
- *diameter 2.7cm*
- **£400**   ● AM-PM

Gentleman's Rolex Watch ▼
- *1960*

Gentleman's Rolex Oyster
perpetual explorer wristwatch on
a Rolex Oyster expandable
bracelet.
- *diameter 3cm*
- **£2,400**   ● AM-PM

Hexagonal Watch ▲
- *1920s*

Ladies silver hexagonal
wristwatch with white enamel
dial, auxiliary sweep seconds and
a red number 12.
- *diameter 2cm*
- **£250**   ● AM-PM

Tiffany & Co. Watch ▲
- *1920s*

Ladies Tiffany & Co. Set in 9ct
rose gold white enamelled dial
with Arabic numerals and a red
number 12.
- *diameter 2cm*
- **£500**   ● AM-PM

Rolex Oyster Watch ◄
- *1920s*

Rolex Oyster precision auxiliary
sweep seconds white dial. Two,
four, eight, ten and 12 in Arabic
numerals, set in stainless steel.
- *diameter 1.6cm*
- **£650**   ● AM-PM

Omega Watch ▼
- *1950s*

Swiss made men's Omega 18ct
gold mechanical movement
watch with auxiliary sweep
seconds and a gold dial with gold
hands and gold digits.
- *diameter 3.1cm*
- **£650**   ● AM-PM

Expert Tips

*Pocket watches date back to
1675. Engraved or hand-
painted pictures of rural or
hunting scenes add value, as do
those of classical mythology, so
keep a look out for these.*

Ladies Movado Watch ▼
- *1940s*

Ladies Movado Swiss made 8ct
rose gold wristwatch with a
square face and two-tone dial
with Arabic numerals.
- *diameter 1.9cm*
- **£450**   ● AM-PM

Omega Watch ▼

- **1950s**
Gentleman's Omega watch set in 9ct gold on a white dial with gold Arabic numerals and auxiliary sweep seconds.
- *diameter 2.9cm*
- **£350**
- **AM-PM**

Romer Wristwatch ▲

- **1950s**
Ladies Swiss made Romer wristwatch set in 9ct gold on a 9ct gold bracelet with safety chain. White dial with three, six, nine and 12 in Arabic numerals.
- *diameter 1.2cm*
- **£250**
- **AM-PM**

Vacheron Constantin Watch ▼

- **1960s**
Gentleman's Vacheron Constantin 18ct white gold wristwatch with oblong design black dial with white gold digits.
- *diameter 1.9cm*
- **£1.300**
- **AM-PM**

Bulova Wristwatch ▲

- **1920s**
Ladies Bulova wristwatch set in 18ct gold with white dial. three, six, nine and 12 in Arabic numerals with serrated lugs, on a black leather cocktail strap.
- *diameter 1.1cm*
- **£200**
- **AM-PM**

Universal Geneve ▶

- *circa 1939*
An early 18ct gold Compax two-button chronograph with subsidiary seconds, minute and hour recording dials.
- **£3,900**
- **Anthony Green**

Lemania ▲

- **1953**
An Air Ministry RAF issue, pilots high grade one button chronograph with a steel case. The dial signed "Lemania &" with MOD Arrow, minute recording dial and sweep second dial. The case with fixed bar lugs and back with ordinance marks, "Arrow AM/6B/551 333/53".
- **£1,800**
- **Anthony Green**

Omega Seamaster Watch ▲

- **1950s**
Gentleman's Omega seamaster wristwatch set in stainless steel with a black dial with white Roman numerals. Mechanical movement and a screw back case. Red second hand.
- *Diameter 2.9cm*
- **£300**
- **AM-PM**

Rolex Watch ▼

- *circa 1920s*
Silver Tonneau shaped
gentleman's wristwatch. The
white enamel dial signed Rolex,
with luminous numerals and
hands and subsidiary seconds.
The 3pc case signed Rolex 7
Worlds Records Gold Medal
Geneva Suisse (RWC Ltd)
#64948. The lever movement
signed Rolex Swiss made. 15
Rubies.
  - **£2,550** • **Anthony Green**

Omega Watch ▼

- *circa 1938*
An 18ct gold wrist chronograph
with subsidiary seconds and 30
minute register dial. The main
dial with outer tachymeter scal.
Inner pulsations scale and base
1000 scale. The case signed
Omega & with Swiss control
marks. CS #9174757. The
movement signed Omega Watch
Company. 17 Jls #9388131.C333.
  - **£6,500** • **Anthony Green**

Aviator's Chronograph ▲

- *circa 1968*
An aviator's "Navitimer"
chronograph by Breitling, with
subsidiary dials for sweep seconds,
minute and hour recording. Outer
rotating bezel allowing various
aviation calculations. Case #
1307320 Ref # 806.
  - **£1,800** • **Anthony Green**

Hunting Chronograph ▲

- *1907*
Swiss made Hunting Split
Secondsi Chronograph with
subsidiary minute recording
and sweep second dials.
Case ~ 130519. The white
enamel dial signed S. Smith
& Son 9. The Strand London
Maker to the Admiralty.
142B 68.Non Magnetizable
Swiss Made.
  - **£2,950** • **Anthony Green**

Flightmaster Chronograph ▼

- *circa 1978*
A steel aviator's "Flightmaster"
chronograph by Omega, with
multifunction dial and internal
rotating bezel. This watch comes
with the original box and papers.
  - **£1,800** • **Anthony Green**

Propelling Pencil ▼

- *circa 1920*
French propelling pencil with
timepiece in engine turned body.
With Swiss lever 15 jewelled
movement. French control marks
and struck. 925 monogram to
case "MA".
  - **£1,950** • **Anthony Green**

Gentleman's Pocket Watch ▶

- *circa 1890*
Gold gentleman's pocket by
Balbi, Buenos Aires. With black
Roman numerals on a white face
with a subsidiary second dial. The
front of the case is engraved with
a house with mountains in the
background, surrounded by a
floral design, with diamonds.
  - *2.5cm*
  - **£950** • **Bellum Antiques**

145

Ladies Oyster Watch ▲
- *1930s*

Rolex Oyster precision ladies stainless steel wristwatch with a white dial and trianglular digits.
- *diameter 1.8cm*
- £650 ● AM-PM

Benson Watch ▲
- *1940s*

J.W. Benson ladies wristwatch set in 9ct gold with fancy lugs amd white dial with Arabic numerals.
- *diameter 1.7cm*
- £250 ● AM-PM

Oyster Wrist Watch ▼
- *1950s*

Gentleman's Rolex Oyster Royal watch set in stainless steel with a white mottled dial with three, six, nine in Arabic numerals, Mercedes hands and mechanical movement.
- *diameter 2.6cm*
- £800 ● AM-PM

Rolex Wristwatch ▼
- *1918*

Ladies Rolex wristwatch with white enamelled dial set in 9ct gold. Black Arabic numerals.
- *diameter 2cm*
- £580 ● AM-PM

Gentleman's Longines Watch ▶
- *1930s*

Gentleman's Longines oblong design set in 14ct. rose gold, with white dial set with gold Arabic numerals and auxiliary sweep seconds.
- *diameter 1.8cm*
- £950 ● AM-PM

Fly-Back Chronograph ▲
- *circa 1970*

A rare German air force issue aviator's "Fly-Back" chronograph by Heuer in steel. The black dial with subsidiary seconds and minute recording dial 1 and red "3H" in circle, case # 6445-12-146-3774 and stamped "BUNDWEHR".
- £2,200 ● Anthony Green

Omega Seamaster Wristwatch ▲
- *1940s*

Gentleman's Omega Seamaster wristwatch set in stainless steel automatic movement, two-tone dial with gold digits.
- *diameter 2.9cm*
- £300 ● AM-PM

Rock Crystal Clockwatch ▶

- *1620*

German verge clockwatch with the bell under the dial in a gilt metal and rock crystal case. Simple small silvered dial, with engraved Roman numerals, later single blue steel hand.

- *37mm x 77mm x 35 mm*
- £16,500 • **Pieces of Time**

Gold and Enamel French Cylinder ▲

- *1790*

A French cylinder in a gold and enamel case with protective outer. Polychrome scene of two figures in a garden painted on translucent dark blue enamel over an engine turned ground.

- *diameter 36mm*
- £2,450 • **Pieces of Time**

Turquoise Set Gold French Verge ▼

- *1820*

A French verge with gold cartouche dial in a turquoise set gold case. Decorative gold open face case, the bezels and middle set with turquoise.

- *diameter 41mm*
- £975 • **Pieces of Time**

Silver Explorer's Watch ▼

- *1878*

A 19th century keyless fusee English lever with up and down dial in a watertight silver case. Comes in a green morocco covered travelling case with easel stand.

- *diameter 59 mm*

Small Early English Verge ▼

- *1655*

A pre-balance spring English verge in a silver gilt case deeply chased and engraved with a representation of a mythical animal amongst profuse foliage.

- *27mm x 10mm*
- £8,550 • **Pieces of Time**

Expert Tips

Check that the case of a pocket watch labelled gold really is gold, particularly when purchasing an American watch. Also ensure the mechanism is in good working order.

Ladies Rolex Wristwatch ▼

- *1940*

Ladies 18ct rose gold Rolex wristwatch with original expanding strap with the Rolex symbol on the buckle square face with scalloped lugs. Gold digits on a white face.

- *diameter 2cm*
- **£1,800**   ● AM-PM

Air King Wristwatch ▲

- *1960s*

Gentleman's Rolex Oyster perpetual Air King Model wristwatch in steel and gold. Automatic movement, white dial with gold digits, with a sunburst bezel.

- *diameter 3cm*
- **£1,400**   ● AM-PM

Jaeger Le Coultre Watch ▲

- *circa 1960*

Jaeger Le Coultre Memovox (alarm) Stainless steel wrist watch with silver digits on a silver face and automatic movement.

- *diameter 4cm*
- **£1,500**   ● AM-PM

Ladies Oyster Watch ▼

- *1920s*

Ladies Rolex Oyster wristwatch set in 14ct gold With mechanical movement, a sunburst dial, auxiliary sweep seconds and a white face with gold numbers.

- *diameter 2cm*
- **£1,500**   ● AM-PM

Oyster Speedking Watch ▲

- *1950s*

Boys size Rolex Oyster Speedking. Stainless steel mechanical movement with silver digits and expandable Rolex Oyster bracelet.

- *diameter 2.8cm*
- **£950**   ● AM-PM

Rolex Cushion Watch ▲

- *1920s*

Gentleman's Rolex cushion wristwatch set in 9ct gold. With white enamel dial, auxiliary sweep seconds and a red number 12. Rolex signature underneath the dial.

- *diameter 2.5cm*
- **£950**   ● AM-PM

Ladies Swiss Watch ▶

- *1920s*

Ladies Swiss made wristwatch in 18ct rose gold with enamel dial with old cut diamonds on the bezel, on an expandable 18ct rose gold bracelet.

- *diameter 1.7cm.*
- **£500**   ● AM-PM

Small Gold Hunter Coin Watch

- *circa 1910*

A Swiss cylinder in a small gold full hunter case, the lids formed from the two halves of a French 20 franc coin dated 1908. When closed the watch resembles a stack of three gold coins.

- *diameter 21mm*
- £975   • Pieces of Time

Swiss Digital Dial Lever ▲

- *circa 1895*

Swiss lever with digital dial in a nickle open-face case marked "Acier Garanti" in an oval, gilt winding button.

- *diameter 53mm*
- £775   • Pieces of Time

Gold Half Hunter Wrist Watch ▼

- *circa 1880*

A Swiss cylinder by Patek Philippe in a gold half hunter case with blue enamel chapter ring, applied twisted wire lugs for a cord strap.

- *diameter 32mm*
- £1,900   • Pieces of Time

Gunmetal World Time Watch ▼

- *circa 1910*

A Swiss lever with world time dial in a gunmetal open face case. White enamel dial with gold decoration.

- *diameter 52mm*
- £1,750   • Pieces of Time

French Oignon Watch and Clock Stand ▲

- *circa 1695*

A French verge oignon watch and ormolu and tortoiseshell stand for use as a clock. Standing on four gilt feet the case has an arched door bordered and decorated with gilt metal.

- *57mm x 22mm*
- £5,975   • Pieces of Time

Silver and Tortoiseshell Verge ◄

- *circa 1688*

An English verge by Tompion in silver and tortoiseshell pair cases with silver pendant and stirrup bow.

- *56mm x 18.5mm*
- £7,950   • Pieces of Time

Gold Half Hunter by Benson ▲

- *circa 1899*

An English lever by Benson in a gold half hunter case. Plain 18ct half hunter case with blue enamel chapter ring, maker's mark "JWB" in an oval.

- *diameter 49mm*
- £1,200   • Pieces of Time

Expert Tips

Rolex is not the only sought-after make: watches made by Patek Philippe are just as keenly pursued but are not so readily found.

149

Enamelled Centre Seconds English Verge ◀

- *circa 1789*

An English centre seconds verge in gilt metal and enamel pair cases for the Chinese market. Outer case with engraved gilt bezels, the front set with a row of green paste stones alternating with split pearls.

- *64mm x 15mm*
- **£4,500**   • Pieces of Time

Gold and Enamel Quarter Repeater with Chatelaine ▲

- *circa 1780*

An French quarter-repeating verge in a gold and enamel consular case, decorated with an oval enamel cartouche depicting two cupids. Matching gilt metal and enamel chatelaine.

- *46mm x 11mm*
- **£6,900**   • Pieces of Time

Expert Tips

Pocket watches date from 1675 – look out for hand-painted pictures of rural or hunting scenes.

Gold Minute Repeating Half Hunter ▼

- *circa 1890*

A Swiss minute repeating lever in a gold half hunter case with blue enamel chapter ring, gold slide in the band.

- *diameter 48mm*
- **£3,200**   • Pieces of Time

Silver Swiss Half Hunter ▼

- *circa 1910*

A Swiss lever in a silver half hunter case. White enamel dial with subsidiary seconds, Arabic numerals and blue steel hands.

- *diameter 52mm*
- **£495**   • Pieces of Time

Marine chronometer ▼

- *circa 1870*

A two-day marine chronometer by Dent with a 24 hour dial in a brass bound mahogany box with brass corners. Engraved signed and numbered silvered brass dial with Arabic numerals for 24 hours.

- *175mm x 175mm x 170mm*
- **£4,900**   • Pieces of Time

Miniature Gold and Enamel Turkish Market Verge ▲

- *circa 1780*

An English verge made for the Turkish market in gold and enamel pair cases, the two halves meeting at a scalloped edge, faces decorated in light blue enamel.

- *34mm x 12mm*
- **£4,500**   • Pieces of Time

Trench Guard Watch ▼

• *circa 1915*
A First World War large size officer's wristwatch with original mesh "Trench Guard". The white enamel dial with subsidiary seconds, signed Omega. The case struck Omega Depose No. 9846 case # 5425073. The movement with Swan Neck Micro Reg. Signed Omega # 211504.
• *diameter 4.2cm*
• **£2,250**   • Anthony Green

Cushion-shaped Watch ▼

• *1924*
Gentleman's silver cushion-shaped wristwatch. The movement signed "Rolex 15 Jewels Swiss Made" Cal 507 Rebberg Depose. The case back signed RWC Ltd. (Rolex Watch Company). The case frame # 655. The dial signed "Rolex Swiss Made". Lug size 22.5mm.
• *width 2.3cm*
• **£2,850**   • Anthony Green

Gold Rolex Watch ▲

• *1935*
A 9ct gold gentleman's Rolex wristwatch. The dial signed Rolex Swiss Made, with subsidiary seconds. The case signed Rolex 25 World Records Geneva Suisse R.W.C. Ltd. # 19736 ref # 2356. Movement Sig Rolex Precision 17 Rubis Patented Superbalance Swiss Made.
• **£4,500**   • Anthony Green

Oyster Royal Watch ▲

• *circa 1947*
An Oyster "Royal" waterproof Rolex wristwatch, with centre seconds. The case signed "Rolex Geneve Suisse" with screw down Oyster button and case # 506021. Ref # 4444.
• **£1,550**   • Anthony Green

Pocket Watch ▶

• *circa 1920*
A high grade fully jewelled minute repeating open face pocket watch, with dial with subsidiary seconds. The case with Swiss control marks for 18ct gold and case # 62837. Repeating activated by a slide on the band.
• **£4,800**   • Anthony Green

Peerless Wristwatch ▼

• *1934*
A gentleman's wristwatch, the movement jewelled to the centre signed "Peerless" Swiss Made # 332257 with S & Co Logo. The case # 331618-2 & FB fo Francis Baumgartner Borgelle case designer Enamel dial subsidiary seconds.
• *diameter 3.3cm*
• **£2,750**   • Anthony Green

Rolex Officer's Wristwatch ▼

• *circa 1916*
An early First World War officer's wristwatch. The silvered dial signed Rolex & Swiss Made. The movement # 4636 and signed Rolex Swiss 15 Jls. Case signed with "W & D" for Wilsdorf & Davis, the original founders of the Rolex empire. Case # 769936.
• **£2,500**   • Anthony Green

Scientific Instruments

French Iluminated Globe ▶
- *circa 1950*

French globe made of glass on a wooden stand in teak finish.
- *30cm x 20cm*
- £950   ● **Map House**

Famous Explorers Globe ▲
- 1807

Made by Dudley Adams of London, this globe shows the accomplishments of the most famous late 18th century explorers; for example, the discoveries of Captain Cook are carefully marked. Three stretchers hold a central compass with blued steel needle.
- *58cm x 30cm*
- £16,500   ● **Map House**

Terrestrial and Celestial Globe ▼
- *circa 1820*

Pair of tabletop globes with wooden four-legged stands and cross stretchers made by James Kirkwood of Edinburgh.
- *46cm x 30cm (both)*
- £19,500   ● **Map House**

Desktop Political Globe ▼
- 1918

Political globe by Peter Oestergaard. Warm and cold ocean currents and steamer routes are marked. On wooden stand with a mahogany finish.
- *64cm x 36cm*
- £1,450   ● **Map House**

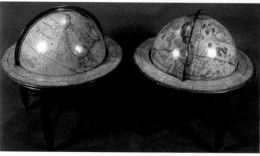

Clock Globe ▲
- *circa 1890*

Globe shows the position and path of the sun over the earth with working clock and calendar ring enclosed in a glass dome. House of Delamarche, France.
- *56cm x 23cm*
- £25,000   ● **Map House**

Terrestrial Globe ▼
- *1824*

Eight-inch terrestrial globe by Delamarche is supported on an ebonised beech stand which has four quadrants giving the names and latitudes of various different cities.
- *height 20cm*
  - £7,500   • Trevor Philip

Travelling Thermometer ▼
- *circa 1810*

Fisherman's or travelling thermometer in original wooden Morocco case. Signed: Richardson, 1 Drury Lane, Holborn, London.
- *height 12cm*
  - £875   • Trevor Philip

Boxwood Nocturnal ▲
- *mid 18th century*

Fine boxwood nocturnal. The central volvelle marked for the Great Bear G and Little Bear L constellations, the centre scale marked with a calendar and hour scale. The reverse of the instrument is marked with the polar distance correction for the Pole star for both the Great and Little Bear constellations when finding the latitude marked Sam Bosswell Fecit on the fiducial arm and David Boswell on the handle.
- *height 25cm*
  - £10,750   • Trevor Philip

Pocket Globe ▼
- *mid 19th century*

Unsigned but probably German. Composed of 12 engraved, hand coloured gores with the continents outlined in primary colours. Housed in a blue card box, the lid marked: "The Earth and its inhabitants". The box contains a folded engraved and hand coloured illustration of 16 males from various parts of the world in their national costumes, labelled in English, French and German.
- *diameter 5cm*
  - £3.500   • Trevor Philip

Noon-Day Cannon Dial ▼
- *early 19th century*

Fine noon-day cannon dial by Boucar, 35 Q de L'Horloge, Paris. The marble base supports a brass cannon, adjustable magnifier and calendar scale. The sun dial graduated from five to 12 to seven, with brass gnomon, correct for latitude 48.5 and 13 minutes.
- *height 26cm*
  - £5,750   • Trevor Philip

Map Measure ▼
- *early 19th century*

Map measure by W. & S. Jones, 30 Holborn, London. The gilt brass case incorporates an enamel dial graduated in Arabic numerals, housed in its original leather case.
- *height 8cm*
  - £3,750   • Trevor Philip

Expert Tips

The original finish is what gives a scientific item its value, so be careful as many instruments have been ruined by the lavish use of metal polishes combined with the buffing wheel.

Admiral Fitzroy Barometer ▶

- *circa 1880*

Simple cased oak Admiral Fitzroy antique barometer with thermometer.
- *91.5cm x 14cm*
- £750
- Rayment

Mahogany Barometer ▼

- *circa 1840*

Mahogany with boxwood and ebony stringing and with thermometer, hygrometer, convex mirror and level dials.
- *96.5cm x 25.4cm*
- £750
- Rayment

Mahogany and Brass Stick Barometer ▲

- *circa 1810*

Mahogany barometer with door over silver engraved brass scales. The scales always signed by a maker or retailer.
- *96.5cm x 10cm*
- £2,650
- Rayment

Dial Barometer ▶

- *1810–1820*

Mahogany barometer with inlay of flowers and shells. Main dial signed by maker.
- *96.5cm x 25.4cm*
- £1,100
- Rayment

Oak Case Barograph ◀

- *circa 1900*

Simple oak case barograph.
- *19cm x 20cm x 35.5cm*
- £850
- Rayment

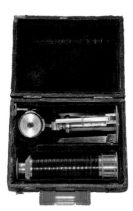

Six-Drawer Telescope ▲

- *1854*

Miniature travelling six-drawer telescope signed: "Baker, 244 High Holborn, London". Housed in its original leather case with extra eye-piece and folding stand.
- *height 9cm*
- £1,550   • Trevor Philip

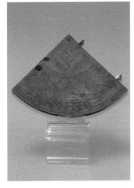

Boxwood Quadrant ▲

- *circa 18th century*

English boxwood quadrant incorporating five star positions.
- *height 12.5cm*
- £6,500   • Trevor Philip

Pocket Globe ▶

- *circa 1834*

Fine three-inch pocket globe by Newton Son & Berry, 66 Chancery Lane, London. Housed in its original simulated fish-skin case. The interior with celestial gores for the northern and southern celestial poles.
- *height 7.5cm*
- £6,500   • Trevor Philip

Sand Glasses ▼

- *mid-17th century–early 19th century*

Group of three sand glasses. Manufactured from glass, brass and wood. Each glass has a different time duration and would have been used for a number of timing uses including marine, business, legal and ecclesiastical use.
- *height 27cm*
- £3,000   • Trevor Philip

French Armillary Sphere ▲

- *late 19th century*

French armillary sphere signed on the enamel charter ring Grivolat Horloger, Paris. The dial is constructed of steel and brass.
- *height 61cm*
- £5,750   • Trevor Philip

Collector's Items

From car boot to old boots, collectables continue to mesmorise and captivate the serious and amateur rummager alike.

In this disposable age, or perhaps because so much is disposable, the artefacts of today are valued more highly by modern collectors than their equivalents were by previous generations, who generally considered anything owned by their parents to be not worth having.

The old saying still holds true that what one throws away today will be collectable tomorrow. From soap packets to mobile phones, all have their place in the collector's market. But beware of fads that start with a splash and are just as soon forgotten. The most collectable items are those that were, in some way, ground-breaking or revolutionary at the time, such as radios, TVs or telephones. Look out, too, for items that are becoming obsolete in the digital age, such as records or cassette tapes. The great advantage when buying collectables is that they need not be especially old or cost a great deal to be considered valuable.

Advertising & Packaging

Castle Polish ▲
- 1930
Red tin of Castle Ballroom floor polish with a picture of a castle.
- *height 11cm*
- £13 • Huxtable's

Bisto Tin ▼
- 1960
Tin of Bisto with a girl wearing a green hat and a boy with a red hat, both sniffing the aroma from a gravy boat.
- *height 19cm*
- £14 • Huxtable's

Pearce Duff's Custard Powder ◄
- 1950
Tin of Pearce Duff's custard powder with a picture of a bowl of custard and pineapple, plums and pears on each side.
- *height 11.5cm*
- £13 • Huxtable's

My Fair Lady Talc ▲
- 1960
Cusson's My Fair Lady talc, showing a photograph of a blonde-haired lady.
- *height 14cm*
- £14 • Huxtable's

Sandwich Tin ▲
• **1930**
Yellow French sandwich tin with
a red handle and trim, showing
Mickey Mouse offering Pluto
some sweets on the lid.
• *8cm x 18cm*
• **£150**   • Huxtable's

Aero Chocolate ▲
• *circa 1930*
Unused bar of Aero chocolate in
a brown wrapper with cream
writing by Rowntrees.
• *width 11cm*
• **£20**   • Huxtable's

Gray Dunn's Biscuits ▶
• **1915**
Yellow ochre bus with red roof
and wheels with figures looking
out of the window and a bus
conductor. With the letters "Gray
Dunn's Biscuits" in red and
"Lands End to John O' Groats".
• *height 9.5cm*
• **£1500**   • Huxtable's

Thorne's Creme Toffee ▲
• **1924**
Royal blue tin with gold scrolling
and the words, "Thorne's Extra
Super Creme Toffee and British
Empire Exhibition Souvenir".
• *height 5.5.cm*
• **£30**   • Huxtable's

Ashtray ▼
• **1955**
Ashtray with "Don't forget your
Anadin tablets" written in white
writing on a red background and
decorated with a two-tone green
Anadin packet.
• *15cm square*
• **£12**   • Huxtable's

Huntley and Palmers Biscuits ▼
• **1927**
A British toy tank containing
Huntley & Palmers biscuits.
• *height 9.5cm*
• **£800**   • Huxtable's

Coffee Packet ▲

- *1920s*
A packet of "delicious coffee",
"fresh roasted" by George
Bowman of 84 Main Street,
Cockermouth. 4oz nett weight.
- *24cm x 19cm*
- £5 • **Keith Old Advertising**

Probyn's Sign ▲

- *circa 1930*
An enamel sign for Probyn's
Guinness's Stout – the Harp
label. From the Argus Brand
showing a picture of two stout
bottles.
- *65cm x 40cm*
- £400 • **Keith Old Advertising**

Cherry Blossom
Shoe Stand ▶

- *circa 1930*
A tin and wood shoe stand
advertising Cherry Blossom shoe
polish in dark tan, with printed
transfer on its sides.
- *height 30cm*
- £150 • **Keith Old Advertising**

McVities & Prices
Digestive Biscuits ▼

- **1930**
Small red tin with a cream lid
and a boy seated on a red tin of
McVitie & Price's Digestive
Biscuits.
- *diameter 8cm*
- £12 • **Huxtable's**

Redbreast Tobacco Tin ▼

- **1930**
Ogden's Redbreast Flake tobacco
tin, made in Liverpool, decorated
with a robin shown perched on a
branch.
- *width 14cm*
- £12 • **Keith Old Advertising**

Pot Lid ▲

- **1890s**
Areca Nut toothpaste for
"Beautiful White Teeth" with
black and white underglazing,
made in London.
- *diameter 6cm*
- £85 • **Keith Old Advertising**

Show Card ▲

- *circa 1890*
Greensmith's Derby dog biscuits
showcard (chrono lithograph)
showing a clown holding a hoop
for a dalmatian to jump through.
- *45cm x 34cm*
- £200 • **Keith Old Advertising**

Book Mark ▼
- *circa 1910*

A book mark advertising
giveaways for Wright's Coal Tar
Soap. The Nursery Soap,
inscribed with the words "The
Seal of Health and Purity".
- *length 15.4cm*
- **£12** • Keith Old Advertising

Player's Ash Tray ▼
- *1930*

Pottery Player's ashtray showing
an interior scene with a man
seated smoking a pipe, a lady in a
green dress, a hound, and the
words "Player's Tobacco Country
Life and Cigarettes".
- *width 11.5cm*
- **£25** • Huxtable's

Golden Leaf Tobacco Tin ▲
- *circa 1912*

Golden leaf navy cut tobacco tin,
manufactured by Louis
Dobbelmann, Rotterdam.
Showing an angel blowing a horn
and flying on wings in the center
of the tin, surrounded by flowers
and the Dutch flag.
- *width 8cm*
- **£60** • Keith Old Advertising

Grimbles Brandy ◀
- *circa 1900*

Grimbles royal cognac brandy of
Albany St, London. 3s per bottle.
Set in a red shield with gold foliate
design.
- *height 45cm*
- **£30** • Michael Laws Antiques

Senior Service Tobacco ▲
- *1940*

Red plaque with the written
inscription "Senior Service
Satisfy – Tobacco at its best".
- *height 28cm*
- **£15** • Michael Laws Antiques

Ceramic Coaster ▼
- *1890s*

A white beer coaster advertising
The Cannon Pale Ale, from the
Cannon Brewery Co Ltd and
bottled by Plowman & Co Ltd,
London.
- *diameter 16cm*
- **£175** • Keith Old Advertising

Bottles

Opaque Bottle ▲
- *circa 1900*
Chinese opaque glass snuff bottle decorated with emerald green flowers and an oriental bird. With a cornelian stopper set within a silver rim.
- *height 7.5cm*
- £175 • Bellum Antiques

Blue Glass Bottle ▲
- *circa 1900*
Blue glass Chinese snuff bottle with green stone stopper set in silver.
- *height 6cm*
- £95 • Bellum Antiques

Porcelain Snuff Bottle ▼
- *circa 1900*
Chinese porcelain snuff bottle with topaz stopper and silver rim.
- *height 7.5cm*
- £65 • Bellum Antiques

Snuff Bottle ▼
- *circa 1900*
Opaque glass Chinese snuff bottle with a stylised sepia leopard chasing its tail.
- *height 6cm*
- £145 • Bellum Antiques

Pagoda Snuff Bottle ▲
- *circa 1900*
Chinese white snuff bottle decorated with crimson fish underneath a pagoda roof. Green stone stopper set in silver.
- *height 7cm*
- £175 • Bellum Antiques

Chinese Bottle ▲
- *circa 1900*
Chinese snuff bottle decorated with a panda and palm trees with a semi precious stone stopper set in silver.
- *height 8cm*
- £95 • Bellum Antiques

Shalimar Scent Bottle ▲

- *1960*

Shalimar clear glass perfume bottle with scrolling and bee design, one of a limited edition of a 100 manufactured.
- *height 20cm*
- £150   • Linda Bee

Saturday Night Lotion ▼

- *1940*

Saturday Night Lotion in clear glass bottle with circular gilt stopper.
- *height 14cm*
- £65   • Linda Bee

Schiaparelli Perfume ▲

- *1960*

Clear glass bottle in the form of a female model. In a moulded glass case.
- *10cm x 6cm*
- £250   • Linda Bee

Eau de Cologne ▲

- *1950*

Scrolling glass bottle with burgundy flame stopper.
- *height 16cm*
- £120   • Linda Bee

Lancôme Bottle ◄

- *1960*

Lancôme perfume bottle with a foliate design on the stopper complete with original box.
- *10cm x 4cm*
- £85   • Linda Bee

Expert Tips

*Sealed bottles with their original
contents and carton are king. Also
inventive forms and good makers.*

Gold Tassle Bottle ▼

- *circa 1920*
Art Deco clear glass perfume
bottle with yellow spots, and
royal blue leaf design around the
base and gilt stopper and gold
tassle.
- *height 15cm*
- £250　　　　　• Linda Bee

Prince Matchabelli Bottle ▼

- *circa 1930*
Prince Matchabelli perfume
bottle in the shape of a ceramic
crown with gilt cross stopper, in
original box.
- *height 4cm*
- £125　　　　　• Linda Bee

Cut Glass Bottle with Black Banding ▶

- *circa 1920*
Art Deco cut glass oval bottle
with black enamel banding.
- *4cm x 11cm*
- £185　　　　　• Trio

Art Deco Bottle ▲

- *circa 1930*
European Art Deco glass bottle
with fine floral and foliate
engraved stopper.
- *height 22cm*
- £250　　　　　• Trio

Black Tassle Bottle ▼

- *circa 1920*
Moulded Art Deco glass bottle
with black circular design and
black tassle.
- *height 14cm*
- £120　　　　　• Linda Bee

Wedgwood Bottle ▼

- *circa 1930*
Wedgwood blue bottle with silver plate stopper.
- *height 4cm*
- £85   • Trio

Silver Bottle ▼

- 1893
Small silver bottle ornately engraved with a floral design.
- *height 5cm*
- £158   • Trio

Ruby Red Bottle ▶

- 1880
Ruby red double-ended perfume bottle with silver stoppers.
- *height 12.5cm*
- £188   • Trio

Candy Stripe Bottle ▲

- *circa 1850*
Candy stripe pink glass perfume bottle with a rose gold stopper.
- *height 6cm*
- £288   • Trio

Ruby Bottle ▶

- 1911
Ruby red perfume bottle with a foliate design engraved in the silver stopper.
- *height 7cm*
- £98   • Trio

Green Double Bottle ▲

- 1880
Green perfume bottle with pinch back stoppers.
- *length 13cm*
- £168   • Trio

Hallmarked Bottle ▶

- **1889**

Dual-ended cut glass Victorian
bottle with silver gilt stopper
hallmarked London, 1889.
- *length 14cm*
- **£245**   • Trio

Victorian Bottle ▲

- *circa 1880*

Purple glass scent bottle with
silver stopper.
- *length 9cm*
- **£245**   • Trio

Joy de Jean Patou
Scent Bottle ▲

- *circa 1950*

Large black plastic bottle, large
red stopper, Joy de Jean Patou.
- *height 15cm*
- **£95**   • Linda Bee

Silver Case ◀

- *circa 1899*

Clear glass perfume bottle inside
a fine silver case.
- *height 4cm*
- **£280**   • Trio

Twisted Glass Bottle ▲
- *1890*

Twisted glass perfume bottle with an opal and diamond stopper.
- *length 6.5cm*
- £550   ● Bellum Antiques

Bloodstone Bottle ▲
- *19th century*

Bloodstone snuff bottle and stopper from China.
- *7.5cm x 3.2cm*
- £220   ● Ormonde Gallery

Cameo Bottle ▼
- *1860*

Thomas Webb cameo bottle in original box.
- *height 11cm*
- £2,750   ● Lynda Brine

Perfume Bottle ▼
- *1870*

Glass perfume bottle with a silver gilt stopper with amethyst stones, inscribed "M.S.V.".
- *height 9cm*
- £425   ● Lynda Brine

Heart Shaped Bottle ▶
- *1870*

Silver heart-shaped bottle with scrolled design.
- *height 9cm*
- £520   ● Lynda Brine

Silver Scent Bottle ▲
- *1760*

Silver lozenge shaped perfume bottle with a foliate design.
- *height 11.5cm*
- £650   ● Lynda Brine

Cranberry Perfume Bottle ▲
- *1870*

Cranberry glass perfume bottle with moulded bubbles with a silver lid.
- *height 10cm*
- £400   ● Lynda Brine

Cameras

Kodak Advertisement

- *circa 1950*

An advertisement in the shape of
a yellow box of film with the
words "Kodak Verichrome Safety
Film" with black and red check
border.
- *41cm x 43cm*
- **£99**
  - Jessop Classic

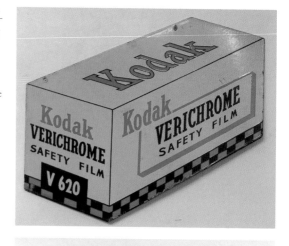

Ikonta Camera ▲

- *circa 1950*

Ikonta model no.524/2. Novur
Lens. F stop 4.5.
- *16cm x 10cm*
- **£149**
  - Jessop Classic

French Sign ▲

- *circa 1940*

Advertisement with a picture of a
camera and the words "*Film
appareils Lumiere – En Vente Ici*".
- *85cm x 80cm*
- **£200**
  - Jessop Classic

Sign for Photos

- *circa 1950*

Cream metal sign with the word
"Photo" in red with red and
yellow border.
- *40cm x 59cm*
- **£50**
  - Jessop Classic

Zeiss Strut Camera ▲

- **1928**

A 4.5 x 6cm Strut-type camera,
with compur shutter.
- *10cm x 9cm*
- **£199**
  - Jessop Classic

Camera Sign

- *circa 1950*

Yellow sign with red writing with
the words "*Appareils Pellicules*" a
sign for cameras and films.
- **26cm x 93cm**
- **£95**
  - Jessop Classic

Retina Kodak Camera ▲
- *circa 1960*
Retina-Xenar F2.8 45mm lens by Kodak.
- *height 8cm*
- £70 • Mac's Cameras

Franke & Heidecke Rolly Camera ▲
- *1921–40*
Frank & Heidecke Braunschweig, Germany, Rolley Heidoscop three lens stereo camera including its own case. 7.5cm F4.5 Tessar Lens.
- *height 17cm*
- £699 • Jessop Classic

Soligor Camera ▲
- *circa 1960*
Soligor 50mm lens, Japanese made auto lens.
- *height 7cm*
- £74 • Mac's Cameras

Expert Tips

When purchasing an antique camera ensure, that it is in good working order and check the quality of the lens. Remember to ask the dealer which film type the camera uses as some films are no longer manufactured.

Robin Hood Camera ▼
- *1930*
Black marbelised bakelite Robin Hood camera with a picture of Robin Hood by Standard Cameras of Birmingham. Takes darkroom loaded single sheets of 45 x 107mm film. Originally came with film, paper and darkroom safelight. Sometimes seen in England, but rarely seen elsewhere.
- *height 5cm*
- £69 • Jessop Classic

Miniature Tessina ▼
- *1960*
Swiss-made miniature Tessina camera in the style of a watch, with meter and strap. It took exposure on 35mm film, which was divided up in special cartridges.
- *width 6.8cm*
- £899 • Jessop Classic

Mamiya ▲
- *1959*
Japanese Mamiya 16 camera.
- *width 11.5cm*
- £49 • Jessop Classic

Contina Zeiss Camer ▲
- *circa 1960*
Zeiss Contina camera with an F2.8 45mm Novica lens.
- *height 7cm*
- £30 • Mac's Cameras

Rajar Bakelite Camera ▼

- **1929**
Rajar black bakelite No.6.
Folding camera. With 120 roll
film, with 6 x 9cm negative size.
- *height 17cm*
- **£49**　　　　• Jessop Classic

Ensign Cupid Camera ▼

- **1922**
Ensign Cupid simple metal-
bodied camera. 4 x 6cm exposures
on 120 film. The design is based
on a 1921 prototype for a stereo
camera, which was never
produced. Mensicus achromatic
F11 lens. Available in black, blue,
grey and some other colours.
- *height 8cm*
- **£89**　　　　• Jessop Classic

The New Special Sybil ▶

- **1914–35**
The new special Sybil. Ross
Xpress F4.5 112mm. N & G
special shutter.
- *height 16cm*
- **£149**　　　　• Jessop Classic

Rolleiflex Camera ▼

- **circa 1955–65**
Rolleiflex camera with a Tessar
1.3.8. F7.5mm lens.
- *height 19cm*
- **£70**　　　• Mac's Cameras

Revere Stereo 33 ▲

- **1950**
Revere Stereo 33 made in the
U.S.A. 35mm F3.5 Amaton.
Complete with its original leather
case.
- *width 19cm*
- **£249**　　　　• Jessop Classic

Tennents Lager Can Camera ▲

- **1980**
Promotional Tennents lager can
camera.
- *length 12cm*
- **£39**　　　　• Jessop Classic

Kodak Camera ▲

- **circa 1960**
Kodak 35 camera with an F4.5
51mm lens.
- *height 6cm*
- **£50**　　　• Mac's Cameras

Weston Master Light Meter ◀

- *circa 1940*

English Weston Master light meter.

- *9cm x 6cm*
- £20 ● Jessop Classic

Speed Graphhic ▲

- *circa 1948*

Miniature "Speed Graphic" camera. Optar Lens 101mm.

- *23cm x 16cm*
- £299 ● Jessop Classic

Lizars Challenge ▶

- *circa 1903*

Lizars Challenge made in Glasgow mahogany frame and brass fittings, Bush and Long Lens.

- *17cm x 21cm*
- £249 ● Jessop Classic

Meopta Admira 8F Camera ▶

- *circa 1960*

Meopta Admira 8F- similar to the A8G but with BIM.

- *16cm x 16cm*
- £30 ● Jessop Classic

Newman Sinclair ▲

- *circa 1946*

A Newman Sinclair, London. Used generally in the Antartic. London 35mm spring-driven movie camera. Polished patterned Duralumin body. Ross Xpres F3.5 lens.

- *24cm x 25cm*
- £2,000 ● Jessop Classic

Bolex H 16 ▶

- *circa 1950*

Swiss-made Paillard Bolex H16 Cine camera still used by students today for animation. Black leather body.

- *23cm x 24cm*
- £299 ● Jessop Classic

Bolex Projector ▲
- *circa 1960*
An M.A. Bolex projector.
- *height 50cm*
- £150 • Mac's Cameras

Kodak Eastman ▲
- *circa 1920*
No.2 Hawkette brown
tortoiseshell effect bakelite
folding camera by Kodak.
- *height 18cm*
- £69 • Jessop Classic

Contax G1 Camera ▲
- *circa 1990*
Contax G1, 35mm camera with
an F2 Planar lens by Carl Zeiss.
- *height 8cm*
- £50 • Mac's Cameras

Ensign Auto-speed Camer ▼
- *1932*
Ensign auto-speed camera
inscribed on the side, 100mm
F4.5 lens, with focal plane shutter
speed of 15–500 sec.
- *height 20cm*
- £199 • Jessop Classic

Newman & Guardia ▼
- *1913*
The ideal Sybil camera by
Newman & Guardia with an
unusual Ross Express 136mm F4.5
Lens. The camera takes 3.25 x
4.25 inch film.
- *height 23.5cm*
- £24 9 • Jessop Classic

Zenit B Camera ▲
- *circa 1960*
Zenit B camera with 300mm lens.
- *height 8cm*
- £69 • Mac's Cameras

Bolex Camera ▼
- *circa 1960*
A Bolex P1 zoom cine camera.
- *height 38cm*
- £149 • Mac's Cameras

Hasselblad 550c Camera

- *circa 1970*
A Hasselblad. Model 500c, 18mm
with 2.8 planner lens.
- *17cm x 10cm*
- **£700** • Jessop Classic

Super Nettle Camera

- *circa 1920*
Zeiss Super Nettel. 11. F2.8.
Black leather covered press
camera.
- *9cm x 14cm*
- **£499** • Jessop Classic

Franke & Heideck Rolleiflex Camera ▲

- *mid 20th century*
A Rolleiflex 2.8F Lens Zeiss,
made by Franke & Heideck.
- *13cm x 12cm*
- **£599** • Jessop Classic

Perkeo Camera ▼

- *circa 1954*
A Perkeo with rangefinder Color
Skopar lens in Prontor SVS
shutter. Voigtlander.
- *6cm x 12cm*
- **£199** • Jessop Classic

Expert Tips

*The condition of a camera body
and its shutter mechanism is
very important. Likewise, the
lenses must be free of scratches
for them to be worth collecting.*

Nikon Red Spot Camera ▼

- **1965**
Nikon F known as Red Spot.
Lens 50mm F1.4.
- *height 14cm*
- **£349** • Jessop Classic

Petie Vanity Camera and Compact ▶

- *circa 1956*
Petie camera housed in a make up
compact. Front door opens to
reveal mirror and powder. One
top knob contains a lipstick,
another provides storage for an
extra roll of film. Beautiful Art
deco marblelized finish in either
red, green or blue made by Kreher
and Bayer Offenbach, Germany.
Kigu a British make of powder
compacts. Highly collectable.
- *8cm x 10cm*
- **£499** • Jessop Classic

Chess Sets

Silver and Enamel Chess Set ◄

- *circa 1940*
A fine Austro-Hungarian silver and enamel chess set.
- *height 8cm*
- £5,500　　• G. Coleman

Dieppe Bone Chess Set ▼

- *circa 1790*
A polychrome bone "Dieppe" bust set. The pawns and bishops having lacquered paper hats.
- *height 7.5cm*
- £6,800　　• G. Coleman

Indian Chess Set ▲

- *circa 1835*
Chess set by John Co. Rooks from India.
- *height 11cm*
- £3,950　　• G. Coleman

Ebony Fruitwood Chess Set ▲

- *circa 1805*
Rare inverted lyon French chess set, made of ebony and fruitwood with carved bone mounts and horses heads.
- *height 8cm*
- £2,450　　• G. Coleman

Ivory Chess Set ◄

- *circa 1830*
Finely carved ivory Indian chess set.
- *height 12cm*
- £1,950　　• G. Coleman

Napoleon & Frederick the Great Chess Set ◄

- *circa 1850*
Rare German cast iron figural chess set of Napoleon verses Frederick the Great.
- *height 6.7cm*
- £2,350
- G. Coleman

South East Asian Ivory Chess Set ▲

- *circa 1880*
South East Asian natural and red stained figural ivory chess set.
- *height 4cm*
- £5,500
- G. Coleman

Blue and Green Bakelite Chess Set ◄

- *circa 1930*
Unusual blue and green Bakelite chess men with board and box.
- *height 7cm*
- £680
- G. Coleman

Puzzle Ball Chess Set ▼

- *circa 1880*
Cantones ivory Puzzle Ball chess set with a lacquer stand.
- *height 13.5cm*
- £2,500
- G. Coleman

Mysore Chess Set ▼

- *circa 1845*
Superb quality carved sandalwood and rosewood Indian Mysore chess set on a Hindu theme.
- *height 7cm*
- £6,850
- G. Coleman

War of Independence Chess Set ▲

- *circa 1830*
A French monobloc ivory American War of Independence polychromed figural chess set.
- *height 10cm*
- £15,500
- G. Coleman

Expert Tips

The very earliest chess sets were made in India in 600 AD or earlier. By 1000 AD the game had spread through Europe and as far as Scandinavia.

Coins & Medals

German Long Service Cross ▶

- *1936-1945*
NSDAP Long Service Cross, German Third silver for 25 years. GVF
- *Diameter 5cm*
- £225 ● Gordons

WWI Iron Cross ▲

- *1870*
Iron Cross 2nd class, maker's mark "KO" which denotes it as a rare WWI made piece.
- *Diameter 4cm*
- £295 ● Gordons

Order of the Bath ▶

- *1867–68*
A fine civil order of the Bath and Abyssinian campaign group of three consisting of Civil 1st type gold with gold pin buckle, Coronation 1902 in silver, and Abyssinian War Medal 1867-68 . All mounted for wear by Spink & Son London.
- *Diameter 6cm*
- £285 ● Gordons

Third Lufwaffe ◀

- *1936-45*
German Third Lufwaffe Wireless Operator Air Gunners' Badge.
- *Diameter 3cm*
- £225 ● Gordons

Kitzbuhel Shooting Badge ▲

- *1943*
Attractively enameled Kitzbuhel shooting badge, maker's mark 'Ges Gesch' and the inscription Meisterklasse Kitzbuhel
- *Diameter 4cm*
- £165 ● Gordons

Naval Service Medal ▲

- *1914–19*

Naval Distinguished Service medal with GVR bust, as awarded to: A8654. J. Crorkran. Sea. R.N.R. Mediterranean Service, 23 March, 1918. This award was mentioned in the London Gazette on 7.8.1918, and was approved for services in action with enemy submarines.

- *diameter 4cm*
- **£395**　　　● Gordon's

DSO Miniature Medal Group ▲

- *1895–1902*

An unattributable contemporary group of three miniatures comprising: Distinguished Service Order, VR Gold Type, Delhi Durbar medal 1902, and India General Service medal with 3 clasps; Punjab Frontier 1897–98, Samana 1897, Tirah 1897–98. Medals mounted for wear with attachment pin by Spink & Son, London.

- *diameter 6cm*
- **£145**　　　● Gordon's

Khedive's Star ▼

- *circa 1890*

Khedive's star dated 1882. Unnamed as issued.

- *diameter 4cm*
- **£55**　　　● Gordon's

Purple Heart Award ▼

- *1932–present*

Purple heart medal of the Vietnam period. This is awarded for gallantry, the wounded or those killed in action in the service of the military forces of the United States of America.

- *diameter 4cm*
- **£24**　　　● Gordon's

British Victory Medal ▲

- *1914–19*

British Victory medal, as awarded to Lieutenant J.C Holmes RAF, and Ceylon Planters Rifle Corps medal. Inscribed on rim with: "Marathon Race, L.C.P.L.J.C. Holmes Kandy 1913". This man was killed in action on Sunday the first September 1918 in Egypt, aged 29. Having served in the Ceylon Planter's Rifle Corps, transferred on 17/11/1915 to the Yorkshire Regiment, was later commissioned as a second Lieutenant and joined the Royal Flying Corps and latterly the Royal Air Force.

- *diameter 12cm*
- **£325**　　　● Gordon's

Military Cross ▲

- *1914–19*

Military Cross, GVR, unofficially named on reverse: A. Melville Kennedy. 8th BN. Royal Scots Fusiliers June 1917.

- *diameter 4cm*
- **£395**　　　● Gordon's

Inter-Allied Victory Medal ◀

- *1914–19*

Inter-allied Victory medal for the Great War, this is the Italian version, with maker's mark: "Sacchimi – Milano".

- *diameter 4cm*
- **£14**　　　● Gordon's

Indian Army Long Service Medal ▶

- **1910–1936**
Indian Army Long Service and Good Conduct Medal for Indians. GVR Kaisar-i-hind bust.
- *Diameter 4cm*
- £30
- Gordon's

Naval Reserve ▲

- **Pre-1914**
Royal Naval Reserve Decoration, GV type with pre-1914 plain green ribbon.
- *Diameter 3cm*
- £25
- Gordon's

Q.S.A. ▲

- **1899**
Q.S.A. with two fixed clasps, O.F.S. swivel suspension, and contact marks.
- *Diameter 4cm*
- £25
- Gordon's

Lapland Shield ▼

- **1939–45**
Lapland shield made from zinc on a cloth backing.
- *Diameter 3cm*
- £295
- Gordon's

Efficiency Decoration ▶

- **1936–1952**
The Efficiency Decoration, GV1, with second award long service bar, territorial top bar, and Honourable Artillery Company ribbon.
- *Diameter 3cm*
- £40
- Gordon's

Volunteer Officer Medal ▼

- **1897**
Volunteer Officer's Decoration V.R. cypher complete with top bar pin and hallmarks for London 1897–98.
- *Diameter 3cm*
- £95
- Gordon's

Third Lufwaffe ▼

- **1936–45**
German Third Lufwaffe Wireless Operator Air Gunners' Badge.
- *Diameter 3cm*
- £225
- Gordon's

Royal Air Force Brooches ▼
- *circa 1918*
Pair of Royal Air Force
sweetheart brooches made from
15 carat gold, with original box.
- £200   • James Vanstone

Masonic Collar Jewel ▼
- *1920*
Thirtieth degree Masonic collar
jewel with hinged crown above a
double-headed phoenix clutching
a double-edged sword.
- £60   • James Vanstone

Edward VII Florin ▼
- *1802*
Edward VII florin. A scarce
example in enamel, centred with
Britannia.
- £150   • James Vanstone

George IV Shilling ▲
- *1826*
A George IV shilling. Unusual
because both sides are enamelled.
- £250   • James Vanstone

Masonic Jewel ▲
- *1930*
St John's Lodge whole Masonic
jewel. This hallmarked jewel
bears a good quality enamel of St
John the Martyr.
- £70   • James Vanstone

Victoria Crown ▲
- *1845*
1845 crown with the head of the
young Queen Victoria, centred
with enamel bearing the Royal
Standard.
- £100   • James Vanstone

Grand Master Jewel ▼
- *1850*
A jewel of the Grand Master's
Masonic Lodge, with a face with
rays of light radiating behind,
within an enamel blue circle.
- £50   • James Vanstone

Half Crown ▼
- *1854*
Enamel Victorian half crown
with the Royal Standard within a
laurel border.
- £35   • James Vanstone

Rose Cross ▼
- *1900*
Fifteen carat gold exceptionally
rare Rose Cross with coloured
jewel and a swan within degrees
and dividers surmounted by a
hinged crown with seven stars.
- £350   • James Vanstone

Boer War Medal ▼
- *1899–1900*

Queen's South Africa medal, 1899–1900 with six clasps; Relief of Kimberley, Paardeberg, Driefontein, Johannesburg, Diamond Hill, Wittebergen, as awarded to: 82180 Bomb: WHLR: H. BlissEett. "P" BTY: R.H.A. This man was wounded during a Victoria Cross action at Nooitedacht on the 13th of December 1900.
- *diameter 4cm*
- **£375**   • **Gordon's**

Campaign Service Medal ▼
- *1970–82*

Campaign Service medal with one clasp; Northern Ireland, South Atlantic medal 1982, with rosette, UN Cyprus medal (UNFICYP), as awarded to: 24501637 Gunner J.C Howe Royal Artillery. Group mounted court style for wear.
- *diameter 12cm*
- **£345**   • **Gordon's**

Victorian Crown ▼
- *1887*

Mounted example of a Victorian crown with fine enamels.
- **£95**   • **James Vanstone**

Air Force Cross ▲
- *1960–present*

US Airforce, Air Force cross.
- *diameter 5cm*
- **£43**   • **Gordon's**

Distinguished Service Medal ▲
- *1970–present*

US Defence Distinguished Service medal.
- *diameter 5cm*
- **£43**   • **Gordon's**

Victoria Half Crown ▲
- *1876*

Enamel half crown commemorating the reign of Queen Victoria with fine enamels.
- **£250**   • **James Vanstone**

Five Mark ▼
- *1875*

Unusual five mark coin. Well-defined example centred with the Habsburg Eagle.
- **£350**   • **James Vanstone**

George II Crown ▼
- *1743*

Rare example of George II crown with fine enamels representing England, Scotland and Ireland.
- **£400**   • **James Vanstone**

British Medal ▼
- *1890–97*

British South Africa Company medal without clasp. Inscribed on the reverse: Rhodesia, 1896. As awarded to: 93593 Shoeg.Smith W.Didoe. 10.B.Y.R.A. Died in South Africa on 26th May, 1900.
- *diameter 4cm*
- **£295**   • **Gordon's**

Military Cross ▶

- **1910–1936**
The Military Cross, GV, with
inscribed name on reverse N.P.
Spooner.
- *Diameter 4cm*
- £35 • Gordon's

Sede Vacante ▼

- **1758**
Silver coin from the Papal states,
Sede Vacante 1 Scudo from the
Rome Mint.
- *Diameter 3.5cm*
- £400 • Pavlos Pavlou

Cyprus Coin ▶

- **circa 1928**
First Colonial Crown Cyprus
coin, 45 Piastres.
- *Diameter 3.5cm*
- £120 • Pavlos Pavlou

Cape Colony Medal ◀

- **1902**
South African Cape Colony
Medal – Coldstream Guards.
- *Diameter 4cm*
- £75 • Gordon's

Crimea Medal ▲

- **1854–56**
Crimea Medal with no clasp,
issued without a name.
- *Diameter 4cm*
- £95 • Gordon's

Victoria Cross ▼

- **2003**
A modern example of a Victoria
Cross in good condition.
- *Diameter 4cm*
- £30 • Gordon's

SS Long Service ▼

- **1936–45**
German World War Two SS Long
Service Medal for eight years.
Bronze with original blue moire
silk ribbon.
- *Diameter 4cm*
- £345 • Gordon's

Expert Tips

*Condition: FDC (mint), UNC
(uncirculated), EF (extremely
fine), VF (very fine), F (fine).
"Fine" coins have considerable
wear but you can still see the
main features and inscriptions.*

179

Zodiameterc Wheel Coin ▼
- **238–161 AD**
Copper drachma coin from
Roman Egypt featuring Antonius
Pius with zodiacmeterc wheel on
reverse.
- *Diameter 2.5cm*
- **£3,750** • Pavlos Pavlou

Alexander the Great Coin ▶
- **336–323 BC**
Gold coin with the head of
Alexander the Great from the
Mileus Mint.
- *Diameter 1.5cm*
- **£1,650** • Pavlos Pavlou

Bithynian Kingdom Coin ▼
- **124–94 BC**
Bithynian Kingdom silver
tetradrachm coin, featuring
Nicomedes III
- *Diameter 1.5cm*
- **£500** • Pavlos Pavlou

Roman Gaius Coin ◀
- **24–37 AD**
Copper Roman coin, Gaius
Caligula Dupondius, from the
Rome Mint.
- *Diameter 2.5cm*
- **£400** • Pavlos Pavlou

Ptolemaic Empire Coin ◀
- **30–81 BC**
Copper 80 drachna coin from the
Ptolemaic Empire Egyptian Mint,
Alexandria.
- *Diameter 1.5cm*
- **£1,300** • Pavlos Pavlou

Roman Crispina Coin ▼
- **177–192 AD**
Roman coin featuring Crispina,
wife of Commodus Sestertius,
from the Rome Mint.
- *Diameter 3cm*
- **£180** • Pavlos Pavlou

Maurice Tiberius Flollis Coin ▶
- **582–602 AD**
Maurice Tiberius flollis coin from
the Constantin Mint.
- *Diameter 2cm*
- **£30** • Pavlos Pavlou

Constantine VII Coin ▶

- **945–9 AD**
Constantine VII and Romanus II
AV Solidus. from the
Constantinople Mint.
- *Diameter 1.5cm*
- **£265** • Pavlos Pavlou

Crusader coin ▲

- **1275–1297 AD**
Crusaders of Tripoli coin,
Bohemond VII.
- *Diameter 2cm*
- **£90** • Pavlos Pavlou

Peter III Gold Coin ▼

- **1336–1387**
Spanish gold coin from Barcelona
featuring Peter III.
- *Diameter 2cm*
- **£225** • Pavlos Pavlou

German Third
Spanish Cross ◀

- **1939–45**
Bronze German Spanish cross
with swords, no maker's mark.
- *Diameter 4cm*
- **£465** • Pavlos Pavlou

Islamic Coin ▼

- **1201–1230 AD**
Rulers of Mardin al-Nasir Idirhm.
- *Diameter 2cm*
- **£40** • Pavlos Pavlou

Ottoman Coin ▼

- **157–495 AD**
Murad III Sultani coin from
Gidrekipsine Mint.
- *Diameter 1.5cm*
- **£75** • Pavlos Pavlou

Spanish Coin ◀

- **1556–1598 AD**
Spanish coin, Phillipe II, from
the Seville Mint.
- *Diameter 3cm*
- **£475** • Pavlos Pavlou

Expert Tips

*Beware! There is more damage
done cleaning coins than
by anything else. If you
absolutely have to wash coins,
use slightly soapy water, never
use metal polish. A scratch
can cost you a mint!*

Knight Templar Collar ▲
- **1850**

Unusual Knight Templar's collar jewel with enamelled double cross in silver, gold, red, black and white.
- **£100**   • James Vanstone

Founder Jewel ▲
- **1940**

Hallmarked silver founder jewel with Masonic symbols painted on the enamel, set between two pillars
- **£40**   • James Vanstone

George IV Shilling ▲
- **1820**

Attractive example of the George IV shilling with enamel centre, with the Crown and Lion.
- **£40**   • James Vanstone

Victorian Shilling ▼
- **1897**

Victorian shilling with enamel standard and the date 1897.
- **£25**   • James Vanstone

Diamond Jubilee Medal ▼
- **1897**

Commemorative medal for the Diamond Jubilee of Queen Victoria decorated in silver, gilt and paste settings. The central cartouche of Queen Victoria is set within 24-paste diamonds, within the angle and the divider.
- **£60**   • James Vanstone

Canada General Service Medal ▼
- **1866–70**

Canada General Service medal 1866–70, with one clasp; Fenian Raid 1866, as awarded to: 311 Pte. A. Carroll, 7th Bn. Royal Fusiliers.
- *diameter 4cm*
- **£295**   • Gordon's

Gold Post Master Jewel ▲
- **1930**

Nine carat gold Post Master jewel representing the guild of Freeman Lodge, decorated with the City of London's coat of arms.
- **£140**   • James Vanstone

Burmese Rupee ▲
- **1920**

Burmese rupee centred with a peacock. Whilst of exceptionally high quality this example is one of the more common seen on the market.
- **£120**   • James Vanstone

Victorian Crown ▲
- **1897**

A Victorian crown with a strong depiction of George and the dragon highlighted in enamel. Reasonably common example.
- **£60**   • James Vanstone

WWI Death Plaque ▲
- *1917*

World War One Death Plaque for
Albert James Donovan 35th
Battalion, Australian Infantry.
- *Diameter 4cm*
- £65 • Pavlos Pavlou

Royal Red Cross ▲
- *1913*

Royal Red Cross, second class
(Associate), ARRC, GVR initials
engraved on the reverse. In
Garrad and Co. titled case of
issue, with wearing pin.
- *Diameter 4cm*
- £100 • Pavlos Pavlou

Order of Medjidiek ▶
- *1916–17*

Order of Medjidie together with
Royal Society of Arts Silver
Medal awarded to A. J. Todd,
Professor of the Khedivial School
of Law.
- *Diameter 4cm*
- £385 • Pavlou

Imperial Service Medal ▼
- *1901–1910*

Early star-shape EVII Imperial
Service Medal, unnamed in case
of issue.
- *Diameter 4cm*
- £75 • Pavlos Pavlou

Luftschutz Cross ◀
- *1938*

Luftschutz Cross, first class, in
gold with original loop and ring
suspender and pin-back ribbon.
Rare, with less than 150 awarded.
- *Diameter 4cm*
- £675 • Pavlos Pavlou

Order of the War Cross ▲
- *1936–39*

Order of the War Cross "Cruz de
guerra", second class, breast star
in silver, awarded during the
Spanish Civil War of 1936–39. In
deluxe box of issue with the
makers name, "Insustrias Egana"
Motrico.
- *Diameter 4cm*
- £200 • Pavlos Pavlou

Sports Badge ▲
- *circa 1937*

Weightlifting bronze athlete's
sports badge.
- *Diameter 3cm*
- £325 • Pavlos Pavlou

War Merit Cross ▼

- **1939**

War Merit Cross, first class, with maker's mark.
- *Diameter 4cm*
- **£75** • **Pavlos Pavlou**

Khartoum Medal ▼

- **1897**

Khedive's Sudan Medal with one clasp.
- *Diameter 4cm*
- **£100** • **Pavlos Pavlou**

Jubilee Medal ▶

- **1897**

Silver jubilee medal in Wyon of Regent Street case, complete with wearing pin.
- *Diameter 4cm*
- **£100** • **Pavlos Pavlou**

Hitler Youth Medal ▶

- **1939**

Hitler Youth Kreisseiger 1939 bronze and enamel medal, maker's mark H. Aurich, Dresden.
- *Diameter 4cm*
- **£195** • **Pavlos Pavlou**

German Red Cross ▲

- **1934**

German Red Cross, second class, white enameled cross with eagle in black and without swastika. The ribbon is in the style of a lady's bow.
- *Diameter 4cm*
- **£125** • **Pavlos Pavlou**

German Iron Cross Bar ▶

- **1939**

Second-class Bar badge of an eagle clutching a wreath.
- *Diameter 4cm*
- **£160** • **Pavlos Pavlou**

Army Roll of Honour Clasp ▼

- **1941–45**

Very rare Army Roll of Honour Clasp. An actual presentation award piece, the clasp is a superb fire-gilt tombak swastika in very high relief with slight wear.
- *Diameter 3cm*
- **£850** • **Pavlos Pavlou**

Commemorative Ware

Patriot Jug
- *circa 1855*
Crimean War Royal Patriot jug by Hill Pottery.
- *height 21cm*
- £300   • Hope & Glory

Queen Victoria Earthenware Mug
- *circa 1887*
Golden Jubilee earthenware mug to commemorate Queen Victoria. Made for Cardiff Sunday school children, presented by the Mayor.
- *height 8.5cm*
- £80   • Hope & Glory

Doulton Beaker
- *circa 1897*
Royal Doulton Queen Victoria Diamond Jubilee beaker.
- *height 9.5cm*
- £130   • Hope & Glory

Corn Laws Plate
- *circa 1845*
Small hexagonal ceramic plate to commemorate the abolition of the corn laws, with the inscription "Our bread untaxed our commerce free".
- *diameter 11cm*
- £120   • Hope & Glory

Diamond Jubilee Chinaware Mug
- *circa 1897*
A bone chinaware mug celebrating the Diamond Jubilee with a portrait of Queen Victoria with all the Commonwealth countries inscribed.
- *height 9cm*
- £125   • Hope & Glory

Boer War Pin Tray
- *circa 1900*
Carlton Ware circular pin tray to commemorate the Boer War depicting Lord Kitchener, Lord Robert, and Buller.
- *diameter 11cm*
- £110   • Hope & Glory

Doulton Beaker
- *circa 1887*
Unusual-shaped bone china beaker to commemorate the Golden Jubilee of Queen Victoria.
- *height 10cm*
- £110   • Hope & Glory

Golden Jubilee Plate
- *circa 1887*
Royal Worcester blue and white earthenware plate of Queen Victoria's Golden Jubilee.
- *diameter 27cm*
- £125   • Hope & Glory

Mason's Jug ▼

• **1935**
Mason's ironstone jug commemorating King George and Queen Mary, a limited edition of 1,000. With King George and Queen Mary in profile within a wreath border.
• *height 19cm*
• **£275** • Hope & Glory

Memorial Plaque ▶

• **1972**
An oval basalt plaque of the Duke of Windsor in memoriam.
• *8.3cm x 10.8cm*
• **£48** • Hope & Glory

Commemorative Plaque ▼

• **1914–15**
Bone china plaque commemorating the alliance between Germany and Austria, Kaiser Wilhelm II and Franz Joseph.
• *diameter 23.5cm*
• **£170** • Hope & Glory

Royal Albert Commemorative Mug ▲

• **1935**
Bone china Royal Albert commemorative mug of the Silver Jubilee of King George V and Queen Mary.
• *height 7cm*
• **£58** • Hope & Glory

Loving Cup ▼

• **1936–37**
Loving cup to commemorate the proposed Coronation of Edward VIII.
• *height 25.3cm*
• **£135** • Hope & Glory

Copeland Mug ▼

• **1936–7**
Earthenware mug for the proposed Coronation of Edward VIII, made by Copeland for Thomas Goode of London.
• *height 9.8cm*
• **£95** • Hope & Glory

Wedgwood Mug ▼

• **1939**
Wedgwood mug to commemorate the visit of King George and Queen Elizabeth to America with the inscription "Friendship makes Peace".
• *height 10cm*
• **£165** • Hope & Glory

Jubilee Jug ▼
- 1897

Doulton commemorative jug of Queen Victoria's Diamond Jubilee with a silver rim and olive green cartouches showing Queen Victoria.
- *height 16cm*
- £240   • Hope & Glory

Doulton Mug ▼
- 1901

Doulton bone china mug depicting Queen Victoria in memoriam with purple decoration around the rim, and decorated with a prayer book, inscribed below with the words, "She wrought her people lasting good".
- *height 7.6cm*
- £475   • Hope & Glory

Diamond Jubilee Beaker ▲
- 1897

Goss white bone china beaker celebrating Queen Victoria's Diamond Jubilee.
- *height 9.7cm*
- £110   • Hope & Glory

Royal Wintonia Mug ▲
- 1911

Royal Wintonia earthenware mug for the Investiture of Edward Prince of Wales made for the City of Cardiff.
- *height 8cm*
- £90   • Hope & Glory

Royal Doulton Beaker ▼
- 1902

Royal Doulton earthenware King's coronation beaker celebrating the coronation of Edward VII in rare purple.
- *height 9.8cm*
- £95   • Hope & Glory

Princess Mary Mug ▼
- 1929

Earthenware mug to commemorate the visit of Princess Mary Viscountess Laschelles to Castleford.
- *height 8.6cm*
- £175   • Hope & Glory

Coronation Mug ▼
- 1911

Green and white coronation mug of George V. Manufactured by Booths.
- *height 7.5cm*
- £70   • Hope & Glory

Balance of Payments Plate ▶

- *1887*

Octagonal earthenware Golden Jubilee plate commemorating the Balance of Payments.
- *diameter 24cm*
- £130 • Hope & Glory

Joseph Chamberlain Plate ▲

- *1904*

Ridgeway earthenware plate commemorating Joseph Chamberlain.
- *diameter 25cm*
- £70 • Hope & Glory

King Edward Coronation Earthenware Jug ▲

- *1902*

Royal Doulton earthenware jug from the Lambeth factory to commemorate the Coronation of King Edward VII.
- *height 21cm*
- £150 • Hope & Glory

King's Beaker ▼

- *1902*

Royal Doulton beaker commemorating the King Edward VII's Coronation Dinner, with a silver hallmarked rim, presented by His Majesty.
- *height 10cm*
- £130 • Hope & Glory

Child's Plate ▼

- *1897*

A child's plate commemorating Queen Victoria's diamond jubilee.
- *diameter 16cm*
- £65 • Hope & Glory

Princess of York Mug ▼

- *1937*

Royal Doulton bone china mug depicting a picture of Princess Elizabeth as a young girl.
- *height 9cm*
- £400 • Hope & Glory

William Gladstone Charger ▼

- *1898*

Commemorative charger of William Gladstone with a cartouche of Hawarden Church and of his home Hawarden Castle.
- *diameter 25cm*
- £75 • Hope & Glory

Edward VII Earthenware Mug ▼

- *1910*

An earthenware mug to commemorate the demise of Edward VII.
- *height 10cm*
- £110 • Hope & Glory

King George & Queen Mary Beaker ▲

- *circa 1911*
Enamel on tin beaker to commemorate the Coronation of King George V and Queen Mary and also the investiture of the Prince of Wales.
- *height 10cm*
- £70 • Hope & Glory

Lions' Heads Beaker ▲

- *2002*
Limited edition beaker of 2500 from the Royal Collection to commemorate the Golden Jubilee of Queen Elizabeth II.
- *height 22cm*
- £50 • Hope & Glory

Booths Coronation Mug ▲

- *circa 1911*
Ceramic coronation mug to commemorate King George V and Queen Mary, by Booths.
- *height 9cm*
- £60 • Hope & Glory

Prince William Bone China Mug ▲

- *2003*
Royal Collection English bone china mug to commemorate the 21st birthday of Prince William.
- *height 15cm*
- £21 • Hope & Glory

Loving Cup ◄

- *1977*
Limited edition of 250 loving cup for the Silver Jubilee of Elizabeth II.
- *27cm x 37cm*
- £1250 • Hope & Glory

Paragon Mug ▼

- *circa 1935*
Silver Jubilee bone china paragon mug of George V and Queen Mary.
- *height 8cm*
- £75 • Hope & Glory

Hammersley Bone China Mug ▼

- *circa 1935*
Bone china mug to commemorate the Silver Jubilee of King George V and Queen Mary – transfer with enamel colours.
- *height 10cm*
- £95 • Hope & Glory

Prince William Porcelain Mug ◄

- *1982*
Porcelain mug by J. & J. May to commemorate the birth of Prince William depicting a pram with the royal crest.
- *height 9cm*
- £65 • Hope & Glory

Expert Tips

Check that the painting or transfer has not been defaced in any way by harsh cleaning or chips on the porcelain. Also check the provenance as this contributes to the item's value.

Brass Shield Plaque ▼
- 1897

Brass plaque of Queen Victoria in the shape of a shield to commemorate the Diamond Jubilee of Queen Victoria.
- 43cm x 32cm
- £175 • Hope & Glory

Imperial Beer Stein ▼
- 1870

Imperial half-litre size beer stein with attractive painted enamelled panel of Ulanen, of the Imperial Lancers, hunting in a mountainous landscape. Inscribed with the following undamaged lettering: "Zur Erinnerung an meine Dienstzeit".
- height 24cm
- £495 • Gordon's

Blue and White Plaque ▲
- 1898

Blue and white plaque of William Gladstone to commemorate his death. Maker Burgess and Lee.
- 39cm x 25.8cm
- £230 • Hope & Glory

Gordon Highlanders ▲
- 1890

One of a pair of Gordon Highlander commemorative plates. Decorated with a picture of a soldier standing guard, with the words "Gordon Highlander" inscribed around the figure.
- height 21cm
- £75 • Gordon's

Crown Devon Jug ▼
- 1937

Crown Devon jug musical "Super Jug" to commemorate the coronation of King George VI and Queen Elizabeth. Limited edition. With a lion handle.
- height 30.5cm
- £2,250 • Hope & Glory

German Knight ▼
- 1918

German bronzed spelter figure of a knight in armour on a stained wood plinth, with a dedication plate on the side to Major Niemann from his brother officers of the 39 Field Artillery Regiment, 22 March to 16 November, 1918.
- height 45.5cm
- £325 • Gordon's

Wall Plaque ◄
- 1938

German black ash wall plaque with metal relief of Artillery crew serving their gun, and metal label reading: "Res. battr. Opel 39.8.38. 11.10.38".
- 23cm x 32.5cm
- £115 • Gordon's

Fans

Ostrich Feather Fan ▶

- *circa 1900*
Ivory fan with fine ostrich feathers.
- *26cm x 41cm*
- **£56** • Cekay

Child's Fan ▲

- *circa 1920*
Child's cream lace fan with sequins at the centre of the flower and a bone handle with gilt-scrolling.
- *14cm x 25cm*
- **£45** • Cekay

Romantic Spanish Fan ▲

- *circa 1900*
Hand-painted Spanish or French fan of two ladies and a gentleman holding a garland of roses in a pastoral setting.
- *26cm x 49cm*
- **£110** • Cekay

Dancing Figures Fan ▲

- *circa 1920*
Small ivory fan with a pierced ivory foliate design and featuring a silhouette of two figures dancing.
- *13cm x 23cm*
- **£28** • Cekay

Pink Feather Fan ▲

- *1920*
Pink feather fan with ivory handle, painted with birds and floral design.
- *22cm x 30 cm*
- **£25** • Cekay

Union Castle Cruise Fan ▼

- *circa 1900*
Hand-painted flowers on parchment with delicate wood frame inscribed "Union Castle Line souvenir".
- *21cm x 35cm*
- **£23** • Cekay

Benedictine Fan ◀

- *1920*
An advertisement fan featuring a figure in red holding a lamp sitting beside a bottle of Benedictine.
- *23cm x 34cm*
- **£23** • Cekay

Spanish Fan ▲

- *circa 1920*
Satin Spanish silk fan with ivory stick featuring a hand-painted romantic man giving a rose to a lady.
- *24cm x 29cm*
- **£56** • Cekay

Gentlemen's Accessories

Maiden with Rifle
Tobacco Jar ▶

- *circa 1890*

A very rare German Conta and Boheme porcelain jar modelled as a young woman standing before a drum holding a rifle.
- *26cm x 18cm*
- £850   ● E. Bradwin

Laughing Cavelier
Tobacco Jar ▲

- *circa 1880*

Conta and Boheme porcelain jar modelled as a cavelier seated on a half-barrel holding a goblet.
- *25cm x 14cm*
- £740   ● E. Bradwin

Devil Tobacco Jar ▼

- *circa 1900*

Terracotta devil head tobacco jar by Johann Maresch.
- *14cm x 18cm*
- £390   ● E. Bradwin

Entertainer Tobacco Jar ▼

- *circa 1880*

Porcelain jar modelled as an entertainer, sitting on a large drum, his dog beside him.
- *height 38cm*
- £640   ● E. Bradwin

Girl on Trunk
Tobacco Jar ▼

- *circa 1880*

Conta and Boheme porcelain jar modelled as a young woman with trumpet in hand seated on a trunk.
- *height 26cm*
- £640   ● E. Bradwin

Victor Hugo
Tobacco Box ▼

- *circa 1890*

Conta and Boheme porcelain figural tobacco box.
- *height 35cm*
- £580   ● E. Bradwin

Bloch Tobacco Jar ◀

- *circa 1900*
Polychrome and painted
terracotta jar from a series
produced by Bernhard Bloch of a
black man at the races.
- *height 33cm*
- £1,550   • E. Bradwin

Jack Russell Tobacco Jar ▲

- *circa 1910*
Part polychrome painted
terracotta jar modelled as a barrel
with a black and white Jack
Russell forming the lid. Maker
Johann Maresch.
- *height 20cm*
- £675   • E. Bradwin

Expert Tips

*Tobacco jars were mostly made in
the nineteenth century from terracotta or majolica, but rare versions
come in bronze or wood.*

Jack on Guard
Tobacco Jar   ▼

- *circa 1890*
Appealing polychrome painted
terracotta figure of a golass-eyed
begging dog wearing a straw hat.
- *39cm x 27cm*
- £3,300   • E. Bradwin

Frog Tobacco Jar   ▲

- *circa 1900*
Tobacco jar of Phylias Fogg seated
in a top hat holding a book by
Bernhard Bloch.
- *37cm x 15cm*
- £1,450   • E. Bradwin

Pair of Monteiths   ▲

- *circa 1810*
A pair of Regency red tole
monteiths decorated with
classical urns, swags and vine
leaves.
- *11cm x 27.5cm x 20cm*
- £6,500   • Mallett

Folding Bagatelle Table   ▲

- *circa 1890*
Victorian mahogany folding
games table with green baize
interior, complete with a cue, cue
rest and a set of balls.
- *13cm x 92cm x 51cm*
- £275   • D. Hume

Mother-of-Pearl Desk Set ▶

- *circa 1810*
A fine quality Palais Royal
mother-of-pearl and gilt-bronze
inkstand having elaborately
scrolling handles and a base
enriched with tiles of mother-of-
pearl.
- *9cm x 24cm*
- 16,500   • Mallett

Top Hat ▲

- *circa 1940*

Grey top hat by Army and Navy, London.

- *height 14cm*
- £45
- Julian Smith

Shaving Brush ▲

- *1903*

Gentlemen's travelling silver shaving brush.

- *length 14.5cm*
- £400
- Bentleys

Spirit Flasks ▶

- *1920*

Pair of silver-plated spirit flasks housed in original leather case.

- *height 15cm*
- £300
- Bentleys

Travelling Mirror ▲

- *1930*

Travelling mirror in original leather case with the letter H.R.B. inscribed on the lid.

- *diameter 23cm*
- £40
- Julian Smith

Bowler Hat ◀

- *circa 1930*

Black bowler hat with original box from James Lock & Co. Ltd., 6 St James Street, London SW1.

- *height 32cm*
- £45
- Julian Smith

Miniature Tool Kit ▲

- *1920*

Miniature travelling tool kit in a leather case with "Bonsa" on flap.

- *width 14.5cm*
- £300
- Bentleys

Grey Top Hat ▲

- *1930*

Grey top hat with original box by Herbert Johnson of New Bond St, London.

- *height 16cm*
- £75
- Julian Smith

Horn Beakers ◀

- *1873*

Nest of six horn beakers with hall marked solid silver collars in original leather case.

- *height of case 14,5cm*
- £2,000
- Bentleys

Handbags

Pink Velvet Bag ▶

- *circa 1820*
Pink velvet ladies evening bag, with ormolu ornate foliate frame and rosette base.
- *10cm x 8cm*
- £75 • Hilary Proctor

Victorian Leather Handbag ▲

- *circa 1860*
Rare and unusually small Victorian fine leather handbag with silver frame and clasp in excellent condition.
- *15cm x 16cm*
- £160 • Hilary Proctor

Austrian Silver Tapestry Bag ▲

- *1850*
Black tapestry bag with rose pink floral pattern, a fine Austrian silver frame with unusual figures of ladies entwined in the scrolling.
- *25cm x 26cm*
- £275 • Hilary Proctor

Dogs Head Clasp Handbag ▼

- *circa 1920*
Silver lame rose fabric with lilac silk lining and an unusual dog's head clasp with ruby eyes.
- *21cm x 20cm*
- £106 • Hilary Proctor

Gold Scrolling Purse ▼

- *circa 1860*
Cream felt purse with gold embroidered scrolling design.
- *height 21cm*
- £145 • Red Roses

Buffalo Skin Purse ▼

- *1903*
Art Deco buffalo skin purse with a silver chain and frame, hallmarked with unusual silver circular ring handle for use with a chatelaine.
- *9cm x 10cm*
- £75 • Hilary Proctor

Chinese Silk Purse ◀

- *1920*
Delicate rose Chinese silk and gold thread overlay handbag with enamel and green stone clasp.
- *26cm x 25cm*
- £95 • Hilary Proctor

Blue Beaded Bag ▼
• *circa 1940*
Blue beaded circular bag with an
unusual gilt ball clasp and
generous beaded looped handle.
• *diameter 16.5cm*
• **£295** • **Beauty and the Beasts**

Bakelite Bag ▼
• **1950**
American silver grey bakelite bag
with lucite top. With a flower and
foliate design standing on ball
feet.
• *height 15cm*
• **£265** • **Beauty and the Beasts**

Pink Sequinned Bag ▼
• **1960**
English baby pink beaded and
sequinned small evening bag.
• *width 22cm*
• **£160** • **Beauty and the**

Two Owls Bag ▲
• **1930**
Brown leather bag with strap
decorated with two owls with
beaded glass eyes, surrounded by a
foliate design.
• *width 21cm*
• **£145** • **Beauty and the Beasts**

Leather Handbag ▶
• **1930**
Brown leather handbag with
chrome and orange bakelite clasp.
• *width 21cm*
• **£295** • **Beauty and the Beasts**

Cream Beaded Bag ▲
• **1880**
Victorian cream beaded bag
depicting a basket of pink flowers
with emerald green and pink
beaded tassels, gilt clasp and
chain handle.
• *height 21cm*
• **£695** • **Beauty and the Beasts**

Laurel Leaf Handbag ▼
- *18th century fabric and 19th century frame*
Woven silk bag with a gilt laurel leaf design frame inset with pearls.
- *27cm x 21cm*
- £265   • Hilary Proctor

Coral Clasp Purse ▶
- *circa 1780*
Tapestry bag with gilt and delicate coral inlay, cameo glass clasp and gilt chain.
- *25cm x 25cm*
- £265   • Hilary Proctor

Cocktail Mirror Bag ▼
- *circa 1950*
Ladies black cocktail oval silk bag with handle and small square mirrored sides.
- *8cm x 15cm*
- £60   • Red Roses

Beaded Roses Purse ▲
- *circa 1850*
Large beaded bag with rose design and a gilt frame with chain.
- *30cm x 28cm*
- £365   • Hilary Proctor

Tapestry Bag ▼
- *circa 1760*
Early romantic tapestry bag of birds and crest on one side and a floral and foliate cartouche with the portrait of a young handsome gentleman on the reverse – silver frame and handle.
- *18cm x 15cm*
- £150   • Hilary Proctor

Belgian Crewell Handbag ▼
- *1910*
Belgian crewell work of pink roses and purple flowers with a blue scrolling design on black silk and a floral gilt frame and jewelled clasp.
- *19cm x 20cm*
- £160   • Hilary Proctor

Black Beaded Bag ▼
- *1890*

Fine black beaded Victorian bag
with floral design of pink roses,
blue cornflowers and daisies, with
a filigree frame and paste jewels.
- *height 25cm*
- £495 • Beauty and the Beasts

Clear Perspex Bag ▼
- *circa 1950*

Clear perspex American bag with
foliate design on the lid.
- *height 111cm*
- £248 • Lynda Brine

Petit Point Handbag ▶
- *circa 1940*

A handbag with black petit point
background decorated with
flowers in a vase.
- *width 21cm*
- £275 • Beauty and the Beasts

Moiré Silk Evening Bag ▲
- *circa 1940*

Brown moiré silk evening back
with a geometric gilt clasp by
Josef.
- *height 17cm*
- £265 • Beauty and the Beasts

Wicker Bag ▼
- *1950*

Wicker bag made by Midas of
Miami, decorated with birds, and
green, orange and blue sequins.
- *width 37cm*
- £135 • Beauty and the Beasts

Velvet Bag ▲
- *circa 1860*

Black velvet bag with cut steel
beading of a heraldic design.
With metal clasp and chain.
- *height 28cm*
- £895 • Beauty and the Beasts

Red Plastic Bag ▲
- *1930*

Red plastic bag with a gold and
black geometrical design, with a
gilt chain handle.
- *width 19cm*
- £395 • Beauty and the Beasts

Velvet Strawberries Purse ▼
- *circa 1960*

Plastic cream wicker bag with handle with pink and red velvet strawberries on the lid, pearls set in the green velvet leaves and pink velvet and gold trim.
- *18cm x 26cm*
- £130 • **Hilary Proctor**

Pink Beaded Bag ▼
- *circa 1930*

Very unusual soft pink beaded bag with circular beaded tassels.
- *height 25cm*
- £115 • **Hilary Proctor**

Beaded Deco Purse ▲
- *circa 1920*

Black Art Deco silk ladies bag with a scrolling design of silver and black jet beads.
- *11cm x 17cm*
- £65 • **Hilary Proctor**

Chrome Velvet Bag ▶
- *circa 1960*

Velvet ladies evening bag with chrome stripes and handle.
- *height 25cm*
- £125 • **Red Roses**

Flowers and Butterflies Handbag ▶
- *circa 1960*

Woven wool bag with butterflies and floral design with carrying handles.
- *27cm x 25cm*
- £75 • **Red Roses**

Plastic Strawberries Purse ▼
- *circa 1950*

Woven wicker bag with plastic strawberries and white flowers on the lid with red velvet trim.
- *height 20cm x 26cm*
- £80 • **Hilary Proctor**

Sequined Bag ▼
- *circa 1930*

Small ladies Art Deco sequined bag with fine cream beaded scrolling and ribbon design.
- *10cm x 14cm*
- £55 • **Hilary Proctor**

Expert Tips

Handbags are now very collectable. Go for top designer names and if it has a famous owner attached, all the better.

Beaded Bag ▲

- *circa 1920*

Gold metal beaded bag with pink lotus flowers and a green and pink geometric design, with a metal clasp and gold and silver looped fringing.

- *height 20cm*
- **£395** • **Beauty and the Beasts**

Bulaggi Bag ▼

- *circa 1950*

Bulaggi plastic bag with gold metal fittings and handle, with the inscription Bulaggi on the right-hand side.

- *width 17cm*
- **£85** • **Lynda Brine**

English Handbag ▶

- *1831*

English leather handbag with floral design. Inside the inscription reads "His Majesty King William the Fourth to his dutiful subject and servant John Singleton Lord Lyndhust AD 1831".

- *width 19cm*
- **£175** • **Beauty and the Beasts**

Brown Bakelite Bag ◀

- *1950*

America brown bakelite bag with lucite cover with faceted foliate design, made by Solar.

- *height 15cm*
- **£395** • **Beauty and the Beasts**

Wicker Bag ▲

- *1950*

Simulated wicker bag with a fabric head of palomino horse made by Atlas of Hollywood.

- *width 32cm*
- **£165** • **Beauty and the Beasts**

Metal Beaded Bag ▼

- *circa 1920*

Metal beaded bag with a blue, pink and gold floral design and a gilt frame and chain.

- *height 22cm*
- **£695** • **Beauty and the Beasts**

Petit Point Bag ◀

- *circa 1940*

Petit point bag decorated with figures on horseback outside a castle, with an opaline beaded and enamel frame.

- *width 21cm*
- **£395** • **Beauty and the Beasts**

Victorian Beaded Bag ▲
- *1890*
Cream Victorian fine beaded bag with pink and yellow roses, with a silver gilt frame and pink and green glass beaded tassels.
- *height 25cm*
- **£495** • Beauty and the Beasts

Ken Lane Handbag ▲
- *1960*
Ken Lane brown handbag with a dramatic coral circular diamante handle.
- *height 15cm*
- **£295** • Beauty and the Beasts

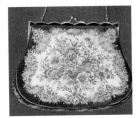

Floral Handbag ▲
- *circa 1940*
Petit point floral design bag with black enamel frame with gilt scalloped edge and gilt chain.
- *width 19cm*
- **£295** • Beauty and the Beasts

Clochette Evening Bag ▶
- *circa 1920*
Clochette shaped beaded evening bag, with rows of blue and pink with a black metal filigree clasp and silver and black handle.
- *height 18cm*
- **£395** • Beauty and the Beasts

Chain Link Bag ▼
- *1900*
Gilt chain link bag with an Art Nouveau lady on the rim inset with sprays of berries inset with red stones and foliate design.
- *height 14cm*
- **£395** • Beauty and the Beasts

Velvet Bag ▼
- *circa 1860*
Victorian cream velvet evening bag with a silver filigree frame, and fine cut-steel looped fringing.
- *height 23cm*
- **£495** • Beauty and the Beasts

French Beaded Bag ▼
- *circa 1950*
French beaded bag decorated with pink roses and a gold and white beaded frame inset with enamel roses.
- *width 22cm*
- **£695** • Beauty and the Beasts

Silk Evening Bag ▲
- *circa 1920*
Black silk evening bag decorated with flowers in blue, red and green with steel chips decoration.
- *height 18cm*
- **£295** • Lynda Brine

Pink Suede Purse ▼

- *circa 1960*
Pink suede handbag with gilt oval clasp.
- *height 26cm*
- £165 • **Red Roses**

Chain Coin Purse ▲

- *circa 1900*
A fine chain mail coin purse with expanding clasp.
- *height 6cm*
- £75 • **Hilary Proctor**

Silver Mesh Bag ▼

- *circa 1930*
Silver mesh bag with a delicate pink and orange floral design, a silver foliate design frame and chain handle.
- *height 18cm*
- £225 • **Red Roses**

Belgian Art Deco Purse ▲

- *circa 1920*
Belgian Art Deco silk leaf design with gold overlay and gilt foliate. The styled frame is inset with green stones and the purse has a blue stone clasp.
- *19cm x 20cm*
- £175 • **Hilary Proctor**

Whiting & Davis Purse ▲

- *circa 1920*
Art Deco chain-mail bag with pink, blue, and cream design and a grey and silver frame by Whiting and Davis.
- *height 16cm*
- £20 • **Red Roses**

Amethyst Clasp Handbag ▼

- *circa 1910*
Art Nouveau ladies evening bag of finely woven material with delicate silver scrolling frame, silver chain handle and an amethyst clasp.
- *18cm x 19cm*
- £165 • **Hilary Proctor**

Kitchenalia

Bakelite Cruet ▶
- **1960**
Salt and pepper pots made from Bakelite styled as a red pepper and green chilli.
- *height 9cm*
- **£10**   • **Manic Attic**

Kenwood Mixer ▲
- **1952**
Classic design steel Kenwood "Chef" food mixer with red dial and red lid, together with a steel bowl.
- *36cm x 37cm*
- **£60**   • **Manic Attic**

Kosy Kraft Teapot, Sugar Bowl, and Water Jug ▲
- **1958**
Pale pink china and stainless steel teapot, sugar bowl, and water jug. Unused in their original with "Kosy Kraft Ever-Hot: The Greatest Name in Thermal Tableware" box and wrapper.
- *35cm x 35cm*
- **£75**   • **Manic Attic**

Expert Tips

Bakelite is a synthetic plastic with properties that make it ideal for kitchenware. It was very popular in the 20s, 30s and 40s.

Milk Shake Mixer ▼
- **circa 1940**
Classic stainless steel café milk shake mixer, with wood handle and metal stand.
- *height 47cm*
- **£75**   • **Manic Attic**

Bovril Cup ▲
- **1960**
Red plastic cup with "Bovril warms and cheers" in white writing.
- *height 9cm*
- **£20**   • **Manic Attic**

Weighing Scales ▲
- **1950**
Beige Salter ten lb kitchen scale.
- *height 24cm*
- **£12**   • **Manic Attic**

Enamel Coffee Pot ▼

• *1890*
White enamel coffee pot in two
sections with purple flowers and
red banding.
• *height 33cm*
• £70   • **Rookery Farm**

Enamel Utensil Rack ▼

• *1890*
French utensil rack painted red
and black with a shaped top,
white tray, and grey utensil.
• *height 54cm*
• £65   • **Rookery Farm**

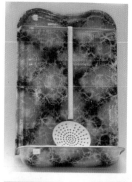

Metal Weighing Scales ▲

• *1890*
Metal kitchen weighing scales
with metal base and copper scoop
and weights, inscribed "To weigh
2lbs".
• *height 22cm*
• £98   • **Rookery Farm**

Worcester Ware Cake Tin ▲

• *1950*
Worcester Ware tin with a red lid
and "Cakes" in red letters on the
front and "Worcester Ware made
in England" on the base.
• *diameter 22cm*
• £28   • **Rookery Farm**

Copper Dish ▲

• *1920*
Medium size copper dish with
cover and brass handles.
• *9cm x 22cm*
• £58   • **Rookery Farm**

Small Iron ▲

• *circa 1920*
Small iron with a moulded base
made by W. Cross and Son.
• *length 12cm*
• £18   • **Michael Laws**

Sucre and Café Pots ◄

• *1920*
French enamel blue and white
marbled pots printed in black
with the words "sucre" and "café".
• *height 23cm*
• £45   • **Rookery Farm**

Metal Weighing Scale ▶

- *1950*
Metal Hanson five lb.weighing scale.
- *height 25cm*
- **£55** • **Rookery Farm**

Storage Jar ▼

- *1930*
Hanging enamelled storage jar with a wooden lid and flue and white check design.
- *height 24cm*
- **£38** • **Rookery Farm**

French Enamel Rack ▼

- *1890*
French pale blue enamel utensil rack with shaped top and blue and white sunshine border with two pale blue utensils.
- *height 52cm*
- **£70** • **Rookery Farm**

Porcelain Jars ▶

- *1910*
Five French cream pottery storage jars in three different sizes for cafe, sucre, farine and poivre, each one decorated in blue with wild flowers.
- *height 22cm*
- **£95** • **Rookery Farm**

Enamel Storage Tin ▶

- *1890*
French enamel storage tin with yellow and blue marbled pattern.
- *height 15cm*
- **£22** • **Rookery Farm**

Blue and White Coffee Pot ▲

- *1890*
French enamel coffee pot, white with blue banding and a white scrolling pattern.
- *height 29cm*
- **£78** • **Rookery Farm**

Bread Board ▼

- *circa 1940*
Circular wood bread board with the inscription "Bread" and a foliate design surrounding a central flower.
- *diameter 28cm*
- **£28** • **Michael Laws**

Large Brass Kettle ▼

- *1920*
Oversized brass English kettle.
- *height 20cm*
- **£68** • **Rookery Farm**

Plastic Container Set ▶
- *circa 1959*

A set of flour, sugar, rice, tea and coffee containers in variegated sizes, each one having a figurative design, and also a set of five smaller containers on a plastic shelf.
- *height 26cm*
- £85 • **Manic Attic**

Cornish Ware Jug ▲
- *1959*

Blue and white-striped Cornish Ware milk jug
- *height 18cm*
- £85 • **Manic Attic**

Set of Egg Cups ▶
- *circa 1930*

A set of four green Bakelite egg cups on a circular tray.
- *height 8cm*
- £12 • **Manic Attic**

Bakelite Egg Cups ▼
- *circa 1950*

A set of four Bakelite egg cups: two yellow, one blue and one red.
- *6cm x10cm*
- £7 • **Manic Attic**

Spice Containers ▲
- *circa 1950*

A set of five cream Australian Bakelite spice containers with red lids on a shelf.
- *height 8cm*
- £90 • **Manic Attic**

Sputnik Egg Cups ◀
- *circa 1950*

Set of red, yellow, grey, black, blue, and green Sputnik egg cups with matching spoons.
- *height 3cm*
- £20 • **Manic Attic**

Expert Tips

Most kitchenalia is nineteenth and twentieth century and a good start for collectors with a budget.

Fruitwood Flour Scoop ▶

- **1940**

Fruitwood flour scoop carved from one piece of wood with a turned handle.
- *length 28cm*
- £20 • **Michael Laws**

Enamel Casserole Dish ▲
- **1910**

French enamel casserole dish with painted cornflowers and variegated blue, white and turquoise, with white handles.
- *height 18cm*
- £68 • **Rookery Farm**

Art Deco Allumettes ▲
- **1920**

Art Deco allumettes storage box decorated with a purple floral and geometric design with red spots.
- *height 13cm*
- £45 • **Rookery Farm**

French Water Jug ▶
- **1880**

Large white French enamel water jug with red banding and a red pattern of squares and a central diamond with four gold bands.
- *height 29cm*
- £55 • **Rookery Farm**

Green Thermos ▲
- **1950**

Green Vacwonder metal thermos painted with a selection of sportsmen including runners, cyclists, shot putters and swimmers, made to commemorate the Olympic Games.
- *height 27cm*
- £65 • **Manic Attic**

Butter Press ▲
- **circa 1890**

Wooden butter press with an oak leaf mould.
- *height 19cm*
- £58 • **Michael Laws**

Blue Enamel Candleholder ▶
- **1880**

French blue enamelled candleholder with gold-banding on the handle.
- *diameter 16cm*
- £20 • **Rookery Farm**

Peugeot Frères Coffee Grinder ▲
- **1950**

Wooden coffee grinder with the makers mark in brass, Peugeot Frères Valentigney (Doubs) with a large metal handle and wood knob.
- *height 19cm*
- £50 • **Rookery Farm**

Hoover Janitor ◄
- *circa 1950*

Classic metal and cloth Hoover Janitor.
- *height 106cm*
- £35 • **Manic Attic**

Kitchen Material ▲
- *circa 1950*

Unused kitchen curtain fabric with red coffee grinders and assorted containers and floral arrangements in baskets on a white background.
- *width 94cm*
- £75 • **Manic Attic**

Sputnik Butter Dish ▼
- *circa 1950*

Red plastic Sputnik-style butter dish with white spots, standing on three legs.
- *height 12cm*
- £9 • **Manic Attic**

Tea Towel Rail ▲
- *circa 1960*

Metal tea towel rail coated with yellow plastic.
- *length 16cm*
- £8 • **Manic Attic**

Sugar Shaker ▼
- *circa 1950*

Glass sugar shaker with metal lid and spout.
- *height 18cm*
- £10 • **Manic Attic**

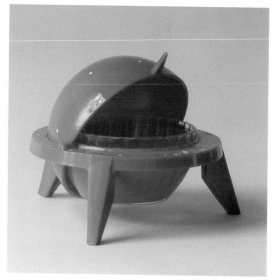

Cheese Dish ►
- *circa 1950*

Clear plastic cheese dish with plastic stand and geometric plastic handle.
- *10cm x 18cm*
- £18 • **Manic Attic**

English Sugar Jar ▲
- 1950

English white porcelain sugar jar with a circular wood lid with a royal blue geometric design with the words "Sugar" in black.
- *height 17cm*
- £28   • Rookery Farm

Porcelain Wall Box ▲
- 1950

Porcelain wall box with wooden lid and decorated with fruit and blue banding with "Allumettes" in gold writing.
- *height 15.5cm*
- £45   • Rookery Farm

Bread Bin ▲
- 1890

French enamel red and white marbling bread bin with handles each side and a handle on the cover.
- *height 23cm*
- £50   • Rookery Farm

Metal Salad Sieve ▲
- 1920

Metal salad sieve with handles and two feet.
- *height 24cm*
- £15   • Rookery Farm

Ham Stand ▼
- 1910

English white pottery ham stand.
- *height 20cm*
- £45   • Rookery Farm

Enamel Utensil Rack ◄
- 1880

French Royal and light blue enamel wall hanging utensil rack, with two utensils.
- *height 52cm*
- £75   • Rookery Farm

Copper Kettle ▼
- 1850

Large English rose copper kettle with original patina.
- *height 30cm*
- £125   • Rookery Farm

Toast Rack ▶

- *circa 1950*
Yellow plastic toast rack with black spots.
- *length 12cm*
- £8　　　● Manic Attic

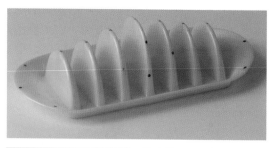

Metal Saucepans ▲

- *circa 1940*
Blue and grey metal saucepan with lid.
- *height 30cm*
- £15　　　● June Victor

Pink Pyrex Dish ◀

- *circa 1950*
Pink Pyrex casserole dish with snowflake design, set on a metal stand with two burners.
- *15cm x 36cm*
- £12　　　● June Victor

Ceramic Cruet Set ▼

- *circa 1960*
White ceramic cruet decorated with pink fish.
- *height 16cm*
- £15　　　● June Victor

Dessert Knives ▲

- *circa 1960*
A set of six pink, green, blue, purple, white and yellow Sheffield stainless steel dessert knives.
- *length 22cm*
- £12　　　● June Victor

Sugar Shaker ▲

- *circa 1950*
Pale blue plastic sugar shaker with star-pierced design on the lid and handle.
- *height 10cm*
- £7　　　● June Victor

Caldor Ware ▶

- *circa 1950*
Green ceramic casserole dish with white lid decorated with a yellow cooker, blue sink, whisk, spatula, blue kettle and a frying pan.
- *height 13cm*
- £55　　　● June Victor

Rocket Ice Crusher ▶
- *1950*

American rocket ice crusher made from aluminium with red plastic handle and container. Made by Fortuna.
- *height 32.5cm*
- *£150*   •Manic Attic

Enamel Coffee Pot ▲
- *1890*

French cornflower blue enamelled coffee pot with turned fruitwood side-handle.
- *height 22cm*
- *£70*   • Rookery Farm

Scales ▲
- *1920*

European cast iron weighing scales with copper pans and iron weights.
- *height 32cm*
- *£45*   • Michael Laws

Café and Chicorée Pots ▲
- *1920*

Café and chicorée brown enamelled pots with white writing and banding.
- *height 20cm*
- *£45*   • Rookery Farm

Enamel Funnel ▶
- *1890*

French blue and white enamel funnel.
- *height 12cm*
- *£12*   • Rookery Farm

Wood Butter Pat ▲
- *1910*

Wood butter pat moulded one side with a handle.
- *length 19.5cm*
- *£10*   • Rookery Farm

Small Metal Mould ▲
- *1890*

Small metal mould in the shape of a fish.
- *length 9.5cm*
- *£12*   • Rookery Farm

French Storage Jar ▼
- *1920*

French hanging storage jar with a wood lid with red and white panels and the word "Sel" in black.
- *height 27cm*
- *£65*   • Rookery Farm

211

Wagon Train Teapot, Sugar Pot, and Milk Jug ▶

- *circa 1958*

Teapot, sugar pot and milk jug stylised to represent vehicles from the Wagon Train TV programme
- *height 14cm*
- £130   • June Victor

Diamond-cut Honey Jar ▲

- *1820*

Heavily diamond-cut honey jar and cover with star-cut foot.
- *height 16.5cm*
- £495   • C. Bridge

Herb Chopper ▲

- *19th century*

A lovely herb chopper, steel and brass with horn handle.
- *width 15cm*
- £70-£100   • T. Murland

Cut Star and Vine Engraving Cream Jug ▼

- *1870*

Charming English cream jug with cut star and fruiting vine engraving.
- *height 15.3cm*
- £225   • C. Bridge

Victorian Pastry Roller ▼

- *1860*

Victorian pastry roller and pie crimper.
- *length 15cm*
- £50-£80   • T. Murland

Bristol Blue Egg Cups ▼

- *1800*

Two rare "Bristol Blue" eggcups with gilded rim.
- *height 8.9cm*
- £195 for pair   • C. Bridge

Fox-shaped Vegetable Chopper ▲

- *Early 19th century*

A European vegetable chopper in the form of a fox. Original horn and brass handle and complete with original brass eye.
- *length 34.3cm*
- £500-£700   • T. Murland

Luggage

Foxcroft Suitcase ▶
- *circa 1950*
Cream plastic suitcase with
leopard skin print on one side by
Foxcroft.
- *45cm x 77cm*
- £75   • Manic Attic

Antler Vanity Case ▲
- *circa 1950*
Plastic leopard skin design vanity
case by Antler with carrying
handle.
- *height 30cm*
- £68   • Manic Attic

Leather Briefcase ▶
- *circa 1900*
Leather briefcase with brass
fittings and "M. D Amoso" on the
lock.
- *26cm x 36cm*
- £120   • Jean Guiller

Leather and Hide
Vanity Case ▶
- *circa 1970*
Morocco leather and hide vanity
case.
- *32cm x 23cm*
- £90   • June Victor

Leather Suitcase ▼
- *circa 1940*
Leather suitcase with two straps
and covered with labels of various
destinations.
- *42cm x 74cm*
- £50   • June Victor

Teenage Case ◀
- *circa 1950*
Blue and white plastic teenage
case with figure of a young girl
wearing jeans and a blue-check
shirt using the telephone.
- *30cm x 35cm*
- £75   • June Victor

Expert Tips

*Highest prices are paid for top
quality, top maker, unusual
function and all original fittings
and accessories intact.*

Snakeskin Hat Box
- *1912*

Lady's hardrock python snakeskin hat box with snakeskin handle, made in London for a family in Brunei.
- *23cm x 33cm*
- £1,500
- Julian Smith

Leather Suitcase
- *1930*

Brown leather suitcase with leather straps.
- *width 73cm*
- £120
- Julian Smith

Gladstone Bag
- *1930*

Lady's gladstone leather bag with brass fittings and leather handle.
- *width 37cm*
- £75
- Julian Smith

Army & Navy Hat Box
- *1910*

Leather and canvas top hat box made by Army and Navy outfitters, comes with original top hat.
- *height 33cm*
- £200
- Julian Smith

Gentleman's Hat Box
- *1910*

Leather gentleman's top hat box with leather handle, brass lock and leather strap.
- *height 23cm*
- £160
- Julian Smith

Crocodile Skin Case
- *1930*

Indian crocodile skin case with handles at each end and silver nickel locks.
- *32cm x 61cm*
- £450
- Julian Smith

Tapestry Case ▶

- *circa 1950*
Circular zip-action tapestry case, with labels of Rome, Casablanca and Brussels.
- *diameter 40cm*
- £75   • Girl Can't Help It

Black Circular Case ▲

- *circa 1950*
Black circular vanity case with zip-action and black plastic carrying handle.
- *diameter 42cm*
- £55   • Girl Can't Help It

Tartan Plastic Case ▲

- *circa 1950*
Tartan plastic case with black plastic trim and handle.
- *diameter 35cm*
- £95   • Girl Can't Help It

Fruitwood Case ◀

- *circa 1920*
Fruitwood gentleman's carrying case.
- *30cm x 42cm*
- £120   • Hilary Proctor

Black Crocodile Case ◀

- *circa 1920*
Black crocodile ladies vanity case relined with blue Moiré silk.
- *25cm x 32cm*
- £350   • Hilary Proctor

Brown Crocodile Case ▲

- *circa 1920*
Brown crocodile vanity case – relined with a new handle.
- *35cm x 40cm*
- £850   • Hilary Proctor

Leather Briefcase ▲
- *circa 1920*

Leather brief case with circular brass fitting and leather straps and handle.
- *length 40cm*
- £500   • Bentleys

Louis Vuitton Case ▲
- *1920*

Louis Vuitton case with leather trim and handle with brass fittings.
- *width 70cm*
- £1,000   • Bentleys

Cricket Case ▼
- *1930*

Tan leather cricket case with brass fittings and leather handle, the interior fitted with leather straps for holding a tennis racket, by Finnigans of Bond Street, London.
- *length 73cm*
- £800   • Bentleys

Expert Tips

There is a steady rise in auctions of original Louis Vuitton luggage, leather hat boxes and picnic hampers, with their quality and durability guaranteeing their popularity.

Dispatch Satchel ▲
- *circa 1900*

Leather dispatch satchel with a good patina, one main leather shoulder strap and three smaller straps.
- *width 61cm*
- £800   • Bentleys

Tan Hat Box ▼
- *1930*

Tan leather hat box with nickel fittings and a leather handle.
- *diameter 41cm*
- £700   • Bentleys

Hat Box ▶
- *circa 1890*

Tan leather top hat bucket with brass fittings and leather handle.
- *height 23cm*
- £500   • Bentleys

Crocodile Hat Box ▶
- *circa 1920*
Crocodile skin hat box with gilt over brass locks, with brown Moiré silk lining.
- *26cm x 41cm*
- **£4,000**   ● Bentleys

Crocodile Case ▲
- *circa 1900*
Small crocodile case with handle and nickle fittings, with the letters L.T. on the lid.
- *width 35cm*
- **£650**   ● Bentleys

Attaché Case ▲
- *circa 1900*
Rare moulded Norfolk hide attaché case with original brass fittings, a leather handle, and a green leather interior.
- *10cm x 47cm x 32cm*
- **£1,000**   ● Bentleys

Goyard Hat Case ▶
- *1920*
Goyard canvas hat case with a painted chevron pattern and a tan leather trim with small brass nails, leather handle and brass fittings.
- *25cm x 49cm*
- **£1,500**   ● Bentleys

Lady's Travelling Case ▶
- *circa 1930*
Lady's green leather travelling case in two separate sections, fitted with a silk interior incorporating a turquoise enamel brush set, boxes with silver gilt lids and a travelling clock.
- *width 32cm*
- **£600**   ● Julian Smith

Gladstone Bag ◀
- *1890*
Small leather Gladstone bag with brass fittings and leather handle.
- *24cm x 34cm*
- **£500**   ● Bentleys

Mechanical Music

Rock-Ola Princess ▲
- **1946**
American Rock-Ola Princess
No.1422, manufactured in 1946,
plays 20, 78 R.P.M. records. In
good original condition with
pheonilic pilasters and a central
panel with decorative metal
scrolling.
- *149cm x 54cm*
- **£5,200**   • **Juke Box Services**

Eight Air Musical Box ▲
- **circa 1885**
Swiss eight air music box with
five bells and drum by Paillard, in
an inlaid rosewood case with
brass handles each side standing
on square ebonised feet.
- *23cm x 68cm*
- **£4,000**   • **Vincent Freeman**

Singing Bird Autometer ▼
- *circa 1880*
Rare French singing bird
autometer in a brass and gilded
cage with moving chicks and
singing bird. The cage with
foliate design and gilded
panelling around the base. Coin-
operated and in perfect working
order.
- *58cm x 21cm*
- **£6,800**   • **Vincent Freeman**

Heart Musical Box ▼
- **1950**
Heart-shaped musical manicure
box, lined with pink silk, with a
circular mirror on the inside of
the lid and a couple in evening
dress dancing. Fitted with pink
manicure set and two small
circular metal boxes.
- *diameter 23cm*
- **£48**   • **Manic Attic**

Ami Continental ▲
- **1961**
American Ami Continental juke
box, which has push button
electric selection and plays both
sides. In good working condition
and fully restored.
- *170cm x 70cm*
- **£6,500**   • **Juke Box Services**

Seeburg HF100R ▲
- **1954**
Seeburg H.F. 100R. Holds 60
records with push button
electric selection. Plays both
sides. Considered by many to
be the best design of a series
of jukeboxes made by Seeburg
in the 50s and 60. Made in the
U.S.A.
- *158cm x 87cm*
- **£7,000**   • **Juke Box Services**

American Music Box ▲
- 1895

Regina music box cased in light oak with two rows of beading. On the inside of the lid is a central figure of a lady surrounded by cherubs playing instruments.
- 28cm x 55cm
- £4,300 • Vincent Freeman

Zodiac ▲
- 1971

A Zodiac multi selector model 3500 phonograph, manufactured by the Wurlitzer Company, Tonawanda, New York, U.S.A. with the slogan "Music for Millions".
- 138cm x 74cm
- £1,000 • Juke Box Services

Swiss Music Box ▲
- circa 1890

Unusual Swiss music box with convex glass lid by Mermod Freres.
- 27cm x 76cm
- £4,000 • Vincent Freeman

Rock-Ola 1454 ▼
- 1956

Rock-Ola 1454 juke box in original condition. The cabinet styling is based on a Seeburg M100 from 1954.
- 143cm x 77cm
- £4,000 • Juke Box Services

Rock-Ola Princess ▼
- 1962

Rock-Ola Princess stereophonic juke-box, Model 1493. Takes 50 records. Stereo and auto mix, (plays with or without centres). In original condition. Made in the U.S.A.
- 124cm x 76cm
- £4,000 • Juke Box Services

Swiss Music Box ▶
- circa 1875

Swiss music box playing ten airs with 16-reed organ by Bremond.
- 29cm x 69cm
- £5,000 • Vincent Freeman

Ami H ▲
- 1957

American Ami H, one of the first of the car influenced style of jukebox with a wrap around glass. It holds 100 records, with orange and blue push button electric selection, and plays both sides. Fully restored and in original condition.
- 159cm x 80cm
- £7,000 • Juke Box Services

Singing Bird Autometer ▲
- circa 1900

French singing bird, sitting on a brass rail with white flowers in a brass cage. Standing on a circular base with foliate scrolling decoration.
- height 53cm
- £4,600 • Vincent Freeman

219

Bal-Ami S100 ▲
- *1960*
The Bal-Ami Jukebox, made in Britain by Balfoure. Engineering, using *High Tech* parts manufactured in the U.S.A by Ami, to overcome import ban on luxury goods after the Second World War.
- *147cm x 80cm*
- £3,500 • Juke Box Services

Key-Wind Musical Box ▲
- *1858*
Nicole Frères key-wind musical box playing six operatic airs by Bellini, in an inlaid rosewood case. No.37625.
- *11cm x 56cm*
- £2,600 • Vincent Freeman

Líepee Music Box ▲
- *circa 1880*
Six bell music box by Líepee, playing eight operatic airs in an inlaid rosewood case.
- *22cm x 58cm*
- £4,000 • Vincent Freeman

Ami J 200 ▼
- *1959*
Ami J.200. Holds 100 records. With pink plastic push-button electric selection, playing both sides. Made in U.S.A. Fully restored.
- *152cm x 83cm*
- £5,800 • Juke Box Services

Birdcage Autometer ▼
- *1870*
French birdcage with two singing birds in rustic setting with roses, standing on a circular gilded base with a leaf design and circular feet. In perfect working order.
- *height 61cm*
- £5,600 • Vincent Freeman

German Symphonion ▲
- *1895*
German symphonion in a rococo walnut case carved with cherubs and a courting couple on the lid, with carved foliate design. Standing on bracket feet.
- *height 30cm*
- £6,000 • Vincent Freeman

Musical Jewellery Box ▲
- *1960*
Red plastic musical jewellery box in the form of a radiogram with turn-table that rotates when music plays, Blue interior, red drawers and a gold *fleur de lis*.
- *height 11cm*
- £55 • Manic Attic

Music Box ▲
- *circa 1875*
Music box by Nicole Frères playing eight operatic airs.
- *12cm x 58cm*
- £2,500 • Vincent Freeman

Photographs

Film Makers ▲
- *1960*

Three Italian neo-realist filmmakers, from l to r; Vittorio de Sica (1901–1974), Roberto Rossellini (1906–1977) and Federico Fellini (1920–1993) on the set of de Sica's film, "Generale delle Rovere". Black and white fibre, silver gelatin photograph. Limited edition: one of only four signed by the photographer Slim Aarons. Printed from original negative in Getty Images darkrooms.
- *length 25.4cm*
- **£1,500** • **Getty Images**

Bacall and Bogart ▶
- *24th December 1951*

American actor Humphrey Bogart (1899–1957) with Lauren Bacall and their son Stephen at their home in Beverly Hills on Christmas Eve. Black and white fibre, silver gelatin photograph from a limited edition: one of only four signed by the photographer Slim Aarons. Printed from original negative in Getty Images darkrooms.
- *length 61cm*
- **£1,500** • **Getty Images**

Take It ▼
- *September 1970*

Painter Salvador Dali (1904–1989) in a pose with his trademark walking stick, with some of his works at Port Ligat, Costa Brava, Spain. Colour Lambda photograph. Limited edition: one of only four signed by photographer Slim Aaron.
- *50.8cm x pro*
- **£2,400** • **Getty Images**

Groucho Marx ▼
- *circa 1954*

American comic Julius "Groucho" Marx (1895–1977), member of the Marx brothers, in bed with a joke cigar in Beverly HillS. Black and white, fibre silver gelatin photograph, from a limited edition: one of only four signed by the photographer Slim Aarons. Printed from original negative in Getty Images darkrooms.
- *length 61cm*
- **£1,500** • **Getty Images**

Capucine ▲
- *1957*

French actress Capucine, (Germaine Lefebvre) (1933–90) fanning herself at a New Years Eve party held at Romanoffs in Beverly Hills. By Photographer Slim Aarons. Black and white fibre, silver gelatin photograph. Limited edition: one of only four signed by the photographer. Printed from original negative in Getty Images darkrooms.
- *length 50.8cm*
- **£1,500** • **Getty Images**

Kings of Hollywood ▲
- *31st December 1957*

Film stars (left to right) Clark Gable (1901–1960), Van Heflin (1910–1971), Gary Cooper (1901–1961) and James Stewart (1908–1997) enjoy a joke at a New Year's party held at Romanoff's in Beverly Hills. A black and white, fibre silver gelatin photograph. Limited edition: one of only 250 signed by the photographer.
- *length 50.8cm*
- **£2,000** • **Getty Images**

Jackie K ▼
- **circa 1959**

Jacqueline Kennedy (Jackie Onassis 1929–1994), wife of Senator Jack Kennedy at an "April in Paris" ball. Colour Lambda photograph. Limited edition: one of only four signed by the photographer.
- *50.8cm x pro*
- **£2,400**
- Getty Images

Sea Drive ▶
- **1967**

Film producer Kevin McClory takes his wife and family out in an "Amphicar" in the Bahamas. Colour Lambda photograph. Limited edition: one of only four signed by the photographer
- *length 1.52m*
- **£3,500**
- Getty Images

The Rolling Stones ▼
- **January 1967**

British rock group The Rolling Stones; from left to right, Bill Wyman, Brian Jones (1942–1969), Charlie Watts, Keith Richards and Mick Jagger. Photographer: Keystone Collection. Modern black and white, fibre silver gelatin archival photograph printed in Getty Images Darkrooms. Limited edition: 300.
- *length 50.8cm*
- **£225**
- Getty Images

Man"s Work ▲
- **1960**

Hugh Hefner working at his typewriter surrounded by "bunny" girls. Publisher Hugh M Hefner at the Playboy Key Club in Chicago. He founded adult magazines, *Playboy*, *VIP* and *Oui*. Colour Lambda photograph. Limited edition: one of only four signed by the photographer.
- *length 50.8cm*
- **£2,400**
- Getty Images

Victoria Bridge ▲
- **1859**

Victoria Bridge – Special limited edition. A lone man sitting on the Victoria Railway Bridge over the St Lawrence River in Montreal, during its construction. Photographer: William England/London Stereoscopic Company. PLATINUM Photograph. Modern platinum print made from original glass negative by Studio 31. Platinum Limited edition: ten only.
- *paper size: 40.7cm x 30.5cm*
- *image size: 23cm x 20.4cm*
- **£500**
- Getty Images

Hitchcock Profile ▼
- **July 1966**

Film director Alfred Hitchcock (1889–1980) during the filming of "The Torn Curtain" by photographer Curt Gunther/BIPs Collection. Modern black and white, fibre silver gelatin archival photograph, printed in Getty Images Darkrooms. Limited edition: 300.
- *length 50.8cm*
- **£225**
- Getty Images

Night Time New York ▼
- **1936**

Paramount Building in Times Square, New York, towers over Schenley's Chinese Restaurant. Photographer: Fox Photos Collection. Modern black and white, fibre silver gelatin archival photograph, printed in Getty Images darkrooms. Limited edition: 300.
- *length 50.8cm*
- **£225**
- Getty Images

Chrysler Building ▲
- **3rd May 1957**
The Chrysler Building in New York by Photographer: Phil Burcham, Fox Photos. Modern black and white, fibre silver gelatin archival photograph, printed in Getty Images darkrooms. Limited edition: 300.
- *length 50.8cm*
- **£225**   • Getty Images

Taylor Reclines ▲
- **1954**
American actress Elizabeth Taylor reclining in bed by the photographer Baron. Modern black and white, fibre silver gelatin archival photograph, printed in Getty Images darkrooms. Limited edition: 300.
- *length 50.8cm*
- **£225**   • Getty Images

John Lennon Profile ▼
- **26th June 1967**
John Lennon (1940–1980), singer, songwriter and guitarist with the Beatles by photographer Peter King, Fox Photos. Modern black and white, fibre silver gelatin archival photograph, printed in Getty Images darkrooms. Limited edition: 300.
- *length 50.8cm*
- **£225**   • Getty Images

Ali In Training ▼
- **August 1966**
American heavyweight boxer Muhammad Ali in training in London for his fight against Brian London. Photographer: R.McPhedran, Express Collection. Modern black and white, fibre silver gelatin archival photograph, printed in Getty Images darkrooms. Limited edition: 300.
- *length 50.8cm*
- **£225**   • Getty Images

Commissionaire's Dog ◄
- **22nd October 1938**
A hotel commissionaire talking to a small dog in London. Photographer: Kurt Hutton, Picture Post. Modern black and white, fibre silver gelatin archival photograph, printed in Getty Images darkrooms. Limited edition: 300.
- *length 40.7cm*
- **£185**   • Getty Images

The Beatles ▲
- **10th January 1964**
Paul McCartney, Ringo Starr, John Lennon (1940–1980) and George Harrison (1943–2001) of the Beatles. Photographer: Terry Disney, Express Collection. Modern black and white, fibre silver gelatin archival photograph, printed in Getty Images darkrooms. Limited edition: 300.
- *length 50.8cm*
- **£225**   • Getty Images

Gorbals Boys ▲
- **31st January 1948**
Two boys in the Gorbals area of Glasgow. The Gorbals tenements were built quickly and cheaply in the 1840s. Conditions were appalling; overcrowding was standard and sewage and water facilities inadequate. The tenements housed about 40,000 people with up to eight family members sharing a single room, 30 residents sharing a toilet and 40 sharing a tap. By the time this photograph was taken 850 tenements had been demolished since 1920. Photographer: Bert Hardy, Picture Post. Modern black and white, fibre silver gelatin archival photograph, printed in Getty Images darkrooms. Limited edition: 300.
- *length 40.7cm*
- **£185**   • Getty Images

Fair Fun ▲
- **8th October 1938**
Two young women enjoying themselves on a roller coaster at Southend Fair, England by the photographer Kurt Hutton, Picture Post. Modern black and white, fibre silver gelatin archival photograph, printed in Getty Images Darkrooms. Limited edition: 300.
- *length 50.8cm*
- **£225**   • Getty Images

Bright Lights ▲
- **1970**
Aerial view of the Manhattan skyline at night, looking southeast down Fifth Avenue, from the RCA Building Rockefeller Center, New York City by photographer: Lawrence Thornton. Modern black and white, fibre silver gelatin archival photograph, printed in Getty Images Darkrooms. Limited edition: 300.
- *length 50.8cm*
- **£225**   • Getty Images

Snow in the Park ▼
- **1947**
A man trudging through Central Park West, New York City, in a blizzard by photographer: Nat Fein/Courtesy of Nat Fein's Estate. Exclusive. Black and white, fibre silver gelatin archival photograph, printed from original negative in Getty Images darkrooms.
- *length 50.8cm*
- **£485**   • Getty Images

Fonda in Town ▼
- **1951**
Film star Henry Fonda (1905–1982) on a balcony overlooking a street in New York by photographer Slim Aarons. Black and white, fibre silver gelatin photograph, printed from original negative in Getty Images darkrooms. Limited edition: 300.
- *paper: 40.7cm x 30.5cm*
image: 30.5cm x 30.5cm
- **£185**   • Getty Images

Jazz Scooter ▶
- **1949**
Lucille Brown takes control of the Vespa scooter as her husband Louis Armstrong (1898–1971) displays his musical appreciation of the ancient Coliseum in Rome. Black and white fibre, silver gelatin photograph, from a limited edition of 300 by photographer Slim Aarons. Printed from original negative in Getty Images darkrooms.
- *length 50.8cm*
- **£225**   • Getty Images

Walking in the Rain ▲
- **circa 1955**
A man and his dog walking in the rain in Central Park, New York City by photographer: Nat Fein/Courtesy Of Nat Fein's Estate. Black and white, fibre silver gelatin archival photograph, printed from original negative in Getty Images darkrooms. Exclusive.
- *length 40.7cm*
- **£415**   • Getty Images

Guggenheim Window ▲
- **circa 1955**
The Guggenheim Museum of Modern and Contemporary Art in New York. Photographer: Sherman, Three Lions Collection. Black and white fibre, silver gelatin photograph, printed from original negative in Getty Images darkrooms. Limited edition: 300.
- *length 61cm*
- **£250**   • Getty Images

Portrait Miniatures

Richard Cosway ▶

- *circa 1790*
A portrait of Sir Charles
Cockrell, in original gold frame,
the reverse with gold monogram
CC on blond plaited hair within
gold mount and blue glass border.
- *height 5cm*
- **£8,000**   • **Ellison Fine Art**

Kenneth Macleay ▲

- *circa 1835*
A miniature of Lt. John Ure
Donaldson wearing scarlet
uniform with gold epaulettes and
collar, white cross band with gold
plate XLVI within laurel wreath
and crown.
- *height 11 cm*
- **£1,950**   • **Ellison Fine Art**

Expert Tips

*Get to know your medium –
miniatures can be executed in
many forms: silvette, block
painting on glass, en-grisie,
enamel, watercolour, gouache.*

Samuel Shelley ▶

- *circa 1790*
A miniature of Captain Edward
Herriman of the HEICS, wearing
blue uniform with black facings
and gold lace, yellow waistcoat,
his powdered hair en queue. Set
in a gold frame.
- *height 7.5cm*
- **£6,500**   • **Ellison Fine Art**

Collector's Items

Expert Tips

The seventeenth century method of making glass pictures uses prints. The print is soaked, placed on the glass, dried and then the thin paper is removed to leave a print that is hand-coloured.

Christian Richter ▶

- *circa 1705*
Queen Anne, wearing ermine robes over a golden dress, a blue sash and order around her neck. On vellum, set in the original gold coloured frame with pierced spiral cresting.
- *height 7.5cm*
- £5,850   • Ellison Fine Art

Charles Hayter ▼

- *circa 1790*
A portrait of a lady with powdered wig, wearing white dress, fichu and matching turban. Set in the original gold frame with shaped border, the reverse with locks of hair tied with split pearls and gold wire on ivory ground.
- *height 7.5 cm*
- £2,700   • Ellison Fine Art

Andrew Plimer ▲

- *circa 1810*
Portrait miniature of Miss Abrams possibly Eliza (1772–1830) the sister of Harriet and Theodosia by artist Andrew Plimer. Set in the original ivory frame with gold mount and plaited hair reverse.
- *height 7cm*
- £6,500   • Ellison Fine Art

George Engleheart ▶

- *circa 1790*
A miniature of a young lady with powdered hair wearing white dress with turquoise trimmings, ruff collar and pearl necklace, a turquoise ribbon entwined in her hair. Gold oval frame with plaited hair reverse.
- *height 6cm*
- £6,850   • Ellison Fine Art

Posters

Salamander Brandy

- *circa 1950*

Advertising poster for Salamander Brandy with a view of a village and the sea in the background and a cartouche of the factory, a large bottle of cognac, and a bunch of grapes in the foreground.

- *41cm x 36cm*
- £145   • Dodo

Ovaltine Nightcap

- *circa 1950*

An Ovaltine advertisement of a young smiling lady holding a cup and saucer with the words "Ovaltine – The World's Best Nightcap".

- *37cm x28cm*
- £75   • Dodo

Marcella Cigars

- *circa 1950*

Poster of a hand holding five Marcella cigars and the words "A Grand Shilling's Worth".

- *42cm x 36cm*
- £120   • Dodo

Metrovick Lamps

- *circa 1950*

Advertising poster of a lady wearing a cream dress leaning over a red chair advertising Metrovick Lamps for Metropolitan.

- *48cm x 36cm*
- £75   • Dodo

Grapefruit Breakfast

- *circa 1950*

Gentleman in a suit and bowler hat seated on a grapefruit with the slogan "Start the day on a Grapefruit".

- *26cm x 46cm*
- £55   • Dodo

Expert Tips

Poster collecting is now a major activity. Two tips: top condition and old film stars.

Monarch Whisky

- *circa 1950*

The Monarch Old Scotch Whisky advertising poster.

- *37cm x 23cm*
- £65   • Dodo

Way Out West ▼
- 1937
"Way Out West" with Laurel and Hardy.
- *28cm x36cm*
- £650   • Cine Art Gallery

Ice Cold in Alex ▼
- 1958
"Ice Cold in Alex" with John Mills and Sylvia Syms. Directed by Bruce Robinson.
- *height 1.02m*
- £350   • Cine Art Gallery

The Untouchables ▲
- 1987
"The Untouchables", with Kevin Costner, Sean Connery and Robert De Niro.
- *28cm x 36cm*
- £75   • Cine Art Gallery

Blade Runner ▲
- 1982
"Blade Runner" with Harrison Ford.
- *1.04m x 58cm*
- £400   • Cine Art Gallery

Apocalypse Now ◀
- 1979
"Apocalypse Now" with Marlon Brando. German double panel.
- *85cm x 1.18m*
- £1,300   • Cine Art Gallery

Sherlock Holmes Faces Death ▲
- 1951
"Sherlock Holmes Faces Death". Spanish one sheet.
- *1.04m x 29cm*
- £450   • Cine Art Gallery

The Birds ▲
- 1963
"The Birds" by Alfred Hitchcock, with Tippi Hedren and Rod Taylor.
- *1.02m x 79cm*
- £500   • Cine Art Gallery

Goldfinger ▲
- 1964
"Golfinger" starring Sean Connery.
- *28cm x 36cm*
- £325   • Cine Art Gallery

Cycles Favor Motos

- *circa 1950*

Advertisement for Cycles Favor
Motos featuring a mechanic
wearing a cap and blue overalls,
holding a bicycle in one hand
and a motor bike in the other.

- *46cm x 50cm*
- £75
- Dodo

Jaws II

- *1961*

U.S. linen-backed "Jaws II" poster
with art work by Mick McGinty.

- *1.04m x 69cm*
- £500
- Reel Poster

Bay of Naples

- *1950*

Lady holding a guitar seated on a
boat, with the words "A trip thro'
the Bay of Naples".

- *48cm x 54cm*
- £45
- Dodo

Cruising West Indies

- *circa 1960*

"Southampton to the West
Indies" travel poster showing a
cruise liner, tropical fruit, and the
words "French Line – A Service
of Distinction".

- *80cm x 48cm*
- £85
- Dodo

Night of the Demon

- *circa 1960*

"The Night of the Demon"/"La
notte del demonio" Italian linen-
backed poster.

- *1.4m x 99cm*
- £1,500
- Reel Poster

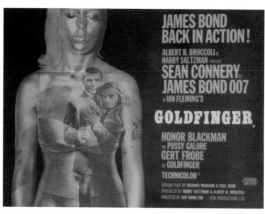

Goldfinger ◄

- *1964*

"Goldfinger" poster with Sean Connery as James Bond and Honor Blackman as Pussy Galore.
- *76cm x 1.01m*
- **£2,800** • **Cine Art Gallery**

Withnail and I ▼

- *1987*

"Withnail and I" starring Richard E. Grant and Paul McGann.
- *height 1.03m*
- **£400** • **Cine Art Gallery**

High Society ▼

- *1956*

"High Society" with Frank Sinatra, Grace Kelly and Bing Crosby.
- *28cm x 36cm*
- **£120** • **Cine Art Gallery**

Brigitte Bardot ▲

- *1963*

"Le Mepris", with Brigitte Bardot.
- *height 1.58m*
- **£1,500** • **Cine Art Gallery**

The Godfather ▲

- *1972*

"The Godfather" and "Italian Photobusta".
- *45cm x 65cm*
- **£350** • **Cine Art Gallery**

Alfie ▲

- *1966*

"Alfie", with Michael Caine.
- *28cm x 36cm*
- **£95** • **Cine Art Gallery**

Goldfinger ▼

- *1967*

"Goldfinger" with Sean Connery.
- *56cm x 1.02m*
- **£1,200** • **Cine Art Gallery**

Persona
- *1966*

Swedish linen-backed poster for Ingmar Berman's "Persona" with Bibi Andersson and Liv Ullmann.
- *99cm x 69cm*
- £1,800   • Reel Poster

Deserto Rosso
- *1964*

Italian linen backed poster for "Deserto Rosso".
- *2.01m x 1.4m*
- £2,500   • Reel Poster

Czerwona Pustynia
- *1964*

Polish "Il Deserto Rosso"/ "Czerwona Pustynia" poster with art by Witold Janowski.
- *84cm x 58cm*
- £600   • Reel Poster

Badlands
- *1974*

British linen-backed film poster for "Badlands".
- *76cm x 1.02m*
- £375   • Reel Poster

Expert Tips

Posters of the early twentieth century were not intended to last and were printed on very thin paper. Make sure the central image is unaffected by stains, folds and fading, though small tears are not a big problem.

Sporting Life
- *1963*

British linen-backed poster for "This Sporting Life" with art by Renatop Fratini.
- *1.04m x 69cm*
- £300   • Reel Poster

French Cancan ▶

- **1955**

Linen-backed "French Cancan" poster with art by Rene Gruau.

- *1.6m x 1.19m*
- **£2,250**
- **Reel Poster**

Battleship Potemkin ▲

- **1925**

Poster for first Japanese release of "The Battleship Potemkin".

- *76cm x 51cm*
- **£600**
- **Reel Poster**

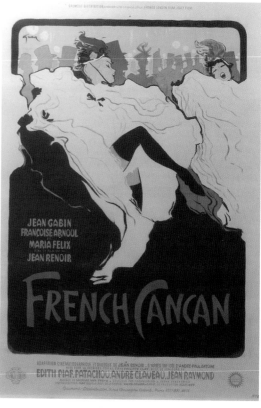

Forbidden Planet ▲

- **1956**

American linen-backed poster for landmark science fiction film "Forbidden Planet" with Leslie Nielson.

- *1.04m x 69cm*
- **£7,500**
- **Reel Poster**

Italian Rififi ▶

- **1955**

Italian linen-backed poster for "Rififi" by Jules Dassin.

- *1.40m x 99cm*
- **£1,250**
- **Reel Poster**

Apocalypse Now ◀

- **1979**

Australian linen-backed poster for "Apocalypse Now".

- *1.02m x 69cm*
- **£350**
- **Reel Poster**

Pyscho ▲
- **1962**
"Pyscho" 1962 re-issue U.S. sheet.
- *width 29cm*
- **£600** ● Cine Art Gallery

Gilda ▲
- **1946**
"Gilda", American insert.
- *92cm x 35cm*
- **£1,600** ● Cine Art Gallery

Love is My Profession ▼
- **1959**
"Love is My Profession", starring
Brigitte Bardot.
- *83cm x 60.5cm*
- **£350** ● Cine Art Gallery

Breakfast at Tiffany's ▼
- **1961**
"Breakfast at Tiffany's", starring
Audrey Hepburn.
- *28cm x 36cm*
- **£475** ● Cine Art Gallery

Manhattan ▼
- **1979**
"Manhattan" Lobby Carl.
- *28cm x 36cm*
- **£95** ● Cine Art Gallery

Revenge of the Creature ▲
- **1955**
"Revenge of the Creature" U.K.
Quad John Agar Laurie Nelson.
- *1.02m x 60.5cm*
- **£850** ● Cine Art Gallery

My Fair Lady ▲
- **1965**
"My Fair Lady" with Audrey
Hepburn and Rex Harrison.
- *75cm x 1.37m*
- **£450** ● Cine Art Gallery

The Enforcer ▲
- **1977**
"The Enforcer" with Clint
Eastwood as Dirty Harry.
- *28cm x 36cm*
- **£95** ● Cine Art Gallery

Yellow Submarine ▼

- *1969*
"Yellow Submarine" with the
Beatles. U.S. One sheet.
- *height 1.04m*
- £12,500 • Cine Art Gallery

Thunderball ▶

- *1965*
"Thunderball" with Sean
Connery.
- *41cm x 27cm*
- £1,100 • Cine Art Gallery

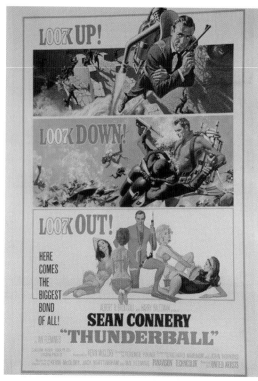

The Italian Job ▲

- *1969*
"The Italian Job" with Michael
Caine. U.K. Mini Quad.
- *31cm x 41cm*
- £5 • Cine Art Gallery

Expert Tips

*If you decide to start collecting
posters, it is best to start with
the posters that depict your
favourite old films and stars.
As an amateur antique
collector, posters are a good
starting point because their cost
is fairly reasonable.*

The Apartment ▶

- *1960*
"The Apartment" starring Jack
Lemmon and Shirley McLaine.
- *28cm x 36cm*
- £85 • Cine Art Gallery

Bullitt ▲

- *1969*
"Bullitt" with Steve McQueen.
U. S. One sheet.
- *27cm x 21cm*
- £680 • Cine Art Gallery

Midnight Cowboy ▼

- *1969*
"Midnight Cowboy" with Dustin
Hoffman. U.K. Quad.
- *76cm x 1.02m*
- £190 • Cine Art Gallery

Radios

Decca Gramaphone ▲
- *1951*
Children's gramophone in original box with nursery rhyme pictures on each side and carrying handle.
- *18cm x 32cm*
- £150   • Manic Attic

Dansette Portable Radio ▲
- *1961*
Grey plastic Dansette portable radio with beige plastic handle and large circular dial.
- *14cm x 21cm*
- £45   • Manic Attic

Isis Plastic Radio ▲
- *circa 1960*
Isis white plastic radio in the form of the word "radio".
- *7cm x 25cm*
- £55   • Manic Attic

Calypso Radio ▲
- *circa 1960*
Grey plastic Calypso radio with circular dial.
- *18cm x 23cm*
- £28   • Manic Attic

Kidditune Record Player ▲
- *1962*
Red plastic battery-operated record player by Marx Toys in original box complete with original records.
- *13cm x 26cm*
- £65   • Manic Attic

Wrist Radio ▲
- *1960*
Panasonic blue plastic radio worn around the wrist.
- *17cm x 18cm*
- £50   • Revenance

Panasonic Novelty Radio ▲
- *1960*
Yellow plastic wrist radio by Panasonic.
- *17cm x 18cm*
- £50   • Revenance

Roberts Metal and Teak Radio ▲
- *1968*
Roberts radio with metal and teak case and carrying handle.
- *23cm x 38cm*
- £38   • Revenance

P.Y.E. Record Player ▲

- **1955**

P.Y.E. record player in a bow-fronted teak case with cream turntable. Holds ten records on stack.
- *height 26cm*
- **£100**   • Manic Attic

Radio and TV Diary 1957 ▲

- **1957**

Radio and TV Diary for 1957 with photographs on each page of actors and musicians. Showing a photograph of David Attenborough.
- *height 12cm*
- **£10**   • Manic Attic

P.Y.E. Record Player ▼

- **1955**

P.Y.E. record player in a grey with white polka dot case, with unusual curved sides, white plastic carrying handles and a black and gold sparkling grill.
- *height 25cm*
- **£75**   • Manic Attic

Perdio Transistor ▶

- **1962**

Perdio Super Seven Transistor radio, inscribed with "Real Morocco leather made in England", on the back, with a dial for an aerial and phone or tape, and a large brass dial and gold writing.
- *height 12.5cm*
- **£38**   • Manic Attic

E.A.R. Triple Four ◀

- **1958**

E.A.R. Triple four record player in a blue and grey Rexine case with cream piping and handles.
- *height 27cm*
- **£80**   • Manic Attic

Hacker ▲

- **1964**

Hacker record player in a black and grey case with metal fittings.
- *height 27cm*
- **£50**   • Manic Attic

Roberts Radio ▲

- **1958**

Roberts radio in original condition with red Rexine case and handle and brass dials and fittings.
- *height 15cm*
- **£68**   • Manic Attic

Rock & Pop

Record Bag

- *circa 1950*

Plastic multi-coloured bag for carrying 45rpm records with various musical instruments.
- *diameter 24cm*
- £26   • Revenance

ABBA Mirror

- *circa 1970*

Mirror with photograph of the band ABBA.
- *24cm x 20cm*
- £16   • Revenance

Record Case

- *circa 1950*

White plastic carrying case for 45rpm records with jazz and dancing design.
- *diameter 26cm*
- £28   • Revenance

Sex Pistols

- *circa 1980*

Sex Pistols T-shirt with a picture of the Queen and the words "God Save the Queen".
- *50cm x 42cm*
- £25   • Revenance

Top Pop Stars

- *circa 1950*

"Book of Top Pop Stars" with Cliff Richard on the cover.
- *28cm x 24cm*
- £14   • Revenance

Pat As I See Him ▲
- 1966

"Pat As I See Him", a pen and ink portrait on an envelope by Joe Meek of his lover. Annotated in verso "Pat was Meek's boyfriend and was present at the landlady's shooting and Meek's subsequent suicide".
- £5,250   • Music and Video

Michael Jackson Doll ▼
- 1995

A singing Michael Jackson doll wearing a white shirt and black trousers in original box.
- £47   • Music and Video

Stone Age ◄
- 1971

"Stone Age" by The Rolling Stones.
- £580   • Music and Video

Instant Karma Lennon ▲
- 1971

John Ono Lennon "Instant Karma" produced by Phil Spector.
- £117   • Music and Video

Andy Warhol ◄
- 1967

Andy Warhol- "Andy Warhol's Index Box". First hardback edition-Random House USA complete and in working order including the velvet underground flexi-disc. Reed's eye has not even popped!
- £1,500   • Music and Video

Bob Dylan ◄
- **1961**
Bob Dylan's first recording produced by John Hammond.
- **£735**   • **Music and Video**

Beatles Lady Madonna ▲
- **1968**
"The Inner Light, Lady Madonna" by The Beatles.
- **£72**   • **Music and Video**

Agogo ▲
- **1963**
"Agogo", with Ray Charles, The Supremes, Petula Clark, and The Everly brothers.
- **£35**   • **Music and Video**

Time Will Pass ▲
- **1977**
"Time Will Pass" by the Spriguns. Distributed by The Decca Record Company Limited, London.
- **£175**   • **Music and Video**

Equinoxe 4 ▼
- **1979**
"Equinoxe 4", an album by Jean Michel Jarre, with a signed autograph in black biro on front cover.
- **£60**   • **Music and Video**

Yellow Submarine ▼
- **1960s**
The Beatles "Yellow Submarine and Eleanor Rigby".
- **£72**   • **Music and Video**

The Monkees ▲
- **1968**
The Monkees. Original motion picture sound track "Head".
- **£95**   • **Music and Video**

Status Quo ▲
- **1970**
"In my Chair/Gerdundula" Status Quo.
- **£72**   • **Music and Video**

The Beatles ▶

- *circa 1960*
"The Beatles:, An Illustrated
Record" by R. Carr and T. Tyler.
- *23cm x 30cm*
- £20　　　　• Revenance

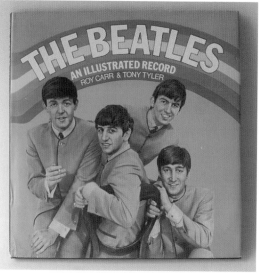

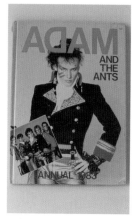

Adam Ant ▲

- *circa 1970*
Annual of Adam and the Ants.
- *24cm x 20cm*
- £14　　　　• Revenance

Slade in Flame ▼

- *circa 1970*
Rare album and cover of Slade in
Flame.
- *42cm x 42cm*
- £20　　　　• Revenance

Donny Osmond ▼

- *circa 1970*
Teen Pin-Ups dynamite colour
comic featuring Donny Osmond.
- *23cm x 28cm*
- £10　　　　• Revenance

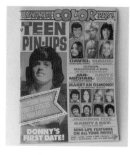

Latin a la Lee ▼

- *circa 1950*
Peggy Lee album and cover.
- *width 42cm*
- £7　　　　• Revenance

The Police Box ▼
- **1997–87**
"The Police Box" (Sting, Stewart Copeland and Andy Summers) from 1977 to 1987.
- **£150**   • **Music and Video**

Elvis ▼
- **1971**
"You'll Never Walk Alone" by Elvis. Manufactured and Distributed by RCA Limited.
- **£1,800**   • **Music and Video**

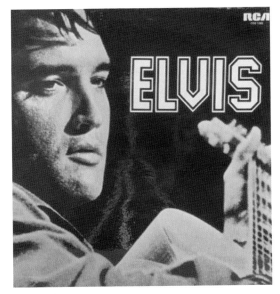

H. M. S. Donovan ▲
- **1971**
"H.M.S. Donovan" produced by Donovan Engineered by Mike Bobak at Morgan Studios London. All paintings by Patrick.
- **£130**   • **Music and Video**

Sticky Fingers: Rolling Stones ▲
- **1972**
"Sticky Fingers", an album by The Rolling Stones.
- **£220**   • **Music and Video**

Whitehouse Present Total Sex ▼
- **circa 1980**
Whitehouse present "Total Sex".
- **£125**   • **Music and Video**

The Velvet Underground ▼
- **circa 1967**
Andy Warhol presents the "The Velvet Underground and Nico", original German Issue with Erice Emmerson Sleeve (No Banana).
- **£248**   • **Music and Video**

Roy Harper Sophisticated ▼
- **1966**
Roy Harper "Sophisticated Beggar" Strike JHL 105. Test pressing. W/Proff Sleeve in excellent condition.
- **£550**   • **Music and Video**

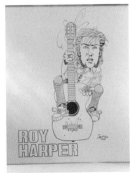

Sewing Items

Wicker Sewing Bag ▶

- *1880*

Wicker sewing bag with green wool panels, decorated with pink silk flowers and lined with green silk.

- *26cm x 20cm*
- £175   • M. Williamson

Silver Thimble ▲

- *1912*

Silver thimble made in Birmingham.

- *height 2cm*
- £45   • Cekay

Needle Case ▲

- *circa 1900*

Hand-carved ivory needle case.

- *height 7cm*
- £78   • Cekay

Mother-of-Pearl Bobbin ◀

- *circa 1900*

Small ivory bobbin with mother-of-pearl.

- *height 3.5cm*
- £45   • Cekay

Needle Case ▼

- *circa 1900*

Ivory needle case.

- *height 7cm*
- £56   • Cekay

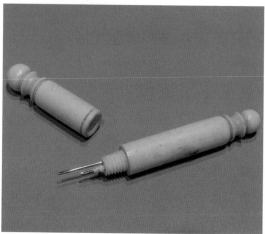

Expert Tips

Thimbles are great fun to collect, before you start view collections ahead and decide what type to collect.

Musical Sewing Box ◀

- *circa 1850*

Palais Royale tortoiseshell and ivory-faced musical sewing box with a reverse glass painted pastoral scene on the lid, enclosing original inkwells, needle case, screw top pencil, scissors, thimble and other sewing implements. Most with the Palais Royale insignia. The music box is in working order.
- *10cm x 19cm*
- £3,450   • J. & T. Stone

English Thimble ▶

- *circa 1880*

English mother-of-pearl thimble set inside case with velvet lining and clasp.
- *height 2cm*
- £220   • Arca

Silver Bear Pincushion ▼

- *1908*

English silver articulated bear pincushion from Birmingham.
- *height 8cm*
- £850   • Arca

Silver Filigree Case ▲

- *circa 1780*

French silver filigree case enclosing pincushion and blue glass bottle.
- *length 5cm*
- £1,150   • Arca

Filigree Scissor Case ▶

- *circa 1840*

Delicate silver filigree scissor case with scrolling.
- *length 6.5cm*
- £480   • Arca

Sewing Box ▶

- *circa 1820*

Chinese export black lacquer sewing box with a scene showing a family group with a pagoda and landscape in the background, with fitted interior, standing on gilt claw feet.
- *34cm x 23.5cm x 14cm*
- £2,000   • O.F.Wilson

Collector's Items

Silk Winder
- *circa1890*
Chinese carved hardwood double
silk winder.
- *18cm x 2.5cm*
- £32   • Jocelyn Chatterton

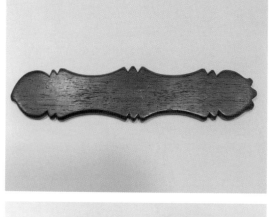

Ivory Pin Cushion ▲
- *circa 1900*
Small urn-shaped ivory pin
cushion holder.
- *height 6cm*
- £67   • Cekay

Plum Blossom Silk Winder ▼
- *circa 1890*
Chinese hardwood silk winder
carved with a plum blossom, a
symbol of winter.
- *15cm x 4cm*
- £25   • Jocelyn Chatterton

Red Lacquer Winder ▲
- *circa 1890*
Carved Chinese festive red
lacquer winder with gilded
flowers.
- *13cm x 8cm*
- £25   • Jocelyn Chatterton

Chinese Scissors ▲
- *circa 1860*
Steel Chinese sewing scissors.
- *height 11cm*
- £95   • Jocelyn Chatterton

Ivory Needle Case ▼
- *circa 1870*
Fine ivory needle case with
original needle packets and the
inscription "T.H." on the cover.
- *height 11cm*
- £495 • Arca

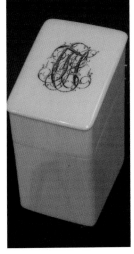

Gold Egg Sewing Case ▲
- *circa 1880*
French gold filigree case in the
shape of an egg and lined with
the original red velvet. With
gold thimble scissors, needle case
and pick.
- *height 8cm*
- £700 • Arca

English Bodkin Case ▲
- *circa 1780*
English lilac enamel bodkin case
in two sections with a bird
cartouche.
- *length 15cm*
- £520 • Arca

Oval Tortoiseshell Case ▼
- *circa 1880*
Oval tortoiseshell sewing case,
complete with gold scissors,
thimble, pick needle case and
pencil.
- *length 12.5cm*
- £950 • Arca

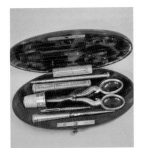

Pig Pincushion ▲
- *circa 1880*
Ivory pig with brown velvet
pincushion on the back.
- *height 3cm*
- £360 • Arca

Tortoiseshell Box ▲
- *circa 1880*
Tortoiseshell needle case, with
hinged cover.
- *height 5cm*
- £330 • Arca

Bodkin Case ◄
- *circa 1780*
Purple bodkin case with white
hexagonal spot design and six
landscape cartouches, with gold
banding.
- *length 15cm*
- £980 • Arca

Fruitwood Winder ◄

- *circa 1900*

Finely carved fruitwood Chinese silk winder.

- *height 24cm*
- £28   • Jocelyn Chatterton

Lacquered Needle Case ▶

- *circa 1870*

Carved wood red and gold lacquer needle case in the form of a flower.

- *12cm x 8cm*
- £100   • Jocelyn Chatterton

Chinese Thimble ▲

- *circa 1860*

Silver Chinese thimble engraved with trailing blossom, worn as a ring.

- *diameter 1.5cm*
- £95   • Jocelyn Chatterton

Silver Needle Case ▶

- *circa 1890*

Needle case of silver with trailing foliate banding.

- *length 8cm*
- £95   • Jocelyn Chatterton

Carved Needle Case ▲

- *circa 1930*

Carved fruitwood winder and needle case.

- *length 26cm*
- £95   • Jocelyn Chatterton

Satinwood Table Workbox ▶

- *circa 1820*

English hexagonal sewing workbox having triangular lidded compartments with small knob handles on either side of a central rectangular pin cushion.

- *7.5cm x 18.5cm x 28cm*
- £500-£1,00   • J. Collins

Silver Scissors ◄

- *circa 1880*
Victorian silver case with scissors.
- *length 9.5cm*
- £260　　　　　　　　• Arca

French Etui ▲

- *circa 1880*
French ebonised etui with silver gilt fitting.
- *length 12cm*
- £550　　　　　　　　• Arca

Silver Boot Pincushion ▼

- *circa 1870*
Silver boot pincushion.
- *height 5cm*
- £280　　　　　　　　• Arca

Gothic Chair Pincushion ▲

- *circa 1900*
Gothic silver metal chair the red velvet seat being a pincushion.
- *height 6.5cm*
- £135　　　　　　　　• Arca

Silver Wool Winder ▼

- *circa 1780*
Silver wool winder in the shape of a ball made of fine foliate filigree, with small flowers on each leaf.
- *circumference 18cm*
- £850　　　　　　　　• Arca

Walnut Sewing Case ▶

- *circa 1840*
French walnut sewing case in the form of a nut, lined with red satin and containing small scissors, thimble, needle case and pick.
- *width 5cm*
- £690　　　　　　　　• Arca

Gold Chatelaine ▶

- *circa 1780*
French gold five piece sewing chatelaine, with heavily engraved design of flowers in baskets, ribboning, and scrolling joined by linked chains to a central foliate scrolled hook.
- *length 18cm*
- £1,350　　　　　　　• Arca

Snuff Boxes & Smoking Equipment

Horn Box ◄

- *circa 1890*
Horn snuff box with inlaid silver foliate design.
- *length 8cm*
- £65   • **Michael's Boxes**

Expert Tips

Tobacco was regarded by doctors as a valuable medicine and, particularly during the plague of 1665, both smoking and snuff-taking proliferated. The earliest snuff boxes are Irish, where the habit of snuff-taking – know as "smutchin" – took off long before it became popular in England.

Hampton Court Snuff Box ◄

- *circa 1890*
Oblong silver snuff box with Hampton Court on the lid, by G. Smith and Sons.
- *length 5cm*
- £65   • **Michael's Boxes**

Miniature Snuff Box ▲

- *circa 1890*
Miniature papier mâché snuff box with silver inlay of fleur-de-lys.
- *length 2cm*
- £30   • **Michael's Boxes**

Table Snuff Box ▲

- *circa 1890*
Table snuff box with the words "Help yourself" on the lid.
- *4cm x 13cm*
- £100   • **Michael's Boxes**

Huntsmen and Hounds Snuff Box ◄

- *circa 1890*
Silver snuff box by Fribourg and Treyer of London with huntsmen and foxes on the lid.
- *length 5cm*
- £55   • **Michael's Boxes**

French Gold Snuff Box ◀

- *circa 1750*
French oval snuff box with a
tooled striped pattern of gold over
tortoiseshell, and a roped effect
around the rim.
- *length 7cm*
- £1,980 • Arca

Burr Walnut Snuff Box ▲

- *circa 1870*
Burr walnut circular snuff box,
with a painted landscape scene
on the lid and gold banding.
- *diameter 6.5cm*
- £250 • Arca

Silver Gilt Snuff Box ▶

- *circa Louis XIV*
French silver gilt snuff box with
shell design on the top and a
pastoral scene with a bird at the
bottom.
- *length 8cm*
- £980 • Arca

Painted Snuff Box ▶

- *circa 1890*
English oval papier mâché
snuff box painted with the head
of a young man on a red
background.
- *length 7cm*
- £460 • Arca

Ebonised Snuff Box ▲

- *circa 1870*
Circular ebonised snuff box,
painted with a portrait of a
woman shown against a blue
background, by L. Fischer.
- *diameter 8.5cm*
- £980 • Arca

Circular Painted
Snuff Box ▶

- *circa 1790*
Circular tortoiseshell painted
snuff box showing a lady seated
playing a harp.
- *diameter 8cm*
- £1,750 • Arca

Mother-of-Pearl Snuff Box ◀

- *circa 1890*
Oblong black lacquer snuff box with inlaid banding of mother-of-pearl pink.
- *length 7cm*
- **£40** • **Michael's Boxes**

Silver Flower Snuff Box ▼

- *circa 1880*
Horn snuff box with ivory banding and silver foliate design.
- *length 4cm*
- **£65** • **Michael's Boxes**

Horn Mull Snuff Box ▲

- *circa 1880*
Horn snuff box with silver banding and shield with the initials "L.M".
- *length 9cm*
- **£275** • **Michael's Boxes**

Chinoiserie Snuff Box ◀

- *circa 1890*
Oval silver snuff box with chinoiserie scene featuring a pagoda and trees on the lid.
- *diameter 5cm*
- **£65** • **Michael's Boxes**

Expert Tips

Collecting snuff boxes is one area where there are very few period fakes or improvements – nothing reasonably and economically could be turned into a snuff box. However, during the eighteenth century, snuff boxes were sometimes turned into vinaigrettes, portable containers for vinegar to be used as a suppressant of bad smells and as a disease deterrent, by the addition of a grill under the lid. These are now rare and highly collectable.

Silver and Enamel Cigarette Case ▶

- *circa 1896*
Silver cigarette case with an enamel picture showing a circus ring, with a lady in a pink dress astride a white horse, with a clown turning towards her.
- *length 9cm*
- £1,350 • Arca

Tortoiseshell and Silver Snuff Box ▲

- *circa 1780*
An oval tortoiseshell snuff box with a silver floral and geometric design, with a mother-of-pearl background.
- *diameter 6.5cm*
- £240 • Arca

Japanese Cigar Box ▲

- *circa 1880*
Japanese export cigar box with a dragon and Japanese characters on the lid characterising longevity and good fortune.
- *5cm x 18cm*
- £120 • Younger

Mother-of-Pearl Snuff Box ▼

- *circa 1750*
Small bulbous snuff box with mother-of-pearl sections and silver banding.
- *height 5cm*
- £750 • Arca

Satinwood Humidor ▲

- *circa 1910*
An elegant English rectangular satinwood humidor, with ivory banding and a fitted interior.
- *12.5cm x 23cm*
- £495 • A.I.G

Dog Tobacco Jar ▲

- *circa 1900*
Carved mahogany tobacco jar in the shape of a comical dog with glass eyes, wearing a hat with a tassel and a bow tie.
- *height 18cm*
- £600 • Arca

Telephones

Call Exchange Telephone ◀

- *circa 1950*

Black telephone cast in Bakelite with large central rotary dial and small drawer.
- *20cm x 26cm*
- £135   • Duffield

Black Bakelite Telephone ▲

- *circa 1930*

Black Bakelite telephone with large dial and drawer.
- *18cm x 25cm*
- £165   • Duffield

Expert Tips

The trimphone is now popular with collectors because it was so unpopular with users.

Red G.P.O. Telephone ▲

- *circa 1960*

Unusual G.P.O. telephone cast in red.
- *14cm x 18cm*
- £53   • Duffield

Trimphone ▶

- *circa 1970*

Two tone beige trimphone with push-button dialing.
- *10cm x 19cm*
- £55   • Duffield

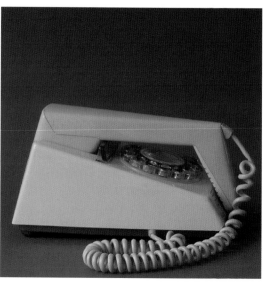

Two Toned Telephone ▶

- *circa 1970*
Two toned, adjustable volume stone coloured British GPO telephone in plastic.
- *12cm x 10cm*
- **£48**   • Genie

English Telephone ▲

- *circa 1950*
Cream Bakelite telephone with nickel rotary dial and black numerals, inscribed Portobello 4559, rare in any colour but black.
- *height 15cm*
- **£290**   • Old Cinema

Belgian Desk Telephone ▼

- *circa 1950*
European ivory desk telephone with large numerals and clear plastic rotary dial.
- *height 12.5cm*
- **£75**   • Old Cinema

Candlestick Telephone ▲

- *circa 1920*
Candlestick telephone with Steal handle with black bakelite top and brass and separate wood and brass ring box.
- *44cm x 15cm*
- **£395**   • Duffeld

Ericsson Telephone ◀

- *circa 1950*
Cream bakelite Ericsson telephone with original handset and cord and large rotary dial with black numerals.
- *height 14cm*
- **£185**   • Old Cinema

Bakelite Telephone ▶

- *circa 1950*

Black bakelite British G.P.O. telephone with ringing bell.
- *16cm x 24cm*
- £105   • Genie

Gecophone Telephone ▼

- *circa 1930*

Gecophone black bakelite telephone with bell ringing.
- *18cm x 24cm*
- £185   • H. Duffeld

Genie Telephone ▼

- *circa 1970*

Red "Genie" designer telephone by A. P. Besson manufactured by British Telecom, with push button dial.
- *11.5cm x 22cm*
- £65   • Old Cinema

Red Telephone ▲

- *circa 1960*

Red plastic British GPO telephone.
- *13cm x 24cm*
- £45   • Genie

Pyramid Telephone ▼

- *circa 1930*

Black bakelite pyramid telephone with drawer and bell ringing.
- *16cm x 23cm*
- £185   • H. Duffeld

Green Plastic Telephone ◀

- *circa 1960*

Green plastic British GPO telephone. Slightly older than telephone # 9965.
- *13cm x 24cm*
- £45   • Genie

Expert Tips

Ivory or coloured bakelite telephones were more expensive for the subscriber to rent and are therefore now rarer and more valuable to the present day collector.

Tools

Plumb Board ▶
- **1866**
A pine plumb board, probably
Austrian, displaying punch
decorations.
- *length 56cm*
- £100–£200 • T. Murland

Expert Tips

*Although the best place to buy
antique tools is from a good
dealer, they can be very
expensive in country auctions.
You may have to buy a large lot,
however, in order to acquire the
one tool you want.*

Router ▼
- **Early 19th century**
A European carved fruitwood
router with flamboyant carved
detail.
- *length 30.4cm*
- £200–£300 • T. Murland

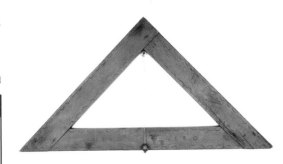

Ebony-handled Hammer ▲
- **18th century**
Unusually-formed ebony-handled
hammer with pleasing decoration.
- *length 17.8cm*
- £80–£120 • T. Murland

Iron Saw ▼
- **18th century**
An iron saw with ivory and ebony
handle and iron ferrule.
- *length 51cm*
- £300–£500 • T. Murland

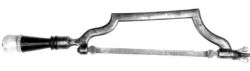

Bronze Brace ▼
- **18th century**
Bronze brace with fruitwood
handles and ivory head button.
- *length 30.4cm*
- £800–£1,200 • T. Murland

Leatherworkers' Punch ▲
- **Early 19th century**
Beautiful leatherworkers' punch.
- *length 11.4cm*
- £30–£50 • T. Murland

Brass Trammels ▲

- *19th century*
A quality pair of steel-tipped brass trammels with keeps.
- *length 20.32cm*
- £70–£100   • T. Murland

Medical Forceps ▼

- *Early 19th century*
A pair of rare medical forceps with blackwood handles.
- *length 33cm*
- £50–£100   • T. Murland

Brass Bevel ▲

- *18th century*
A beautifully engraved brass and rosewood bevel.
- *length 17.8cm*
- £300–£500   • T. Murland

Shoe Rule ▲

- *19th century*
A boxwood shoe rule, nicely marked "Thomas Webb".
- *length 20.3cm*
- £80–£100   • T. Murland

Combination Tool Kit ▼

- *1850*
An extremely high quality gentlemen's tool kit by Timmins, figured rosewood handles and original carrying case.
- *10cm x 4cm*
- £300–£500   • T. Murland

Pump Drill ▼

- *17th century*
A primitive, stone and wood pump drill, extremely rare.
- *height 1m*
- £100–£20   • T. Murland

Bronze Dividers ◄

- *17th century*
A pair of steel tipped bronze dividers with a rare circular design.
- *length 12.7cm*
- £200–£400   • T. Murland

Chamfer Plane ▶

- *1890*

A solid boxwood chamfer plane with lovely patina.
- *length 15cm*
- £80–£120 • T. Murland

Smooth Plane ▲

- *19th century*

A classic Scottish smoothing plane with cove front, double pierced lever cap and hardwood infill.
- *length 25cm*
- £300–£500 • T. Murland

Beech Plough ▲

- *1880*

A beech plough by Mosely with the rare internal stem adjustment feature.
- *length 25cm*
- £300–£500 • T. Murland

Fiddlemakers Clamps ▲

- *19th century*

Eight hardwood Violinmakers "Fiddlemakers" clamps.
- *length 20cm*
- £20–£40 • T. Murland

Drawing Instrument Set ▼

- *1910*

A quality set of drawing instruments with two ivory rulers, an ivory parallel rule, and brass protractor.
- *15cm x 20cm*
- £100–£150 • T. Murland

Inuit Knife ▲

- *19th century*

An Inuit bone knife, typically decorated with scrimshaw moose.
- *length 20cm*
- £80–£120 • T. Murland

Stanley Plane ▶

- *1925*

A Stanley 85 plane with original decal.
- *length 20cm*
- £500–£700 • T. Murland

Planishing Hammer ▶

- **18th century**

A rare planishing hammer with a few age cracks to the handle.
- *length 30cm*
- £40–£60 • T. Murland

Blueing Pan ◀

- **1880**

An extremely rare early Georgian watchmakers' blueing pan used for the oxidization of watch parts.
- *length 20cm*
- £500–£800 • T. Murland

Beech Ogee ◀

- **1910**

A little used handled beech ogee by T. Hall, Newcastle.
- *length 7.6cm*
- £60–£90 • T. Murland

Bridle Plough ▲

- **1870**

A unique solid Brazilian rosewood Mathieson brass stemmed bridle plough.
- *length 30cm*
- £3,000–£5,000 • T. Murland

Styled Hammer ▶

- **Late 17th – early 18th century**

Silversmiths' or Goldsmiths' hammer of wonderful style with replaced ebony handle.
- *length 26cm*
- £300–£500 • T. Murland

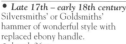

Veterinary Tools ◀

- **19th century**

A travelling set of veterinary instruments including some nice horn-handled knives.
- *20cm x 30cm*
- £50–£100 • T. Murland

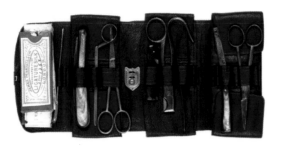

Expert Tips

Many craftsmen, particularly cabinet makers, made their own tools. An expert can identify the provenance by the workmanship, but often there is a maker's mark.

Walking Sticks

Hand Holding Whistle Cane ▲

- *circa 1890*
Small carved ebony hand holding a metal whistle (probably for calling the dog), plain silvered collar, on ebonised hardwood shaft.
- *length 92cm*
- £340 • M. German

Ivory Fighting Dogs Cane ▲

- *circa 1870*
Carved Victorian ivory handle depicting two fighting dogs artistically positioned. Plain silver collar mounted on dark brown hardwood shaft with light horn ferrule.
- *length 92cm*
- £1,250 • M. German

Silver Gold Head System Cane ▲

- *circa 1880*
Golf club handle mounted on a fine snakewood shaft opens to reveal a compartment for cigarettes and is engraved with the monogrammed initials "EP".
- *length 90cm*
- £1,800 • M. German

Jewelled Rock Crystal Cane ◀

- *circa 1890*
Rock crystal handle inset with a curtain of small gold set rubies in art nouveau taste, the wide gold collar overlaid with dark red guioche enamel, on ebonised hardwood shaft with light horn ferrule.
- *length 91cm*
- £2,200 • M. German

Silver Vinaigrette ▲

- *circa 1880*
Rare scottish silver handle containing a vinaigrette. The hinged top covers a pierced silver gilt grill which lifts out by means of a small ring.
- *length 89cm*
- £1,600 • M. German

Cane Display Stand ▲

- *circa 1880*
Polished Victorian cast iron cane stand, with a large decorative fretted back, and fitted with a removable drip tray.
- *71cm x 36cm*
- £650 • M. German

Parrot Cane ▼
- *1870*

Oversized head of a parrot carved from fruitwood, with fine detail, mounted on a hardwood shaft, with ornate gilt collar.
- **£850**   • **Michael German**

English Walking Stick ▼
- *1870*

Country walking stick with a carved wood handle, modelled as a hare with large glass eyes and silver collar, mounted on a briar wood shaft.
- **£580**   • **Michael German**

Ebony Cane ▲
- *1840*

Ebony cane with the handle carved as the head of a Negro with ivory teeth and boxwood hat and collar, mounted on a rosewood shaft.
- **£480**   • **Michael German**

Stag Horn Cane ▲
- *1860*

Country walking stick carved as a grotesque with a beard and glass eyes, mounted on a knotted wood shaft, with a silver collar and an antler handle.
- **£390**   • **Michael German**

Victorian Cane ▼
- *1860*

Elegant Victorian cane with a well carved handle depicting a hunting dog with a bird, mounted on a partridge wood shaft, with a gilt collar.
- **£1,100**   • **Michael German**

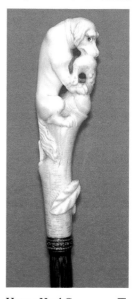

Hussar Head Cane ▼
- *1860*

A painted and carved wood cane with the handle modelled as a Continental hussar, with a plumed helmet.
- **£950**   • **Michael German**

Decorative Arts

The term "decorative arts" is ambiguous and can be loosely defined as "the modelling or carving of stone, wood and bronze."

Decorative arts, as collected, tend to follow Oscar Wilde's maxim that "all art is completely useless", because decorative arts are those items that have no practical application whatsoever, but are there to be admired. Art for art's sake, in fact.

There is no doubt that collecting these items – particularly those relating to the excesses of the Victorian era – is often tinged with a degree of irony. Many would not be regarded today with quite the same reverence they had then and some are frankly hilarious.

On the other hand, items of the sheerest beauty, of wonderful craftsmanship and unique quality are to be found and, particulary in our eclectic age when homogeny is no longer regarded as a *sine qua non* of decoration, such beautiful objects of any period find themselves very much in demand. Interior designers have definitely enhanced the market for these items.

Another aphorism of Oscar's would now be seen as only partly true: "For there is no art where there is no style, and no style where there is no unity, and unity is of the individual."

Figures & Busts

Gnome with Axe ▶

- *circa 1900*
Delightful polychrome painted terracotta gnome chopping wood, Austrian.
- *height 47cm*
- **£1,750**   • Bradwin

Art Nouveau Maiden Bust ◀

- *circa 1890*
Fine quality bisque porcelain bust of a stunning Nouveau maiden heightened with gilt and rouge, signed Andre Traggia.
- *height 31cm*
- **£1,695**   • Hickmet

Gardening Gnome ▼

- *circa 1900*
Gnome holding a top hat with a rabbit, one of three.
- *height 58cm*
- **£5,700**   • Bradwin

Augustus Caesar ▼

- *circa 1850*

Italian marble bust of Augustus Caesar raised on a marble plinth. This is taken from the bronze full-length figure of Augustus, circa 20 BC in the Vatican Museum. The breastplate is richly carved with mythological and historical scenes and the bust is supported on a panelled and moulded marble plinth of tapering form.
- *height 2.08m*
- **£9,800** • **Anthony Outred**

Bronze Centaur ▼

- *circa 1850*

Italian bronze of a centaur fighting a ram on marble.
- *height 17cm*
- **£895** • **Gavin Douglas**

Pair of Maidens ▶

- *circa 1730*

One of a pair of white marble busts of maidens in the antique manner, attributed to Michael Rysbrach (1694–1770). With finely carved robes pinned at the shoulder with a brooch, the hair flowing loosely over one shoulder, supported on later Portoro marble socles.
- *76cm x 36cm*
- **£33,000** • **Anthony Outred**

Marley Horses ▲

- *circa 1880*

A small pair of French Marley horses after the model by Costeau. On black marble bases decorated with patinated friezes.
- *height 28cm*
- **£1,075** • **Gavin Douglas**

Napoleon ▼

- *circa 1850s*

A fine well-finished momento mori of Napoleon in bronze from the mid-19th century.
- *height 13cm*
- **£475** • **Gavin Douglas**

Maternity ◀

- *circa 1880*

A fine patinated, cold-painted parcel gilt bronze of a mother feeding an infant from the breast while holding a sleeping toddler, by Paul Dubois (1829–1905). Cast by the F. Barbedienne Foundry.
- *height 49cm*
- **£3,950** • **Gavin Douglas**

Grand Tour Bronze ▲

- *circa 1860*
Unusual and small Italian grand tour bronze of a man about to use a sling.
- *height 12cm*
- **£425**   • Gavin Douglas

Stone Roundels ▼

- *circa 1850*
A pair of Italian carved stone roundels in the Renaissance manner, each with a carved head, one depicting Benvenuto Cellini (1500–1571), Florentine sculptor, goldsmith and amorist. The other depicts Giulio Romano (1499–1546), painter and architect, one of the creators of Mannerism, and chief assistant of Raphael.
- *diameter 102cm*
- **£12,000**   • Westland & Co

Bronze Bust ▼

- *circa 1880*
Fine pair of bronze busts of Albrecht Durer & Paul Romaine, with two colour patination, standing on bases of red and black reeded marble, after the style of Salmson.
- *height 40cm*
- **£2,950**   • Gavin Douglas

Marble Statue ▲

- *circa 1890*
An attractive Italian marble statue of a young girl leaning against a fountain playing a set of panpipes. Signed "Pittaluga".
- *height 80cm*
- **£8,750**   • Gavin Douglas

Italian Bronze Boy ▶

- *1904*
A fine Italian bronze of a naked young boy playing with kittens. He holds one up while cuddling the other. The bronze is signed "Marcuse, Roma 1904". On a chamfered marble base.
- *height 73cm*
- **£5,950**   • Gavin Douglas

Beaux Arts Figure ▲

- *circa 1890*
French Beaux Arts statuary marble figure of a young woman emblematic of spring. Signed "F. Palla".
- *76cm x 23cm*
- **£6,500**   • Westland & Co

Venus ▲

- *circa 1860*
A Victorian re-constituted stone figure of Venus by the Farnley Co. Standing by a pillar in flowing chiffon, her hair dressed in a chignon, on a rectangular plinth.
- *1.34m x 55cm*
- **£750**   • Westland & Co

Boy Archer ▶

- *circa 1925*
Carved ivory figure of a naked
young boy holding a bow raised
on onyx base, signed "Ferdinand
Preiss".
- *height 15cm*
- £3,800   • Hickmet

Wolfhound Bronze ▲

- *circa 1920*
French cast of Gayrad's peaceful
wolfhound, from the Susse Frères
foundry.
- *8cm x 16cm*
- £1,070   • Bradwin

Tiger Hunt Bronze ▲

- *circa 1890*
Cold-painted Austrian bronze of
an elephant and a tiger.
- *height 24cm*
- £5,800   • Bradwin

Bronze Spaniel Bookends ▲

- *circa 1930*
Cold-painted Austrian bronze
spaniels, one black and the other
liver and white.
- *13cm x 8cm*
- £780   • Bradwin

Parrot on a Branch ▼

- *circa 1900*
Cold-painted Austrian bronze of
a parrot perched on a branch.
- *height 28cm*
- £3,300   • Bradwin

Arab on a Camel ▼

- *circa 1830*
Superb bronze model of an Arab
on a camel.
- *height 30cm*
- £4,800   • Bradwin

Nue Debout ▼

- *circa 1920*
Exquisite hand-carved ivory
figure of a standing nude lady
raised on a rouge marble base,
signed "Joe Descomps".
- *height 27cm*
- £3,800   • Hickmet

Austrian Hare Bronze ◄

- *circa 1890*
Bronze with original paint of a
hare with punishment in mind,
aiming a stick at a youngster
being held up by one ear.
- *height 4cm*
- £700   • Bradwin

Mouse with Biscuit ▼

- *circa 1890*
Viennese novelty of a small
mouse guarding the remains of a
biscuit.
- *height 2cm*
- £540   • Bradwin

Robin in a Basket ▲

- *circa 1890*
Austrian bronze of a pretty robin
sitting in an oak-leaf basket, with
original paint.
- *14cm x 16cm*
- £780   • Bradwin

Ram with Horns ▲

- *circa 1890*
Austrian bronze of a ram with
head down, huge horns, and
undocked tail – with original
paint.
- *5cm x 13cm*
- £720   • Bradwin

Hare Musician ▼

- *circa 1890*
Austrian bronze of a hare playing
a double base.
- *height 8cm*
- £700   • Bradwin

Stag Bronze ▲

- *circa 1900*
Model of a standing stag with a
good show of antlers and original
paintwork.
- *height 10cm*
- £640   • Bradwin

Maribou and Chicks ▲

- *circa 1900*
Austrian bronze figures of a
family group of birds, a mother
with her young, with original
paint.
- *height 10cm*
- £1,100   • Bradwin

Winning Greyhound Bronze ▶

- *circa 1870*

Striking bronze figure of a winning greyhound with rich brown patina and excellent detail, signed by Paul Comolera.
- *height 36cm*
- £3,600 • Bradwin

French Rabbit Bronze ◀

- *circa 1880*

Charming model of a rabbit by sculptor Isidore Bonheur. Cast by his brother-in-law Peyrol, signed and stamped.
- *height 5cm*
- £1,400 • Bradwin

Poodle on a Cushion ▼

- *circa 1830*

A bronze French poodle on a cushion, after the original by Thomire.
- *height 30cm*
- £2,300 • Bradwin

Bronze Duck ▶

- *1560*

Small finely cast bronze duck.
- *height 2cm*
- £100 • Marko Pollo

Gilt Bronze Cat ▶

- *circa 1920*

Delightful gilt bronze model of a seated cat signed by Thomas Carter.
- *15cm x 13cm*
- £1,400 • Bradwin

Napoleon III's Dogs ◀

- *circa 1900*

Napoleon III adored his two dogs. Ravagout and Ravageole, here depicted by E. Fremiet and cast by Barbedienne.
- *16cm x 17cm*
- £3,800 • Bradwin

Bronze Dancer ▶

- *circa 1890*
French bronze figure of a naked nymph with fine smooth surface raised on rouge marble, signed "August Moreau".
- *height 21cm*
- £1,850   • Hickmet

Maiden with Scroll ▲

- *circa 1890*
Gilt bronze figure of a semi-clad maiden holding a scroll and quill. Signed by "George Baeau" and inscribed.
- *height 27.5cm*
- £2,950   • Hickmet

Expert Tips

Another way to tell spelter from bronze is simply to hold it in your hand. If it warms up quickly it is probably spelter.

Dachshund and Pups Bronze ◀

- *circa 1880*
Superb Clovis Masson bronze group of dachshund and pups with excellent detail and rich brown patination sign.
- *height 19cm*
- £5,800   • Bradwin

Bronze Study of Rhinoceros ◀

- *circa 1920*
Detailed study of a rhinoceros on a rectangular base. Madlestickse of Germany.
- *6cm x 8cm*
- £840   • Bradwin

Bronze Eagle ▶

- *13th century*
Fine bronze eagle standing on a circular stand with a star-shaped base.
- *height 15cm*
- £800   • Marko Pollo

Alex Falguiere ▲

- *circa 1880*
Gilt bronze figure of a coy young lady on a marble base, signed and stamped with Siot foundry.
- *height 16cm*
- £1,450   • Hickmet

Lighting

Column Table Lamp ▶

- **1870**
Tall English facet-cut column
table lamp with cut font and
gilded mounts.
- *height 56cm*
- **£1,800**   • C. Bridge

Student Lamp ▲

- *circa 1900*
Crossbanded student lamp in
gilded brass fitted with a marble
plinth and bell-shaped
crossbanded glass shade.
- *63cm x 15cm*
- **£1,200**   • **Turn On Lighting**

Expert Tips

*René Lalique dominated the
glass market in the 1920s and
1930s as the master of what
became known as Art Deco. He
used glass in architectural
settings and for light fixtures.
There are many pseudo-Lalique
light fittings on the market, but
they are generally of easily
identifiable poorer quality.*

Wedgwood Lamp ▼

- *circa 1925*
Wedgwood desk lamp fitted with
a trough-shaped shade and
circular stepped base.
- *38cm x 23cm*
- **£1,300**   • **Turn On Lighting**

Tiffany Lamp ▼

- **20th century**
Bronze lamp with caged green
glass shade stamped "Tiffany
Studio".
- *height 50cm*
- **£5,900**   • C. Bridge

Chrome Wall Lights ▼

- *circa 1925*
Set of six wall lights in chromed
brass fitted with coolie-shaped
shades.
- *20cm x 15cm*
- **£2,500**   • **Turn On Lighting**

"Go To Bed" Candlestick ▲

- *circa 1850*
Victorian Tunbridge Ware and
rosewood "go to bed" candlestick,
and taper holder. The lid rises to
reveal storage for candles and
tapers.
- *height 11cm*
- £365 • Period Pieces

Italian Gilded Candlesticks ▲

- *circa 1880*
One of a pair of Italian gilded
bronze candlesticks, with three
foliate scrolled branches.
- *height 74cm*
- £2,950 • Poppets

Victorian Table Lamp ▼

- *1880*
Victorian brass pedestal lamp
with a pink and glass shade with a
cherry blossom painted design.
- *height 49cm*
- £895 • Turn On Lighting

French Student Lamp ▼

- *circa 1899*
French highly decorative
adjustable library lamp with a
frosted glass shade, standing on a
reeded Corinthian column with
laurel leaf decoration, standing
on a rouge royale marble base.
- *height 65cm*
- £1,200 • Turn On Lighting

French Chandelier ◀

- *circa 1880*
French ormolu and cut-glass bag
and waterfall eight-branch
chandelier.
- £2,400 • Mora Upham

Victorian Bijou Lamp ▲

- *1880*
Victorian adjustable reading lamp
with a pink glass tulip shade,
metal rim and a curved brass
stand, on a circular wooden
base.
- *height 24cm*
- £700 • Turn On Lighting

Silver-Plated Table Lamp ▲

- *circa 1895*
Late Victorian silver-plated table
lamp, fitted with feathered white
glass lampshade, standing on a
moulded silver column and base.
- *height 36cm*
- £895 • Turn On Lighting

Branch Chandelier ▲
- *circa 17th–18th century*
Chandelier with ten large
branches and five smaller ones
from the 17th century with some
later additions.
- *height 1.86m*
- £6,800 • Augustus Brandt

French Prichet Sticks ▲
- *1780*
One of a pair of French prichet
sticks standing on three feet.
- *height 55cm*
- £950 • Heytesbury

Black Tôle Lamp ▲
- *1870*
Black tôle lamp with gilt vases
and floral swags around the base,
and sprays of corn around the
central column, with original
patination.
- *height 74cm*
- £580 • Augustus Brandt

Victorian Ceiling Pendant ▼
- *circa 1889*
Victorian gas ceiling pendant in
brass, fitted with two branches
with acid-edged cranberry glass
shades.
- *height 90cm*
- £1,100 • Turn On Lighting

Cast Brass Table Lamp ▼
- *circa 1890*
English cast brass table lamp
fitted with a hand-painted glass
lampshade decorated with a scene
of birds and trailing foliage,
supported by brass arms.
- *height 48cm*
- £1,100 • Turn On Lighting

Glass Wall Lights ▶

- *circa 1950*
Set of three Italian moulded glass
wall lights fitted with vertical
chrome bands.
- *20cm x 16cm*
- £1,500 • **Turn On Lighting**

Dutch Brass Six-Arm Chandelier ▲

- *circa 1900*
Brass chandelier with six arms
attached to central shaft
terminating in a sphere and hoop.
- *53.3cm x 50.8cm*
- £1,250 • **O. F. Wilson**

Swedish Brass and Glass Chandelier ▲

- *circa 1850*
Ornate chandelier with brass
arms terminating in candle
holders and tear-shaped glass
pendants.
- *78.7cm x 61cm*
- £3,000 • **O. F. Wilson**

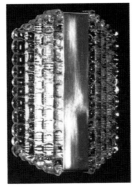

French Brass and Glass Chandelier ▼

- *circa 1850*
Chandelier with 16 light fittings
profusely decorated with hanging
faceted crystals.
- *1.07m x 63.5cm*
- £4,000 • **O. F. Wilson**

Brass Chandelier ▼

- *circa 1880*
A European six-armed chandelier
with globe-shaped reservoir and
curved foliate arms.
- *53.3cm x 71cm*
- £1,800 • **O. F. Wilson**

Bronzed Gas Wall Light ▼

- *circa 1865*
An important English bronzed gas wall light fitted with opal glass gas shade with decorative motives.
- *height 45cm*
- £1,200   • **Turn On Lighting**

French Chandelier ▼

- *circa 1890*
One of a pair of gilt brass French Gothic revival chandeliers.
- *62cm x 91cm*
- £3,500   • **Westland & Co**

Three Light Ceiling Pendant ▶

- *circa 1899*
Edwardian three light ceiling pendant in brass, fitted with acid-edged cranberry glass shades.
- *height 43cm*
- £1,500   • **Turn On Lighting**

Wall Appliqués ▲

- *circa 1860*
A pair of gilt brass Neo-Classical wall appliqués.
- *length 81cm*
- £1,500   • **Westland & Co**

Brass Wall Lamp ▲

- *circa 1880*
One of a pair of English decorative gas brass wall lamps fitted with cut and acid-edged glass shades.
- *height 20cm*
- £995   • **Turn On Lighting**

French Candelabra ▼

- *circa 1840*
One of a pair of French four branch ormolu candelabra with a snake circling a tapered column, with scrolled acanthus leaf and shell decoration and a flame finial, the whole on a solid platform base.
- *height 60cm*
- £3,850   • **O. F. Wilson**

Brass Lanterns ▼

- *1850–60*
A pair of English 19th century brass lanterns with conical roofs ending in brass hoops for hanging.
- *32cm x 15.2cm*
- **£550** ● **Heritage Antiques**

Wall Lantern ◄

- *circa 1880*
Wall lantern of copper and sheet iron, made by Faucon Frères, Paris.
- *58.4cm x 24cm x 30cm*
- **£850** ● **O. F. Wilson**

Tôle Lamp ▲

- *circa 1920*
One of a pair of French tôle lamps, cream with gilt decoration.
- *71cm x 35.5cm*
- **£1,850** ● **O. F. Wilson**

Column Lamps ◄

- *circa 1880*
One of a pair of bronze fluted French column lamps.
- *height 52cm*
- **£3,950** ● **O. F. Wilson**

Bouillotte Lamp ▲

- *circa 1840*
Red French tôle bouillotte lamp with two snuffers, painted later.
- *50.8cm x 38.1cm*
- **£1,250** ● **O. F. Wilson**

English Gas Wall Lamp ▲
- *circa 1875*
One of a pair of decorative glass brass wall lamps fitted with acid-edged glass shades.
- *33cm*
- **£995** • **Turn On Lighting**

Victorian Wall Lamp ▲
- *circa 1895*
One of a pair of Victorian gas wall lamps fitted with moulded peach-coloured glass shades.
- *34cm*
- **£895** • **Turn On Lighting**

Electric Wall Lamp ▲
- *circa 1900*
One of a pair of decorative cast brass electric wall lamps fitted with blue vaseline glass shades.
- *20cm*
- **£895** • **Turn On Lighting**

Wall Lamp ▶
- *circa 1890s*
One of a pair of English bronzed electric wall lights. Fitted with cut crystal glass shades.
- *height 28cm*
- **£1,800** • **Turn On Lighting**

French Silver Plated Obliques ▲
- *circa 1860*
French silver plated three branch wall obliques with cut glass storm shades, mounted on a silver stylised shield with scrolled shell design.
- **£3,400** • **Mora Upham**

English Wall Lamp ▲
- *circa 1880*
One of a pair of English decorative cast brass gas wall lamps fitted with acid-edged glass shades.
- *35cm*
- **£995** • **Turn On Lighting**

Gas Wall Lamp ▲
- *circa 1875*
One of a pair of highly decorative cast glass gas wall lamps fitted with cut glass shades.
- *22cm*
- **£995** • **Turn On Lighting**

Expert Tips

Try to buy from a reputable dealer who will have rewired the gas lamp fittings with new electric cables, and check that the shades are not broken.

Metalware

Brass Ewers

- *circa 1805*

Fine pair of patinated brass and overlay ewers by Naurio.
- *height 28cm*
- £6,750 • Gavin Douglas

Victorian Tôle Coal Box ▶

- *circa 1850*

Victorian tôle coal box with gilt chinoiserie and pattern decoration on a most unusual malachite background.
- *54cm x 48cm x 33cm*
- £850 • Dudley Hume

Bird Cage ▲

- *circa 1900*

Rare late 19th century triple singing birds in cage, having a penny-in-the-slot mechanism.
- *58.5cm x 25.5cm x 25.5cm*
- £8,750 • R. Gardner

Alex Vibert Ewer ◀

- *circa 1890*

Art Nouveau gilt bronze ewer with raised decoration of a naked nymph fishing in a pool.
- *height 44cm*
- £4,450 • Hickmet Fine

Frog Candlesticks ▼

- *circa 1870*

Superb pair of bronze candlesticks with tri-form frogs to the base and lily bud sconces. Signed by August Cain.
- *height 36cm*
- £2,400 • Elizabeth Bradwin

Pair of Bronze Hunting Trophy Lidded Vases ▼

- *circa 1870*

Fine pair of bronze hunting trophy lidded vases attributed to Auguste Cain (1822–1894) and decorated front and back with animal trophies in bold relief. Ormolu handles terminated in retriever heads.
- *height 45.5cm*
- £2,950 • R. Gardner

Ormolu Ewers ▲

- *circa 1795*

A pair of French Directoire period patinated bronze and finest original ormolu ewers. Of slender ovoid form, the sinuous lip continuing to an SOR-scroll arm with finely chased griffin and satyrs mask terminal, on a circular base with stiff leaf and engine turned decoration, resting on a square plinth.
- *height 38cm*
- **£11,250** • Gavin Douglas

Ormolu Tazza ▼

- *circa 1815*

A fine quality fire gilded ormolu tazza or dish set on a porphry base. Almost certainly Swedish from early 19th century. With fine quality work to tazza and original ormolu.
- *25cm x 25cm*
- **£2,250** • Gavin Douglas

Bronze Dolphins ▼

- *1880*

A pair of English stylized bronze dolphins with mounted seashells resting on their tails, on a rectangular marble base.
- *height 16cm*
- **£1,650** • Heytesbury

Bronze Lady ▼

- *circa 1880*

Bronze lady with a pensive expression, one arm over a chair and the other at her spinet.
- *height 53cm*
- **£720** • John Clay

Gothic Revival Splint Holders ▲

- *circa 1850*

An attractive pair of gothic revival splint holders in the style of Pugin. With fine original ormolu in superb condition. Probably French.
- *height 20.5cm*
- **£1,750** • Gavin Douglas

Bronze Girl with Dragonfly ▲

- *circa 1880*

Painted spelter figure of a young laughing girl with a bow in her hair, one arm outstretched and the other holding a bowl with a dragonfly. Standing on a foliate rustic mound and circular wood base.
- *height 49cm*
- **£220** • John Clay

Expert Tips

While condition is important, rust on ironwork is not a problem; it can be stripped, treated with an antirust agent and sympathetically repainted with metal paint.

French Empire Candlesticks ▼

- *circa 1815*

A fine pair of patinated bronze and original ormolu French Empire candlesticks. In the form of a classically draped vestal standing holding an oil lamp in her arms, with a very well formed candleholder on her head, with round ormolu socle.
- *height 38cm*
- **£3,950**   • Gavin Douglas

Bronze Young Girl ▼

- *circa 1880*

Bronze classical figure of a young girl semi-clad, holding her robe in one hand.
- *height 52cm*
- **£1,320**   • John Clay

Reclining Nude Plaque ▲

- *circa 1880*

Reclining nude with her head resting on her hand and Cupid at her feet.
- *width 51cm*
- **£275**   • John Clay

Boy Water Carrier ▲

- *circa 1870*

Gilt on bronze boy carrying two ewers on a yoke, standing on a circular bronze base, signed "Moreau".
- *height 23cm*
- **£1,250**   • John Clay

Orient ▶

- *circa 1900*

A good quality early 20th century French bronze bust of a woman inscribed "Orient", and stamped: E Villanis.
- *51cm x 34cm*
- **£2,750**   • John Riordan

Bronze Figures ▲

- *circa 1870*

Very attractive pair of patinated bronze figures of negro slaves carrying produce. Produced and signed by Susse Frères from models by Charles Cumberworth an American born artist working in Paris. On reeded onyx bases.
- *height 50cm*
- **£4,750**   • Gavin Douglas

Fire Jambs ▶

- *1820–40*
Pair of bell metal fire jambs.
English or American.
- *18cm x 16.5cm x 14cm*
- **£380** • **Heritage Antiques**

Fire Tools ◀

- *circa 1840*
Set of English polished steel fire
tools, comprising a shovel with
pierced lattice-work, poker and
tongs.
- *height 76.2cm*
- **£450** • **Heritage Antiques**

Expert Tips

*Brass in the seventeenth and
early eighteenth century was
raised from the hammered sheet.
Later brass was made from
thin, rolled sheets giving a
smooth finish.*

Brass Fender ▼

- *1780–1800*
Late 18th century English cast
brass fender with lattice design
raised on paw feet.
- *16.5cm x 20.3cm x 1.12m*
- **£395** • **Heritage Antiques**

Fire Screen ▲

- *1890–1910*
Late 19th century or early 20th
century French fan fire screen in
brass with fine lattice work.
- *7cm x 15cm x 99cm*
- **£650** • **Heritage Antiques**

Dutch Brass Andirons ▼

- *circa 1840*
Pair of Dutch cast brass andirons
with ornate bases incorporating
male head and crest.
- *45.7cm x 12.7cm x 26.7cm*
- **£750** • **Heritage Antiques**

Coal Scuttle ▼

- *1860–70*
English Brass repoussée coal
scuttle with original turned ebony
handles, foliate and scrolled
motifs and lion heads.
- *45.7cm x 32cm x 44.5cm*
- **£390** • **Heritage Antiques**

Bacchante ▼

- *circa 1880*

A fine quality 19th century
French bronze figure of
Bacchante. Signed "Clodion".
Also stamped with the
Barbedienne foundry stamp.
- *55cm x 54cm*
- **£2,995** • John Riordan

The Kiss ▶

- *circa 1875*

A superb 19th century French
bronze bust of a couple kissing.
Signed "Houdon".
- *46cm x 39cm*
- **£4,950** • John Riordan

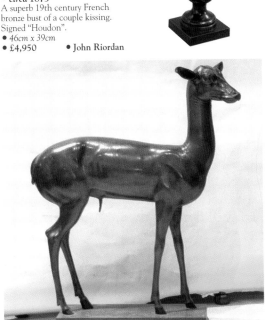

Celinius ▲

- *circa 1800*

Bronze figure of Celinius and the
infant Bacchus.
- *height 59cm*
- **£3,750** • John Riordan

Robert the Bruce ▼

- *circa 1890*

Impressive spelter figure of
Robert the Bruce wearing armour
and holding a shield, standing on
a square green marble base.
- *height 83cm*
- **£1,500** • John Clay

Bronze of David ▼

- *circa 1880*

Bronze figure of David with the
head of Goliath. Stamped and
signed "A. Mercie Barbedienne
foundry".
- *height 70cm*
- **£4,950** • John Riordan

Bronze Chinese Roe Deer ◀

- *circa 1880*

Bronze study of a Chinese Roe
deer from the Chiurazzi foundry,
Naples.
- *height 56cm*
- **£7,800** • Wakelin Linfield

Lion Chimney Ornaments ▼

- *1840–60*
Pair of English cast iron chimney ornaments as recumbent lions on pedestals.
- *11.4cm x 2.54cm x 18cm*
- £85 • Heritage

Boot Chimney Ornaments ▲

- *1850–60*
Pair of curious English cast bronze or bell metal chimney ornaments as buttoned boots.
- *13.3cm x 2.5cm x 12.7cm*
- £180 • Heritage Antiques

Brass Wall Pocket ◄

- *1840–50*
Nineteenth century English brass wall pocket in a pleasing curved and pierced design.
- *16cm x 6.4cm x 23.5cm*
- £220 • Heritage Antiques

Brass Skimmer ◄

- *1910–20*
Early 20th century English brass skimmer with pierced eagle motif and lattice handle.
- *53.3cm x 20.3cm*
- £220 • Heritage Antiques

Lion Tool Rests ▲

- *1860–70*
Pair of English Victorian cast iron and brass fire tool rests figured as lions on brass egg and dart bases on eight-sided pedestal.
- *35.5cm x 17.8cm x 25.4cm*
- £950 • Heritage Antiques

French Brass Andirons ◄

- *circa 1880*
Large French 19th century cast brass andirons with original backs and scrolled and foliate bases.
- *63.5cm x 44.5cm x 30.5cm*
- £850 • Heritage Antiques

Furniture

The chest or coffer is the earliest form of furniture, made from planks and sometimes reinforced with iron bandings.

Almost since man started to use furniture in his home there has been another man who has made a career of trying to enhance it to increase the value. Because collecting furniture is something of a minefield, in this area more, perhaps, than any other it is most important to genuinely like the pieces that you buy. Then, when they turn out to be not quite what you thought they were, at least you don't mind living with them. Buying from reputable dealers is your best guarantee of authenticity, but it is always worth making your own checks.

Furniture should be worn from use. Anything that seems unnecessarily distressed in unlikely places should be avoided. Similarly, anything that suggests uneven proportions should be treated with care – although taste will probably steer you away from it anyway. It may have been cut down or "married". When in doubt, trust your instincts.

Beds

Mahogany Bed ►
- **1920**
Large, elaborately carved, mahogany bed with pointed headboard and footboard and posts with finial decoration.
- *width 1.96m*
- **£4,250**   • Bruschweiler

Mahogany Four Poster Bed ▲
- *19th century*
Four poster bed with moulded and carved headboard and footboard and turned and fluted columns.
- *width 1.53m*
- **£2,500**   • Bruschweiler

Walnut Louis Style Bed ►
- *late 19th century*
An unusual French walnut Louis style bed in very good condition with quarter veneer design to the head and foot, carved mouldings, and detailed cabriole feet.
- *1.57m x 1.98m x 1.52m*
- **£2,100**   • Swans

French Empire Bedstead ▼

- *circa 1870*

French empire flame mahogany bedstead with pilaster moulding, cross banded and inlaid designs with ormolu mounts.
- *width 1.53m*
- £6,500 • Sleeping Beauty

French Mahogany Bedstead ▼

- *circa 1880*

French mahogany Louis XVI bed with a moulded headboard with a gilt torchière in the centre with two cherubs below, and gilt finials.
- *length 1.78m*
- £5,500 • Sleeping Beauty

Mahogany French Bedstead ▶

- *circa 1860*

Flame mahogany Louis XV bedstead with highly decorative floral and ribbon ormolu mounts.
- *width 1.37m*
- £6,000 • Sleeping Beauty

French Louis XV Bedstead ▲

- *circa 1880*

French Louis XV solid walnut single bed with moulded and carved headboard and footboard.
- *length 1.84m*
- £4,200 • Sleeping Beauty

Bow-Fronted Bedstead ▼

- *19th century*

Upholstered bow-fronted and padded Louis XV bedstead with original green paintwork.
- *1.48m*
- £1,295 • Sleeping Beauty

Walnut Louis XVI Bedstead ◀

- *circa 1880*

Large French solid walnut Louis XVI bed with carved ribboning on the headboard, and floral swags footboard, with fluted posts.
- *length 1.79m*
- £6,750 • Sleeping Beauty

Expert Tips

If you come across a pair of period bed posts for a four poster bed, snap them up. It is simple to make your own bed as long as you have the genuine posts.

Louis Style Painted Bed ▲

- *late 19th century*
A good quality late 19th century
French Louis style painted bed
with a fitted base.
- *1.37m x 1.90m*
- £1,150   • Swans

Mahogany Wall Bed ▲

- *late 19th century*
A French mahogany wall bed
with a beautifully carved super
top rail from left to right at each
end and mouldings that continue
down the side columns.
- *length 2.06m*
- £1,150   • Swans

Scroll End Upholstered Bed ▲

- *late 19th century*
A French scroll end upholstered
bed with original rails, mouldings,
and gilding to highlight. The
upholstery is in good condition.
- *1.19m x 1.60m x 1.98m*
- £2,250   • Swans

Painted Empire Bed ▼

- *late 19th century*
French kingsize Empire Henri
style bed restored and repainted
in its original style with carved
guilded mouldings. Part of a suite
with a pair of matching bedside
cabinets and a triple door armoire.
- *1.37m x 2.08m x 1.50m*
- £2,750 for suite   • Swans

Regency Four Poster Bed ◄

- *circa 1810*
Decorated and giltwood Regency
period four poster bed attributed
to Thomas Hope.
- *2.97m x 1.88m x 2.18m*
- £65,000   • M. Norman

Italian Bombe Bed ▲

- *early 20th century*
An unusual Italian "bombe" bed
made in solid walnut with
marquetry inlay incorporating
tireless attention to detail.
- *1.63m x 1.83m x 2.24m*
- £3,350   • Swans

Cane Bergère Bed ▲

- *late 19th century*
A French solid walnut framed
cane bergère bed with beautiful
carving on the frame and cane in
excellent condition.
- *2.13m x 1.55m*
- £1,950   • Swans

Louis XV Bedstead ▲

- *19th century*

Upholstered Louis XV pink velvet button backed bedstead with solid walnut frame and bow fronted base, standing on cabriole legs.
- *length 2.22m*
- **£1,495** • Sleeping Beauty

Louis XV Bedstead ▲

- *1880*

Painted, padded and upholstered Louis XV bedstead with original gilding to headboard and base.
- *length 1.85m*
- **£4,500** • Sleeping Beauty

Walnut Louis XV Bedstead ▲

- *circa 1880*

French solid walnut Louis XV bedstead with carved floral swag and moulded decoration.
- *width 1.53m*
- **£4,200** • Sleeping Beauty

Renaissance Style Bedstead ▶

- *circa 1880*

Extended Renaissance style walnut bedstead with wreath and torchière ormolu mounts.
- *width 2.22m*
- **£6,950** • Sleeping Beauty

Victorian Bedstead ▼

- *1895*

Victorian brass and black-painted iron bedstead with unusual tubular brass top and central linked plaques on both the headboard and base.
- *length 2.22m*
- **£2,500** • Sleeping Beauty

Cottage Bedstead ▼

- *1880*

Victorian hand-forged black iron cottage bedstead.
- *length 2.22m*
- **£1,495** • Sleeping Beauty

Victorian Bedstead ▲

- *1885*

Victorian black cast iron bedstead with brass rail and ball finials.
- *length 2.22m*
- **£1,295** • Sleeping Beauty

zSpanish Bedstead ▲

- *1850*

A Spanish hand-forged iron bedstead with large ornate cast brass ornamentation.
- *length 1.83m*
- **£2,600** • Sleeping Beauty

Bookcases

George IV Mahogany Bookcase ▲

- *circa 1825*

A George IV cream-painted and parcel-gilt mahogany bookcase in the manner of William Kent. The rectangular moulded cornice above an egg and dart dentilled lower cornice above a foliate swagged frieze centred by a female mask and flanked by shells. There are four glazed panelled doors below, between Ionic pilasters. The base section with four panelled doors between plain panelled uprights, each enclosing an adjustable shelf.

- *3.08m x 2.1m*
- **£48,000** • **Anthony Outred**

Mahogany Bookcase ▲

- *circa 1840*

Fine flame mahogany secretaire bookcase with two glazed doors and fitted interior and two cupboards below on a square base.

- *2.36m x 1.04m*
- **£10,500** • **Butchoff**

Mahogany Bookcase ▼

- **1880**

Unusually large breakfront bookcase with mahogany and satinwood cross-banded decoration, swan neck pediment, galleried and moulded designs, raised on a plinth base.

- *2.33m x 3.13m*
- **£28,000** • **Butchoff**

Glazed Bookcase Cabinet ▼

- *circa 1760*

An early George III mahogany glazed bookcase cabinet. With a broken, moulded dentil work pediment, each door composed of two astragal glazed octagonal panels with glazing bars connecting to the door frames, the interior lined and fitted with glass shelves. The cabinet with figured timber, the doors each with a shaped fielded panel defined by ribbon and flower-head moulding. The cabinet fitted with a moulded lip at the base above.

- *2.33m x 1.17m*
- **£24,500** • **Anthony Outred**

Mahogany Bookcase ▼

- **1880**

Victorian Walnut Bookcase ▲

- *circa 1880*

Victorian walnut bookcase with moulded flat top pediment, glazed doors enclosing five shelves, two deep drawers above two moulded doors, standing on moulded bracket feet.

- *height 2.51m*
- **£2,850** • **Hill Farm**

Secretaire Bookcase ▲

- *circa 1820*

Regency secretaire bookcase with Gothic glazed upper section, the fall opens to reveal a well fitted interior above matched flame veneer doors, the whole raised on splayed feet with shaped apron.

- *2.62m x 1.2m*
- **£18,750** • **Serendipity**

Mahogany Revolving Bookcase ▶

- *circa 1900*
Mahogany inlaid revolving bookcase with marquetry rosette.
- *68.6cm x 46cm x 46cm*
- **£1,750** • Manser Antiques

Mahogany Waterfall Bookcase ▲

- *circa 1800*
Regency mahogany waterfall bookcase, the shelves over two drawers, with its original brasses and legs.
- *1.1m x 25cm x 76cm*
- **£3,750** • R. Gardner

Mahogany Breakfont Bookcase ▲

- *circa 1780*
A fine George III mahogany breakfront bookcase. Provenance – made for Harborough House, signed "J. Johnson Price".
- *3.22m x 57cm x 4.34m*
- **£58,950** • M. Norman

Book Carrier ▲

- *circa 1820*
Regency period mahogany book carrier on wheeled feet.
- *43cm x 24cm x 82cm*
- **£3,950** • M. Norman

Regency Mahogany Bookcase Cabinet ▼

- *circa 1815*
A fine Regency period highly figured mahogany bookcase cabinet with surmounting Grecian style moulded cornice above two glazed doors, unusually fitted with brass astragal glazing bars enclosing three adjustable shelves, the base with two panelled cupboard doors on four square tapered peg feet.
- *2.18m x 44cm x 1.01m*
- **£11,750** • R. Gardner

George III Breakfront Bookcase ▼

- *circa 1790*
George III mahogany breakfront bookcase, the moulded cornice with a flame-mahogany veneered frieze surmounted by a broken arch pediment, above four gothic glazed doors, the base section with a projecting top with a moulded edge above a narrow frieze, above four panelled cupboard doors. Provenance: Lord Oakley – JAT Bartsow, Esq, DSO TD.
- *2.61m x 54cm x 2.51m*
- **£48,500** • R. Gardner

George I Bureau ▼

- *circa 1715*
George I walnut veneered double domed bureau cabinet, replacement glass plates and brass wear.
- *2.04m x 58.5cm x 1.02m*
- **£48,500** • M. Norman

Walnut Book Cabinet ◀

- *circa 1720*
George I walnut veneered bureau book cabinet, incorporating mirrored door.
- *2.02m x 48cm x 76cm*
- **£16,500** • M. Norman

Mahogany Bookcases
- *circa 1800*

A rare pair of English mahogany bookcases of small size, with open upper shelves above a pair of small panelled doors.
- *1.1m x 32cm x 63.5cm*
- **£48,000** • **Mallett**

Bamboo Chiffonier ▶
- *circa 1870*

Victorian bamboo chiffonier with lacquer and anaglypta paper panels.
- *1.8m x 41cm x 74cm*
- **£950** • **D. Hume**

Burr Walnut Bookcase ▲
- *circa 1720*

Tall George I bookcase with two large mirrored doors with brass key escutcheons. The interior has numbered folio shelves and is stamped in two places on the base GR VI surmounted by a crown.
- *2.58m x 67cm x 1.29m*
- **£265,000** • **Mallett**

Oak Bookcase ▼
- *circa 1870*

Large Victorian bookcase with gothic influence, four shelves above two deeper base shelves with ledge.
- *2.3m x 40.6cm x 2.5m*
- **£5,950** • **Manser Antiques**

Rosewood Bookcase or Display Cabinet ▲
- *circa 1840*

French rosewood bookcase or display cabinet with a shaped scroll pediment, two glazed doors with cast gilt brass decorative edging, and a rosewood veneered lined drawer above two smaller glazed doors.
- *2.37m x 47.5cm x 1.1m*
- **£20,000–£30,000** • **J. Collins**

Secretaire Bookcase ▲
- *mid 20th century*

Mahogany breakfront secretaire with brass fittings surmounted by glass-fronted bookshelves.
- *2.1m x 36cm x 1.7m*
- **£4,750** • **Manser Antiques**

George II Mahogany Bookcase ▲

- *circa 1750*
George II mahogany bookcase, the bold swan neck pediment with foliate and rosette carving, above two astragal glazed doors opening to reveal a fitted interior. The lower section with sloping fall opening to reveal a finely fitted interior. The whole on bracket feet.
- *2.28m x 1m*
- **£27,500**   • Wakelin Linfield

Regency Bookcase ▲

- *circa 1810*
English Regency period two door chiffonier/bookcase in a mixture of pine and fruit wood with galleried and turned designs.
- *1.07m x 63cm*
- **£2,950**   • Wakelin Linfield

George III Bureau Bookcase ▼

- *circa 1765*
George III mahogany bureau bookcase, the astragal glazed doors enclosing adjustable shelves with fall front and well fitted interior of tulip wood. With letter slides and drawers.
- *width 1.09m*
- **£7,900**   • Salem Antiques

Satinwood Secretaire Bookcase ▼

- *circa 1780*
Excellent secretaire bookcase of small elegant proportions. The whole veneered in satinwood heightened with cross banding in tulip wood, with shaped cornice and urn finials surmounting a corbelled frieze above two doors with moulded gothic glazing bars retaining their original glass.
- *1.94m x 52cm x 23cm*
- **£85,000**   • Wakelin Linfield

Victorian Mahogany Bookcase ▲

- *circa 1880*
One of a pair of mahogany bookcases with open shelves and storage cupboards below, enclosed by bow-fronted doors.
- *1.35m x 13cm*
- **£1,850**   • R. & S. Antiques

Regency Bookcase ▲

- *circa 1835*
Regency rosewood bookcase with glazed doors and two panelled doors below, standing on a plinth base.
- *1.93m x 84cm x 36cm*
- **£3,250**   • The Swan

Boxes

Jewellery Table Cabinet ▶

• *circa 1825*
Dutch mahogany jewellery table
cabinet with hinged lid that
opens to reveal a full-sized velvet
lined interior and six small
drawers fitted with small ivory
knob handles.
• *30.5cm x 23cm x 32cm*
• £1,000–£2,000   • J. Collins

Mother-of-Pearl Coffret ▲

• *circa 1670*
Spa lace box with walnut ground
inlaid with mother-of-pearl and
silvered metal flowers and
animals.
• *2.5cm x 24cm x 33cm*
• £19,500   • Mallett

Expert Tips

*"Tea caddy" is a late eighteenth
century term derived from the
Malay word, "Kati" – a unit of
weight slightly over 1lb.*

Oval Lacquer Casket ▼

• *circa 1690*
A fine Japanese oval casket
decorated on all sides with panels
of raised lacquer depicting a
fenced garden and rockeries.
Nashiji interior mounted on an
ormolu base in the rococo
manner.
• *22cm x 21cm x 39.5cm*
• £16,000   • Mallett

Regency Tea Caddy ◀

• *circa 1820*
Regency maple wood tea caddy
with two divisions and a mixing
bowl inside.
• *43.2cm x 38cm x 78.7cm*
• £850   • D. Hume

Red Casket ▲

• *1870*
Flashed ruby red Bohemian
casket well-engraved with spa
towns.
• *30cm x 15cm*
• £1,200   • C. Bridge

Wig Box ▶

• *circa 1780*
French wig box with a domed lid
hand-painted with floral garlands
centred by a classical folly in a
heart shaped cartouche, flanked
by a lady to the right and a
gentleman to the left.
• *16cm x 30cm*
• £1,050   • O. F. Wilson

Document Box ▲

• *circa 1880s*
Late Meiji period sugi wood
cabinet for documents, in six
sections.
• *71cm x 46cm*
• £1,395   • Gordon Reece

Box on Stand ▼

• *circa 1870*
Leather lacquered box on stand
with original brass lockplate with
"ruyi" head mounts and fittings.
Ex- Shanxi.
• *36cm x 48cm*
• £570   • Eastern Interiors

Jewellery Case ▲

• *circa 1880*
Black lacquered jewellery box
with a red interior and
polychrome paintings of flora and
fauna. Inside the lid is a folding
mirror. Ex Fuzhou.
• *20cm x 24cm*
• £390   • Eastern Interiors

Blackwood Box ▼

• *circa 1870*
Small box with a mirror fitted
under the lid, with double
handles, chrysanthemum-shaped
mounts and brass lockplate
fashioned as a butterfly. Ex
Shanghai.
• *10cm x 24cm*
• £280   • Eastern Interiors

Chinese Hat Box ▼

• *circa 1880*
Red lacquered cylindrical
Chinese hat box with original
brass fittings, the interior fitted
with two sandalwood plates for
the storage of hats.
• *41cm x 34cm*
• £430   • Eastern Interiors

Tortoiseshell Box ◀

- *1909*
A tortoiseshell and silver ring box with floral piqué.
- *height 3cm*
- £235   • A. & K. Stacey

Tortoiseshell Trinket Box ▼

- *circa 1850*
An English miniature tortoiseshell trinket box with pagoda top.
- *3.8cm x 4.5cm x 6.3cm*
- £390   • A. & K. Stacey

Trinket Box ▶

- *circa 1860*
An English miniature tortoiseshell trinket box.
- *3cm x 3cm x 6.3cm*
- £315   • A. & K. Stacey

Tortoiseshell Domed Box ▲

- *circa 1875*
A small English tortoiseshell dome topped box with silver feet.
- *2.5cm x 2.5cm x 7cm*
- £285   • A. & K. Stacey

Ring Box ◀

- *1906*
A silver and tortoiseshell ring box with swag inlay "H Matthews", Birmingham.
- *height 3.8cm*
- £330   • A. & K. Stacey

George III Ivory Tea Caddy ▲

- *circa 1790*
A George III ivory tea caddy with tortoiseshell stringing and mother-of-pearl inlay.
- *11.5cm x 8.9cm x 15cm*
- £5,200   • A. & K. Stacey

Blonde Tortoiseshell Box ◀

- *circa 1860*
A miniature blonde tortoiseshell trinket box with ivory edging, English.
- *3.8cm x 5cm x 7.6cm*
- £330   • A. & K. Stacey

Ash Tea Caddy ▶

- *circa 1850*

Tea caddy made from Mongolian ash, with lead receptacles and an oval enamel plaque with a painted cherub. This was a wedding present in 1869, and at that date tea cost 10/- per lb.
- *height 11cm*
- £2,800
- J. & T. Stone

Red Merchant's Trunk ▼

- *circa 1880*

Lacquered merchant's trunk with a moulded hinged lid over a conforming body, decorated with intricate brass-work of faceted and smooth rounded nails. The front lock is a large stylised butterfly – the symbol of longevity. Ex-Fuzhou.
- *27cm x 24cm*
- £400
- Eastern Interiors

Tortoiseshell Tea Caddy ▼

- *circa 1800*

Rare George III red tortoiseshell single tea caddy with ebony line stringing. The cover and interior lid have the original silver-plated ball handles, with original silver-plated lock and hinges.
- *height 10cm*
- £5,580
- Period Pieces

Regency Rosewood Tea Caddy ▶

- *circa 1810*

Regency rosewood tea caddy with brass foliate inlay, with a cushion moulded cover on a tapering body, standing on brass ball feet. The interior is fitted with the original cut glass mixing bowl and two brass inlaid tea containers.
- *height 21cm*
- £1,325
- Period Pieces

Tortoiseshell Box ▼

- *circa 1760*

Tortoiseshell Anglo Dutch box with ivory stringing and silver mounts, on silver bun feet.
- *16cm x 28cm x 20cm*
- £3,000
- O. F. Wilson

Satinwood Tea Caddy ▼

- *circa 1790*

A George III oval satinwood tea caddy with bats wing pattern to the front and cover and original axe head handle to lid.
- *height 12cm*
- £1,950
- Period Pieces

George III Cutlery Urn ▲

- *circa 1790*

One of a pair of George III mahogany cutlery urns, with chequered line stringing and barbers pole edging. The stepped lid with ivory finial rises to reveal the original fitted interior for twelve place settings. Standing on a platform base with barber's pole stringing.
- *height 66cm*
- £10,980
- Period Pieces

Expert Tips

A tortoiseshell tea caddy is worth more if it is not restored. Sometimes slight wear and tear at the corners makes the tea caddy more valuble.

George III Mahogany Tea Caddy ▼

- *circa 1790*
A George III mahogany and inlaid oval tea caddy.
- *11.5cm x 9cm x 15cm*
- **£2,000**   • A. & K. Stacey

Belgian Tea Caddy ▲

- *circa 1830*
A wonderful Belgian Spa pen work sycamore single cube tea caddy.
- *11.5cm x 10cm x 11.5cm*
- **£1,700**   • A. & K. Stacey

Ivory Tea Caddy ▼

- *circa 1790*
A rare George III ivory tea caddy, strung in horn and mounted with three Wedgwood blue and white Jasper cameos. The centre cameo surrounded by silver piqué-clouté.
- *9.5cm x 7cm x 11.4cm*
- **£10,515**   • A. & K. Stacey

Holly Tea Caddy ▲

- *circa 1795*
A Georgian mahogany tea caddy with holly oval panels and barber pole stringing.
- *11.5cm x 11.5cm x 11.5cm*
- **£650**   • A. & K. Stacey

Cube Tea Caddy ▼

- *circa 1800*
A George III satinwood cube tea caddy with incised decoration.
- *12cm x 10cm x 12.7cm*
- **£1,460**   • A. & K. Stacey

Green Tortoiseshell Tea Caddy ▲

- *circa 1825*
A rare green tortoiseshell double compartment tea caddy with pewter stringing and silvered ball feet, English.
- *14.5cm x 10cm x 17.7cm*
- **£9,015**   • A. & K. Stacey

Tea Chest ▲

- *circa 1840*
A Victorian mahogany double tea chest, English.
- *16.5cm x 15cm x 30.5cm*
- **£650**   • A. & K. Stacey

Mahjong Set ▲
- **1920**

Impressive and imposing Mahjong set of the highest quality in a solid oak case with extensive brass work decoration to the sides and top. With solid brass handle and sliding front panel revealing five similarly decorated drawers containing solid ivory tiles, game sticks and dice. Provenance: The Right Honourable The Viscount Leverhulme, K. G. of Thornton Manor.
- *29cm x 32cm*
- **£5,950**　　• **J. & T. Stone**

Apothecary Box ▲
- *circa 1830*

Georgian mahogany apothecary box with an almost complete set of original bottles, some with original contents. With lower drawer with original scales, weights, mortar, pestle and key.
- *13cm x 19cm*
- **£1,950**　　• **J. & T. Stone**

Tortoiseshell Tea Caddy ▶
- *circa 1775*

Exceptional red tortoiseshell tea chest with ivory stringing, silver ball feet and top handle, the interior with three original glass canisters with silver plate lids and original key.
- *height 14cm*
- **£29,500**　　• **J. & T. Stone**

Georgian Knife Boxes ▼
- *circa 1790*

One of a pair of superb flame mahogany Georgian knife boxes with original interiors, silver plate ring pulls and escutcheons.
- *height 48cm*
- **£6,950**　　• **J. & T. Stone**

Regency Chinoiserie Box ▼
- *circa 1820*

English Regency penwork box with trailing floral designs around a central panel depicting a group of hand-painted Chinese figures.
- *height 16cm*
- **£1,650**　　• **O. F. Wilson**

Scholar's Parchment Box ▲
- **19th century**

Scholar's leather parchment box embossed with the design of the Buddhist swastika, the cover designed with the character of "Long Life". Ex-Shanghai.
- *18cm x 28cm*
- **£465**　　• **Eastern Interiors**

Tea Tins ▲
- **1880**

Set of six cylindrical tea tins with covers and a central cartouche of a classical ruin surrounded by a foliate design, each with a gilt shield and numerals.
- *height 48cm*
- **£2,500** • **Goodison Paraskeva**

Regency Tea Caddy
- *circa 1820*
A Regency tortoiseshell tea caddy
with canted corners and double
cavetto top, English.
- *14cm x 8.9cm x 14cm*
- £3,880   • A. & K. Stacey

Shagreen Box
- *circa 1920*
An English Art Deco geometric
shagreen box with ivory stringing.
- *5cm x 10cm x 12.5cm*
- £450   • A. & K. Stacey

Tortoiseshell Tea Caddy
- *circa 1830*
A blonde tortoiseshell tea caddy
with ivory stringing and horn
edging, English.
- *14.6cm x 8.9cm x 15cm*
- £3,525   • A. & K. Stacey

Satinwood Tea Caddy
- *circa 1790*
A satinwood tea caddy with
conch shell inlays, chequer and
rosewood bandings, ebony
stringing.
- *12cm x 10.8cm x 19cm*
- £1,700   • A. & K. Stacey

Mother-of-Pearl
Tea Caddy
- *circa 1875*
Late Victorian mother-of-pearl
double tea caddy with abalone
banding.
- *8.5cm x 8.5cm x 14cm*
- £1,650   • J. & T. Stone

Rosewood Tea Caddy
- *circa 1850*
A Victorian rosewood tea caddy
with mother-of-pearl inlay,
relined with hand-made paper.
- *17.8cm x 12.7cm x 24cm*
- £420   • A. & K. Stacey

Expert Tips

*Some of the most exquisite
boxes were produced during the
eighteenth century as containers
for snuff, patches or tobacco.
Price is usually determined by
quality and materials used.
Boxes of wood or papier mâché
are the most affordable and
generally available.*

Bombe-shaped Tea Caddy ▶

- *circa 1830*
A bombe-shaped tortoiseshell tea caddy with pewter stringing and ivory edging.
- *15cm x 10cm x 19cm*
- £4,720   • A. & K. Stacey

Indian Box ◀

- *circa 1860*
An Indian tortoiseshell Vizagapatam box with bone edging and feet.
- *5cm x 6.4cm x 11.5cm*
- £235   • A. & K. Stacey

Indian Box with Ivory Veneer ◀

- *circa 1780*
An Indian Vizagapatam box, ivory veneered on sandalwood, engraved with architectural scenes.
- *8.9cm x 22.8cm x 30.5cm*
- £3,945   • A. & K. Stacey

Regency Tea Chest ▼

- *circa 1830*
A large Regency blonde tortoiseshell tea chest with lion claw feet and lion head handles.
- *17cm x 12.7cm x 28cm*
- £6,800   • A. & K. Stacey

Vizagapatam Box ◀

- *circa 1785*
A very rare late 18th century Vizagapatam engraved and etched ivory tea caddy with floral banding and architectural scene on the lid.
- *width 12cm*
- £4,750   • J. & T. Stone

Georgian Tea Caddy ▲

- *circa 1790*
A rare Georgian fluted ivory octagonal single tea caddy with tented top and silver adornments, horn stringing and interior facing.
- *12cm x 7.5cm x 10.5cm*
- £6,950   • J. & T. Stone

Stag Horn Double Caddy ◀

- *circa 1800*
A very rare late 18th century stag horn double caddy with ivory hunting scene panels, ivory stringing and claw feet. The interior with rustic lids. Probably Austrian.
- *width 20cm*
- £9,000   • J. & T. Stone

Pagoda Top Tea Caddy ◀

- *circa 1835*
A fine William IV tortoiseshell tea caddy with inverted front and pagoda top.
- *12.7cm x 10cm x 17cm*
- **£3,645** • **A. & K. Stacey**

Regency Tea Caddy ▶

- *circa 1830*
A very rare late Regency mother-of-pearl veneered tea caddy of polygonal form with white metal and abalone engraved floral inlay and ivory banding to the interior with twin subsidiary covers. The base on six carved mother-of-pearl-feet.
- *width 18.4cm*
- **£18,500** • **J. & T. Stone**

Spa Tea Caddy ▼

- *circa 1820*
A very rare early 19th century painted Spa tea caddy of inverted rectangular shape with cut out canted corners, each panel painted with scenes of the town, the top panel of an interior scene of a minstrel serenading a maiden. The interior with two compartments, each with a painted cover of a spa scene.
- *width 23cm*
- **£7,750** • **J & T Stone**

"Melon" Tea Caddy ▲

- *circa 1790*
Late 18th century painted melon fruitwood tea caddy with original stalk.
- *12cm x 12cm x 12cm*
- **£14,500** • **J. & T. Stone**

"Aubergine" Tea Caddy ▲

- *circa 1840*
Mid 19th century Chinese aubergine single tea caddy with screw top.
- *height 19cm*
- **£9,950** • **J. & T. Stone**

"Pear" Tea Caddy ▲

- *circa 1790*
Very fine late 18th century George III fruit wood pear tea caddy with original escutcheon.
- *height 18cm*
- **£6,950** • **J. & T. Stone**

Belgian Spa Tea Caddy ▶

- *circa 1800*
Late 18th century Belgian Spa single oval tea caddy in mint condition, the lid and four panels with hand-painted scenes of the town.
- *10cm x 10cm x 16cm*
- **£4,950** • **J. & T. Stone**

Tunbridge Ware Tea Caddy ▶

- *circa 1860*
Excellent Tunbridge Ware marquetry inlaid single tea caddy with stick marquetry roses on lid.
- *width 13.5cm*
- £495　　• J. & T. Stone

Tortoiseshell Jewel Casket ▼

- *circa 1860*
High quality 19th century French tortoiseshell jewel casket with bowed panels, extensive ormolu decorative mounts and original silk lined interior. The lustre effect of this casket is the result of a rare technique of gilding behind the tortoiseshell.
- *width 35cm*
- £7,950　　• J. & T. Stone

Edwardian Stationery Box ◀

- *1904*
Unusual Edwardian slope front stationery box with 1904 Birmingham hall marked silver decoration, probably by John Angel.
- *26cm x 17cm x 24cm*
- £995　　• J. & T. Stone

Book Box ▲

- *circa 1900*
Italian inlaid book box with secret compartments.
- *11.4cm x 12.7cm x 23cm*
- £185　　• Millers Antiques

Regency Double Tea Caddy ▼

- *circa 1830*
A sarcophagus-shaped Regency beech double tea caddy with high quality hand painted decoration on every panel, the interior with matching subsidiary lids and original painted inner lid. All on decorative brass feet with matching brass side handles.
- *width 22cm*
- £3,950　　• J. & T. Stone

Bohemian Box ▼

- *circa 1770*
Bohemian box with panelled top opening to reveal a simple interior, the front with split balusters and moulded decoration containing traces of the original flower decorated pattern.
- *58.4cm x 47.6cm x 75.6cm*
- £3,600　　• Hallidays

Brass-bound Military Coffer ▼

- *circa 1890*
Box strengthened with brass inlay on all edges, brass carrying handles and lock and key.
- *45.7cm x 37cm x 66cm*
- £565　　• Millers Antiques

Military Instrument Box
- *circa 1890*
Wooden box with brass corners and handles.
- *49.5cm x 29cm x 38cm*
- £345   • Millers Antiques

Oak and Brass Jewellery Box
- *circa 1870*
Late Victorian oak and brass mounted box originally for letters now converted for jewellery, with lined interior. Bears Edinburgh maker's plaque.
- *width 20.3cm*
- £395   • Barham Antiques

William IV Box
- *circa 1835*
William IV rosewood and maple marquetry box converted for jewellery.
- *length 35cm*
- £325   • Barham Antiques

Regency Card Boxes
- *circa 1830*
Pair of Regency lacquer card boxes.
- *length 9cm*
- £110   • Barham Antiques

Anglo Indian Box
- *circa 1830*
Early 19th century Anglo-Indian ivory mounted box.
- *length 25.5cm*
- £695   • Barham Antiques

Mahogany Stationery Case
- *circa 1880*
Sloped stationery case with hinged compartments and original escutcheon.
- *33cm x 27cm x 37cm*
- £395   • Millers Antiques

Expert Tips
Dates and inscriptions to famous people enhance value – the reverse is true of those who history has forgotten.

Glove Box
- *circa 1835*
William IV rosewood and satin birch marquetry glove box with original interior.
- *length 20cm*
- £185   • Barham Antiques

Bureaux

George I Bureau Bookcase ◀
- *circa 1720*

A walnut veneered oak bureau bookcase, with bevelled mirrors and original brass furniture.
- *2.3m x 1.07m*
- **£75,000** • **Haughey Antiques**

Georgian Chippendale Bureau Bookcase ▶
- *circa 1760*

Mahogany bookcase with glazed doors enclosing four shelves above a bureau with a sloping fall.
- *2.24m x 56.5cm x 1.13m*
- **£20,000–£30,000** • **J. Collins**

William & Mary Walnut Bureau ▼
- *circa 1690*

Walnut bureau with fall opening to reveal an interior with a well and two secret compartments over three frieze drawers.
- *96.52cm x 58.4cm x 96.5cm*
- **£28,500** • **S. Cook**

French Bureau Plat

- *circa 1850*

French ebony, tortoiseshell and brass inlaid bureau plat. The antique leather top with a massive moulded gilt bronze edge, above a large recessed central drawer flanked by two smaller drawers. Supported on four cabriole legs, mounted above the knees with a satyr's mask, and terminating in hoof feet. With chased and gilt bronze mounts. The central drawer is mounted with a large mask of Bacchus.
- *79cm x 2.02m*
- £65,000 • Anthony Outred

Swedish Bureau ▼

- *1780*

Swedish bureau with original paintwork and fall front with stepped interior above three long drawers, standing on original scrolled bracket feet.
- *1.04m x 94cm x 54cm*
- £6,200 • Heytesbury

Druce of London Bureau ▲

- *circa 1880*

George III style mahogany bureau with fall front, fitted interior and original brass fittings, standing on moulded bracket feet, with a brass plate bearing the inscription, "Druce & Co, Baker St, London" inside the top drawer.
- *height 1.13m*
- £3,500 • Hill Farm

Regency Secretaire ▲

- *circa 1805*

A Regency mahogany secretaire cabinet enclosed by a pair of astragal glazed doors. Fitted with a secretaire drawer and an arched frieze drawer below, on square tapering legs terminating in spade feet.
- *1.6m x 75cm*
- £12,500 • Great Grooms

French Secretaire ▼

- *circa 1810*

Secretaire desk with serpentine front, original paint, three long drawers with oval iron handles, brass escutcheon plates and a fall front enclosing fourteen small drawers, the whole raised on gilded feet.
- *1.08m x 1.21m*
- £9,000 • Augustus Brandt

Walnut Secretaire ▲

- *circa 1880*

Fine Swedish secretaire, heavily carved with a burr walnut veneer. The fall front enclosing an architectural fitted interior, above three long drawers.
- *1.47m x 1.09m*
- £6,500 • Hatchwell

George I Walnut Bureau ▽

- *circa 1720*

George I walnut bureau, with a fitted interior veneered in walnut with line inlay.

- *1.05m x 51cm x 92cm*
- **£11,500**   • R. Gardner

Queen Anne Walnut Veneered Bureau ▽

- *circa 1710*

A bureau with fitted interior and later mirrored plate, with a secret well.

- *98cm x 43cm x 68cm*
- **£18,000**   • Hallidays

Burr Walnut Bureau Bookcase ▲

- *1920*

Bureau bookcase with upper doors enclosing shelves and drawers above a bureau and base.

- *2.34m x 56cm x 1.12m*
- **£4,750**   • Bruschweiler

Cylinder Bureau ▶

- *circa 1880*

A Louis XVI style gilt bronze mounted mahogany bureau with a pierced gallery above three drawers over a tambour retracting cylinder front. The bureau has three tiers of letter compartments above a sliding leather writing surface.

- *1.2m x 80cm x 1.52m*
- **£30,000**   • Adrian Alan

Cabinets

George III Secretaire ▶
- *circa 1775*
A George III satinwood secretaire abattant decorated on all sides with panels of Chinese and Japanese lacquer and standing on carved feet enriched with foliate decoration.
- *1.42m x 41cm x 1.04m*
- **£55,000** • Mallett

George III Bedside Cabinets ▲
- *circa 1790*
A pair of George III mahogany bedside cabinets, the tray tops with pierced carrying handles above a single cupboard door with brass drop handle, raised on square tapering legs.
- *77cm x 33cm x 46cm*
- **£30,000** • Mallett

Coromandel Cabinets ▶
- *circa 1808*
A pair of coromandel wood side cabinets with brass star and scroll decoration in the Egyptian style
- *1.07m x 39cm x 91.5cm*
- **£38,000** • Haughey Antiques

Mysore Table Cabinet ◀
- *1898-1905*
Solid rosewood and ivory inlaid "Mysore" table cabinet, made in India. Features a shaped pediment surmounted by three urn-shaped finials above two panelled doors enclosing a full-sized interior divided and a full-width drawer below.
- *78cm x 24cm x 45.5cm*
- **£3,000-£5,000** • J. Collins

Macassar Sideboard ▼
- *1929-30*
Art deco period Heal's Macassar ebony veneered sideboard having top panels of green shagreen and sides and front veneered in boldly figured timber supported on ivory feet.
- *89cm x 152.5cm x 51cm*
- **£29,500** • Mallett

George III Bedside Table ◀
- *circa 1765*
A large mahogany bedside table raised on square chamfered legs, with pierced carrying handles and pull-out commode section with dummy drawer front.
- *81.5cm x 56cm x 51.5cm*
- **£10,500** • Mallett

Mahogany Bow Fronted Georgian Sideboard ▲
- *circa 1790*
Sheraton period sideboard with a skirting board overhang above three drawers fitted with brass lion mask ring handles.
- *89.5cm x 61cm x 96.5cm*
- **£5,000-£7,000** • J. Collins

Expert Tips

"China cabinets" are not strictly cabinets. A cabinet should be a case fitted with small drawers or cupboards, and with doors. The correct term for this glazed-fronted display case is "china cupboard".

Victorian Cabinet ▼

- *circa 1890*

Victorian walnut and planewood bedside cabinet, with moulded cupboard doors, raised on a plinth base.
- *height 85cm*
- £450   • Hill Farm Antiques

Chinese Medicine Cabinet ▶

- *circa 19th century*

One of a pair of black lacquer Chinese medicine cabinets with forty-five drawers with circular ring handles.
- *height 2.06m*
- £1,800   • Younger

English Corner Cupboard ▲

- *1780*

English painted wall-mounted, corner cupboard, with carved moulded door panels and original blue paintwork.
- *1.08m x 81cm*
- £2,800   • Heytesbury

Continental Painted Cabinet ▼

- *circa 1880*

Continental fruitwood display cabinet with circular moulded pediments, two glazed doors, flanked by bevelled glass, below two cupboard doors painted with ribbons and flowers, surmounted with a pierced brass rail, standing on small cabriole legs.
- *1.75m x 1.35m*
- £3,500   • Hill Farm

Walnut Bedside Cabinet ▼

- *circa 1880*

One of a pair of Louis XV style walnut bedside cabinets with one single drawer above a carved and moulded cupboard door, raised on cabriole legs.
- *height 88cm*
- £1,650   • Hill Farm Antiques

Small Chinese Cabinet ◀

- *1880*

Small Chinese cabinet from Zhejiang Province, decorated with carvings of a phoenix and lotus plants.
- *81cm x 55cm*
- £550   • Lotus House

Bow Fronted Sheraton Double Corner Cupboard ▲

- *circa 1790*
A two-part Sheraton double
corner cupboard with
two Gothic arched glazed doors
enclosing three fixed shelves. A
pull-out mahogany slide
surmounts the base with two
additional bow-fronted doors.
- *2.26m x 61cm x 95.5cm*
- £20,000–£30,000 • **J. Collins**

Domed Walnut Cabinet ▲

- *circa 1930*
Pretty walnut cabinet with
domed bookcase, raised on
cabriole legs.
- *60cm x 40.6cm x 58.4cm*
- £2,250 • **Manser Antiques**

Pot Cupboard ▶

- *19th century*
A mahogany pot cupboard
having inlaid marble top
- *71.1cm x 35.6cm*
- £880 • **Dorking Desk**

Queen Anne Cabinet on Chest ▲

- *circa 1710*
Cabinet on chest with bevelled
mirrored door opening to reveal
ten chevron banded drawers and
a bookshelf. The lower section
with a secretaire drawer and three
further drawers.
- *2m x 48.3cm x 76.2cm*
- £45,000 • **S. Cook**

Painted Walnut Cabinet ▲

- *circa 1930*
Fine quality walnut cabinet with
painted panel set into the door of
still life with roses.
- *73.6cm x 43.2cm x 1.143m*
- £3,250 • **Manser Antiques**

Open-fronted Walnut Cabinet ▼

- *circa 1930*
Open-fronted walnut corner
display cabinet with shaped
moulded pediment.
- *1.85m x 68.6cm*
- £1,850 • **Manser Antiques**

Walnut Sideboard ▼

- *circa 1930*
Pretty serpentine-fronted walnut
cabinet and sideboard with
moulded panel doors.
- *81.3cm x 40.6cm x 81.3cm*
- £2,250 • **Manser Antiques**

Dutch Walnut Display Cabinet ▲

- *circa 1780s*

A slim Dutch walnut display cabinet profusely decorated with floral and foliate motifs in marquetry, the shaped cornice above shaped glazed doors and canted corners to the upper section. The lower section of bombe form, the whole on turned and ebonised bun feet.

- *2.37m x 1.70m*
- **£22,500** • Wakelin Linfield

Dutch Display Cabinet ▲

- *circa 1780*

Dutch walnut display cabinet with foliate inlay and glass panels to front and doors.

- *height 85cm*
- **£4,850** • Paul Hopwell

Japanese Lacquer Cabinet ▶

- *circa 1880*

Japanese lacquer cabinet with two doors decorated with mother-of-pearl floral inlay, two small drawers and one long drawer inlaid with boxwood.

- *39cm x 29cm*
- **£450** • Younger

Mahogany Chiffonier ▼

- *circa 1840*

Flame mahogany chiffonier with single long drawer, above two gilt brass grills with door silks, flanked by turned pilasters, raised on turned feet.

- *93cm x 91.5cm x 41cm*
- **£3,200** • O. F. Wilson

Two Part Kortan Cabinet ▼

- *circa 1800*

A kortan cabinet of two parts made from elm, with four drawers above two cupboard doors with brass mounts.

- *1.45m x 1.05m*
- **£2,950** • Wakelin Linfield

George IV Display Cabinet ▲

- *circa 1825*

George IV mahogany display cabinet, the top section with two glazed doors, above a lower section with four octagonal tapering legs decorated with stylised palmetto.

- *1.91m x 94cm*
- **£8,750** • Wakelin Linfield

Swedish Mahogany Cupboard ▲

- *circa 1890s*

Swedish Louis XVI style mahogany cupboard with two doors, above one long single drawer, with moulded apron and gilt ormulu mounts, on tapering slender legs.

- *1.06m x 59cm*
- **£1,950** • Rupert Cavendish

Walnut Display Cabinet ▲

- *circa 1920*
Walnut display cabinet with
doors opening to reveal shelves,
scrolled apron with central finial
on turned legs with double
stretcher
- *1.55m x 28.1cm x 99cm*
- **£3,950** • Manser Antiques

Regency Side Cabinet ▲

- *circa 1825*
A rosewood breakfront dwarf side
cabinet in the manner of Gillows
of Lancaster with four pleated
panel and glazed doors enclosing
adjustable shelves to a plinth base
with beadwork mouldings.
- *99cm x 36cm x 1.55m*
- **£9,800** • R. Gardner

Red Lacquer Corner Cupboard ▼

- *Early to mid 18th century*
Red lacquer bow-fronted corner
cupboard in chinoiserie style with
three waterfall display shelves.
- *1.27m x 33cm x 48.3cm*
- **£2,250** • Manser Antiques

Black Lacquer Cabinet ▶

- *Early 20th century*
English lacquer cabinet in the
Chippendale style incorporating
fine peacock design, the whole
surmounted by a galleried
cornice.
- *1.80m x 43.2cm x 68.6cm*
- **£2,950** • Manser Antiques

Regency Chiffonier ◀

- *circa 1820*
Regency rosewood two door
chiffonier, the white marble top
with a reeded edge, above a pair
of pleated silk doors flanked by
spiral twist columns.
- *85.5cm x 33cm x 87cm*
- **£8,400** • R. Gardner

Walnut Credenza ▲

- *circa 1870*
French walnut credenza with
inlayed oval artwork, fine gilt
mouldings and glazed display
cupboards at each side.
- *1.02m x 40.6cm x 1.65m*
- **£6,950** • Manser Antiques

Sheraton Revival Satinwood Side Cabinet ◀

- *circa 1900*
A Sheraton revival satinwood
cabinet of semi-elliptical form
inlaid and crossbanded
throughout. One central door
with circular decorative panel
encloses a single shelf.
- *91.5cm x 45.5cm x 99.5cm*
- **£9,400** • R. Gardner

Expert Tips

*Large cabinets can have a
chequered past; quite often they
are "marriages". The two parts
may be from the same period,
but very often they have been
coloured in.*

Regency Rosewood Side Cabinet ▲

- *circa 1810*

A Regency rosewood and boxwood strung side cabinet with canted front corners incorporating two frieze drawers above twin glazed and pleated doors.

- *91.5cm x 38cm x 75cm*
- **£4,850**   • R. Gardner

Pine Table Cabinet ▼

- *Late 19th century*

A small, decorated table cabinet used for storing scrolls and books. Pine with dark burgundy stain and carved and gilded door panels depicting birds and flowers. The doors close to a central, removable post and internally there are two drawers at the base. Original brassware.

- *45cm x 65cm x 55cm*
- **£295** • Orient Expressions

George III Mahogany China Cabinet ▼

- *circa 1770*

China cabinet with swan-neck pediment and single arched astragal glazed door enclosing shelves with panelled cupboard door below.

- *2.04m x 1.14m x 51cm*
- **£23,500**   • R. Gardner

Regency Period Chiffonier ◀

- *circa 1820*

Regency ebonised chiffonier with double cupboard and silk panel doors, one drawer and two display shelves with scrolled edges, fine gilding and ball feet.

- *1.44m x 40.6cm x 90cm*
- **£9,850**   • M. Norman

Decorated Lacquer Cabinet ▲

- *Late 19th century*

Four-door cabinet, pine with red lacquer and gilded, carved panels. Decoration and brassware are original.

- *1.65m x 1.24m x 54cm*
- **£1,600** • Orient Expressions

Satinwood Display Cabinet ▲

- *circa 1900*

A satinwood cabinet with a crossbanded frieze which features panel of decorative feathery veneers. The two glazed doors each have a lower panel with a distinctive oval motif in West Indian show-wood.

- *1.76m x 38cm x 1.1m*
- **£13,750**   • R. Gardner

Regency Rosewood Chiffonier ▲

- *circa 1820*

Regency period rosewood veneered chiffonier having raised super-structure with shelf and original brass gallery mirror. Supported on brass turned uprights below a two-door cupboard.

- *1.30m x 34cm x 1.08m*
- **£14,000**   • Hallidays

Expert Tips

Backs of cabinets were not designed to be seen and are relatively crudely made. They should be dry and untouched and probably show some signs of shrinkage.

Regency Chiffonier ▼
- *circa 1820*

Regency mahogany chiffonier with silk panel doors, a pierced gallery and one long mirror, with two Corinthian columns, lions head ring handles and brass ormulu mounts.
- *1.18m x 1m*
- £1,650 • R. Macklin Smith

Mahogany Corner Cupboard ▼
- *circa 1890*

Mahogany corner cupboard with double moulded panel doors, above three drawers with turned knob handles.
- *width 1.16m*
- £1,585 • The Swan

Victorian Cabinet ▲
- *circa 1880*

Victorian mahogany cabinet with two panelled doors, enclosing two small drawers with turned handles, raised on a plinth base.
- *width 1.34m*
- £1,175 • The Swan

George III Dressing Stand ▲
- *circa 1795*

George III mahogany gentleman's dressing stand with original mirror, and brass fittings.
- *89cm x 51cm*
- £825 • The Swan

Mahogany Chiffonier ▼
- *circa 1880*

Victorian mahogany chiffonier, with one long single drawer above two moulded panelled doors, flanked with carved pilasters.
- *1.05m x 1.14m*
- £1,350 • The Swan

Biedermeier Style Cupboard ▼
- *circa 1899*

Danish Biedermeier style cupboard in birchwood, with a central oval inlay in rosewood and satinwood of an urn with a spray of flowers.
- *1.28m x 55cm*
- £5,600 • Rupert Cavendish

Swedish Sideboard ◄
- *circa 1800*

Louis XVI Gustavian painted pine sideboard with two centrally carved diamond panels on the doors.
- *98cm x 1.07m*
- £4,500 • Rupert Cavendish

Campaign Furniture

Travelling Games Table ▶
- *circa 1830*
George IV mahogany campaign
games table that dismantles to fit
neatly into its folding chess board
box top.
- *72.4cm x 33cm x 38.1cm*
- **£1,250** • Christopher Clarke

E. Ross Dining Chairs ▲
- *Mid 19th century*
Pair of mahogany Ross chairs
with a stencilled maker's mark.
- *87.6cm x 50.5cm x 45.7cm*
- **£1,150** • Christopher Clarke

Campaign Cradle ◀
- *Early 19th century*
Mahogany campaign cradle that
completely dismantles for travel.
- *1.23m x 63.5cm x 1.143m*
- **£2,200** • Christopher Clarke

Low Table ▼
- *Late 19th century*
Teak campaign low table by S.W.
Silver & Co. Flat packs for travel.
- *58.4cm x 61cm x 61cm*
- **£595** • Christopher Clarke

Folding Armchair ◀
- *Third quarter 19th century*
Colonial folding teak armchair
with brass straps.
- *73.7cm x 53.3cm x 52cm*
- **£795** • Christopher Clarke

Campaign Double Mirror ▼
- *Early 19th century*
Mahogany oval campaign double
mirror with both a standard and a
magnifying looking glass.
- *1.9cm x 15.2cm x 23.5cm*
- **£195** • Christopher Clarke

Powder Box ◀
- *Early 19th century*
Black powder box with copper
canisters and double protective
caps. This box would have
provided safe storage for gun
powder in between filling up a
powder horn for everyday use.
- *23cm x 18.4cm x 28.6cm*
- **£1,450** • Christopher Clarke

Railway Companion ▶

- *Late 19th century*
Railway companion with
sandwich tin and decanter with
the drinking glass forming the
bottle stop.
- *18.4cm x 7.6cm x 10.2cm*
- **£345** • **Christopher Clarke**

Campaign Commode ◀

- *Second quarter 19th century*
Campaign commode in
mahogany with leather seat and
lead plumbing. Stamped
"Bonneels".
- *48.3cm x 53.3cm x 61cm*
- **£2,750** • **Christopher Clarke**

Portable Desk ▲

- *Early 19th century*
Three section portable desk with
brass strapwork and secret
drawers.
- *15.2cm x 24.8cm x 34.3cm*
- **£575** • **Christopher Clarke**

Travel Flask ◀

- *Early 20th century*
Travel flask with four beakers in a
two-part leather case.
- *19.7cm x 5.1cm x 8.9cm*
- **£195** • **Christopher Clarke**

Folding Cutlery Set ▲

- *Late 18th to early 19th century*
Prisoner-of-war bone and horn
folding cutlery set.
- *2.54cm x 4.4cm x 20.3cm*
- **£195** • **Christopher Clarke**

Campaign Cutlery ◀

- *Second quarter 19th century*
French campaign silver cutlery in
leather barrel case.
- *13.2cm x 7.6cm x 7.6cm*
- **£1,150** • **Christopher Clarke**

Canterburies

Mahogany Canterbury ◄

- *circa 1870*

Victorian mahogany canterbury with three compartments. The side drawer with turned knob handles, finials and supports, with original porcelain castors.
- *height 62cm*
- **£995**   ● A.I.G.

Mahogany Canterbury ▶

- *circa 1830s*

Early Victorian mahogany galleried and tiered dumb waiter, with turned supports and single drawer with turned handles, the whole standing on bulbous turned legs with brass castors.
- *1m x 38cm*
- **£2,200**   ● Old Cinema

Rosewood Canterbury ▼

- *circa 1790*

Mahogany canterbury comprising four sections with a single side drawer with circular ring handle, raised on square tapered legs with original brass castors.
- *height 39cm*
- **£1,950**   ● John Clay

Victorian Canterbury ▲

- *circa 1880*

Victorian walnut canterbury of four sections, with pierced scrolled decoration above a lower shelf, on upturned scrolled legs.
- *height 55cm*
- **£1,195**   ● The Swan

Walnut Canterbury ▶

- *circa 1880*

Victorian walnut canterbury with four sections with heavily carved and pierced floral designs, turned handles, and a single side drawer, the whole raised on turned legs with brass castors.
- *height 54cm*
- **£1,295**   ● The Swan

Chairs

Commode Armchair ▶

- *circa 1780*

George III mahogany commode armchair with rounded shield back above a slip-in upholstered seat with shaped and concaved moulded arms. Attributed to Gillows.

- *99cm x 44.5cm x 56cm*
- £1,000–£2,000 • J. Collins

Metamorphic Library Chair ▲

- *circa 1815*

A Regency period metamorphic library chair made by Morgan and Saunders, specialists who patented the design in 1811.

- *91.5cm x 63.5cm x 58.5cm*
- £18,000 • Haughey

Queen Anne Gilt Chinoiserie Side Chairs ▲

- *circa 1700*

Side chairs with caned rear panels and stuffed overseat standing on cabriole legs with stretcher.

- *height 1.09m*
- £2,950 • S. Cook

Mahogany Regency Chairs ▼

- *circa 1815*

A set of eight Regency period mahogany dining chairs (six singles and two with arms) in the style of Thomas Hope, featuring sabre legs and top rails decorated with Greek key patterns of boxwood inlay.

- *84cm x 47cm x 56cm*
- £17,500 • Haughey

Arts and Crafts Chair ▼

- *circa 1880*

Mahogany hall chair by Liberty & Co with original paper label still under the seat.

- *height 95cm*
- £1,250 • D. Hume

Pair of Walnut Chairs ◀

- *circa 1870*

Pair of French walnut chairs with floral pattern seats and backs.

- *96.5cm x 48cm x 51cm*
- £2,750 • Manser Antiques

Expert Tips

The price of a set of chairs rises exponentially with quantity. Beware of sets made up of parts of originals.

Rosewood Chairs ▶

- *circa 1800*

A rare pair of French rosewood chairs with undecorated rectangular backs with square section upright supports. The shaped arms with low relief carved decoration to the upper surface, terminating in very well carved rams heads above scrolled supports with low relief carved decoration to the front. With a straight seat rail above an apron.
- *1m x 59.5cm*
- **£15,500** • **Anthony Outred**

Regency Mahogany Chair ▼

- *circa 1810*

Regency mahogany elbow chair, with curved arms and turned legs and leather seat.
- *height 89cm*
- **£995** • **Old Cinema**

Elbow Chair ▼

- *1890*

One of a pair of mahogany elbow chairs with foliate carving on slender turned legs with cane back and set.
- *height 97cm*
- **£1,450** • **Old Cinema**

Victorian High Chair ▲

- *circa 1860*

Victorian ash and elm child's high chair, with turned decoration.
- *height 99cm*
- **£395** • **The Swan**

French Walnut Chair ▲

- *1890*

French walnut chair with carved mask decoration, standing on a cross stretcher base.
- *height 87cm*
- **£595** • **Old Cinema**

Child's Chippendale Chair ▼

- *circa 1890*

Chippendale-style mahogany child's chair, with pierced back splat, serpentine top rail and raised on straight tapered legs.
- *height 78cm*
- **£475** • **The Swan**

Victorian Nursing Chair ▼

- *1880*

Victorian nursing chair with a circular padded seat and a padded back.
- *height 74cm*
- **£550** • **Old Cinema**

Wing Back Chair ▼
- *circa 1900*
Oak framed wing armchair, re-upholstered in Watts of Westminster fabric.
- *1.04m x 71cm x 71cm*
- **£2,450** • Manser Antiques

Leather Desk Chair ◄
- *circa 1920*
Walnut desk chair with leather upholstery.
- *94cm x 48cm x 58.4cm*
- **£950** • Manser Antiques

Hepplewhite Armchair ▲
- *circa 1780*
Painted and decorated English Hepplewhite ebonised armchair, shield back with urn detail, curved arm supports and straight tapered legs with hand-painted designs of trailing foliage and ribboning.
- *97cm x 57cm*
- **£4,450** • O.F. Wilson

Empire Bergère ▲
- *circa 1815*
French mahogany Bergère chair with turned top rail and curved, padded arms.
- *92cm x 61cm*
- **£2,850** • O.F. Wilson

Pair of Decorated Fauteuils ▲
- *circa 1760*
One of a pair of French beechwood painted and gilt decorated fauteuils stamped "Premy" with oval backs.
- *94cm x 61cm*
- **£7,800** • O.F. Wilson

Library Bergère ◄
- *circa 1815*
Rare Regency period Irish library Bergere in burr yewwood with scroll arms standing on panelled legs decorated with Amthenions and reeded feet into brass cup castors, covered in black hide.
- *95.5cm x 73.5cm x 99cm*
- **£11,500** • R. Gardner

Louis XV Fauteuil ▲

- *circa 1750*
Louis XV French giltwood
fauteuil, with carved floral
designs raised on cabriole legs.
- £1,250   • Mora Upham

Swedish Armchair ▲

- *circa 1880*
Swedish armchair, with gilded
floral decoration to the back rail,
carved and gilded supports to the
arms and original neutral paint.
Part of a set comprising a sofa,
armchair and four single chairs.
- *height 1.06m*
- £18,500 set   • Wakelin

Mahogany Chair ▼

- *circa 1870*
Set of six mahogany and brass
inlaid dining chairs in the
manner of Gillows.
- £3,200   • Mora Upham

Swedish Dining Chair ▼

- *circa 1880*
Swedish dining chair, with lyre
shaped back, gilded with floral
designs, raised on straight tapered
front legs, with swept back legs.
- *height 83cm*
- £18,500   • Wakelin Linfield

English Hepplewhite
Chairs ◄

- *circa 1780*
English Hepplewhite oval back
chairs, with three Prince of Wales
feathers carved into the back
splat, above a shaped front rail,
raised on elegant cabriole legs,
with floral and shell motifs.
- *height 84cm*
- £5,500   • Mora Upham

Directoire French Chair ▲

- *circa 1880*
One of a pair of French,
mahogany directoire style open
armchairs with carved finial
decoration, raised on tapered,
reeded legs.
- £1,850   • Mora Upham

George I Walnut Chair ▲

- *circa 1715*
One of a pair of George I walnut
side chairs with vase shaped
splats, the front cabriole legs and
back legs united by a turned wavy
stretcher.
- *height 96cm*
- £6,800   • Wakelin Linfield

Sheraton Armchair ▶
- *circa 1880*

Sheraton revival decorated armchair of very good quality with interlaced splats, labelled for Druce & Co of Baker Street, with finely painted floral decoration.
- *85cm x 52cm x 55cm*
- **£2,750**   • R. Gardner

Georgian Dining Chairs ▲
- *circa 1800*

Set of eight (six chairs two carvers) late Georgian mahogany dining chairs. Having many interesting features.
- *84cm x 48.5cm x 51cm*
- **£14,500**   • R. Gardner

George II Dining Chairs ▼
- *circa 1740*

Two chairs from a set of four George II dining chairs in red walnut, on cabriole front legs to pad feet, front and back.
- *height 93.5cm*
- **£3,300**   • R. Gardner

George III Mahogany Dining Chairs ▶
- *circa 1790*

Two from a fine set of twelve Hepplewhite design mahogany dining chairs, each with moulded top rails and uprights with leaf carved decoration, standing on tapering square section legs.
- *92.5cm x 43cm x 51cm*
- **£57,500**   • R. Gardner

Cockfighting Chair ▼
- *circa 1835*

William IV oak and leather desk/ cockfighting chair, with padded button back.
- *90cm x 61cm*
- **£1,950**   • R. Gardner

Yew Wood Open Armchairs ▼
- *circa 1800*

Two from a set of six late George III armchairs, each with a pierced serpentine top rail with ball finials above a simulated-bamboo filled rectangular back and a pair of out-curved arms, the seat covered in green ribbed velvet.
- *96.5cm x 49cm x 61cm*
- **£12,750**   • R. Gardner

Expert Tips

When buying any chair it is a good idea to stand back and assess its proportions. A good chair should "stand well" when looked at from all angles. Some are not at all well-proportioned and should be avoided. A good chair should be comfortable as well, so try it out.

Hepplewhite Armchair ▼
- *1785*

Hepplewhite mahogany armchair, with shield back and shaped arm rests with scrolled terminals on wavy supports, the whole raised on square tapered legs.
- *98cm x 57cm*
- **£26,000** • Wakelin Linfield

Court Chair ▼
- *circa 1810*

One of a pair of Chinese court chairs of simple elegant form.
- *1m x 61cm*
- **£3,100** • Gordon Reece

Victorian Mahogany Chair ▶
- *circa 1860*

Victorian mahogany button back chair, with scrolled arms and cabriole legs.
- *height 1.1m*
- **£1,350** • In Vogue

French Desk Chair ▲
- *circa 1880*

French mahogany desk chair in the Louis XV style, with gilt ormolu mounts and carved front rail.
- *height 95cm*
- **£1,950** • Hatchwell

Horse Shoe Back Chair ▲
- *18th century*

One of a pair of Chinese antique horseshoe back chairs, each bearing a moon symbol.
- *97cm x 24cm x 18cm*
- **£2,680** • Gordon Reece

Elmwood Chairs ▼
- *19th century*

A pair of Chinese elmwood chairs.
- *1.02m x 56cm*
- **£890** • Gordon Reece

Lancashire Spindle Back Chair ▼
- *circa 1880*

One of a set of ten Harlequin Lancashire rush seat spindle back chairs.
- *height 98cm*
- **£6,750** • Gerald Brodie

French Louis XV Suite ▼
- *1870*

French Louis XV suite with two armchairs and one sofa.
- *1.06m*
- **£10,500** • Butchoff

Georgian Wing-Back Armchairs ◀

- *circa 1760*

Georgian mahogany wing-back armchairs, raised on square chamfered legs, with an "H" stretcher, upholstered in a woven silk damask.
- *height 1.19m*
- £3,450   • R.S. Antiques

Georgian Fruitwood Chairs ▼

- *circa 1760*

Georgian fruitwood chairs of the Chippendale period, with unusual rosewood splat and square chamfered legs. Original colour and patina.
- *height 95cm*
- £485   • R.S. Antiques

Regency Armchair ▲

- *circa 1880*

Regency revival armchair with mahogany frame carved with honeysuckle and harebell motifs, raised on moulded bun feet.
- *83cm x 54cm*
- £1,395   • R.S. Antiques

Italian Walnut Chair ▲

- *circa 1740*

One of a pair of Italian armchairs. The walnut framwork carved with scrolled and moulded decoration, raised on cabriole legs with escargot feet.
- *height 1.14m*
- £14,000   • O. F. Wilson

French Walnut Bergère ▼

- *circa 1880*

French 2nd Empire bergère with a heavily carved walnut frame incorporating floral swags and fruit motifs, raised on cabriole legs.
- *height 1.01m*
- £2,200   • O. F. Wilson

Windsor Chair ▲

- *circa 1860*

Oak Windsor chair, with carved vase shaped back splat, turned supports and shaped seat.
- *height 1.07m*
- £750   • Poppets

Victorian Lacquered Chair ▲

- *circa 1860*

Small Victorian black lacquered chair with mother-of-pearl inlay, wicker back and seat and elongated arms, standing on turned legs with brass castors.
- *height 75cm*
- £995   • Serendipity

Painted Fauteuil ▼

- *circa 1760*
One of a pair of beechwood
fauteuils with oval backs and gilt
foliate designs over cream paint.
Stamped "Premy".
- *height 83cm*
- £7,800   ● O. F. Wilson

Regency Chair ▼

- *circa 1820*
One of a pair of Regency faux
rosewood chairs, with turned and
gilded designs, raised on sabre
legs.
- *height 82cm*
- £2,750   ● O. F. Wilson

Ebonised Beechwood Chair ▲

- *circa 1880*
One of a pair of ebonised
beechwood chairs with rush seats,
influenced by William Morris.
- *height 84cm*
- £220   ● O. F. Wilson

French Louis XV Fauteuil ▲

- *circa 1760*
One of a pair of Louis XV
fauteuils with curved top rail,
inverted arm supports and
serpentine front rail, raised on
cabriole legs.
- *height 84cm*
- £5,250   ● O. F. Wilson

Mahogany Armchair ◀

- *1880*
One of a pair of mahogany
Chippendale-style armchairs,
with a heavily carved serpentine
top rail and pierced back splat,
raised on carved cabriole legs.
- *height 95cm*
- £8,800   ● Butchoff

Directoire Armchair ▼

- *circa 1795*
Fine directoire mahogany
armchair, with scrolled top rail,
pierced back splat, and turned
arm supports.
- *height 86cm*
- £2,500   ● O. F. Wilson

Empire Bergère ▼

- *circa 1815*
Mahogany Empire bergère, with
turned top rail and curved,
padded arms.
- *height 94cm*
- £2,8501   ● O. F. Wilson

Expert Tips

*When buying antique furniture
always try to buy the item in
pristine condition and from a
good dealer, as restoration costs
could be a shock.*

Adam-style Chairs ▶
- *circa 1785*
Pair of George III Adam-style
carved mahogany elbow chairs
with anthemion carved splats and
foliate rails, on moulded legs with
miniature florets.
- *94.5cm x 61cm x 59.5cm*
- £3,850　　• R. Gardner

Regency Hall Chairs ▲
- *circa 1815*
A pair of Regency mahogany hall
chairs with scrolled and leaf
carved backs to platform seats on
turned and fluted front supports.
- *90cm x 48.5cm x 44.5cm*
- £2,250　　• R. Gardner

Mahogany Library Chair ▶
- *circa 1835*
William IV mahogany library
chair with beautifully shaped
back, recently re-leathered.
- *1.09m x 91.5cm x 71cm*
- £4,350　　• R. Gardner

"Drunkards" Chairs ▶
- *circa 1775*
A matched pair of George III
mahogany hall chairs, sometimes
referred to as "drunkards" chairs.
- *86.5cm x 58.5cm 61.5cm*
- £3,400　　• R. Gardner

Corner Chair ▼
- *circa 1835*
William IV buttoned hide chair
on three turned legs, very
unusual, designed for a corner.
- *height 87.5cm*
- £2,900　　• R. Gardner

Regency Dining Chair ◀
- *circa 1815*
Set of twelve Regency period
decorated dining chairs with cane
backs and fine gilding.
- *84.5cm x 48cm x 43cm*
- £68,500　　• M. Norman

Queen Anne Desk Chair ▼

- *circa 1705*

Queen Anne walnut single desk chair with interesting and boldly shaped front legs and back splat.
- *1.02m x 40cm*
- **£1,750** • **Wakelin Linfield**

French Fauteuil ▼

- *circa 1840*

A well proportioned French fauteuil. The carved beech frame retaining traces of original painted decoration.
- *1m x 73cm*
- **£5,500** • **Wakelin Linfield**

Ash Dining Chair ▲

- *18th century*

One of a set of ten ash dining chairs, decorated with floral marquetry and birds. The shaped top rail over a serpentine splat with shaped serpentine fronted seat rails and cabriole legs with pad feet.
- *92cm x 51cm*
- **£22,500** • **Wakelin Linfield**

English Windsor Chair ▲

- *circa 1750s*

Unusual rustic, mid 18th century, Windsor chair made from elm, with turned supports and solid seat, with good warm patina.
- *1m x 53cm*
- **£3,850** • **Wakelin Linfield**

Venetian Chair ◄

- *1820*

Venetian Rococo style carved fruitwood armchair, in original condition.
- *1.04m x 84cm*
- **£8,000** • **Augustus Brandt**

Directoire Side Chair ▼

- *1780*

One of a set of four French giltwood directoire dining chairs, with original cream paintwork and gilt pastel pink covers.
- *89cm x 43cm*
- **£6,800** • **Augustus Brandt**

Elm Elbow Chair ▼

- *circa 1890s*

One of a pair of late 19th century elbow chairs in elm from southern China, of sculptural ox-bow form, from a good merchant's house.
- *1.25m x 60cm*
- **£6,000** • **Wakelin Linfield**

Ladder-back Chair ▲
- *circa 1780*
Well proportioned 18th century ladder-back chair made from elm with rush seat and good patina.
- *1.06m x 57cm*
- £1,750 • Wakelin Linfield

English Elbow Chair ▲
- *circa 1900*
One of a stylish pair of English elbow chairs in an Egyptian style, with carved heads and paw feet and hand-worked signed tapestry upholstery in the Regency manner.
- *95cm x 62cm*
- £4,500 • Wakelin Linfield

Country Armchair ▶
- *circa 1700*
A rare traditional English country armchair, with two vase-shaped backsplats, down-swept arms on two turned supports, solid seat and turned front legs.
- *1.2m x 55cm*
- £7,850 • Wakelin Linfield

Chinese Armchair ▼
- *circa 1850s*
One of a pair of Chinese armchairs in padouk wood with original seats, from the Meiji period.
- *height 90cm*
- £3,950 • Wakelin Linfield

Yew-wood Rocking Chair ▼
- *circa 1820s*
Yew-wood early 19th century rocking chair, with carved and turned decoration.
- *1.05m x 49cm*
- £1,750 • Wakelin Linfield

Blade & Gilt Dining Chair ▲
- *circa 1840*
One of a set of eight harlequin blade and gilt japanned dining/salon chairs, with shaped seat rails, turned baluster legs, the black ground with pilwork depicting flowers, foliage and birds.
- *90cm x 46cm*
- £5,800 • Wakelin Linfield

Hepplewhite Chair ▲
- *1785*
Hepplewhite mahogany chair. The shield back with pierced decoration above a concave leather upholstered seat, raised on square tapered legs.
- *98cm x 57cm*
- £26,000 • Wakelin Linfield

George IV Hall Chair ▼

- *circa 1825*

A pair of George IV, mahogany
hall chairs, with original painted
armorials to the shaped and
reeded backs, raised on reeded
front legs with outswept rear legs.
- *85cm x 42.5cm*
- £4,950   • Wakelin Linfield

Tub/Desk Chair ▶

- *circa 1880*

French flame mahogany "klismos"
shaped tub/desk chair, the
downswept arms decorated with
gilt ormolu palmettos and
supported by winged swans, raised
on square tapered legs.
- *1.09m x 68cm*
- £4,500   • Wakelin Linfield

English Regency Chair ▲

- *circa 1830*

English Regency mahogany chair,
with a shield back and a
"klismos" shaped seat, with
carved and reeded designs.
- £3,500   • Mora Upham

Set of Dining Chairs ◀

- *circa 1835*

A set of eight William IV period
mahogany dining chairs.
Stamped: J. Porter, Cabinet
Chairs & Sofa Manufacturer,
Upholsterer, 166 High Street,
Camden Town. Each consisting
of a panelled klismos tablet back,
supported by shaped uprights
which are in the form of stylised
ionic columns with leaf motifs to
capitals. With turned reeded legs
and sabre back legs.
- *89.4cm x 44cm*
- £16,500   • Anthony Outred

George I Dining Chair ▲

- *circa 1720*

Set of walnut George I dining
chairs, with shaped top rail, vase
shaped back splat and moulded
seat and rail, raised on cabriole
legs, with turned cross rails.
- *97cm x 47cm*
- £14,000   • Wakelin Linfield

William IV Library Chair ▲

- *circa 1835*

Outstanding William IV
gentleman's library chair. The
massive mahogany frame heavily
carved with C scrolls and
acanthus leaf designs. Supported
on large brass castors.
- *1.02m x 98cm*
- £7,950   • Wakelin Linfield

Regency Hall Chairs ▲

- *circa 1820*

Pair of Irish mahogany hall chairs from the Regency period, with shell backs and acanthus carved rail and sabre legs.
- *81.5cm x 48.5cm x 39.5cm*
- £3,100 • R. Gardner

George I Sidechairs ▲

- *circa 1725*

Pair of George I walnut sidechairs, veneered splat and rails, with old leather covers.
- *98cm x 40.5cm x 49.5cm*
- £2,750 • R. Gardner

Hepplewhite Sidechairs ◀

- *circa 1790*

A pair of Hepplewhite hoop back side chairs, having saddle seats and rope carving to the back and to the front legs.
- *94cm x 52.5cm x 54cm*
- £2,200 • R. Gardner

Wing Armchair ▶

- *circa 1890*

Late 19th century Georgian style mahogany wing armchair of good proportions.
- *1.09m x 71cm x 84cm*
- £1,950 • R. Gardner

Walnut Wing Chair ◀

- *circa 1740*

George II red walnut wing chair with scrolled arm rests and cabriole legs.
- *1.16m x 78cm x 69.8cm*
- £6,850 • M. Norman

Walnut Armchair ▲

- *circa 1750*

George II solid walnut armchair, pierced splayed splat, upholstered seat on cabriole legs with pad feet.
- *95cm x 59.5cm x 56cm*
- £3,250 • M. Norman

Pair of Swan Armchairs ◀

- *circa 1880*
Pair of 19th century gilt wood
and decorated continental swan
armchairs.
- 85cm x 67cm x 58.5cm
- £17,500   • M. Norman

Regency Dining Chairs ▶

- *circa 1815*
Set of six Regency period
mahogany dining chairs, raised
on turned legs.
- 81cm x 48cm x 40cm
- £5,850   • M. Norman

Regency Library Chair ◀

- *circa 1820*
Regency period mahogany library
chair with olive leather
upholstery.
- 84cm x 53cm x 68.5cm
- £3,500   • M. Norman

Mahogany Library Chair ▲

- *circa 1820*
Early 19th century French
mahogany library chair with
scrolled arms and leather
upholstery.
- 95cm x 63.5cm x 56cm
- £7,850   • M. Norman

Mahogany Dining Chair ▶

- *circa 1830*
Set of eight William IV
mahogany dining chairs, richly
carved front legs on scroll feet.
- 95cm x 48cm x 43cm
- £22,500   • M. Norman

French Library Chairs ▲

- *circa 1850*
A stylish pair of continental
mahogany library chairs, with
plumed escutcheon, on sabre legs.
- 94cm x 45.7cm x 56cm
- £2,750   • Walter Moores

Folding Campaign Chair ▲

- *circa 1870*
A mid-Victorian folding
campaign chair made from
mahogany with cane seat.
- *70cm x 37cm*
- £395 • Old Cinema

Hepplewhite Carver ▲

- *1880*
One of a set of eight mahogany
Hepplewhite-style, dining chairs
including two carvers.
- £11,000 • Butchoff

Arts & Crafts Chair ▶

- *circa 1890*
Russian Arts & Crafts chair of
triangular outline, with a tablet
back, profusely inlaid with
numerous wood specimens
including walnut, mahogany,
satinwood and harewood in
geometric patterns. Above a
shaped back splat decorated with
inlaid woods, with decorated arms
issuing from tablet back, leading
to an overstuffed shaped brown
leather seat. Raised on turned
legs of alternate specimen woods.
- *86.5cm x 58.5cm*
- £3,400 • Anthony Outred

Oak Elbow Chair ▼

- *circa 1890*
Oak elbow chair from the late
Victorian period, with padded
and buttoned top rail.
- *90cm x 55cm*
- £395 • Old Cinema

Regency Chair ▼

- *circa 1830*
Regency rosewood chair with
scrolled top rail, splayed back legs
and turned front legs.
- *84cm x 51cm*
- £980 • The Lacquer Chest

Oak Dining Chair ▲

- *circa 1890*
One of a set of four late Victorian
oak dining chairs, in the
Chippendale style, raised on
square straight legs.
- *1m x 50cm*
- £695 • Old Cinema

Windsor Armchair ▲

- *circa 1810*
Beechwood Windsor armchair
with elm seat, hooped back and
arms, standing on turned legs.
- *87cm x 55cm*
- £435 • The Lacquer Chest

Flemish Carved Walnut Chairs ▶

- *circa 1670*

A pair of 17th century Flemish carved walnut chairs. The carved crested top supported by twist uprights and caned back and seat with unusual carved decoration to the seat rails.

- *1.21m x 40.5cm x 53.3cm*
- £8,880 • Hallidays

Rush Seated High Chair ▼

- *circa 1890*

Simple country-style child's rush seated high chair.

- *height 84cm*
- £295 • Millers Antiques

Regency High-backed Bergère ◀

- *circa 1815*

A Regency period mahogany framed Bergère chair with swept high back, supported by a reeded mahogany frame and with turned reeded columns joining the arms to the ring turned front legs.

- *height 1.42m*
- £8,800 • Hallidays

Elm Lady's Chair with Carved Panel ▲

- *Late 19th century*

A lady's chair made in the traditional style of a five-legged round stool with back. The back splat is divided into carved panels, the central one depicting a lady standing in a pavilion. Elm, stained to simulate hardwood, with caned seat.

- *height 95cm*
- £275 • Orient Expressions

George III Wing Chair ▶

- *circa 1800*

A mahogany framed wing chair, with shaped back and wings and a single cushion. Supported on square taper and reeded front legs, with plain square swept legs to the back, joined by stretchers.

- *1.11m x 58cm x 76cm*
- £5,800 • Hallidays

Grape and Leaf Carved Dining Chairs ▲

- *circa 1840*

A set of ten single solid rosewood dining chairs. with unusual panelled back with grape and leaf carving to the ears. Moulded shaped uprights joined by a leaf carved stretcher, contain later caned seats.

- *86cm x 40cm x 45cm*
- £15,000 • Hallidays

Chinese Rocking Chair ▲

- *Early 20th century*

A rocking chair with turned legs and arm supports showing a very Western-influenced style. Blackwood with cane seat and back, with a simple floral motif carved into the back rail.

- *height 1.1m*
- £490 • Orient Expressions

Italian Chair ▲

- *circa 1870*

One of a pair of Italian walnut chairs, heavily carved with depictions of Pan, ram's heads, and griffins, raised on claw feet.

- *height 1.54m*
- £18,000   ● Hatchwell

Ladder Back Chair ▲

- *circa 1820*

One of a pair George IV ash and elm ladder back chairs, with domed top rail above four graduated ladders, on turned legs standing on pad feet.

- *height 94cm*
- £1,075   ● Great Grooms

Court Chairs ▲

- *circa 1810*

Pair of Chinese court chairs of simple elegant form.

- *1m x 61cm*
- £3,100   ● Gordon Reece

Horseshoe Shaped Chair ▲

- *circa 1800*

A single low horseshoe shaped back rail chair. Originally low in construction.

- *82cm x 57cm*
- £1,480   ● Gordon Reece

Syrian Folding Chair ▲

- *circa 1890*

Attractive and decorative, folding, Syrian chair with inlaid ivory stars, profusely carved with scrolled, foliate designs throughout.

- *height 1.05m*
- £485   ● Elyot Tett

Regency Dining Chairs ◀

- *circa 1820*

One of a set of eight Regency mahogany dining chairs, with pierced back splats, raised on turned legs.

- *height 84cm*
- £12,000   ● Barry Cotton

Cherry Dining Chair ▶

- *circa 1920*
One of six Provençal dining chairs in cherrywood with rush seats.
- *height 96.5cm*
- **£1,295** • Millers Antiques

Balloon Back Chair ▲

- *circa 1920*
One of six balloon back chairs with cane seats.
- *89cm x 38cm x 40.6cm*
- **£765** • Millers Antiques

Sabre Leg Chair ▲

- *circa 1820*
One of an attractive set of four regency mahogany sabre leg chairs.
- *height 92.7cm*

Lion's Head Chairs ▶

- *circa 1880*
English chairs standing on carved lion mask headed cabriole legs terminating in hairy paw feet. The open arms are finely shaped and terminate in eagles' heads, expressive of power and victory.
- *1.09m x 51cm x 74cm*
- **£14,500** • Butchoff Antiques

Edwardian Child's Chair ▼

- *circa 1910*
Simple country-style chair with shaped armrests, turned legs and cross rails, with good patina.
- *75cm x 34cm x 38cm*
- **£185** • Millers Antiques

Neo-classical Armchair ▶

- *circa 1880*
A satinwood inlaid and brass stung chair with a lyre-shaped back, upholstered seat, and square tapered legs terminating in spade feet. The cresting is finely inlaid with mother-of-pearl, ivory and brass decoration.
- *97cm x 52cm x 52cm*
- **£5,500** • Butchoff Antiques

Regency Chair ▼

- *circa 1810*
One of a pair of Regency chairs with sabre legs and new upholstery.
- *86.4cm x 45.7cm x 47cm*
- **£645** • Millers Antiques

Tub Chair with Cabriole Legs ▲

- *circa 1860*
A Victorian rosewood tub chair on cabriole legs, the arms terminating in carved scrolls.
- *91.4 cm x 53.3cm x 66cm*
- **£1,650** • Walter Moores

English Bamboo Chair ▲
- *circa 1830*

One of a set of four English faux bamboo chairs, with cane seats, and splayed front legs.
- *85.5cm x 44.5cm x 38cm*
- £2,750   • O. F. Wilson

French Walnut Chair ▼
- *circa 1780*

One of a pair of French walnut upholstered open bergère chairs, standing on cabriole legs.
- £3,800   • Mora Upham

Elm and Beech Chair ▼
- *circa 1890*

Elm and beech kitchen chair.
- *height 97cm*
- £65   • Nicholas Mitchell

First Empire Chair ▲
- *circa 1810*

French First Empire, giltwood chair in the manner of Dellenge, with carved stylised floral decoration.
- £3,800   • Mora Upham

Mahogany Hall Chairs ▲
- *circa 1775*

One of a pair of English mahogany hall chairs inspired by designs from Chippendale's pattern books, the circular carved and pierced backs in the form of spoked wheels, the dished seats shaped to reflect this pattern, the turned front legs decorated with ring turning.
- *95cm x 35cm*
- £10,500   • Wakelin Linfield

Gothic Revival Style Leather Library Armchairs ▶

- *circa 1900*

Library chairs upholstered in deep buttoned burgundy leather with slightly out-curved arms, resting on "C" scroll arc-shaped supports. Cabriole legs support the chair, terminating in pad feet.
- *99cm x 61cm x 69cm*
- **£12,500** • Butchoff Antiques

Biedermeier Style Satin Birchwood Arm Chairs ▲

- *19th century*

Armchairs with plume shaped top rails terminating in an ebonised fan shaped splat, above a stepped stretcher. The scrolling arms supported on "C" scrolls with ebonised ball finials.
- *97cm x 51cm x 61cm*
- **£7,500** • Butchoff Antiques

Black Lacquer Folding Chair ▲

- *Early 20th century*

A pair of folding chairs, black lacquer over elm with cane seat and back. Made in Shanghai, where a more Westernised style was popular.
- *height 90cm*
- **£395** • Orient Expressions

Sheraton-style Side Chairs ▼

- *circa 1870*

A pair of satinwood and painted chairs with pierced petal shaped and decorated splats forming an eight pointed flower within the chair backs, centred with charming and romantic paintings of young ladies.
- *97cm x 41cm x 46cm*
- **£10,500** • Butchoff Antiques

SOH Armchairs ▼

- *Mid 19th century*

One of a pair of elm wood "southern official's hat" chairs with original black lacquer, much of which has worn from the seat and footrest. The back splat has a carved medallion and the seat is paneled.
- *1.01m x 47cm x 60cm*
- **£1,200** • Orient Expressions

Horseshoe Back Chair ▼

- *Late 19th century*

A cross-legged armchair in elm with black lacquer and a caned seat. The back splat is carved with a cloud design and inlaid with bone figures.
- *height 85cm*
- **£475** • Orient Expressions

Indian Parcel Gilt Silvered Throne ▼

- *circa 1880*

The throne of His Highness The Thakore Saheb of Limbdi, with a shaped rectangular padded back and seat, surmounted by a coat of arms and gilt urn finials. Silvered recumbent lions guard each side, above a serpentine apron, centred to the front by a gilt lion's head.
- *1.49m x 69cm x 39cm*
- **£30,000** • Butchoff Antiques

Hall Chair ▼

- **1890**
One of a pair of mahogany hall
chairs, with carved shield back
and oval padded insert, raised on
cabriole legs.
- *height 87cm*
- **£875**   ● **Elyot Tett**

Walnut Armchair ▲
- *circa 1880*
George I, Chippendale-style
walnut armchair with pierced
back rest with scrolled designs,
supported by shaped, scrolled
arms above a serpentine front
rail, with scalloped motifs, raised
on cabriole legs with claw and
ball feet.
- *height 95cm*
- **£1,600**   ● **Elyot Tett**

George II Irish Armchair ▲
- *circa 1730*
A rare and exquisite George II
Irish mahogany open armchair of
outstanding quality and design.
The chair is beautifully carved
throughout and in exceptional
condition for its age.
- *height 98cm*
- **£6,500**   ● **Freshfords**

Walnut Chair ▲
- **1880**
One of a pair of fine George I-
style walnut chairs with pierced
backsplat and scrolled back,
raised on cabriole legs with
scalloped designs and claw and
ball feet, with original leather
and good patina.
- *height 95cm*
- **£1,750**   ● **Elyot Tett**

William IV Rosewood Armchair ◀
- *circa 1830.*
William IV colonial rosewood
armchair, formerly the property
of Major Arthur Annesley.
- *height 89cm*
- **£3,850**   ● **Freshfords**

Small Swedish Chair ▶

- *1780*

Small Swedish pine nursing chair in original condition with moulded oval back, standing on turned legs.
- *height 92cm*
- £850   • **Augustus Brandt**

Oak Hall Chair ▼

- *1870*

Victorian oak hall chair with an architecturally carved back, raised on turned legs with good patina.
- *height 84cm*
- £375   • **Elyot Tett**

Regency Mahogany Bergères ▶

- *circa 1820*

One of a fine pair of Regency mahogany bergères decorated with ebony mouldings and turnings, with later cane and hide coverings.
- *width 66cm*
- £21,500   • **Freshfords**

Recumbent Easy Chair ◀

- *circa 1830*

One of a pair of rare matched English Regency "Daws" patent "Recumbent Easy Chairs", both bear the maker's stamp, with one chair bearing an original label for Bantings of Pall Mall.
- *height 79cm*
- £18,500   • **Freshfords**

French Fauteuil ▲

- *circa 1870*

One of a pair of French fauteuils, with a high padded back and wings, with carved and gilded foliate decoration to the back and arms, raised on turned legs.
- *height 1.49m*
- £1,850   • **Elyot Tett**

Chests of Drawers & Commodes

George III Mahogany Bow Fronted Chest of Drawers ▶
- *circa 1790*
A small bow-fronted chest of
drawers of the Sheraton period
with four full-width oak and pine
lined cockbeaded graduated
drawers with decorative brass
circular plate ring handles.
- *93.5cm x 56cm x 80cm*
- **£3,000–£5,000** • J. Collins

Bachelors Chest of Drawers ▶
- *circa 1780*
Mahogany chest of drawers with
Georgian veneered and
crossbanded caddy top over a
fitted brushing slide with four
graduated drawers all retaining
the original handles, standing on
original bracket feet.
- *78.7cm x 47cm x 86.4cm*
- **£6,750** • S. Cook

Welsh Oak Cwpwrdd Deuddarn ◀
- *mid 18th century*
A Welsh Oak Cwpwrdd
Deuddarn from Cardiganshire the
upper section with turned
pendants and three panelled
doors over frieze drawers with
conforming cupboards below.
- *1.80m x 58.4cm x 1.5m*
- **£14,500** • S. Cook

George III Tallboy ▼
- *circa 1780*
Tallboy with eight drawers having
original ram's head plate handles
and standing on bracket feet.
- *1.85m x 53.3cm x 1.22m*
- **£28,500** • S. Cook

William & Mary Walnut Chest on Stand ◀
- *circa 1690*
Walnut chest with veneered top
and three crossbanded drawers
standing on a three-drawer
Gothic arched base with cup and
cover turning to wavy stretchers.
- *1.55m x 53.3cm x 1.04m*
- **£16,950** • S. Cook

Expert Tips
*In the antiques world, bigger
does not always mean better.
Small chests of drawers from the
eighteenth century consistently
command three times the price
of larger pieces.*

Venetian Commode ▶

- *circa 1760*

Superb Venetian commode with trailing foliate painted design overall, two deep drawers large metal handles painted marble top, with moulded carved apron on cabriole legs.
- *35cm x 1.01m*
- **£18,750** • C. Preston

Gustavian Commode ▲

- *circa 1800*

Louis XVI Swedish Gustavian commode with three long drawers and original brass handles, standing on square legs.
- *86cm x 1.03m*
- **£6,700** • Rupert Cavendish

Indian Brass Chest ▲

- *circa 1890*

An Indian repoussé and engraved, floral, banded design brass chest with teak interior. The slightly domed lid decorated with studded bands interspersed with repoussé floral stripes, flanked by stripes decorated with diamonds. The lid with brass inscribed catch; the front panel of grid design with repoussé decorated squares within a banded frame, standing on concealed wooden wheels.
- *70cm x 97cm*
- **£3,500** • Anthony Outred

Ash Cupboard ▶

- *1870*

One of a small Hungarian pair of pot cupboards, disguised as a chest of drawers.
- *height 66cm*
- **£1,995** • A.I.G.

George III Chest ▲

- *circa 1750*

George III mahogany chest of drawers, of small proportions, with four graduated drawers and original brass handles, raised on bracket feet.
- *86cm x 77cm*
- **£4,950** • Barry Cotton

Small Chest of Drawers ▼

- *circa 1780*

George III small chest of oak two small and two long drawers standing on moulded bracket feet.
- *height 50cm*
- **£5,500** • Paul Hopwell

Japanese Chest ▼

- *circa 1880*

Large standing Meiji period Japanese chest, possibly for futon storage.
- *1.71m x 1.8m*
- **£4,995** • Gordon Reece

William & Mary Chest of Drawers ▲

- *circa 1690*
William & Mary chest of two short and three long drawers on turned bun feet, the whole in oyster laburnum with broad cross-banding to the side, top and drawer fronts.
- *84cm x 94cm x 26cm*
- £24,500 • Wakelin Linfield

Mahogany Chest of Drawers ▲

- *circa 1860*
Flame mahogany, marble-topped chest of drawers with good colour and patination, one long single drawer above three deep drawers, standing on scrolled bracket feet.
- *92cm x 74cm*
- £1,850 • Drummonds

Himalayan Kist ▶

- *circa 17th century*
Fine Himalayan pine chip slab Kist (chest) with deeply carved designs, from the Indian state of Himachal Pradesh.
- *56cm x 1.3m*
- £780 • Gordon Reece

French Commode ▲

- *1880*
French marquetry commode of small proportions, with serpentine top and fine gilt ormolu mounts.
- *79cm x 74cm*
- £5,500 • Butchoff

Biedermeier Tallboy ▶

- *1820–1830*
A rare narrow Swedish mahogany Biedermeier tallboy with one narrow and five wider drawers with ormulu mounts, standing on gilt paw feet.
- *1.36m x 67cm*
- £4,500 • Rupert Cavendish

Wellington Chest ▼

- *circa 1835*
Unusually tall rosewood Wellington chest with finely figured rosewood, the rectangular top with moulded lip, with eight drawers with wooden pulls, with hinged and locking stile, the whole raised on a plinth.
- *56.5cm x 53cm*
- £5,500 • Anthony Outred

Kusuri Dansu ▼

- *circa 1890s*
A Japanese Kusuri Dansu (storage chest) with small drawers, from the Meiji period.
- *50cm x 43cm*
- £1,495 • **Gordon Reece**

Burr Walnut Tallboy ▶

- *circa 1740*
A good George II period burr-walnut tallboy with original metalwork. The top surmounted with a canted concave cornice above three short drawers and three graduated long drawers, all drawers having herringbone inlay and cross-banded with panels of distinctively figured walnut and fitted with open brass plate handles, with fluted canted corners terminating in an ogee point. The lower section with moulded lip above three long graduated drawers flanked by canted fluted corners headed and terminating in ogee points.
- *1.91m x 1.09m*
- £25,500 • **Anthony Outred**

Mahogany Chest of Drawers ◀

- *circa 1890*
One of a pair of small Victorian mahogany chest of four drawers.
- *height 93cm*
- £1,380 • **The Swan**

Bombe Commode ▲

- *circa 1890*
Swedish serpentine-fronted, walnut bombe commode, with cross-banded designs and gilt brass mounts raised on splayed legs.
- *82cm x 92cm x 20cm*
- £2,250 • **Hatchwell**

Biedermeier Tallboy ▲

- *1842-1843*
Biedermeier birchwood tallboy with a gentleman's chest, interior signed and dated: Carl Christian Hoff, Trondhjem, Norway.
- *1.4m x 1.18m*
- £8,800 • **Rupert Cavendish**

Brass Bound Chest of Drawers ▼

- 1890
Mahogany and brass-bound
military-style chest of drawers
- *width 87cm*
- £750　　• **Bruschweiler**

Scottish Chest ▼

- 1880
Large Scottish mahogany chest of
drawers with large wide drawers
surmounted by five smaller ones.
- *width 1.3m*
- £875　　• **Bruschweiler**

George I Burr Walnut Chest of Drawers ▲

- *circa 1725*
Chest of drawers with quarter
veneered and banded top over
two short and three long chevron
banded drawers, the sides walnut
veneered and banded standing on
bun feet.
- *91.4cm x 55.9cm x 1.02m*
- £12,500　　• **S. Cook**

Shaped Front Chest of Drawers ▼

- *circa 1920*
Walnut shaped front chest of
drawers of lovely faded colour.
- *50.8cm x 40.6cm x 69cm*
- £3,950　　• **Manser Antiques**

Mahogany Chest on Chest ▲

- *circa 1790*
Fine mahogany inlaid chest on
chest.
- *2.11m x 58.4cm x 1.194m*
- £14,750　　• **Manser Antiques**

Expert Tips

*Drawer linings are usually of
oak or pine. During the
seventeenth century they tended
to be chunky – the later the
piece the thinner the drawer
lining. Up until 1770, the
drawer lining runs from front to
back, from 1780 onwards it
runs from side to side.*

Walnut and Fruitwood Commode ▼

• *circa 1770*
North Italian walnut and fruitwood three drawer serpentine commode retaining its original locks and brasses, with a poplar carcass, probably Piedmont or Lombardy.
• *81.5cm x 40.5cm x 96.5cm*
• £6,750   • R. Gardner

George III Commode ▶

• *circa 1770*
A George III figured mahogany serpentine fronted commode of three long drawers with shaped apron on splayed bracket feet.
• *83cm x 49.5cm x 99cm*
• £18,500   • R. Gardner

William and Mary Oyster Chest ▼

• *circa 1695*
William and Mary chest with two short and two long drawers, veneered throughout in olivewood oyster pieces, the top drawer fronts outlined in boxwood, the top decorated with circles forming a flower.
• *84cm x 58.5cm x 96cm*
• £23,000   • R. Gardner

Walnut Chest of Drawers ◀

• *circa 1930*
Walnut chest of drawers on cabriole legs.
• *86.4cm x 50.8cm x 76.2cm*
• £2,750   • Manser Antiques

Expert Tips

As a rule, the more dovetail joints on the corners of drawers, the later the piece. Fine eighteenth century drawers may have six dovetails, seventeenth century pieces may have three.

Victorian Chest of Drawers ▲

• *circa 1860*
Victorian walnut chest of drawers in lovely condition.
• *86.4cm x 50.8cm x 91.4cm*
• £3,250   • Manser Antiques

Dutch Chest of Drawers ▶

- *circa 1725*

An excellent early 18th century Dutch chest of drawers of serpentine form, with four graduated long drawers. The top quarter veneered and walnut strung. This is an exceptionally small example of this type of furniture.

- *75cm x 79cm*
- **£18,750** • Wakelin Linfield

Collector's Chest ▲

- *circa 1880*

Mahogany collector's chest of eight small drawers with wooden bar with lock and key.

- *28cm x 33cm*
- **£170** • The Lacquer Chest

Louis XV Style Commode ▲

- *circa 1880*

Louis XV style bombe commode, with violet marble top with three long drawers, veneered in rosewood and mahogany with marquetry panels, profusely gilded with foliate bronze ormolu mounts.

- *1.02m x 1.15m*
- **£5,500** • Hatchwell

George III Oak Chest of Drawers ▶

- *circa 1817*

George III chest of drawers with two short and three long drawers, with boxwood banding and brass handles, standing on shaped bracket feet.

- *90cm x 88cm*
- **£1,425** • Rushlight

English Mahogany Chest of Drawers ▼

- *circa 1780*

Fine English mahogany chest of two small and three long drawers standing on plain bracket feet.

- *height 1.06m*
- **£2,550** • C. Preston

Oak Coffer ▲

- *circa 1780*

George III oak chest with carving to the front standing on square straight legs.

- *height 56cm*
- **£6,850** • Paul Hopwell

Mahogany Chest of Drawers ▲

- *circa 1880*

A late Victorian mahogany chest of drawers, consisting of three deep drawers with original brass swan neck handles, on low bracket feet.

- *85cm x 1.15m*
- **£1,500** • Drummonds

Mahogany Chest of Drawers ◀

- **1790**

One of a pair of small mahogany chests of drawers with three drawers with ebony moulding, brass handles, standing on bracket feet.
- *height 66cm*
- **£1,750**   • A.I.G.

Chest on Chest ▼

- *circa 1760*

Fine George III beautifully figured mahogany chest on chest, with dentil moulded cornice above an upper section of two short and six long drawers, supported on ogee bracket feet.
- *1.95m x 1.02m*
- **£12,750**   • Wakelin Linfield

Georgian Chest of Drawers ▲

- *circa 1790*

Georgian chest of two short and three long drawers, with swan neck handles, standing on bracket feet,
- *1.13m x 98cm*
- **£1,475**   • The Swan

Walnut Chest of Drawers ▲

- *circa 1820*

Walnut chest of four drawers standing on bracket feet, with original handles.
- *height 98cm*
- **£4,800**   • Denzil Grant

French Mahogany Commode ▲

- *circa 1840*

French flame mahogany commode with original marble top and one long and three deep drawers on a straight base with small plain bracket feet.
- *width 1.12m*
- **£2,250**   • C. Preston

Walnut Chest on Stand ◀

- *circa 1920*
Pretty walnut chest with seven drawers on cabriole legs.
- *1.27m x 43cm x 76.2cm*
- **£2,450** • **Manser Antiques**

George I Walnut Chest on Stand ▲

- *circa 1715*
George I chest on stand, the upper part with a cross grained cavetto cornice above five boxwood and ebony chevron inlaid drawers. The stand comprising a long central and two short side drawers, standing on walnut cabriole legs.
- *1.56m x 58.5cm x 1.06m*
- **£13,200** • **R. Gardner**

William & Mary Walnut Chest on Stand ▲

- *circa 1700*
A walnut veneered chest on stand, the upper section with two short and three long drawers on a stand with one long central drawer flanked by two deep drawers above an arched apron.
- *1.58m x 56cm x 1.04m*
- **£14,850** • **R. Gardner**

Walnut and Marquetry Chest of Drawers ▼

- *circa 1695*
Late 17th century walnut and marquetry chest of drawers, with two short and three long drawers. Fine ornate scrolled designs on front and top, raised on moulded bracket feet.
- *89cm x 54.6cm x 96.5cm*
- **£12,850** • **M. Norman**

Chippendale Chest on Chest ▲

- *circa 1760*
Chippendale period mahogany chest on chest with dentil moulded cornice and finely carved frieze above an upper section of two short and six long drawers, supported on ogee bracket feet.
- *1.79m x 54.6cm x 1.11m*
- **£8,850** • **M. Norman**

George III Chest of Drawers ▶

- *circa 1810*
Satinwood bow front chest of four drawers on a moulded apron with slay bracket feet and original fittings.
- *99cm x 58.4cm x 1.08m*
- **£13,850** • **M. Norman**

George I Walnut Veneered Chest of Drawers ▶
- *circa 1720*

George I chest of drawers with a well figured quartered top with chequered stringing and cross-banding. Five chequered strung standing on a plinth base with restored bracket feet.
- *95.3cm x 52.7cm x 95.3cm*
- **£13,500** • **Hallidays**

Oak Chest of Drawers ▼
- *circa 1760*

Mid 18th century chest of drawers of good proportions on ogee feet with very good original ormolu handles in the rococo taste.
- *81cm x 52cm x 92cm*
- **£4,950** • **John Beazor**

Mahogany Chest of Drawers ▼
- *circa 1750*

Chest of four graduated drawers with re-entrant corners, a brushing slide, and replacement handles. Unusually small and good colour.
- *74cm x 46cm x 76cm*
- **£4,450** • **John Beazor**

Olivewood Chest of Drawers ▲
- *circa 1860*

William and Mary oyster olivewood chest of drawers having a top with matching oysters and geometric circles of holly inlay. Two short and three long drawers similarly decorated supported on bun feet.
- *79cm x 54.6cm x 85cm*
- **£29,000** • **Hallidays**

Chest On Chest ◀
- *circa 1760–70*

A chest on chest of the Chippendale period with original shaped swan neck handles and escutcheons; the top with reed canted sides and dentil cornice.
- *79cm x 55cm x 1.3m*
- **£5,750** • **John Beazor**

Expert Tips

From the eighteenth century drawer fronts are flat with overlapping ovolo moulding. From c.1735 cock beading was introduced. Herringbone crossbanding was used from c.1690–1720 as was inlaid boxwood decoration.

Davenports

Victorian Davenport ▶
● *circa 1870*
An unusual Victorian burr walnut rising top davenport, enclosing a fitted interior and pull out ratcheted writing slope.
● *90cm x 60cm*
● **£4,350**   ● **Amandini**

Regency Davenport ▲
● *circa 1820*
A Regency style faux rosewood davenport with pen drawer to right hand side and a removable fire screen.
● *98cm x 51cm*
● **£995**   ● **Clarke & Denny**

Walnut Davenport ▲
● *circa 1860*
Fine walnut Victorian davenport with original leather, inlaid with satinwood, with four side drawers, pierced brass rail and maple interior.
● *height 88cm*
● **£1,950**   ● **Old Cinema**

Burr Walnut Davenport ▼
● *circa 1860*
Burr walnut davenport with piano lid, central cupboard flanked by eight small side drawers with turned wood handles.
● *98cm x 62cm*
● **£3,750**   ● **The Swan**

Rosewood Davenport ▼
● *circa 1820*
Small Regency rosewood davenport, with pierced brass gallery and pen drawer to the side of a writing slope with unusual side action.
● *88cm x 34cm*
● **£3,995**   ● **W. John Griffiths**

Expert Tips

The name davenport came from an entry in the book of Captain Davenport in the 1790s. Look out for the following:

fine veneer in walnut
panelled back
original inkwells
pen trays
mother of pearl escutcheons
secret drawers

Up to 1840 their style was quite plain, but after 1840 davenports tended to be more feminine, with scrolled supports.

Walnut Davenport ◀
● *circa 1840*
An English figured walnut davenport with stunning matched sunburst veneers. The sliding top is fitted with a hinged pen and inkwell drawer raised above four graduated drawers and four dummy panel drawers supported on a shaped plinth base.
● *79cm x 46cm*
● **£7,500**   ● **Freshfords**

Piano Front Davenport ▼

- *19th century*

A walnut piano front davenport
with a rising stationery
compartment, having four
drawers, behind a cupboard door,
to the right-hand side.
- *91.4cm x 63.5cm x 58.4cm*
- **£5,850** • **Dorking Desk**

Victorian Walnut Davenport ▼

- *1860*

Davenport with green inlayed top
and four drawers.
- *height 96cm*
- **£1,050** • **Bruschweiler**

William IV Davenport ▶

- *circa 1835*

William IV satinwood veneered
davenport in the Gillows manner
with a galleried sliding top and
front and rear panelling all
standing on lobbed feet with
recessed castors.
- *85cm x 57cm x 52cm*
- **£8,250** • **R. Gardner**

Rosewood Davenport ▲

- *19th century*

A Rosewood davenport having
five drawers and decorative
carvings
- *1.19m x 30.5cm x 50.8cm*
- **£2,850** • **Dorking Desk**

Mahogany Davenport ▼

- *19th century*

Mahogany davenport desk with
brass top columns and old leather
top.
- *78.7cm x 53.3cm x 53.3cm*
- **£2,700** • **Dorking Desk**

Expert Tips

*The handles of davenport
drawers should always be of
turned, wooden knobs.*

George IV Rosewood Davenport ◀

- *circa 1825*

A rosewood davenport in the
manner of Gillows, the sliding
top with brass gallery and secret
pen drawer and the pedestal with
four fluted corner pilasters.
- *90cm x 58cm x 52.5cm*
- **£8,450** • **R. Gardner**

Desks

Bonheur du Jour ▼
- *circa 1890*

Bonheur du jour with pierced brass rail and two small drawers, flanked by cupboards with circular inlay panels and a gallery single drawer, standing on slender tapering legs.
- *1.04m x 73cm*
- £1,150
- The Swan

Victorian Dressing Table ▼
- *circa 1870*

Fine quality Victorian burr walnut dressing table and mirror supported by scrolled carving.
- *height 1.74m*
- £2,800
- Hill Farm

George IV Bonheur du Jour ▲
- *circa 1825*

George IV rosewood writing table in solid and veneered rosewood. With pierced gallery drawers and moving writing slide supported by twist columns.
- *height 1.22m*
- £7,800
- Gerald Brodie

Sheraton Bonheur du Jour ▲
- *circa 1790*

Fine Sheraton period bonheur du jour, with harewood inlay fold-over tops, enclosing a rising nest of drawers and pigeonholes.
- *89cm x 1.14m*
- £22,500
- John Bly

Victorian Dressing Table ▲
- *circa 1880*

Victorian mahogany dressing table with central mirror and drawer, flanked by eight small drawers.
- *height 1.67m*
- £2,350
- C. Preston

Bonheur du Jour ▼
- *circa 1890*

Late Victorian mahogany bonheur du jour with satinwood stringing, a roll top cover, the interior fitted with five pigeonholes and a central small drawer, above a pull-out writing slope and two drawers, the whole on straight legs.
- *1.03m x 72cm*
- £1,500
- Macnaughton-Smith

Chippendale Style Bonheur du Jour ▼
- *circa 19th century*

Chippendale-style bonheur du jour in the style of Angelica Kauffman, decorated with floral designs and classical scenes in the finest satin wood. Shield style bevelled glazed mirror with urn finial, standing on delicate turned legs.
- *1.65m x 1.07m*
- £24,500
- J. & T. Stone

Louis XVI Desk ▲

- *circa 1800*

A Louis XVI Swedish Gustavian desk, with long drawer, plain gilt ring handle, raised on slender tapered legs.
- *75cm x 80cm*
- **£1,950** • **Rupert Cavendish**

Mahogany Partner's Desk ▲

- *circa 1825*

A historically important George IV mahogany partner's desk by Robert Lawson for Gillows of Lancaster. With a central drawer above the kneehole flanked by a bank of four drawers. Each pedestal with vertical reeded pilasters. The pedestals supported on plinth bases with gilded castors, all locks original.
- *79cm x 1.83m*
- **£95,000** • **Anthony Outred**

Louis XV Bureau Plat ▲

- *circa 1900*

Fine French Louis XV style mahogany bureau plat with gilt bronze mounts.
- *80cm x 1.45m x 76cm*
- **£9,500** • **Hatchwell**

Satinwood Writing Table ▼

- *1870*

Satinwood and ormolu writing table. The top with egg and dart moulded rim, above two side drawers, raised on four reeded legs on original brass castors, by Wright & Mansfield.
- *74cm x 1.1m*
- **£10,500** • **Butchoff**

Satinwood Desk ▼

- *circa 1890*

Sheraton revival high quality Victorian inlaid satin wood pedestal desk with two side compartments. The base containing single drawer, stamped "Maple & Co.".
- *1.24m x 1m*
- **£12,500** • **J. & T. Stone**

Georgian Mahogany Desk ▶

- *circa 1820s*

Georgian kneehole mahogany desk with leather top, two long and two small drawers, original laurel wreath brass handles.
- *79cm x 1.01m*
- **£1,350** • **Old Cinema**

George II Partner's Desk ▲

- *circa 1755*

George II ebony-inlaid mahogany partners pedestal desk with a rich, untouched patina. The rectangular leather inset top above three mahogany-lined frieze drawers to each side and two simulated drawers with carrying-handles to each. Raised on a plinth base.
- *80.5cm x 1.4m*
- **£68,000** • **Anthony Outred**

Birchwood Desk ▲

- *circa 1890s*

Swedish free-standing veneered Biedermeier style birchwood desk. The top with leather insert and three drawers, above two pedestals with panelled doors.
- *76cm x 1.43m*
- **£5,900** • **Rupert Cavendish**

Double-sided Desk ▶
- *19th century*
A rare decorative double-sided
Continental pedestal partners
desk having pull-out slides to
either end with dummy drawers
and working cupboards to the rear.
- *1.68m x 91.4cm*
- **£7,500**   • **Dorking Desk**

Kidney-shaped Pedestal Desk ▲
- *circa 1840*
Kidney-shaped pedestal desk, by
Gillow of Lancaster, finished in
mellow English oak, with brown-
oak, cross-banded inlays, and
mahogany drawer linings.
- *72.5cm x 76cm x 1.36m*
- **£39,000**   • **Freshfords**

Shoolbred Desk ▲
- *19th century*
A fine oak swivel pedestal desk
by J. A. S. Shoolbred.
- *89cm x 71cm x 1.5m*
- **£6,800**   • **Dorking Desk**

Golden Oak Desk ▲
- *19th century*
Golden oak panelled kneehole
desk with flush fitted brass
handles, hide leather top, slides
and moulded drawers.
- *1.37m x 86.4cm*
- **£3,200**   • **Dorking Desk**

Oak Office Desk ▼
- *20th century*
An all-in-one oak office desk,
having seven drawers.
- *1.14m x 68.6cm*
- **£375**   • **Dorking Desk**

Marquetry Desk ◀
- *19th century*
An exceptional early 19th
century double sided pedestal
desk having fine inlaid detail to
all sides.
- *1.50m x 89cm*
- **£12,500**   • **Dorking Desk**

Georgian Slope Top Desk ▶

- *Late 18th – early 17th century*
A fine Georgian slope top writing desk having tapered legs and a single cockbeaded drawer with an early solid brass handle.
- *86.3cm x 45.72cm x 55.88cm*
- £880 • Dorking Desk

S-shaped Roll Top Desk ▼

- *19th century*
A 19th century oak S-shaped roll top desk with well fitted interior.
- *1.32m x 81.3cm x 1.27m*
- £2,500 • Dorking Desk

Expert Tips

The best kneehole desks, dating from the mid-eighteenth century, have six bracket feet. Those with only four feet may have been cut down from chests of drawers.

Regency Writing Table ▼

- *1811 – 1830*
A superb quality Regency mahogany writing table having three drawers to the front and three to the rear with original turned knobs stamped "M Willson 68 Great Queen Street".
- *1.52m x 96.5cm*
- £12,500 • Dorking Desk

Knee-hole Desk ▼

- *19th century*
A mahogany display serpentine knee-hole desk with polished lift-up top and four bracket feet.
- *1.07m x 58.42cm*
- £6,500 • Dorking Desk

Walnut Lady's Desk ▼

- *1870*
Victorian burr walnut lady's desk with inlay and green leather insert.
- *80cm x 121cm x 152cm*
- £1,950 • Bruschweiler

Wooten Desk ▼

- *19th century*
A well fitted solid walnut Wooten desk with rare provenance.
- *1.52m x 68.6cm x 99cm*
- £6,500 • Dorking Desk

Walnut Cabriole Leg Desk ◀

- *Early 20th century*
Fine walnut leather-topped
writing desk raised on cabriole
legs, with curved front, the
central drawer flanked by two
deep drawers.
- *71cm x 61cm x 1.22m*
- **£1,950** • **Manser Antiques**

Walnut Kidney Shaped Pedestal Desk ▲

- *circa 1845*
A pedestal desk with an inset
leather writing surface with brass
gallery, above three frieze drawers,
the right one concealing a
mechanism allowing the top to
swivel revealing secret recess.
- *78.5cm x 66.5cm x 1.34m*
- **£67,500** • **R. Gardner**

Mahogany Writing Desk ◀

- *circa 1820*
Early 19th century mahogany
writing desk from Gillow model.
- *94cm x 61cm x 56cm*
- **£12,500** • **M. Norman**

Mahogany Twin Pedestal Partner's Desk ▼

- *circa 1830*
A partner's desk having a gilt
tooled green leather top with
each pedestal comprising drawers
to one side and a cupboard to the
other.
- *76cm x 1.09m x 1.85m*
- **£23,750** • **R. Gardner**

Carlton House Mahogany Desk ▶

- *circa 1890*
An English George III style
kidney-shaped Carlton House
mahogany desk with brass gallery
and legs terminating in wheels.
- *1.04m x 81cm x 1.39m*
- **£11,000** • **Adrian Alan**

Tambour Front Writing Table ▲

- *circa 1800*
A superb George III mahogany
tambour front writing table with
roll top. Interior fitted with
pigeon holes above a kneehole
flanked by nine drawers with
brass swan-necked handles.
- *1.01m x 1.37m x 78.7cm*
- **£12,850** • **M. Norman**

George III Writing Table ◄

- *circa 1800*

George III mahogany writing table on tapered legs with brass castors, incorporating a raised writing slide.

- *77.5cm x 95.3cm x 64cm*
- **£4,750** • **M. Norman**

Walnut Kneehole Desk ▶

- *circa 1715*

George I desk having a quartered top and cross-banded moulded edge. Below is a single drawer supported by three drawers to either side with cock-beaded edges and herringbone decoration and original furniture.

- *73.6cm x 54.6cm x 86.4cm*
- **£19,000** • **Hallidays**

Lady's Kneehole Writing Desk ▲

- *1735-40*

A George II lady's kingwood writing desk with a figured surface above a full length drawer. In between sets of three short drawers is a cupboard with moulded panel door and a false drawer with blind fret carving.

- *85cm x 47cm x 83cm*
- **£29,000** • **Hallidays**

Pedestal Desk ▲

- *19th century*

A superb pedestal desk having nine drawers to the front and two cupboards to the rear with original turned knobs and a full hide leather top. Formerly owned by Sir Admiral A.H. Markham.

- *1.49m x 83.8cm*
- **£12,500** • **Dorking Desk**

Mahogany Kneehole Desk ◄

- *circa 1910*

A mahogany desk of large size, standing on ogee bracket feet and retaining original handles.

- *width 1.37m*
- **£1,850** • **Walter Moores**

Mahogany Desk ▲

- *circa 1900*

Early twentieth century kneehole desk with new leather inlay, raised on a plinth base.

- *76cm x 80cm x 1.5m*
- **£1,475** • **Millers Antiques**

Dressers

Oak Dresser Base ▶

- *circa 1780*

George III oak dresser base with central panelled door flanked by two sets of three long drawers with original brass handles, and standing on bracket feet.
- *height 1.1m*
- **£14,750** • **Paul Hopwell**

George II Oak Dresser ▲

- *circa 1750*

George II oak dresser with panelled back, two shelves with three small drawers with turned handles and two cupboards below standing on straight square legs.
- *height 2.45m*
- **£11,750** • **Paul Hopwell**

Victorian Sideboard ▲

- *circa 1880*

Impressive sideboard with a deep central drawer, centered with a raised ivory classical plaque, flanked by two deep large cupboards, standing on two pedestals with bun feet.
- *90cm x 1.98m*
- **£4,850** • **Drummonds**

George III Plate Rack ▲

- *circa 1780*

George III open oak plate rack with pierced rail and architectural side columns.
- *height 1.02m*
- **£3,750** • **Paul Hopwell**

Pine Open Dresser ◀

- *circa 1880*

Open back pine dresser with four shelves. The base with three long drawers above three panelled cupboard doors, with alloy handles and fittings.
- *2.75m x 1.7m*
- **£850** • **Drummonds**

French Dresser ▼

- *circa 1820*

French provincial fruitwood galleried four shelf dresser with two long drawers and cupboards below.
- *width 1.27m*
- **£3,850** • **C. Preston**

Breakfront Sideboard ▲

- *circa 1800*

Mahogany breakfront D-shaped
sideboard, one cellaret drawer
and a shallow centre drawer over
a linen drawer. Raised on four
front finely reeded legs and two
turned back legs.
- *94.5cm x 1.68m x 66.5cm*
- **£16,500** • **Wakelin Linfield**

George III Oak Rack ▲

- *circa 1790*

George III oak wall-mounted
dresser with moulded and shaped
cornice and three shelves flanked
either side with additional
shelving.
- *height 97cm*
- **£3,250** • **Paul Hopwell**

Pine Glazed Dresser ▲

- *circa 1840*

Pine dresser with three glazed
doors enclosing three shelves, with
two long drawers and cupboards
below with brass knob handles.
- *2.35m x 1.7m*
- **£1,600** • **Drummonds**

Oak Dresser Base ▲

- *circa 1786*

George III oak dresser base. Carved
drawers with geometric designs,
with brass drop handles, the
whole raised on turned front legs.
- *height 97cm*
- **£22,500** • **Paul Hopwell**

Pine Dressers ▶

- *circa 1820*

One of a pair of unusual narrow
pine dressers or bookcases with
panelled backs and adjustable
shelves.
- *width 67cm*
- **£3,350** • **C. Preston**

Miniature Dresser ◀

- *circa 1890*

Miniature English oak dresser
with moulded gallery, turned
supports all above carved panel
doors and turned bun feet.
- *height 47cm*
- **£225** • **Great Grooms**

Oversized Dresser ▲

- *circa 1840*

Large pine dresser painted pea
green, with moulded pediment
and two central cupboards
flanked by four deep long drawers
with brass handles, standing on a
straight base.
- *height 4.25m*
- **£3,650** • **Drummonds**

Dumb Waiters & Whatnots

Mahogany Whatnot ▶
- *circa 1880*
Mahogany whatnot with five
graduated serpentine tiers with
turned finials and barley twist
supports.
- *height 1.25m*
- £350   • The Swan

William IV Dumbwaiter ▲
- *1825*
One of a pair of mahogany
dumbwaiters with brass gallery,
three well figured shelves, raised
on carved supports with bun feet.
- *1.17m x 1.24m*
- £16,500   • Butchoff

Brass Cake Stand ▼
- *1890*
Victorian lacquered brass cake-
stand with two circular tiers
embossed with an organic
repeating design, raised on
scrolled legs with hoof feet.
- *height 88cm*
- £295   • A.I.G.

Oriental Cake Stand ▶
- *1880*
Oriental cake stand with three
circular tiers carved with six-leaf
shaped receptacles, around a
central circular design, within a
carved frame.
- *height 82cm*
- £110   • Poppets

George II Washstand ▲
- *circa 1750*
George II mahogany two tier
washstand with fan carving to the
sides, and a small drawer standing
on slender legs and pad feet.
- *height 85cm*
- £3,850   • John Bly

Walnut Whatnot ▼
- *1880*
Victorian burr walnut whatnot
with pierced gallery and turned
finials, three well-figured tiers,
with turned supports the lower
section with single drawer and
wood knob handles, on turned
legs with original castors.
- *height 1.22m*
- £2,200   • Salem Antiques

Four Tier Walnut Whatnot ▲

- *circa 1880*

Four tier walnut corner whatnot inlaid with boxwood and burr walnut, with acorn finial and turned supports.
- *height 1.37m*
- £875　　　• The Swan

Satin Birch Whatnot ▲

- *circa 1840*

An English satin birchwood whatnot with three shelves, the lower section with a single drawer with barley-twist supports, stamped "Mills Cabinetmakers", raised on gadrooned feet with original brass castors.
- *99cm x 53cm x 39.5cm*
- £4,250　　　• O. F. Wilson

George III Whatnot ◄

- *circa 1790*

Unusual mahogany George III whatnot. The rising with ratcheted bracket and four shelves below. The whole on square section legs and square caped castors.
- *height 1.14m*
- £6,500　　　• John Bly

Cake Stand ▲

- *circa 1880*

Mahogany cake stand with satin wood banding, incorporating three graduated circular shelves, within wood frame, open at one side, surmounted by a ball finial, raised on splayed legs.
- *height 93cm*
- £280　　　• John Clay

Walnut Whatnot ◄

- *circa 1870*

A Victorian walnut three-tier whatnot with carved scrolled pierced gallery and elaborately turned supports.
- *height 1.32m*
- £1,950　　　• The Swan

Mahogany Washstand ▲

- *circa 1860*
Mahogany washstand inset with a circular pink marble top and two shelves, supported by pillared turned legs on a triangular base, raised on shallow bun feet.
- *85cm x 32cm*
- **£980** • **The Lacquer Chest**

Mahogany Plant Stand ▲

- *circa 1870s*
Fine Victorian mahogany plant stand, with a slender baluster column on three curved legs with drop turned finial.
- *90cm x 29cm*
- **£495** • **Old Cinema**

Walnut Whatnot ▼

- *circa 1870s*
Victorian walnut whatnot, the scrolled gallery with turned finials, above four graduated triangular tiers, with carved apron and turned supports.
- *1.3m x 57cm*
- **£550** • **Old Cinema**

Teak Whatnot ▼

- *1890*
Victorian corner whatnot made from teak with scrolled gallery, above four graduated tiers, supported by turned Solomonaic columns.
- *height 1.27m*
- **£450** • **Salem Antiques**

Regency Rosewood Whatnot ▲

- *circa 1825*
English Regency rosewood whatnot of small proportions with three well-figured tiers, raised on finely turned supports, the middle tier having a fitted drawer with small brass circular handles.
- *1.02m x 38cm*
- **£4,650** • **Freshfords**

French Etagère ▲

- *1890*
French etagère with pierced brass gallery, single narrow drawer with brass handle and two shelves below, on ebonised shaped legs.
- *height 94cm*
- **£675** • **Vale Antiques**

Mirrors

Mahogany Dressing Mirror ▶
- *circa 1770*
George III dressing mirror hung between two scratch stock moulded tapered supports with adjustable brass thumb side screws and small brass urn finials. The stepped base is fitted with three oak lined drawers.
- 63cm x 20.5cm x 42.5cm
- £1,000–£2,000 • J. Collins

Gilt Mirror ▲
- *circa 1880*
Fine Victorian oval mirror with original gilt.
- 1.63m x 1.6m
- £3,250 • Manser Antiques

Cheval Mirror ▲
- *circa 1815*
Regency mahogany cheval mirror with satinwood inlaid panels, with turned supports and stretchers.
- 1.64m x 58.5cm x 66cm
- £3,500 • R. Gardner

Giltwood Convex Mirror ▼
- *circa 1820*
A circular convex mirror with a carved acanthus leaf crest, cornucopia mounted shoulders, and carved scrolling acanthus leaves to the base.
- 1.38m x 82.5cm
- £15,000 • J. Collins

Gilded Wood Pier Mirror ▼
- *circa 1790*
A late eighteenth century Italian carved and gilded wood pier mirror in an English design.
- 1.83m x 86.5cm
- £7,800 • Haughey

Overmantle Mirror ▼
- *Early 19th century*
Regency overmantle mirror with gilt wood frame and foliate mouldings.
- 1.29m 1.35m
- £1,650 • Manser Antiques

George II Mirror ◀
- *circa 1730*
A George II mirror with a swan neck pediment, tasselled drapery and a later ho-ho bird. The frame is covered in fine gesso carving with a ring-punched ground typical of the first quarter of the 18th century.
- 1.81m x 87cm
- £25,500 • R. Gardner

Giltwood Oval Mirrors ▲

- *circa 1840*
One of a pair of finely carved oval
English mirrors with carved
giltwood vine leaves and grapes
with bead and red moulding, and
original plate glass.
- *1.08m x 90cm*
- £8,000 ● O. F. Wilson

French Giltwood Mirror ▲

- *circa 1890s*
Oval French giltwood mirror with
carved roses placed intermittently
on a moulded wood frame.
- *82cm x 51cm*
- £1,300 ● Looking Glass

Regency Overmantle Mirror ▲

- *circa 1820*
Regency giltwood overmantle
mirror, with architectural designs,
surmounted by a frieze depicting
the procession of Jupiter.
- *length 1.39m*
- £3,500 ● Great Grooms

Mercury Plate Mirror ▶

- *circa 1800s*
Rectangular Austro-Hungarian
water-gilt looking-glass with a
scrolling floral border and
original plate glass.
- *96.5cm x 81cm*
- £5,350 ● Looking Glass

Regency Toilet Mirror ▼

- *circa 1810*
Regency mahogany toilet mirror
with three drawers, cross-banded
in satinwood with boxwood and
ebony stringing.
- *height 68cm*
- £1,150 ● Barry Cotton

French Oval Mirror ▼

- *circa 1850*
Small oval French mirror with
elaborate carved foliate and
acorn border.
- *53.4cm x 46cm*
- £1,400 ● Looking Glass

Victorian Mirror ▶

- *circa 1870*
Victorian oval gilt framed mirror
with triple candle sconce and
beaded rim, surmounted by a
scrolled finial.
- *height 75cm*
- £685 ● The Swan

French Mirror ▲

- *circa 1860*
A fine, imposing French gilt
wood and gesso looking-glass in
the Louis XV manner. The
arched framed headed by a foliate
and shell cresting.
- *1.94m x 1.32m*
- £1,950 ● Westland & Co

Italian Mirror ▼

- *circa 1780*

An 18th century Italian mirror with egg and leaf design, cavetto and a Rococo shell at the base.

- *1.32m x 86.5cm*
- **£5,500**   ● R. Gardner

Napoleon III Marginal Frame Mirror ▲

- *circa 1850*

One of a pair of French Napoleon III carved and giltwood marginal frame mirrors in the 18th century Regency style.

- *2.76m x 1.73m*
- **£88,000**   ● Adrian Alan

George II Gilt Framed Mirror ▲

- *circa 1740*

A gilt framed mirror with bevelled plate bordered with bead and reel and leaf moulded decoration. The apron decorated with Prince of Wales feathers and rosettes, surmounted by a swan neck pediment.

- *1.35m x 64cm*
- **£15,800**   ● R. Gardner

Gesso Mirror ▼

- *circa 1890*

An ornately carved French rococo giltwood and gesso mirror.

- *1.24m x 84cm*
- **£8,500**   ● Adrian Alan

Breman Oval Giltwood Mirror ▲

- *circa 1820*

A German Breman oval mirror, with the plate flanked by guilloched cornucopia issuing flowers and fruit. The cresting applied with a foliate spray and the apron with eagle heads, flanking a foliate band.

- *87cm x 78cm*
- **£4,600**   ● Adrian Alan

Chinoiserie Overmantle Mirror ◄

- *circa 1815*

Mirror in the "Brighton Pavilion" style carved with umbrellas and a cavetto-moulded cornice with dolphins, with one standing and two seated Chinamen above.

- *1.70m x 1.45m*
- **£47,000**   ● Adrian Alan

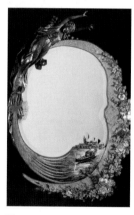

Venetian Mosaic and Carved Walnut Mirror ▲

- *circa 1880*

A Venetian mirror depicting day and night, with a walnut maiden with outstretched arms to the left and blossoming foliage and a shooting star that encircles a Venetian scene to the right.

- *1.45m x 1.01m*
- **£68,000**   ● Adrian Alan

Regency Mirror ▲

- *circa 1830*

A small giltwood Regency mirror of rectangular shape.
- *51cm x 1.13m*
- **£1,850**   • **Westland & Co**

William & Mary Mirror ▲

- *circa 1690*

Fine William & Mary cushion frame mirror, decorated with floral and bird motifs including stained ivory.
- *1.09m x 92cm*
- **£22,500**   • **Wakelin Linfield**

Giltwood Mirror ▼

- **1870**

French carved giltwood mirror on red bouille, with moulded rim.
- *height 1.17m*
- **£650**   • **Augustus Brandt**

Victorian Gilt Mirror ▲

- *circa 1860s*

A mid-Victorian circular mirror, verre eglomisé, with swept arch, surmounted by a large carved eagle motif.
- *89cm x 43cm*
- **£1,750**   • **Looking Glass**

Adam Style Gilt Mirror ◄

- *circa 1880*

English Adam-style gilt mirror surmounted by an urn finial above a strung lyre, flanked by foliate swags. The base with swept berried and bunched laurel bracket carving.
- *1.56m x 71cm*
- **£12,800**   • **Anthony Outred**

Italian Carved Mirror ▲

- *circa 1810*

Giltwood mirror with a carved, scrolled floral border, surmounted by a scallop shell and a head of a young girl at the base.
- *99cm x 68.5cm*
- **£3,600**   • **Looking Glass**

Regency Convex Mirror ▲

- *circa 1820s*

Fine Regency giltwood convex mirror with ebonised slip and ball-encrusted frame, surmounted by an eagle suspending a ball on a columned finial.
- *99cm x 56cm*
- **£3,950**   • **Looking Glass**

George II Walnut Mirror ▶

- *circa 1735*
George II walnut and giltwood
mirror with fine gilded swan neck
pediment culminating in a
central golden bird and gilded
foliate carved decorations to the
sides.
- *1.32m x 3.8cm x 63.5cm*
- **£6,850**   • **M. Norman**

Walnut and Giltwood Wall Mirror ▲

- *circa 1735*
George II walnut fret-cut mirror
with gilded motif and inner slip.
- *1.04m x 46.4cm*
- **£2,250**   • **M. Norman**

Victorian Wall Mirror ▲

- *circa 1860*
A Victorian gilt composition oval
wall mirror with a later glass and
fine carved, scrolled floral border.
- *1.6m x 1.02m*
- **£4,800**   • **House of Mirrors**

Regency Cheval Mirror ▼

- *circa 1825*
Regency period mahogany cheval
mirror with candle arms.
- *1.84m x 61cm x 83cm*
- **£9,500**   • **M. Norman**

Regency Giltwood Convex Mirror ▼

- *circa 1820*
One of a pair of Regency convex
mirrors, fine carved foliate
decoration and beading
surmounted by an ebonised eagle.
- *1.33m x 6.4cm x 83cm*
- **£37,500**   • **M. Norman**

Chippendale Mirror ▼

- *circa 1760*
Chippendale carved walnut and
giltwood looking glass.
- *71cm x 44.5cm*
- **£950**   • **M. Norman**

Expert Tips

*Mirror glass made before the
1780s was small. Large mirrors
were made up of several pieces.*

Cushion Mirror ◀

- *circa 1710*
Eighteenth century walnut
veneered cushion mirror with
beaded edges.
- *58.4cm x 54.6cm*
- **£3,950**   • **M. Norman**

William IV Giltwood Mirror ▲

- *circa 1835*

William IV period giltwood and gesso convex mirror with a carved frame depicting acorns and foliage, surmounted by a crest in the form of a seated deer upon a rocky ground, the mirror fitted with sconces in the form of serpents.

- *1.12m x 76cm*
- **£7,500** • **Anthony Outred**

Irish Mirror ▶

- *circa 1850s*

Irish oval mirror with a blue and gold strip border on the mirror.

- *71cm x 46cm*
- **£2,500** • **Looking Glass**

Venetian Giltwood Mirror ▲

- *circa 1780*

Venetian giltwood mirror with lion, armorial crest and trophies, with trailing foliate designs to the rim, with original plate glass.

- *84cm x 47cm*
- **£3,800** • **O. F. Wilson**

Italian Giltwood Mirror ▼

- *circa 1780*

Italian giltwood swept mirror with carved scrolling, in the form of decoration depicting trailing ivy and small pink roses.

- *49cm x 44cm*
- **£650** • **Augustus Brandt**

Venetian Mercury Plate Mirror ▼

- *circa 1850s*

Small mid 19th century Venetian blue oval glass mirror, etched with floral sprays, with original mercury plate mirror.

- *56cm x 43cm*
- **£2,250** • **Looking Glass**

Regency Girandole Mirror ▲

- *circa 1820s*

Regency giltwood convex mirror, with ebonised slip surrounded by ropework design, surmounted by a giltwood deer and grapevines, at the base stylised leaf designs flanked by two scrolled candle holders of candle holders.

- *1.04m x 56cm*
- **£4,250** • **Looking Glass**

Victorian Mirror ▲

- *circa 1870s*

One of a pair of rectangular giltwood mirrors with arched top surmounted by a stylised acanthus leaf, flanked by giltwood urn finials, and a carved border with foliate swag decoration.

- *94cm x 53cm*
- **£3,250** • **Looking Glass**

Gooderson Mirror ▶

- *circa 1730*
Eighteenth century giltwood
mirror in the manner of
Gooderson.
- *1.55m x 90cm*
- **£15,500**   • M. Norman

Victorian Overmantle Mirror ▲

- *circa 1880*
A Victorian gilt composition
overmantle mirror with old glass
and ornate foliate carving.
- *94cm x 1.29m*
- **£2,350**   • House of Mirrors

Gilt Overmantle Mirror ▲

- *circa 1880*
A fine classical inspired Victorian
gilt composition overmantle
mirror with old glass,
architectural pediment and
scrolled elements to the base.
- *1.70m x 1.57m*
- **£3,600**   • House of Mirrors

Expert Tips

*Unlike modern glass, mirrors
from the eighteenth century
project a dark and shadowy
image. It will have oxidised
in places and become
non-reflective. Resist the
temptation to restore.*

Victorian Overmantle Mirror ▼

- *circa 1880*
A Victorian gilt composition
overmantle mirror with old glass,
rounded corners, surmounted by
ornate scrolled element.
- *137cm x 122cm*
- **£2,630**   • House of Mirrors

George III Bird and Leaf Mirror ▼

- *circa 1760*
An early George III mahogany
framed mirror crested with a
gilded ho-ho bird and scrolling
leaf work, attractive carved leaf
drops to either side with gilded
slip holding the original plate.
- *1.18m x 52cm*
- **£7,600**   • Hallidays

Victorian Overmantle Mirror ▼

- *circa 1880*
A Victorian gilt composition
overmantle mirror, with central
gilt scallop shell and foliate
scrolled elements and ornate
gilded columns to the sides.
- *1.27m x 1.63m*
- **£5,430**   • House of Mirrors

Landscape Wall Mirror ▶

- *circa 1870*
Victorian gilt composition
landscape wall mirror with
original gilding and glass.
  - *1.2m x 1.45m*
  - **£6,600** • **House of Mirrors**

Glass and Ormolu Wall Bracket ▲

- *circa 1850*
One of a pair of mirrored glass
and ormolu wall brackets with
double candle sconce with ornate
blue and gold scrolled designs.
  - *52cm x 23cm*
  - **£3,750** • **M. Norman**

"Old French" Giltwood Overmantle Mirror ▲

- *circa 1830*
A carved giltwood overmantle
mirror in the "Old French" or
neo-Rococo style with bold
scrolled acanthus leaf decoration
and reeded columns.
  - *2.03m x 1.53m*
  - **£13,500** • **Freshfords**

Victorian Overmantle Mirror ▼

- *circa 1880*
A Victorian gilt composition
overmantle mirror with old glass,
rounded top with carved
pediment, turned and decorated
columns to the sides with vase
finials.
  - *1.63m x 1.53m*
  - **£5,100** • **House of Mirrors**

Victorial Oval Gilt Mirror ▲

- *circa 1880*
A Victorian gilt composition
overmantle mirror with old glass.
Oval design with beaded edge,
surmounted by ornate scrollwork.
and crest carving.
  - *1.24m x 1.12m*
  - **£2,700** • **House of Mirrors**

Oval Girandole Mirror ▼

- *circa 1880*
A Victorian gilt composition oval
girandole mirror with a later
glass.
  - *1.37m x 71cm*
  - **£3,400** • **House of Mirrors**

Miscellaneous

Library Steps ▼
• **1770**
French library steps made from
walnut consisting of four steps,
with turned and carved
decoration.
• *99cm*
• **£4,850**   • **Augustus Brandt**

Music Stand ▼
• *circa 1825*
Regency rosewood music stand
with lyre shaped design. The
reeded column with turned and
gadrooned decoration raised on a
tripod base with bun feet.
• *height 1.08m*
• **£3,600**   • **O. F. Wilson**

Tôle Plant Holder ▲
• **1850**
One of a pair of painted English
tôle plant holders decorated with
hand painted chrysanthemums
and peonies. With pierced gilt
foliate rail around the top,
flanked by brass lion handles.
• *height 34.5cm*
• **£1,250** • **Goodison Paraskeva**

Victorian Washstand ▼
• *circa 1870*
Victorian burr-walnut washstand
with a grey and white marble top
above three drawers and a
moulded cupboard, standing on a
straight moulded base.
• *85cm x 1.24m*
• **£850**   • **Hill Farm**

Chinese Pot Stand ▼
• *18th century*
One of a pair of simple boldly
executed pot stands of country
craftsman construction, from
Southern China.
• *81cm x 50cm*
• **£2,950**   • **Gordon Reece**

Towel Rail ◀
• *circa 1870*
Victorian satin birchwood towel
rail with carved and turned
decoration.
• *height 90cm*
• **£220**   • **Nicholas Mitchell**

Knife Cleaner ▲
• *circa 1900*
Circular pine knife sharpener,
with the maker's name "Kent's",
on cast iron frame support, with
a wood and metal handle.
• *1.2m x 75cm*
• **£475**   • **Drummonds**

Birdcage ▲
- *circa 1850s*
Mid 19th century French
birdcage, modelled on Notre
Dame cathedral.
- *2.1m x 1.1m*
- £6,950 • Wakelin Linfield

Cast Iron Trivet ▲
- *circa 1830s*
Early Victorian cast iron trivet
with a scrolled design within a
lattice border.
- *26cm x 42cm*
- £295 • Old Cinema

French Plant Holder ▲
- *1880*
Dark green French circular tôle
plant holder, standing on gilt paw
feet with a laurel wreath design
around the lip, and a cartouche of
a hand-painted classical scene.
- *height 49cm*
- £495 • Goodison Paraskeva

Georgian Tray ▼
- *circa 1820*
Georgian oval tray, with
fruitwood inlay around the rim,
brass handles and a central shell
design.
- *length 54cm*
- £275 • Salem Antiques

Mahogany Piano Stool ▼
- *circa 1880s*
An ornate Victorian mahogany
piano stool with a music
compartment under seat with
turned and scrolled decoration.
- *56cm x 51cm*
- £550 • Old Cinema

Luggage Rack ▼
- *circa 1870*
Yew-wood luggage rack, standing
on four tapered square legs with
shaped apron.
- *45cm x 72cm*
- £1,250 • John Clay

Rosewood Music Stand ▲
- *circa 1820s*
Early 19th century rosewood
music stand with candle holders,
supported by a turned column on
a tripod base with scrolled feet.
- *height 1.5m*
- £2,200 • Old Cinema

Torchère Stand ▲
- *circa 1890*
A Regency style torchère stand
decorated with three female
busts, with stylized acanthus leaf
designs, surmounted by a black
marble top on a tripod base
standing with gilt paw feet.
- *height 1.14m*
- £450 • Vale Antiques

Mahogany Gallery Tray ▶

- *circa 1890*
Edwardian mahogany tray with a
fretted gallery surround
incorporating handles.
- *58cm x 41cm*
- £475 • D. Hume

Regency Tôle Tray ▲

- *19th century*
Regency tôle tray featuring ducks
bathing. The back is also
decorated in a primitive style
simulating wood.
- *82cm x 59cm*
- £3,200 • D. Hume

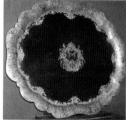

Gilded Tray ▼

- *1865*
Large English papier mâché tray,
gilded with mother-of-pearl inlay.
- *78.8cm x 59.7cm*
- £1,865 • C. Bridge

Papier Mâché Tray ◀

- *circa 1850*
Shaped Victorian papier mâché
tray, with scalloped decoration.
- *80cm x 67cm*
- £675 • D. Hume

Ironstone Footbath ▲

- *circa 1830*
Ironstone footbath by Hicks
Meigh & Johnson in good
condition.
- *20cm x 32cm x 52cm*
- £3,200 • D. Hume

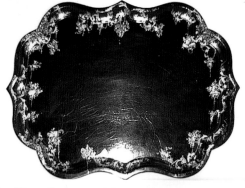

Yew Library Step ▼

- *20th century*
A hand-made solid yew library
step with brass fittings.
- *88.9cm x 38.1cm*
- £820 • Dorking Desk

Goats Beneath Trees Centrepiece ▲

- *circa 1890*
Centrepiece of carved wood
centrepiece of goats beneath an
oak tree with original glassliner.
- *height 37cm*
- £3,670 • Bradwin

Mahogany Corner Bar ◀

- *Early 20th century*
Elaborately carved panelled and
canopied corner bar, with
medallion decoration and scrolled
moulding below a moulded
cornice.
- *width 1.52m*
- £4,750 • Bruschweiler

Oak Canopy Bar ▶
- *Early 20th century*
Oak canopy bar with carved panels and galleried and turned designs and etched mirrors. The moulded cornice with leaded glass decorative panels.
- *width 1.22m*
- £4,500 • Bruschweiler

Plate Bucket ▲
- *circa 1780*
A fine 18th century mahogany plate bucket with brass banding and handle.
- *38.1cm x 35.5cm*
- £1,950 • M. Norman

Mahogany Library Steps ▲
- *circa 1825*
A set of early 19th century mahogany library steps.
- *77.5cm x 56cm x 40.6cm*
- £2,250 • M. Norman

Iron Bound Chest ▼
- *circa 1860*
Nineteenth century Indian teak iron bound chest with brass studs and iron carrying handles.
- *54cm x 62cm x 89cm*
- £950 • D. Hume

George III Linen Press ▶
- *circa 1800*
A George III mahogany and inlaid linen press in the manner of Gillows of Lancaster still retaining its original brass "bail handles".
- *2.13m x 1.32m*
- £10,500 • Freshfords

Papier Mâché Tray ◀
- *circa 1850*
Mid 19th century papier mâché tray on a later stand.
- *71cm x 42cm x 73cm*
- £2,250 • M. Norman

Oak Canted Corner Bar ▼
- *Early 20th century*
Highly decorated oak canted corner bar; a hybrid of architectural elements, panelled with scrolled and turned columns and mirrored rear.
- *height 2.2m*
- £5,250 • Bruschweiler

Paris Porcelain and Tulipwood Armoire ◀
- *circa 1850*
Ormolu-mounted parcel armoire surmounted by four finial urns. The breakfront pediment has panels depicting playing putti and the front is centred by a bevelled mirrored cupboard door.
- *2.51m x 63cm x 2.31m*
- £230,000 • Adrian Alan

Expert Tips
Wherever possible, check the thickness of veneer. Eighteenth and early nineteenth century veneers were cut by hand, so anything thinner than 1/16th of an inch thick is later than that.

Screens

Sparrow and Bamboo Screen ▶

- *Edo period 18th–19th century*
A six-fold Japanese paper screen painted in ink and colour on a gold ground with sparrows amongst bamboo. Kano School.
- *94.5cm x 2.9m*
- **£9,800** • **Gregg Baker**

Bijin and Sakura Screen ▼

- *Taisho period 20th century*
A two-fold silk screen painted in ink and colour on a buff ground with two young bijin (beauties) beside a palanquin and beneath a flowering sakura (cherry tree). One is making a garland from the fallen blossoms she is collecting whilst the other looks on.
- *1.72m x 1.73m*
- **£8,000** • **Gregg Baker**

Birds and Cherry Tree Screen ▲

- *Edo period 18th century*
A two-fold paper screen painted in ink and colour on a buff and gold ground with two birds in flight and a hato (dove) perched in a cherry tree in full bloom above a turbulent river.
- *1.59m x 1.89m*
- **£16,900** • **Gregg Baker**

Waterfall Screen ▲

- *20th century*
A two-fold Japan paper screen painted in ink on a gold ground with a taki (waterfall), signed by Kunsai.
- *1.67m x 1.68m*
- **£9,800** • **Gregg Baker**

Clothes Rack Screen ▶

- *Meiji Period 19th century*
A four-fold paper screen painted in ink and colour on a gold ground with kimono and obi folded and hanging from the rails of two lacquer clothes racks.
- *54cm x 1.72m*
- **£8,500** • **Gregg Baker**

Weeping Cherry Screen ◀

- *Edo period 17th/18th century*
A paper furosaki screen painted in ink and colour on a gold ground with birds, a snow covered shidare-zakura (weeping cherry) and daffodils in a river landscape in early spring.
- *67cm x 1.58m*
- **£5,500** • **Gregg Baker**

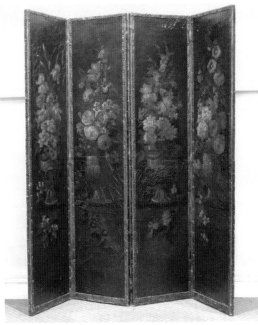

Victorian Screen ◀

- 1870

A good size painted leather four fold screen in the 18th century style, painted with floral arrangements.
- 1.6m x 1.53m
- £4,200
- Butchoff

Chinese Fire Screen ▲

- *circa 1860*

Chinese fire screen embroidered with peonies, chrysanthemums, butterflies and birds, in silk with gold threads. Supported by a mahogany stand.
- 78cm x 62cm
- £385
- Younger

Victorian Beadwork Screen ▼

- *circa 1840*

One of a pair of excellent Victorian pole screens in walnut carved frames containing fine examples of beadwork of the period.
- height 1.4m
- £4,500
- Wakelin Linfield

Soolmaker Screen ▲

- 1690

Dutch six-fold screen by Soolmaker, with a painted romantic landscape of an impression of Italy.
- 1.26m x 2.44m
- £3,800
- Butchoff

Expert Tips

Original needlepoint or tapestry must be in good condition and there should not be any wear or tears on the picture.

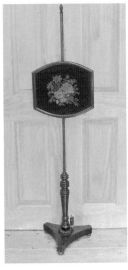

Regency Rosewood Screen ▲

- *circa 1820*

Regency rosewood pole screen with floral tapestry panel, on a turned pedestal and tri-partite platform base.
- height 1.43m
- £545
- R. S. Antiques

Settees & Sofas

Victorian Chaise Longue ▶

- *circa 1860*

Victorian mahogany chaise longue with curved button back and scrolled arm, standing on turned legs with original brass castors.
- *length 1.5m*
- £1,375   • The Swan

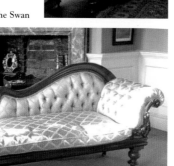

Mahogany Chaise Longue ▲

- *circa 1840*

Victorian mahogany chaise longue with feather padded button back, gold damask upholstery and carved, turned decoration.
- *length 1.89m*
- £1,650   • The Swan

French Chaise Longue ▶

- *circa 1900*

Mahogany walnut Louis XVI-style meridienne.
- *length 84cm*
- £1,650   • French Room

Rosewood Chaise Longue ◀

- *circa 1860*

Mid Victorian rosewood chaise longue, with finely carved rose decoration, scrolled arms, moulded serpentine apron and original porcelain castors.
- *length 1.86m*
- £2,800   • Drummonds

Victorian Chaise Longue ▲

- *circa 1870*

Recently upholstered chaise longue dating from the Victorian period. Presented with original marble castors and brass fittings.
- *length 2.13m*
- £1,900   • Gabrielle de Giles

Louis XVI Chaise Longue ▲

- *circa 1890*

Double-ended chaise longue in Louis XVI-style.
- *length 1.7m*
- £2,700   • North West 8

Double Scroll End Sofa ▶

- *circa 1810*

Regency period rosewood and cut brass inlaid double scroll end sofa, the shaped back inlaid with cut brass quatrefoils and large brass paterae. The frame profusely decorated with foliate brass inlay.

- *85cm x 62cm x 2.03m*
- **£15,750**   • R. Gardner

George II Settee ◀

- *circa 1750*

A George II settee of delightfully small proportions, with acanthus and scroll front legs in walnut, the whole on an oak, ash and beech frame. A photograph of the frame is available.

- *94cm x 67.5cm x 1.3m*
- **£16,250**   • R. Gardner

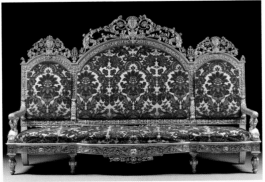

Regency Style Canapé ▲

- *circa 1850*

A French canapé surmounted by a carved cresting and flanked to the sides by foliage and mythological beasts, above an arched-shaped padded back. The seat is flanked by arm-rests supported by sphinxes.

- *width 2.7m*
- **£14,000**   • Adrian Alan

Victorian Sofa ◀

- *19th century*

A fine Victorian sofa with walnut frame, restored and upholstered to the highest quality.

- *length 1.4m*
- **£3,850**   • Manser Antiques

Walnut Framed Settee ▲

- *circa 1900*

A late Victorian walnut-framed two-seater settee, finely carved with leaf scrolls and flowers, on four cabriole supports, in the French taste.

- *76cm x 68.5cm x 1.23m*
- **£3,250**   • R. Gardner

George I Sofa ▲

- *circa 1720*

A George I arched-back sofa with scrolled arms and serpentine front raised on walnut cabriole legs with pad feet to the front and swept walnut legs to the rear, upholstered in 19th century tapestry fabric.

- *91.5cm x 78.5cm x 1.59m*
- **£22,500**   • R. Gardner

Expert Tips

Original framework, which should usually be of beech, will show signs of old tack holes.

Carved and Giltwood Chaise Longue ◀

- *circa 1880*

Chaise longue attributed to Fourdinois with floral and ribbon-carved frame, scrolled back, and acanthus-clasped armrest supported by winged putti. The padded back, cushions are covered in floral damask.

- *1.04m x 79cm x 1.83m*
- **£18,000**   • Adrian Alan

Mahogany Framed Sofa ▲

- *circa 1820*

A Regency period mahogany framed sofa. The scroll ends with fine carved reeded decoration and the two scrolling arms are supported by a swept back with central gadroon carved cresting and brass inlay.
- *91.4cm x 65cm x 2.03m*
- £8,800 • Hallidays

Regency Rosewood and Beechwood Sofa ▲

- *circa 1815*

An English Regency sofa beautifully worked with cut brass inlays and carved decoration, of classical inspiration, very much influenced by the designs of Thomas Hope.
- *width 1.78m*
- £9,850 • Freshfords

Pair of Window Seats ▲

- *circa 1880*

Pair of 19th century decorated window seats with scrolled arms and gilded decoration.
- *70cm x 53.3cm x 1.05m*
- £6,850 • M. Norman

Banquette de Croisée ▲

- *circa 1880*

A fine carved gilt wood Louis XV-style banquette de croisée, with armrests and serpentine frieze, decorated with acanthus leaf and flowers.
- *54cm x 49cm x 1.1m*
- £5,600 • Butchoff Antiques

Scroll End Couch ▲

- *circa 1830*

A fine late Regency mahogany double scroll end couch, with finely carved decorative back.
- *99cm x 61cm x 2.01m*
- £5,250 • Walter Moores

George IV Window Seat ▽

- *circa 1825*

Window seat in the form of a chaise longue with scroll ends and seat rail decorated with carved acanthus and lotus leaf. The turned, fluted and tapered legs headed with carved anthemion patera.
- *79cm x 79cm x 1.53m*
- £16,500 • Butchoff Antiques

Lion's Head Settee ▲

- *circa 1880*

English sofa with waisted back and seat set in matching narrow moulded frames with carved lion mask headed cabriole legs terminating in hairy paw feet. The open arms are terminated in eagles' heads.
- *1.07m x 66cm x 1.53m*
- £9,500 • Butchoff

High Back Settee ▼

- *circa 1880*

A late Victorian mahogany high back settee with scrolled high arched and sides, standing on cabriole legs.
- *1.07m x 88cm*
- **£3,200**   • John Clay

French Sofa ▲

- *circa 18th century*

French sofa with a high back and curved sides, standing on turned Doric legs on ball feet, with a straight stretcher.
- *height 1.18m*
- **£8,800**   • Augustus Brandt

Gustavian-style Sofa ▲

- *circa 1899*

Swedish Louis XVI and Gustavian-style birchwood sofa, open in form and upholstered in calico with noticeable carved and scrolled armrests and moulded back, the whole resting on carved scrolled feet.
- *1.35m x 1.58m*
- **£3,400**   • Rupert Cavendish

High Back Oak Settee ▼

- *circa 1840*

Oak high back four-panelled settee with moulded arms and padded seat, standing on cabriole legs with pad feet.
- *82cm x 1.89m*
- **£1,875**   • Drummonds

Biedermeier Sofa ▲

- *circa 1820*

Biedermeier birchwood sofa with serpentine back and front and carved decoration to the apron, on turned and fluted legs.
- *95cm x 1.99m*
- **£5,600**   • Rupert Cavendish

Expert Tips

Always check that the legs are in good condition, especially on a Victorian chaise longue or day bed, where the delicate sabre legs are often broken through heavy wear and tear. Check that the back is secured firmly to the base as often these have been broken and not restored correctly.

High Button-Back Sofa ▲
- *circa 1860*

Victorian rosewood button-back sofa with moulded top rail, sides and arms and four cabriole legs, splayed legs to the rear.
- *length 1.56m*
- £2,400   ● Drummonds

Regency Sofa ▲
- *circa 1810*

Regency beech wood faux rosewood sofa with double scroll arms and a carved moulded back with scrolling, inlaid with brass decoration.
- *93cm x 1.95m*
- £5,250   ● R. S. Antiques

Walnut Sofa ▶
- *circa 1890s*

Small late Victorian sofa with arched padded button back and carved walnut frame with small scrolled arms, the whole on slender turned legs.
- *94cm x 1.33m*
- £1,200   ● John Riordan

Chesterfield Sofa ▼
- *circa 1860*

Victorian Chesterfield sofa upholstered in Venetian damask, with padded moulded back and seat, standing on turned legs.
- *length 1.97m*
- £1,950   ● The Swan

French Louis XVIII Sofa ▲
- *circa 1780*

French Louis XVIII sofa with painted and moulded carved wooden frame, curved back and a padded seat and small padded arm rests, by D. Julienne.
- *82cm x 1.91m*
- £6,200   ● Augustus Brandt

Italian Hallbench ▶
- *circa 1790*

Italian pine hallbench with a straight back swept arms, heavily carved apron and short cabriole legs.
- *82cm x 1.93m*
- £4,700   ● Anthony Sharpe

Stools

Regency X-Frame Stool ▶
- *circa 1820*
Regency mahogany X-frame stool
with wooden saddle seat.
- *48cm x 33cm x 51cm*
- £1,800   • D. Hume

Victorian Footstools ▲
- *circa 1880*
Pair of Victorian mahogany
footstools with rose fabric.
- *15.2cm x 25.4cm x 33cm*
- £695   • Manser Antiques

Mahogany Footstool ▲
- *circa 1825*
Early 19th century mahogany
foot stool on turned and carved
splayed legs.
- *54.6cm x 47cm x 48.3cm*
- £650   • M. Norman

Anglo-Indian Stool ▼
- *circa 1850*
Mid 19th century stool with
carved and pierced stretcher.
- *45cm x 42.5cm x 80cm*
- £1,450   • R. Gardner

Oval Footstool ▶
- *circa 1725*
Early 18th century walnut
veneered oval footstool featuring
three figures on the olive
upholstery.
- *45.7cm x 45.7cm x 61cm*
- £6,850   • M. Norman

Floral Footstools ▼
- *circa 1880*
Pair of Victorian walnut
footstools, recovered with
embroidered floral pattern.
- *15.2cm x 30.5cm x 38.1cm*
- £850   • Manser Antiques

William IV Ottoman ◀
- *circa 1835*
William IV rosewood upholstered
ottoman of waisted form, with
hinged lid.
- *47cm x 49.5cm x 49.5cm*
- £1,250   • R. Gardner

Louis XVI Footstool ▼

- *circa 1780*
Louis XVI giltwood footstool
with carved acanthus moulding
and foliate legs.
- *height 14cm*
- £2,900   ● O. F. Wilson

Walnut Footstool ▼

- *circa 1880*
Small walnut footstool with
circular re-upholstered padded top
standing on small cabriole legs.
- *width 36cm*
- £290   ● Salem Antiques

Rustic Stool ▼

- *circa 1840*
Rustic oak child's stool standing
on four turned legs.
- *20cm x 31cm*
- £85   ● The Lacquer Chest

Tapestry Stool ▶

- *1880*
Fine walnut tapestry Queen
Anne-style stool raised on
cabriole legs carved with
acanthus leaf designs, with claw
and ball feet.
- *48cm x 51cm*
- £3,500   ● Butchof

Birchwood Stool ▲

- *1820–1830*
One of a pair of Swedish
Biedermeier birchwood stools
raised on splayed legs.
- *39cm x 35cm*
- £3,400   ● Rupert Cavendish

Mahogany Stool ◀

- *circa 1880*
Mahogany oblong country oak
stool standing on square straight
legs, with scrolls at each corner.
- *56cm x 34cm*
- £495   ● Macnaughton-Smith

George I Walnut Stool ◀

- *circa 1720*
George I walnut stool with cabriole legs, carved at each knee with a carved shell.
- *height 54cm*
- £22,500   • John Bly

Mahogany Stool ▶

- *circa 1890*
Miniature mahogany stool fashioned as a small table.
- *22cm x 33cm*
- £89   • The Swan

Piano Stool ▲

- *circa 1880*
Walnut revolving piano stool with circular padded seat on cabriole legs with claw feet.
- *height 49cm*
- £500   • Nicholas Mitchell

Piano Stool ▲

- *circa 1830s*
William IV piano stool on adjustable reeded and carved column, on a platform base with scroll end feet and original tapestry seat.
- *height 54cm*
- £495   • The Swan

Ebonised Stool ◀

- *circa 1860*
Ebonised stool with a rush seat, with faux bamboo designs and gilding with curved rails connected by gilded balls.
- *42cm x 40cm*
- £220   • The Lacquer Chest

Gustavian Bench ▲

- *circa 1800*
Louis XVI Swedish Gustavian pine bench seat painted white with carved arms, raised on turned feet.
- *37cm x 1.09m*
- £2,900   • Rupert Cavendish

Beechwood Piano Stool ▶

- *circa 1825*

Regency period beechwood revolving piano stool with circular leather padded seat and pierced leaf carved back splat.
- *56cm x 35.5cm*
- **£2,950**   • **M. Norman**

Carved Walnut Stool ▲

- *circa 1900*

Early 20th century stool on "H" frame stretcher with central finial and carved, turned legs; new upholstery.
- *52cm x 36.8cm x 89cm*
- **£595**   • **Millers Antiques**

William and Mary Long Stool ▲

- *circa 1920*

A William and Mary style upholstered long stool with early 18th century tapestry covering. On turned legs with pad feet, joined by shaped moulded stretchers with three turned finials.
- *17cm x 18cm x 60cm*
- **£4,600**   • **Hallidays**

Chippendale Footstool ▼

- *circa 1760*

Chippendale period mahogany footstool with English needlework of the George II period embroidered on canvas with silks and wools.
- *45.7cm x 43cm x 53cm*
- **£8,850**   • **M. Norman**

Piano Stool in Walnut ▼

- *circa 1900*

Early 19th century walnut piano stool with cabriole legs and carved floral motifs.
- *53.3cm x 40.6cm*
- **£395**   • **Millers Antiques**

Saddle Stool ◀

- *circa 1890*

Simple country stool with square legs and well-worn patina.
- *53.3cm x 30.5cm x 45.7cm*
- **£235**   • **Millers Antiques**

Expert Tips

Rosewood, predominantly used during the Regency period, can be identified by its black streaks.

Mahogany Stool ◀

- *circa 1850*

Mid 19th century mahogany stool with cabriole legs standing on whirl feet.
- *50.8cm x 53.3cm x 90cm*
- **£2,570**   • **M. Norman**

Hessian Ottoman

- *circa 1910*
Ottoman covered in cross-stitch hessian with red and blue floral patterns.
- *61cm x 53.3cm x 98cm*
- **£345** • **Millers Antiques**

Rosewood George IV "X" Frame Stool

- *circa 1825*
A rosewood "X" frame stool with acanthus leaf carving, upholstered in leather and terminating on hairy paw feet.
- *36cm x 44cm x 50cm*
- **£5,800** • **Butchoff Antiques**

Serpentine Giltwood Single Stool

- *circa 1880*
Stool of serpentine form with cabriole legs crested with satyr's mask ending in scroll feet joined by an scrolling X stretcher. The seat rail is pierced with shells and acanthus foliage.
- *41cm x 43cm x 61cm*
- **£2,850** • **Butchoff**

Meditation Stool

- *Mid 19th century*
Large fruitwood stool with recessed waist above a simply carved apron with double-mitred braces. Legs end in hoof feet.
- *52cm x 45cm x 90cm*
- **£320** • **Orient Expressions**

Rococo-style Giltwood Stool

- *circa 1880*
Ornate stool with cabriole legs crested with satyr masks and joined by waved stretchers, ending in scroll feet. The double serpentine seatrail, centred with pierced shells, is surrounded by acanthus foliage.
- *41cm x 41cm x 1.07m*
- **£5,500** • **Butchoff**

Pair of Ningbo Stools

- *Late 19th century*
A pair of waisted stools in traditional Ningbo style, using an elm frame with huali (rosewood) floating seat panel and waist. Simple hump back stretchers join legs ending in hoof feet.
- *45cm x 30cm x 55cm*
- **£250** • **Orient Expressions**

Pair of Square Stools

- *Mid 19th century*
A pair of square elm stools with decorative bracing and hump back stretchers above straight base stretchers. Legs end in hoof feet.
- *40cm x 40cm x 40cm*
- **£275** • **Orient Expressions**

Tables

Pier Table ▶
- *circa 1790*
One of a pair of giltwood side table of fluted legs with carved wood frieze of anthemion decoration. The tops are veneered in the finest West Indian satinwood, cross-banded in kingwood with boxwood lines.
- *89cm x 44cm x 1.45m*
- **£120,000** • **Haughey**

Rosewood Sewing Table ▶
- *circa 1840*
Fine rosewood sewing table with drawer, standing on claw feet.
- *76.2cm x 46cm x 61cm*
- **£3,500** • **Manser Antiques**

Irish Mahogany Pie Crust Table ▲
- *circa 1780*
Pie crust table with shaped and moulded two-plank top on a fluted column meeting a tripod base with ball and claw feet.
- *73.7cm x 1.07m*
- **£16,500** • **S. Cook**

George III Red Walnut Dish Top Tripod Table ◀
- *circa 1770*
Walnut table with one piece tilt top raised on a ring turned barrel column with a shallow vase design, supported by three tripod legs of traditional design.
- *71cm x 68.5cm*
- **£2,000–£3,000** • **J. Collins**

Rosewood Sutherland Table ▼
- *circa 1850*
Rosewood table with two hinged serpentine leaves, each supported on a single strut, which swing out on a wooden knuckle hinge.
- *73cm x 16.5cm x 1.07m*
- **£1,000–£2,000** • **J. Collins**

Regency Mahogany Coaching Table ▼
- *circa 1820*
English coaching table with a solid mahogany rectangular folding top raised on four shaped legs united at the middle and base by three turned stretchers.
- *73cm x 44cm x 89cm*
- **£1,000–£2,000** • **J. Collins**

Russian Centre Table

- *circa 1790*

A fine Russian oval centre table, the cobalt blue glass top surmounted by a three quarter brass gallery above a brass reeded edge. The frieze fitted with a drawer and decorated with fluted panels alternating with brass-edged square panels and lozenges on fluted turned tapering legs with beaded collars and sabots.
- *81cm x 93cm*
- £28,500   • Anthony Outred

Victorian Occasional Table

- *circa 1860s*

A Victorian rosewood and marquetry inlaid occasional table.
- *64cm x 50cm*
- £440   • Old Cinema

William IV Table

- *circa 1830s*

William IV mahogany table with brass drop handles and single drawer, raised on turned, tapering, candy twist legs.
- *76cm x 56cm*
- £750   • Macnaughton-Smith

Louis XVI Night Table

- *circa 1790*

Louis XVI night table with a pierced brass rail and three small drawers in purple heart and satinwood banding.
- *height 86cm*
- £4,250   • O. F. Wilson

Light Oak Side Table

- *circa 1870*

Victorian light oak side table with moulded back and scrolled designs, with side drawers, standing on turned tapering legs.
- *height 1.1m*
- £950   • Hill Farm Antiques

Tilt Top Table

- *circa 1890*

Mahogany tilt top table with turned support raised on a tripod base with splayed legs.
- *height 83cm*
- £295   • Great Grooms

Regency Pembroke Table

- *circa 1810*

Fine quality Regency period mahogany and ebony inlaid Pembroke table. Standing on a twin double "C"- scrolled supports joining out swept legs, with brass caps and castors.
- *73cm x 104cm x 51cm*
- £10,950   • Wakelin Linfield

Mahogany Writing Table

- *circa 1870s*

Nineteenth century mahogany writing table with tooled leather writing surface and reeded, turned and tapered legs.
- *75cm x 1.1m*
- £1,675   • Shirley Knight

Mahogany Console Table ▼

- *circa 1810*

A console table with a rectangular top with an ebonised moulded edge over a frieze inlaid with repeated brass sunburst motifs on an ebonised background, raised on a pair of columns joined to the panelled back with an arcaded profile. The whole raised on a concave plinth base leading to gilt paw feet, the front two facing forward, the back two to the side.

- *89cm x 95cm*
- £9,800   • Anthony Outred

George III Table ▼

- *circa 1800*

George III small mahogany birdcage table, with well-shaped baluster tripod support on splayed legs.

- *height 79cm*
- £2,500   • Great Grooms

Victorian Table ▶

- *circa 1870*

Victorian walnut and marquetry table on a pedestal base with carved gadrooned decoration and carved splat legs, by Taylor & Son, Dover St, London.

- *height 1.37m*
- £9,800   • Butchoff

Peachwood Centre Table ▲

- *circa 1820*

A rare peachwood centre table with turned legs and bamboo skirting.

- *81cm x 1.75m*
- £8,200   • Gordon Reece

Oval Table ▲

- *circa 1800s*

Small oval table with a George III tray with a scalloped edge on four splayed legs joined by a "X" frame stretcher.

- *height 56cm*
- £695   • Old Cinema

Rosewood Table ▲

- *circa 1835*

William IV rosewood sewing/games table with trestle supports and bun feet.

- *73cm x 61cm*
- £2,600   • Salem Antiques

Victorian Dressing Table ▲

- *circa 1885*

Victorian mahogany dressing table with an oval mirror with heavily carved decoration, above six fitted drawers and turned front legs on bun feet.

- *height 1.3m*
- £4,500   • Sleeping Beauty

Victorian Games Table ▲

- *circa 1850*

Victorian mahogany inlaid walnut games table with inlaid chessboard and heavily turned column, standing on a tripod base with carved legs.

- *height 82cm*
- £875   • Hill Farm

Expert Tips

During the mid-eighteenth century the tea gardens around London were regarded as vulgar, and it therefore became fashionable to invite friends to drink tea at home. Cabinet makers turned their attention to designing suitable ornamental tables for the occasion.

Victorian Washstand ▼
- *circa 1840*

Victorian mahogany washstand with two drawers with turned handles and side table, in excellent original condition.
- *width 98cm*
- £595   • The Swan

Side Table ▼
- *circa 1880*

Mahogany table with moulded serpentine top supported by two turned columns, joined by a turned stretcher above heavily carved legs with leaf designs.
- *height 89cm*
- £695   • Macnaughton-Smith

Mahogany Serving Table ▶
- *circa 1795*

English serving table, of breakfront "D"-shaped form, surmounted by the original brass gallery, the frieze fitted with a long oak lined drawer, with a finely flamed mahogany front. The rounded corner panels and side panels of the frieze finished in a similar manner each panel flanked by finely carved urns heading the six elegant fluted tapering legs.
- *82cm x 2.9m*
- £28,000   • Anthony Outred

Sewing Table ▲
- *1870*

Victorian rosewood sewing table with single drawer standing on a pedestal base with turned feet.
- *88cm x 84cm*
- £1,995   • Flower Antiques

Mahogany Jardinière ▲
- *1830*

Rare William IV mahogany occasional table stamped Freemans on a carved and turned column raised on a tripod base, resting on bun feet.
- *76cm x 44cm*
- £4,500   • Butchoff

Victorian Tilt Top Table ▼
- *circa 1880*

Victorian mahogany tilt top table with turned baluster pedestal base, raised on splayed legs.
- *height 74cm*
- £580   • Nicholas Mitchell

Mahogany Side Table ▼
- *circa 1830*

Mahogany side table with square top single long drawer with brass handle, standing on four straight square legs.
- *height 82cm*
- £475   • John Clay

Console Table ◄
- *circa 1825*

One of a pair of George IV mirror backed console tables in rosewood. The marble tops above a rococo carved frieze supported by carved and giltwood acanthus decorated "S" scroll uprights.
- *96cm x 75cm x 36cm*
- **£18,750**   • **Wakelin Linfield**

Cricket Table   ▼
- **1790**

Oak cricket table with circular top standing on three splayed legs, joined by a square, panelled sretcher.
- *59cm x 66cm*
- **£1,275**   • **Rushligh**

Burr Walnut Table   ▲
- *circa 1880*

Victorian burr walnut table with a circular top inlaid with boxwood foliate design and carved leaves around the rim, with a turned pedestal standing on a tripod base.
- *height 69cm*
- **£875**   • **A.I.G**

Games Table   ▲
- *circa 1860*

Victorian mahogany games table with inlaid chess board on a circular top, pedestal column and three splat legs.
- *height 75cm*
- **£1,200**   • **The Lacquer Chest**

Console Table   ▲
- *circa 1870*

Empire style console figured maple wood table with a pink marble top, central winged brass motif, on a single drawer flanked by ebonised pillars with oriental busts.
- *91cm x 92cm*
- **£2,400**   • **Old Cinema**

Empire Writing Table   ▶
- **1810–1820**

Swedish mahogany Empire writing/console table. The top with fitted drawers and gallery, above a central drawer, raised on four turned columns, with a solid stretcher base.
- *72cm x 74cm*
- **£3,700**   • **Rupert Cavendish**

Inlaid Mahogany Card Table ▶
- *circa 1900*
Fine inlaid mahogany card table on tapered legs with brass castors.
- *76.2cm x 43cm x 48cm*
- **£3,950** • **Manser Antiques**

Sheraton Lady's Writing Table ▶
- *circa 1795*
Sheraton rosewood lady's writing or work table with rising screen with fine boxwood and satinwood line inlays, the top banded in purpleheart, with pen and ink drawer to the side of the writing drawer.
- *76cm x 47cm x 56cm*
- **£5,850** • **R. Gardner**

George III Reading Table ◀
- *circa 1770*
A mahogany table, the top fitted with a removable bookrest, rising on a ratcheted adjustable stand, above a line inlaid frieze with a drawer at each end, all raised on a turned column with spiral knop.
- *77.5cm x 47cm x 63cm*
- **£5,900** • **R. Gardner**

Nested Occasional Tables ◀
- *circa 1890*
A nest of three burr walnut and crossbanded occasional tables with ring turned spindle supports.
- *68.5cm x 27.5cm x 53.5cm*
- **£2,450** • **R. Gardner**

Walnut Side Table ▼
- *circa 1920*
Walnut drop-leaf side table with drawer on barley twist legs and curved cross stretcher.
- *68.6cm x 35.5cm x 96.5cm*
- **£1,750** • **Manser Antiques**

George IV Console Table ▼
- *circa 1825*
George IV console table, the Verdie Alpie marble top above carved and gilded lions paw and acanthus front supports. The frieze, panelled inset back, and concave fronted plinth all veneered in rosewood.
- *91.5cm x 56cm x 99cm*
- **£7,200** • **R. Gardner**

Expert Tips

Elegant and plain George II card tables were often "improved" in the early 1900s to enhance their value. Look for carving at the knees and shells and scrolls at the feet.

Walnut Sofa Table ◀
- *circa 1930*
Walnut sofa table with two side extensions, standing on a turned stretcher, drawers and feet with brass fittings.
- *71cm x 56cm x 73.7cm*
- **£2,750** • **Manser Antiques**

Mahogany Night Table ▲

- *1800*

Dutch mahogany night table with tambour front, and small brass round handles and brass handles each side.
- *66cm x 47cm*
- £995   • A.I.G.

Sutherland Table ▲

- *circa 1835*

Walnut Sutherland table with satinwood and boxwood inlay.
- *height 72cm*
- £450   • The Swan

Rosewood Occasional Table ▼

- *circa 1860s*

A good quality Victorian rosewood occasional table with a barley twist column.
- *73cm x 45cm*
- £550   • Old Cinema

Mahogany Tripod Table ▼

- *circa 1760*

Mahogany tilt-top, birdcage table with turned support raised on splayed legs.
- *height 69.5cm*
- £4,800   • O. F. Wilson

Burr-Walnut Card Table ▲

- *circa 1870*

Burr-walnut Victorian card table with marquetry inlay, serpentine basket base and scrolled legs with upturned finial.
- *height 87cm*
- £3,750   • The Swan

Oak Side Bookstand ▲

- *circa 1890s*

Late Victorian oak side table/bookstand with carved scrolled supports.
- *63cm x 57cm*
- £695   • Old Cinema

Irish Side Table ◄

- *circa 1890*

Irish mahogany side table with a gadrooned edge above a plain frieze, the decorative, shaped apron centred by a lion-head mask within a rope twist border, flanked by stylised birds with feathered wings and foliate decoration. Raised on cabriole legs with handsome ball and claw feet decorated at the knees with low relief carved decoration of stylised birds.
- *81cm x 1.58m*
- £12,500   • Anthony Outred

George I Lowboy ▶

- *circa 1720*

A walnut veneered lowboy with quartered panels surrounded by herringbone and cross-banded inlay with a moulded edge. Below is a single cross-banded drawer all standing on cabriole legs.

- *71cm x 43cm x 76cm*
- £4,800 • Halllidays

Walnut Lamp Table ▲

- *circa 1900*

Square walnut two-tier table on turned legs.

- *65cm x 42.5cm x 42.5cm*
- £165 • Millers Antiques

Low Elm Table ▲

- *circa 1860*

One of a pair of simple country style two-tier tables with straight legs and stretcher.

- *66cm x 28cm x 43.2cm*
- £1,145 • Millers Antiques

Small Carved Table ▼

- *circa 1910*

A pretty two-tier table with scroll and lotus carved detail and carved foliate edge.

- *68.6cm x 33cm x 33cm*
- £165 • Millers Antiques

Rosewood and Brass Inlaid Work Table ▼

- *circa 1820*

A continental work table having a figured top with brass stringing and a rosewood-lined drawer, with a cupboard bag underneath. The piece supported on lyre stiles on trestle feet, joined by turned stretcher.

- *73.7cm x 40cm x 57.8cm*
- £8,800 • Halllidays

Regency Pembroke Worktable ▼

- *circa 1820*

A Pembroke worktable with twin flaps and a single drawer below with dummy drawer to the reverse and gadrooned beading. The workbag supported on hooped supports, joined by a turned stretcher.

- *71cm x 43.2cm x 86.4cm*
- £6,800 • Halllidays

Tripod Table ▶

- *circa 1860*
Circular table with figured
mahogany top, pedestal column
standing on three splayed legs.
- *65cm x 52.5cm*
- **£530** • **The Lacquer Chest**

Regency Table ▲

- *circa 1820*
Adjustable Regency mahogany
table, with a central tan hide top,
standing on a tall central pedestal
and a tripod base.
- *height 1.04m*
- **£1,395** • **A.I.G**

Oak Cricket Table ▲

- *circa 1860*
Oak cricket table with circular
top, single shelf, standing on
three turned pillared legs.
- *70cm x 38cm*
- **£780** • **The Lacquer Chest**

Walnut Table ▼

- *1880*
Small octagonal Victorian walnut
table, on a heavily moulded cross-
banded stretcher.
- *height 55cm*
- **£595** • **Old Cinema**

Small Tripod Table ▼

- *circa 1780*
Small rustic oak table with inlaid
flower in the centre standing on a
tripod base.
- *57cm x 40cm*
- **£395** • **The Swan**

Table with Ormolu Mounts ▼

- *1870*
Two tier mahogany table with
inlaid shaped top, with ormolu
pierced mounts and curved legs.
- *height 88cm*
- **£1,395** • **Old Cinema**

Portuguese Rosewood Table ▼

- *circa 1700*
A solid rosewood table, the top
with a decorative bead moulded
edge, the frieze with chevron
pattern decoration, raised on
spiral-twist legs with discs and
bulbous turnings, with similar
stretchers, joined at the corners
with decorative pegs.
- *79cm x 1.12m*
- **£6,800** • **Anthony Outred**

Expert Tips

*The foreruners of the tripod
table were the small round
topped tables designed to
support a lantern or candlestick,
which were popular during the
second half of the seventeenth
century. These tables were an
English phenomenon. They
were also popular in America,
but not on the Continent.*

Calamander Sofa Table

- *circa 1810*

A small calamander veneered sofa table, the top crossbanded with amboyna. Below is a decorative frieze containing two real and two dummy drawers with tulipwood bandings.

- *68.5cm x 61cm x 1.22m*
- £23,000 • R. Gardner

Japanned and Giltwood Work Table

- *circa 1815*

Regency period japanned and giltwood work table with hinged table top on platform base with carved acanthus leaves on a four scroll legged pedestal.

- *1.03m x 61cm x 96.5cm*
- £8,850 • M. Norman

Lacquer Tripod Table

- *circa 1810*

Regency period lacquer tripod table with eight-sided table top on turned candy twist column and with gilt ball feet.

- *76.2cm x 30cm*
- £1,750 • M. Norman

George III Serpentine Lady's Dressing Table

- *circa 1770*

An 18th century rosewood dressing table by John Cobb with a rectangular hinged divided top enclosing an interior with ratcheted sliding mirror, eight lidded compartments and two further compartments.

- *78cm x 54cm x 62cm*
- £16,500 • R. Gardner

Regency Mahogany Hunt/ Wine Table

- *circa 1810*

Regency mahogany hunt/wine table, the semi-circular top with removable semi-circular inset above a plain frieze on ring turned legs with original brass caps and castors.

- *71cm x 63.5cm x 1.76m*
- £7,250 • R. Gardner

Colonial Sutherland Tables

- *circa 1860*

A rare matched pair of Colonial oval Sutherland tables, the tops inlaid with radiating exotic specimen woods with a leaf carved moulded edge, the solid ebony base profusely carved with leaf and scrolls.

- *63cm x 15cm x 61cm*
- £14,850 • R. Gardner

New Jersey Lowboy ▶
- *circa 1735*
American walnut New Jersey
lowboy with paintbrush feet
topped by wristers mouldings.
- *74cm x 52cm x 86.4cm*
- **£58,500**   • **M. Norman**

Penwork Decorated
Work Table ▶
- *circa 1820*
Regency penwork decorated work
table with drop leaf table
standing on trestle supports and
bun feet.
- *77.5cm x 38cm x 52cm*
- **£3,500**   • **M. Norman**

Mahogany Urn Table ▲
- *circa 1785*
Late 18th century mahogany urn
table with pierced top rail on
square tapered and fluted legs.
- *77.5cm x 28cm x 28cm*
- **£2,950**   • **M. Norman**

Mahogany Tea Table ◀
- *circa 1815*
Regency mahogany tea table on
turned supports raised on
outswept legs, with brass caps
and castors joined by a solid
inlaid stretcher.
- *47cm x 49cm x 99cm*
- **£3,950**   • **M. Norman**

Mahogany Games Table ▼
- *circa 1760*
An 18th century mahogany
games table on cabriole legs with
claw feet.
- *71cm x 36.8cm x 66cm*
- **£3,950**   • **M. Norman**

Triple Top Card Table ▶
- *circa 1750*
A George II period mahogany
triple top card table. The shaped
top lifts to reveal a tea table, a
card table, a back-gammon and
chessboard, which opens to
reveal a reading slope with a
compartment below.
- *75cm x 39.4cm x 81.3cm*
- **£9,500**   • **Hallidays**

Sheraton Writing and Work Table ▼

- *circa 1790*

Sheraton rosewood writing and work table with sliding pleated silk needlework compartment, single drawer with hinged, leather-topped writing slide on square tapered legs with original brass castors.

- *78cm x 47.6cm x 56cm*
- **£4,750**   • M. Norman

George III Centre Table ▶

- *circa 1780*

George III mahogany circular centre table with good patina on a turned pedestal with three splayed legs on a tripod base with brass caps and castors.

- *73.7cm x 1.13m*
- **£5,250**   • M. Norman

Rosewood Veneered Writing Table ▶

- *circa 1815*

A rosewood veneered writing table. The surface has green tooled leather and rosewood cross-banding. Below are two drawers with two dummy drawers to the reverse with original brass pull handles.

- *71cm x 66cm x 1.17m*
- **£9,900**   • Hallidays

Games and Tea Table ◀

- *circa 1750*

George II solid red walnut triple top games and tea table.

- *76.2cm x 43.2cm x 83.8cm*
- **£5,750**   • M. Norman

Regency Work and Writing Table ▲

- *circa 1820*

Regency rosewood work and writing table with hinged writing slide and inlaid and brass-banded demi-lune side compartments, scrolled feet with gilt ormolu mounts and turned stretcher.

- *71cm x 42cm x 73cm*
- **£5,850**   • M. Norman

Mahogany Kettle Stand with Gallery ▲

- *circa 1750*

Circular mahogany kettle stand with gallery on a heavily turned pedestal, standing on a splayed tripod base.

- *58.4cm x 30.5cm*
- **£6,850**   • M. Norman

Expert Tips

A good eighteenth century pedestal table always has a very substantial support. If the legs look delicate and short rather than handsome, then they may have been redrawn. This is a difficult alteration to detect – use your judgement.

Walnut Writing Table ▶

- *circa 1910*

Writing table with leather inlay, two side drawers on carved cabriole legs.

- *76.2cm x 53.4cm x 89cm*
- **£565** • **Millers Antiques**

Three-drawer Side Table ▼

- *Late 18th century*

Mahogany bow fronted three-drawer side table, the drawers with their original brass handles; lovely colour and patination.

- *74cm x 48cm x 84cm*
- **£3,450** • **John Beazor**

Victorian Side Table ▼

- *circa 1860*

A Victorian gilt composition side table with original marble.

- *89cm x 58cm x 185cm*
- **£10,500** • **House of Mirrors**

Mahogany Wine Table ▼

- *circa 1840*

Mahogany circular table with good patina on turned pedestal and tripod base.

- *71cm x 39.4cm*
- **£445** • **Millers Antiques**

Regency Rosewood and Brass-inlaid Card Table ▼

- *circa 1820*

Regency card table by John Wellsman. The brass marquetry has been etched and inlaid "contrepartie", and unusually depicts huntsmen inset in a running border of scrolled acanthus leaf with fruiting vines.

- *73.6cm x 45.7cm x 91.4cm*
- **£8,750** • **Freshfords**

Regency "Penwork" Games Table ◀

- *circa 1830*

The chequerboard top with its frieze drawer is raised on a tulip pedestal with a quatreform base, ending with bun feet and concealed castors.

- *73.4cm x 58.4cm*
- **£6,500** • **Freshfords**

George III Three-part Dining Table ▶

- *circa 1810*

George III period dining table in three parts, made from Cuban mahogany and retaining all original leaves.
- *72.5m x 1.68m x 4.46m*
- **£75,000** • **Haughey Antiques**

Regency Twin Pillar Dining Table ▲

- *circa 1810*

A mahogany twin pillar table, the top with a swivel mechanism allowing the two leaves to be supported on a frame. Each leaf with a triple reeded edge and held together with original lacquered brass clips.
- *72cm x 1.27m x 2.54m*
- **£46,000** • **R. Gardner**

George III Tilt-top Breakfast Table ▶

- *circa 1790*

George III mahogany tilt-top rectangular breakfast table crossbanded with rosewood and satinwood enhanced with ebony stringing. Has rare brass wagon-wheel castors with elongated prongs.
- *76cm x 1.06m x 1.39m*
- **£18,500** • **R. Gardner**

Drop Leaf Dining Table ▼

- *circa 1750*

George III mahogany drop leaf dining table on shaped cabriole legs terminating in pointed toes, lovely colour and patina.
- *72cm x 1.295m x 1.07m*
- **£3,350** • **R. Gardner**

William IV Library Table ◀

- *circa 1830*

A late Regency rosewood and brass mounted library table with superb "S" scrolled lyre ends and carved throughout with acanthus leaf, honeysuckle and lotus leaf decoration.
- *73.7cm x 56cm x 1.22m*
- **£26,000** • **Freshfords**

Oak Refectory Table ▲

- *circa 1680*

Refectory table with single-plank top over an arcaded frieze with inverted baluster legs ending in block feet.
- *73.7cm x 76.2cm x 2.26m*
- **£24,950** • **S. Cook**

Circular Walnut Table ▲

- *circa 1870*

Fine walnut pedestal table supported by three feet.
- *diameter 1.27m*
- **£4,950** • **Manser Antiques**

Regency Mahogany Breakfast Table ▶

- *circa 1820*

A fine breakfast table with rounded corners and inlaid band on a turned pedestal with four splayed legs ending in brass caps and castors.
- *74cm x 1m x 1.32m*
- **£6,850**   • **M. Norman**

Regency Coromandel Breakfast Table ▼

- *circa 1815*

An unusual table in coromandel wood with rounded corners on a fluted pedestal with four scrolled feet; decorated with fine inlaid brass banding.
- *71cm x 1.12m x 1.51m*
- **£10,850**   • **M. Norman**

Regency Rosewood Breakfast Table ▲

- *circa 1815*

A Regency period rosewood veneered brass inlaid breakfast or hall table.
- *71.8cm x 1.25m x 1.25m*
- **£16,500**   • **Hallidays**

Rosewood Circular Table ▶

- *circa 1815*

Rosewood circular table on central pedestal and platform base, with well-figured faded top.
- *74cm x 1.03m*
- **£6,250**   • **John Beazor**

Rosewood & Marquetry Centre Table ▼

- *circa 1840*

Centre table with circular snap top, centred with a panel of a butterfly amidst exotic flowers within a superb rosewood field. The deep border separated by stringing is decorated with six floral panels.
- *diameter 1.27m*
- **£26,000** • **Butchoff Antiques**

Regency Extending Dining Table ▲

- *circa 1825*

A mahogany telescopic-action dining table attributed to Gillow of Lancaster. In original condition with four leaves and castors & clips stamped "Copes Patent". Seats up to fourteen comfortably.
- *3.71m x 1.32m*
- **£25,500**   • **Freshfords**

William IV Dining Table ▼

- *circa 1835*

William IV mahogany circular dining table of large size, standing on a triform base and carved scroll feet.
- *72.4cm x 1.37m*
- **£4,500**   • **Walter Moores**

Expert Tips

Damaged table tops are sometimes replaced. Observe the direction of the grain; on an original top the grain runs across the depth of the table rather than along its width.

Large Wine Table ▶

- *Early 19th century*

Elm wood wine table with original black lacquer. Round section recessed legs are joined by beaded apron and spandrels. The humpback stretchers back and front have a simple carved fungus detail.
- *87cm x 58cm x 1.07m*
- **£1,500** • **Orient Expressions**

Elm Half Table with Carved Apron ▲

- *Mid 19th century*

An elm wood half table in a waisted design with simple carved apron, the pieces ending in stylized dragons' heads.
- *82cm x 48cm x 96cm*
- **£450** • **Orient Expressions**

Regency Mahogany Breakfast Table ▶

- *circa 1820*

A Regency breakfast table with rosewood crossbanded top, retains excellent colour and figure.
- *74cm x 76.2cm x 1.37m*
- **£8,000** • **Freshfords**

Scholar's Table ▲

- *Early 19th century*

A low fruitwood Regency table with cloud shaped low-relief carving to the apron.
- *36cm x 26cm x 1.17m*
- **£550** • **Orient Expressions**

Altar Table ▲

- *Early 19th century*

Northern Chinese table with everted ends and recessed beaded legs joined with a pierced carved panel. The apron and spandrels are elaborately carved with an open scrollwork design.
- *96cm x 43cm x 2.1m*
- **£2,500** • **Orient Expressions**

Pair of Tea Tables ◀

- *Early 19th century*

A pair of hardwood tea tables with drawers and traditional ridged top. The base stretchers incorporate an ice crack lattice framework and the central shelves are simply panelled.
- *80cm x 39cm x 39cm*
- **£850** • **Orient Expressions**

Wardrobes

Architectural Breakfront Wardrobe ▶

- *circa 1850*

One of a pair of ebonised wardrobes by Anthony Salvin for Peckforton Castle. Each with moulded cornice above a central cupboard, revealing five slides, with ebonised fascia, over two short and two long drawers, flanked by lined hanging compartments each with brass rail fixtures. Each door with decorative panelling, and Arts and Crafts style brass strap hinges, engraved with an asymmetric design, the escutcheons follow the same design.

- *2.21m x 2.58m*
- **£28,000** • **Anthony Outredd**

Georgian Display Cupboard ▲

- *circa 1780*

Georgian cupboard with two doors enclosing an arched and pillared interior and two cupboards below.

- *height 2.4m*
- **£1,850** • **Drummonds**

Victorian Wardrobe ▶

- *circa 1880*

Victorian single-door wardrobe with central mirror, moulded pediment and one long deep drawer with turned handles. The whole standing on a moulded square base.

- *height 2.07m*
- **£995** • **Old Cinema**

Lacquered Corner Cupboard ◀

- *circa 1770*

Dutch black lacquered corner cupboard, with a raised gilt Chinoiserie design of figures, pagodas and birds, with brass butterfly hinges.

- *height 1.1m*
- **£3,950** • **O. F. Wilson**

Dutch Corner Cupboard ◀

- *circa 1850*

Dutch Chinoiserie painted corner cupboard with stylised butterflies, birds and figures, with three green painted interior shelves, original brass butterfly hinges and a moulded base.

- *92cm x 59.5cm x 40cm*
- **£5,500** • **O. F. Wilson**

Expert Tips

Features to look for in wardrobes and tallboys include: original handles, feather banding to drawers, canted corners to top section, and cross banding decoration.

Louis XVI Cupboard ▲

- 1800–10
Swedish Louis XVI Gustavian cupboard in two sections, with architecturally styled pediment and doors to top chest, and the lower chest with two panelled doors, the whole standing on small bracket feet.
- 1.88m x 1.13m
- £2,700 • Rupert Cavendish

Mahogany Linen Press ▲

- circa 1780
Mahogany linen press with moulded dentil course and two doors with inlaid oval panels concealing original trays. The lower section with two short and two long drawers.
- 2.12m x 1.22m x 58cm
- £10,950 • Wakelin Linfield

Indian Linen Press ▼

- circa 1880
Indian linen press with panelled doors carved with central pleated medallions and corner spandrels, above two long drawers raised on bracket feet.
- height 1.75m
- £2,500 • Hatchwell

French Provincial Cupboard ▼

- circa 1780
French painted Provincial cupboard in three parts, with heavily panelled doors on the top cupboard fitted with two serpentine shelves, and elongated hinges.
- 2.23m x 1.72m
- £4,300 • Anthony Sharpe

Black Lacquer Cupboard ▶

- 1880
Small Chinese black lacquer cabinet with fitted interior of one long and seven other drawers. With brass fittings at each corner with curved edges. Flanked by brass carrying handles.
- 37cm x 40cm x 28.5cm
- £2,250 • O. F. Wilson

Mahogany Wardrobe ▲

- circa 1880
Fine Victorian figured mahogany moulded two-door wardrobe with scrolled moulding below a moulded pediment. Standing on a straight base.
- height 2.06m
- £1,850 • Hill Farm

George III Commode ▲

- circa 1790
George III mahogany tambour-door commode with square tapering legs.
- 79cm x 53cm x 49cm
- £3,450 • Serendipity

William IV Linen Press ▲

• *circa 1835*
William IV mahogany linen press
retaining its old trays, with two
finely figured panelled doors
decorated with beading. The
lower section with figured drawer
fronts and original handles. The
whole raised on turned and
gadrooned feet.
• *2.14m x 1.2m x 50cm*
• **£8,750** • Wakelin Linfield

Pedestal Cupboard ▲

• *circa 1810*
Swedish Louis XVI Gustavian
cream-painted pine pedestal
cupboard with two doors and
square moulded and painted
green base.
• *1.47m x 1.07m*
• **£2,900** • Rupert Cavendish

Flame Mahogany Wardrobe ▶

• *circa 1890*
Flame mahogany Victorian
wardrobe with central pediment
above bow-fronted doors, with
four drawers flanked by long
cupboards with oval mirrors.
• *width 2.4m*
• **£2,650** • Drummonds

Linen Press ▲

• *circa 1800*
Elegant mahogany linen press in
original condition, with oval
panels of matching veneers and
satinwood cross-banded doors.
• *height 2.25m*
• **£8,950** • Barry Cotton

Corner Cupboard ▼

• *circa 1790*
George III bow-fronted
mahogany corner cupboard, fitted
with four shelves and two small
drawers, with shell inlay to frieze
and Greek key-moulded cornice.
• *height 1.05m*
• **£2,450** • Serendipity

Mahogany Linen Press ◀

• *circa 1860*
Mahogany linen press, having
two arched panelled door
enclosing three sliding drawers
and two long and two short
drawers below.
• *width 1.25m*
• **£2,450** • The Swan

Expert Tips

*Georgian bookcases were
usually made in pine when they
were going to be gessoed; gesso
is a plaster-like substance
applied to carved furniture
before gilding. The bookcase
would then be painted to
complement the decor in the
room or library.*

Glass

The inherent fragility of glass makes it highly prized, if not widely collected. This fragility also ensures its rarity value.

Notwithstanding the above, glass is still an area where a keen eye is required to eliminate the substantial quantity of items on the market which may deceive the casual collector. Some of these items have undoubtedly been made or altered with the intention to fool buyers and enhance prices. Nevertheless, many more are just honest reproductions.

One difficulty with glass is that it tends to be difficult to date. It is worthwhile visiting museums to view their glass collections as they often house a wide range of examples from different periods, allowing you to familiarise yourself with the styles and distinctive features of glass items through the ages. Collectors' societies are also a valuable source of information and often give you the opportunity to handle the objects. The best source, though, are reputable dealers who, incidentally, by supplying a proper descriptive receipt, bind themselves to their honest opinion and will make amends should they be proved wrong.

Tall Bohemian Blue Vase ▼
- *circa 1880*

Tall slender cobalt blue vase engraved with an interlaced stylised leaf pattern, raised on a domed foot.
- *height 42cm*
- £290 • Mousa

Green Wine Glass ▲
- **1760**

Green wine glass with elegant air twist stem.
- *height 18cm*
- £3,000 • Somervale

Glass Match Striker ▼
- *circa 1890*

Circular glass match container with silver mounts. The body incised with a grooved pattern which functions as a striking surface.
- *height 8cm*
- £160 • H. Gregory

Expert Tips

Gilding is applied both to the inside and to the surface of glasswares in the form of paint, powder and foil, usually on the surface of plain glass.

Wine Glasses ▼
- *1860*
Two green Bristol glass wine glasses.
- *height 12cm*
- £45   • Somervale

Green Wine Glasses ▲
- *1825*
Set of bowl-shaped green wine glasses with raspberry encrustation applied to the stems, raised on circular bases.
- *height 17cm*
- £600 set of three • Somervale

Bristol Spirit Decanter ▼
- *circa 1825*
Bristol blue spirit decanter inscribed with "Brandy" in gilt lettering, with a lozenge-shaped stopper.
- *height 28cm*
- £400   • Somervale

Toasting Glass ▲
- *circa 1700*
Toastmaster's glass with bell-shaped bowl, large circular knop stem with enclosed tear drop.
- *height 12cm*
- £1,800   • Somervale

Cream Skimmer Bowl ▲
- *circa 1800*
Large shallow glass cream skimmer bowl with central boss and moulded rim.
- *diameter 51cm*
- £500   • Somervale

Tall Bohemian Vase ▼
- *circa 1880*
Tall fluted vase with borders of red overlay heavily engraved with gilt scrolled decoration, raised on a domed foot with a shaped edge.
- *height 42cm*
- £480   • Mousa

Bohemian Decanter with Bowl ▼
- *circa 1880*
Bohemian bottle shaped decanter and dish with jewelled decoration of pink and blue stylised flowers with red beading and gilding.
- *height 28cm*
- £600   • Mousa

Square Spirit Decanters ▼
• **1900**
Good pair of well-cut square
English spirit decanters with
original facet ball stoppers.
• *height 22.9cm*
• **£250**   • C. Bridge

Opaline Vases ▼
• **1820**
Splendid pair of opaline boulle de
Savon urn vases in gilded
mounts.
• *height 44.5cm*
• **£4,000–£6,000**   • C. Bridge

Red Glass Dishes ▼
• **1860**
Splendid set of ten red glass
dishes, each with cut-shaped rim
and base and exceptional gilding.
• *diameter 30cm*
• **£200–£350 each**   • C. Bridge

Green Bowl ▲
• ***circa 8th–10th century AD***
A green glass Islamic bowl from
Afghanistan with an overall
dimple effect.
• *diameter 20cm*
• **£300**   • Mazar

Green Glass Decanters ▲
• **1840**
Three square-cut green glass
decanters with gilded labels for
Rum, Brandy and Hollands (gin),
in silver-plated stand with
original stoppers.
• *height 28cm*
• **£500–£1,000**   • C. Bridge

Strawberry-Cut Piggin ▲
• **1820**
Large heavily strawberry-cut
piggin (cream bowl) and under
dish.
• *width 20.3cm*
• **£900**   • C. Bridge

Cut Glass Cornucopia ▲
• **1830**
A fine pair of French cut glass
cornucopia in gilded bronze
mounts on marble bases.
• *height 19cm*
• **£3,600**   • C. Bridge

Expert Tips

*A diamond-shaped mark, with a
date and "parcel number" may
identify glass made in Britain
between 1852 and 1883.*

Ogee Bowl ◀
• **1800**
Very large English ogee bowl
rummer-shaped punch serving
glass on plain stem.
• *height 30cm*
• **£950**   • C. Bridge

Balustroid Glass ▶

- *1740*

Balustroid wine/ale glass with central ball knop and tall bell bowl.

- *height 20.3cm*
- £1,200   • C. Bridge

Posy Vase ▲

- *1880*

Charming horn-shaped posy vase in a glass stand on a mirrored base.

- *height 18cm*
- £320   • C. Bridge

Bristol Blue Decanters ▲

- *1800*

Pair of mallet-shaped Bristol Blue decanters with gilded labels reading "Rum" and "Brandy".

- *height 24cm*
- £580 for pair   • C. Bridge

Gin Glass ▶

- *1740*

Small English inverted baluster stem gin glass with tear inclusion on folded foot.

- *height 12cm*
- £1,400   • C. Bridge

Ship's Decanter ▼

- *1830*

English ship's decanter with flat slice cutting, four neck rings and target stopper.

- *height 25.4cm*
- £1,250   • C. Bridge

Green Cup Bowl ▼

- *1880*

English cup bowl of green champagne glass on knop stem.

- *height 10.2cm*
- £88   • C. Bridge

Cranberry Glass Bowl ▼

- *1880*

Large English cranberry glass bowl, with clear pull up leaf rim on a silver-plated stand.

- *height 28cm*
- £1,250   • C. Bridge

Georgian Decanter ▼

- *1830*

Half-sized Georgian decanter, with basal flutes, flat cutting and triple neck rings.

- *height 22.9cm*
- £155   • C. Bridge

Bohemian Glass Bowl ▲

- *circa 1880*
Bohemian amber-coloured glass bowl.
- *height 18cm*
- £200 • Sharif

English Vase ▲

- *circa 1870*
English clear cylindrical glass vase engraved with birds amongst foliage and geometric designs, with a star-cut base.
- *height 38cm*
- £680 • Mousa

Red Sweet Dish ▼

- *circa 1890*
Red Bohemian sweet dish painted with alternating panels of portraits and white diamond patterns, within gilt foliage, supported on a white overlay stem with a circular base.
- *height 34cm*
- £1,300 • Mousa

Blue Decanter ▼

- *circa 1880*
Bohemian bottle-shaped glass decanter with blue overlay, painted with red and yellow designs amongst clear glass flowers, made for the Middle Eastern market.
- *height 25cm*
- £370 • Mousa

Bohemian Red Candle Vase ▲

- *circa 1880*
Red Bohemian chalice-shaped vase, with white overlay and a gilt band painted with a floral frieze, above a knopped stem supported on a splayed foot with gilt banding.
- *height 27cm*
- £580 • Mousa

Bohemian Style Vase ▲

- *circa 1880*
One of a pair of green Bohemian style English vases of baluster form with an asymmetric rim, decorated with gilding, with a clear glass shield cartouche.
- *height 30.5cm*
- £780 • Mousa

405

Red Bohemian Glass Vase ▼

- *circa 1880*

Red Bohemian glass vase with
white panels painted with bull
rushes, above a knopped stem
raised on a splayed foot decorated
with panels of bullrushes within
gilt borders.
- *height 31cm*
- £380   • Mousa

Amethyst Cream and Sugar Bowls ▲

- *1800*

Amethyst baluster cream and
sugar bowls with gilt writing.
- *height 12cm*
- £600   • Somervale

French Opaline Bottle ▼

- *circa 1880*

French opaline bottle and
stopper, gilded, with a moulded
rim. The body decorated with
trailing roses and turquoise foliate
designs, raised on a circular base.
- *height 25cm*
- £300   • Mousa

Blue and Gold Bohemian Bottle ▼

- *circa 1890*

Bohemian azure blue glass bottle
with gilt floral and leaf designs,
surmounted by an oversized
lozenge-shaped stopper.
- *height 27cm*
- £490   • Mousa

Bohemian Centrepiece ▲

- *circa 1880*

Bohemian red glass centrepiece,
with a circular clear glass dish on
a red stem, engraved with a
trailing foliate pattern.
- *height 38cm*
- £1,400   • Mousa

Red Glass Candlesticks ▲

- *circa 1880*

Red Bohemian glass candlesticks,
each with a scalloped rim,
tapered stem on a circular star-cut
base with a shaped edge.
- *height 23cm*
- £650   • Mousa

Georgian Decanters

- *circa 1800*
Fine pair of English decanters
with geometric cutting design
and knopped stems.
- *height 23cm*
- £350 • Manser Antiques

Bowl and Cover ▼

- *circa 1820*
Georgian bowl and cover cut
with combs, steps and panels. Has
a ball-knop stem, star-cut foot
and stepped lid with cut
mushroom knob.
- *height 15cm*
- £75 • Antique Glass

Spirit Decanter ◄

- *circa 1840*
Fine panel-cut green spirit
decanter with single ring neck
and spire stopper.
- *height 36cm*
- £240 • Antique Glass

Magnum Decanters ▲

- *circa 1790*
Pair of Georgian magnum
decanters with panel-cut neck
and shoulders, comb-cut bases
and associated lozenge stoppers.
- *height 32cm*
- £1,200 • Antique Glass

Two-handled Wine Flask ▶

- *19th century*
Dutch two-handled wine flask,
beautifully trailed, engraved and
"bronzed".
- *height 23.5cm*
- £95 • Antique Glass

Four-Bottle Tantalus ▼

- *circa 1880*
Unusual and rare four-bottle
tantalus using the Janitor
Chapman's patent, No. 765.
- *height 32.5cm*
- £2,300 • R. Gardner

Globular Flask ▼

- *19th century*
Trailed globular flask with loop
handles, engraved and gilded
with fruiting vine.
- *height 23cm*
- £135 • Antique Glass

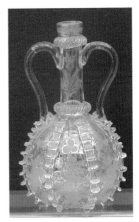

J. Jacobs Bowl and Dish ▶

- *circa 1810*

Bristol Blue bowl and dish with
gilt key pattern design around the
rim of the bowl, and a gilt stag in
the centre of the plate. Signed on
the base of each "J. Jacobs,
Bristol", in gilt.
- *height of bowl 9cm*
- **£1,000** • Somervale

Amethyst Cream Jug ▲

- *1820*

Pear-shaped amethyst cream jug
with "Be canny with the cream"
inscribed on the body, trails of
gold enamelling, a loop handle,
splayed lip and plain base.
- *height 14cm*
- **£300** • Somervale

Newcastle Goblet ▼

- *circa 1750*

Newcastle goblet with a finely
engraved foliate design, central
air beaded and ball knops to the
stem and domed foot.
- *height 19cm*
- **£1,800** • Somervale

Jacobite Wine Glasses ▼

- *circa 1750*

Fine pair of Jacobite wine glasses
with engraved bowls showing the
Jacobite Rose and two buds, on
double knopped, multiple spiral
air-twist stems and domed bases.
- *height 16cm*
- **£2,200** • Somervale

Cordial Glass ▲

- *circa 1720*

A cordial wine glass with flared
trumpet bowl, knopped stem and
air-folded conical foot.
- *height 17cm*
- **£800** • Somervale

German Liquor Set ▲

- *circa 1890*

German Moser hexagonal
decanter and four glasses chased
with gilt paisley designs
surrounding clear red glass
windows, surmounted by a spire-
shaped stopper.
- *height decanter 24cm*
- **£580** • Mousa

Nailsea Glass Cloche ▲

- *circa 1800*

Clear glass bell-shaped garden
cloche by Nailsea.
- *height 34cm*
- **£400** • Somervale

Green Wine Glass ▲

- *circa 1830*
One of a set of twelve green wine
glasses, with conical-shaped
bowls, bladed knop stems and a
circular base.
- *height 11cm*
- £896 • Somervale

Bohemian Vase
for Candles ▲

- *circa 1880*
One of a pair of dark green
Bohemian candle holders, with
white overlay panels painted with
pink roses within gilt borders,
raised on a conical stem and
circular base.
- *height 34cm*
- £980 • Mousa

Posset Pot ▼

- *circa 1740*
Posset pot with a trumpet bowl
and a carved spout, flanked by
two scroll handles, on a plain
conical foot.
- *height 7cm*
- £995 • Somervale

Nailsea Container ▼

- *circa 1860*
Nailsea double container of clear
glass with white pull-up
decoration, and emerald green
rims.
- *height 21cm*
- £160 • Somervale

Mallet-shaped Decanter ▲

- *circa 1780*
Mallet-shaped decanter engraved
with "Port" within an oval
cartouche, flanked by trailing
vine and grapes.
- *height 31cm*
- £1,000 • Somervale

Amber Glass Cane ▼

- *circa 1810*
Amber glass barley twist cane
with knob.
- *length 1m*
- £150 • Somervale

Large Green Goblet ▲

- *circa 1800*

Large dark green goblet with cup-shaped bowl.

- *height 19cm*
- £1,200 • Somervale

Set of Spirit Bottles ▲

- *1840*

A fine set of spirit bottles in amethyst, blue and green glass, with silver foliate bands around the neck and grape finials, resting in a pierced silver stand on three leaf shaped feet.

- *height 36cm*
- £980 • Somervale

Bohemian Bottles ▼

- *circa 1880*

Pair of Bohemian bottles with a white bulbous body with pink roses and blue cornflowers, orange flowers painted over red glass, a slender fluted neck, a red lozenge-shaped stopper and gilding.

- *height 22cm*
- £780 • Mousa

Bristol Blue Oil Bottle ▼

- *1840*

Bristol Blue bottle inscribed with "Oil" in gilt lettering within a gilt foliate cartouche, with a painted chain around the neck.

- *height 12cm*
- £200 • Somervale

Bohemian Lustre ▲

- *circa 1880*

One of a pair of Bohemian green lustres with white overlay and gilt borders, decorated with clear cut-glass hanging pendants.

- *height 30cm*
- £1,000 • Mousa

William III Glass ▲

- *circa 1780*

Irish wine glass with a cigar-shaped stem and engraved with the figure of King William on horseback with the inscription "The Glorious Memories of William III".

- *height 15.5cm*
- £4,000 • Somervale

Glass Twisted Cane ▼
- *circa 1810*
Turquoise twisted glass walking stick.
- *length 1m*
- £150　　　• Somervale

Glass Barrel Decanters ▼
- *1820*
Set of three Bristol Blue glass barrel decanters inscribed with "Rum", "Whiskey" and "Brandy" in gilt lettering within gilt banding. Each decanter has a gilt ball stopper.
- *height 20cm*
- £1,400　　　• Somervale

Bristol Rum Decanter ▼
- *1800*
Rum decanter inscribed with "Rum" in gilt lettering on the body and "R" on the lozenge-shaped stopper.
- *height 28cm*
- £280　　　• Somervale

Victorian Epergne ▲
- *circa 1890*
One of a pair of Victorian épergnes, with a central flute flanked by matching hanging baskets, suspended on spiral branches.
- *height 48cm*
- £2,200　　　• Sinai

French Opaline Vase ▲
- *circa 1880*
Opaline pink glass vase with jewelled beading and gilt decoration with an eastern inspiration.
- *height 48cm*
- £850　　　• Sinai

Jacob Sang Wine Glass ▼
- *circa 1759*
Composite air twist stem wine glass, engraved with a scene showing the Customs House in Amsterdam and cargo being unloaded, marked "Jacob Sang 1759", on the foot.
- *height 23.5cm*
- £8,000　　　• Somervale

Ale Glass ▼
- *circa 1760*
Ale glass with a round funnel bowl engraved with hops and barley and a double series twist stem, standing on a plain foot.
- *height 21cm*
- £580　　　• Somervale

Newcastle Glass Goblet ▼

- *circa 1810*

Large bowl-shaped goblet engraved with a horse and carriage, scrolling foliate and grape design and the words "Newcastle to York", on a domed base.

- *height 24cm*
- £800 • Somervale

Baluster Cream Jug ▼

- *circa 1800*

Blue baluster cream jug with pinched lip and barley twist design.

- *height 12cm*
- £155 • Somervale

Bohemian Vases ▲

- *circa 1870*

A pair of Bohemian cranberry glass vases with gilt leaf decoration and central cartouches showing portraits of a lady in a wedding dress and a lady in country dress.

- *height 39.5cm*
- £5,500 • Sinai

Match Holder ▼

- *circa 1890*

Ovoid match holder with a silver rim and etched glass body.

- *height 8cm*
- £150 • H. Gregory

Blue Decanter ▼

- *circa 1790*

Club-shaped Bristol Blue spirit decanter with a plain lozenge-shaped stopper.

- *height 32cm*
- £220 • Somervale

Green Georgian Wine Glasses

• *early 19th century*
Set of six Georgian green wine glasses with rib-moulded bowls on drawn stems and large feet.
• *height 12cm*
• **£360**   • **Antique Glass**

Ribbed Decanter ▲

• *circa 1875*
Subtly ribbed decanter, the four-sided dimpled body with applied pincer-worked ribs and the neck with milled collar. Original diagonally ribbed stopper with applied pincer-worked edge.
• *height 33.6cm*
• **£475**   • **Laurie Leigh**

Amethyst Cream Jug ◄

• *circa 1820*
Georgian amethyst cream jug with pincer-worked handle.
• *height 10.2cm*
• **£295**   • **Laurie Leigh**

Bristol Blue Tankard ▼

• *circa 1820*
Georgian Bristol Blue tankard with waisted body and pincer-worked handle.
• *height 8.9cm*
• **£185**   • **Laurie Leigh**

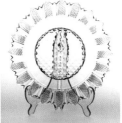

Regency Glass Plate ▲

• *circa 1820*
One of a pair of Regency plates, the centres cut with diamonds, the scalloped rims cut with cross-cut diamonds and prisms.
• *diameter 23cm*
• **£350**   • **Laurie Leigh**

Irish Canoe Bowl

- *circa 1790*
Irish canoe bowl with trefoil rim above a row of large slice-cut strawberry diamonds on scalloped "lemon squeezer" foot.
- *width 35.6cm*
- **£2,250**　　• Laurie Leigh

Kettledrum Bowl

- *circa 1810*
Georgian Irish kettledrum bowl cut with saw tooth rim over a band of large strawberry diamonds on knopped stem and circular foot.
- *height 33cm*
- **£975**　　• Laurie Leigh

Green Victorian Wine Glasses

- *circa 1890*
Unusual pair of Victorian wine glasses with green conical bowls on clear stems with annular collars, blade knops and clear feet.
- *height 13.3cm*
- **£135**　　• Laurie Leigh

Table Lustres

- *circa 1790*
Pair of Georgian table lustres, the sconces cut with diamonds below trefoil rims, the pans also with trefoil rims on cut baluster stems and octagonal feet.
- *height 24cm*
- **£1,650**　　• Laurie Leigh

Blue Ice Jug

- *circa 1880*
Unusual Victorian blue "ice glass" baluster shaped ice jug or ewer with ice pocket and rope twist handle.
- *height 29.2cm*
- **£295**　　• Laurie Leigh

Georgian Decanters with Neck Rings

- *circa 1820*
Pair of Georgian barrel-shaped decanters with three annular neck rings over cut broad shoulder flutes and a broad band of diamonds above a row of vertical blazes and basal broad flutes.
- *height 35cm*
- **£875**　　• Laurie Leigh

Georgian Tapered Decanter

- *circa 1780*
Georgian tapered decanter cut with large shoulder and basal zigzags and engraved with stars between two bands of stars, ovals and zigzags. Lozenge stopper.
- *height 30cm*
- **£495**　　• Laurie Leigh

Victorian Ice Jug

- *circa 1880*
Unusual Victorian ice glass baluster-shaped ice jug or ewer with ice pocket and rope twist handle.
- *height 29.2cm*
- **£275**　　• Laurie Leigh

Small Victorian Wine Glasses ▼

- *circa 1900*

Two of a set of six Victorian small wine glasses with everted rims cut in the Roman style with three rows of small oval lenticles or "printies" over a row of basal circular lenticles, on fluted stems.
- *height 12cm*
- £595 • Laurie Leigh

Bristol Blue Cream Jug ◀

- *circa 1800*

Georgian Bristol Blue cream jug decorated all over with diamond moulding. Pincer-worked handle.
- *height 10.2cm*
- £325 • Laurie Leigh

Green Champagne Glasses ▲

- *circa 1870*

Rare pair of Victorian sea green champagne glasses with double ogee bowls on baluster stems. Designed by T. G. Jackson.
- *height 12cm*
- £350 • Laurie Leigh

Ruby Trailing Wine Glasses ▲

- *circa 1880*

Two of a set of six Victorian wine glasses, the cup-shaped bowls decorated with applied ruby trailing on plain stems and feet.
- *height 12cm*
- £485 • Laurie Leigh

Ship's Decanter and Coaster ▲

- *circa 1800*

Very rare plain Georgian broad-based ship's decanter with three neck rings and original target stopper on its original turned mahogany coaster resting on three tiny castors with leather rollers.
- *height 23cm*
- £1,550 • Laurie Leigh

Expert Tips

The revival of the Venetian glass industry in the 1840s coincided with a demand for honest copies of artefacts from their ancient past. Many items purporting to come from the sixteenth century were in fact made between 1840 and 1880.

Irish Barrel-Shaped Decanter ▶

- *circa 1820*

Georgian Irish barrel-shaped decanter with three annular neck rings over engraved festoons, bows and florets above moulded basal flutes. The decanter is embossed "WATERLOO C CORK".
- *height 27.3cm*
- £925 • Laurie Leigh

Jewellery

The quality of jewellery is defined more by the quality of design and manufacture than the materials.

For many centuries jewellery-makers would invariably vye with each other to incorporate as many jewels into a piece of precious metal as the item could reasonably hold without becoming cumbersome. This technique was deemed to be an indication of the quality of the jewellery-maker's workmanship as well as a statement of the wealth of the eventual wearer of the piece.

During the early twentieth century, Art Nouveau designers challenged these accepted methods, favouring a more sculptural value and eschewing the intrinsic value of the precious stones. The products of both approaches to jewellery-making have retained their value remarkably well but the latter tends to be less influenced by the fluctuations in the value of precious metals.

Early Victorian Earrings ▼

- *circa 1840*

Early Victorian rock crystal and diamond earrings set in silver and gold.
- *length 3cm*
- £2,850 • Wimpole Antiques

Etruscan style Earrings ▶

- *circa 1875*

Victorian 15ct gold Etruscan revival-style earrings with an applied globular design.
- *length 2cm*
- £875 • Wimpole Antiques

Salvador Dali Brooch ▼

- 1950

Eighteen carat gold stylised leaf brooch in the form of a hand with red painted nails, signed "Dali" on the right-hand leaf.
- *length 6.5cm*
- £3,750 • N. Bloom

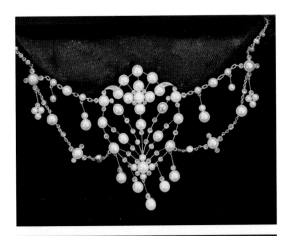

Pearl and Diamond Necklace ◄

- *circa 1905*
Edwardian pearl and diamond necklace with droplets and swag designs.
- *length 6cm*
- **£3,950** • **Wimpole Antiques**

Victorian Gold Bracelet ▼

- *circa 1880*
Victorian gold bracelet in the Etruscan revival style with architectural designs, set with pearls.
- *length 8cm*
- **£2,250** • **Wimpole Antiques**

Gold Brooch/Pendant ▼

- *circa 1875*
Victorian 15ct gold brooch/pendant with natural pearls and floral enamel designs.
- *length 8cm*
- **£1,275** • **Wimpole Antiques**

Pearl Necklace ▲

- *circa 1900*
Fifteen carat gold necklace with half pearls and a second row of swagged pearls between floral droplets.
- *length 4cm*
- **£2,955** • **Wimpole Antiques**

Art Deco Diamond Clasp ►

- *1920*
Art Deco jade and diamond clasp together with a re-strung twisted cultured pearl necklace.
- *clasp 4cm*
- **£3,950** • **N. Bloom**

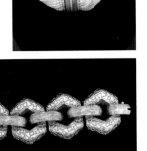

American Gold Bracelet ◄

- *1950*
American heavy-textured gold link bracelet with geometric engraving on some of the links.
- *4cm/link size*
- **£3,300** • **N. Bloom**

Flower Head Earrings

- *circa 1910*
Sapphire and diamond earrings
set in a flower head design of
platinum and gold.
- *length 3cm*
- £4,850 • Wimpole Antiques

Diamond Earrings

- *1920*
Pair of diamond earrings with
oval, circular and rectangular
diamonds within gold settings.
- *length 2.5cm*
- £4,400 • N. Bloom

Gold Victorian Earrings

- *circa 1875*
Victorian Etruscan revival 15ct
gold earrings with a central wheel
motif.
- *width 1cm*
- £875 • Wimpole Antiques

Diamond Leaf Earrings

- *circa 1925*
Mille grain set in platinum
diamond earrings in the form of a
leaf.
- *length 2cm*
- £3,475 • Wimpole Antiques

Victorian drop Earrings

- *circa 1880*
Fifteen carat gold articulated
lozenge- shaped earrings.
- *length 5cm*
- £1,295 • Wimpole Antiques

Expert Tips

*Bear in mind that the majority
of items of jewellery are second
hand and will have been subject
to some wear and tear.*

Silver Gilt Brooch

- *1940s*
American large silver gilt and
cut-glass sapphire floral brooch.
- *7cm x 6cm*
- £95 • Linda Bee

French Pearl and Diamond Earrings

- *circa 1875*
French enamel, gold and
platinum earrings set with
diamonds and natural pearls.
- *length 3cm*
- £2,650 • Wimpole Antiques

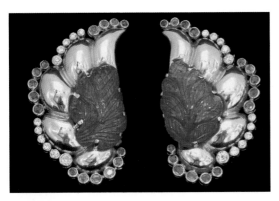

Pair of Ruby Clasps ◀

- *1940*

Pair of ruby and diamond clasps set in stylised gold leaf.
- *length 5cm*
- £2,500 • N. Bloom

Austrian Violet Brooch ▼

- *1950*

Austrian violet brooch with diamonds and jade leaves, set in silver.
- *height 6.5cm*
- £1,650 • N. Bloom

Pearl and Diamond Earrings ▼

- *circa 1925*

Pendulous natural pearl and diamond earrings set in 18ct gold and platinum.
- *length 3.5cm*
- £3,785 • Wimpole Antiques

Edwardian Jade Earrings ▲

- *1910*

Edwardian circular jade earrings set in plain gold with two bands of roping.
- *width 1.5cm*
- £1,200 • N. Bloom

Glass Italian Necklace ▼

- *circa 1990*

Hand blown glass necklace, made from blue, gold, red, green and clear glass squares.
- *length 37cm*
- £135 • Francesca Martire

Emerald Pearl Pendant ▲

- *circa 1890*

French polished emerald set in 18ct gold with floral and swag designs, with diamonds and a single pearl.
- *length 8.5cm*
- £1,975 • Wimpole Antiques

French Art Deco Bracelet ◀

- *1920*

French Art Deco sapphire and diamond bracelet by Trabert and Hoeffer, Mauboussin.
- *length 19cm*
- £44,500 • N. Bloom

Zuni Needlepoint ▶

- *circa 1920*
Unusual antique bracelet from
Zuni, Arizona. Needlepoint with
"Sleeping Beauty" turquoise.
- *width 8cm*
- **£850**   • Jessie Western

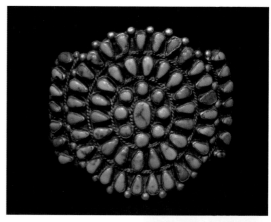

Navajo Bracelet ▲

- *circa 1950*
Antique Navajo American
turquoise and coral feather
shadow box design with the
artist's initials etched into the
bracelet "ML Fowler".
- *width 3cm*
- **£500**   • Jessie Western

Silver and Turquoise Necklace ▼

- *circa 1920*
Unusual Navajo necklace with
five silver and turquoise drops
from Arizona.
- *length 44cm*
- **£395**   • Jessie Western

Butterfly Belt ▲

- *circa 1920*
Silver Navajo butterfly belt with
green turquoise conchos stamped
"AJC" on the belt buckle, from
Arizona.
- *length 83cm*
- **£1,390**   • Jessie Western

Zuni Bow-guard ▶

- *circa 1920*
Pendant or pin and bow-guard,
petit point design by Zuni Native
American Indians.
- *height 6cm*
- **£299**   • Jessie Western

Expert Tips

*Replacing missing precious stones
substantially enhances the value
of antique jewellery items, as
long as the replacement stone
matches the originals in cut,
quality and colour.*

Thunderbird Earrings ▲

- *circa 1950*
Zuni Thunderbird earrings with
turquoise petit point design.
- *height 7cm*
- **£180**   • Jessie Western

Art Deco Feather Pin ◄

- 1920

Art Deco peacock feather pin encrusted with diamonds on each side.
- *length 8cm*
- £4,500　　　　• N. Bloom

Zuni Cuff ▼

- 1950

"Sleeping Beauty" Zuni cuff with 33 turquoise stones set in silver in a traditional design.
- *diameter 9cm*
- £1,200　　　• Wilde One's

Zuni Turquoise Pin ▼

- 1920

Zuni pin flower design with 30 turquoise stones, set on a silver base.
- *diameter 8cm*
- £799　　　　• Wilde One's

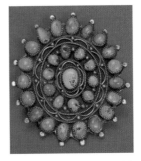

English Silver Brooch ▼

- 1940s

English silver and enamel brooch modelled as a butterfly.
- *6.5cm x 3cm*
- £125　　　• Linda Bee

Sterle Coral Earrings ▲

- 1960

Coral earrings set in gold with gold balls.
- *height 8cm*
- £6,600　　　• N. Bloom

Vic Blister Pearl Heart ▼

- 1920

Vic Blister heart-shaped pearl pendant set with diamonds.
- *width 2cm*
- £2,950　　　• N. Bloom

Gold Linked Bracelet ◄

- *circa 1870*

Gold 15ct linked bracelet with a design of bars with chain link borders.
- *length 15cm*
- £1,475　• Wimpole Antiques

Turquoise Bow-guard ◀

- *circa 1940*

Navajo silver and turquoise bow-guard on its original leather.
- *length 9cm*
- £350
- Jessie Western

Victorian Choker ▲

- *circa 1880*

Black Victorian jet choker.
- *height 6cm*
- £350
- Jessie Western

Zuni Bracelet ▶

- *circa 1930*

Zuni turquoise bracelet with petal design set on silver. There are arrow heads to each side and a hopi cactus and bird engraving.
- *length 14cm*
- £370
- Jessie Western

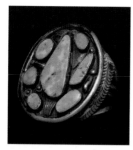

Men's Bracelet ▲

- *circa 1940*

Navajo men's seven stone bracelet with unusual silver setting with a feather one side.
- *diameter 7cm*
- £799
- Jessie Western

Silver Belt ◀

- *circa 1930*

Second-stage concho belt with turquoise stones.
- *length 97cm*
- £2,500
- Jessie Western

Butterfly Pendant ▲

- *circa 1950*

Navajo silver butterfly pendant with turquoise stone.
- *height 5cm*
- £189
- Jessie Western

Gold Chainlink Bracelet

- *circa 1940*
Gold 18ct double chainlink
bracelet with light and dark gold
linkages.
- *length 15cm*
- £1,350 • Wimpole Antiques

Opal and Ruby Necklace

- *circa 1900*
Opal and ruby necklace with oval
opals set in 15ct gold, hanging
from a gold chain with ruby
linkages.
- *length 47cm*
- £3,985 • Wimpole Antiques

Peridot Necklace

- *circa 1900*
Peridot and pearl Edwardian
necklace set in 15ct gold with
lozenge and circular peridots
linked by pearls.
- £1,785 • Wimpole Antiques

Boucheron Diamond Pin

- *1920*
Diamond-encrusted pin in the
shape of a tie by Boucheron.
- *length 4cm*
- £11,500 • N. Bloom

American Earrings

- *1950*
American turquoise glass earrings
by Tiffany, modelled as flower
petals within gold settings.
- *3.5cm x 3.5cm*
- £85 • Linda Bee

Amethyst Necklace

- *circa 1890*
Large amethyst necklace with
stones of graded size set in 15ct
gold, with gold double linkages.
- *length 47cm*
- £3,550 • Wimpole Antiques

Austrian Bracelet

- *1920*
Austrian Art Deco diamond
bracelet set with a large central
diamond surrounded by emeralds.
- *length 16cm*
- £15,00 • N. Bloom

Glass Fruit Necklace ▶

- *20th century*
Venetian glass orange, lemon and
strawberry necklace.
- *length 50cm*
- £150   • Western

Silver-wrapped Crystal Beads ▲

- *circa 1900*
Unusually large and long silver-
wrapped crystal beads. The
graduated facetted crystals are
each wrapped in silver ropework
baskets.
- *length 72cm*
- £470   • Rowan & Rowan

Necklace with Detachable Brooch Pendant ▲

- *circa 1950*
Dramatic white paste necklace
with closed back silver setting,
and detachable pendant with
brooch fittings.
- *length 43cm*
- £550   • Rowan & Rowan

Victorian Paste Heart ▼

- *circa 1900*
Lovely plump white paste heart
brooch with closed-back silver
setting.
- *6cm x 3.5cm*
- £350   • Rowan & Rowan

Lanvin Pendant ▼

- *circa 1950*
Large circular black plastic
pendant with red circular disc by
Lanvin.
- *diameter 5cm*
- £150   • Linda Bee

Expert Tips

*Replacing missing precious
stones substantially enhances the
value of antique jewellery items,
as long as the replacement stone
matches the originals in cut,
quality and colour.*

Victorian Scottish Agate Brooch ▼

- *circa 1860*
Victorian silver brooch set with
multi-coloured Scottish agates.
- *diameter 5.5cm*
- £280   • Rowan & Rowan

Butterfly Ruby and Diamond Brooch ▶
- *Late 19th century*
A late Victorian ruby and diamond brooch in the form of a butterfly, with the wings set *en tremblant*.
- *5cm x 6cm*
- £29,500 • Bentley & Skinner

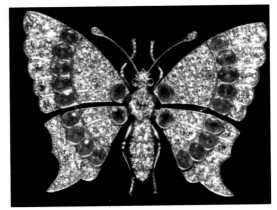

Dragonfly Brooch ▲
- *circa 1900*
A brooch in the form of a dragonfly with enamel and ruby wings set with rose-cut diamonds at the top and tip. The body with a bouton pearl above two diamonds, the tail of shaded enamel, all mounted on yellow gold.
- *6cm x 6.5cm*
- £9,750 • Bentley & Skinner

Emerald Brooch ▼
- *circa 1870*
A Victorian brooch with the central emerald set within a border of old-cut diamonds, set against a red enamel border, and 18 principal old-cut diamonds, with green enamel detail and a pearl at each compass point.
- *3.5cm x 3cm*
- £29,750 • Bentley & Skinner

La Cloche Pendant Watch ◀
- *circa 1930*
A diamond and gemset pendant watch – the rectangular watch back set with brilliant-cut diamonds, suspended by a run of diamonds, and the top and base embellished with carved rubies, sapphires and emeralds.
- *length 11.5cm*
- £42,250 • Bentley & Skinner

Art Deco Diamond Brooch ◀
- *circa 1915*
Diamond brooch with a circular plaque depicting a stylised rising sun over water, the lower section of undulating form with an old brilliant-cut diamond sun above.
- *diameter 4.1cm*
- £12,500 • Bentley & Skinner

Art Nouveau Flower Pendant ▲
- *circa 1900*
An American Art Nouveau pendant with a shaded blue, white and yellow enamelled flower head with brilliant-cut diamond centre, a fan of enamelled leaves to each side below set with pearls.
- *10cm x 8cm*
- £22,500 • Bentley & Skinner

Diamond and Garnet Brooch ▼

- *1850*

Large Victorian oval gold filigree pendant with a central ruby surrounded by medium-size and smaller diamonds, three ruby lozenge-shaped droplets and mounted by a diamond-encrusted platinum ribbon.
- *length 9cm*
- **£16,000**   • N. Bloom

Snake Brooch ▲

- *circa 1900*

English gilt brooch modelled as a snake with stone settings.
- *6cm x 3cm*
- **£150**   • Linda Bee

Venetian Earrings ▲

- *1950s*

Venetian glass earrings modelled as sugared oranges and lemons.
- *2.5cm x 2.5cm*
- **£45**   • Linda Bee

French Gold Necklace ▼

- *1960*

Fine French gold necklace with a graduated design of icicles.
- *length of largest drop 4cm*
- **£2,400**   • N. Bloom

Expert Tips

Abrasion during cleaning of jewellery can be injurious to metal and soft stones. The simplest method for cleaning jewellery is by soaking the item in a strong solution of washing up liquid and then gently rinsing afterwards.

Necklace and Bracelet Set ▼

- *1930s*

Rare interlinked diamante necklace and bracelet set by DRGM, Germany.
- *necklace length 36cm bracelet length 18cm*
- **£350 for the set**   • Linda Bee

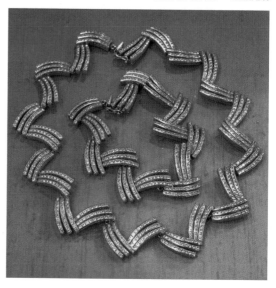

Fly Brooch ▶

- *circa 1850*

A Victorian sapphire, pearl and diamond fly brooch with the body of a sapphire and a pear-shaped natural pearl, the wings set with old brilliant-cut diamonds and the legs with rose-cut diamonds.

- *length 4cm*
- £8,250 • Bentley & Skinner

Art Nouveau Tiara ▼

- *circa 1900*

An Art Nouveau enamel, diamond and pearl ivy spray tiara. The ivy spray with ten green enamel leaves each with rose-cut diamonds, alternately set with six natural baroque pearls and two natural blister pearls.

- *length 18cm*
- £59,750 • Bentley & Skinner

Wasp Brooch ◀

- *circa 1890*

A late Victorian enamel and diamond brooch in the form of a wasp, having rose-cut diamond encrusted wings and head, a finely textured yellow gold body and abdomen with black enamel striped markings.

- *length 2cm*
- £2,750 • Bentley & Skinner

Peacock Diamond Brooch ▲

- *circa 1880*

A Victorian diamond brooch in the form of a peacock, set throughout the body and tail feathers with graduated old-cut and old brilliant-cut diamonds.

- *6.5cm x 6cm*
- £36,000 • Bentley & Skinner

Gemset Peacock Brooch ▼

- *circa 1890*

An Art Nouveau enamel and gemset peacock brooch, the gold head and body enamelled in shades of blue and green with an emerald set plume above the tail of shaded mauve and a single brilliant-cut diamond suspended below.

- *5.5cm x 6cm*
- £29,750 • Bentley & Skinner

Floral Cluster Tiara ▼

- *circa 1880*

A Victorian diamond tiara of floral cluster design, the 11 foliate clusters alternately spaced by graduated scroll work motifs, set throughout with old brilliant-cut diamonds. Can be worn as a tiara or necklace.

- *length 42cm*
- £37,500 • Bentley & Skinner

Ruby and Diamond Necklace ▶

- *circa 1880*

A late Victorian ruby and diamond necklace, the locket pendant set with a central ruby and eight pear shaped rubies in petal formation suspended from a graduated necklace of 28 ruby and diamond links.

- *length 40cm*
- **£47,500** • Bentley & Skinner

White Gold Sardonyx Cameo Ring ▲

- *circa 1930*

A man's ring crafted of 14ct white gold and set with a hand-carved sardonyx cameo depicting a Roman god profile. The stone is layered white and ebony and the profile is in distinct relief.

- *1.95cm x 1.55cm*
- **£270** • Old Cities

Expert Tips

Look out for American jewellery of the 1940s and 1950s. Jewellery manufacturers from France, Belgium and the Netherlands fled from the Nazis, taking a wealth of expertise and materials with them. For the first time America led the world market and the centre of the industry shifted permanently from Europe.

Greek God Cameo Ring ▼

- *1920*

Fourteen carat yellow gold men's ring set with four high quality diamonds in the laurel wreath surrounding the god's head cameo.

- *2.35cm x 2.15cm*
- **£600** • Old Cities

Fabergé Sunray Brooch ▼

- *late 19th century*

A Fabergé brooch, the slightly concave disc with deep blue guilloché enamel of sunray design embellished to one side with a four-leaf clover.

- *length 2.5cm*
- **£12,500** • Bentley & Skinner

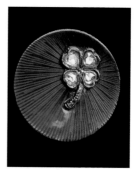

Black Pearl and Diamond Brooch ◀

- *circa 1935*

A brooch crafted of yellow and white gold and set with a highly iridescent Tahitian pearl of a rich metallic ebony colour. Surrounding the pearl are 46 round, pear and oval cut diamonds.

- *length 4.5cm*
- **£950** • Old Cities

Gold Oval-Cut Amethyst Ring ◀

- *circa 1920*

A ring crafted of 14ct yellow gold and set with a mixed oval-cut African amethyst, a vibrant violet in colour.

- *2.35cm x 1.9cm*
- **£360** • Old Cities

Boxer Brooch ▼
- *circa 1900*
French gold "Boxer" dog brooch pendant.
- *length 3cm*
- £1,100 • Harvey and Gore

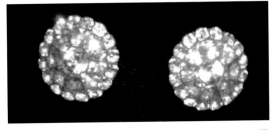

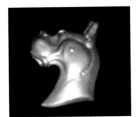

White Paste Buttons ▲
- *circa 1785*
Pair of white paste buttons, close-backed.
- *diameter 3cm*
- £600 each • Harvey and Gore

Gold and Coral Suite ▼
- *circa 1860*
Gold and coral suite of brooch and pendant earrings with original case from Naples, Italy.
- *length 10cm*
- £3,000 • Harvey and Gore

Gold Floral Bracelet ▲
- *circa 1910*
French carved gold bracelet with flowers in oval panels.
- *length 18cm*
- £925 • Harvey and Gore

Pearl and Diamond Bracelet ▼
- *circa 1870*
English natural bouton-shaped pearl and diamond cluster bracelet with circles and heart, expandable chain.
- *length 16cm*
- £17,500 • Harvey and Gore

Enamel and Paste Clock ▲
- *circa 1770*
English red and white paste clock with blue enamel and white pastes to either side. Possibly by James Cox, the movement by William Ballantine.
- *length 9cm*
- £6,000 • Harvey and Gore

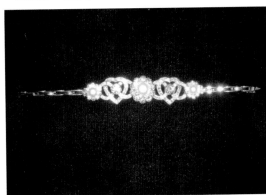

Deco Lapis Bracelet ▶

- *1950*

Art Deco bracelet with circular lapis lazuli discs with gold links and rectangular enamels with dragon designs.
- *length 19cm*
- **£4,500**   • N. Bloom

Swiss Balainot Bracelet ◀

- *1960*

Swiss gold bracelet by Balainot from the "Sheet Range".
- *height 6cm*
- **£3,950**   • N. Bloom

Snake Bracelet ▼

- *1930*

Gilt bracelet styled as a coiled serpent with a spiralled chainlink, body and scale design to the head and tail.
- *8cm x 8cm*
- **£85**   • Linda Bee

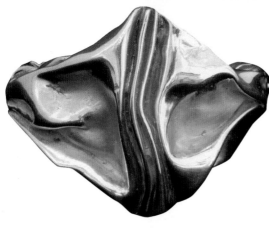

Coral and Diamond Earrings ▼

- *circa 1910*

Carved coral ball and lozenge-shaped earrings set in platinum and 18ct gold with a diamond bow linking the upper and lower sections.
- *length 5.5cm*
- **£2,475**   • Wimpole Antiques

Bear Claw Belt Buckle ▲

- *1950*

Bear claw set in silver foliate design with two flowers of coral and turquoise. Stamped "E. King" and found on an Apache reservation.
- *diameter 7cm*
- **£699**   • Wilde One's

Jade Earrings ▼

- *1930*

Carved flower jade earrings set in 14ct gold.
- *width 2.5cm*
- **£1,150**   • N. Bloom

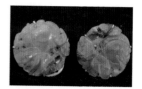

Expert Tips

It is advisable to test all joints in bracelets and necklaces for play, and brooch clasps for security, whilst ring shanks should not be too thin as they can snap.

French Jade Brooch ▶

- *1940*

French jade carved dragon bar brooch set in gold with gold scrolling.
- *length 9cm*
- **£2,400**   • N. Bloom

Ruby and Emerald Pendant ▶

- 1950
French ruby and emerald flower pendant with diamonds and pearls.
- *length 9.5cm*
- £19,500   ● N. Bloom

Santa Domingo Earrings ▲

- 1960
Pair of oval Santa Domingo turquoise and black earrings from Arizona.
- *length 4cm*
- £129   ● Wilde One's

Navajo Green Bracelet ▲

- 1930
Navajo silver bracelet with two rosettes each side of a large green stone.
- *length of stone 6cm*
- £459   ● Wilde One's

Metal Enamel Pin ▲

- circa 1930
English metal enamel pin by Dismal Desmond, with a seated black dog with a purple bow around its neck.
- *7.5cm x 2.5cm*
- £75   ● Linda Bee

Ruby Heart Locket ▼

- 1850
Ruby enamelled heart-shaped locket with central gold star of diamonds and a single pearl, surrounded by scrolling set with diamonds and a gold ring clasp on a velvet neck ribbon.
- *width 2.5cm*
- £8,950   ● N. Bloom

Zuni Ceremonial Ring ▲

- 1920
Lady's Zuni traditional ceremonial ring set with 17 turquoise stones in a flower design.
- *diameter 5cm*
- £269   ● Wilde One's

Expert Tips

Recently, with the return of retro design in both fashion and furniture, jewellery from the 1960s and 1970s has become popular.

431

Tiger's Head Brooch ▶

- *circa 1875*
Onyx, gold and reverse crystal
tiger's head brooch.
- *diameter 3.5cm*
- **£2,800** • Harvey and Gore

Indian Diamond Earrings ▲

- *late 19th–early 20th century*
North Indian diamond earrings in
the shape of flowers and leaves on
a vine in gold.
- *10.5cm x 4.5cm*
- **£11,400** • Samina

Diamond Baazuband ▼

- *early 18th century*
An Indian diamond baazuband
(upper arm bracelet) with a
centre section set with five flat
cut diamonds and folding outer
sections to fit on any arm, wrist
or neck.
- *10cm x 3.8cm*
- **£47,300** • Samina

French Tortoiseshell Compact ▼

- *late 1920s*
French celluloid tortoiseshell
lady's head powder compact.
- *diameter 8.4cm*
- **£120** • Sheryl's Art Deco

Seven Strand Necklace ▼

- *18th century*
A "satlara" necklace set on seven
strings of natural pearls with
central pendants of rubies and
emeralds in stylised floral motifs
and smaller pendants of yellow
sapphires, rubies and emeralds.
- *length 32cm*
- **£9,600** • Samina

Gold Crescent Brooch ◀

- *circa 1880*
French gold crescent brooch with
diamond-set wisteria and gold
bow within.
- *length 3.5cm*
- **£2,900** • Harvey and Gore

Stratton Powder Compact ▶

- *1920s*
English Stratton powder compact,
with celluloid lid depicting
stylised lady and two borzois on a
gold-toned engine-turned back
case.
- *diameter 7cm*
- **£130** • Sheryl's Art Deco

Rectangular Tortoiseshell Compact ▶

- *1920s–30s*
Rectangular tortoiseshell enamel powder compact with trigger-action lid and stylised motif to the front.
- *6cm x 9cm*
- **£100** • **Sheryl's Art Deco**

Pink Enamel Compact ◀

- *1920s–30s*
American pink enamelled handbag compact, with silvered link chain, engine-turned back for rouge and powder, stamped with the maker's mark "E.A.M."
- *5cm x 6.5cm*
- **£130** • **Sheryl's Art Deco**

Compact with Yacht Decoration ◀

- *circa 1928*
English Gwenda powder compact in pink enamel with celluloid trigger-action lid depicting a yacht in foil finish.
- *4.5cm x 8cm*
- **£95** • **Sheryl's Art Deco**

Red and Yellow Enamel Compact ▲

- *1920s–30s*
American red and yellow compact for powder, rouge and lipstick, with fine gilded interior detailing, engine-turned rear case and red and yellow enamelled lid suspended on silvered link chain.
- *5.5cm x 7.5cm*
- **£130** • **Sheryl's Art Deco**

Deere Power Compact ▲

- *late 1920s*
American Deere powder book compact with geometric enamelled lid in black, white, gold, red and green with "Deere" written on the spine of the book.
- *5cm x 7cm*
- **£120** • **Sheryl's Art Deco**

Federal Building Compact ◀

- *1934*
Green enamel powder compact with metal lid from the World's Fair, Chicago, 1934 depicting the Federal Building.
- *diameter 8cm*
- **£120** • **Sheryl's Art Deco**

Combination Compact ▶

- *circa 1926*
Combination compact in green
enamel with marbled lid detail
and yellow diagonal band.
Sections for powder, cigarettes
and money with additional pull-
out lipstick holder with attached
original tassle.
- *10cm x 5cm*
- **£130** • **Sheryl's Art Deco**

Gold Tone Powder Compact ▲

- *circa mid-1920s*
Gold tone powder compact with
enamelled lid depicting lady and
fan.
- *diameter 5cm*
- **£125** • **Sheryl's Art Deco**

Lady Diver Brooch ▲

- *mid-1930s*
Art Deco red enamel and chrome
lady diver brooch, made in
Czechoslovakia and still on its
original card.
- *6cm x 4cm*
- **£65** • **Sheryl's Art Deco**

Expert Tips

*The mid-eighteenth century saw
a change in stone-setting
techniques. Settings earlier than
that were open, with the reverse
of the stone revealed. After
that period, settings tend
usually to be closed, with a
solid metal backing.*

Lady and Mirror Compact Case ▶

- *early 1930s*
French chromed lady and mirror
powder compact with engine-
turned back case inscribed
"MUGUET DE MAI".
- *4.8cm x 4.8cm*
- **£130** • **Sheryl's Art Deco**

Organ Grinder and Monkey Brooch ▶

- *circa 1928*
American Art Deco brooch of an
organ grinder and monkey linked
by a chain with separate pin
holders for each.
- *height 5.5cm*
- **£68** • **Sheryl's Art Deco**

Aeroplane Brooch ◀

- *mid-1930s*
Celluloid black and white Art
Deco aeroplane brooch.
- *5cm x 5cm*
- **£85** • **Sheryl's Art Deco**

Lady and Dog Brooch ◀

- *circa 1922*
American Art Deco lady and
dog brooch made of white
metal.
- *height 6cm*
- **£78** • **Sheryl's Art Deco**

Scottie Dog Brooch ▶
- *early 1930s*
Art Deco Scottie dog brooch
made of celluloid on chrome.
- *height 5cm*
- £38   • Sheryl's Art Deco

Arrow Brooch ▲
- *early 1920s*
Art Deco sterling silver arrow
brooch by Neja.
- *7cm x 2cm*
- £125   • Sheryl's Art Deco

Stylized Art Deco Brooch ▼
- *late 1920s*
French Art Deco celluloid brooch
of a stylized man and woman
leaning against each other.
- *4cm x 9cm*
- £85   • Sheryl's Art Deco

Lady Golfer Brooch ◀
- *early 1930s*
American Art Deco gold tone
metal brooch of a stylised lady
golfer.
- *height 6cm*
- £25   • Sheryl's Art Deco

Yacht Brooch ▲
- *early 1930s*
Art Deco German celluloid and
chrome yacht brooch.
- *6.5cm x 6cm*
- £58   • Sheryl's Art Deco

Vogue Brooch ▼
- *early 1920s*
Art Deco brooch of a flapper with
a dog, given as a gift with a year's
subscription to *Vogue* magazine.
Metal with red detailing.
- *5cm x 7cm*
- £58   • Sheryl's Art Deco

Scottie Dog Brooch ▼
- *late 1920s*
Art Deco chrome and red enamel
Scottie Dog brooch.
- *6cm x 5cm*
- £38   • Sheryl's Art Deco

Flapper and Dog Brooch ▼
- *early 1920s*
American white metal Art Deco
brooch of a flapper lady with a
dog tugging at the leash.
- *6cm x 5cm*
- £68   • Sheryl's Art Deco

Marine Items

Marina antiques provide a rich field of study, dependent on history more than condition.

Marine antiques depend for their value and collectability more on their history than their condition. That is not to say that with two items of equal historical merit the more pristine would not be more valuable, although perhaps its provenance might be more questionable. Bells, blocks, lights, clocks, chronometers, compasses, model ships, bosun's calls, clasp knives and sailor's cap ribbons are just some of the items that fall within this fascinating area, but the sub-divisions are bewildering. There are, for instance, more than 70 different types of bosun's call, ranging in value from £75 to £300.

Collectors of marine items tend to fall into two categories. Those who have an active passion for the sea, and often seek to adorn their yachts with mementoes of the sea, and those who simply appreciate the precision and fine craftsmanship of the instruments.

Model of East Indiaman Ship ▼
- *circa 1860*
A well-made model of an East Indiaman ship.
- *88.9cm x 33cm x 1.17m*
- **£8,500** • **Langfords Marine**

Ship's Saloon Chairs ▼
- *circa 1900*
A pair of English ship's saloon chairs on cast iron stands. The mahogany backs have hand-painted insets depicting a three-masted vessel flanked by mermaids.
- *height 88.9cm*
- **£1,600** • **Langfords Marine**

Chronometer by Breguet ▶
- *circa 1865*
A Breguet chronometer No. 885 in mahogany box with brass fittings. The clock has a brass casement with silver face and roman numerals.
- *17.8cm x 16.3cm x 16.3cm*
- **£4,950** • **Langfords Marine**

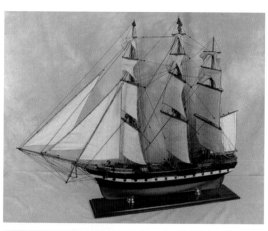

Napoleonic Model Ship ▶
- *circa 1805*
A handsome Napoleonic prisoner of war model ship made of bone. This third rate ship of the line has carved stern detail.
- *29.2cm x 11.43cm x 34.3cm*
- **£9,600** • **Langfords Marine**

Sextant by Whitbread ▲
- *circa 1850*
Sextant by G. Whitbread, in original oak box with brass fittings.
- *width 27cm*
- £1,650 • Langfords Marine

Celestial Globe ▲
- *circa 1950*
Celestial globe with brass fittings, and original oak box with carrying handle.
- *height 28cm*
- £1,280 • Langfords Marine

Octagonal Telescope ▲
- *circa 1780*
Fine octagonal fruitwood telescope with brass single draw and lens housing.
- *length of case 31cm*
- £800 • Langfords Marine

Marine Chronometer ▲
- *circa 1840*
Two-day marine chronometer by Parkinson & Frodsham, Change Alley, London 1705. Housed in a mahogany double-tier case.
- *height 16cm*
- £7,000 • T. Philip & Son

Steam Yacht ▼
- *circa 1910*
Model steam yacht complete with planked hull, working steam engine, brass funnel prop and lights and eight portholes.
- *length 1m*
- £8,000 • Langfords Marine

Chinese Dish from the Ship "Diana" ▼
- *circa 1817*
Chinese porcelain blue and white dish from the ship "Diana" which sank near Malacca on 4 March, 1817.
- *diameter 28cm*
- £185 • Langfords Marine

Weichert Chronometer ▼
- *circa 1860*
Two-day chronometer by Weichert, in a coromandel box with brass inlay and handles.
- *height 20cm*
- £4,300 • Langfords Marine

Tulip Frame Sextant ▶

- *circa 1860*
Tulip frame sextant in original oak box lined with green base, brass handle and fittings.
  - *width 28cm*
  - **£1,250**   • **Langfords Marine**

Pond Yacht ▲

- *circa 1900*
Pine pond yacht with three sails and brass fittings modelled as a pilot cutter.
  - *width 1.64m*
  - **£1,500**   • **Langfords Marine**

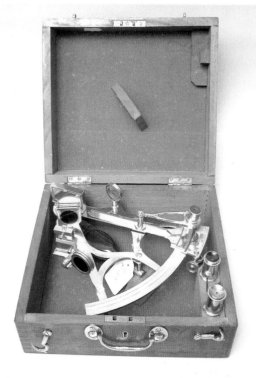

Bone Beaker Aberdeen Schooner ▲

- *circa 1880*
Bone beaker with the inscription; "Succefs to the Aberdeen Schoone Proto", below an engraved schooner in full sail.
  - *height 9.5cm*
  - **£320**   • **Langfords Marine**

Dry Land Compass ▼

- *circa 1800*
Gimballed dry land compass in brass case.
  - *diameter 11.5cm*
  - **£1,150**   • **Langfords Marine**

Georgian Coconut Cup ▲

- *circa 1810*
Georgian coconut cup with silver mounts raised on splayed legs with paw feet.
  - *height 13.5cm*
  - **£690**   • **Langfords Marine**

Half-Boat ◀

- *circa 1900*
Half-boat racing yacht, made from fruitwood for use as a boatbuilder's model.
  - *width 87cm*
  - **£1,600**   • **Langfords Marine**

Small Brass Barometer ▶

- *circa 1800*
Barometer H. M. S. Britannia Prize, by Coomes Devenport in original leather box.
- *diameter 5.5cm*
- £850   • **Langfords Marine**

Model of S.S. "Rallus" ▲

- *circa 1900s*
A builder's scale model of the S.S. "Rallus", which was built for the Cork Steam Ship Co Ltd, Cork, Ireland by Swan Hunter & Wigham Richardson Ltd. Masts, derricks and rigging with scale ivorine and nickel plated blocks, deck details including anchor winches, fairleads, bollards, ventilators, deck rails, hatches, and deck winches. The superstructure with lifeboats.
- *67cm x 2.34m*
- £9,500   • **Anthony Outred**

Nelson's Last Signal ◀

- *circa 1910*
Nelson's last signal, "England expects that every man shall do his duty."
- *38cm x 57cm*
- £430   • **Langfords Marine**

Parallel Brass Rule ▲

- *circa 1920*
Brass parallel rule.
- *length 46cm*
- £120   • **Langfords Marine**

Model of the Queen Mary ◀

- *circa 1940*
Model of the Queen Mary by Bassett-Lowke, with display case.
- *width 32cm*
- £400   • **Langfords Marine**

Musical Instruments

Some musical instruments are now purely decorative. Those that are still musical are to be preferred.

The development of musical instruments is inextricably linked to the development of music. As new contexts for music-making arose, so new instruments were devised in response. Some instruments became obsolete altogether, while others evolved to accommodate the developments. Music was then written specifically for the new instruments. The cycle continues to the present day.

Musical instruments have also evolved because of extraneous factors – by the beginning of the nineteenth century,

for instance, the violin had acquired a longer neck and fingerboard, a larger bass bar and a thicker soundpost. This type of development was due, at least in part, to the need for louder noises that could be heard easily in larger rooms.

Every musical instrument is unique, but expensive mistakes can be made by collectors who are ignorant about what makes a musical instrument collectable. For example, pianos and grand pianos can vary wildly in price, depending on their maker and date of construction.

Single Action Square Piano ◄
- 1783
A square piano by John Broadwood. Five octaves, single action, with brass underdampers. Mahogany case with string inlay, raised on trestle support.
- 1.63m x 57.2cm
- £7,200 • Music Room

Dolmetsch Spinet ▼
- 1915
Five-octave Arnold Dolmetsch spinet in red, gold and black decorated by the Omega Workshop.
- 1.17m x 78cm
- £7,000 • Robert Morley

Grecian Harp ▼
- circa 1821
Forty-three string S & P Erard Grecian harp in black and gold.
- 1.7m x 80cm
- £9,575 • Robert Morley

Schwieso and Erard Harp ◄
- circa 1820
A double-action harp in full playing order. The black lacquer body with gilt line decoration, the fluted column surmounted by gilt gesso Grecian terms. Eight pedals and with louvres intact.
- height 1.73m
- £9,500 • Music Room

Gretsch Guitar ▼
● *1957*
Gretsch guitar. Model 6120, with
original white cowboy case.
S/N:22080
● *height 1.05m*
● **£5,545**   ● **Vintage Guitars**

Gibson Guitar ▼
● *1953*
Gibson Model SJ200. Sunburst
finish. S/N A17263.
● *height 1.05m*
● **£5,850**   ● **Vintage Guitars**

Gibson Guitar ▲
● *1960*
Gibson. Model Les Paul Special.
Finish TV Yellow. S/N O 1432.
● *height 1m*
● **£3,850**   ● **Vintage Guitars**

Gibson Guitar ▲
● *1960*
Gibson. Model: ES330. Sunburst
finish. Dot neck. Factory order
No. R29523.
● *height 99cm*
● **£2,850**   ● **Vintage Guitars**

Fender Guitar ▼
● *1959*
Fender. Model: Esquire. Blond
finish. S/N 40511.
● *height 95cm*
● **£5,500**   ● **Vintage Guitars**

Fender Guitar ▼
● *1959*
Fender. Model: Jazzmaster.
Sunburst finish. Original tweed
case. S/N 31596.
● *height 1.04m*
● **£2,095**   ● **Vintage Guitars**

Fender Guitar ▲

- *1952*
Fender. Model: Esquire with original thermometer case. S/N 4047.
- *height 98cm*
- **£7,500**   • **Vintage Guitars**

Gibson Guitar ▲

- *1949*
Gibson. Model: SJ200. Maple back and sides stained and a new scratch guard added by Gibson in the mid-1960's. S/N A3487.
- *height 1.05m*
- **£4,950**   • **Vintage Guitars**

Epiphone Guitar ▼

- *1958*
Epiphone. Model: Coronet. Refinished in black.
- *height 96cm*
- **£1,895**   • **Vintage Guitars**

Martin Guitar ▼

- *1965*
Martin. Model: D28. Brazilian rosewood. Replaced fingerboard. S/N 201923.
- *height 1.03m*
- **£2,300**   • **Vintage Guitars**

Martin Guitar ▲

- *1965*
Martin. Model: O18. S/N: 208 916.
- *height 99cm*
- **£1,895**   • **Vintage Guitars**

Epiphone Guitar ▲

- *1967*
Epiphone. Model: casino. Long scale model. Near mint condition. Original card case.
- *height 1.08m*
- **£2,500**   • **Vintage Guitars**

Broadwood Six Octave Piano ◄

- *1827*

Square piano by Broadwood in fine mahogany case with turned reeded legs, the instrument has six octaves and is fully restored.
- *1.73m x 63.5cm*
- £7,700 • Music Room

Broadwood Square Piano ▲

- *1802*

A restored square piano by Broadwood with five and a half octaves, single action, and brass underdampers. Mahogany case raised on square tapered legs.
- *1.63m x 60cm*
- £5,850 • Music Room

Longman and Broderip ▲

- *circa 1795*

A restored square piano by Longman and Broderip. Five octaves with double action. Mahogany case raised on square tapered legs, the nameboard with floral swags to the enamel nameplate.
- *1.58m x 53.3cm*

Stodart Square Piano ▼

- *circa 1823*

A square piano by Stodart. A fine double-action instrument in mahogany case with rosewood crossbanding and brass trim, two music drawers and supported on six turned reeded legs.
- *1.7m x 62cm*
- £7,500 • Music Room

Adam Beyer Piano ▲

- *1788*

A fully restored square piano by Adam Beyer. Five octaves with single action, in a mahogany case supported on a trestle stand with pedal to operate the swell mechanism.
- *1.58m x 56cm*
- £8,250 • Music Room

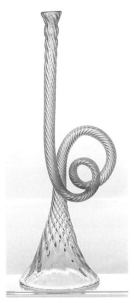

Expert Tips

Wooden-framed pianos of the late nineteenth century are pretty but impossible to tune.

Glass Bugle ▶

- *late 18th–early 19th century*
Georgian wrythen bugle made from glass with a double-loop to the tube.
- *length 28cm*
- £90 • Antique Glass

Concert Grand Piano ▶
- *1935*

Model D concert grand in a very
unusual mahogany high gloss
polish (most concert grands are
black). Fully rebuilt by Steinway
and Sons.
- *length 2.7m*
- **£58,500**　　　• Steinway

Mahogany Cased Organ ▲
- *1805*

Rare organ by Broderip &
Wilkinson, London, in full
working order, complete with six
barrels each with up to eight
different tunes.
- *height 2.26m*
- **£24,500**　　• Anthony Outred

Rickenbacker Guitar ▲
- *1967*

Rickenbacker. Model: 365.
Fireglow finish. S/N GC1415.
- *height 98cm*
- **£1,895**　　　• Vintage Guitars

Fender Guitar ▼
- *1969*

Fender. Model: Jazzbase. Sunburst
finish. Original case. S/N 283918.
- *height 1.15m*
- **£2,250**　　　• Vintage Guitars

Gretsch Guitar ▲
- *1962*

Gretsch. Model: 6120. Original
case. S/N 67410.
- *height 1.09m*
- **£2,500**　　　• Vintage Guitars

Tomkinson Square Piano ▶
- *circa 1815*

Square double-action piano by Tomkinson. The case of rosewood with satinwood crossbanding and satinwood legs, with three music drawers.
- *1.68m x 61cm*
- **£12,500**   • **Music Room**

Broadwood Grand Piano ◀
- *circa 1868*

John Broadwood and Sons of London grand piano with rosewood case and carved legs.
- *length 1.75m*
- **£4,820**   • **Robert Morley**

Erard Paris Gothic Harp ▲
- *1896*

Forty-six string Erard Paris gothic harp made of rosewood and gold.
- *1.7m x 90cm*
- **£15,600**   • **Robert Morley**

Harp Lute ▼
- *circa 1810*

Light harp lute with painted black case decorated with gold work and raised detailing on the pillar.
- *height 83.5cm*
- **£2,525**   • **Robert Morley**

Erard Gothic Harp ▲
- *circa 1859*

Forty-six string Erard gothic harp made in Paris of maple and gold with decorated pillar.
- *length 2.16m*
- **£15,000**   • **Robert Morley**

Rosewood Gothic Harp ◀
- *circa 1896*

Erard Paris gothic harp with 46 strings made of rosewood and gold.
- *1.76m x 94cm*
- **£15,600**   • **Robert Morley**

Expert Tips

The provenance of a musical instrument is often of more consideration than its manufacture. Jimi Hendrix's Woodstock guitar is worth about 300 times more than a similar Fender Stratocaster.

445

Silver & Pewter

**Antique silver seems to be out of fashion right now –
but it won't be for ever.**

Silver prices have fallen to an all time low at the moment, which means that for collectors this really should be a good time to buy before prices start to rise again.

On the whole, decorative silver has remained in its original form since the time of manufacture, so it is important to beware of reproductions. Fortunately, fake silver items are not common simply because the workmanship involved in making fine silver pieces makes it uneconomical. Fake hallmarks have been known to appear on the market from time to time, though, so always make sure that you take a dealer's receipt when buying items. Utilitarian pieces, however, have often evolved, so look out for jugs that may have started out as saucepans or mugs.

Child's Whistle ▶
- *early 18th century*
Very unusual child's silver whistle with pierced engraving of tulips circling the mouthpiece.
- *length 10cm*
- £995   • Ian Roper

Heart-shaped Mirror ▲
- **1896**
This unusual heart-shaped mirror was made in London by William Comyn. The mirror has decorations of flowers and cherubim for ornamentation, and an easel back, while the glass itself swivels to suit the person using it.
- *47cm x 37cm*
- £2,250   • Langfords

Dressing Set ◀
- *circa 1875*
A first quality French silver dressing set made by Aucoc et Cie in Paris. The set has perfume bottles, powder jars and a soap box sitting in a fitted wooden case.
- *height 15cm*
- £12,500   • Langfords

Silver Wall Sconce ▶
- **1912**
This silver wall sconce was made by L A Crichton in London in a style that would have been popular during the reign of Charles II. The decoration shows two cherubim amid flowers and birds with the two candleholders having gadroon borders.
- *30cm x 20cm*
- £1,800   • Langfords

Archibald Knox Candlestick ◀

- *circa 1900*

One of a pair of pewter candlesticks by Archibald Knox for Liberty, with a tulip design, on a large circular base.
- *height 19cm*
- **£3,000**   • **Victor Arwas**

Silver Cruet Set ▲

- *circa 1880*

Silver cruet set with salt, mustard and pepper pot with lobed lower bodies and gadrooned borders.
- *height 11cm*
- **£190**   • **H. Gregory**

French Liquor Set ▼

- *1880*

French liquor set of 12 silver cups with foliate scrolling and matching tray, engraved with the initials "J. C."
- *height of cup 5cm*
- **£575**   • **Tagor**

Loving Cup ▲

- *circa 1900*

Tudric pewter loving cup with double handles with "honesty flower" design and a cartouche with the inscription "For Old Times Sake", by Veysey for Liberty.
- *height 20cm*
- **£650**   • **Victor Arwas**

Silver Centrepiece ▲

- *1865*

A silver centrepiece with finely chased figures of "romantic" children by The Barnards. Fully hallmarked.
- *height 33cm*
- **£5,750**   • **Percy's**

Silver Salts ▶

- *circa 1760*

Pair of Georgian silver salts with beaded decoration and blue glass liners.
- *height 7cm*
- **£675**   • **Barrett & Towning**

Basket Centrepiece ▶

- *1918*

A silver three-basket centrepiece made by Sharman Dermott Neill in Chester. The centre bowl would have been used for fruit or flowers while the side baskets, which are detachable, would contain nuts, fruit or sweets.
- *30cm x 22cm*
- £3,000 • Langfords

Victorian Decanter Set ▲

- *1880*

A Victorian silver-plated and gold-plated barrel decanter set made in Sheffield. This piece would have generally been used for whisky and brandy and is still in very good working order.
- *29cm x 27cm*
- £2,385 • Langfords

Victorian Coffee Pot ▲

- *1840*

Victorian silver coffee pot made by EE & JW Barnard of London. This pot is finely chased with floral designs, an insulated handle, and a chrysanthemum finial.
- *height 30cm*
- £1,850 • Langfords

Victorian Cake Basket ▼

- *1843*

Victorian silver cake basket with hand-chased floral decorations and a scroll border, made by William Brown in London.
- *21cm x 26.5cm*
- £1,950 • Langfords

Victorian Inkstand ▼

- *1867*

A Victorian silver inkstand made in London by D & C Hands. The stand has a leaf and floral design and a removable inkwell with hinged cover.
- *8cm x 17cm*
- £785 • Langfords

Pair of Silver Candlesticks ▶

- *1911*

Pretty pair of silver candlesticks of George II design, made in Sheffield.
- *height 16cm*
- £875 • Manser Antiques

Edwardian Photo Frame ▼

- *1903*

A beautiful Edwardian pierced and embossed photo frame, decorated with lion mask, cherubs, birds, foliage and wild beasts. The frame was made by WJ Myatt & Co. in Birmingham and has a dark blue velvet backing.
- *13cm x 9cm*
- £585 • Langfords

Georgian Candle Snuffer and Tray ▼

- *1806*

A Georgian silver candle snuffer and tray made in London – the snuffer by William Barratt in 1806 and the tray by Tim Renou in 1792. It is not unusual for items of this type to be of separate dates and makers and subsequently put together over the years.
- *24cm x 9cm*
- £1,450 • Langfords

Silver Teapot with Bee ▶

- *circa 1900*

Silver teapot with unusual foliate and insect design with a bee finial and stylised bamboo spout and handle.
- *height 16cm*
- £1,500　　　　　• Tagor

Continental Pewter Plate ▼

- *circa 1790s*

Continental pewter plate with a rifle stamp on the border and a single reeded rim.
- *diameter 25.5cm*
- £70　　　　　• Jane Stewart

Victorian Silver Cruet ◀

- 1867

A fine solid silver cruet comprising ten items, with pierced scrolled sides and scrolled central handle, by G Angel, London.
- *25cm x 30cm*
- £3,750　　　　　• Percy's

Art Nouveau Frame ▲

- *circa 1900*

Silver and enamel Art Nouveau picture frame by William Connell.
- *height 23cm*
- £2,800　　　　　• Victor Arwas

Tudric Jug ▲

- *circa 1900*

Tudric Liberty pewter "fish and the sea" jug with brass handle, and the inscription "U. C. C."
- *height 19cm*
- £680　　　　　• Victor Arwas

Liberty Biscuit Tin ▲

- *circa 1900*

Pewter tudric box by Archibald Knox with floral design.
- *height 12.5cm*
- £1,200　　　　　• Victor Arwas

Expert Tips

On most coasters one must look out for a hallmark on the lower rim, which overlaps the wooden base.

Asprey Square Waiter ▶
- *1927*
A small square salver/waiter with serpentine corners to the raised border, on four hoof feet. Made in London by Asprey & Co.
- *17.5cm x 17.5cm*
- **£295**   • **Hayward & Stott**

Hester Bateman Sugar Tongs ▲
- *1776*
A fine pair of George III brightcut sugar tongs, made in London by Hester Bateman.
- *length 13.5cm*
- **£225**   • **Hayward & Stott**

Pair of Scottish Toast Racks ▼
- *1937*
A pair of Scottish five piece toast racks of rectangular form with celtic knot lug handles. Made in Edinburgh by Hamilton & Inches.
- *length 10cm*
- **£275**   • **Hayward & Stott**

Bettridge Vinaigrette ▼
- *1833*
Lightly gilded vinaigrette with engine turned decoration to base and lid, enclosed within a foliate border. Gilded interior, with hinged pierced floral grille. Made in Birmingham by Joseph Bettridge.
- *3.4cm x 2.4cm*
- **£320**   • **Hayward & Stott**

Sovereign Case with Sovereign ◀
- *1900*
A fine sovereign case cum Vesta/match safe; initialled "CE" and well decorated. The case was made in Birmingham by Constantine & Floyd and holds a 1914 gold sovereign.
- *length 7.6cm*
- **£245**   • **Hayward & Stott**

Smith Vinaigrette ▼
- *1843*
A vinaigrette engraved and initialed "AR". Silver hinged grill and gilded interior base and cover. Made in Birmingham by Edward Smith.
- *3.5cm x 2.4cm*
- **£325**   • **Hayward & Stott**

Irish Lighthouse Sugar Castor ▼
- *1896*
Victorian Irish lighthouse-shaped sugar duster or castor, with embossed floral designs on lid and body, standing on a circular pedestal foot. Made in Dublin by Charles Lambe.
- *height 10.5cm*
- **£275**   • **Hayward & Stott**

Victorian Sovereign Case ◀
- *1898*
A fine engine-turned sovereign case, initialled "HR" within a gartered cartouche which includes an 1887 half sovereign. Made in Birmingham by Deakin & Francis.
- *diameter 3.5cm*
- **£225**   • **Hayward & Stott**

Art Nouveau Sauceboat ▶

- *circa 1900*
German Art Nouveau pewter
sauceboat with fixed base
designed by Orovit.
- *height 12cm*
- £300 • **Victor Arwas**

Salts with Shell Feet ▲

- *1913*
Pair of silver circular salts with
a serpentine scalloped rim,
standing on three scalloped
feet.
- *diameter 7.5cm*
- £395 • **Barrett & Towning**

Scrolled Silver Box ▼

- *1840*
Oblong silver box with embossed
scrolling and floral designs and a
cartouche inscribed with the
name "Hilda".
- *length 13cm*
- £175 • **Barrett & Towning**

Silver Pepper Castor ▲

- *circa 1860*
Silver pepper castor of baluster
form with a pierced and engraved
cover surmounted by a finial lid.
- *height 19cm*
- £325 • **Barrett & Towning**

Silver Milk Jug ▶

- *circa 1940*
Silver milk jug with a lobed body,
engraved and embossed
decoration and a reeded handle.
- *height 11cm*
- £300 • **Barrett & Towning**

Silver Tea Set ◀

- *circa 1851*
Three-piece silver tea set with
large scrolled handle standing on
small paw feet.
- *height/teapot 17cm*
- £540 • **H. Gregory**

Pair of Victorian Salt Cellars ▶

- *1866*

Pair of Victorian salt cellars of compressed circular form, each with beaded rim, embossed foliate design and three hoof feet. Made in London by Robert Hennell III.
- *diameter 5cm*
- £165   • Hayward & Stott

Pair of Pierced Napkin Rings ▲

- *1879*

Pair of elegant pierced napkin rings with raised beaded rims and vacant cartouches. Made in Birmingham by Frederick Elkington.
- *3cm x 4cm*
- £145   • Hayward & Stott

George III Child's Mug ▲

- *1819*

George III child's mug of tapering cylindrical form, with beaded rim and foot and reeded bands. Made in London by William Eaton.
- *diameter 5.5cm.*
- £295   • Hayward & Stott

Pepper Castor ▼

- *1765*

A George III pepper castor of plain baluster form on spreading foot, with beaded rims and spiral knop finial. Made in London by John Delmester.
- *height 12cm*
- £425   • Hayward & Stott

Edinburgh Fish Slice ◀

- *1820*

A George IV fish slice with fiddle pattern and a pierced blade and scroll border, initialled "GMæ". Features two maker's marks: Charles Robb and D McL. Made in Edinburgh.
- *length 32cm*
- £275   • Hayward & Stott

Chick Pepperette ▼

- *1908*

A finely modelled chick pepperette, sitting on a flat base with pierced removable head. Import marks for Chester; imported by Berthold Muller.
- *4cm x 4cm*
- £195   • Hayward & Stott

Cherub Place Name Holders ▼

- *circa 1880*

A set of four silver place name holders depicting cherubs holding a plate of fruit aloft. Probably made in Germany.
- *9cm x 6cm*
- £325   • Hayward & Stott

Grape Scissors ▼

- *circa 1880*

A fine pair of plated grape scissors or shears with decorated stems.
- *length 16.5cm*
- £95   • Hayward & Stott

Edwardian Porringer Christening Cup ▲
- **1906**
An Edward VII porringer christening cup, circular with everted rim, embossed with gadroons and flutes, with reeded strap handles. Inscribed "Pamela Ann Sutherland, 1906". Made by C J Vander Ltd.
- 7.5cm x 14.5cm
- £365   • Hayward & Stott

Aeroplane Cruet Stand ▼
- *circa 1930*
A rare and fine early 20th century silver-plated cruet stand in the form of an aeroplane, with four bottles, salt container and toothpick holder.
- 25.5cm x 38cm x 35.5cm
- £5,600   • R. Gardner

Afternoon Tea Pot ▲
- **1782**
A George III afternoon teapot of slightly compressed bullet form, later embossed with roses and trailing foliage, with wooden "mushroom" finial, scrolled fruitwood handle and curved spout.
- 10cm x 21cm
- £495   • Hayward & Stott

Aeroplane Desk Set ▲
- *circa 1930*
Exceptionally fine early twentieth century silver-plated desk set in the form of an aeroplane.
- 16.5cm x 36cm x 37cm
- £4,800   • R. Gardner

Horse's Hoof Cigar Lighter ▼
- *circa 1908*
A rare and unusual cigar lighter in the shape of a horse's hoof, in tortoiseshell and silver. The hunting horn unscrews to reveal a reservoir. A small wick would go up through the horn to light cigars.
- height 10cm
- £1,450   • R. Gardner

Silver Book Mark ▲
- *circa 1899*
Unusual boxed silver book mark with ship anchor and motto "Here I cast".
- length 10cm
- £980   • R. Gardner

William and Mary Silver Clothes Whisk ▲
- **1693**
William and Mary sterling silver clothes whisk of conical shape. A family coat of arms is engraved just above the hallmark and is currently being researched.
- height 16.7cm
- £4,400   • Sanda Lipton

Expert Tips

Pierced silver often has a leather backing, making it hard to clean without staining the leather or damaging the delicate silver. Once you have cleaned it, use a preservative spray.

Dutch Urn ▼

- *circa 1800*

A Dutch urn and cover with an embossed floral leaf design and a wood knob finial.

- *13cm x 10cm*
- £65   • Jane Stewart

Pewter Ladle ▼

- *circa 1780*

English pewter soup ladle with shallow bowl and plain thumb piece.

- *length 32cm*
- £50   • Jane Stewart

Butter Dish ▲

- *circa 1900*

German pewter Art Nouveau butter dish on raised feet, with foliate and tulip designs, by Kayserzinn.

- *height 13cm*
- £300   • Victor Arwas

Silver Salt and Pepper Pot ▲

- *circa 1923*

Matching silver salt and pepper pot, of octagonal baluster form with finial lid, from E. Johnson & Son Ltd., Derby.

- *height 9cm*
- £240   • Barrett & Towning

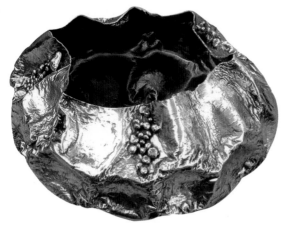

Continental Pewter Bowl ▼

- *18th century*

Continental pewter deep dish, with floral engraving to the centre, and a single reeded rim.

- *diameter 23cm*
- £70   • Jane Stewart

Cigarette Case ▼

- *circa 1920*

Silver cigarette case with meshed effect and lines of gold inlay.

- *length 12cm*
- £65   • H. Gregory

Pewter Continental Bowl ▼

- *circa 1900s*

Continental pewter bowl with a wide border and moulded rim.

- *diameter 30cm*
- £120   • Jane Stewart

Silver Bowl ◄

- *1930*

Silver "Crumpled Paper" bowl with fruit decoration.

- *height 16cm*
- £1,100   • S. Kalms

French Silver Bowl

- *circa 1890*
Silver punch bowl/wine cooler with elaborate chasing and foliate designs, four scrolled handles, acanthus leaf swags and ribboning.
- *height 47cm*
- £32,500   • S. Kalms

Silver and Glass Jar

- *1945*
Glass cosmetic container with a silver cover and a bone moon shaped thumbpiece, made in London.
- *height 9cm*
- £150   • Evonne Antiques

Silver Bon-Bon Dish

- *1901*
Liberty & Co. cymric silver bon-bon dish designed by Oliver Baker. Hallmarked "Birmingham 1901".
- *9cm x 10.5cm*
- £1,500   • Liberty

Art Nouveau Mirror

- *circa 1930*
Art Nouveau silver mirror with elaborate scrolling and a young lady holding a light in the shape of a lily.
- *height 59cm*
- £4,500   • S. Kalms

Condiment Set

- *1911*
Condiment set comprising two glass bottles with faceted stoppers, on a silver stand with extended ring handle, supported on silver ball feet.
- *height 21cm*
- £240   • Evonne Antiques

Hunt & Roskell Butter Shells ▶

- *1889*

A pair of Victorian sterling silver butter shells by Hunt & Roskell made in the shape of clam shells and supported by three feet in the shape of snail or cockle shells.

- *10.4cm x 10.7cm*
- **£680**   • **Sanda Lipton**

Silver Wax-jack ▲

- *circa 1769*

Silver wax-jack, or taper stand by John Carter II. Consists of a six-sided pierced base with a gadroon border. A silver vertical pillar rises from the centre of the base and ends in a detachable flame finial.

- *15.2cm x 10.67cm*
- **£2,500**   • **Sanda Lipton**

Hester Bateman Silver Sugar Basket ▼

- *1789*

Unusual George III sterling silver sugar basket by Hester Bateman made without a handle. The boat-shaped body is plain and the rim of the body has an applied reeded moulding.

- *9.9cm x 16.26cm x 10.67cm*
- **£1,950**   • **Sanda Lipton**

Pewter Teapot ▼

- *mid-19th century*

Pewter squat teapot with mother-of-pearl knob.

- *height 10.8cm*
- **£75**   • **Early Oak**

Justis Brandy Warmer ◀

- *1761*

George III brandy warmer by William Justis with a bowl-shaped body that flares outwards at the rim. The handle is partly silver but continues as a plain, turned wooden handle to facilitate a cool grip of the pan.

- *6.1cm x 19.3cm*
- **£2,400**   • **Sanda Lipton**

George III Silver Shoe Horn ▲

- *1817*

George III sterling silver shoe horn with a simple backward curving shape. The plain cast handle is joined to the body of the shoe horn with a clearly visible seam.

- *17.5cm x 4.7cm*
- **£1,245**   • **Sanda Lipton**

Victorian Silver Owl Pepper Pot ▲

- *1854*

Victorian novelty pepper pot in the shape of a seated owl. The head pulls off so that the body can be filled with pepper and the top of the head is pierced with scroll-shaped holes.

- *8.9cm x 3.1cm*
- **£1,500**   • **Sanda Lipton**

Pair of Electroplate Double Salt Cellars ▲

- *circa 1850*

A pair of Victorian salt cellars in the form of two open cowrie shells. The inside of the shells is silver gilt and the shells are mounted on branches of coral supported on the back of a dolphin.

- *7.6cm x 14.5cm x 9.4cm*
- **£2,875**   • **Sanda Lipton**

George II Sugar Nips

- *circa 1740*

One of a pair of George II silver gilt cast rococo sugar nips. The nips have shell-like decoration on the bowls and on the central pin and leaf decoration on the arms and the finger grips.
- *length 12.7cm*
- £315 • Sanda Lipton

Victorian Table Cigar Lighter ▲

- *1871*

Victorian table cigar lighter with oval curved body rising to a domed centre. At both ends of the lighter's body are cast ram's heads which hold a detachable torch with flame finial and circular cage terminal.
- *12.2cm x 12.2cm x 8.9cm*
- £1,400 • Sanda Lipton

Half-gill Tankard ▲

- *late 19th century*

English pewter half-gill measure tankard.
- *height 6.4cm*
- £40 • Early Oak

Pewter Half-pint Measure ▲

- *19th century*

Half-pint pewter measure stamped "VR" with slight nick to rim.
- *height 8.9cm*
- £50 • Early Oak

Victorian Sweetmeat Dish ▼

- *1841*

Victorian sweetmeat dish in the shape of an open oyster shell by William Moulson. Apart from around the edges, the silver is smooth both on the front and on the back.
- *9.1cm x 7.9cm*
- £670 • Sanda Lipton

Gill Tankard ▼

- *18th century*

English pewter one-gill measure tankard with hallmarks on the rim of a stamp, a crown, and the letters "C", "V" and "R".
- *7.5cm x 6.3cm*
- £35 • Early Oak

George III Sauceboat ▼

- *1811*

Irish George III sauceboat by James Le Bas. The plain body is oval and has a strong band of reeding while the body is supported by three cast shell and hoof feet and also has a cast flying scroll handle.
- *10.7cm x 17cm x 8.6cm*
- £1,750 • Sanda Lipton

Pewter Vases ▼

- *circa 1890*

Pair of nineteenth-century hammered pewter vases on square bases by T.W. & S.
- *height 21cm*
- £60 • Early Oak

Pewter Half-pint Tankard ▼

- *19th century*

English half-pint tankard with small hole to base by Yates & Birch, Isle of Man.
- *height 9cm*
- £40 • Early Oak

Large Pewter Charger ▼

- *18th century*

A charger of simple proportions, flat-rimmed and undecorated.
- *diameter 51.5cm*
- £295 • Early Oak

English Half-pint Tankard ▲

- *18th century*

Pewter tankard with hallmarks on the rim: James Yates, Castle Stamp, Letters No. 6, Crown over Letters V R over Numbers 154, Number 36.
- *9.3cm x 7.5cm*
- £35 • Early Oak

Pewter Charger ▲

- *18th century*

English pewter charger initialled "E.H." on reverse.
- *diameter 37.5cm*
- £180 • Early Oak

Silver Soup Tureen ▲

- *late 17th century*

An exceptional Baltic parcel-gilt soup tureen, possibly from Estonia, cornucopia-shaped handles, stylised fruit ball feet and moulded garland decoration centred with classical heads.
- *22.8cm x 40.6cm*
- £145,000 • Partridge

Pewter Pint Tankard ▼

- *early 19th century*

English pewter pint tankard by James Yates.
- *height 11.4cm*
- £50 • Early Oak

Pewter Plate ▼

- *18th century*

Plain pewter flat-rimmed plate, the only decoration being a single incised band to the interior.
- *diameter 22.9cm*
- £75 • Early Oak

George I Silver Etui ▼

- *circa 1725*

Silver étui case containing a variety of implements including a knife, fork, spoon, scissors, a ruler, a pair of dividers, tweezers, a pencil and ivory tablets.
- *height 9.5cm*
- £6,200 • Partridge

Silver Goblets ▶

- **1970**

Set of four silver goblets with silver gilt interiors with rusticated stems on circular bases, by Christopher Lawrence.
- *height 15cm*
- **£1,000** • **Themes**

French Measures ▼

- *circa 1850*

Set of French pewter jug measures from demi-litre to demi-decilitre.
- *17cm x 12cm*
- **£200** • **Jane Stewart**

Pewter Coffee Pot ▼

- *circa 1860*

Coffee pot by James Dickson of Sheffield of baluster form with scroll handle and acorn leaf finial.
- *23cm x 23cm*
- **£70** • **Jane Stewart**

Cigar Case ▲

- *circa 1920*

Silver cigar case with three compartments allowing for half coronas.
- *length 12cm*
- **£160** • **H. Gregory**

English Quart Tankard ▼

- *circa 1860*

Pewter quart tankard with strap handle and banded decoration.
- *18cm x 13cm*
- **£100** • **Jane Stewart**

Continental Pewter Plate ▲

- *circa 1780s*

Continental pewter plate with single reeded rim.
- *diameter 25cm*
- **£70** • **Jane Stewart**

Georgian Silver Basket ◀

- *circa 1799*

Oval Georgian sweetmeat basket, with a swing handle, pierced foliate designs and apron support.
- *11cm x 38cm*
- **£4,000** • **Barrett & Towning**

Adam Style Teapot ◄

- *circa 1860*
English Adam style pewter teapot
with floral and swag decoration,
surmounted by ivory finial.
- *16cm x 25cm*
- £65 • Jane Stewart

Silver Perfume Spray ▼

- *circa 1910*
Silver perfume spray on a faceted
glass circular bottle.
- *height 17cm*
- £175 • Barrett & Towning

Glass Sugar Shaker ▼

- *circa 1906*
Glass sugar castor of baluster
form, with a pierced silver cover,
engraved floral designs and ball
finial.
- *height 16.5cm*
- £225 • Barrett & Towning

Pepper Castor ▲

- *circa 1800*
English pewter pepper castor of
baluster form with acorn finial.
- *height 12cm*
- £30 • Jane Stewart

English Pewter Ladle ▼

- *circa 1820*
English pewter ladle with a wide
circular bowl.
- *length 33cm*
- £50 • Jane Stewart

Georgian Silver Candlesticks ◄

- *1782*
A superb set of four Georgian
silver candlesticks, fully
hallmarked by John Parsons,
Sheffield, England.
- *height 34cm*
- £10,750 • Percy's

Regency Silver Coasters ▶

- **1823**
A set of four coasters, finely chased with flowers and shells. Made in Sheffield by T & J Settle.
- *width 17.5cm*
- **£5,750**   • Percy's

Dutch Nautilus Cup ▼

- *circa 1875*
A rare Dutch nautilus cup in the seventeenth century style. The shell is finely engraved with classical scenes.
- *height 25cm*
- **£5,250**   • Percy's

Teak Cigarette Box ▶

- **1903**
Teak cigarette box within a silver frame with "Cigarettes" in silver on the lid.
- *width 13cm*
- **£260**   • H. Gregory

Cigarette Box ▼

- *circa 1900*
Sheffield silver cigarette box with a diamond pattern lid and plain panel, the interior containing two compartments.
- *width 17cm*
- **£180**   • H. Gregory

"Neff" Model Ship ▶

- *circa 1875*
A German solid silver model of a mythical vessel.
- *height 28cm*
- **£2,750**   • Percy's

Parcel-gilt Beaker ▲

- *circa 1570*

An early and rare French beaker by Steffan Vesuch, the base engraved with initials "I.H. 6 1/2 lot", divided into two main registers, the top decorated with intricate arabesque design and the lower half with beaten and incised roundel motifs.

- *height 7.6cm*
- **£34,000**   • Partridge

Set of Four Victorian Salts ▲

- *1874–5*

Victorian silver salts by Charles Favell & Co with spoons by J. A. Rhodes.

- *height 9.2cm*
- **£2,200**   • Partridge

George II Cream Jug ◄

- *1747–8*

Silver cream jug by Edward Wakelin, London, with scrolling feet and moulded foliate decoration.

- *height 14cm*
- **£12,000**   • Partridge

German Silver Snuff Box ▼

- *1717–18*

Circular snuff box by Philip Stengelin, Augsburg, the lid depicting a seascape set in a cartouche and scrolling arabesque decoration.

- *diameter 7cm*
- **£7,000**   • Partridge

Victorian Sugar Bowl ▼

- *1880–1*

Highly unusual silver sugar bowl by R. Martin and E. Hall with hand-hammered or martelé finish.

- *height 10.8cm*
- **£3,950**   • Partridge

Odiot Parcel-gilt Salts ▲

- *circa 1820*

Set of four salts by Odiot, Paris in the form of dolphins with intertwined tails supporting shells, stamped "ODIOT" under base.

- *height 10.16cm*
- **£35,000**   • Partridge

Régence Snuffer Tray ▲

- *1718*

French Regency snuffer tray by Toussaint Bingeant, profuse beading decoration to the rim on four claw feet.

- *length 22.2cm*
- **£9,200**   • Partridge

Pair of Charles II Covered Vases ▲

- *circa 1670*

Silver-gilt covered vases or ginger jars decorated with putti amongst scrolling acanthus foliage and arabesques.

- *height 40.3cm*
- **£135,000**   • Partridge

Silver Vesta Box ▲
- *circa 1880*
Small silver vesta box with floral engraving and a ring at the side.
- *length 3.5cm*
- **£70**　　　● **H. Gregory**

English Charger ▼
- *circa 1740*
Georgian English pewter charger, of plain design with a single reeded rim.
- *diameter 46cm*
- **£350**　　　● **Jane Stewart**

Silver Cruet Set ◄
- *circa 1930*
Silver Art Deco cruet set consisting of mustard, salt and pepper in the style of tankards.
- *height 5cm*
- **£360**　　　● **H. Gregory**

Silver Vesta Box ▲
- *circa 1880*
Ladies' silver vesta box with floral engraving and a plain shield panel, ring to the side.
- *length 5cm*
- **£70**　　　● **H. Gregory**

Vesta Box ▲
- *circa 1880*
Plain silver vesta box with hinged lid and striker on the base.
- *length 5.5cm*
- **£72**　　　● **H. Gregory**

Four-section Cigar Case ▲
- *circa 1930*
Four-section silver plate cigar case.
- *length 13cm*
- **£49**　　　● **H. Gregory**

Georgian Silver Tureen ▶
- *circa 1825*
Georgian oval entrée dish of plain design with banded decoration, surmounted by a handle in the form of a coiled snake.
- *length 28cm*
- **£895**　　● **Barrett & Towning**

George II Chocolate Pot ▼

- *1753-4*

Chocolate pot in silver and fruitwood incorporating a chinoiserie plaque and maker's mark of Thomas Heming.
- *height 29.2cm*
- **£22,000**   • **Partridge**

Fiddle Soup Ladle ▼

- *1800*

George III sterling silver fiddle pattern soup ladle, hallmarked in London by Eley & Fearn.
- *length 33cm*
- **£325**   • **I. Franks**

Victorian Tea Set ▲

- *1879-80*

Three-piece tea set by Richard Martin and Ebenezer Hall in silver and parcel gilt. A very rare British essay into the hand-finished or martelé silver that was being produced in America at this time.
- *height 14.6cm*
- **£14,500**   • **Partridge**

George III Tea Caddy ▲

- *1780*

George III sterling silver tea caddy with original crest and bead detail, hallmarked in London.
- *height 10cm*
- **£3,275**   • **I. Franks**

Silver Pheasant ▲

- *1966*

Hand chased sterling silver pheasant, hallmarked "London".
- *length 19cm*
- **£975**   • **I. Franks**

George II Tea Urn ▼

- *1729-30*

George II Scottish tea urn by Hugh Gordon, Edinburgh, with maker's marks and slightly later Baring arms.
- *height 33.6cm*
- **£52,000**   • **Partridge**

Harris Silver Salver ▼

- *1892*

Victorian sterling silver salver with bead detail, hallmarked in London by Charles Stuart Harris.
- *diameter 15cm*
- **£275**   • **I. Franks**

George II Sauceboat ▼

- *1748*

George II sterling silver sauceboat with fine scroll decoration and standing on three shell feet.
- *height 11cm*
- **£975**   • **I. Franks**

Silver Ashtray ▶

- **1900**
Silver ashtray made in London
with five recesses within the
border.
- *width 8cm*
- £1,900   • H. Gregory

Silver Art Nouveau Vase ▼

- **1850**
Silver Art Nouveau vase with
green glass lining and profuse
pierced decoration.
- *height 34cm*
- £1,850   • Tagor

Silver Soap Box ▲

- *circa 1888*
Victorian silver soap box of plain
design with curved corners.
- *width 8cm*
- £225   • Barrett & Towning

Four Silver Salts ▼

- *circa 1808*
Set of four urn-shaped silver salts
with gadrooned and fluted
decoration, made in London.
- *height 6cm*
- £475   • Barrett & Towning

Claret Jug ▲

- *circa 1880*
Victorian claret jug with silver
spout and collar with scrolled
decoration, made in London.
- *height 21cm*
- £1,350   • Tagor

Georgian Silver Salt ▲

- *circa 1794*
Elegant silver Georgian salt with
a fluted body and scrolled
handles, on a square base.
- *height 8cm*
- **£210** • Barrett & Towning

Set of Four Salts ▶

- *1883*
Set of four silver salts embossed
with bird and floral designs and
four silver spoons with gilt bowls
in original box finished in velvet
and silk.
- *width of box 21cm*
- **£675** • Barrett & Towning

Art Nouveau Creamer ▼

- *circa 1936*
Art Nouveau silver cream jug,
with moulded lip, strap handle
and raised on a square moulded
base.
- *height 8.5cm*
- **£160** • Barrett & Towning

Continental Pewter Dish ▼

- *circa 1790*
Continental dish with single
reeded rim and the owner's
initials "I.F.B." on the front and
rear.
- *diameter 35cm*
- **£200** • Jane Stewart

Stamp and Cigarette Case ▼

- *circa 1910*
Silver stamp and cigarette case
with blue enamel lid.
- *width 9cm*
- **£275** • Barrett & Towning

Silver Cocktail Shaker ◀

- *circa 1910*
Art Deco silver cocktail shaker
with plain sides and banded
decoration.
- *height 22cm*
- **£575** • Barrett & Towning

George III Teapot ▶
- *1784*

George III sterling silver teapot decorated with fine bright-cut engraving, hallmarked in London by Samuel White.
- *height 13cm*
- **£1,595**   • I. Franks

George III Sugar Basket ◀
- *1796*

George III sterling silver sugar basket, bright-cut, engraved and hallmarked by Urquart & Hart.
- *height 16cm*
- **£975**   • I. Franks

Silver Toast Rack ▼
- *1895*

Victorian unusual sterling silver toast rack, hallmarked in London.
- *height 10cm*
- **£465**   • I. Franks

Silver-chased Bowl ▲
- *1845*

Victorian sterling silver-chased bowl, hallmarked in London by Angel & Savory.
- *diameter 15cm*
- **£545**   • I. Franks

Hancock Silver Bowl ▲
- *1911*

Sterling silver bowl with cut card decoration, hallmarked in London by George Hancock.
- *diameter 12cm*
- **£365**   • I. Franks

Sheffield Pierced Dish ▼
- *1919*

Sterling silver pierced dish, hallmarked in Sheffield by William Hutton.
- *width 26cm*
- **£995**   • I. Franks

Silver Coffee Pot ▲
- *1774*

Silver coffee pot made in London by William Collings, with replacement handle.
- *height 31cm*
- **£2,650**   • D & B Dickinson

Edwardian Candlesticks ▲
- *1905*

Edwardian pair of sterling silver square based candlesticks, hallmarked.
- *height 22cm*
- **£1,425**   • I. Franks

Vignelli Carafe ▶
- **1970**

Christofle and Venini silver
carafe and six shots, designed by
Vignelli. Stamped "Christofle,
Italy".
- *height of carafe 22.5cm*
- **£2,000** ● Themes

Silver Photograph Frame ▲
- **1935**

Silver photograph frame with a
concave design.
- *height 26cm*
- **£350** ● Evonne Antiques

Pair of Decanters ▶
- **1910**

Pair of glass decanters with silver
mounts and handle, made by
Walker and Hall.
- *height 23cm*
- **£3,900** ● S. Kalms

Twenties Toastrack ▼
- *circa 1929*

Silver Art Deco toastrack with
six bays, canted corners and a
pierced apron.
- *height 6cm*
- **£190** ● Barrett & Towning

Archibald Knox Barrel ◀
- **1902**

Tudric pewter biscuit barrel
designed by Archibald Knox,
with blue and green enamelling.
- *15cm x 13cm*
- **£1,500** ● Liberty

Embossed Mustard Pot and Spoon ▼

- *1826*
Embossed silver mustard pot, made in London by Thomas Ballam. The whole is ornately decorated with cartouches and scrolling foliate designs.
- *height 7.5cm*
- **£895**   • D & B Dickinson

Lion's Head Salt Cellar ▼

- *1895*
Silver salt cellar with lion head decoration and paw feet. Made in London by John Bodman Carrington.
- *height 5.5cm*
- **£695**   • D & B Dickinson

Leaf Dish ▼

- *1900*
Silver leaf-shaped dish with curled rim and vein pattern. Made in Birmingham by Joseph Gloster.
- *length 17.5cm*
- **£125**   • D & B Dickinson

Silver Mustard Pot ▲

- *1864*
Made in Birmingham by Hirons, Plante & Co, the body is of a pierced lattice design and the lid flips open with the aid of a scalloped shell motif.
- *height 7cm*
- **£350**   • D & B Dickinson

Silver Salt Cellar ▲

- *1824*
One of a pair of salt cellars made in London by Charles Fox of a stylised acanthus leaf form on a pedestal base.
- *height 5cm*
- **£975**   • D & B Dickinson

Pair of Sauceboats ▼

- *1888*
Late Victorian sauceboats, made in London by John Marshall Spink with scalloped decoration.
- *height 10cm*
- **£650**   • D & B Dickinson

Oval Mustard Pot ▼

- *1804*
Oval silver mustard pot made in London by Peter, Ann & William Bateman. The round bowl condiment spoon has matching marks.
- *height 7cm*
- **£695**   • D & B Dickinson

Expert Tips

Long-term cleaners or foaming preparations which can be applied by sponge are best for cleaning your silver. When cleaning, always protect the hallmark with your thumb and use a cloth especially kept for the purpose. Any proprietary cleaner is bound to remove a little of the surface silver, so use it sparingly and infrequently.

Whisky Measure ◄

- *1876*
Silver whisky measure in the shape of a thimble with the motto "Just a thimbleful" along the rim. Made in Birmingham in by Hilliard & Thomason.
- *height 5.5cm*
- **£275**   • D & B Dickinson

Liberty & Co. Tea Set   ◄

- *1903*

Pewter tudric tea set with turquoise enamel mount, and tray designed by Archibald Knox for Liberty & Co.
- *length 42cm*
- £4,500   • Liberty

Silver Pierced Dish   ▼

- *1950*

Silver dish with pierced border, supported on a pedestal base with banded decoration.
- *height 15cm*
- £175   • S. Kalms

Silver Gilt Heron Cigarette Box   ▲

- *circa 1909*

Silver gilt heron standing on a silver box, the mechanism opens the cover for the heron to bend and pick out a cigarette. Made by W. H. Sparrow of Birmingham.
- *height 30cm*
- £4,250   • S. Kalms

Set of Salts   ►

- *1880*

Set of six silver gilt salts with individual spoons with original presentation box.
- *width 24cm*
- £1,100   • S. Kalms

Polar Bear Inkwell   ◄

- *circa 1900*

Continental silver polar bear inkwell and tray, with a pair of silver candlesticks, together with silver letter opener.
- *18cm x 29cm*
- £2,250   • S. Kalms

Pair of Match Strikers ◀

- 1897

Pair of glass match strikers with silver rims, made in Birmingham.
- *height 10.5cm*
- £750   • Evonne Antiques

Victorian Pewter Cup ▼

- *circa 1870*

Victorian engraved pewter cup with floral engraving, scrolled handle and banded decoration, inscribed with the name "Maude".
- *7.5cm x 10cm*
- £50   • Jane Stewart

Silver Tea Strainer ▼

- *circa 1920*

Silver tea strainer made in Sheffield, England, with pierced and engraved decoration and lattice handle.
- *length 13cm*
- £160   • Barrett & Towning

Sheffield Silver Dish ▼

- 1937

Octagonal silver dish with double handles of ivory, made in Sheffield, England.
- *diameter 30cm*
- £180   • Evonne Antiques

Expert Tips

Regular cleaning of antique silver produces a patina quite different from that of new silver, and one which cannot be accelerated or reproduced artificially.

Silver and Glass Bowl ▶

- 1920

Ladies' melon-shaped glass bowl with a silver banded collar and tortoiseshell insert.
- *diameter 15cm*
- £280   • Evonne Antiques

Caddy Spoon ▼
- **1847**

Made in Sheffield by Aaron Hadfield, this caddy spoon is of an irregular scallop-shaped form with elaborate scrolled handle.
- *length 15cm*
- **£425**   • D & B Dickinson

Castletop Vinaigrette ◀
- **1837**

Silver vinaigrette with decorated lid of a castletop mansion. Made by Taylor & Perry, Birmingham.
- *3.5cm x 2.2cm*
- **£750**   • B. Silverman

Silver Horse Figurine ▲
- **1903**

Silver figure of a horse in motion with mouth open and flowing mane and tail, by Nereisheimer in Chester.
- *17cm x 23cm*
- **£2,500**   • B. Silverman

Lily Pattern Flatware ▼
- **1865**

Set of lily pattern flatware by George Adams, London, including large and small ladles, three types of spoon and two types of fork.
- *length 15cm*
- **£8,000**   • B. Silverman

Irish Dish Ring ▲
- **1916**

Irish silver dish ring decorated with foliage, flowers, birds and animals by Weir of Dublin.
- *8cm x 19cm*
- **£2,700**   • B. Silverman

Expert Tips

Photograph and catalogue your silver, and keep valuations up to date. Insurance companies prefer accurate descriptions.

Pair of Silver Wine Coasters ▶
- **1820**

Silver wine coasters by Charles Fox, London, with wooden bases and scrolling acanthus leaf decoration.
- *diameter 15cm*
- **£3,500**   • B. Silverman

Silver Tureen and Stand ▼
- *1788*
Silver soup tureen with two large side handles and lid on a gently curving stand, by Fogelberg & Gilbert.
- *37cm x 55cm*
- £30,000   • B. Silverman

Four Scofield Candlesticks ▲
- *1783*
A set of four silver candlesticks supported on circular patterned bases by John Scofield, London.
- *height 30cm*
- £19,000   • B. Silverman

Venison Dish ▼
- *1845*
Large silver venison dish supported on four feet with two handles and a large domed lid, by Hamilton & Co.
- *35cm x 65cm x 47cm*
- £27,000   • B. Silverman

Storr Silver Salts ▲
- *1814*
Set of four silver salts with out-turned embossed rims raised on four ornate feet by Paul Storr, London.
- *6cm x 8.5cm x 7cm*
- £12,000   • B. Silverman

Storr Fish Slice ▲
- *1820*
Silver fish slice with decorated handle by Paul Storr, London.
- *length 24cm*
- £2,300   • B. Silverman

Vinaigrette with Flowers ▲
- *1819*
Silver vinaigrette by Betteridge with an outer raised floral border surrounding an inner rectangular pattern of stylised flowers.
- *2.7cm x 1.8cm*
- £600   • B. Silverman

Horse Hooves Ink Well ▶

• *circa 1900*
Silver writing set made of two
horse hooves, set in silver with
two ink wells with silver covers,
standing on a silver base on ball
feet.
• *width 46cm*
• £900   • S. Kalms

Small Silver Teapot ▼

• *circa 1904*
Edwardian silver teapot of small
proportions with bone handle
and finial lid.
• *height 15cm*
• £240   • Evonne Antiques

William Commings Frame ▼

• *1899*
Silver William Commings
hourglass frame decorated with
cherubs and foliage.
• *height 22cm*
• £450   • Evonne Antiques

Letter Rack ▲

• *1937*
Silver letter rack, with a double
circle design, mounted on a
mahogany base.
• *height 17cm*
• £350   • Evonne Antiques

Victorian Sauceboat ◀

• *circa 1891*
Victorian silver sauceboat with
vacant panel within embossed
decoration raised on a splayed
foot.
• *height 9.5cm*
• £240   • Barrett & Towning

Sporting Items

Collecting sporting memorabilia is irresistible, but it pays to keep an eye on the future before spending lavishly.

So much of sporting memorabilia is desperately ephemeral. At the time of writing, Jonny Wilkinson's right boot, with which he kicked the drop goal that won the 2003 Rugby World Cup for England, must be virtually priceless. Geoff Hurst's 1966 Football World Cup winner may not be quite as financially glossy as it once was – who knows? What will happen if we win several more Rugby World Cups? Or when the memory of Wilkinson is known only to the students of arcanity, when rugby has long been outlawed as too dangerous?

The safest investments in sport are probably ones that do not feature as the most romantic at the moment. For example, a well-made fishing reel or rare tennis racquet may stand the financial test of time better than the boots of any Golden Boy of sort. What price now for one of Henry Cooper's Lonsdale Belts? Henry who?

General

Child's Football Boots ▶
- **1930**
Child's leather football boots in original condition.
- *length 18cm*
- **£125**   • Sporting Times

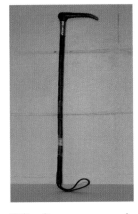

Riding Crop ▲
- *circa 1930*
Bamboo riding crop with 13 crosses on the bone handle, above a silver collar, engraved with the letters "H. S."
- *length 61cm*
- **£65**   • Sporting Times

Bowling Balls ▼
- **circa 1900**
Pair of lignum bowling balls with ivory central plaques, on a stand.
- *diameter 12cm*
- **£110**   • Henry Gregory

Trophy Cap ▲
- **1923–4**
Black velvet cap with gold braiding and tassel with the letters "S. S. O. B." in gold.
- *medium*
- **£45**   • Sporting Times

Snow Shoes ▲
- *circa 1900*
Canadian snow shoes made from
wood with leather mesh base and
fasteners.
- *length 1.03m*
- £95　　　• Sporting Times

Bamboo Shooting Stick ▶
- *circa 1920*
Bamboo shooting stick with a
folding rattan seat, with metal
spike and brass fittings.
- *length 75cm*
- £195　　　• Sporting Times

Leather-cased Thermos ▼
- *circa 1900*
Brass thermos with original
leather case with the inscription
"B. R." and a long leather carrying
handle with leather buckle.
- *height 38cm*
- £125　　　• Sporting Times

Leather Football Boots ▼
- *1930*
Leather football boots in
excellent condition appointed by
Stanley Matthews.
- *length 30cm*
- £125　　　• Sporting Times

Goggles ▲
- *1940*
Goggles with brass and metal rim
on a leather backing with
adjustable rubber straps.
- *width 18cm*
- £28　　　• Sporting Times

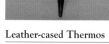

Billiard Scorer ◀
- *circa 1910*
Wall-mounted mahogany billiard
scorer, with brass numerals and
sliding markers.
- *92cm x 35cm*
- £280　　　• Henry Gregory

Leather Riding Boots ▼
- *1930*
Pair of gentleman's brown leather polo boots with laces, three straps with brass buckles and wood shoe trees.
- *height 61cm*
- £170 • **Sporting Times**

Leather Football ▼
- *circa 1940*
Novelty miniature leather football.
- *miniature*
- £20 • **Sporting Times**

Child's Riding Seat ▶
- *1880*
A child's saddle made from wicker, with curved base and leather fasteners, to fit on a pony.
- *height 57cm*
- £275 • **Sporting Times**

Expert Tips

Hesitate before buying an over-polished sporting item such as a saddle bag or football, as this can decrease the value of the condition item.

Leather Gaiters ▲
- *circa 1920*
Pair of leather gaiters with leather straps and metal buckles.
- *length 29cm*
- £28 • **Sporting Times**

Saddle Bags ▲
- *circa 1930*
Brown leather saddle bags in fine condition with leather straps and brass buckles.
- *length 18cm*
- £155 • **Sporting Times**

Football Trophy ▼
- *1956*
Football trophy presented to Mr. and Mrs. Clarke of Berkhampstead Football Club 1956.
- *height 17cm*
- £45 • **Sporting Times**

Leather Gaming Bag ▼
- *circa 1900*
Leather gaming bag in original condition with brass clasp and leather carrying strap.
- *width 30cm*
- £125 • **Sporting Times**

Travelling Primus Stove ▲
- *circa 1890*

Travelling primus in a circular leather case with leather strap.
- *diameter 13cm*
- £155 ● Sporting Times

French Boules ▼
- *circa 1900*

Pair of French boules with original leather carrying strap.
- *diameter 20cm*
- £32 ● Sporting Times

Child's Skis ▼
- *1920s*

Child's wooden skis with matching poles and bindings.
- *1.05m x 8cm*
- £120 ● Henry Gregory

B C F C Cap ▼
- *1933*

B C F C velvet blue and maroon football cap with silver braiding and tassel. On the inside "English manufactured Christys, London, Horton Stephens, Ltd., The Shops Brighton College and Ward 1933–45".
- *diameter 20cm*
- £45 ● Sporting Times

Riding Whip ▶
- *circa 1900*

Leather riding whip, with silver collar.
- *length 1.70m*
- £140 ● Henry Gregory

Travelling Sandwich Tin ▲
- *circa 1890*

Travelling leather case, the interior enclosing a sandwich tin and flask.
- *15cm x 15cm*
- £155 ● Sporting Times

Cribbage Board ▼
- *circa 1900*

Marchline tartanware cribbage board box.
- *26cm x 10cm*
- £310 ● Henry Gregory

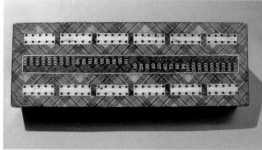

Fishing

Brass Gaff ▶
- **1880**
A Hardy telescopic brass gaff with lignum handle.
- *length 35cm*
- £100–£200 • **T. Murland**

Trout Priest ▲
- **1910**
An unusual trout priest in staghorn, carved in the form of an eagle with a dragonfly motif.
- *length 30cm*
- £200–£300 • **T. Murland**

Perfect Fly Reel ▲
- **1920–1**
Rare Hardy "Perfect" duplicated MK-2 salmon fly reel with smooth alloy foot held with two screws, ivorine handle, nickel silver line guide and duplicated check.
- *diameter 10.8cm*
- £120–£180 • **B. J. Ayers**

Expert Tips

Fishing reels proliferate but usually only the good ones have survived. If in doubt, at least make sure it works.

Uniqua Fly Reel ▶
- **circa 1923**
Hardy "Uniqua" duplicated MK-2 trout fly reel with horseshoe latch, ivorine handle, smooth brass foot and retaining most of the black lead finish.
- *diameter 7.3cm*
- £130–£150 • **B. J. Ayers**

Allcocks Reel ◀
- **circa 1920–40**
Wood fishing reel by Allcocks with brass fittings and ebonised handles.
- *diameter 9cm*
- £50 • **Sporting Times**

Fishing Flies ▼
- **1920**
A case of 45 fishing flies.
- *15cm x 10cm*
- £100–£200 • **T. Murland**

Cased Flies ▲
- **1920**
A case of 70 fishing flies.
- *15cm x 10cm*
- £100–£200 • **T. Murland**

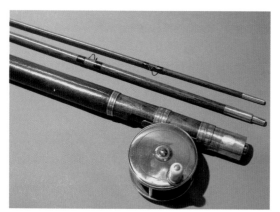

Fly Rod ◄
- *circa 1880*
Green heart trout rod of three sections, with brass reel and ivory handle.
- *length 2.8m*
- £190 • Henry Gregory

Fly Box ▼
- *circa 1915*
Leather lined box with 12 glass and alloy containers for flies, with original tweezers and pocket.
- *13cm x 10cm*
- £90 • Henry Gregory

Small Fishing Reel ◄
- *circa 1920–40*
Small wood fishing reel with a brass plate and turned decoration.
- *diameter 7cm*
- £25 • Sporting Times

Fishing Reel ▼
- *circa 1920–40*
Wood fishing reel with brass handles and plate with turned decoration.
- *diameter 10cm*
- £45 • Sporting Times

Leather Fly Wallet ▼
- *circa 1920–40*
Leather fly wallet with eight compartments.
- *width 16cm*
- £28 • Sporting Times

Wood Fishing Reel ▼
- *circa 1920–40*
Wood fishing reel with banded decoration, brass fittings and ebonised double handles.
- *diameter 8cm*
- £35 • Sporting Times

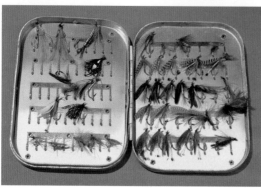

Hardy Fly Box ◄
- *circa 1920*
Hardy alloy fly box, includes collection of trout flies.
- *13cm x 10cm*
- £110 • Henry Gregory

Nottingham Walnut Reel ▶

- **1912**

Rare Hardy Nottingham reel made of seasoned walnut, with patent lever "Silex" action, fitted with twin cow horn handles on elliptical brass seats and Bickerdyke line guide.
- *diameter 10.2cm*
- £150   • **B. J. Ayers**

Bernard & Sons Reel ▲

- *circa 1928*

J. Bernard & Sons salmon fly and trolling or harling reel with a fixed calliper check, strap over rim mounted tension adjuster and unventilated drum with ivorine handle.
- *diameter 12.7cm*
- £80–£100   • **B. J. Ayers**

St George Fly Reel ▲

- **1935**

Hardy "St George" fly reel with ridged brass foot, three screw drum release, grey agate line and ebonite handle.
- *diameter 8.6cm*
- £100–£140   • **B. J. Ayers**

Sea Fishing Reel ▶

- *Early 20th century*

A Nottingham sea fishing reel made of walnut with twin bulbous handles on elliptical brass seats, brass cross on the back with sliding on/off check button and fitted with a brass Bickerdyke line guide.
- *diameter 14cm*
- £25–£80   • **B. J. Ayers**

Wide Drum Perfect Reel ▼

- *circa 1955*

Hardy wide drum salmon "Perfect" fly reel fitted with revolving nickel silver line guide, and duplicated check and ridged brass foot reel.
- *diameter 9.5cm*
- £120–£160   • **B. J. Ayers**

Nottingham Fly and Trolling Reel ▶

- *circa 1900*

Hardy Nottingham fly and trolling reel with twin horn handles on elliptical brass seats, Bickerdyke line guide and early spring steel calliper.
- *diameter 12.7cm*
- £100–£150   • **B. J. Ayers**

Hercules Fly Reel ▲

- *early 20th century*

Hardy "Hercules" raised-face brass fly reel with ivoreen handle, wasted and ventilated foot, and oval logo.
- *diameter 10.2cm*
- £150   • **B. J. Ayers**

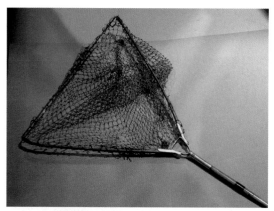

Hardy Landing Net ◀

- *circa 1890*
Hardy's triangular folding landing net with brass fittings.
- *1.15m x 48cm*
- **£230** • Henry Gregory

Starback Fishing Reel ▲

- *circa 1920–40*
Starback wood fishing reel with turned decoration and brass fittings.
- *diameter 12cm*
- **£55** • Sporting Times

Willow Creel ▼

- *circa 1900*
Small willow fishing creel with leather strap handle.
- *25cm x 19cm*
- **£90** • Henry Gregory

Starback Reel ▲

- *circa 1920–40*
Starback wooden fishing reel with brass fittings and double handles.
- *diameter 9cm*
- **£58** • Sporting Times

Hardy Fishing Reel ▲

- *circa 1930*
Hardy platewind fishing reel. Silex no 2.
- *diameter 10cm*
- **£280** • Henry Gregory

Brass Reels ▲

- *circa 1910*
Three brass fly fishing reels.
- *7cm/left; 5.5cm/centre; 5cm/right*
- **£35–£50** • Henry Gregory

Wood Reels ▶

- *circa 1920*
Two wooden fly fishing reels with brass cross backs.
- *9cm/left; 9cm/right*
- **£45–£90** • Henry Gregory

Dry Fly Tin ◀

- *1900*
A Hardy black japanned dry fly tin with lift lid and ivorine pencil inside lid.
- *15cm x 10cm*
- **£100–£200** • T. Murland

Shooting

Leather Gun Case ▼
- *circa 1890*
Leather leg of mutton gun case
with leather shoulder strap and
carrying handle.
- *length 79cm*
- £125   • Sporting Times

Magazine Case ▲
- *circa 1920*
Ammunition case with brass
fittings and leather straps by
Penry Williams, Middlesbrough.
- *41cm x 16cm*
- £950   • Holland

Holland & Holland Rifle ▼
- *2001*
Holland & Holland 375 H&H.
New bolt-action magazine rifle.
- *length 1.19m*
- £15,615   • Holland

Cartridge Case ▲
- *circa 1890*
Gannochy loader canvas
cartridge case with holders for
30 rounds of ammunition.
- *26cm x 13cm*
- £1,500   • Holland

Magazine Box ▲
- *circa 1890*
Leather magazine box with strap,
buckle and a lock, by James
MacNaughton, Gun and Rifle
Maker, Edinburgh.
- *23cm x 24cm*
- £650   • Holland

Brass Powder Flask ▲
- *circa 1875*
Brass black powder flask with
embossed decoration.
- *10cm x 19cm*
- £48   • Holland

Royal Rifle ◀

- *1945*

Holland & Holland Royal model 300 back-action double rifle, with sights.
- *length 1.14m*
- **£32,000**   • Holland

Cartridge Case ▲

- *circa 1890*

Gannochy loader leather cartridge case with canvas shoulder strap, made by McArthur and Prain.
- *25cm x 9cm*
- **£1,200**   • Holland

Four-Bore Shotgun ▲

- *1928*

Holland and Holland four-bore shotgun with black powder only.
- *length 1.5m*
- **£5,500**   • Holland

Gun Case ▼

- *circa 1890*

Leather gun case with brass reinforced corners and leather carrying handle.
- *30cm x 82cm*
- **£380**   • Henry Gregory

Bullet Mould ▼

- *circa 1895*

Sixteen-bore brass bullet mould. Paradox stock.
- *27cm x 8cm*
- **£550**   • Holland

Flintlock Pistol ▲

- *circa 1840*

Flintlock percussion double-barrel pistol with back-action locks, engraved lockplates and trigger guards.
- *25cm x 10cm*
- **£430**   • Holland

Twenty-Bore Shotgun ▶

- *2001*

Holland & Holland sporting over and under 20-bore single-trigger shotgun.
- *length 1.15m*
- **£25,000**   • Holland

Expert Tips

When purchasing firearms it is important to ensure that they come with a proofing certificate of fireworthiness.

Taxidermy

Photographers often use stuffed animals for advertisements because of their lifelike and naturalistic poses.

The art of taxidermy as a technique for keeping animals, birds, insects and fish in a preserved state is of great importance to both the scientist, academic researcher and sportsmen alike. Taxidermy has always been a popular and desirable way of preserving a trophy, especially at the turn of the century when big game was hunted in Africa and India.

Nowadays however, it is more usual to find a smaller stuffed animal, such as your Aunt Betty's favourite dog, than to find a large stuffed lion in someone's house. These wilder and more exotic animals can now be found decorating a film set or photo shoot, where they are being used more and more, not only because they don't move, but also because it is a lot safer and cheaper than working with the real thing.

In the past, before the advent of photography and television, the majority of people would not have known what a polar bear, tiger or chameleon looked like, except from drawings or paintings.

Albino Cobra ▼
- *20th century*
Albino cobra shown in an aggressive pose.
- *60cm x 28cm*
- **£195**   • **Get Stuffed**

Mallards ▲
- *20th century*
Two male mallards, one shown standing and the other recumbent.
- *40cm x 64cm*
- **£295**   • **Get Stuffed**

Hooded Crow ▼
- *20th century*
Hooded crow shown perched on a branch and mounted on a plinth base.
- *57cm x 28cm*
- **£125**   • **Get Stuffed**

Bullfrog Skeletons ◄
- *20th century*
Bullfrog skeleton in sections with documentation.
- *30cm x 40cm*
- **£140**   • **Get Stuffed**

Tawny Owl ▼
- *20th century*
Tawny owl naturalistically posed
and mounted on a circular base,
with original glass dome.
- *55cm x 27cm*
- £395
- Get Stuffed

Eagle Owl ▼
- *20th century*
Eagle owl in fine condition with a
good expression mounted on a
circular base.
- *65cm x 35cm*
- £550
- Get Stuffed

Sparrowhawk ▼
- *20th century*
Sparrowhawk with wings pinned
back.
- *27cm x 35cm*
- £190
- Get Stuffed

Yorkshire Terrier ▲
- *20th century*
Yorkshire terrier seated with a
curious expression and a red
ribbon.
- *30cm x 20cm*
- £245
- Get Stuffed

Tropical Birds ▲
- *circa 1880*
Victorian glass dome containing
various tropical birds.
- *54cm x 36cm*
- £650
- Get Stuffed

Roach ▼
- *1996*
Roach in a bow-fronted case with
natural grasses and weeds, with
gilt lettering documenting the
catch.
- *32cm x 50cm*
- £385
- Get Stuffed

Barn Owl ▼
- *20th century*
Barn owl with wings outstretched
at the point of take off, mounted
on a branch.
- *70cm x 70cm*
- £275
- Get Stuffed

Red Fox ▼
- *20th century*
Red fox vixen shown recumbent
with head slightly raised.
- *35cm x 57cm*
- £200
- Get Stuffed

Textiles

A fascinating area of collection and study, where the original artists may have been amateur, but accurately reflect the tastes and skills of their time.

London is particularly rich in museums exhibiting textiles and costumes throughout the ages, but there are very good museums across the country with experts who will help you in this fascinating area of antique study and collection. Textiles are of particular interest to the historian because they so accurately reflect the social and industrial history of their time. Every textile, with the exception of felt, is produced by weaving – the interlinking of the "warp" and "weft" thread on a loom. However, the richer the society the more that textiles are patterned during this process, or are decorated afterwards, either by a needle, as in embroidery, or by painting or printing. Although early tapestries and sixteenth and seventeenth century needlework command prices of thousands of pounds, nineteenth century samplers can be obtained for only a few hundred.

Chinese Evening Coat ▶

- **1918**
Chinese black ladies' coat embroidered with pink yellow and blue floral design and lined with white rabbit.
- *full length*
- **£2,000**   ● **Red Roses**

Cloche Hat ▶

- **1920**
Brown silk cloche hat with velvet brim and a large gold silk flower and leaf.
- *height 23cm*
- **£195**   ● **Red Roses**

Pink Cocktail Dress ◀

- *circa 1950*
Short pink satin cocktail dress.
- *length 1.06m*
- **£225**   ● **Red Roses**

Art Deco Evening Dress ▼

- **1920**
Black Art Deco silk chiffon evening dress with silver beading.
- *full length*
- **£900**   ● **Red Roses**

Blue Evening Dress ▼
- *circa 1930*
Royal blue net evening dress.
- *full length*
- £175 • **Red Roses**

Silk Cape ▼
- *circa 1910*
Silk cape decorated with red
chrysanthemums within a trailing
foliate design.
- *length 96cm*
- £165 • **M. Williamson**

Short Velvet Jacket ▲
- *circa 1920*
Pale pink velvet short evening
jacket.
- *length 44cm*
- £125 • M. Williamson

Silk Day Dress ▲
- *circa 1940*
Silk day dress with lace design
background and stripes of pink,
yellow and green with matching
bow.
- *full length*
- £135 • **Hilary Proctor**

Pink Chiffon Dress ▼
- *circa 1960*
Pale pink chiffon layered evening
dress with large pink satin ribbon.
- *full length*
- £175 • **M. Williamson**

Silver Lurex Dress ▼
- *circa 1965*
Silver lurex hand-crocheted
dress.
- *mid-length*
- £125 • **Hilary Proctor**

Patchwork Quilt ▼
- *circa 1840–70*

Victorian patchwork quilt made up of predominantly pink and white hexagonal patches dating from the mid nineteenth century.
- *2.5m sq*
- £895   • Sheila Cook

Patchwork Quilt ▼
- *circa 1950*

Patchwork quilt with a bold, multi-coloured and patterned geometric design.
- *1.6m x 1.56m*
- £195   • Sheila Cook

Silk Smoking Hat ▲
- *circa 1870*

Brown silk smoking hat with trailing foliate embroidery of small white flowers.
- *size 6*
- £125   • Sheila Cook

Tartan Umbrella ▲
- *circa 1930*

Tartan umbrella with a handle in the shape of a swan with glass eyes.
- *length 67cm*
- £65   • Sheila Cook

Cream Child's Dress ▶
- *circa 1880*

Cream cotton child's dress with lace trim and navy blue ribboning on the hips and collar.
- *small*
- £265   • Sheila Cook

Victorian Cushion Cover ▼
- *circa 1880*

Cut pile cushion cover with a red and black diamond geometric design.
- *40cm x 45cm*
- £95   • Sheila Cook

Gentleman's Slipper Cut Out ▼
- *circa 1880*

Gentleman's unused embroidered slipper "cut out" with a diamond design of cream, beige and variegated reds within black borders.
- *size 9*
- £95   • Sheila Cook

Expert Tips

Be careful when buying vintage clothes to look out for rips and tears in the fabric as they might be difficult to repair, although some wear is inevitable.

Welsh Patchwork Quilt ▲

- *circa 1880*

Welsh patchwork quilt with a white and lilac diamond design centered with lilac floral sprays.
- *80cm x 80cm*
- **£650** • Sheila Cook

Smoking Hat ▲

- *circa 1880*

Black velvet smoking hat with white embroidered floral design, a central yellow silk button, pink gold and white tassel, with original box in good original condition.
- *size 7*
- **£165** • Sheila Cook

Cut Pile Cushion Cover ▼

- *circa 1880*

Cut pile Victorian cushion cover with a red, green and pink geometric design.
- *42cm x 30cm*
- **£95** • Sheila Cook

Ivory Fan ▼

- *circa 1904*

Cream silk fan with a trailing design of pink and yellow apple blossom mounted on carved ivory spines.
- *length 35cm*
- **£125** • Sheila Cook

Slipper Pattern ▼

- *circa 1850*

Fine continental unused beaded slipper "cut out" pattern, with a turquoise background, pink and yellow flowers and two deer by a river.
- *length 22cm*
- **£225** • Sheila Cook

Purple Silk Kimono ▲

- *circa 1900*

Purple silk kimono with trailing pink apple blossom design.
- *medium*
- **£295** • Sheila Cook

Gentleman's Smoking Hat ▲

- *circa 1880*

Black velvet gentleman's smoking hat with trailing foliate designs of pink and blue flowers, surmounted by a red satin-covered button on the top with a trailing green, white and red tassel.
- *size 6*
- **£110** • Sheila Cook

Beaded Pelmet ◀

- *circa 1880*

Beaded cream pelmet with red tassel design below a gold and red diamond design.
- *length 3.2m*
- **£495** • Sheila Cook

Gold Cocktail Dress ▶

- *circa 1960*
Hand-beaded gold cocktail dress with gold beading and topaz stones.
- *mini*
- £130   ● **Hilary Proctor**

Rafia Cocktail Dress ▲

- *circa 1960*
Pink hand-crocheted raffia sleeveless shift dress.
- *short*
- £130   ● **Hilary Proctor**

Navy Blue Cocktail Dress ▲

- *circa 1960*
Navy blue strapless cocktail dress with white frill.
- *mid-length*
- £100   ● **Red Roses**

Strapless Cocktail Dress ▼

- *circa 1950*
Yellow and white cotton strapless cocktail dress by Frank Usher with swathed bodice detail and gathered skirt.
- *mid-length*
- £100   ● **June Victor**

Nylon Flower Dress ▼

- *circa 1960*
Nylon flower power print dress with smock detail on the hips and interesting orange belt.
- *long dress*
- £75   ● **Hilary Proctor**

Silk Floral Hat ▼

- *circa 1950*
A summer hat lavishly decorated with silk faux flowers and leaves intertwined with fine veiling.
- *length 22cm*
- £49   ● **Red Roses**

Lilac Petal Hat ▶
- *circa 1950*
Faux lilac petals and lilac wire
and mesh "leaves" arranged to
form a decorative summer
headpiece.
- *diameter 22cm*
- £22   • Red Roses

Military Breeches ▲
- *circa 1910*
Gentleman's war-issue military
tweed breeches.
- *medium*
- £95   • Red Roses

Pink Mini Dress ▼
- *circa 1960*
Pink floral silk mini dress with
chiffon sleeves and a matching
hat.
- *mid-length*
- £150   • Red Roses

Black Mortarboard ▲
- *1940*
Black mortarboard by Ede &
Ravenscroft, by appointment to
the King and Queen, 93 & 94
Chancery Lane, London.
- *circumference 17cm*
- £30   • June Victor

Straw Boater Hat ▶
- *1930*
Gentleman's straw boater with
black band, by Falcon.
- *circumference 32cm*
- £27   • June Victor

Silk Top Hat ▲
- *1910*
Black silk top hat by Battersby,
Northumbland Av, Trafalgar
Square, London.
- *circumference 17cm*
- £75   • June Victor

Mother-of-Pearl Fan ▲

- *circa 1910*
Cream silk lace fan covered with
cream floral lace and a mother-of-
pearl handle.
- *length 29cm*
- £275   • Sheila Cook

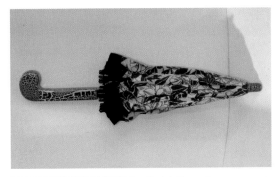

Lady's Red Hat ▲

- *circa 1920*
Lady's red soft silk mesh hat by
Pauline Louy's, decorated with
red felt flowers.
- *medium*
- £145   • Sheila Cook

Lace Fan ▼

- *circa 1905*
Cream lace fan with silk backing
and cream ivory handle with a
cartouche of a raised lily.
- *length 32cm*
- £375   • Sheila Cook

Lady's Parasol ▲

- *circa 1920*
Lady's parasol with a black floral
design and a handle with a black
and beige geometric pattern.
- *length 53cm*
- £95   • Sheila Cook

Child's Shoes ◄

- *1870*
Child's leather shoes with black
studs and metal fittings.
- *length 13cm*
- £65   • Sheila Cook

Italian Allegorical Panel ▼

- *1763*
Rare set of Italian silk-work
allegorical panels signed
"Gaetano Pati, Rome". Part of a
set of eight panels composed of
fine silk threads, arranged and
pressed into wax. The facial and
body detailing is hand painted
onto finely woven silk. The tonal
detailing and intricacy is very
fine.
- *34cm x 27cm*
- £32,000   • Anthony Outred

Russian-Style Cape and Hat ▲

- *circa 1950*
Dramatic red Russian-style cape
with black embroidery and white
fur lining, with matching hat.
- *medium*
- £695   • Sheila Cook

Panama Hat
- **1940**
Gentleman's Panama hat with
black band.
- *circumference 21cm*
- **£32**   • **June Victor**

Miriam Hunt Sampler ▲
- **1722**
Sampler worked by Miriam Hunt
with polychrome silk threads on
linen which features the Lord's
Prayer surrounded by a border of
flowers and berries.
- *22cm x 32cm*
- **£2,850**   • **Maureen Morris**

Jean Smith Sampler ▲
- **1807**
Polychrome silk threads on
tammy sampler by Jean Smith
featuring a house guarded by a
black man in a folly, surmounted
by a band of flowers and Adam
and Eve below.
- *44cm x 52cm*
- **£7,850**   • **Maureen Morris**

Ann Chapman Sampler ▼
- **1839**
Pictorial sampler by Ann
Chapman depicting a country
house and garden with people,
surmounted by a verse and
various motifs. Polychrome silk
threads on tammy.
- *44cm x 32cm*
- **£7,950**   • **Maureen Morris**

Elenor Dickenson Sampler ▶
- **1749**
Sampler signed "This is The
Work of Elenor Dickinson in The
11th Year Of Her Age 1749"
depicting alphabets, numerals,
verses, flowers and foliage
surrounded by an intricately
worked border.
- *22cm x 32cm*
- **£4,500**   • **Maureen Morris**

Expert Tips
*Early samplers were in long
narrow strips and dates, names
and ages all add value.*

Isabella Blacklin Sampler ▼
- **late 18th century**
Sampler by Isabella Blacklin with
a naive interpretation of a goat
surrounded by a man sitting
beneath a tree, a rural cottage
scene and bordered by stylised
flowers.
- *28cm x 41cm*
- **£2,500**   • **Maureen Morris**

Blue Silk Kesi ▼
- *late 18th–early 19th century*
A Japanese blue silk ground Kesi
(priest's robe) with gold Kinran
cloud designs.
- *2.18m x 1.2m*
- £4,800   ● **Brandt**

Chinese Court Robe ▶
- *circa 1870*
An embroidered silk court robe
worked in couched gold thread in
multi coloured satin stitch. The
upper half with dragons and
Buddhist emblems, the attached
apron with 12 dragon roundels.
- *medium*
- £9,000   ● **Brandt**

Silk Kesi ▲
- *19th century*
A fine Japanese silk Kesi (priest's
robe) cleverly constructed using
an eighteenth century Chinese
blue and gold brocade dragon
robe on a gold brocade ground.
- *2.28m x 1.14m*
- £4,500   ● **Brandt**

Chiné Woven Silk Polonaise ◀
- *circa 1780*
Silk polonaise with a cream silk
ground woven with a satin stripe
with pink roses and green leaves.
The square necked bodice and
elbow sleeves trimmed with wide
pleated ruffle.
- *depth 23cm*
- £2,500   ● **Meg Andrews**

Shibori Kimono Designs ▼
- *circa 1920*
A bold set of nine Japanese blue
and white designs for kimono
decorated in Shibori, stylised
from traditional designs. Framed
and glazed.
- *48cm x 79cm*
- £2,800   ● **Brandt**

Manchu Woman's Fuschia Jacket ▼
- *1875–99*
Jacket with satin ground applied
with jui shapes around and
embroidered with flowers. Lined
with light blue silk, the piece has
golden engraved buttons.
- *small*
- £750   ● **Meg Andrews**

Crewel Wool Work Hanging ▼

- *mid-17th century*

Hanging with fine twill weave ground (wool and linen) embroidered in shades of mid-green, blue, forest and dark green wools with thick stems from which acanthus-style leaves hang.
- *1.93m x 54.6cm*
- £2,500   • Meg Andrews

Silkwork Picture ▲

- *circa 1800*

Silkwork picture of a young woman gazing at a rose, worked in a variety of stitches in shades of soft yellow through green with black highlighting. Her face and the sky are painted.
- *28cm x 21.6cm*
- £500   • Meg Andrews

Brussels Wedding Veil ▲

- *19th century*

A wedding veil of Brussels lace.
- *1.36m x 1.2m*
- £475   • J & B Mendes

Lace Lawn Shawl ▼

- *19th century*

Lawn shawl with a lace border and applied lace motifs throughout.
- *2.3m x 1.2m*
- £275   • J & B Mendes

Scarlet Crinoline Frame ▼

- *1865–68*

Thomson's Empress crinoline frame for a young girl, with shaped red cotton waistband with central oval and wide red patterned attached to 11 steel hoops.
- *waist 56cm*
- £600   • Meg Andrews

Expert Tips

Honiton Lace from Devon: look for designs which include a rose, shamrock and thistles and with crosshatched centres to flowers.

Maltese Lace Handkerchief ▼

- *19th century*

Handkerchief in silk with a Maltese lace surround.
- *28cm x 28cm*
- £18   • J & B Mendes

Bobbin Lace ▼
- *19th century*
A flounce of Duchesse applied
bobbin lace.
- *3m x 62cm*
- £250   • J & B Mendes

Edwardian Parasol ▲
- *1880*
Black Edwardian parasol with
bone handle and gilt scrolled
band with shield.
- *height 87cm*
- £85   • Hilary Proctor

Olive Green Parasol ▲
- *1920*
Olive green silk parasol with
black netting overlay, gold thread
roses and an ivory handle. Black
engraved with an eagle and tiger's
eye.
- *height 75cm*
- £180   • Hilary Proctor

Evening Waistcoat ▲
- *1820*
Gentleman's evening waistcoat,
pink silk with leaf pattern of gold
thread.
- *medium*
- £395   • Red Roses

Chinese Silk Jacket ◀
- *circa 1960*
Cream cotton Chinese design
jacket with wide burgundy silk
lapels and belt.
- *full length*
- £60   • Red Roses

Orange Silk Dressing Gown ▶
- *circa 1980*
Orange silk dressing gown with
design, by Georgina Von Ernodof.
- *full length*
- £195   • Red Roses

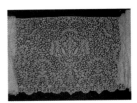

Milanese Lace ▲
- *17th or 18th century*
Fine piece of Milanese lace
displaying very interesting fillings
and designs.
- *3.2m x 32cm*
- £580   • J & B Mendes

Paisley Silk Dressing Gown ▲
- *circa 1930*
Gentleman's black and gold
paisley design silk dressing gown.
- *full length*
- £125   • Red Roses

Gleneagles Coat ▲

- *circa 1980*
Gentleman's single-breasted three-quarter length cream light wool coat.
- *three-quarter length*
- £120 • **Red Roses**

Burgundy Scarf ▲

- *circa 1940*
Burgundy paisley silk gentleman's scarf with gold and burgundy tassels.
- *length 1.1m*
- £28 • **Red Roses**

Tweed Suit ▶

- *20th century*
Gentleman's Harris tweed suit with matching waistcoat.
- *medium*
- £150 • **Red Roses**

Velvet Waistcoat ▼

- *circa 1970*
Velvet waistcoat with broad paisley pattern and wide lapels.
- *length 60cm*
- £95 • **Red Roses**

Silk Evening Scarf ▲

- *circa 1920*
Cream silk evening scarf with black and white wool tassels.
- *length 1.3m*
- £30 • **Red Roses**

Expert Tips

Look for 18th century designs that have bizarre and strange abstract patterns – study pattern books and check out styles.

Corduroy Breeches ▲

- *circa 1920*
Olive green corduroy breeches with side lacing below the knee and cotton with buttoning. Two large angled pockets and one smaller.
- *length 1m*
- £100 • **Red Roses**

Animal Print Scarf ▲

- *circa 1950*
Burgundy wool gentleman's scarf with ethnic print of figures, animals and flowers.
- *length 70cm*
- £30 • **Red Roses**

Toys, Games & Dolls

Until the 1940s the largest producers of toys were based in Germany, where they also created special versions of toys for export.

Toy collecting has grown in stature over recent years with many collectors tucking away new toys in pristine boxes in the hope of a good profit – dream on! Old toys are valuable because they were used and very rarely survived in good condition. It wasn't until the eighteenth century that parents realised that their children could learn through play. When William Hamley opened his doors in 1760 the trend started. The industrial revolution created inexpensive production techniques and the new middle classes the demand. Now any pre-war toy in good condition will fetch high prices and examples from the eighteenth century are very rare. Most collectors collect specific categories and become expert in identification, price and the difference condition can make to value. Collectors can tell the difference between signs of love and signs of abuse, and love is a market winner.

Gold Cadillac ▲

- *circa 1950*
American gold cadillac with red interior and chromed fittings, made by Bandai, Japan.
- *length 29cm*
- £150 • P. McAskie

Fred Flintstone ▼

- 1960
Tin plate "Fred Flintstone" sitting astride his dinosaur "Dino", made by Louis Marks in Japan.
- *length 2cm*
- £265 • P. McAskie

Smiley of the Seven Dwarfs ▲

- *circa 1930*
Padded soft toy of "Smiley", one of the dwarfs from the children's story, "Snow White and the Seven Dwarfs".
- *height 27cm*
- £160 • Glenda

Huntley & Palmers Van ◄

- *circa 1920*
Brown toy van with a hinged lid to store biscuits and the gilt inscription, "Huntley & Palmers Ltd, Reading Biscuits" and a Royal Crest above.
- *19cm x 25cm*
- £875 • P. McAskie

Bru Walker Doll ▲

- *circa 1880*
Bru "Kiss throwing walker doll"
with long auburn hair and brown
glass eyes, wearing a cream cotton
and lace dress, a bonnet with lilac
bows and brown leather shoes.
- *height 62cm*
- **£3,750**   • Glenda

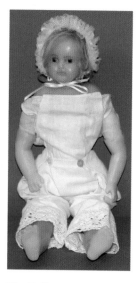

Wax Doll ▲

- *circa 1900*
Wax girl doll with blonde hair,
blue eyes and a painted face,
wearing a linen top and
pantaloons with lace embroidery,
and a lace cap.
- *height 48cm*
- **£475**   • Glenda

Tin Plate Racing Car ▼

- *circa 1930*
English tin plate cream racing
car, with a red radiator grill and
red line decoration, bonnet
straps, and the number five on
the side and on the tail back.
- *length 38cm*
- **£265**   • P. McAskie

Noddy ▼

- *1980*
Noddy wearing a red shirt, yellow
spotted scarf and blue hat with a
yellow pom-pom, in his yellow
rubber car with red fenders.
- *19cm x 27cm*
- **£30**   • P. McAskie

Japanese Motor Launch ▼

- *circa 1950*
Japanese red, yellow, orange and
blue motor launch with driver in
a helmet, and hand crank.
- *length 21cm*
- **£73**   • P. McAskie

Drummer Boy ▲

- *1930*
Drummer boy with a tin plate
body, legs and arms, and a
celluloid head, with the makers
name "Fecuda", Japan.
- *24cm*
- **£275**   • P. McAskie

Red Double Decker Bus ▲

- *1960*
Red bus with "Mobilgas" and
"Double Decker Bus" decals on
the side, in fine condition.
- *height 22cm*
- **£145**   • P. McAskie

Spanish Racing Car ▼

- *circa 1920*
Blue and yellow racing car with
driver and passenger, and the
number seven on the side.
Manufactured by Paya in Spain.
- *length 27cm*
- **£225**   • P. McAskie

Mickey Mouse ▼
- *circa 1930*
Velvet padded Mickey Mouse with a large smiling expression.
- *height 33cm*
- £110　　　　　　• Glenda

Heubach Boy Doll ▼
- *circa 1890*
Heubach jointed porcelain boy doll with a painted face, wearing a matching beige and cream outfit with hat.
- *height 25cm*
- £395　　　　　　• Glenda

Ferrari Pedal Car ▲
- *1970*
Red Ferrari pedal car with the number three on the side.
- *length 1.17m*
- £250　　　　　• C.A.R.S.

Steiff Owl ▲
- *circa 1950*
Steiff owl with large glass eyes and a menacing expression.
- *height 14cm*
- £49　　　　　　• Glenda

Tri-ang Red Racing Car ▼
- *1950*
Red Tri-ang Mimic racing car with driver, the car bearing the number three.
- *length 15cm*
- £45　　　　　• P. McAskie

Dream Baby ▲
- *circa 1920*
Porcelain jointed black "Dream Baby", in perfect condition.
- *height 28cm*
- £398　　　　　　• Glenda

Expert Tips

Any toys associated with popular books or films today, for example the Harry Potter series, are worth investing in now for the future.

Petrol Tanker ▶

- *1930*

Red lead petrol tanker by Taylor and Barrett.
- *length 10cm*
- £85
- P. McAskie

Alfa Romeo ▼

- *circa 1960*

Red Alfa Romeo 1900 "Super Sprint", made by Dinky, no. 85, with original box.
- *length 10cm*
- £62
- P. McAskie

Oriental Baby Doll ▼

- *circa 1930*

Small oriental porcelain jointed baby doll with brown glass eyes and a painted face.
- *height 18cm*
- £300
- Glenda

Austin Seven ▲

- *circa 1940*

Cornflower-blue Austin Seven, 35 series with pneumatic tyres.
- *height 3cm*
- £38
- P. McAskie

Horse and Milk Float ▲

- *1950*

Matchbox horse-drawn red milk float with driver.
- *height 3cm*
- £18
- P. McAskie

Kestner Doll ▼

- *circa 1900*

Porcelain jointed doll by Kestner with blue glass eyes and long auburn hair, wearing linen and lace dress and brown leather shoes.
- *height 38cm*
- £595
- Glenda

Chad Valley Teddy ▼

- *1950*

Chad Valley padded teddy with glass eyes and a pleasant expression.
- *height 44cm*
- £250
- Glenda

German Fire Engine ◄
- **1950**
Red German fire engine with
fireman, manufactured by
Gamma.
- *length 43cm*
- **£110**   • P. McAskie

Mummy Bear ▼
- *circa 1930*
Padded jointed bear with glass
eyes and cloth paws.
- *height 39cm*
- **£85**   • Glenda

XK Yellow Jaguar ▲
- *circa 1950*
XK yellow Jaguar with a bottle
green top, and chromed bumper,
made by Hoku.
- *length 25cm*
- **£225**   • P. McAskie

Ovaltine Van ►
- *circa 1950*
Blue Dinky Bedford 10cwt
Ovaltine van, inscribed "Ovaltine"
and "Ovaltine Biscuits" on the
side, with original box.
- *length 8cm*
- **£65**   • P. McAskie

Mickey Mouse ▲
- **1950**
Mickey Mouse puppet carved
from wood with yellow
composition feet, by Pelham.
- *height 29cm*
- **£75**   • P. McAskie

Tri-ang Blue Van ►
- **1950**
Tri-ang Mimic navy-blue London
and North Eastern Railway van.
- *length 18cm*
- **£225**   • P. McAskie

Terrafish ◄
- *1960*

Green Terrafish with yellow spots and large white eyes, from the Gerry Anderson TV show, by Lakeside Toys, Japan.
- *length 23cm*
- £275 • P. McAskie

Shoe-Shine Panda ▼
- *circa 1960*

Shoe-shine soft panda, battery-operated, sitting with a pipe in its mouth and a brush in each paw, wearing red dungarees.
- *height 25cm*
- £80 • P. McAskie

American Racing Car ▲
- *1930*

Red and silver racing car and driver, made from an interesting combination of metals, die cast and cast iron, probably by Hubbly American. No. 22 on the side.
- *length 25cm*
- £67 • P. McAskie

Bobby Bear ▶
- *1950*

Padded "Bobby Bear" made by Pedigree, in good overall condition.
- *height 44cm*
- £89 • Glenda

Yellow Milk Float ▼
- *circa 1960*

Rare yellow Dinky promotional milk float, with "Jobs Dairy" inscribed on the front and rear, with red interior and hubs.
- *length 7cm*
- £145 • P. McAskie

Orober Fire Engine ◄
- *1920*

Fire engine set of two vehicles with a driver on a pumper, and three figures on the fire engine carrier, complete with red garage, made by Orober in Germany.
- *19cm x 33cm*
- £650 • P. McAskie

Playing Card Box ▲

- *circa 1875*

Late Victorian mother-of-pearl playing card and games box containing two sets of original playing cards and a cribbage board.

- *length 22cm*
- **£1,950**   • **J & T Stone**

Dutch Silk Plush Bear ▲

- *1950s*

Dutch brown art silk plush bear in superb original condition with bulging cheeks, black and white plastic eyes, brown plastic nose, black stitched mouth, white plush pad, and excelsior filling.

- *height 43.2cm*
- **£65**   • **Baba Bears**

Backgammon and Chess Board ▲

- *circa 1860*

Mid-nineteenth century mahogany folding backgammon and chessboard with backgammon counters, dice and shakers.

- *52cm x 36cm*
- **£995**   • **J & T Stone**

Golden Blonde Mohair Bear ▲

- *circa 1910*

Early American golden blonde mohair bear, probably by Harman. Brown glass eyes, black fabric nose, black stitched mouth and claws, peach felt pads, excelsior filling, humped back and front final seam.

- *height 49.5cm*
- **£685**   • **Baba Bears**

Blonde Mohair Bear ▶

- *circa 1920*

English blonde mohair bear with glass eyes, black stitched nose and mouth, original linen pads (extensively darned), inoperative tilt growler, excelsior filling and pronounced humped back.

- *height 50.8cm*
- **£325**   • **Baba Bears**

Gold Mohair Bear ▲

- *circa 1918*

A dark gold German short bristle mohair bear with black boot button eyes, black stitched nose and mouth, replaced tan felt pad, and excelsior filling.

- *height 36cm*
- **£285**   • **Baba Bears**

Daimler Ambulance ▲

- *circa 1950*

Primrose-yellow Dinky Daimler ambulance, no. 253, with a red cross on the side, red hub plates and original box.
- *height 4cm*
- **£45**   • P. McAskie

Matchbox Fire Engine ▲

- *1950*

Red Matchbox fire engine with driver.
- *height 3cm*
- **£22**   • P. McAskie

Expert Tips

Look out for finely made jointed porcelain dolls by French makers such as G Vichy, or ballet dancers by Lambert, as these are very rare and highly collectable items.

Nestlé's Austin Van ▲

- *circa 1950*

Red Austin van inscribed with "Nestlé's" in gold letters on the side, made by Dinky, no. 471.
- *length 9cm*
- **£125**   • P. McAskie

Baby Doll ▼

- *circa 1900*

Porcelain jointed baby doll with blue eyes, blonde hair and painted face, wearing a matching hat and outfit.
- *height 26cm*
- **£298**   • Glenda

Telstar Kaleidoscope ▼

- *1960*

Telstar kaleidoscope with a rocket, stars and satellite and a blue background, made by Green Monk of England.
- *height 17cm*
- **£20**   • P. McAskie

MG Midget TD ▼

- *1950*

Matchbox yellow MG Midget TD with red interior, driver, grey wheels and a wheel on the boot.
- *height 2cm*
- £24　　　　　　　• P. McAskie

Scalextric Green BRM ▼

- *1960*

Scalextric tin plate green BRM with racing driver. No. Three on the side.
- *length 15cm*
- £95　　　　　　• P. McAskie

Vespa and Driver ▲

- *1960*

Green Vespa with a driver wearing red, made in England by Benbros.
- *height 5cm*
- £22　　　　　　• P. McAskie

Velam Bubble Car ◄

- *1960*

French cream Velam bubble car with grey roof, made by Quiralu, with original box.
- *height 4cm*
- £78　　　　　　• P. McAskie

Pintel & Godchaux Doll ▲

- *circa 1900*

French porcelain jointed doll with blonde hair, blue eyes and painted face, wearing a lace dress, with a pink satin bow and lace socks, made by Pintel and Godchaux.
- *height 43cm*
- £595　　　　　　• Glenda

Cottage Doll ▲

- *circa 1950*

Small padded "Cottage Doll" made by Glenda O'Connor, with blonde plaits, blue eyes and a pleasant expression, wearing a pink gingham dress, green hat, top and shoes.
- *height 21cm*
- £58　　　　　　• Glenda

Folding Games Board ▶

- *circa 1675*

Rare ivory inlaid, ebony and
ebonised, south German folding
games board, the interior having
a backgammon board and two
panels of hunting scenes. One
side of the exterior having a
chessboard, the other with Nine
Men's Morris board.
- *16cm x 99cm x 56cm*
- £17,500   • R. Gardner

Silver King Locomotive ▼

- **1953–54**

Hornby Dublo EDL11 Silver
King locomotive.
- *length 28cm*
- £68   • Toycellars

Tri-ang Hornby Tank Loco ▲

- **1967–70**

Triang Hornby R754 0-4-4 Class
M7 Tank Locomotive. Complete
with instructions, service sheet
and crew.
- *length 15cm*
- £70   • cbTOYS

Hornby Dublo Signal Home ▲

- **1950s**

Rare Hornby Dublo 5065 Single
Arm Signal Home, an electrically
operated signal.
- *length 8cm*
- £45   • cbTOYS

Tri-ang Tank Locomotive ▶

- **1961–67**

Tri-ang TT Railways T99 2-6-2
Class 4MT Tank Loco in
excellent boxed condition with
internal packing and oil bottle.
- *length 14cm*
- £75   • cbTOYS

Tri-ang Hornby Train Station ▲
- *1965–71*
Tri-ang Hornby R459 train station set, part of their range of accessories and rolling stock with "Picture Boxes".
- *32cm x 19cm*
- £95 • cbTOYS

Wrenn Locomotive ▲
- *1976–89*
Wrenn W2221 Cardiff Castle locomotive in excellent condition with box.
- *length 25cm*
- £100 • cbTOYS

Hornby Duplo Train ▶
- *1962–64*
Hornby Dublo 2234 Deltic Diesel Electric 2 Rail train in excellent condition with box.
- *length 25cm*
- £150 • cbTOYS

Minic Red Steam Lorry ▼
- *1966–68*
Minic Motorway M1564 Red Steam Lorry to compliment and run with Tri-ang OO scale railways.
- *length 7cm*
- £175 • cbTOYS

Topsy-Turvy Doll ◀
- *1930s*
A British Topsy-Turvy doll which changes from black to white when turned upside down. The heads are composition with painted features.
- *height 30cm*
- £150 • cbTOYS

Tri-ang Accessories ▲
- *1960s*
Tri-ang TTRailways T27 signal box.
- *length 9cm*
- £40 • cbTOYS

Staunton Chess Set ▶

- *early 20th century*
Early twentieth century ivory
tournament size Staunton chess
set, with leather folding board.
- *height 6cm*
- **£3,100**   • R. Gardner

Tinplate Fire Engine ▲

- *circa 1960*
Tinplate clockwork fire engine
with three-piece extending
ladder. Made in Japan and
marked with "K" trademark.
- *length 33cm*
- **£145**   • Toycellars

Twin Rotor Helicopter ▼

- *circa 1960*
ALPS Japanese tinplate battery-
driven twin rotor helicopter with
plastic rotors.
- *length 35cm*
- **£180**   • Toycellars

Coal Truck ▲

- *1931–36*
Hornby "O" gauge Meccano coal
truck.
- *length 17cm*
- **£88**   • Toycellars

Tinplate Crane ▲

- *circa 1950*
Tinplate tower three function
crane N.B.L., made in Western
Germany.
- *height 42cm*
- **£85**   • Toycellars

LNER 504 Locomotive ▶

- *circa 1930*
Bing for Bassett Lowke 4-4-0
George V LNER Locomotive
504, with clockwork, "O" gauge.
- *length 42cm*
- **£375**   • Toycellars

CN Budd Dummy Railcar ◀

- *1965–71*
Rare r352cn CN Budd Dummy
unpowered locomotive.
- *length 25cm*
- **£40**   • cbTOYS

Expert Tips

*Pre-war Dinky toys have no
model names or numbers, white
tyres and plain metal hubs.*

Treen

The most mundane item was not beneath the notice of imaginative craftsmen, and the ordinary in their hands quickly became a work of art.

Treen applies to those items which are carved from wood, and encompasses a wide range of items, from the simple napkin ring to the highly decorative and heavily carved oak plaque. The word treen actually means "made from trees" and therefore the beauty of collecting treen lies in the variety of artefacts that are available. Occasionally objects dating back to the seventeenth century arrive on the market, with the workaday items, such as cups and other vessels being fashioned from hardwoods such as sycamore and holly, while the more important were carved from lignum vitae, which had to be imported into England.

If you are about to embark on your first journey to collect treen it is worth noting that boxes and love tokens are amongst the most desirable types of treen. Look out for burr walnut or rosewood snuff boxes, which attract the collector with their sleek lines and simple design.

As a new collector treen is a good place to start as some of the items are still relatively inexpensive.

Rosewood Box ▼
- *circa 1825*
Small rosewood box with a silver plaque with the letters "E. M."
- *4cm x 7cm*
- **£225** • **Rupert Gentle**

Pressed Wood Box ▼
- *circa 1840*
Pressed circular wood box with a carving of a boy and sword beside a dog jumping.
- *diameter 6cm*
- **£550** • **Rupert Gentle**

Fruitwood Box ▲
- *1830*
Small fruitwood box with gold foliate banding between bands of gold leaves on a black background.
- *2cm x 8cm*
- **£275** • **Rupert Gentle**

Tunbridge Ware Box ▲
- *circa 1850*
Tunbridge Ware box by Burrows. From Tunbridge Wells.
- *8cm square*
- **£140** • **Jasmin Cameron**

Carved Deer Heads ▼
- *circa 1860*
One of a pair of continental carved reindeer with red paint and genuine horns.
- *height 64cm*
- **£1,800** • **Anthony Sharpe**

French Carved Stand ▼

- *1780*

One of a pair of French carved stands, with scrolled foliate designs and seven giltwood flowers on a moulded serpentine base.

- *height 93cm*
- £1,450 • Heytesbury

Four Egg Cups ▲

- *circa 1840*

A set of four turned mahogany egg cups.

- *height 9cm*
- £375 • Rupert Gentle

Yew Wood Coaster ▲

- *circa 1840*

Yew wood coaster with a raised diamond flower in the centre and a linked border, with maker's name, M. Scott.

- *diameter 17cm*
- £650 • Rupert Gentle

Rosewood Snuff Box ▲

- *circa 1780*

Circular snuff box with the inscription "A. C. B. to J. G. B. 1821".

- *diameter 9cm*
- £380 • Rupert Gentle

Burr-Walnut Snuff Box ▲

- *circa 1770*

Burr-walnut snuff box with a vacant silver plaque on the lid.

- *length 8.5cm*
- £380 • Rupert Gentle

Austrian Stamp Box ▲

- *1860*

Small Austrian stamp box with carved relief of oak leaves.

- *1.5cm x 5cm*
- £35 • Jasmin Cameron

Pipe Taper with Royal Charter ▼

- *circa 1780*

Pipe taper with a "Royal Charter" label on the base.

- *length 7.5cm*
- £350 • Rupert Gentle

Tribal Art

Even the creators of these works of art didn't choose to share their houses with them; today people are making money doing just that.

Tribal art is often considered to be something of a macabre field of collection. It is surrounded by fetish and the worship of ancestor gods, extending from the fetish figures, through chieftain's stools carved in the shape of a kneeling figure, to dance masks that were often truly horrific.

The god figures, which were often carved from ironwood and polished with sand, would usually be kept in dark huts or caves. It was only on festive occasions, religious rituals or, perhaps, prior to a war, that these items would be brought out and put on view. They would be sprinkled with blood while descendant tribesmen would dance themselves into a frenzy, some going into trances in order to speak to their distant ancestor gods.

All this might seem to be deep, dark stuff, but tribal art is markedly appreciating in value. Collectors should be wary of modern copies, though, which are proliferating in response to growing tourism.

Zuni Fetish Frog ▼
- **1930**
Large Zuni fetish circular silver pendant with a central turquoise styled frog flanked by silver leaves.
- *length 4.5cm*
- **£59**   • **Wilde One's**

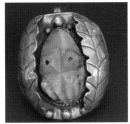

Kple Kple Mask ▲
- *circa 1920*
Kple Kple junior mask of the Golidance, one of the most abstracted masks of Africa, from a collection in France.
- *height 43cm*
- **£5,500**   • **Gordon Reece**

Nigerian Delta Region ◄
- *circa 1910*
Spirit mask from the Nigerian Delta region, the head crowned by four men and a boat, with classical red pigmentation. The figures, originally white, have been overpainted black.
- *height 53cm*
- **£1,100**   • **Gordon Reece**

Suku Fetish ▼
- *circa 1900*
Suku finely carved figure used as a fetish with additional fibre, beads and feathers, from Northern Zaire.
- *height 43cm*
- **£950**   • **Gordon Reece**

Buffalo Helmet Mask ◄

- *circa 1920*

Kanos buffalo carved wood mask from the Ivory coast of Africa.
- *height 38cm*
- £1,400   • Gordon Reece

M'Bun Currency ▼

- *unknown*

M'Bun status currency in throwing knife form.
- *48cm x 39cm*
- £720   • Gordon Reece

Guardian of the Spirits ▼

- *circa 1820*

West Nepalese bronze figure of a village guardian of the spirits.
- *height 22cm*
- £720   • Gordon Reece

Pulley Guro Bete ▲

- *circa 1890*

Figure of a pulley Guro Bete.
- *height 19cm*
- £490   • Gordon Reece

Man Betu Gabon ▼

- *circa 1890*

A cephalomorphic ceramic from the Man Betu, Gabon, used only in court art.
- *height 42cm*
- £630   • Gordon Reece

Igbo Tribe Figure ▲

- *circa 1910*

One of a pair of figures from the Igbo tribe. A terracotta seated ancestral couple, with typical central crested headdress and multiple anklets, bracelets and necklaces symbolising wealth.
- *height 54cm*
- £6,500   • Gordon Reece

Bhutan Nepal Mask ◄

- *circa 1700*

Early mask of dynamic primitive form relying on simplicity, from Bhutan on the Nepalese border. Very rare and in excellent condition.
- *height 33cm*
- £1,380   • Gordon Reece

Dan-Karan Mask ▲
- *circa 1900*
Fine heavily patinated Dan-Karan mask, a powerful and abstracted mask from the Ivory Coast. From a collection in France.
- *height 25cm*
- £3,600   • Gordon Reece

Himalayan Tribal Mask ▲
- *unknown*
Himalayan tribal mask with heavy patination on the inside, the exterior has been constantly painted with red, black and cream paint. Origin unknown.
- *height 28cm*
- £620   • Gordon Reece

Apache Smoking Pouch ▼
- *1950*
Apache Indian smoking pouch with a red, white and black butterfly, and an orange background made from glass beads sewn on leather.
- *12cm x 7cm*
- £160   • Wilde One's

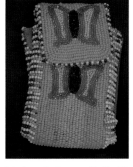

Mask with Cowrie Shells ▼
- *circa 1910*
Mask with applied cowrie shells on the nose and cheeks, iron rings through the nose and ears, and erect hair.
- *height 36cm*
- £3,200   • Gordon Reece

Yonba Maternity Figure ▲
- *circa 1910*
Yonba carved wood maternity figure of a seated woman with a child at her breast.
- *height 59cm*
- £1,700   • Gordon Reece

Kul Status Currency ▲
- *unknown*
Kul status currency in abstract human form, from West Africa.
- *height 51cm*
- £320   • Gordon Reece

Tshokwe-Mbuna ◄
- *circa 1910*
Striking Tshokwe-Mbuna mask with natural patination and fibre additions.
- *height 37cm*
- £400   • Gordon Reece

Twentieth-Century Design

The designers Charles Eames and Eero Saarinen were the first to experiment with moulded plywood, fibreglass and plastic.

From the 1900s the design of furniture and ceramics took on an exciting futuristic vibrancy, with designers experimenting with moulded plywood, fibreglass, plastic and leather. The famous Eames chair, successfully manufactured from the 1950s by the Herman Miller Company, with its moulded rosewood veneer and steel base, exemplifies this. These new materials completely changed the way furniture design was viewed, and the moulded organic shape became popular, with the innovators Eames and Saarinen winning prizes for their prototype chairs at the Organic Design in Home Furnishings Exhibition held at the Museum of Modern Art in New York in 1940. This exhibition was to have a profound effect on post war ceramic design.

Roy Midwinter designed two startling ranges of ceramics known as "Stylecraft" and "Fashion" in the new curving shapes, and commissioned innovative new ranges of patterns from the resident designers Jessie Tait and Terence Conran.

Ceramics

Italian Fishbone Vase ▲
- *1970*
Grey Italian flask-shaped vase with a raised grey fishbone design on a burnt orange ground.
- *height 33cm*
- £95   • Goya Hartogs

Owl by Goldscheider ▼
- *1890*
Owl by Goldscheider, with menacing glass eyes, standing on two books.
- *height 32cm*
- £700   • Heytesbury

Totem ▶
- *circa 2000*
"Giogold" by E. Sottsass, a vase of cylindrical form with dark blue and gold banding above a blue circular base.
- *height 38cm*
- £380   • Francesca Martire

Goldscheider Wall Mask

- *circa 1930*

An Italian Art Deco wall mask, executed in the Goldscheider style, of a young woman with stylized turquoise ringlets.
- *height 27cm*
- £375　　• 20th Century

Royal Dux Centrepiece

- *circa 1910*

An Art Nouveau Royal Dux centrepiece of two nude maidens intertwined amongst the waves.
- *20cm x 40cm*
- £595　　• 20th Century

Beswick Wall Mask

- *circa 1930*

An English Art Deco wall mask by Beswick depicting a young lady in profile.
- *height 27cm*
- £395　　• 20th Century

Expert Tips

As with everything else in Art Deco, it is still possible to pick up quality ceramics at reasonable prices if one is prepared to look for the lesser-known names, notably from the French Robj factory and Shelley of Staffordshire.

Art Deco Wall Mask

- *circa 1930*

An Art Deco terracotta coloured wall mask of a woman with black hair and turquoise collar. Marked "Kunstkeramik Adolf Prischl Wien".
- *height 25cm*
- £145　　• 20th Century

Goldscheider Figure

- *circa 1930*

An Art Deco figure by Goldscheider, designed by Claire Herezy, of a young lady in a blue dress profusely decorated with flowers.
- *height 35cm*
- £795　　• 20th Century

Katzhutte Figure

- *circa 1930*

An Art Deco figure by Katzhutte of a woman in a pink floral dress.
- *height 26cm*
- £445　　• 20th Century

Doulton Art Nouveau Jug

- *circa 1905*

Doulton jug with pink and green Art Nouveau design with brown edging.
- *height 19cm*
- £225　　• 20th Century

Torso by Zaccagnini ▼

- *circa 1940*
Ceramic torso of a nude lady by
Zaccagnini.
- *height 61cm*
- £1,050   • Vincenzo

Tissue and Cotton Jars ▼

- *circa 1950*
Italian jars by Fornasetti for
cotton and tissues with mermaids,
scallop shells and gilt banding.
- *height 23cm*
- £250   • Vincenzo

Taurus ▶

- *1950*
Blue stylised bull "Taurus"
standing on all fours with head
bowed and tail up by Gambone.
- *height 25cm*
- £2,000   • Themes

Retino ▲

- *circa 2000*
"Retino" by E. Sottsass, container
of conical form, with a design of
turquoise and gold banding above
a gilded circular base.
- *height 16cm*
- £250   • Francesca Martire

French Grey Vase ▲

- *1950*
Small French vase of conical form
with a textured finish and a black
geometric design with a large red
dot.
- *height 16cm*
- £55   • Goya Hartogs

Valaurido Plate by Capron ▼

- *1970*
Plate by Roger Capron for
Valaurido with a red and orange
design within borders of matt
grey.
- *diameter 22cm*
- £85   • Goya Hartogs

Basket Pattern ▼

- *1956–7*
Basket pattern Poole pot designed
by Anne Read.
- *height 19cm*
- £220   • Richard Dennis

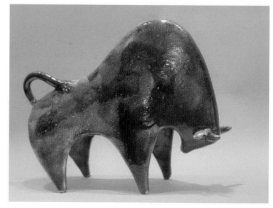

Cheese Dish ▲
- *circa 1940*

Cream-coloured cheese dish and cover with a floral design and moulded rim.
- *14cm x 20cm*
- £30   ● Old School

Poole Pottery Vase ▲
- *circa 1930*

Poole pottery bulbous vase with stylised yellow lilac flowers and green foliage.
- *height 13cm*
- £75   ● Richard Dennis

Lambeth Vase ▼
- 1900

Lambeth vase with green foliate design and pale blue flowers on a dark grey background, by Francis Pope.
- *height 30cm*
- £1,900   ● Richard Dennis

Poole Vase ▼
- *circa 1930*

Poole vase of ovoid form with yellow, blue and green design.
- *height 26cm*
- £400   ● Richard Dennis

Rosenthal Pottery ◄
- *circa 1950*

Peynet vase of conical form designed by Rosenthal Pottery entitled "The Marriage".
- *height 29cm*
- £300   ● Richard Dennis

Poole Floral Vase ▲
- *circa 1930*

Poole pottery vase with stylised yellow and purple flowers and a purple, green and lilac design around the rim.
- *height 20cm*
- £200   ● Richard Dennis

Peynet Design Plate ▲
- *circa 1950*

Rosenthal Germany pottery plate, showing spring with a couple on a bridge.
- *height 30cm*
- £200   ● Richard Dennis

Expert Tips

An important influence in Italian postwar design was surrealism, which can be clearly seen in the prolific designs of Piero Fornasetti in the 1950s.

Gouda Vase

- *circa 1900*
A Dutch Gouda vase profusely decorated with stylised flowers.
- *height 16.5cm*
- £120　　• 20th Century

Katzhutte Figure

- *circa 1930*
An Art Deco figure by Katzhutte, posing in a pink dress, with Katzhutte marks.
- *height 26cm*
- £545　　• 20th Century

Terracotta Wall Mask

- *1930s*
An Art Deco terracotta wall mask, in the German/Austrian style, of a woman with black glazed hair, a mottle glazed face, and orange lips.
- *height 27cm*
- £155　　• 20th Century

Goldscheider Art Deco Figure

- *circa 1930*
An Art Deco figure by Goldscheider of a young girl posing tending to a small fawn.
- *height 15cm*
- £395　　• 20th Century

Katzhutte Art Deco Figure

- *circa 1930*
A German Katzhutte Art Deco figure of a stylish woman dancing in a multi-coloured dress.
- *height 29cm*
- £475　　• 20th Century

Ernst Wahliss Dish

- *circa 1900*
An Art Nouveau dish by Ernst Wahliss with a young woman emerging from under three waterlilies.
- *width 33cm*
- £995　　• 20th Century

Lorenzl Art Deco Figure

- *circa 1930*
An Art Deco figured designed by Lorenzl of a stylish young woman posing in a grey lace effect dress.
- *height 30cm*
- £595　　• 20th Century

Butter Container ▼
- *circa 1940*
Cream ceramic butter dish with a lattice and apple blossom design in relief.
- *12cm x 18cm*
- £30　　　　● Old School

De Morgan Plate ▼
- *circa 1900*
William de Morgan designed pottery, decorated with a yellow bird with a trailing cornflower design on a turquoise border, painted by Charles Passenger.
- *diameter 20cm*
- £200　　　● Richard Dennis

Ovoid Vase ▲
- *circa 1920*
Italian bottle-shaped vase with yellow, green and brown abstract design.
- *height 29cm*
- £250　　　　● Iconastas

English Cup and Saucer ▲
- *circa 1920*
English cup, saucer and plate with a cartouche of a painted bird within gilt borders, surrounded by pink roses and cornflowers.
- *height 7.5cm*
- £38　　　● A. Piotrowski

Cigarette Holder ▼
- *1950*
Circular cigarette holder with push-action lid to extinguish the cigarettes.
- *height 21cm*
- £38　　　● Ventesimo

Janice Tchlenko Vase ▼
- *circa 1999*
Poole pottery vase of baluster form with a vibrant candy strip design by Janice Tchlenko.
- *height 37cm*
- £200　　● Richard Dennis

Dutch Jar ◄
- *circa 1923*
Dutch jar with cover by Corona Gouda, designed by W. P. Harispring.
- *height 11cm*
- £280　　● Pieter Oosthuizen

Shelley Tea Plate ▲
- *1927*

Shelley tea plate with orange border, black trees and green woodland border.
- *diameter 16cm*
- £20　　　● Susie Cooper

Vase Tulip Pattern ▲
- *1934*

Vase of baluster form, hand-painted by Clarice Cliff with a "tulip" pattern and green and red banding on a blue ground.
- *height 12cm*
- £650　　　● Susie Cooper

Butterfly Charger ▲
- *2001*

Charger with painted butterflies by Tania Pike for Dennis China Works.
- *diameter 37cm*
- £445　　　● Richard Dennis

Highland Stoneware Vase ▼
- *circa 2000*

Highland stoneware vase of baluster form with a narrow neck and splayed lip painted with trout underwater.
- *height 31cm*
- £145　　　● Richard Dennis

Alan Caiger Smith Goblet ▼
- *circa 1963*

Lustre glaze goblet by Alan Caiger Smith, the bowl with swirled designs above a knopped stem, raised on a circular base.
- *height 14cm*
- £100　　　● Richard Dennis

Ocelot Vase ▼
- *2000*

Catherine Mellor vase with a design of a leopard in blue on a leopard spot ground.
- *height 24cm*
- £411　　　● Richard Dennis

Shelley Bon-Bon Dish ▼
- *1927*

Bon-bon dish with a serpentine rim, orange centre and four black trees.
- *diameter 11cm*
- £65   • Susie Cooper

Shelley Cake Plate ▼
- *1927*

Shelley cake plate with a scalloped border and bold black trees within an orange border.
- *diameter 24cm*
- £65   • Susie Cooper

Carp Charger ▲
- *circa 2000*

Pottery charger with a design of two carp on a green background, by Dennis China Works.
- *diameter 36cm*
- £540   • Richard Dennis

Ocelot Design Vase ▶
- *2000*

Dennis China Works pottery vase of a leopard on a leopard spot background, painted by Catherine Mellor.
- *height 24cm*
- £411   • Richard Dennis

Bulb Vase ▼
- *1936*

Clarice Cliff bulb vase with metal rim from the "Citrus Delicier" collection.
- *diameter 20cm*
- £350   • Susie Cooper

Nuage by Clarice Cliff ◀
- *1935*

"Nuage" bowl by Clarice Cliff, with hand painted flowers and leaves with an orange centre on a green ground.
- *diameter 19cm*
- £950   • Susie Cooper

Keramik Wall Mask ▶

- *1930s*

A terracotta Gmundner Keramik
wall mask made in Austria and
printed with flowerpot mark.
- *height 20cm*
- £165   • 20th Century

Leather Texture Bowl ▼

- *1960s*

Oval stoneware bowl by
Rorstrand with dark brown
leather-textured glaze, with
incised parallel lines.
- *19cm x 16cm*
- £80   • Cabinet

Gunnar Nylund Vase ▼

- *1950s*

A vase by Gunnar Nylund for
Rorstrand, incised "R" and three
crowns. Stoneware with a brown
and black glaze.
- *height 17cm*
- £110   • Cabinet

Poole Vase ▼

- *early 1950s*

Poole carafe designed by Alfred
Read made of hand-thrown white
earthenware with a pattern of
purple stripes and the rim in red.
- *height 30cm*
- £340   • Cabinet

Poole Butterfly Pattern Vase ▼

- *1956–7*

Poole vase designed by Alfred
Read and decorated by Gwen
Haskins. Hand-thrown white
earthenware decorated with
purple and red butterflies.
- *height 21cm*
- £200   • Cabinet

Rorstrand Miniature Vase ▼

- *1950s*

Miniature stoneware vase by
Gunnar Nylund for Rorstrand
with a matte white glaze with
stripes of brown.
- *height 8cm*
- £110   • Cabinet

Hand Painted Wall Plaque ▶

- *1930s*

A quality china wall plaque hand
painted in pastel colours and
unsigned, but most likely a
Beswick piece.
- *27.9cm x 20.3cm*
- £280   • Sheryl's Art Deco

Furniture

Red Leather Chair ▲

- *circa 1960*

One of a pair of Italian chairs, one red and the other black leather, with teak legs and back rest.

- *height 98cm*
- £800   • Vincenzo

Wine Table ▲

- *1900–15*

Edwardian wine table with a circular top, satinwood banding and a central flower, the whole standing on a turned column with a tripod base.

- *47cm x 26cm*
- £169   • Amandini

English Hall Cupboard ▼

- *circa 1900*

English hall cupboard in medium oak with marquetry panel of a Dutch genre scene. With copper strapwork, hinges and escutcheons.

- *83cm x 62cm*
- £1,500   • Liberty

Reclining Armchair ▼

- *circa 1900*

One of a pair of oak reclining armchairs of solid design with slated side panels, raised on square tapered legs.

- *90cm x 70cm*
- £900   • Old Cinema

Arts and Crafts Chair ▲

- *circa 1905*

One of three Arts and Crafts single chairs with moulded top rail and curved splat with fruitwood inlay standing on straight square legs.

- *88cm x 44cm*
- £2,250   • Liberty

Dieter Rams Armchairs ▼

- *1962*

Armchairs by Dieter Rams, for Vitsoe, made from green leather on a white fibreglass base.

- *69cm x 86cm*
- £2,900   • Themes

SP4B Armchair ▼
- *circa 1931*
An SP4B armchair by Oliver
Bernard for PEL, the seat fully
upholstered in green rexine and
supported on a canterlevered
chrome frame.
- *height 71cm*
- £195   • 20th Century

Teak Chair ▼
- *circa 1960*
One of a set of four Danish teak
chairs with black vinyl seats.
- *height 80cm*
- £160   • 20th Century

Ercol Occasional Table ▲
- *20th century*
An Ercol occasional table, the
elm top supported on a beech
frame.
- *49.5cm x 84cm*
- £125   • 20th Century

Teak and Glass Coffee Table ▼
- *1950s*
A teak and glass coffee table, the
boomerang-shaped legs and cross
stretchers supporting a circular
glass top.
- *40.5cm x 73.5cm*
- £65   • 20th Century

Supporto Office Chair ▼
- *circa 1979*
A Supporto office chair, by Fred
Scott for Hille, with grey enamel
finish and black cloth upholstery.
- *height 1.24m*
- £275   • 20th Century

Cleopatra Sofa ▼
- *1970s*
"Cleopatra" sofa designed by
Geoffrey Harcourt, produced by
Artifort. Has a Urethane-padded
metal frame on castors, with
original black stretch fabric.
- *68cm x 1.80m*
- **£950**   • Cabinet

Italian Lounge Chair ▶
- *1960s*
"Lady" lounge chair designed by
Marco Zanuso, made by Arflex.
Wood and fibreglass frame, on
tubular brass legs with black
ferrules, fully upholstered in
yellow fabric.
- *78cm x 78cm x 78cm*
- **£650**   • Cabinet

"Reigate" Rocker ◀
- **1965**
William Plunkett rocker and
footstool with coated steel frame,
aluminium seat and arms, rubber
webbing and cushions
upholstered in original orange
tweed fabric.
- *92cm x 56cm x 84cm*
- **£700**   • Cabinet

Hans Wegner Daybed ▲
- *1960s*
Danish daybed designed by Hans
Wegner and upholstered in
oatmeal tweed. Has a dark oak
frame and the back lifts up to
reveal storage and a canvas roll-
out cover to protect sofa whilst
sleeping.
- *1.95m x 86cm x 76cm*
- **£800**   • Cabinet

Jason Stacking Chairs ▲
- *1950*
A set of five "Jason" stacking
chairs designed by Carl Jacobs for
Kandya. Formed plywood seat
section over a turned beech base.
- *74cm x 52cm x 38cm*
- **£700 for set**   • Cabinet

Expert Tips
*Chairs are for sitting on more
than looking at. Always try
them for comfort as well as
inspecting their design.*

Swedish Desk ▶

- *1920–30*
Gustavian-style Swedish free-standing desk.
- 76cm x 1.44m
- £2,900 • Rupert Cavendish

Arts and Crafts Table ▼

- *circa 1910*
Arts and Crafts oak table of solid construction with straight supports and circular stretcher.
- 52cm x 69cm
- £280 • Old Cinema

Edwardian Three-Tier Stand ▲

- *circa 1905*
An unusual wrought iron and copper Edwardian three-tier stand with scrolled decoration.
- 95cm x 25cm
- £135 • Old Cinema

Oak Hallstand ▲

- *circa 1880*
A very good quality Arts and Crafts hallstand and two matching hall chairs by "Minton Hollins and Co. Patent Tile Works, Stoke-on-Trent".
- 2.08m x 1.28m
- £1,850 • Old Cinema

Art Nouveau Bureau ▼

- *circa 1905*
Art Nouveau oak bureau with folding writing slope above a single drawer with organically designed copper metalwork.
- 1.2m x 90cm
- £565 • Old Cinema

Nursery Chest ▲

- *circa 1930*
Heal's oak nursery chest with double and single panelled doors, three short drawers and two long drawers.
- 1.5m x 1.15m
- £1,850 • Old Cinema

Arts and Crafts Lamp Table ▲

- *circa 1905*
Arts and Crafts mahogany occasional table with three supports and carved and pierced decoration.
- 69cm x 43cm
- £220 • Old Cinema

Art Deco Occasional Table ▲

- *1930s*

Art Deco occasional circular table with a quartered veneered top in an attractive warm "golden" burr walnut and a quartered sectioned base in differing heights.
- *60cm x 58.5cm*
- **£390**　• **Deco World**

Plywood Coffee Table ▲

- *1930s*

A circular two-tiered coffee table made by "Gerald Summers, Makers of Simple Furniture". Made of birch plywood, formed and stained.
- *41cm x 68cm*
- **£550**　• **Cabinet**

Expert Tips

An *"antique of the future" must show not only excellence of manufacture and pleasing lines, but originality. The pieces on here demonstrate this. They will be antiques; the best reproductions will always be reproductions.*

Magistretti Coffee Table ◀

- *1964*

Low coffee table by Vico Magistretti in ebonised wood with end drawers, drop flap sides, a central storage well and brass top.
- *1.28m x 96cm*
- **£500**　• **Cabinet**

French Bedside Cabinet ▶

- *1930s*

Art Deco French bedside cabinet with heavily figured walnut veneers and almost organic shape.
- *58.5cm x 60cm x 32cm*
- **£255**　• **Deco World**

Italian Leather Chair ▲

- *1930s*

Very rare large Italian Art Deco leather chair. In excellent condition with little sign of wear.
- *78cm x 1.16m x 92cm*
- **£285**　• **Deco World**

French Chinese-style Chair ▼

- *circa 1920*
One of a pair of French oak chairs with a strong Chinese influence and a distressed paint effect, standing on straight square legs.
- *height 74cm*
- **£1,250** • Anthony Sharpe

Art Deco Cabinet ▼

- *circa 1930*
Art Deco figured mahogany walnut cocktail cabinet of circular design with pull-out mixing surface.
- *1.61m x 85cm*
- **£995** • Old Cinema

Art Deco Three-Piece Suite ▶

- *circa 1930*
A very rare and unusual Art Deco upholstered leather three-piece suite.
- *86cm x 95cm*
- **£5,330** • Old Cinema

Red Stereophonic Chair ▼

- *circa 1960s*
Red moulded fibreglass egg chair on a circular metal base, with grey and white wool-padded upholstery and leather-padded seat cover and back rest, with fitted stereo and matching ottoman, designed by the Lee Co. of California for a commission.
- *1.29m x 86cm*
- **£4,200** • Country Seat

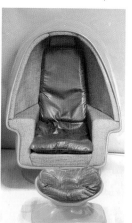

Dressing Table ◀

- *circa 1950*
Modernist oak dressing table with two columns of graduated drawers and single drawer above knee hole.
- *1.65m x 1.22m*
- **£225** • Old Cinema

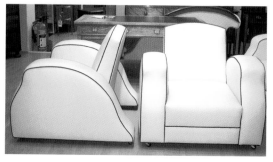

Leather Armchair ▲

- *1970s*
Danish leather armchair with formed beech frames and upholstered in grey leather with buttoned back and seat.
- *76cm x 57cm x 60cm*
- **£200** • Cabinet

Walnut Bureau ▲

- *circa 1940*
A very good early twentieth century figured walnut bureau in the George II style.
- *1.04m x 84cm*
- **£1,895** • John Riordan

French Leather Chairs ▼
- **1977**
Pair of chairs by Michel Cadestin and George Laurent for the Library of the Centre Pompidou Beaubourg, made from wire with leather seat and back. Illus: Les Années 70, by Anne Bony.
- *height 74.5cm*
- **£1,200**   • Themes

Arts and Crafts Dining Chair ▼
- *circa 1905*
One of a pair of oak Arts and Crafts carvers with scrolled arms and turned supports.
- *1.05m x 58cm*
- **£550**   • Liberty

Japanese Chest ▲
- *circa 1920s*
Special Japanese Isho Dansu (storage chest) for fabrics. The wood has not been sealed or lacquered first.
- *1.02m x 54cm*
- **£2,650**   • Gordon Reece

Chrome Dining Chair ▲
- **1975**
One of a set of four dining chairs with grey leather and chrome, by Prebenfabricus & Dorgen Kastholm for Alfred Kill.
- *height 70cm*
- **£2,200**   • Themes

Mahogany Dining Chair ▼
- *circa 1950s*
One of a set of six mahogany dining chairs with pierced backsplat, drop-in seat cushion and cabriole legs.
- *1m x 48cm*
- **£1,250**   • Old Cinema

Stool by Verner Panton ▼
- *circa 1960*
Wire stool with original circular suede padded cover, by Verner Panton Danish.
- *height 43cm*
- **£745**   • Country Seat

Harlow Chairs ◀
- **1971**
Set of four "Harlow" chairs with red wool-padded seats and backs, standing on aluminium bases and stands, by Ettore Sottsass for Poltronova.
- *height 82cm*
- **£3,500**   • Themes

Modernist Chest of Drawers ▶

- **1930s**

Art Deco modernist style chest of drawers. The underwood is mahogany which has been grained in a blonde colour, surrounding the front edging is walnut feather banding. There are six graduated drawers.
- *96cm x 38cm x 50cm*
- **£585**   • Deco World

Cocktail Cabinet ▲

- **1930s**

Art Deco cocktail cabinet in figured walnut, shaped like a half drum. The top part of the cocktail cabinet has an all-mirrored interior and internal light. The doors to the top and base storage areas roll open and shut.
- *1.38m x 1.14m x 35cm*
- **£1,100**   • Deco World

Bird's Eye Circular Coffee Table ▲

- **1930s**

Art Deco pale blonde bird's eye maple circular coffee table. This rare table features grained maple veneers and a classic Deco circular base with walnut feather banded decoration.
- *56cm x 73cm*
- **£545**   • Deco World

Burr Walnut Table ▼

- **1930s**

Art Deco burr walnut table featuring a beautifully grained walnut veneered top, with a second tier underneath and four tapering ebonised legs.
- *59cm x 80cm x 52cm*
- **£225**   • Deco World

Savoy Trolley ▼

- **1930s**

English Art Deco circular "Savoy" hostess trolley with three walnut shelves, frame and castors.
- *78cm x 70cm x 43cm*
- **£345**   • Deco World

Cocktail Table ▼

- **1930s**

Art Deco walnut cocktail table featuring a central compartment in the top, accessed by sliding open two covers. Octagonal in shape, this piece also has two shelves and a ribbed pattern on the side panels.
- *62cm x 60cm*
- **£375**   • Deco World

Expert Tips

Fashionable in the 1930s, large pieces of Art Deco furniture, veneered pale to be less overpowering, were expensive at the time but are good value today.

U-Base Table ◀

- **1930s**

Original Art Deco U-base occasional table in a figured burr walnut with two walnut columns and glass top for protection.
- *62cm x 70cm x 70cm*
- **£475**   • Deco World

Black Leather Armchair ▼

●*circa 1960*
Black leather armchair with
padded seat and back, with metal
and leather arms, standing on a
rotating star-shaped metal base.
●*height 89cm*
● £750   ● Country Seat

Butterfly Chair ▲

●*circa 1950*
One of a pair of plastic mock
snakeskin butterfly chairs on a
early tubular frame, manufactured
by Knoll.
●*height 1m*
● £550   ● Country Seat

Eames Armchair ▲

●*circa 1975*
One of a pair of Eames padded
brown armchairs with aluminium
arms and base.
●*height 1.01m*
● £1,450   ● Country Seat

Edwardian Chest of Drawers ▼

●*circa 1905*
Edwardian chest of two small and
two long drawers, with metal
foliate handles standing on
straight legs.
● *82cm x 1.08m*
● £240   ● Old School

Leather Rotating Chair ▲

●*1970*
Tan leather rotating and
adjustable desk chair with padded
seat and back, and metal legs on
wheels.
●*height 74cm*
● £495   ● Country Seat

White Folding Bench ▲

●*circa 1920*
Continental pine folding bench,
painted white, on metal legs and
arms.
● *90cm x 1.25m*
● £220   ● Old School

Walnut Buffet ▶

●*1930*
Art Deco breakfront walnut
buffet with solid supports and
moulded decoration.
● *84cm x 1.06m*
● £650   ● Old Cinema

Glass

Cameo Glass Vase ▶

- *circa 1905*

A large Art Nouveau cameo glass vase by Richard, the body carved and etched with a landscape.

- *height 33cm*
- £875
- 20th Century

Kosta Paperweight ▲

- *1955–63*

A Kosta paperweight, the teardrop shape consisting of internal cranberry pink glass surrounded by a controlled pattern of bubbles encased in clear glass.

- *height 8cm*
- £75
- 20th Century

Lalique Bowl ▼

- *1920s*

An opalescent Lalique bowl in the "Poisson" pattern, marked "R.LALIQUE FRANCE".

- *diameter 24cm*
- £550
- 20th Century

Orrefors "Ariel" Vase ▼

- *1972*

A strikingly beautiful Orrefors "Ariel" vase designed by Ingeborg Lundin. A thick slightly flaring vase with a continuous design, the inner in olive green glass, the whole cased in clear glass.

- *height 18cm*
- £1,550
- 20th Century

Art Deco Decanter ◀

- *circa 1930*

Art Deco conical ruby cased decanter cut to clear with horizontal bands of broad flutes. Original clear conical stopper cut with broad flutes.

- *height 23cm*
- £425
- Laurie Leigh

Expert Tips

René Lalique (1860–1945) mass-produced glass. Although it is avidly collected and expensive, it is not especially hard to find.

Abstract Glass Structure ▲

- *circa 1990*

Orange and black abstract glass vase of cylindrical form with gold flaked inclusions, by Nichetti for Murano.
- *height 27cm*
- £380　　● Francesca Martire

Mosaic Vase by Ferro ▲

- *1998*

Mosaic Murano glass vase by Ferro, for the Venice Biennale 1998.
- *height 29cm*
- £1,200　● Francesca Martire

Tiffany Centrepiece ▶

- *circa 1930*

L. Tiffany's gold iridescent centrepiece with organic designs.
- *diameter 25cm*
- £4,000　　● Victor Arwas

Glass Paperweight Abstract Sculpture ▼

- *circa 1960*

Italian orange, red, black and white abstract glass sculpture.
- *height 16cm*
- £125　　● Francesca Martire

Murano Paperweight ▼

- *circa 1960*

Murano paperweight of compressed globular form with an abstract pattern of blue, white, lime green, pink and gold.
- *diameter 23cm*
- £325　　● Francesca Martire

Blue Cactus Vase ▼

- *circa 1950*

Blue glass "Cactus" vase by Recardo Licata for Murano.
- *height 44cm*
- £1,200　　● Francesca Martire

Lalique Box Lid ◀
- **1920s**
An opalescent Lalique box lid, marked "R.LALIQUE". This lid was used on a presentation set by Houbigant 1928–1930.
- *diameter 14cm*
- **£145** ● 20th Century

Cordonato d'Oro Vase ▲
- **1950s**
"Cordonato d'Oro" vase of red glass in a tapering ribbed shape above a bulbous body, with gold leaf.
- *height 26.5cm*
- **£300** ● Cabinet

Expert Tips

Modern vases showcase the influence of contemporary trends in their form and decoration.

Red and Yellow Murano Vase ▼
- **1950s**
Murano sommerso vase, red and yellow cased in clear glass, with original label.
- *height 11cm*
- **£65** ● Antique Glass

Toso Glass Vase ▲
- *contemporary*
Heavy clear glass vase by Stefano Toso of Murano with swirls of orange and blue.
- *height 22cm*
- **£350** ● Cabinet

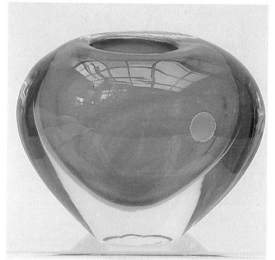

Large Murano Glass Vase ▲
- *contemporary*
A large glass vase designed by Stefano Toso of Murano with dominant colours of green, yellow and red.
- *height 38cm*
- **£450** ● Cabinet

Green and Yellow Murano Vase ▶

- *1950s*
Murano sommerso vase, emerald green and lemon yellow cased in heavily facetted clear glass.
- *height 7.5cm*
- £65 • **Antique Glass**

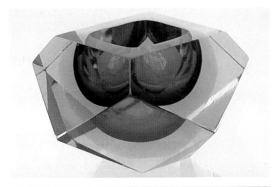

Art Deco Lemonade Set ▲

- *circa 1930*
Art Deco "lemonade" set consisting of a tall jug with an amber handle and six matching glasses with amber stems and feet, all engraved with vertical lines.
- *height 24cm*
- £195 • **Laurie Leigh**

Set of Conical Goblets ▼

- *circa 1930*
Two of a set of six Art Deco conical goblets decorated in intaglio with stylised zigzag pattern on conical uranium green feet.
- *height 20.3cm*
- £495 • **Laurie Leigh**

Gilded Glass Bowls ▲

- *early 20th century*
Three of a set of ten dimple-ribbed bowls and stands gilded with rural scenes.
- *diameter 15cm*
- £300 • **Antique Glass**

Art Deco Candelabra ▼

- *circa 1935*
Pair of American Art Deco candelabra with ribbed arms and icicle drops suspended on rectangular bases cut underneath with diamonds.
- *height 19.7cm*
- £695 • **Laurie Leigh**

Cameo Glass Vase ▲

- *circa 1920*
Le Verre Français cameo glass vase, acid-etched, with an orange and green design on a yellow ground, applied with the Millifiori cane mark.
- *height 30cm*
- £795 • **20th Century**

Mosaic Murrina Vase ▼

- *1998*

Mosaic vase of baluster form, with blue and yellow organic design by "Murrina".
- *height 29cm*
- £1,500 • Francesca Martire

Amber Bowl ▼

- *circa 1970*

Amber glass bowl on a clear stand by Cevedex.
- *height 23cm*
- £500 • Themes

Fish in Glass by Cenedese ▲

- *1950*

Glass object with a seascape design including a tropical fish with underwater plants, by Cenedese for Murano.
- *width 14cm*
- £225 • Francesca Martire

Green Vase with Cactus ▲

- *circa 1950s*

Green "Cactus" vase by Recardo Licata for Murano.
- *height 44cm*
- £1,200 • Francesca Martire

Hutton Vase ▼

- *circa 1920*

Clear glass vase by Oroffords and etched by John Hetton.
- *height 33cm*
- £1,000 • Victor Arwas

Italian Glass Fish ▼

- *1960*

Italian glass object fashioned as a stylised coiled fish.
- *height 24cm*
- £285 • Ventesimo

Small Daum Jug ◄

- *circa 1900*

Small Daum variegated amber to pink jug with "Bleeding Heart" floral overlay.
- *6cm x 12cm*
- £2,200 • The French

Cranberry Glass Vases ▲

- *circa 1900*

A pair of Bohemian cranberry glass vases with engraved decoration depicting castles and a forest setting with a leaping deer, on a faceted and moulded base.
- *height 44cm*
- £4,200   • Sinai

Vase by Baxter ▲

- *circa 1969*

Whitefriars kingfisher-blue vase by Baxter with an abstract design and textured finish.
- *height 29cm*
- £235   • Country Seat

Martini Jug by Baxter ▼

- *circa 1962*

Whitefriars kingfisher-blue Martini jug with a clear handle. A "Whitefriars Studio" range by Peter Wheeler.
- *height 36cm*
- £95   • Country Seat

Silvio Vigliaturo Sculpture ▼

- *1999*

Glass "Ikomos" series sculpture by Silvio Vigliaturo, signed and dated.
- *height 40cm*
- £1,200   • Francesca Martire

Tall Italian Vase ▲

- *1982*

Italian tall glass vase with a moulded lip, cerulean blue variegated to paler blue with moulded banding within the glass.
- *height 63cm*
- £1,000   • Themes

Red Bubble Ashtray ▲

- *1958*

Ruby red lobed bubble ashtray with an organic moulded design by Harry Dyer.
- *diameter 13cm*
- £25   • Country Seat

Whitefriars Vase ▶

- *circa 1969*
Rare Whitefriars ovoid brown
and orange vase. "Studio Range"
by Peter Wheeler.
- *height 22.5cm*
- £245   • Country Seat

Glass Vase by Laura Diaz ▼

- *1990–1*
"Incalmo" ink-blue glass vase,
with a cane pattern neck and
white glass wheel carved bulbous
base by Laura Diaz, Ref: *il vetro a
venezia* by Marino Baronier.
- *height 30cm*
- £1,800   • Themes

Swedish Translucent Vase ▼

- *1955–6*
Swedish translucent tall glass
vase with white trailing lines and
one red line made for Kosta.
- *height 38cm*
- £2,200   • Themes

Tangerine Vase ▶

- *1969*
Tangerine vase with concentric
circular design and a textured
finish by Baxter.
- *height 18cm x 17cm*
- £140   • Country Seat

Glass Vase ▲

- *1973*
Glass vase with circular design by
Olle Alerius. Orrefors Co. 1973,
Expo A 248, signed and
illustrated by Lilane.
- *height 20cm*
- £2,200   • Themes

Guitar Mirror ▼

- *1950*
Guitar-shaped metal mirror.
- *length 83cm*
- £120   • Goya Hartogs

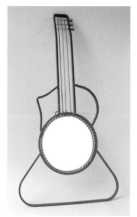

Lighting

French Desk Lamp ▶
- **1955–65**
French chromed steel desk lamp with light green painted shade and base.
- *height 35cm*
- **£60**   • **Cabinet**

Art Deco Lady Lamp ▲
- **1930s**
Art Deco figural lamp featuring a semi-naked female holding a white glass globe shade. The figure is white metal and has been gilded on top in copper and gold tones. She rests on an oval alabaster base.
- *40cm x 22cm x 12cm*
- **£525**   • **Deco World**

Sepia Chrome Lamp ▲
- **1930s**
Art Deco chrome lamp with an all chrome base and a rare sepia coloured segmented shade with slivered detailing.
- *38cm x 12.5cm*
- **£285**   • **Deco World**

Chrome Table Lamp ▼
- **1930s**
Art Deco original chrome table lamp with square-sided marbled cream and brown glass shade which gives off a warm sepia toned glow. Fully rewired.
- *42cm x 12.5cm*
- **£165**   • **Deco World**

Desk Lamp ▼
- **1950–60**
A steel blue metal desk lamp by "Elekthermax" with chrome stem and finial.
- *42cm x 42cm*
- **£250**   • **Cabinet**

Skyscraper Lamp ▼
- **1930s**
Art Deco chrome lamp featuring a skyscraper frosted glass shade in a wonderful sepia colour.
- *height 45cm*
- **£255**   • **Deco World**

Pink and Brown Marbled Lamp ▶

- *1930s*

Art Deco original chrome table lamp with glass shade marbled dusty pink and brown. Fully rewired and in excellent condition.
- *40cm x 12cm*
- £235　● Deco World

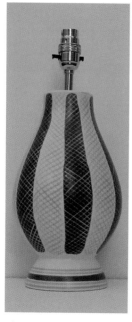

Blue-stripe Freeform Lamp ▲

- *1954–7*

Poole pottery lamp with a cross-hatched abstract design.
- *height 24cm*
- £275　● G. Harris

Patterned Freeform Lamp ▲

- *1954–7*

Poole lamp with brown and black abstract design, a brown band to the upper and lower edges.
- *height 12cm*
- £125　● G. Harris

Poole Vine Lamp ▼

- *1954–7*

Poole pottery lamp base, the body of bulbous form decorated with a leaf ribboned pattern.
- *height 24cm*
- £275　● G. Harris

Aeroplane Lamp ▼

- *1930s*

French Art Deco figural lamp featuring a classic brass aeroplane sitting on a soft brown veined marble base.
- *16cm x 23cm x 10cm*
- £135　● Deco World

Solid Freeform Lamp ▼

- *1954–7*

Poole lamp with attractive ice green glaze.
- *height 24cm*
- £95　● G. Harris

Tubular Lamp ▲

• **1950**
Italian chrome graduated tubular
lamp with coiled decoration.
• *height 44cm*
• **£250**　　　　• **Ventesimo**

Italian Gold Mesh Lamp ▲

• *circa 1940*
Table lamp with mesh lampshade
supported on a black and white
marble base.
• *height 49cm*
• **£900**　　　　• **Vincenzo**

Expert Tips

*Italian designers were at the
forefront of early postwar
lighting producing stylish,
sophisticated lamps in
organic shapes.*

Art Deco Verdigris Lantern ▼

• *circa 1930*
Art Deco bronze lantern of
tapered form, each side centred
by a moulded oval motif below a
stepped fan cresting, fitted with
replaced glass, the sides at the
base of the lantern centred by
scrolls issuing palmettes, with
s-scroll brackets leading to a
lower suspended bracket.
• *94cm x 41.5cm sq*
• **£6,500**　　• **Anthony Outred**

Yellow Sunhat Lamp ▼

• *circa 1960*
Large yellow Italian sunhat lamp
with a green ribbon and assorted
floral design.
• *diameter 44cm*
• **£290**　　　　• **Castello**

Murano Glass Lamps ▲

• *circa 1960*
Murano Italian glass lamp with
yellow and orange ribbed body.
The metal covers are ashtrays.
• *height 32cm*
• **£450**　　　　• **Vincenzo**

Pan-pipes Lamp ▲

• *circa 1970*
Italian pan-pipes table lamp with
chrome and perspex columns
surmounted by lights.
• *height 85cm*
• **£1,000**　　　　• **Themes**

Rye Sphere Lamp ▼

- *1950–60*

Spherical Poole pottery lamp
with yellow glaze, very minimal
in style.
- *height 15cm*
- **£60**   ● **G. Harris**

Poole Atlantis Lamp ◄

- *1972–7*

Poole pottery lamp with a brown
and beige glaze.
- *height 36cm*
- **£195**   ● **G. Harris**

Slim Bottle Lamp ▲

- *1954–7*

Poole freeform lamp with
negative leaf design on striped-
coloured ground.
- *height 26.5cm*
- **£195**   ● **G. Harris**

Stylised Clown Lamp ▲

- *1930s*

French mood lamp of spelter with
two stylised clowns who have
fallen asleep on top of the
original crackle-glaze shade,
mounted on a pink marble base
tall.
- *29.2cm x 30.5cm*
- **£950**   ● **Sheryl's Art Deco**

Candy Stripe Lamp ▲

- *1950–60*

A red and white glaze striped Rye
lamp.
- *height 16.5cm*
- **£60**   ● **G. Harris**

Peanut Lamp ▲

- *1954–7*

Poole freeform lamp with
negative leaf design on striped
background of green, mauve and
brown.
- *height 27cm*
- **£215**   ● **G. Harris**

Poole Helios Lamp

- **circa 1964**
Poole pottery square-shaped lamp
of an abstract geometric design
with moss green glaze.
- *12cm x 10cm*
- £40 • G. Harris

Patterned Poole Helios Lamp

- **circa 1964**
A bluish grey/white glaze
decorated Poole lamp of grid-style
design.
- *height 12cm*
- £50 • G. Harris

Celtic Lamp

- **circa 1960**
Pottery lamp decorated with a
yellow and black stylised dragon
pattern, swirls and black banding
to the upper and lower registers.
- *height 35cm*
- £95 • G. Harris

Small Carafe Lamp

- **1957**
Sky blue glazed lamp by Poole in
a carafe shape.
- *height 27cm*
- £95 • G. Harris

Spelter Lady Lamp

- **early 1920s**
A spelter Egyptian-themed
French lady lamp, possibly by
Voliente although very Chiparus
in detail. This lamp is with a
crackle-glass shade and is
mounted on an ovular red marble
base with pebbled detail.
- *35.5cm x 29.2cm*
- £740 • Sheryl's Art Deco

Conical Lamp

- **1930s**
Large French metal ceiling lamp
in conical form with green
patinated ring detailing and
chrome outer ring.
- *45.7cm x 61cm*
- £595 • Sheryl's Art Deco

Perspex Lamp ▼
- 1970

Italian U-shaped perspex lamp on a metal base by Stilnovo.
- *38cm x 32cm*
- £1,200   • Themes

Brancusi Standing Light ▼
- 1990

Brancusi standing light made from Japanese paper with a metal base, by Tom Dixon.
- *height 2.8m*
- £1,600   • Themes

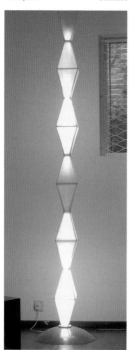

Art Deco Lamp ▲
- *circa 1930*

Art deco lamp with a twisted metal stand and a white glass lampshade with a grey geometric pattern.
- *height 47cm*
- £75   • Old School

Italian Light ▲
- *circa 1950*

Italian light with a white conical shade supported on a black circular base.
- *height 40cm*
- £280   • Francesca Martire

Wall Light by Vemini ▼
- *circa 1950*

One of a pair of abstract Italian glass wall lights with a design of assorted squares with amber, tobacco and clear glass, by Vemini.
- *31cm square*
- £1,280   • Francesca Martire

Cube Floor Light ▼
- 1970

Free-standing floor light made from three white and yellow glass cubes, connected by metal bands with a circular metal top and handle.
- *height 1.15m*
- £1,100   • Themes

Large Classical Lady Lamp ▶
- *1920s–30s*

Large lamp made of green patinated spelter featuring a woman standing bare breasted and wearing a short brown skirt, on a black marble top-hat base.
- *height 69cm*
- **£1,195** • **Sheryl's Art Deco**

"Vers l'Oasis" Lamp ▲
- *late 1920s*

"Vers l' Oasis", a signed spelter lamp by Fayral of a woman holding a yellow glass urn mounted on a Portorro base.
- *height 47cm*
- **£1,395** • **Sheryl's Art Deco**

Arctic Scene Lamp ▼
- *mid-1930s*

An enormous spelter polar bear and a pair of penguins sitting either side of an iceberg lamp on a base of cream and pale green onyx.
- *33cm x 81cm x 22.9cm*
- **£1,695** • **Sheryl's Art Deco**

Lady Pastille Burner Lamp ▲
- *1925*

A spelter lamp with two ladies on stepped tapering columns sitting on either side of a globe. Both women hold a container with removable lids which appear to be pastille burners.
- *25.4cm x 36.8cm*
- **£1,285** • **Sheryl's Art Deco**

Lorenzl Spelter Lady Lamp ▼
- *mid-1920s*

Spelter lamp of a woman in her under-clothes with a silvered enamel patina and peach coloured hightlights. Mounted on a Portorro Extra marble base, unsigned by Lorenzl.
- *28cm x 15.3cm*
- **£650** • **Sheryl's Art Deco**

Alabaster and Spelter Lamp ▼
- *circa 1925*

Gold patinated lady-lamp with base of cream onyx, nude woman figure of spelter, and steps and urn shade – which glows when lit – of alabaster.
- *18cm x 25.4cm*
- **£495** • **Sheryl's Art Deco**

Italian Globe Lamp ▼
- *circa 1960*

One of a pair of clear and ripple effect globe table lamps with a white band running through the body.
- *height 54cm*
- **£300**　　　• **Vincenzo**

Kodak Lampshade ▲
- *1970*

Plastic lampshade with the lettering "Kodak" in red on a deep yellow background.
- *height 25cm*
- **£149**　　　• **Jessops**

Art Deco Lamp ◄
- *1930*

French Art Deco chrome table lamp with a domed shade, curved stand and circular base.
- *height 32cm*
- **£250**　　　• **Ventesimo**

Italian Wall Light ▼
- *circa 1970*

Italian wall light by Marlotta, with a perspex background with metal tubes projecting from it in a variety of sizes, the whole on a square metal frame.
- *60cm x 60cm*
- **£1,600**　　　• **Themes**

Italian Table Lamp ▼
- *1950*

Black Italian table lamp of baluster form with blue, yellow and red dots, within a white graffiti-patterned border.
- *height 15cm*
- **£50**　　　• **Manic Attic**

Baccarat-Style Chandelier ◄
- *20th century*

One of a pair of Baccarat-style cranberry glass chandeliers with scrolled moulded decoration and numerous crystal glass droplets, with 36 arms.
- *height 2.08m*
- **£20,000**　　　• **Sinai**

Raised Band Lamp ▼
- *circa 1950*
Pink Poole pottery lamp of
pleasing proportions.
- *height 16cm*
- £60   • G. Harris

Seal Lamp ▼
- *mid-1920s*
French Art Deco spelter seal
lamp by Carvin mounted on a
marble base.
- *27cm x 31cm*
- £295   • Sheryl's Art Deco

Art Deco Gymnast Lamp ▼
- *1923*
French Art Deco spelter lamp
featuring a woman doing the
splits supporting a globe, signed
by Balleste.
- *28cm x 36cm*
- £760   • Sheryl's Art Deco

Art Deco Lady Lamp ▲
- *early 1930s*
French Art Deco spelter lamp of
a woman supporting a globe,
mounted on a Portorro marble
and onyx base.
- *height 45.7cm*
- £495   • Sheryl's Art Deco

Spelter and Alabaster Lamp ▲
- *early 1930s*
English Art Deco lamp of a
woman supporting a globe with
one hand. Made of gold patinated
spelter and mounted on an
alabaster triangular base.
- *height 40cm*
- £440   • Sheryl's Art Deco

Silvered Bronze Lamp ▼
- *1923*
Art Deco silvered bronze lady
lamp mounted on a Verdigris
marble base, made by the French
artist Janle and signed on the
bottom of the figure.
- *40cm x 30cm*
- £1,595   • Sheryl's Art Deco

Crouching Woman Lamp ▼
- *late 1920s*
Art Deco lamp of a woman in a
crouched position supporting the
fixture. Made of spelter with a
gold enamelled patina.
- *height 38cm*
- £495   • Sheryl's Art Deco

Bronze Art Deco Lamp ▼
- *early 20th century*
French Art Deco bronze lamp by
Molins-Balleste. The lamp shade
is made of hand-made glass fruit
and flowers sitting in an alabaster
basket.
- *45cm x 50cm*
- £2,945   • Sheryl's Art Deco

Metalware

Art Deco Lady ▼

- *circa 1930*

Bronze and ivory figure of a lady in theatrical costume. Excellent colour and detail, signed "Josef Lorenzi".
- *height 26cm*
- £2,800 • Hickmet

Young Girl in Bronze and Ivory ▼

- *circa 1925*

Highly detailed gilt bronze and ivory figure of a young girl, signed and inscribed "Etling, Demetre Chiparus, Romania".
- *height 19cm*
- £3,300 • Hickmet

Robin Hood Figure ▲

- *1934*

French spelter and ivorine figure of a male archer modelled on Robin Hood.
- *height 68cm*
- £995 • Sheryl's Art Deco

Dancing Maiden Figure ▲

- *circa 1930*

Bronze figure of a young lady dancing in striking pose, signed "Georges Angerle", raised on an onyx base.
- *height 24cm*
- £950 • Hickmet

Paul Philippe Bronze ▼

- *circa 1920*

Striking bronze figure of a young lady with arms outstretched with a golden patination standing on a circular marble plinth, signed by Paul Philippe.
- *height 46cm*
- £3,950 • Hickmet

Bronze Flute Player ▼

- *circa 1920*

Bronze figure of a young girl in a seductive dancing pose with golden patination, signed "Claire Colinet".
- *height 48cm*
- £4,800 • Hickmet

Bronze Vase ▼
- *circa 1900*

Two-colour patinated gilt bronze with cats' heads around the rim and field mice, wheat and poppies encircling the body, signed by Leopold Savine, L. Colin and Cie. With Paris founder's mark.
- *height 27cm*
- **£6,500**   • **Victor Arwas**

Italian Seal ▼
- *1950*

Italian silver torpedo-shaped seal stamp with base by Murini.
- *height 18cm*
- **£120**   • **Ventesimo**

Fugare Spelter Figure ▲
- *circa 1893*

Gilded spelter figure of winged Mercury engraved "A. Recompense by Fugare" and exhibited in Paris in 1893.
- *height 34cm*
- **£430**   • **Hayman**

Bronze Lady ▲
- *1911*

Gilt bronze figure of a lady with a parasol by H. Varenne.
- *height 20cm*
- **£2,500**   • **Victor Arwas**

Letter Rack ▼
- *circa 1950*

Black wire cat letter rack, the body in the form of a spring with plastic eyes and rotating eye balls.
- *height 14cm*
- **£45**   • **Francesca Martire**

Italian Chrome Teapot ▼
- *circa 1950*

Round chrome teapot with cork stopper for the spout.
- *height 19cm*
- **£65**   • **Castello**

Chrome Coffee Pot ▼
- *circa 1950*

Italian circular chrome coffee pot.
- *height 24cm*
- **£50**   • **Castello**

Draped Bronze Dancer ▼
- *circa 1925*
Fine bronze and ivory figure of a
beautiful young lady in dancing
pose, stamped and signed "Paul
Philippe".
- *height 24cm*
- £4,950   • Hickmet

Etling Bronze ▲
- *circa 1925*
Detailed gilt bronze and ivory
figure of a young girl, signed and
inscribed "Etling".
- *height 19cm*
- £3,300   • Hickmet

Josef Lorenzi Bronze ▼
- *circa 1930*
Austrian bronze figure of a dancer
with carved ivory head, raised
onyx base and signed "Josef
Lorenzi".
- *height 24cm*
- £1,950   • Hickmet

Pantalon Dancer Bronze ▼
- *circa 1935*
Bronze cold-painted figure of a
young lady dancing in a stylised
pose by Josef Lorenzi.
- *height 24cm*
- £1,450   • Hickmet

Exotic Dancer Figure ▲
- *circa 1920*
A bronze figure of a young
woman in exotic dress with rich
green patina on cream marble
base by Samuel Lypchytz.
- *height 33cm*
- £1,795   • Hickmet

Uriano Rock-man Figure ▲
- *late 1920s*
Large green and bronze patinated
spelter male figure with base of
black and Portorro Extra marbles.
In excellent condition with
original partina, by Uriano,
unsigned.
- *38.1cm x 73.6cm*
- £760   • Sheryl's Art Deco

Scarf Dancer Bronze ▼
- *circa 1930*
Cold-painted gilt and brown
Austrian bronze figure of a young
lady dancing with a scarf, signed
"Joseph Lorenzij".
- *height 28cm*
- £1,850   • Hickmet

La Liseuse Figure ▶

- *circa 1920*
Figure of a lady in medieval dress seated on a chair with a book in one hand, signed on the skirt "Dominique Alon".
- *height 26cm*
- £3,650 ● Hickmet

Bird Brass Charger ▲

- *20th century*
One of a pair of brass chargers of aesthetic movement design, this one depicting a bird on a branch.
- *diameter 31cm*
- £600 ● 20th Century

Le Gauyard Wallplaque ▲

- *circa 1900*
A French Le Gauyard metal wallplaque depicting a reclining nude maiden.
- *length 39cm*
- £235 ● 20th Century

WMF Centrepiece and Liner ▲

- *circa 1900*
An Art Nouveau WMF centrepiece and liner with an Art Nouveau maiden's face in profile and typical whiplash handles.
- *length 31cm*
- £295 ● 20th Century

Fish Brass Charger ▼

- *20th century*
One of a pair of brass chargers of aesthetic movement design, this one depicting a leaping fish with water lilies.
- *diameter 31cm*
- £600 ● 20th Century

WMF Fruit-knife Stand ▼

- *circa 1905*
WMF fruit-knife stand with an Art Nouveau maiden in profile, containing 12 knives.
- *height 30cm*
- £295 ● 20th Century

Alphonse Saladin Bronze ▼

- *circa 1910*
Gilt bronze figure of a young naked woman holding a posy of flowers, signed and raised on a plinth.
- *height 31cm*
- £2,250 ● Hickmet

Pop Art Metal Tray ▼

- *circa 1970*
A pop art metal tray decorated in typical 1970s colours and design. Made in Great Britain and marked "Worcester Ware".
- *diameter 38cm*
- £45 ● 20th Century

Expert Tips

Art Deco is avidly collected for its innovation and craftsmanship, but also because of the exciting jazz and Hollywood era which it evokes. Whether the same will be true of the 1950s and 1960s remains to be seen. You shouldn't spend on personal nostalgia and expect to make a profit.

Liberty Bombvase ▼

- *circa 1905*
A Liberty bombvase by Knox in polished pewter with a open-work tendril design
- *height 17cm*
- £700 • 20th Century

Silvered Bronze Dancer ▼

- *early 20th century*
A silvered bronze lady dancer by J.D. Guirande sitting on a wooden stepped base.
- *53cm x 57.2cm*
- £3,640 • Sheryl's Art Deco

Dianne Figure ▶

- *1928*
Large French "Dianne" figure in spelter by De Marco of the quality and weight of a bronze, and mounted on a Portorro Extra wedge-shaped marble base.
- *73.6cm x 32.5cm x 11.4cm*
- £1,095 • Sheryl's Art Deco

Chromed Dancer Figure ▲

- *late 1930s*
Tall Art Deco figure of a stylish lady, based on a 1920s dancer. Chromed on top.
- *height 40cm*
- £155 • Deco World

Lady on a Bridge Figure ▼

- *1928*
A signed figure of a lady and a deer on a metal slabbed bridge over a stream of green onyx with ribbed waterfall detail and a black marble river bank to either side.
- *36.8cm x 78.7cm*
- £1,485 • Sheryl's Art Deco

Lady and Deer Figures ▼

- *early 20th century*
"The Gift" by D.H. Chiparus, a spelter figure of a lady and deer group.
- *24cm x 49.5cm x 11.3cm*
- £960 • Sheryl's Art Deco

Nude Spelter Figure ▼

- *early 1930s*
Green patinated pointing figure of spelter, "Look'", by Joe De Roncourt, mounted on a Belgian black marble base and signed on the right-hand end.
- *48.3cm x 53.3cm*
- £545 • Sheryl's Art Deco

French Bon-bon Dish ◀

- *circa 1900*
French gilt bronze bon-bon dish
with a young girl on the lid, by
A. Charpentiers.
- *16cm x 29cm*
- £3,500 • **Victor Arwas**

Circular Electric Fan ▲

- *circa 1960*
Salmon-pink circular metal
electric fan standing on metal
legs.
- *diameter 65cm*
- £120 • **Country Seat**

La Musicienne ▼

- *1912*
French gilt bronze of a lady with a
Sistrum, by Muller.
- *height 18.5cm*
- £2,500 • **Victor Arwas**

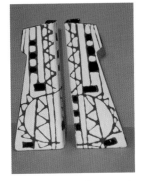

World War I Frame ▲

- *circa 1914*
Iron sculpture of a winged angel
of Mercury and a soldier with a
lion, fashioned as a picture frame.
- *height 47cm*
- £285 • **Hayman**

Metal Door Handles ▲

- *1950*
Metal door handles with ceramic
and enamel yellow and brown
geometric design.
- *26cm x 10cm*
- £155 • **Francesca Martire**

Benson Tea Set ▶

- *circa 1900*
Copper and brass tea set designed
and made by W.A.S Benson.
Stamped "Benson".
- *42cm x 18cm*
- £895 • **Liberty**

"Puppet Dancer" Bronze ▼

- *1927*

A bronze by Ignacio Gallo of a nude dancer holding a jester puppet in her hand. She has a silvered finish with golden hair and a signed base made of Portorro Extra and Sienna marbles.
- *44.5cm x 12.7cm*
- £1,995 • Sheryl's Art Deco

Spelter Mother and Child ▲

- *late 1920s–mid 1930s*

An unusual French spelter and ivoreen mother and child group by Menneville. The lady has an ivorine face and hands and is mounted on a signed ovular Portorro marble and onyx base.
- *28cm x 66cm*
- £840 • Sheryl's Art Deco

Japanese Bronze Peacock ▲

- *circa 1930*

A Japanese Showa period hakudo bronze peacock on original black lacquer stand decorated with inlaid abalone shell and the signature of the artist, Kano Seiun, on the reverse.
- *35.5cm x 53.3cm*
- £1,900 • Phoenix

Spelter Archer ▲

- *mid 1920s*

French green patinated male archer figure, signed by the artist Mellani, with original bow and mounted on a black and white marble base.
- *45.7cm x 61cm*
- £695 • Sheryl's Art Deco

Rivière Nude Bronze ▶

- *1920s*

"Balance", a silvered bronze nude athletic woman balancing on a brown marble ball by Guiraud Rivière Beautiful. Her toes are spread for balance and she has a very stylised bobbed Deco hair detailing, all on a tapered base.
- *49.5cm x 10.2cm x 10.2cm*
- £4,095 • Sheryl's Art Deco

Toga Dancer Figure ▲

- *1927*

A signed, green patinated spelter toga dancer figure by Carlier set on a pyramid marble base.
- *height 39.4cm*
- £575 • Sheryl's Art Deco

Bronze and Marble Figure ▶

- mid-1920s
French silvered bronze and chrome
figure on a base of figured verdigris
and black marbles with lovely
verdigris columns.
- 30.5cm x 45.7cm x 25.4cm
- £4,380 • Sheryl's Art Deco

Diana the Huntress Figure ◀

- 1928
French spelter figure of Diana the
Huntress with brown skin tone
and a bronzed scarf wrapped
around her. Signed on the right-
hand end of the marble base by
Dauvergne.
- length 83.8cm
- £875 • Sheryl's Art Deco

Uriano Spelter Pair ▶

- 1930
A spelter figure of a woman and a
dog, unsigned but by Uriano. The
woman has a natural skin patina
and a blue and gold dress. The
walled base is made of black
marble, Portorro Extra and onyx
sections.
- 43.2cm x 45.7cm
- £740 • Sheryl's Art Deco

Hunter and Leopard Figures ▼

- early 1930s
A French spelter man and
leopard group mounted on a base
of Portorro and brown marble and
onyx, with a ziggurat back wall in
brown marble and onyx. The
man wearing enamel shirt and
trousers, and holding a shield and
chrome spear.
- 43cm x 63.5cm
- £1,145 • Sheryl's Art Deco

Reclining Maiden Bronze ▲

- circa 1920
Bronze Art Deco figure of a
naked young woman reclining,
signed "Amadeus Generalli".
- height 24cm
- £2,950 • Hickmet

Circus Figure ▲

- 1926
A large figure of a woman in
circus costume juggling hoops.
The base brown marble and
cream onyx with circles and semi-
circles of green onyx and brown
marble.
- 55.8cm x 55.8cm
- £1,180 • Sheryl's Art Deco

Spelter Woman and Peacock ▲

- early 1930s
Large French spelter figure of a
woman feeding a peacock with
berries, the base of green onyx
and black and brown marble.
- 30.5cm x 78.7cm
- £765 • Sheryl's Art Deco

Life-size Bronze Torso ▶

- *circa 1930*

Emotive life-size bronze torso by
Hubert Yenge from the foundry of
Alexis Rudier, Paris founder to
Rodin.

- *71cm x 55cm*
- £8,750   • Country Seat

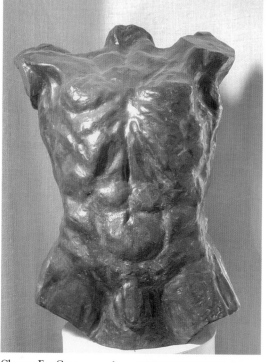

Figure by H. Varenne ▲

- *1912*

Figure of a lady with a large hat
by H. Varenne, founder's mark
Susse Frères.

- *height 19cm*
- £2,500   • Victor Arwas

Chrome Egg Cups ▶

- *circa 1950*

Pair of Italian chrome egg cups
with covers.

- *height 11cm*
- £50   • Castello

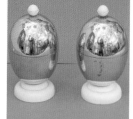

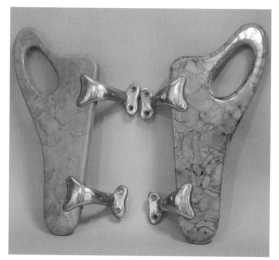

Expert Tips

*Women were the most popular
subjects for bronzes; not the
pre-First World War seductress,
but the newly independent self
possessed female.*

Turquoise Door Handles ◀

- *circa 1960*

Italian stylised pallette-shaped
metal door handles with
turquoise marbled enamel overlay
and large brass mounts.

- *length 33cm*
- £320   • Francesca Martire

"The Lesson" Spelter Figure ▽

- *1928*

"The Lesson" by Limousin, a huge French figural group of a black patinated spelter man giving his son a lesson in how to shoot an arrow. The base is of black marble with white striations, and is signed by the artist.

- *71cm x 76.2cm*
- **£995** • **Sheryl's Art Deco**

Spelter Male Hunter Figure ▲

- *late 1920s*

A male hunter figure made of spelter and signed by the artist Joe De Roncourt, sitting on a canted edged brown marble base.

- *38.1cm x 55.8cm x 17.8cm*
- **£795** • **Sheryl's Art Deco**

"Group Atlante" Spelter Figure ▽

- *1920s–30s*

"Group Atlante", a spelter figure of Diane hunting a leaping gazelle on a granite stone base by De Marco.

- *76.2cm x 96.5cm*
- **£1,695** • **Sheryl's Art Deco**

Mother and Child Spelter Group ▲

- *late 1920s–early 30s*

A signed figural group by Menneville, made in France of spelter and ivorine on a black Belgian marble and onyx base.

- *33cm x 58.4cm*
- **£1,140** • **Sheryl's Art Deco**

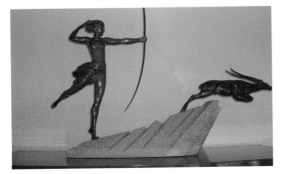

Painted Silver Art Deco Bronze ▲

- *circa 1930*

Art Deco cold-painted silver bronze figure of a sensuous naked young lady.

- *height 35cm*
- **£950** • **Hickmet**

Wine-related Items

The ultimate antiques for daily use where collections can be started for a few pounds.

When the daily newspapers are regularly running stories about the amount of money that city traders are happy to spend on wine in restaurants and when the nation's taste for fine wines seems to be developing across the board, it is no surprise to find that wine-related silver is sitting at the top table of the market at the moment. Coasters, labels, corkscrews and funnels are all performing well and attracting good prices. Equally, at the other end of the scale, wine coolers are in great demand.

One area that does not seem to have benefited from the interaction of the wine merchants and the money-makers is that of the Victorian decanter and claret jug. Surprisingly, it is still possible to pick up a cut-glass decanter made by a reputable manufacturer for less than £300 while a silver and glass claret jug can usually be obtained for no more than twice that price. For collectors, this certainly looks like a good area of the wine-related market to consider investing in at the moment.

Champagne Corkscrew ▼

- *circa 1900*

Rare and unusual boxwood champagne corkscrew made by McBindes.
- *length 11cm*
- **£295** • Jasmin Cameron

Wine Funnel ▲

- *circa 1820*

Clear glass wine funnel.
- *diameter 10cm*
- **£75** • Jasmin Cameron

Brass Cocktail Shaker ▼

- *circa 1930*

Brass cocktail shaker with screw lid.
- *height 20cm*
- **£48** • H. Gregory

Victorian Claret Jug ▼

- *1888*

A rare claret jug, the body cut with an unusual design, The Barnards, London.
- *height 40cm*
- **£4,750**   • **Percy's**

Magnum Claret Jug ▼

- *1872*

An extremely rare Victorian magnum claret jug, with beautiful engraving, the cast silver mount with dragon handle, by Stephen Smith, London.
- *height 40cm*
- **£8,750**   • **Percy's**

Queen Anne Shilling Ladle ▲

- *circa 1777*

Eighteenth century punch ladle with whalebone handle and a Queen Anne shilling incorporated in the base of the bowl.
- *length 33cm*

Rosewood Corkscrew ▲

- *circa 1850–80*

Rosewood corkscrew with grip shank and brush.
- *length 13cm*
- **£120**   • **Jasmin Cameron**

Rosewood Corkscrew ▼

- *circa 1850*

Rosewood gripshank corkscrew.
- *length 13cm*
- **£180**   • **Jasmin Cameron**

Small Silver Coaster ▼

- *circa 1820*

Old Sheffield silver-plated wine coaster with lattice work decoration.
- *diameter 12cm*
- **£95**   • **Jasmin Cameron**

Staghorn Corkscrew ▼

- *circa 1890*

Staghorn corkscrew with brush.
- *length 15cm*
- **£120**   • **Jasmin Cameron**

William IV Mahogany Wine Cooler ▶

- *circa 1835*

A fine mahogany wine cooler on a pedestal base with four elaborately carved paw feet.
- *88.9cm x 48.3cm x 53.3cm*
- **£7,250**   • **M. Norman**

Wine Cooler ▲

- *early 19th century*

Regency period mahogany open brass bound wine cooler with original lead lining; important lion mask ring handles.
- *39cm x 48cm x 74cm*
- **£4,850**   • **John Beazor**

Sheffield Plated Wine Coolers ▼

- *circa 1820*

A pair of campana (bell) shaped plated wine coolers with shell and gadroon borders with removable capes at the top.
- *23cm x 27cm*
- **£3,650**   • **Langfords**

Scottish Wine Label ▼

- *circa 1845*

An unusual wine label in the form of a cut out letter "S" with foliate chasing. Made in Edinburgh by Alexander Wigful.
- *height 3.5cm*
- **£245**   • **Hayward & Stott**

Regency Period Oval Wine Cooler ▼

- *circa 1825*

A very rare oval mahogany wine cooler, exquisitely decorated with inlaid marquetry garland design, carved and moulded paw feet and gadrooned edging.
- *62cm x 63.5cm x 93cm*
- **£39,500**   • **M. Norman**

Silver Campana ▼

- *1838*

An early Victorian silver campana-shaped presentation wine goblet with a fine inscription and gilded bowl. Made by Benjamin Smith.
- *23.5cm x 14.5cm*
- **£695**   • **Hayward & Stott**

Thistle-shaped Cup ◀

- *1880*

An unusual thistle-shaped dram cup with gilded bowl on a curved stem with a well decorated foot inscribed "DINNA FORGET". Made in Edinburgh.
- *height 9cm*
- **£395**   • **Hayward & Stott**

Expert Tips

Wine coolers are generally oval in shape with short legs. Octagonal and hexagonal, lead-lined, static wine containers with longer legs are, correctly, "cellarets."

Oak Handle Corkscrew ▼
- *circa 1880*

Oak handle corkscrew with a metal screw and brush.
- *length 13cm*
- £96
- H. Gregory

Wine Strainer ▲
- *circa 1820*

Silver-plated wine strainer.
- *height 14cm*
- £220
- Jasmin Cameron

Claret Jug ▲
- *1890*

English claret jug with floral engraving and a silver handle and lid.
- *height 30cm*
- £620
- Jasmin Cameron

Rum Label ▼
- *1830*

Silver rum label, made in London.
- *length 5cm*
- £68
- H. Gregory

Spirit Labels ▼
- *1910*

Spirit labels on chains. Port, Shrub, and Madeira.
- *length 5cm*
- £45
- H. Gregory

Victorian Port Decanter ▲
- *circa 1890*

Victorian circular port decanter with faceted design on the body.
- *height 30cm*
- £55
- H. Gregory

Ice Bucket ▲
- *circa 1930*

Silver-plate ice bucket with plain moulded handles to the sides.
- *height 21cm*
- £185
- H. Gregory

Pair of George III Goblets ▼

George III silver-gilt goblets by Richard Morson and Benjamin Stephenson, decorated with crest and rampant lions.
- *height 17cm*
- **£8,500**   • **Partridge**

George IV Wine Cooler ▼

- *1828–9*

Set of four wine coolers by Robert Garrard, London, highly decorated with scrolling foliate motifs, centred cartouches, cornucopias and acanthus leaves.
- *height 25.4cm*
- **£250,000**   • **Partridge**

Double-action Corkscrew ▶

- *19th century*

An English Thomason type double-action corkscrew with turned bone handle, ringed brass barrel with patent tablet marked "PATENT" between lion and unicorn supporters. Helix worm.
- *19.7cm x 8.5cm*
- **£395**   • **Bacchus**

George IV Sherry Label ▼

- *1824*

A George IV sherry label with its original chain. Made in Birmingham by Joseph Willmore.
- *4cm x 2.5cm*
- **£115**   • **Hayward & Stott**

Italian Lever Corkscrew ◀

- *20th century*

All brass Italian lever corkscrew making use of the cog and ratchet principle. Rosati's patent. Archimedian worm, crown cork opener in handle and marked "ITALY" below.
- *17.5cm x 7cm*
- **£130**   • **Bacchus**

George III Corkscrew ▲

- *circa 1790*

A corkscrew in the finest condition initialled "ML" on the cap of the screw sheath, along with the maker's mark. Made in Birmingham by Samuel Pemberton.
- *length 9.5cm*
- **£875**   • **Hayward & Stott**

George III Scottish Silver Wine Goblet ▲

- *1807*

Made in Edinburgh by John McKay, the vase-shaped body is mainly plain and stands on a circular foot with applied reeded rim and curved stem. The top of the bowl has a band of engraved bright-cut decoration of grapes and vine leaves.
- *17.3cm x 9.7cm*
- **£1,900**   • **Sanda Lipton**

Farrow and Jackson Corkscrew ▼

- *19th century*

A fine brass Farrow and Jackson corkscrew (unmarked) with helix worm.
- *17.8cm x 7.4cm*
- £375　　　　　• Bacchus

Heeley King's Screw ▼

- *19th century*

An English narrow rack King's Screw with turned bone handle (no brush and hairline cracks), shaped steel side handle, ringed bronze barrel with unusual gilt tablet marked "HEELEY & SONS". Helix worm.
- *20.5cm x 10.5cm*
- £575　　　　　• Bacchus

King's Screw with Bell Collar ▲

- *19th century*

A fine English four-pillar narrow rack King's Screw with shaped bone handle, bell collar, turned steel side handle and helix worm.
- *21.7cm x 11cm*
- £625　　　　　• Bacchus

Victorian Claret Jug ▲

- *1878*

Victorian sterling silver claret jug, with Bacchus detailed mount, hallmarked in London by Charles Boynton.
- *height 28cm*
- £2,545　　　　• I. Franks

King's Screw ▼

- *19th century*

An English narrow rack King's Screw with shaped bone handle, shaped steel side handle, ringed bronze barrel with tablet marked "PATENT" between a lion and unicorn supporters. Helix worm.
- *20.5cm x 11.5cm*
- £500　　　　　• Bacchus

Archimedian Screw Corkscrew ▼

- *19th century*

A three-fingered simple one-piece metal corkscrew with Archimedian screw.
- *14cm x 7.5cm*
- £15　　　　　• Bacchus

Silver Beer Mugs ◄
- *circa 1940*
Silver beer mugs with glass
bottoms and bamboo decoration.
- *height 13cm*
- **£130 the pair** • **H. Gregory**

Cocktail Shaker ▼
- *1920*
Silver-plated cocktail shaker.
- *height 20cm*
- **£68** • **H. Gregory**

Claret Jug ▼
- *circa 1880*
Continental elegant claret jug
with fine engraving around the
body and a silver geometric band
around the neck, standing on a
plain silver circular base.
- *height 29cm*
- **£335** • **H. Gregory**

Pair of Glass Decanters ▲
- *circa 1890*
Pair of glass decanters with
diamond pattern on the body and
stopper.
- *height 27cm*
- **£150** • **H. Gregory**

Spirit Barrels ▼
- *circa 1880*
Three oak spirit barrels with
silver banding and taps, on an
oak stand with silver banding.
- *36cm x 37cm*
- **£1,080** • **H. Gregory**

Oak Water Jug ▶
- *circa 1880*
Oak cordial jug with silver lid
and ball finial, spout with a shield
below standing on three ball feet.
- *height 29cm*
- **£330** • **H. Gregory**

Fluted Wine Funnel ▲

- *circa 1820*
Clear fluted glass wine funnel.
- *diameter 10cm*
- £85   • Jasmin Cameron

Silver Wine Taster ▲

- *1939*
Silver wine taster engraved
"Souvenir of Schroder and
Schyler & Co. Bordeaux
1739–1939".
- *diameter 8cm*
- £145   • Jasmin Cameron

Claret Jug ▲

- *1880*
Victorian claret jug with diamond
faceted body and silver handle
and lid.
- *height 21cm*
- £270   • H. Gregory

Spirit Decanter ▼

- *1890*
Spirit decanter with moulded
body and fluted silver neck and
four spouts, known as a Kluk
Kluk.
- *height 27cm*
- £420   • Jasmin Cameron

Beehive Spirit Decanter ▼

- *1880*
Beehive spirit decanter with
spout.
- *height 24cm*
- £165   • Jasmin Cameron

Spirit Decanter ▲

- *1840*
One of a pair of fine oblong spirit
decanters with faceted shoulders
and lid.
- *height 28cm*
- £540   • Jasmin Cameron

Henley Corkscrew ▲

- *circa 1890*
Steel corkscrew made by Henley.
- *height 16cm*
- £180   • H. Gregory

George III Goblet ▼

- *1795*

George III sterling silver panelled goblet, hallmarked in London by Peter Podio.
- *height 17cm*
- £965 • I. Franks

George III Wine Coasters ▲

- *1797*

Pair of George III sterling silver engraved wine engraved coasters, hallmarked in London by Richard Crossley.
- *diameter 12cm*
- £2,895 • I. Franks

Baluster-shaped Wine Ewer ▼

- *circa 1850*

Baluster-shaped wine ewer decorated with finely engraved vertical bands of flowers and foliage separated by frosted vertical bands cut with polished lines and mitre cuts.
- *height 27.3cm*
- £425 • Laurie Leigh

Victorian Claret Jug ▼

- *circa 1890*

Victorian amphora-shaped "rock crystal" engraved claret jug finely decorated all round in intaglio with birds with foliage, flowers and blackberries, on domed and star-cut foot. Original matching hollow blown stopper.
- *32cm*
- £925 • Laurie Leigh

Victorian Wine Ewer with Ivy ▶

- *circa 1860*

Victorian amphora-shaped wine ewer finely engraved with bands of ivy. The foot is also engraved with ivy. Rope twist handle.
- *height 30.5cm*
- £695 • Laurie Leigh

Helmet-shaped Wine Ewer ◀

- *circa 1870*

Rare Victorian helmet-shaped wine ewer beautifully acid etched with a scene composed of figures preparing for a sacrifice.
- *height 35.5cm*
- £925 • Laurie Leigh

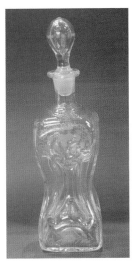

Spirit Decanter ▲
- *1930*

Spirit decanter with moulded body and lozenge-shaped stopper with foliate and bird engraving.
- *height 27cm*
- £320   • Jasmin Cameron

Horn Corkscrew ▲
- *circa 1910*

Corkscrew with a horn handle and metal screw.
- *length 12cm*
- £44   • H. Gregory

Silver Coaster ▶
- *circa 1920*

Silver-plated circular coaster, one of a pair, with scrolled rim and a teak base.
- *diameter 17cm*
- £160   • H. Gregory

Claret Jug ▼
- *1850*

Deeply faceted claret jug, electroplated lip and cover, twisted rope handle and an acorn finial.
- *height 20cm*
- £440   • Jasmin Cameron

Lion-handled Coaster ▼
- *circa 1900*

Silver circular coaster with scrolling to the rim and lion ring handles to the side.
- *height 16cm*
- £70   • H. Gregory

Bone Handle Corkscrew ▲
- *circa 1900*

Bone handle corkscrew with brass end and metal screw.
- *length 14cm*
- £70   • H. Gregory

Wine Coaster ▲
- *circa 1900*

Silver-plate wine coaster with scrolled handles and pierced floral and geometric design.
- *height 57cm*
- £72   • H. Gregory

Key-patterned Wine Ewer ▼

• *circa 1860*
Victorian amphora-shaped wine ewer engraved with anthemion, the Greek key pattern and pennants.
• *height 30.5cm*
• **£695**   • **Laurie Leigh**

Engraved Claret Jug ▼

• *circa 1870*
Victorian claret jug, the silver-plated mount finely engraved with festoons, bows and tassels, the lid surmounted with a rope twist bow, the plaited rope-twist handle terminating with a bow and tassels.
• *height 30.5cm*
• **£650**   • **Laurie Leigh**

Wine Ewer with Cartouches ▲

• *circa 1870*
Tall Victorian wine or champagne ewer engraved with latticework surrounding a cartouche on each side, one containing a bird perched over a pool, the other with a butterfly and an insect.
• *height 28cm*
• **£485**   • **Laurie Leigh**

Silver Wine Coaster ▶

• *1774*
Silver pierced wine coaster made in London by Robert Hennell.
• *height 3.2cm*
• **£1,250**   • **D & B Dickinson**

Victorian Wine Ewer with Teared Handle ▼

• *circa 1880*
Victorian amphora-shaped claret jug engraved with a band of Greek key pattern to the neck and another to the shoulder below etched scroll border and above engraved vertical lines. Engraved foot and "teared" handle.
• *height 33cm*
• **£365**   • **Laurie Leigh**

Silver Madeira Label ◀

• *1852*
Silver leaf-shaped Madeira wine label on a chain. Made in London by Charles Rawlings & Wm. Summers.
• *width 8cm*
• **£125**   • **D & B Dickinson**

Expert Tips

Hand-made decanters are marked on the rim and stopper with a scratched number. These are sometimes hard to discern, but it is worth taking the time to find them and ensure that they are the same.

Works of Art & Sculpture

The Japanese were more prolific than the Chinese in their carving, particularly in the second half of the nineteenth century.

This area of the market is a fascinating one, yet it tends to be fraught with problems for the collector. The most immediate and obvious of these hindrances is that there is no way of knowing what quantities of artefacts were made and have been preserved. This means that inevitabaly some fake items have been allowed to enter the market. Although it is possible to have a piece thermo-luminescence tested to establish its age to within 300 years or so, it is not impossible for the determined criminal to circumvent this process. Then there is exportation and importation and the documentation required for both. All antiques and woks of art can be imported into the United Kingdom, as long as the correct paperwork is completed, but it is not necessarily as easy to export from a country of origin. Of course, all these problems become exacerbated in direct ratio to the value of the artefact purchased, and great pleasure can be derived with little red-tape and risk if your requirements are modest.

Asian/Oriental

Stone Vishnu ▲
- **6th–7th century**
Khmer Phnom Du stone standing Vishnu.
- *height 55cm*
- **£45,000** • Lopburi

Versali Bronze ▲
- **10th century**
Burmese Versali bronze seated figure.
- *height 3cm*
- **£500** • Lopburi

Bronze Geese ▲
- **1868–1912**
A cast pair of Japanese silvered bronze geese from the Meiji period, signed "Masatsune".
- *22.5cm x 25cm*
- **£4,800** • Brandt

Indian Elephants Vase ▲
- **1868–1912**
A bronze Japanese vase of the Meiji period, cast as three standing Indian elephants, with well-modelled heads and carefully rendered hides. Signed "Seiya".
- *height 35cm*
- **£4,200** • Brandt

Malachite Axe Head ▼
- *1600–1000 BC*
Bronze axe head encrusted with
malachite from the Shang
Dynasty.
- *length 20cm*
- £750　　　　• Ormonde

Incense Burner ▼
- *Han Dynasty 206 BC–220 AD*
Incense burner in the shape of a
mountain (representing the Isles
of the Blessed, the abode of the
mortals). The incense burner
rests on a tall tray with a solid
foot hollowed out beneath the
stem.
- *height 21cm*
- £300　　　　• Ormonde

Arite Blue and White Vase ▼
- *early 19th century*
A Japanese Arita blue and white
bottle vase with decoration of
peonies and butterflies potted in
the late seventeenth century
style.
- *height 38.1cm*
- £650　　　　• Phoenix

Machang-type Jar ▲
- *late 3rd or early 2nd
millennium BC*
Machang-type jar of painted
pottery, Gansu or Qinghai
province, with an unusual
circular design and geometric
pattern.
- *height 32cm*
- £650　　　　• Ormonde

Bronze Belt Hook ▲
- *3rd–4th century BC*
Bronze belt hook.
- *length 15cm*
- £150　　　　• Ormonde

Han Dynasty Vase ▲
- *206 BC–220 AD*
Unusual garlic-headed bottle-
shaped vase with original
pigment of pink, white and
crimson with a geometric design
around the neck.
- *height 34cm*
- £750　　　　• Ormonde

Stick Figure ▼
- *206 BC–220 AD*
Stick figure of a man standing,
from the Han Dynasty.
- *height 60cm*
- £1,200　　　　• Ormonde

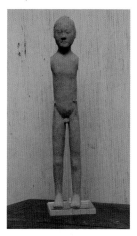

Shaman Beads ▼
- *206 BC–220 AD*
Cream jade beads that once
belonged to a Shaman, from the
Han Dynasty.
- *length 2cm*
- £2,000　　　　• Ormonde

Zodiac Animals ▼
- *7th–9th century AD*
Rare group of pottery Zodiac
animals from the China Tang
Dynasty.
- *height 28cm*
- £550　　　　• Ormonde

Ming Dynasty Vase

- *circa 1450–1500*

A Chinese ironwork vase from the early Ming Dynasty. Hexagonal with individual figures of immortals placed on each surface.
- *height 26.7cm*
- £830 • Phoenix

Double Gourd Vase

- *circa 1900*

A lovely Japanese polychrome patinated double gourd vase, with unusual mottled green, ochre and red patina, signed on the base by the artist.
- *height 26cm*
- £1,040 • Phoenix

Kwannon Incense Burner

- *pre-1900*

A Japanese late Edo/early Meiji period koro depicting the goddess Kwannon seated on a Shi Shi. The figure of Kwannon lifts off to allow access to the incense container in the body of the Shi Shi.
- *33cm x 33cm*
- £1,780 • Phoenix

Witch Doctor

- *Han Dynasty 206 BC–220 AD*

Chinese Han Dynasty witch doctor with large ears and a ferocious face holding a snake.
- *height 1.1m*
- £2,800 • Ormonde

Bronze Chicken

- *late 17th century*

A Japanese cast bronze censer depicting a standing chicken, unusually ornamented with cloud designs. Featuring a lovely soft and glossy chestnut brown patina overlaid with black incense deposits.
- *26.7cm x 24cm*
- £1,125 • Phoenix

Sung Dynasty Lidded Jar

- *1128–1279 AD*

Lidded jar from the Southern Sung dynasty with soft greenish black patina.
- *height 23cm*
- £890 • Phoenix

Tanuki Censer

- *circa 1890*

A small signed Japanese bronze censer from the Meiji period, modelled as a Tanuki with a woven silver lid, silver rings and gold inlaid eyes.
- *length 17.8cm*
- £950 • Phoenix

Terracotta Horse ▲
- **206 BC–220 AD**
Horse and groom standing with
hand extended, from the Han
Dynasty.
- *height of horse 29cm, height of
groom 26cm*
- **£1,200**   • Ormonde

Lacquer Figure ▲
- **206 BC–220 AD**
Wooden figure of a lady with
arms folded, wearing a dress with
red and black lacquer details,
from the Han Dynasty.
- *height 51cm*
- **£1,200**   • Ormonde

Reclining Lion ▲
- **circa 17th century**
Grey selegon jade lion shown in a
reclining position. Ming Dynasty.
- *height 8cm*
- **£850**   • Ormonde

Burmese Table ▼
- **circa 1900**
Carved wood circular table top
with carved legs in the style of an
elephant's head and trunk.
- *70cm x 1m*
- **£1,200**   • Sharif

Bronze Buddha Sakyamuni ▼
- **circa 1800 or earlier**
A large bronze of the Buddha
Sakyamuni, with gently smiling
features. The mandorla is cast
separately, and slots into a lug
cast on the back of the piece.
- *63.5cm x 43cm*
- **£2,055**   • Phoenix

Banshan Pottery Jug ▼
- **mid-3rd millennium BC**
Banshan-type painted pottery jug
from the Gansu or Qinghai
province of Majiayao culture.
- *height 35cm*
- **£1,250**   • Ormonde

Standing Soldier ▲
- **206 BC–220 AD**
One of five soldiers standing,
from the Han Dynasty.
- *height 47cm*
- **£750**   • Ormonde

Dinosaur Egg ▲
- **60–70 million years old**
Dinosaur egg from outer
Mongolia.
- *height 13cm*
- **£300**   • Ormonde

Expert Tips

*Ivories from the Ming dynasty
are usually distinguishable by
extensive surface cracking
caused by oils within the ivory
evaporating over time.*

Marble Buddha Head ▼

- *18th century*
Burmese Shan marble Buddha
head with downcast expression
and traces of pigment.
- *height 35cm*
- £3,000   • Lopburi

Giltwood Dancer ▼

- *19th century*
Burmese Mandalay gilt wood
animated dancing figure in
superbly detailed traditional
costume.
- *height 72cm*
- £2,500   • Lopburi

Buddhist Painting ▲

- *18th–19th century*
Tibetan thangka (painting) of
Buddha with lohans and
guardians and textile border.
- *77cm x 59cm*
- £5,000   • Lopburi

Horse Procession Fragment ▲

- *11th century*
Khmer Baphuon–style tympanum
fragment of procession with
horse.
- *43cm x 90cm*
- £7,500   • Lopburi

Bronze Okimono ▲

- *pre-1920*
Japanese bronze okimono as a
laughing seated Tanuki holding a
ruyi sceptre, symbol of power and
authority.
- *25.4cm x 25.4cm*
- £1,245   • Phoenix

Kneeling Disciple Statues ▲

- *19th century*
Pair of Burmese Mandalay gilt
wood kneeling disciples.
- *height 36cm*
- £2,000   • Lopburi

Wooden Devi Statue ▲

- *19th century*
Burmese carved wood Devi
goddess figure holding a lotus,
traces of green and red pigment.
- *height 92cm*
- £1,250   • Lopburi

Shi Shi Bronze

- *circa 1870*

Large Meiji period Japanese bronze of a seated Shi Shi, the traditional Oriental temple guardian, on original hardwood base with glossy chestnut colour patina.
- *40.6cm x 45.7cm x 28cm*
- £1,700   • Phoenix

Bronze Ikebana Vase ▶

- *17th century*

Rare Japanese engraved and polychrome lacquered bronze ikebana vase decorated with panels depicting Fukurukuju and his deer on one side, and Kwannon riding a Kylin on the reverse.
- *height 23cm*
- £830   • Phoenix

Chinese Burial Object ▲

- *206 BC–220 AD*

Burial object of a well-modelled horse's head, with strong traces of pigment, highlighting a red bridle, from the Han Dynasty.
- *height 15cm*
- £300   • Ormonde

Vietnamese Animal Container ▼

- *18th century or earlier*

A rare Vietnamese bronze food container fashioned in the shape of an elephant-like animal, cast in two pieces, with the legs attached.
- *length 33cm*
- £1,300   • Phoenix

Japanese Cloisonné Vase ▲

- *late 19th century*

A Japanese cloisonné vase, crafted with silver and gold wirework and silver rims depicting birds flying amongst chrysanthemum flowers and leaves.
- *height 30.5cm*
- £1,600   • Phoenix

Meiji Ikebana Vase ▲

- *circa 1880*

A Japanese carved bamboo lotus form ikebana vase from the Meiji period in perfect condition, with a beautiful warm patina.
- *height 38cm*
- £560   • Phoenix

Nagasaki Watercolours ▲
- *1868–1912*
One of three rare Nagasaki school watercolours on paper from the early Meiji period in Japan. Featuring Dutch and Russian families and traders in flamboyant traditional dress.
- *1.24m x 1.24m*
- **£13,500**   • **Brandt**

Terracotta Buddha Head ▲
- *11th century*
Burmese Pagan terracotta head of Buddha, smiling and with downcast eyes.
- *height 22cm*
- **£4,000**   • **Lopburi**

Votive Plaques ▲
- *9th–13th century*
Three Pagan terracotta votive plaques with figures of the seated Buddha with hands placed in various mudra.
- *length 18cm*
- **£500–£1,000 each** • **Lopburi**

Guan Yin Head ▲
- *19th century*
Chinese wooden Guan Yin head with traces of pigment.
- *height 53cm*
- **£950**   • **Lopburi**

Thai Monk Statues ◀
- *18th century*
Pair of Thai gilded bronze Rattanakosin Monks standing on lotus bases in devout pose.
- *height 1.05m*
- **£12,000**   • **Lopburi**

Khmer Buddha Head ▲
- *15th century*
Khmer post-Bayon period bronze Buddha head with fine features, downcast gaze and exceptional "smile".
- *height 26cm*
- **£25,000**   • **Lopburi**

Stone Warrior Head ▲
- *12th century*
Jin Chinese stone guardian warrior head; the carved headdress mirrors the features of the fiercely expressive head.
- *height 42cm*
- **£5,500**   • **Lopburi**

Islamic

Cylindrical Flask ▶
- *7th century BC*
Islamic cylindrical flask with brown, cream and blue marbling.
- *height 13cm*
- £1,200 • Pars

Syrian Table ▲
- *circa 1920*
Hexagonal mother-of-pearl and bone inlay table with pierced masharabi panels on turned legs.
- *49cm x 35cm*
- £200 • Sharif

Syrian Tea Table ▲
- *circa 1910*
A tea table from Damascus with a brass circular top.
- *47cm x 59cm*
- £150 • Sharif

Persian Copper Vase ▼
- *circa 1950*
A Persian copper and brass vase.
- *height 75cm*
- £250 • Sharif

Islamic Chess Pieces ▼
- *9th century BC*
Islamic wooden chess pieces.
- *height 5cm*
- £3,000 • Pars

Vase Bowl and Saucer ▲
- *circa 1910*
Matching blue and turquoise floral pattern vase bowl and saucer.
- *height 37cm*
- £300 • Sharif

Buddha Water Jug ◀

- **12th century**
Small bronze Islamic water jug
with stylized handle and face of
Buddha on the base.
- *height 20cm*
- £1,500 • Marko Pollo

Algerian Brass Teapot ▼

- *circa 1930*
Brass inlay teapot on a tall brass
stand with circular base.
- *length 1.72m*
- £650 • Sharif

Mother-of-Pearl Chair ▲

- *circa 1930*
Mother-of-pearl and bone inlay
chair, with carved top rail and
scrolled arms.
- *93cm x 64cm*
- £500 • Sharif

Mother-of-Pearl Table ▲

- *circa 1920*
Mother-of-pearl and bone inlay
in geometric patterns with
architecturally carved legs.
- *64cm x 44cm*
- £400 • Sharif

Crystal Chess Piece ◀

- **8th–7th century BC**
Clear lozenge-shaped crystal
chess piece.
- *height 4cm*
- £1,000 • Pars

Bronze Gazelle Figure ▶

- *11th century AD*
A green patinated bronze figure
of a gazelle leaping.
- *9cm x 14cm*
- £1,200   • Mazar

Islamic Floor Tile ▲

- *circa 1900*
Islamic glazed mosaic floor tile
with incised geometric design
- *14cm x 14cm*
- £80   • Mazar

Cat Water Vessel ▼

- *10th century AD*
A ceramic water vessel styled
with the face of a cat.
- *height 28cm*
- £700   • Mazar

Small Turquoise Bowl ▼

- *12th century*
Ceramic turquoise glazed bowl
from Afghanistan with scroll
design.
- *height 15cm*
- £600   • Marko Pollo

Expert Tips

*If you cannot find a long
provenance on any Islamic
work of art of significant
value, then it should be
accompanied by a certificate
of authentication from a
museum in its country of
origin and a customs release
document.*

"Saluk" Jug ▲

- *12th century*
Saluk turquoise water jug with
Islamic script.
- *height 20cm*
- £500   • Marko Pollo

Turkish Table ▲
- *circa 1920*

Turkish table with mother-of-pearl and bone inlay on architecturally carved legs.
- *64cm x 44cm*
- £400   ● Sharif

Damascus Table ▲
- *circa 1920*

Side table from Damascus with mother-of-pearl and bone inlay, single small drawer with brass handle, standing on cabriole legs.
- *43cm x 36cm*
- £150   ● Sharif

Persian Charger ▲
- *circa 1940*

Persian oval brass charger or tray.
- *diameter 75cm*
- £200   ● Sharif

Mirror and Stand ▲
- *circa 1900*

Elaborate mother-of-pearl and ivory oblong inlay mirror with scrolled carving, and chest with one long drawer and two smaller, with carved moulded top, and feet, from Damascus.
- *height 2.1m*
- £6,000   ● Sharif

Architectural Table ▶
- *circa 1910*

Mother-of-pearl hexagonal table with geometric patterns and architectural legs.
- *55cm x 43cm*
- £200   ● Sharif

Tiger Bowl
- *12th century*

Islamic ceramic bowl with brilliant turquoise glaze and tigers.
- *height 18cm*
- £2,000   • Marko Pollo

Terracotta House Plaque ▶
- *13th century*

Terracotta Islamic plaque with blue raised Islamic writing and a symbol of a house.
- *25cm x 24cm*
- £11,000   • Marko Pollo

Persian Vases ◀
- *circa 1930*

A pair of fluted Persian blue and turquoise floral pattern vases with two handles on circular bases.
- *height 56cm*
- £200   • Sharif

Bronze Incense Burner ▲
- *12th century*

Bronze Islamic incense burner on three moulded feet inscribed with Islamic writing and surmounted by a bird.
- *height 20cm*
- £1,200   • Marko Pollo

Terracotta Cow Figures ◀
- *12th century*

A pair of terracotta cows of rudimentary form with faint traces of decorative pigment.
- *8cm x 12cm*
- £4,500   • Marko Pollo

Russian

Russian Gilt Enamel Spoon ▶

- *circa 1900*
Silver gilt spoon with pink, blue, red and yellow foliate design.
- *length 18cm*
- £1,000 • Iconastas

Fabergé Hand Mirror ▲

- *1910*
Silver hand mirror by Fabergé, with raised engraved crest.
- *length 21cm*
- £1,400 • Iconastas

Miniature Tankard ▲

- *circa 1787*
Miniature "Charka", or silver tankard, engraved with two eagles above two flowers connected by a ribbon.
- *height 4cm*
- £625 • Iconastas

Moscow Yacht Tankard ▼

- *circa 1871*
Miniature silver tankard with arms of the Moscow Yacht Club.
- *height 6cm*
- £750 • Iconastas

Soviet Pen Tray ▼

- *circa 1930*
Soviet pottery pen tray with a reclining Uzbek reading *Pravda* after Natalia Danko.
- *width 19cm*
- £650 • Iconastas

Fabergé Kovsh ▲

- *1910*
Fabergé ceramic and silver kovsh with set cut amethysts.
Provenance: Princess of Baden, from the Baden collection.
- *height 15cm*
- £5,000 • Iconastas

Enamel Blotter ▼

- *circa 1900*
Enamel blue and pink floral design blotter with gold borders by Semonova.
- *length 14cm*
- £900 • Iconastas

Enamelled Spoon ◀

- *circa 1900*
Silver spoon enamelled with a dark blue, green and pink foliate design on a cream background.
- *length 15cm*
- £1,300 • Iconastas

Silver Gilt and Enamel Spoon ▼

- *circa 1900*
Silver gilt spoon with turquoise, white, green and dark blue, foliate design with an emerald-green border.
- *length 11cm*
- £400　　　• Iconastas

Russian Frame ▶

- *circa 1920*
Russian rosewood picture frame with brass borders and bearing the crest of two eagles with a portrait of Tsar Nicholas II of Russia.
- *28cm x 21cm*
- £1,300　　　• Iconastas

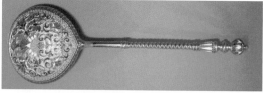

Silver Gilt and Enamel Beaker ▼

- *circa 1885*
Silver gilt beaker with blue scrolling and white flowers.
- *height 11.5cm*
- £1,850　　　• Iconastas

Small Fabergé Mirror ▲

- *1910*
Small Fabergé silver mirror with raised engraved crest.
- *length 17.5cm*
- £1,400　　　• Iconastas

Fabergé Spoon ▼

- *circa 1900*
Silver spoon with gilt bowl, by Fabergé.
- *length 16cm*
- £425　　　• Iconastas

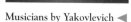

Musicians by Yakovlevich ◀

- *circa 1910*
Pair of terracotta musicians by Golovin Alexander Yakovlevich.
- *height 28cm*
- £5,500 the pair　　• Iconastas

Expert Tips

Any works of art by Fabergé are usually extremely valuable due to the intricate nature of the workmanship involved, their historical importance and their beauty.

Russian Kovsh ▶

- *circa 1900*
Russian enamel kovsh, highly
decorated with blue turquoise
foliate design by Lubwin.
- *length 19cm*
- £1,200 • Iconastas

Soviet Tea Holder ▼

- *1967*
Soviet silver propaganda tea glass
holder with a scene showing a
man in the foreground with a
harvest and a rocket flying into
space and the sun in the
background.
- *height 10cm*
- £80 • Iconastas

Arts and Crafts Spoon ▲

- *circa 1900*
Arts and Crafts silver spoon by
Knox, with a handle fashioned as
a peacock and the bowl as a leaf.
- *length 16cm*
- £800 • Iconastas

Silver Gilt Spoon ▼

- *circa 1900*
Silver gilt spoon with blue flowers
on a cream background with a
green and orange foliate design.
- *length 17cm*
- £750 • Iconastas

Enamel Russian Spoon ▲

- *circa 1900*
Russian silver spoon enamelled
with blue and pink floral design
on gold with a turquoise circular
border design.
- *length 20cm*
- £600 • Iconastas

Silver Gilt Tea Set ▼

- *circa 1875*
Silver gilt tea pot, water jug and
milk jug, with foliate scrolling
and a central cartouche of a
palace, by Ovchinnikov.
- *height 15cm*
- £2,500 • Iconastas

Silver Gilt Engraved Goblet ▲

- *1839*
Silver fluted gilt goblet from
Moscow with foliate design.
- *height 20cm*
- £1,200 • Iconastas

Set of Salts ▼
- *circa 1877*

Set of six circular silver salts on three ball feet with silver spoons by Gachen in original oak box.
- *diameter 18cm*
- £750 ● Iconastas

Opaline Glass Sweet Jars ▲
- *circa 1905*

Opaline glass sweet jars modelled as busts of the Tsar and Tsarina Nicholas and Alexandra, made for the Imperial visit to France.
- *height 35cm*
- £500 the pair ● Iconastas

Baboushka ▲
- *circa 1930*

Soviet white glazed porcelain figure of a baboushka with impressed hammer and sickle mark and initials of Boris Kustodiev (1878–1927) from the Lomonosov factory.
- *height 27cm*
- £1,250 ● Iconastas

Lenin Inkwell ▼
- *circa 1924*

The Lenin inkwell, with facsimile signatures and inscription "Proletariat of the World unite" and anniversary inscription on the cover. By Natalia Danko (1892–1942) from the Lomonosov factory.
- *height 17cm*
- £1,250 ● Iconastas

Stalin ▼
- *circa 1920*

Soviet white glazed porcelain figure of Stalin shown in his youthful revolutionary "Hero" style. Signed.
- *height 36cm*
- £2,450 ● Iconastas

Soviet Inkwell ▶
- *circa 1929*

Soviet pottery inkwell, surmounted by a young lady with a red headscarf reading a book, the lid modelled as books and pamphlets. After Danko.
- *height 16cm*
- £1,250 ● Iconastas

Puss in Boots ▲
- *circa 1930*

A brightly coloured Soviet figure of Puss in Boots, unmarked, probably by Boris Kustodiev.
- *height 23cm*
- £450 ● Iconastas

Lenin ▼
- *circa 1920*
Rare plaster figure of Lenin by
Mauetta.
- *height 34cm*
- £2,450 • Iconastas

Grey Horses with Riders ▲
- *circa 1930*
Pair of grey horses with riders,
one pointing, on a foliate square
base.
- *26cm x 18cm*
- £2,650 • Iconastas

Soviet Porcelain Plate ▲
- *circa 1920*
Russian, Soviet porcelain plate
with floral design and stylised
"CCCP" by Natalya Girshfeld.
- *diameter 23cm*
- £1,650 • Iconastas

Constructivist Plate ◄
- *1928*
Constructivist plate painted with
female skiers in linear form with
strong colours. Signed and dated
1928.
- *diameter 24cm*
- £1,650 • Iconastas

Accordion Player ▼
- *circa 1930*
Soviet white glazed figure of an
accordion player by Boris
Kustodiev.
- *height 23cm*
- £490 • Iconastas

Soviet Bowl ▼
- *circa 1921*
Soviet bowl painted with strong
brush-strokes in vibrant colours
by Rudolf Vilde (1868–1942).
- *diameter 26cm*
- £2,200 • Iconastas

Arctic Rescue Tea Set ◄
- *circa 1925*
Tea set commemorating an
Arctic rescue of the Swedish
Arctic Expedition, led by Nobel,
by the Soviet icebreaker "Krasin".
- *diameter of plate 24cm*
- £2,500 • Iconastas

Tea Caddy Spoon ▶
- *circa 1900*

Silver gilt tea caddy spoon
showing an Imperial Russian
scene and a foliate design.
- *length 8cm*
- £180　　　• Iconastas

Commemorative Tea Holder ▼
- *1970*

Soviet silver tea holder with a
central cartouche showing
Lenin's head, an industrial scene
and the dates "1920–1970",
surrounded by a foliate design.
- *height 10cm*
- £80　　　• Iconastas

Fabergé Picture Frame ◀
- *circa 1890*

Fabergé satinwood picture frame
with silver beading, the gold
initial "A", and four silver roses at
each corner. The photo shows
Tsarina Alexandra.
- *14cm x 11cm*
- £4,500　　　• Iconastas

Expert Tips

*Ex-Soviet works of art are
becoming increasingly popular
and are gaining in value,
especially figures depicting
Lenin in uniform.*

Silver Tankard ▲
- *circa 1900*

A Russian silver tankard made for
political propaganda, with
engraved cartouches showing a
bountiful harvest.
- *height 8cm*
- £1,900　　　• Iconastas

Reclining Man Reading Newspaper ◀
- *circa 1930*

Reclining figure of a man reading
a newspaper dressed in white with
a black and white hat.
- *length 21cm*
- £580　　　• Iconastas

Writing Equipment

The Art Deco period produced some beautifully designed ink pots and pens which are now highly sought after.

The vast range of collectable writing equipment is overwhelmingly Victorian. The Victorians were fervent writers, and as a result an abundance of writing-related items were created in this period. Victorian ink trays were often inlaid with mother-of-pearl and were highly decorative. Some were made of enamel and decorated in a chinoiserie style, which was a very fashionable decorative effect at the time.

If you are a first-time collector, the field of writing equipment is a great place to start with as there is huge scope for the collector and the items can be very affordable, and are also usable. They can make a bold and striking statement on any desk or in a study as they are not only decorative, but are also a great talking point.

Pens are always collectable with the leading brands such as Parker, Mont Blanc and Waterman continuing to attract the highest prices because of their timeless workmanship and superior quality.

Quill Box ▶
- 1920
Quill box made from ebonised wood and quills.
- 5cm x 16cm
- £45   • Sporting Times

Salter Letter Balance ▼
- 1930
Small metal letter balance with a brass dial, with the manufacturer's mark "Salter-and-made in England" on the dial.
- *height 22cm*
- £48   • Rookery Farm

French Inkwell ◀
- *circa 1900*
French Art Nouveau inkwell of a lady reclining on large flowers with a lid concealed in the top of her long hair.
- *height 16cm*
- £1,200   • Victor Arwas

Dog Inkwells

- *circa 1890*
Carved wooden dog with a shaggy coat and an interior concealing two cut-out glass inkwells.
- *height 13cm*
- £2,200 • E. Bradwin

Shell Inkwells

- *circa 1800*
Regency mythological dolphins holding shell inkwells with original patina.
- *height 14cm*
- £5,200 • G. Douglas

Monkey Inkwell

- *circa 1880*
Austrian bronze monkey inkwell. The tree stump contains the inkwell.
- *height 15cm*
- £1,350 • E. Bradwin

Bulldog Inkwell

- *circa 1880*
Austrian bronze bulldog head inkwell with cast insert removable to accommodate a glass reservoir. Locket on the collar has engraved opening doors and recess for a small picture.
- *17cm x 14cm*
- £2,200 • E. Bradwin

Waterwheel Inkwell

- *circa 1880*
Excellent French silvered bronze and ormolu model of an inkwell disguised as a waterwheel. The waterwheel rotates.
- *13cm x 14cm*
- £650 • G. Douglas

Bear Inkstand

- *circa 1890*
Carved wood inkstand with mother bear holding her cub.
- *height 13cm*
- £650 • E. Bradwin

Expert Tips

Inkwells of mahogany, walnut, maple, oak or pine were popular in the mid-nineteenth century.

Rhinoceros Inkwell ◀

- *circa 1880*

Unusual inkwell in the form of a standing rhinoceros, the reservoir concealed by the natural armour of the beast's back. On an oval base with pen stand resting behind.

- *19cm x 29cm*
- £1,100
- E. Bradwin

Crocodile Inkwells ▲

- *circa 1880*

Well cast bronze crocodile double inkwell with original liners.

- *length 26cm*
- £780
- E. Bradwin

Dog Stamp Box ▼

- *circa 1880*

Delightful and rare bronze stamp box modelled as a dog, with a gilded interior.

- *height 2cm*
- £730
- E. Bradwin

Ostrich Inkpot ▼

- *circa 1880*

Bronze ostrich inkwell on a gilt brass oval stand.

- *height 20cm*
- £470
- E. Bradwin

Fox Head Inkwell ▼

- *circa 1900*

Fox mask with tail saucer concealed inkwell with original paint.

- *height 9cm*
- £1,200
- E. Bradwin

Napoleon Bonaparte ▲

- *circa 1850*

An unusual French inkwell featuring Napoleon Bonaparte standing upon a highly decorated plinth with Imperial eagles at each corner. Napoleon folds down by means of a hinge to reveal the inkwell, set on a black marble base.

- *height 23cm*
- £975
- G. Douglas

Double Glass Inkwell ▶

- *circa 1910*
Double glass inkwell with silver
rims around the lids, in a square
oblong container.
- *width 11cm*
- £96   • H. Gregory

Parker Propelling Pencil ▲

- *circa 1930–5*
Mottled green Parker propelling
pencil.
- *length 13cm*
- £220   • Jasmin Cameron

Swirl Glass Inkpot ▼

- *1890*
Swirl glass inkpot with silver-
plated hinged lid with floral
design.
- *height 16cm*
- £640   • Jasmin Cameron

Ebony Ink Tray ▼

- *circa 1820*
Ebony ink tray with two square
inkwells with brass lids, and
central stamp compartment.
- *width 34cm*
- £195   • Hayman

Ball Inkwell ▼

- *1914*
Brass inkwell consisting of four
brass balls resting on each other,
one of which contains the ink,
with a metal and wood base.
- *diameter 17cm*
- £78   • Hayman

Circular Glass Inkwell ◀

- *circa 1890*
Circular inkwell with a brass
hinged lid.
- *height 9cm*
- £270   • H. Gregory

Marquetry Stationery Box ▶

- *circa 1860*

Dutch mahogany case inlaid with floral marquetry within rectangular panels of boxwood stringing. Cedarwood lined interior with pen tray and original glass inkpot with a brass screw top.

- *32.5cm x 16.5cm x 23.5cm*
- £1,000–£2,000 • J. Collins

Bronze Paper Clip ▲

- *circa 1900*

Vienna bronze dog's head paper clip with original paintwork.

- *7.6cm x 14cm x 12.7cm*
- £950 • Heritage Antiques

Pineapple Inkstand ▲

- *circa 1880*

French gilded and patinated green bronze pineapple inkstand.

- *19cm x 19cm x 19cm*
- £550 • Heritage Antiques

Letter Scale ▶

- *1870–80*

English cast brass letter scale.

- *31cm x 11.4cm x 16.5cm*
- £755 • Heritage Antiques

Expert Tips

Early inkwells would often be added to a candleholder by candleholder specialists.

Armadillo Inkstand ▼

- *circa 1860*

Cast brass armadillo inkstand with two wells inside.

- *9cm x 7cm x 17.8cm*
- £390 • Heritage Antiques

Rosewood Writing Slope ▼

- *circa 1820*

Regency rosewood writing slope with rectangular lid which opens to reveal two glass inkpots, a wafer slide, and a dipped removable pen tray. The writing surface is lined in maroon hide with a gilded border.

- *14cm x 22cm x 35cm*
- £500 • J. Collins

Glass Inkwell ▶

- *circa 1901*

Glass inkwell with faceted base and silver hinged lid.
- *height 9cm*
- £290   • H.Gregory

Green Malachite Blotter ▼

- *circa 1860*

Green malachite blotter with knob handle.
- *length 19cm*
- £160   • Hayman

Victorian Writing Tray ◀

- *circa 1870*

Victorian double-handled brass writing tray with two inkwells and a central sander, decorated with C-scrolling and raised on four paw feet.
- *width 27cm*
- £175   • Hayman

Glass Square Inkpot ▲

- *circa 1860*

Square glass inkpot with faceted stopper and moulded shoulders.
- *height 9cm*
- £85   • Jasmin Cameron

Paperweight Inkpot ▼

- *1890*

Victorian circular paperweight inkwell with brass lid.
- *diameter 11cm*
- £48   • Hayman

Butterfly Letter Rack ◀

- *circa 189*

Brass butterfly letter rack standing on a rustic base.
- *height 10cm*
- £238   • Hayman

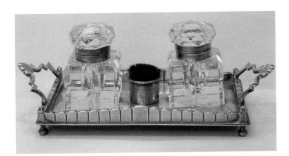

Cut-Glass Inkwell ▼

- *circa 1900*
Cut-glass inkwell with a hinged
silver cover.
- *height 10cm*
- £260 • H. Gregory

Non-Spill Inkpot ▲

- *circa 1900*
Non-spill vaseline glass ink pot of .
ovoid form with a central
teardrop reservoir.
- *height 6cm*
- £24 • Hayman

Brass Inkstand ◀

- *1830*
Double-handled brass inkstand
with scalloped design, holding
two glass inkpots with faceted lids
and brass rims, and a brush in a
brass container.
- *length 21cm*
- £340 • Jasmin Cameron

Silver Inkwell ▲

- *1930*
Small silver circular inkwell with
hinged lid.
- *diameter 9cm*
- £60 • H. Gregory

Satin Glass Inkpot ▲

- *circa 1870*
Satin glass turquoise inkpot with
a white flower and hinged lid.
- *height 11cm*
- £220 • Hayman

Wood Blotter ▲

- *circa 1860*
Wood ink blotter with brass inlay.
- *length 19cm*
- £160 • Hayman

Old Sheffield Inkstand ▶

- *circa 1840*
Old Sheffield silver inkstand with
serpentine border decorated with
floral and leaf design, two faceted
glass inkwells and a central silver
sander.
- *width 27cm*
- £300 • Jasmin Cameron

Ivory Boat Blotter ▶

- *circa 1890*
Ivory boat blotter with knob
handle.
- *length 11cm*
- £175　　• Jasmin Cameron

Victorian Inkpot ▼

- *circa 1830*
Victorian inkpot of ovoid form
with ball stopper.
- *height 7cm*
- £85　　• Jasmin Cameron

Limoges Inkwell ◀

- *1930*
Limoges enamel inkwell with red
flowers on a white ground and
brass banding.
- *height 5.5cm*
- £115　　　　• Hayman

Glass Inkpot ▼

- *circa 1830*
Faceted clear glass inkpot with
star-cut stopper.
- *height 9cm*
- £85　　• Jasmin Cameron

Gutta-percha Writing Set ◀

- *circa 1860*
Ink tray made from gutta-percha
with two inkwells set on a
scrolled base.
- *width 27cm*
- £125　　　　• Hayman

Slide Action Dip Pen ◀

- *1890*
Edward pod slide action
travelling dip pen in "Gothic
design" with rolled gold nib.
- *length 14cm*
- £125　　• Jasmin Cameron

Main Chinese Periods

SHANG DYNASTY	c. 1523 – 1027 BC
CHOW DYNASTY	1027 – 221 BC
WARRING STATES PERIOD	481 – 221 BC
CH'IN DYNASTY	221 – 206 BC
HAN DYNASTY	206 BC – 220 AD
THREE KINGDOMS	220 – 280
SIX DYNASTIES	280 – 589
NORTHERN WEI	385 – 535
EASTERN WEI	535 – 550
WESTERN WEI	535 – 557
NORTHERN CH'I	550 – 577
NORTHERN CHOW	557 – 581
LIU SUNG (SOUTH)	420 – 478
SOUTHERN CH'I	479 – 501
LIANG	502 – 557
CH'EN	557 – 588
SUI DYNASTY	589 – 618
T'ANG	618 – 906
FIVE DYNASTIES	907 – 959
SUNG DYNASTIES	960 – 1280
YUAN DYNASTIES	1280 – 1368
MING DYNASTIES	1368 – 1643
CH'ING DYNASTIES	1644 – 1912

Ming Period

HUNG WY	1368 – 1398
CHIEN WIEN	1399 – 1402
YUNG LO	1403 – 1424
HUNG HSI	1425 – 1425
HSUAN TE	1426 – 1435
CHENG T'UNG	1436 – 1449
CHING T'AI	1450 – 1457
T'IEN SHUN	1457 – 1464
CH'ENG HUA	1465 – 1487
HUNG–CHIH	1488 – 1505
CHENG TE	1506 – 1521
CHIA CHING	1522 – 1566
LUNG CH'ING	1567 – 1572
WAN LI	1573 – 1619

Ch'ing Period

SHUNG CHIH	1644 – 1661
K'ANG HSI	1662 – 1722
YUNG CHENG	1723 – 1735
CH'IENG LUNG	1736 – 1795
CHIA CH'ING	1796 – 1820
TAO KUANG	1821 – 1850
HSIEN FENG	1851 – 1861
T'UNG CHIH	1862 – 1873
KUANG HSU	1874 – 1908
HSUAN T'UNG	1909 – 1912

Japanese Periods

JOMON PERIOD	1000 BC – 200 BC
YAYOI PERIOD	200 BC – 500 AD
TUMULUS PERIOD	300 – 700
ASUKA PERIOD	552 – 645
EARLY NARA PERIOD	645 – 710
NARA PERIOD	710 – 794
EARLY HEIAN PERIOD	794 – 897
HEIAN OR FUJIWARA PERIOD	897 – 1185
KAMAKURA PERIOD	1185 – 1392
ASHIKAGA PERIOD	1392 – 1573
MOMOYAMA PERIOD	1573 – 1615
TOKUGAWA PERIOD	1615 – 1868

Korean Periods

LO LANG	106 BC – 313 AD
PAEKCHE	18 BC – 663 AD
KOGURYO	37 BC – 668 AD
SILLA	57 BC – 668 AD
GREAT SILLA	668 – 936
KORYO	918 – 1392
YI	1392 – 1910

French General Periods

FRANÇOIS–PREMIER	1515 – 1547	Reign of Francis I
HENRI–DEUX	1547 – 1559	Reign of Henri II
	1559 – 1560	Reign of Francis II
	1560 – 1574	Reign of Charles IX
	1574 – 1589	Reign of Henri III
HENRI–QUATRE	1589 – 1610	Reign of Henri IV
LOUIS–TREIZE	1610 – 1643	Reign of Louis XIII
LOUIS–QUATORZE	1643 – 1715	Reign of Louis XIV
LOUIS–QUINZE	1715 – 1774	Reign of Louis XV
LOUIS–SEIZE	1774 – 1793	Reign of Louis XVI
EMPIRE	1799 – 1814	Reign of Napoleon

English General Periods

TUDOR	1485 – 1558	Reigns of Henry VII Henry VIII Edward VI Mary
ELIZABETHAN	1558 – 1603	Reign of Elizabeth I
JACOBEAN	1603 – 1649	Reigns of James I Charles I
COMMONWEALTH	1649 – 1660	Protectorship of Cromwell
CAROLEAN / LATE STUART	1660 – 1689	Reigns of Charles II James II
WILLIAM AND MARY	1689 – 1702	Reign of William and Mary
QUEEN ANNE	1702 – 1727	Reigns of Anne George I
GEORGIAN	1727 – 1820	Reigns of George II George III
REGENCY	1800 – 1830	Reigns of George III George IV
WILLIAM IV	1830 – 1837	Reign of William IV
VICTORIAN	1837 – 1901	Reign of Victoria
EDWARDIAN	1901 – 1910	Reign of Edward VII

English Monarchs since 1066

WILLIAM I	1066 – 1087
WILLIAM II	1087 – 1100
HENRY I	1100 – 1135
STEPHEN	1135 – 1154
HENRY II	1154 – 1189
RICHARD I	1189 – 1199
JOHN	1199 – 1216
HENRY III	1216 – 1272
EDWARD I	1272 – 1307
EDWARD II	1307 – 1327
EDWARD III	1327 – 1377
RICHARD II	1377 – 1399
HENRY IV	1399 – 1413
HENRY V	1413 – 1422
HENRY VI	1422 – 1461
EDWARD IV	1461 – 1470
HENRY VI	1470 – 1471
EDWARD IV	1471 – 1483
EDWARD V	1483 – 1483
RICHARD III	1484 – 1485
HENRY VII	1485 – 1509
HENRY VIII	1509 – 1547
EDWARD VI	1547 – 1553
MARY	1553 – 1558
ELIZABETH	1558 – 1603
JAMES I	1603 – 1625
CHARLES I	1625 – 1649
COMMONWEALTH	1649 – 1660
CHARLES II	1660 – 1685
JAMES II	1685 – 1688
WILLIAM AND MARY	1688 – 1694
WILLIAM III	1694 – 1702
ANNE	1702 – 1714
GEORGE I	1714 – 1727
GEORGE II	1727 – 1760
GEORGE III	1760 – 1820
GEORGE IV	1820 – 1830
WILLIAM IV	1830 – 1837
VICTORIA	1837 – 1901
EDWARD VII	1901 – 1910
GEORGE V	1910 – 1936
EDWARD VIII	1936 – 1936
GEORGE VI	1936 – 1952
ELIZABETH II	1952 –

Not all of the terms that follow appear in this volume, but they may all prove useful in the future.

abadeh Highly-coloured Persian rug.

acacia Dull yellow hardwood with darker markings used for inlay and bandings towards the end of the eighteenth century.

acanthus A leaf motif used in carved and inlaid decoration.

Act of Parliament clock Eighteenth-century English clock, wall mounted and driven by weights, with a large, unglazed dial and a trunk for weights. These clocks often hung in taverns and public places and were relied on by the populace after the Act of Parliament of 1797, which introduced taxation on timepieces.

air-beaded Glass with air bubbles resembling beads.

air-twist Spiral pattern enclosed in a glass stem with air bubbles.

albarello Waisted ceramic drug jar.

alder Wood used for country-style furniture in the eighteenth century.

ale glass Eighteenth-century glass drinking vessel with long stem and tall, thin bowl.

amboyna West Indian wood used for veneers, marquetry and inlays. Light brown with speckled grain.

anchor escapement Late seventeenth-century English invented clock movement, named after the anchor shape of the linkage which moves the escape wheel.

angle barometer Also known as signpost barometers. Barometers where the movement of mercury is shown almost on the horizontal.

andiron Iron support for burning logs.

annulated Ringed (of glass).

apostle spoon Spoon with the figure of an apostle as the finial.

applied Attached or added, rather than modelled or carved as part of the body.

apron The decorative panel of wood between the front legs of a chair or cabinet.

arbor The axle on which the wheel of a clock's mechanism is mounted.

arch (clockmaking) The arch above the dial of a post-1700 longcase clock.

argyle Double-skinned metal pouring jugs and tea and coffee pots.

armoire French wardrobe, linen press or large cupboard.

ash Hardwood used for making country furniture and for its white veneer.

astragal Small semi-circular moulding, particularly used as glazing bar in furniture.

automaton clock A clock where the strike is performed by mechanically operated figures.

backboard The unseen back of wall furniture.

backplate The rear plate supporting the movement of a clock, often the repository of engraved information relating to its manufacture.

baff Knot in rug-making.

balance Device counteracting the force of the mainspring in a clock's movement.

balloon-back chair Popular, rounded-backed Victorian dining or salon chair.

baluster (adj.) Having a dominant convex swell at the base, culminating in a smaller, concave one at the neck. (noun) One of a set of upright posts supporting a balustrade.

banjo barometer Wheel barometer dating from circa 1775-1900, with shape resembling a banjo.

barley-sugar twist Spiral-turned legs and rails popular in the seventeenth century. Colloquial.

bat printed Transfer printed (of ceramics).

beech Hardwood used in the manufacture of country furniture and, when stained, as a substitute for mahogany.

bellarmine Stoneware flagon made in Germany from the sixteenth century.

bergère French for an armchair, used in English to describe a chair with caned back and sides.

bevel Decorative, shaved edge of glass, particularly mirror.

bezel The metal rim of a glass cover or jewel.

bird-cage Support mechanism at the top of the pedestal of some eighteenth-century tilt-top tables.

birch Hardwood used principally for carcassing; occasionally for low-quality veneer.

bird's eye maple Wood of the sugar maple with distinctive figure caused by aborted buds. Used in veneering.

biscuit (bisque) Ceramics fired but unglazed, originating in France in the eighteenth century.

blind fretwork Fretwork carving on a solid background.

block front Front shaped from thick boards allowing for a recessed centre section.

blue-dash Blue dabs around the rim of a delftware plate.

bob The weight at the bottom of a pendulum.

bobbin Turned furniture element, resembling a row of connected spheres.

bocage Foliage, bushes and shrubs supporting, surrounding or standing behind porcelain or pottery figures.

bombé Having an outswelling front.

bone china Clay with bone ash in the formula, almost entirely porcellanous. First produced at the end of the eighteenth century.

bonheur du jour Small, lady's writing desk with a cabinet and drawers above. Originally French, from the mid eighteenth century.

bottle glass Low quality coloured glass for bottles, jars etc.

boulle An eighteenth-century marquetry style employing brass and tortoiseshell.

boxlock Flintlock gun with the mechanism enclosed in the breach.

boxwood Pale yellow, close-grained hardwood used for carving and turning and for inlay and pattern veneers.

bow front Convex curve on the front of chests of drawers.

bracket clock Domestic clock so called because of the necessity of standing it on a bracket to allow its weights to hang down, the term later applied to domestic clocks of the eighteenth and nineteenth centuries regardless of their motive force.

bracket foot Plain foot carved into the rail or stretcher to form an ornamental bracket.

brandy saucepan Miniature, bulbous or baluster shaped saucepan with long handle at right angles to the spout.

breakfront Describing a piece of furniture with a central section which projects forward.

breech Rear end of the barrel of a gun.

breech-loading Gun loaded through an opening in the breech.

bright cut Late eighteenth-century silver engraving technique, making the design brilliant in relief.

Bristol glass Eighteenth century coloured (often blue) glass produced in Bristol.

Britannia metal Form of refined pewter used as a silver substitute in the early nineteenth century.

British plate Silver substitute from the nineteenth century, immediately preceding the introduction of EPNS.

broken arch Arch above the dial of a long-case clock which is less than a semi-circle, indicating an early Georgian date.

broken pediment Pediment with a symmetrical break in the centre, often accommodating an urn or some such motif.

bun foot Flattened spherical foot often found on later seventeenth-century furniture.

bureau Desk with a fall front enclosing a fitted interior, with drawers below.

bureau bookcase Bureau with glazed bookcase above.

burr Veneer used in furniture making, with a decorative pattern caused by some abnormality of growth or knotting in the tree. Usually taken from the base of the tree.

cabriole leg Leg of a piece of furniture that curves out at the foot and in at the top.

Introduced in the seventeenth century.

caddy Tea caddy.

caddy spoon Short-handled, large bowled spoon for extracting tea from the caddy.

calendar / date aperture Window in the dial of a clock displaying day, month or date.

canted corner Decoratively angled corner.

canterbury An eighteenth-century container for sheet music.

carcase/carcass The inner frame of a piece of furniture, usually made of inferior wood for veneering.

card case Case for visiting cards, usually silver, nineteenth century.

carriage clock Portable timepiece, invented in nineteenth-century France, with handle above.

cartel clock Eighteenth-century French wall clock with profusely decorated case.

case furniture Furniture intended as a receptical, e.g. chest of drawers.

caster / castor 1. Sprinkling vessel for e.g. sugar. 2. Pivoted wheel attached to foot.

Castleford ware Shiny white stoneware made in Castleford and elsewhere from circa 1790.

caudle cup Covered cup, often in silver.

cellaret A wine cooler or container, usually eighteenth century.

centrepiece Ornament designed to sit in the centre of a dining table. Often in silver.

chafing dish Serving dish, often in silver, with stand incorporating a spirit lamp to retain heat.

chain fusée The fusée of a clock from which a chain unwinds on to the barrel of the mainspring.

chamfer A flattened angle; a corner that has been bevelled or planed.

chapter ring The ring on a clock dial on which the numbers of the hours are inscribed.

Chesterfield Deep-buttoned, upholstered settee from the nineteenth century.

chest on chest Tallboy having two chests fitting together, the lower with bracket feet, the upper with pediment. From the seventeenth and eighteenth centuries.

chest on stand Known as a tallboy or highboy, a chest of drawers on a stand.

cheval mirror Tall mirror supported by two uprights on swivels.

chiffonnier Side cupboard, originally, in the eighteenth century, with solid doors, but latterly with latticed or glazed doors.

chinoiserie Oriental-style decoration on lacquered furniture or artefacts.

chronometer Precision timepiece, often for navigation.

circular movement Clock movement of circular plates.

cistern Chamber containing mercury at the base of the tube of a barometer.

claw-and-ball foot Foot modelled as a ball clutched in a claw, frequently used to terminate a cabriole leg.

clock garniture Mantelpiece ornamentation with a clock as centrepiece.

close helmet Helmet covering the whole head and neck.

coaster Small, circular tray, often in silver, for holding a bottle.

cockbeading Bead moulding applied to the edges of drawers.

cock bracket Bracket supporting a watch mainspring.

coin glass Early eighteenth-century English drinking glass with a coin moulded into the knop of the stem.

commode High quality, highly decorated chest of drawers or cabinet, with applied mounts.

compensated pendulum Pendulum with mercury reservoir, the mercury rising and falling to compensate for the effects on the pendulum of changes of temperature.

composition Putty-like substance for moulding and applying to e.g. mirror frames, for gilding.

console table Often semi-circular table intended to stand against a wall on the pier between two windows (hence also pier table). Usually with matching mirror above.

cordial glass Glass originating in the seventeenth century, with a small bowl for strong drinks.

corner chair Chair with back splats on two sides and a bowed top rail, designed to fit into a corner.

cornice Horizontal top part of a piece of furniture; a decorative band of metal or wood used to conceal curtain fixtures.

coromandel Wood from India's Coromandel coast, used for banding and inlay.

counter-well The small oval wooden dishes inset into early Georgian card tables for holding chips or cash, hence also guinea-well.

country furniture Functional furniture made outside the principal cities. Also provincial furniture.

countwheel strike Clock mechanism determining the number of strikes per hour.

cow creamer Silver or china cream jug modelled as a cow.

crazing Fine cracks in glaze.

creamware Earthenware glazed in a cream colour giving a porcelain effect, in a widely used technique originally devised by Wedgwood in the 1760s.

credence table Late seventeenth-century oak or walnut table with folding top.

credenza Long Victorian side cabinet with glazed or solid doors.

crenellated Crinkly, wavy.

crested china Ware decorated with heraldic crests; originally by Goss, but subsequently by many Staffordshire and German potteries.

crinoline stretcher Crescent-shaped stretcher supporting the legs of some Windsor chairs.

cross-banding Decorative edging with cross-grained veneer.

cruet Frame for holding condiment containers.

crutch The arm connecting a clock's pendulum to the pallet arbor.

cuirass Breastplate (of armour).

cup and cover Round turning with a distinctly separate top, common on legs until circa 1650.

damascene Inlay of precious metal onto a body of other metal for decorative purposes.

davenport Small English desk, reputedly originally produced by Gillow for a Captain Davenport in 1834. A day-bed or sofa in the USA.

deadbeat escapement Version of the anchor escapement that eliminates recoil and improves accuracy.

deal Sawn pine wood.

delftware Seventeenth- and eighteenth-century tin-glazed earthenware, often decorated in the style of Chinese blue and white porcelain or after Dutch seventeenth-century painting, after the style pioneered by the Delft pottery.

Delft ware Items of delftware which actually emanate from Delft.

dentil Small, block-shaped moulding found under a furniture cornice.

dialplate Frontplate of a clock.

diamond cut (of glass) Cut in diamond shape.

dinanderie Fifteenth-century brass artefact from the factories of Dinant, Belgium.

dished table top Hollowed-out, solid top, particularly of a pie-crust, tripod table.

distressed Artificially aged.

dovetails Interlocking joints used in drawers.

double-action A gun which may be cocked or self-cocking.

douter Scissor-like implement for extinguishing a candle.

dowel Peg holding together wooden joint.

dram glass Small, short-stemmed glass with rounded bowl.

drop-in seat Framed, upholstered seat which sits in the framework of a chair.

drop handle Pear-shaped brass furniture handle of the late seventeenth and early eighteenth centuries.

drop-leaf table Table with a fixed central section and hinged flaps.

drum table Circular writing table on a central pedestal with frieze drawers.

dry-edge With unglazed edges.

dummy drawer False drawer with handle.

Dutch strike Clock chime which strikes the next hour on the half hour.

ebonise To stain a wood to the dark colour of ebony.

ebony Much imitated exotic black hardwood, used as veneer in Europe from the seventeenth century, generally for very high quality pieces.

écuelle Two-handled French soup bowl with cover and stand, often Sèvres.

electroplate The technique of covering one metal with the thin layer of another.

elm Hardwood used in the manufacture of chair seats, country furniture and coffins.

embossing Relief decoration.

enamel Second, coloured glaze fired over first glaze.

endstone In a clock mechanism, jewel on which an arbor pivots.

English dial Nineteenth-century English wall clock with large painted dial, previously a fixture in railway stations.

Engshalskrüge Large German tin-glaze jug with cylindrical neck.

épergne Centrepiece of one central bowl surrounded by smaller ones.

escritoire Cabinet with a fall-front which forms a writing surface. With a fitted interior.

escutcheon Brass plate surrounding the edges of a keyhole.

étuis Small, metal oddments box.

everted Outward turned, flaring (e.g. of a lip).

facet-cut (of glass) Cut criss-cross into straight-edged planes.

faience Tin-glazed earthenware.

fairings Porcelain figures, especially German, made in the nineteenth and twentieth centuries in the mould. Usually comical and carrying descriptive captions.

fall front Flap of a bureau or secretaire that pulls out to provide a writing surface.

famille rose Predominantly pink-coloured Oriental porcelain.

famille verte Predominantly green-coloured Oriental porcelain.

fauteuil Open-sided, upholstered armchair with padded elbows.

feather banding Two bands of veneer laid at opposite diagonals.

field Area of a carpet within its decorated borders.

fielded panel Raised panel with chamfered edge fitting into a framework.

figure Natural pattern created by the grain through the wood.

finial Decorative, turned knob.

flamed veneer Veneer cut at an angle to enhance the figuring.

flatware Plates, knives and forks.

flintlock Gun mechanism whereby the priming in the pan is ignited by a spark created by a flint.

flute glass Glass with tall, slender bowl.

fluting Decorative parallel grooving.

foliate carving Carved flower and leaf motifs.

foliot Primitive form of balance for clock mechanisms.

fretwork Fine pierced decoration.

frieze Long ornamental strip.

frit The flux from which glass is made. An ingredient of soft-paste porcelain.

frizzen The metal which a flint strikes to create a spark in a flintlock mechanism.

fruitwood Generally the wood of apple, cherry and pear trees, used for ebonising and gilding, commonly in picture frames.

fusee The conical, grooved spool from which a line or chain unwinds as it is pulled by the mainspring of a clock movement.

gadroon Carved edge or moulded decoration consisting of a series of grooves, ending in a curved lip, with ridges between them.

Gainsborough chair Deep, upholstered armchair with padded, open arms and carved decoration.

galleried Having a wood or metal border around the top edge.

garniture Set of ornamental pieces of porcelain.

gateleg Leg that pivots to support a drop leaf.

gesso Plaster-like substance applied to carved furniture before gilding and moulded and applied as a substitute for carving.

gilt-tooled decoration Gold leaf impressed into the edges of leather on desk-tops.

gimbal Mounting which keeps a ship's barometer level at all times.

girandole Wall-mounted candle holder with a mirrored back.

gorget Item of armour for protecting the throat.

Goss china Range of porcelain, particularly heraldic, produced in Stoke-on-Trent from 1858.

greave Armour protecting lower leg.

Greek key Ancient key-shaped decoration often repeated in fretwork on furniture.

gridiron pendulum Clock pendulum consisting of rods of a mix of metals positioned in such a way that the dynamics of their behaviour when subjected to heat or cold keep the pendulum swing uniform.

halberd Double-headed axe weapon with projecting spike.

half hunter Watch with an opening front cover with glass to the centre and a chapter ring, giving protection to the glass over the dial.

hallmark The mark by which silver can be identified by standard, place of assay and date.

hard-paste porcelain Porcelain made with kaolin and petuntse in the Chinese fashion, pioneered in Europe at Meissen in the early eighteenth century.

hunter Watch with a hinged, opening front cover in solid metal.

husk Formalised leaf motif.

ice glass Glass with uneven, rippling surface.

Imari Japanese porcelain made in and around Arita from the early eighteenth century and shipped to Europe from the port of Imari. Blue, red and gold coloured.

improved A pejorative term implying that a piece has been altered in order dishonestly to enhance its value.

inlay The decorative setting of one material into a contrasting one.

intaglio Incised design.

ironstone Stoneware patented by Mason in 1813, in which slag from iron furnaces was mixed with the clay to toughen the ware.

istoriato Of some Italian majolica, meaning 'with a story on it'.

japanned Painted and varnished in imitation of Oriental style lacquer work.

jardinière An ornamental pot or vase for plants.

jasper ware Variety of coloured stoneware developed by the Wedgwood factory.

joined Manufactured with the use of mortice and tenon joints and dowels, but without glue.

kabuto Japanese Samurai helmet.

kingwood Exotic, purplish hardwood used in veneer.

kneehole desk Desk with a recessed cupboard beneath the frieze drawer.

knop Rounded projection or bulge in the stem of a glass.

lacquer Resinous substance which, when coloured, provides a ground for chinoiserie and gilding.

ladder-back Chair with a series of horizontal back rails.

lantern clock Clocks made in England from the sixteenth century, driven entirely by weights and marking only the hours. Similar in appearance to a lantern.

lappit Carved flap at the top of a leg with a pad foot.

latten Archaic term for brass.

lead crystal Particularly clear, brilliant glass including lead in the process.

lead-glazed the earliest glaze for Western pottery, derived from glass making.

lever escapement Modification of the anchor escapement for carriage clocks and, particularly, watches.

lion's paw foot Foot carved as a lion's paw. Commonly eighteenth century and Regency.

lock Firing mechanism of a gun.

lockplate Base holding firing mechanism on a gun barrel.

loo table Large Victorian card or games table.

longcase clock The 'grandfather' clock, housed in a tall wooden case containing the weights and pendulum.

loper Pull-out arm that supports the hinged fall of a bureau.

lowboy Small side table with cabriole legs, from the seventeenth century.

lustre ware Ceramic ware decorated with a metallic coating which changes colour when fired.

mahogany The hardwood most used in the production of furniture in England in the eighteenth and nineteenth centuries. Used as a solid wood until the nineteenth century, when its rarity led to its being used for veneer.

majolica Originally tin-glazed earthenware produced in Renaissance Italy, subsequently all nineteenth century wares using the same technique.

mantel clock Clock with feet designed to stand on a mantelpiece.

maple North American hardwood used for its variety of veneers.

marine chronometer Precision clock for use in navigation at sea.

marquetry The use of wooden and other inlays to form decorative patterns.

married Pejorative term applied to a piece of furniture which is made up of more than one piece of the same period.

matchlock Firing mechanism of a gun achieved by lowering a slow match into the priming pan.

mazarine Metal strainer fitting over a dish.

mercury twist Air-twist in glass of a silver colour.

millefiori Multi-coloured or mosaic glass.

moonwork Clock mechanism which computes and displays the phases of the moon.

moquette Heavy imitation velvet used for upholstery.

morion Helmet with upturned front peak.

mortice Slot element of a mortice and tenon joint.

moulding decorative, shaped band around an object or a panel.

mount Invariably metal mounting fitted to a piece of furniture.

mule chest Coffer with a single row of drawers to the base.

musical clock Clock with a cylinder which strikes bells to play a tune.

Nailsea Late eighteenth-century, boldly coloured, opaque glass from Nailsea, near Bristol.

nest of tables Set of three or four occasional tables which slot into each other when not in use.

oak Hardwood which darkens with age, predominant in English furniture manufacture until the middle of the seventeenth century.

obverse The front side of a coin or medal.

ogee An S-shaped curve.

ogee arch Two S-shaped curves coming together to form an arch.

oignon Onion-shaped French watch of the eighteenth century.

ormolu From French *dorure d'or moulu*: 'gilding with gold paste', gold-coloured alloy of copper, zinc, and sometimes tin, in various proportions but usually containing at least 50% copper. Ormolu is used in mounts (ornaments on borders, edges, and as angle guards) for furniture, especially eighteenth-century furniture.

orrery Astronomical clock which shows the position of heavenly bodies. Named after Charles Boyle, fourth Earl of Orrery.

overglaze See **enamel**.

overmantel mirror Mirror designed to hang over a mantelpiece.

ovolo A rounded, convex moulding, making an outward curve across a right angle.

oyster veneer Veneer resembling an open oyster shell, an effect achieved by slanting the cut across the grain of a branch.

pad foot Rounded foot on a circular base, used as termination for cabriole legs.

pair-case A double case for a watch, the inner for protection of the movement, the outer for decoration.

pallet Lever that engages in a clock's escapement wheel in orderb to arrest it.

papier mâché Moulded and lacquered pulped paper used to make small items of furniture and other artefacts.

parian Typically uncoloured, biscuit-style porcelain developed in the nineteenth century by Copeland and named after Parian white marble.

parquetry Veneered pattern using small pieces of veneer, often from different woods, in a geometrical design.

patera Circular ornament made of wood, metal or composition.

patina The layers of polish, dirt, grease and general handling marks that build up on a wooden piece of furniture over the years and give it its individual signs of age, varying from wood to wood.

pearlware White, shiny earthenware, often print decorated.

pedestal desk A flat desk with a leathered top standing on two banks of drawers.

pediment Architectural, triangular gable crowning a piece of furniture or a classical building.

pegged furniture Early furniture constructed with the use of mortice and tenon joints and pegged together with dowels.

pembroke table Small, two-flapped table standing on four legs or a pedestal.

pepperette Vessel, often in silver, for sprinkling pepper.

petuntse Chinese name for the feldspathic rock, an essential element of porcelain, which produces a glaze.

pewter Alloy of tin, lead and often various other metals.

pie-crust Expression used to describe the decorative edge of a dished-top tripod table.

pier glass Tall mirror for hanging on a pier between windows.

pietra dura Composition of semi-precious stones applied to panels of – usually Italian – furniture.

pillar (watchmaking) A rod connecting the dial-plate and backplate of a movement.

pillar rug Chinese rug made to be arranged around a pillar.

pine Softwood used for carcassing furniture.

platform base Flat base supporting a central pedestal and table-top above and standing on three or four scrolled or paw feet.

plinth base Solid base not raised on feet.

pole screen Adjustable fire screen.

pommel Knob at the end of the handle of a dagger.

pontil mark Mark made by the pontil, or blowpipe, on the base of hand-blown glass.

porcellanous Having most of the ingredients or characteristics of porcelain.

porringer Large, two-handled cup with cover.

potboard Bottom shelf of a dresser, often just above the floor.

pounce box A sprinkler for pounce, a powder for drying ink.

Prattware Staffordshire earthenware of the late eighteenth and early nineteenth centuries, decorated in distinctive colours on a buff ground.

print decoration Mass-produced decoration. Not hand painting.

provincial furniture See **country furniture**.

punch bowl Large bowl for the retention and dispensation of punch.

quartered top Flat surface covered with four pieces of matching veneer.

quartetto tables Nest of four occasional tables.

quillon Cross-piece of a sword.

rail A horizontal member running between the outer uprights of a piece of furniture.

rating nut Nut under the bob of a clock's pendulum by which the rate of swing may be adjusted.

redware Primitive eighteenth-century American ware made from a clay which turns red when fired.

reeding Parallel strips of convex fluting.

re-entrant corner Shaped indentation at each corner of a table.

register plate Plate on a barometer with inscriptions to be read against the level of mercury.

regulator Precision timepiece of the eighteenth century.

relief Proud of the surface.

repeating work Mechanism by which the pull of a cord or the press of a button operates the striking mechanism of a clock or watch to the last hour.

repoussé An embossed design which has been refined by chasing.

rosewood Named after its smell when newly cut, rather than its flower or colour, a dark-brown hardwood with an attractive stripe or ripple, used for veneering.

rule joint Hinge on furniture which fits so well that, when open, no join can be detected between two hinged parts.

runners Strips of wood, fitted to furniture, on which drawers slide.

sabre leg Chair leg in the shape of a sabre, typical of the Regency period.

saltglaze Stoneware in which salt is added to the recipe creating a porcellanous, glassy surface. Dates back to the early eighteenth century.

salver A large metal dish or tray for transporting smaller dishes.

satinwood A light golden-coloured, close-grained hardwood used for veneer, panelling and turning from the mid-eighteenth century onwards.

scagiola Composite material resembling marble.

scalloped Having a series of circular edges in the shape of a scallop shell.

scalloped leaf Serpentine flap on some pembroke tables.

sconce 1. Cup-shaped candle holder. 2. Metal plate fixed to the wall, supporting candle holder or light.

scratch blue Eighteenth-century saltglaze decoration where the body is incised and the incisions painted blue.

scroll, scrolling Carving or moulding of a curled design.

seat rail Horizontal framework below the chair seat uniting the legs.

secretaire Writing desk with false drawer front which lets down to reveal a writing surface and fitted interior.

secretaire bookcase Secretaire with bookcase fitted above.

serpent The arm holding the match or flint by which the priming of a gun was ignited.

serpentine Of undulating shape.

settee Upholstered settle.

settle Hard bench seat with back. The earliest form of seating for two or more people.

Sheffield plate Rolled sheet silver placed either side of a layer of copper and fused. Recognised by the Sheffield assay office in 1784, but made elsewhere, notably Birmingham, as well.

shoe piece Projection on the back rail of a chair into which the splat fits.

side chair Chair without arms designed to stand against the wall.

side table Any table designed to stand against the wall.

skeleton clock Clock with the workings exposed.

slipware Earthenware to which mixed clay and water has been added as decoration.

sofa Well-upholstered chair providing seating for two or more people.

sofa table Rectangular table with hinged flaps designed to stand behind a sofa.

soft-paste porcelain Porcelain using frit or soapstone instead of the petuntse of hard-paste porcelain. English, from the eighteenth century.

spade foot Square, tapered foot.

spandrel Pierced, decorative corner bracket found at the tops of legs.

sparrow-beak jug Jug with a triangular spout.

spill vase Container for lighting-tapers.

spindle Thoroughly turned piece of wood. The upright bars of a spindle-back chair.

splat The central upright of a chair back.

sprig Applied or relief ornamentation of any kind on a ceramic artefact.

squab Detachable cushion or upholstered seat of a chair or bench.

standish Inkstand, often in silver.

stick barometer Barometer with a straight, vertical register plate running alongside the mercury tube.

stiles Archaic term for the vertical parts of the framework of a piece of furniture.

stoneware Earthenware that is not porous after firing.

stretcher Rail joining the legs of a table or chair.

strike / silent ring Dial to disengage or re-engage the striking of a clock.

stringing Fine inlaid lines around a piece of furniture.

stirrup cup Cup used for alcoholic refreshment prior to hunting, usually shaped in the head of a fox or, less usually, a hound.

stuff-over seat Chair that is upholstered over the seat rail.

subsidiary dial Small dial, usually showing seconds, within the main dial of a clock or watch. Hence **subsidiary seconds**.

swagged With applied strips formed in a mould (of metal).

swan-neck pediment Pediment with two broken curves.

swan-neck handle Curved handle typical of the eighteenth century.

sycamore Hardwood of the maple family, light yellow in colour, used for veneering.

tang The end of the blade of a sword, covered by the hilt.

tankard Large beer-mug with a hinged lid and thumb-piece.

tazza Italian plate, cup, basin or wide-bowled glass.

teapoy Small piece of furniture designed for holding tea leaves. Usually Anglo-Indian.

tenons The tongues in mortice and tenon joints.

thumb moulding Decorative concave moulding.

thumb-piece Projection attached to a hinged lid which will open the lid when pressure is applied by the thumb.

tine Prong of a fork.

tin-glazed Lead-glazed earthenware to which tin is added, e.g. majolica.

toilet mirror Small dressing mirror with a box base and drawers.

touch mark Individual mark of the maker of a piece of early English pewter.

transfer Ceramic print decoration using colours held in oil.

trefid spoon A seventeenth-century spoon with the handle terminating in the shape of a bud, usually cleft or grooved into two lobes.

trefoil Having three lobes.

trembleuse Cup-stand with feet.

tripod table Small, round-topped table on three-legged base.

tulipwood Pinkish, naturally patterned hardwood used in veneer.

turnery Any wood turned on a lathe.

tureen Large bowl in porcelain or metal, usually with a lid and two handles.

turret clock Clock of any size driven by a weight suspended by a rope wrapped round a drum.

underglaze Colour or design painted below the glaze of a ceramic artefact.

uniface Medal or coin with modelling on one side only.

urn table Eighteenth-century table designed to hold an urn.

veneer A thin sheet of wood laid across a cheaper carcase or used as inlay decoration.

verge escapement Mechanism for regulating a clock movement before the anchor escapement.

Vesta case Match box for Vesta matches, often in silver, from circa 1850.

vinaigrette Small, eighteenth-century box, often silver, to hold a sponge soaked in vinegar to ward off germs and the unpleasant odours of the day.

wainscot chair Joined chair with open arms and a panelled back.

walnut The hardwood used in England for the manufacture of furniture from the Restoration, originally in solid form but mostly as veneer, particularly burr walnut, after the beginning of the eighteenth century.

well Interior of a plate or bowl.

Wemyss ware Late nineteenth-century lead-glazed earthenware originally from Fife, Scotland.

whatnot Mobile stand with open shelves.

wheel-back chair Originally late eighteenth-century chair with circular back with radiating spokes.

windsor chair Wooden chair with spindle back.

yew Tough, close-grained hardwood used for turning, particularly in chair legs, and in veneer.

There follows a list of antique dealers, many of whom have provided items in the main body of the book and all of whom will be happy to assist within their areas of expertise.

20th Century Decorative Arts (ref: 20th Century)
Tel: 0161 4329834
Mob: 07775 675234
www.20thcentury-decorative-arts.co.uk
general-enquiries@20thcentury-decorative-arts.co.uk
Original Art Deco, Art Nouveau, and post war design.

Norman Adams Ltd
8–10 Hans Road
London SW3 1RX
Tel: 020 7589 5266
Fax: 020 7589 1968
www.normanadams.com
antiques@normanadams.com
Eighteenth century fine English furniture, works of art, mirrors, paintings and chandeliers.

After Noah
121 Upper Street
London N1 1QP
Tel: 020 7359 4281
Fax: 020 7359 4281
www.afternoah.com
sales@afternoah.com
Antique furniture, linen and postcards.

After Noah (Kings Road) (ref: After Noah (KR))
261 Kings Road
London SW3 5EL
Tel: 020 7351 2610
Fax: 020 7351 2610
www.afternoah.com
sales@afternoah.com
Antique furniture, linen and postcards.

Adrian Alan
66–67 South Audley Street
London W1K 2QX
Tel. 020 7495 2324
www.adrianalan.net
enquiries@adrianalan.com
English and Continental antique furniture and unique pieces of fine and decorative.

AM–PM
V35 Antiquarius Antique Centre
135 Kings Road
London SW3 4PW
Tel: 020 7351 5654
Antique and modern watches.

Meg Andrews
Tel: 020 7359 7678
www.meg-andrews.com
meg@meg-andrews.com
Antique costumes and textiles.

The Antique and Interiors Group Ltd. (ref: A.I.G)
The Old Cinema
160 Chiswick High Road
London W4 1PR
Tel: 020 8742 8080
Fax: 020 8878 0184
www.antiques-uk.co.uk/theoldcinema/
Antiques in general.

Antique Glass at Frank Dux Antiques (ref: Antique Glass)
at Frank Dux Antiques
33 Belvedere
Lansdown Road
Bath BA1 5HR
Tel: 01225 312367
Fax: 01225 312367
www.antique-glass.co.uk
m.hopkins@antique-glass.co.uk
Antique glassware.

Arca
Roberto Innocenti
Stand 351
Grays Antique Market
58 Davies Street
Mayfair, London WIK 5LP
Tel: 020 7692 729
Innocenti@arcaantiques.freeserve co.uk
Sewing and smoking items.

Victor Arwas Gallery (ref: VictorArwas)
3 Clifford Street
London W1S 2LF
Tel: 020 7734 3944
Fax: 020 7437 1859
www.victorarwas.com
art@victorarwas.com
Art Nouveau and Art Deco, glass, ceramics, bronzes, sculpture, furniture, jewellery, silver, pewter, books and posters, paintings,original graphics, lithographs, etchings and woodcuts.

Ash Rare Books
(ref: Ash Books)
153 Fenchurch Street
London EC3M 6BB
Tel: 020 7626 2665
Fax: 020 7626 2665
www.ashrare.com
books@ashrare.com
Books, maps and prints.

B.J. Ayers
Rivermill House
1 Woodside Court
Usk Montmouthshire
NP15 1SY
Tel: 01291 672710
Fax: 01291 673464
www.vintagefishingtackle.com
bjayers@vintagefishingtackle.
com
*Vintage and collectable fishing
tackle.*

Baba Bears
Windmill Antiques Centre
1 Laureens Walk
Neville Road, Rottingdean
East Sussex
Tel. 01273 248859
www.bababears.co.uk
baba.bears@virgin.net
*Antique and vintage stuffed toys
and bears.*

Bacchus Antiques
(ref: Bacchus)
www.bacchus-antiques.com
corkscrews@bacchus-
antiques.com
*Corkscrews and wine related
items.*

David Baker Oriental Art
(ref: David Baker)
M10/M11
The Mews at Grays
1–7 Davies Mews
Mayfair, London W1Y 2LP
Tel: 020 7629 3788
Tel: 020 8446 0786
Fax: 020 7493 9344
djbming@aol.com
Oriental art.

Gregg Baker Oriental Art
(ref: Gregg Baker)
132 Kensington Church Street
London W8 4BH
Tel: 020 7221 3533
Fax: 020 7221 4410
www.japanesescreens.com
gregg@japanesescreens.com
*Japanese and Chinese works
of art.*

Barham Antiques
83 Portobello Road
London W11 2QB
Tel: 020 7727 3845
Fax: 020 7727 3845
www.barhamantiques.co.uk
info@barhamantiques.co.uk
*Victorian walnut and inlaid
continental furniture, writing
boxes, tea caddies, inkwells and
inkstands, glass épergnes, silver
plate, clocks and paintings.*

Les Barrett & Ian Towning
(ref: Barrett Towning)
Bourbon-Hanby Antiques
Centre
151 Sydney Street
London SW3 6NT
Tel: 020 7352 2106
Fax: 020 7565 0003
www.bourbonhanby.co.uk
l.barrett@btconnect.com
*English ceramics, silver, writing
equipment and antique jewellery.*

Don Bayney
The Mews at Grays
1–7 Davies Mews
Mayfair, London W1Y 2LP
Tel. 020 7491 7200
Fax: 020 8578 4701
Japanese works of art.

Beauty and the Beasts
(ref: Beauty)
Antiquarius Antique Centre
141 King's Road
London SW3 4PW
Tel: 020 7351 5149
Antique handbags.

John Beazor & Sons Ltd
(ref: John Beazor)
78–80 Regent Street
Cambridge CB2 1DP
Tel: 01223 355178
Fax: 01223 355183
www.johnbeazorantiques.co.uk
martin@ohnbeazorantiques.co.
uk
*Eighteenth and early nineteenth
century furniture, barometers,
and decorative items.*

Linda Bee
L18/19
The Mews at Grays
1–7 Davies Mews
Mayfair, London W1Y 2LP
Tel: 020 7629 5921
Fax: 020 7629 5921
*Vintage costume jewellery and
fashion accessories.*

Bellum Antiques
(ref: Bellum)
Bourbon-Hanby Antiques
Centre
151 Sydney Street
London SW3 6NT
Tel: 020 7352 2106
Fax: 020 7565 0003
www.bourbonhanby.co.uk
English ceramics.

Bentley & Skinner
8 New Bond Street
London W1
Tel: 020 7629 0651
Fax: 020 7491 1030
www.bentley-skinner.co.uk
info@bentley-skinner.co.uk
Fine antique jewels, Faberge and silver.

Bentleys
204 Walton Street
London SW3 2JL
Tel: 020 7584 7770
Fax: 020 7584 8182
www.bentleyslondon.com
shop@bentleyslondon.com
Antique luggage and gentlemen's accessories.

Beverley
30 Church Street
Marylebone
London NW8 8EP
Tel: 020 7262 1576
Fax: 020 7262 1576
English ceramics, glass, metal, wood, pottery, collectables and decorative items from 1850–1950.

David Black Oriental Carpets (ref: David Black)
96 Portland Road
London W11 4LN
Tel: 020 7727 2566
Fax: 020 7229 4599
www.davidblack.com
richard@david-black.com
Antique carpets and rugs.

N. Bloom & Son Ltd. (ref: N.Bloom)
12 Picadilly Arcade
London SWIY 6NH
Tel: 020 7629 5060
Fax: 020 7493 2528
www.nbloom.com
nbloom@nbloom.com
Antique jewellery.

John Bly
27 Bury Street
London SW1Y 6AL
Tel: 01442 823030
Fax: 01442 890237
www.johnbly.com
info@johnbly.com
Eighteenth and nineteenth century English furniture, works of art, objets d'art, paintings, silver, glass, porcelain and tapestries.

Joanna Booth
247 Kings Road, Chelsea
London SW3 5RL
Tel: 020 7352 8998
Fax: 020 7376 7350
www.joannabooth.co.uk
joanna@joannabooth.co.uk
Early sculpture, tapestries and Old Master drawings.

Patrick Boyd-Carpenter (ref: Boyd-Carpenter)
Unit 331–332
Grays Antique Market
58 Davies Street
Mayfair, London WIK 5LP
Tel: 020 7491 7623
Mob: 07874 917623
Patrickboyd_carpenter@hotmail.com
Wide range of antiques, sixteenth and eighteenth century sculpture, paintings and prints.

Elizabeth Bradwin (ref: E. Bradwin)
75 Portobello Road
London W11 2QB
Tel: 020 7221 1121
Fax: 020 8947 2629
www.elizabethbradwin.com
eliz@elizabethbradwin.com
Nineteenth and early twentieth Century Animal subjects.

Augustus Brandt
Middle Street
Petworth
West Sussex GU28 OBE
Tel: 01798 344722
Fax: 01798 344772
www.augustus-brandt-antiques.co.uk
brandt@easynet.co.uk
Scandinavian, French, Italian and English eighteenth century furniture, mirrors and lighting and unusual decorative furnishing and objects d'art.

Brandt Oriental Antiques (ref: Brandt)
First Floor
29 New Bond Street
London W1Y 9HD
Tel: 020 7499 8835
Fax: 020 7409 1882
Chinese and Japanese works of art and textiles.

Christine Bridge Antiques (ref: C. Bridge)
78 Castelnau
London SW13 9EX
Tel 020 8741 5501
Mob: 07831 126668
www.antiqueglass.co.uk
christine@bridge-antiques.com
Antique glass, fine eighteenth century collector's glass, Georgian drinking glasses, Nineteenth century Victorian coloured glass, decorative antiques, silkwork, and samples.

Lynda Brine Antiques
Assembly Antiques Centre
5–8 Saville Row
Bath BAI 2QP
Tel: 01225 448488
Fax: 01225 429661
lyndabrine@yahoo.co.uk
Scent bottles and bags.

Gerald Brodie
Great Grooms Antique Centre
Riverside House
Charnham Street
Hungerford
Berkshire RH17 OEP
Tel: 01488 682314
Fine furniture from the eighteenth century.

F G Bruschweiler Antiques Ltd
(ref: Bruschweiler)
41–67 Lower Lambricks
Rayliegh, Essex SS6 7EN
Tel: 01268 772761
www.fgbantiques.com
info@fgbantiques.com
Antique furniture and glasss.

Peter Bunting Antiques
(ref: Peter Bunting)
Harthill Hall
Alport, Bakewell
Derbyshire DE45 1LH
Tel: 01629 636203
Fax: 01629 636190
www.countryoak.co.uk
peterbunting@countryoak.co.uk
Early oak and country furniture, portraits and tapestries.

Butchoff Antiques
(ref: Butchoff)
154 Kensington Church Street
London W8 4BN
Tel: 020 7221 8174
Fax: 020 7792 8923
www.butchoff.com
enquiries@butchof.com
English and continental furniture, decorative items, porcelain and mirrors.

Cabinet
104 Brackenbury Road
London W6 0BD
Tel: 020 8563 2022
www.cabinetinteriors.co.uk
info@cabinetinteriors.co.uk
twentieth and twenty-first century furniture and decorative arts.

Castello Antiques
Bourbon-Hanby Antiques
Centre
151 Sydney Street
London SW3 6NT
Tel: 020 7352 2106
Fax: 020 7565 0003
www.bourbonhanby.co.uk
Specializing in chandeliers of all styles and sizes, and English furniture.

Vincenzo Caffarella
(ref: V. Caffarello)
Alfies Antique Market
13–25 Church Street
London NW8 8DT
Tel: 020 7724 3701
Fax: 020 7724 3701
www.vinca.co.uk
monica@vinca.net
Twentieth century decorative arts and antiques.

Jasmin Cameron
Antiquarias Antiques Market
135 Kings Road
London SW3 4PW
Tel: 020 7351 4154
Fax: 020 7351 4154
Drinking glasses and decanters 1750–1910, vintage fountain pens and writing materials.

C. A. R. S. of Brighton
(ref: C. A. R. S.)
4–4a Chapel Terrace Mews
Kemp Town
Brighton BN2 1HU
Tel: 01273 601960
Fax: 01273 601960
www.eurosuref.com/Cars
cars@kemptown-brighton.freeserve.co.uk
Classic automobilia and regalia specialists and children's pedal cars.

cbTOYS.co.uk
(ref:cbTOYS)
Sandringham
High Street Staithes
Cleveland TS13 5BQ
Tel: 01947 841375
www.cbtoys.co.uk
info@cbtoys.co.uk
Antique and vintage toys and games.

Rupert Cavendish Antiques
(ref: R. Cavendish)
610 Kings Road
London SW6 2DX
Tel: 020 7731 7041
Fax: 020 7731 8302
www.rupertcavendish.co.uk
info@rupertcavendish.co.uk
European twentieth century paintings.

Cekay
Stand 172
Grays Antique Market
58 Davies Street
Mayfair, London WIK 5LP
Tel: 020 7629 5130
Fax: 020 7730 3014
Glass, ceramics, collectables, memorabilia, silver, silver plate, silver collectables, walking sticks.

Jocelyn Chatterton
Grays Antique Market
58 Davies Street
Mayfair, London WIK 5LP
Tel: 020 7629 1971
Fax: 020 7629 1971
Mob: 07798 804853
www.cixi.demon.co.uk
Jocelyn@cizi.demon.co.uk
Antique Oriental textile specialist.

Cine Art Gallery
(ref: Cine Art)
759 Fulham Road
London SW6 5UU
Tel: 020 7384 0728
Fax: 020 7384 0727
www.cineartgallery.com
info@cineartgallery.com
Vintage film posters.

Christopher Clarke Antiques
(ref: Christopher Clarke)
The Fosseway
Stow on the Wold
Glos. GL54 1JS
Tel. 01451 830476
www.campaignfurniture.com
cclarkeantiques@aol.com
Antique campaign furniture.

Clarke and Denny Antiques
(Ref: Clarke & Denny)
Great Grooms Antiques
Centre
Billingshurst
West Sussex RH14 9EU
Tel: 01403 786202
Antique furniture.

Classic Fabrics with Robin Haydock
(Ref: Classic Fabrics)
L1/10 Antiquarius Antiques
Centre
131–141 Kings Road
Chelsea, London SW3 4PW
Tel: 020 7349 9110
Fax: 020 7349 9110
www.robinhaydock.com
robinhaydock@talk21.com
Antique textiles and fabrics.

John Clay Antiques
(ref: John Clay)
263 New Kings Road
London SW6 4RB
Tel: 020 7731 5677
Furniture, objets d'art, silver and clocks from the eighteenth and nineteenth century.

Cohen & Cohen
101b Kensington Church
Street
London W8 7LN
Tel: 020 7727 7677
Fax: 020 7229 9653
www.cohenandcohen.co.uk
info@cohenandcohen.co.uk
Chinese export porcelain works of art.

Garrick D. Coleman
(ref: G. Coleman)
75 Portobello Road
London W11 2QB
Tel: 020 7937 5524
Fax: 020 7937 5530
www.antiquechess.co.uk
106326.2635@compuserve.com
Antiques, fine chess sets and glass paperweights.

J. Collins & Son
(ref: J. Collins)
28 High Street, Bideford
Devon EX39 2AN
Tel: 01237 473103
Fax: 01237 475658
www.collinsantiques.co.uk
biggs@collinsantiques.co.uk
Georgian and Regency furniture, Victorian oil paintings and watercolours.

Sheila Cook Textiles
(ref: Sheila Cook)
14 Addison Avenuec
London W11 4QR
Tel: 020 7603 3003
Fax: 020 7603 4202
www.sheilacook.com
European costume, textiles from the mid-eighteenth century to the 1970s.

Stephen Cook Antiques Ltd
(ref: S. Cook)
58 High Street, Broadway
Worcestershire WR12 7DP
Tel. 01386 854716
www.scookantiques.com
stephen@scookantiques.com
Anitque oak,mahogany and walnut furniture from the seventeenth and eighteenth century.

Susie Cooper Ceramics Art Deco at Gallery 1930
(ref: Susie Cooper)
18 Church Street
Marylebone
London NW8 8EP
Tel: 020 7723 1555
Fax: 020 7735 8309
www.susiecooperceramics.com
gallery1930@aol.com
Twentieth century ceramics.

**Barry Cotton Antiques
(ref: Barry Cotton)**
116 Riverview Gardens
London SW13 8RA
Tel: 020 8563 9899
Mob: 07831 354324
www.barrycottonantiques..com
enquiries@barrycottonantiques.
com
*Fine quality eighteenth and
Nineteenth century period
furniture.By appointment only.*

**The Country Seat
(ref: Country Seat)**
Huntercome Manor Barnv
nr. Henley on Thames
Oxon RG9 5RY
Tel: 01491 6431349
Fax: 01491 641533
www.thecountryseat.com
ferry&clegg@thecountryseat.
com
*Twentieth century furniture,
ceramics and glass.*

**Crowthers of Syon Lodge
(ref: Crowthers)**
Architectural Antiques
for Interior and Exteriors
77/79 Pimlico Road
London SW1 W8PH
Tel: 020 7730 8668
*Architectural antiques and
sculpture.*

**Andrew Dando
(ref: Dando)**
4 Wood Street
Queen Square
Bath BA1 1JQ
Tel: 01225 422702
Fax: 01225 531017
www.andrewdando.co.uk
andrew@andrewdando.uk
English ceramics.

Deco World
Tel: 07745 388908
www.deco-world.com
sales@deco-world.com
*Art Deco funiture, lighting,
telephones and picture frames.*

**Richard Dennis Gallery
(ref: Richard Dennis)**
144 Kensington Church Street
London W8 4BH
Tel: 020 7727 2061
Fax: 020 7221 1283
*Antique and modern studio
ceramics.*

D. & B. Dickinson
The Antique Shop
22 & 22a New Bond Street
Bath, Somerset BA1 1BA
Tel: 01225 466502
www.dickinsonsilver.com
*Antique and twentieth century
jewellery, silver and silver-plated
articles.*

Dodo
Stand F73
Alfies Antique Market
13–25 Church Street
London NW8 8DT
Tel: 020 7706 1545
Fax: 020 7724 0999
*Posters, tins and advertising signs,
1890–1940.*

**The Dorking Desk Shop
(ref: Dorking Desk)**
J.G. Elias Antiques Ltd.
41 West Street, Dorking
Surrey RH4 1BU
Tel: 01306 883327 / 880535
www.desk.uk.com
dorkingdesk@aol.com
Antique desks.

**A. Douch Antiques
(ref: Douch)**
Stand L22-23
The Mews at Grays
1–7 Davies Mews
Mayfair, London W1Y 2LP
Tel. 020 7493 9413
Fax. 020 8947 5773
douch@grays.clara.net
*Eighteenth century jewellery,
silver flatware, fans and glass.*

Gavin Douglas
75 Portobello Road
London W11 2QB
Tel: 020 7221 1121
Fax: 01825 724418
Mob: 07860 680521
www.antique-clocks.co.uk
info@antique-clocks.co.uk
*Clocks, bronzes, sculpture
and porcelain.*

**Drummonds Architectural
Antiques Ltd
(ref: Drummonds)**
78 Royal Hospital Road
Chelsea, London SW3 4HN
Tel: 020 7376 4499
www.drummonds-arch.co.uk
*Restored original and new
bathrooms, reclaimed wood and
stone flooring, fireplaces, statues,
garden features, lighting, gates
and railings, doors and door
furniture, radiators, antique
furniture, windows and large
architectural features.*

**Duffield Antiques
(ref: H. Duffield)**
Unit S054, 2nd Floor
Alfies Antique Market
13–25 Church Street
London NW8 8DT
Tel: 020 7723 2548
*Early twentieth century
telephones.*

Ellison Fine Art
Claudia Hill
7 Ledborough Wood
Beaconsfield, Bucks HP9 2DJ.
Tel: 01494 678880
Portrait miniatures.

Eastern Interiors
Shop 8
Bourbon Hanby Antiques
Centre
151 Sydney Street
London SW3 6NT
Tel: 020 7795 2658
Fax: 020 7565 0003
Mob: 07803 701 778
www.eastern-interiors.co.uk
antiques@eastern-
interiors.co.uk
Oriental boxes and furniture.

**Eastern Satrapy Coin &
Antiquities
(ref: Eastern Satrapy)**
M20/21
The Mews at Grays
1–7 Davies Mews
Mayfair, London W1Y 2LP
Mob: 07956 59705
eastern.satrap@virgin.net
Coins and antiquities.

Evonne Antiques
301 Grays Antique Market
58 Davies Street
Mayfair, London WIK 5LP
Tel: 020 7491 0143
Fax: 020 8998 7790
evonne@grays.clara.net
*Silver collectables and objets
d'art.*

Flower Antiques
Great Grooms Antique Centre
Riverside House
Charnham Street
Hungerford
Berkshire RH17 OEP
Antique furniture.

**I. Franks Antique Silver
(ref: I. Franks)**
London Silver Vaults
Chancery House
Chancery Lance
London WC2A 1QS
Tel: 020 7242 4035
Fax:020 7242 4035
www.ifranks.com
info@ifranks.com
Antiques silver collectables.

**Vincent Freeman Antiques
(ref: Vincent Freeman)**
1 Camden Passage
Stand G 57, Islington
London N1 8EA
Tel: 020 7226 6178
Fax 020 7226 7231
Mob: 07889 966880
*Nineteenth century musical
boxes, furniture and ceramics.*

The Galleries Ltd.
157 Tower Bridge Road
London SE1 3LW
Tel: 020 7407 5371
Fax: 020 7403 0359
*Victorian, Edwardian,
reproduction furniture, babies'
chairs, telephone boxes, and
reproduction leather Chesterfields.*

**The French Glasshouse
(ref: French Glasshouse)**
P14–P16 Antiquarias
Antiques Market
135 Kings Road
London SW3 4PW
Tel: 020 7376 5394
Fax: 020 7376 5394
*Gallé and Daum glassware, and
Japanese works of art.*

The French Room
5 High Street, Petworth
West Sussex GU28 OAU
Tel: 01798 344454
Fax: 01403 269880
*French period furniture and
decorative wares.*

Freshfords
High Street, Freshford
Bath BA2 7WF
Tel: 01225 722111
Mob. 07720 838877
Fax: 01225 722991
www.freshfords.com
antiques@freshfords.com
*Fine antique furniture and works
of art, specialising in dining and
library furniture.*

**Richard Gardner Antiques
(ref: R. Gardner)**
Swan House, Market Square
PetworthGU28 0AH
Tel. 01798 343411
www.richardgardnerantiques.
co.uk
rg@richardgardnerantiques.co.
uk
*Fine period furniture and works
of art.*

Genie
Unit S057/8
Alfies Antique Market
13–15 Church Street
Marylebone
London N W8 8DT
Tel: 020 7723 2548
Fax: 020 7724 0999
www.alfies.com
*Silver-plated items, lamps,
shades, glassware, clocks, china,
wooden items, small furniture,
mirrors, and more.*

**Michael German Antiques
(ref: M. German)**
Dominic Strickland
38b Kensington Church Street
London W8 4BX
Tel: 020 7937 2771
Fax: 020 7937 8566
www.antiquecanes.com
www.antiqueweapons.com
*Antique walking canes, antique
arms and armour.*

Get Stuffed
105 Essex Road
London N1 2SL
Tel: 020 7226 1364
Fax: 020 7359 8253
www.thegetstuffed.co.uk
taxidermy@thegetstuffed.co.uk
*Taxidermy and natural history
artefacts.*

Getty Images
3 Jubilee Place
London SW3 3TD
Tel: 020 7376 4525
Fax: 0207 376 4524
www.getty-images.com
*Photographs from late
nineteenth to twentieth century.*

**The Girl Can't Help It
(ref: Girl Can't Help It)**
Sparkle Moore
Alfies Antique Market
13–25 Church St.
London NW8 8DT
Tel: 020 7724 8984
Fax 0208 809 3923
sparkle@sparklemoore.com
www.sparklemoore.com
*Collectables and memorabilia,
textiles, fabrics, vintage clothing,
jewellery, and accessories.*

Gabrielle de Giles
The Barn at Bilsington
Swanton Lane, Bilsington
Ashford, Kent TN25 7JR
Tel: 01233 720917
Fax: 01233 720156
www.gabrielledegiles.com
gabrielle@gabrielledegiles.com
*Antique and country furniture,
home interiors, designer for
curtains and screens.*

**Glenda Antique Dolls and
Collectables
(ref: Glenda Dolls)**
Grays Antique Market
58 Davies Street
Mayfair, London WIK 5LP
Tel: 020 8367 2441
Fax: 020 8366 5811
glenda@grays.clara.net
Dolls and collectables.

**John Goodison/Chris
Paraskeva Antiques
(Ref: Goodison Paraskeva)**
30 Camden Passage
London N1 8EA
Tel: 020 7226 2423
Mob: 07711 839177
goodison.paraskeva
@tinyworld.co.uk
*Antique lighting and boxes
and decorative items.*

**Gordon's Medals
(ref: Gordon's)**
Stand G14–16
The Mews at Grays
1–7 Davies Mews
Mayfair, London W1Y 2LP
Tel: 020 7495 0900
Fax: 020 7495 0115
Mob: 07971 840642
www.gordonsmedals.co.uk
sales@cocollector.co.uk
*Militaria, uniforms, headgear,
badges, medals and documents.*

**Goya Hartogs
(ref: Goya)**
Stand S002
Alfies Antique Market
13–25 Church Street
London NW8 8DT
Tel: 020 7723 6105
Fax: 020 7586 9031
Mob: 07787 714477
goya@alfies.clara.net
Twentieth century glass.

**Denzil Grant Antiques
(ref: Denzil Grant)**
Drinkston House
Drinkston
Bury St. Edmunds
Suffolk IP30 9TT
Tel: 01449 736576
Fax: 01449 737679
Mob: 07836 223312
denzil@denzilgrant.com
www.denzilgrant.com
*Eighteenth and nineteenth century
country and French provincial
furniture. Specialty French
farmhouse tables.*

**Anthony Green Antiques
(ref: Anthony Green)**
Unit 39
Bond Street Antiques Centre
124 New Bond Street
London W1S 1DX
Tel: 020 7409 2854
Fax: 020 7409 2854
www.anthonygreen.com
*Vintage wristwatches and antique
pocket watches.*

Henry Gregory
82 Portobello Road
London W11 2QD
Tel: 020 7792 9221
Fax: 020 7792 9221
*Silver-plate, silver, sporting goods
and decorative antiques.*

W. John Griffiths
Great Grooms Antique Centre
Riverside House
Charnham Street
Hungerford
Berkshire RH17 OEP
Antique furniture.

Guest & Gray
The Mews at Grays
1–7 Davies Mews
Mayfair, London W1Y 2LP
Tel: 020 7408 1252
Fax: 020 7499 1445
www.chinese-porcelain-art.com
info@chinese-porcelain-art.com
Oriental and European ceramics and works of art, and reference books.

Jean Guiller
Alfies Antiques Market
13–25 Church Street
London NW8 8DT
Luggage.

Gutlin Clocks and Antiques
(ref: Gutlin Clocks)
606 Kings Road
London SW6
Tel: 020 7384 2439
Fax: 020 7384 2439
www.gutlin.com
mark@gutlin.com
Longcase clocks, mantle clocks, furniture and lighting, all eighteenth and nineteenth century.

Hallidays
The Old College
Dorchester-on-Thames
Wallingford
Oxfordshire OX10 7HL
Tel: 01865 340028
www.hallidays.com
antiques@hallidays.com
Oak, walnut and mahogany Antique furniture from the seventeenth to the nineteenth century.

Adrian Harrington
Antiquarian Bookseller
(ref: A. Harrington)
Pierre Lombardini
64a Kensington Church Street
London W8 4DB
Tel: 020 7937 1465
Fax: 020 7368 0912
www.harringtonbooks.co.uk
rare@harringtonbooks.co.uk
Antiquarian, rare and secondhand books on literature, children's illustrated and travel.

Peter Harrington
Antiquarian Bookseller
100 Fulham Road
London SW3 6HS
Tel: 020 7591 02220
Fax: 020 7225 7054
www.peter-harrington-books.com
mail@peter-harrington-books.com
Antique books and maps.

Geoffrey Harris Lighting Ltd
(ref: G. Harris)
537 Battersea Park Road
London SW11 3BL
Tel: 020 7228 6101
Fax: 020 7228 6102
www.geoffreyharris.co.uk
lighting@geoffreyharris.co.uk
1950s and 1960s base lamps and modern lighting.

Harvey and Gore
41 Duke Street, St James's
London SW1Y 6DF
Tel: 020 27839 4033
Fax: 020 7839 3313
www.harveyandgore.co.uk
norman@harveyandgore.co.uk
Jewellery from the seventeenth century to the present.

Hatchwell Antiques
(ref: Hatchwell)
533 Kings Road
London SW10 0TZ
Tel: 020 7351 2344
Fax: 020 7351 3520
hatchwell@callnetuk.com
Period furniture, fine furniture and bronzes.

Haughey Antiques Ltd
(ref: Haughey Antiques)
20–30 Market Street
Kirkby Stephen
Cumbria CA17 4QW
Tel. 01768 371302
Fax. 01768 372423
www.haugheyantiques.co.uk
info@haugheyantiques.co.uk
Seventeenth, eighteenth and nineteenth century oak, walnut and mahogany furniture.

Hayward & Stott Ltd
(ref: Hayward & Stott)
P.O. Box 13828
Penicuik
Midlothian EH26 0YH
Scotland
Tel. 0131 445 3656
www.scottishsilver.com
info@scottishsilver.com
Antique Scottish silver.

**Hayman and Hayman
(ref: Hayman)**
Stand K3 Antiquarius Antique
Centre
135 Kings Road
London SW3 4PW
Tel: 020 7351 6568
Fax: 020 8741 0959
hayman@wahlgren.
demon.co.uk
*Art deco and brass photograph
frames, scent bottles and writing
equipment.*

Heritage Antiques
P.O. Box 2974, Brighton
East Sussex BN1 3QG
Tel: 01273 326850
www.heritage-antiques.com
ahd@heritage-antiques.com
*Dining room antiques and
accessories.*

**Heytesbury Antiques
(ref: Heytesbury)**
PO Box 222, Farnham
Surrey GU10 5HN
Tel: 01252 850893
Fax: 01252 850828
ingall@heytesbury.demon.co.uk
*Eighteenth and nineteenth century
English and Continental furniture
and decorative items.*

**Hickmet Fine Arts
(ref: Hickmet)**
75 Portobello Road
London W11 2QB
Tel: 01342 841508
Mob: 07050 123450
www.hickmet.com
david@hickmet.com
*Antique sculpture and works of
art.*

**Hill Farm Antiques
(ref: Hill Farm)**
at The Old Cinema
160 Chiswick High Road
London W4 IPR
Tel: 020 8994 2998 and 01488
638541/361
beesley@hillfarmantiques.
demon.co.uk
Antique furniture.

**Holland & Holland
(ref: Holland)**
31–33 Bruton Street
London W1J 6HH
Tel: 020 7499 4411
Fax: 020 7409 3283
www.hollandandholland.com
gunroom@hollandandholland.c
om
Antique guns.

Hope & Glory
131a Kensington Church
Street
(entrance in Peel Street)
London W8 7LP
Tel: 020 7727 8424
*Commemorative ceramics
including royal and political
subjects.*

**Paul Hopwell Antiques
(ref: Paul Hopwell)**
30 High Street
Westhaddon
Northamptonshire NN6 7AP
Tel: 01788 510636
Fax: 01788 510044
www.antiqueoak.co.uk
paulhopwell@antiqueoak.co.uk
*Seventeenth and eighteenth
century English oak furniture.*

House of Mirrors
597 Kings Road
London SW6 2EL
Tel. 020 7736 5885
www.houseofmirrors.co.uk
Info@houseofmirrors.co.uk
Antique mirrors

**Jonathan Horne
(ref: J. Horne)**
66c Kensington Church Street
London W8 4BY
Tel: 020 7221 5658
Fax: 020 7792 3090
www.jonathanhorne.co.uk
JH@jonathanhorne.co.uk
*Early English pottery, medieval
to 1820.*

**Dudley Hume Antiques
(ref: D. Hume)**
46 Upper North Street
Brighton, East Sussex BN13FH
Tel: 01273 323461
Mob: 07977 598627
www.dudleyhume.co.uk
dudley@dudleyhume.co.uk
*Antique fruniture, pottery and
porcelain, garden furniture,
lighting, decorative accessories,
mirrors and metalware.*

**Huxtable's Old Advertising
(ref: Huxtable's)**
Alfies Antique Market
13–25 Church Street
London NW8 8DT
Tel: 020 7724 2200
*Advertising, collectables, tins,
signs, bottles, commemoratives
and old packaging from late
Victorian.*

Iconastas
5 Piccadilly Arcade
London SW1Y 6NH
Tel: 020 7629 1433
Fax: 020 7408 2015
www.iconastas.co.uk
Russian fine art.

**In Vogue Antiques
(ref: In Vogue)**
Martin Lister
The Swan Antiques Centre
High Street
Tetsworth, Thame
Oxfordshire OX9 7AB
Tel: 01844 281777
Fax: 01844 281770
Mob: 0773 786103
www.theswan.co.uk
invogueantiques@aol.com
Antique furniture.

**Jessop Classic Photographica
(ref: Jessop Classic)**
67 Great Russell Street
London WC1
Tel: 020 7831 3640
Fax: 020 7831 3956
www.jessops.com/classic
classic@jessops.com
*Classic photographic equipment,
cameras and optical toys.*

Juke Box Services
15 Lion Road
Twickenham
Middlesex TW1 4JH
Tel: 020 8288 1700
www.jukeboxservices.co.uk
enquiries@jukeboxservices.co.uk
Juke boxes.

**Stephen Kalms Antiques
(ref: S. Kalms)**
The London Silver Vaults
53–64 Chancery Lane
London WC2A 1QS
Tel: 020 7430 1254
Fax: 020 7405 6206
www.kalmsantiques.com
stephen@skalms.freeserve.co.uk
*Victorian and Edwardian silver,
silver plate and decorative items.*

Shirley Knight
Great Grooms Antique Centre
Hungerford
Berkshire RG17 0RP
Tel: 01488 6823114
Fax: 01487 8233130
*Antiques and decorative
furnishings.*

**The Lacquer Chest
(ref: Lacquer Chest)**
75 Kensington Church Street
London W8 4BG
Tel: 020 7938 2070
Fax: 020 7376 0223
*Military chests, china, clocks,
samplers and lamps.*

Langfords
Vault 8–10
London Silver Vaults
53 Chancery Lane
London WC2A 1QS
Tel: 020 7242 5506
Fax: 020 7405 0431
www.langfords.com
vault@langfords.com
*Antique and modern silver
and silver plate.*

**Langfords Marine Antiques
(ref: Langfords Marine)**
The Plaza, 535 Kings Road
London SW10 0SZ
Tel: 020 7351 4881
Fax: 020 7352 0763
www.langfords.co.uk
info@langfords.co.uk
Nautical artefacts.

**LASSCO St Michael's
(ref: Lassco)**
Mark Street
London EC2A 4ER
Tel 020 7749 9944
www.lassco.co.uk
st.michaels@lassco.co.uk
Architectural antiques.

Metro Retro
1 White Conduit Street
Islington, London N1 9EL
Tel: 020 7278 4884
Fax: 020 7278 4884
www.metroretro.co.uk
sales@metroretro.co.uk
*Furniture and lighting of postwar
design.*

**Michael Laws Antiques Ltd.
(ref: Michael Laws)**
Bartlett Street Antiques
Centre
Bath BA1 2QZ
Tel: 01225 446322
Fax: 01249 658366
Antique fishing tackle and curios.

**Laurie Leigh Antiques
(ref: Laurie Leigh)**
36 High Street
Oxford OX1 4AN
Tel: 01865 244 197
Fax: 01865 244197
www.laurieleighantiques.com
laurie@laurieleighantiques.com
*Antique glass and antique
keyboard musical instruments.*

Liberty
210–220 Regent Street
London W1R 6AH
Tel: 020 7734 1234
Fax: 020 7578 9876
www.liberty.co.uk
*Twentieth century furniture,
jewellery, ceramics, clothes
and kitchenware.*

Libra Antiques
131D Kensington Church
Street
London W8 7PT
Tel: 020 7727 2990
English ceramics.

Libra Designs
34 Church Strret
London NW8 8EP
Tel: 020 7723 2688
Fax: 020 7286 8518
Mob: 07951 391624
www.libradeco.com
mariegottlieb@btconnect.com
Art Deco pieces.

Sanda Lipton Antique Silver
(ref: Sanda Lipton)
Third Floor, Elliott House
28a Devonshire Street
London W1G 6PS
Telephone: 020 7431 0866
www.antique-silver.com
info@antique-silver.com
Antique silver.

London Antique Gallery
(ref: London Antique)
66e Kensington Church Street
London W8 4BY
Tel: 020 7229 2934
Fax: 020 7229 2934
Meissen, Dresden, Worcester,
Minton, Shelley, Sèvrea, Lalique
and bisque dolls.

Lopburi Art and Antiques
(ref: Lopburi)
5 Saville Row
Bath BA1 2Q
Tel: 01225 322947
www.lopburi.co.uk
mail@lopburi.co.uk
Antique Chinese furniture,
statues and lacquerware, figures
from Thailand, Burma, and
Cambodia, seventeenth to
nineteenth century painted
wooden Tibetan cabinets, chests,
and tables.

Lotus House
Great Grooms Antique Centre
Riverside House
Charnham Street
Hungerford
Berkshire RH17 OEP
Tel: 01488 6823114
Oriental antiques.

Mac's Cameras
(ref: Mac's)
1A Beadon Road
London W6 0DA
Tel: 020 7846 9853
Antique camera equipment.

Joyce Macnaughton-Smith
(ref: Macnaughton-Smith)
The Swan Antique Centre
TetsworthThame
Oxfordshire OX9 7AB
Tel: 01884 281777
Antique furniture.

Manic AtticAntiques
(ref: Manic Attic)
Alfies Antique Market
13–25 Church St.
London NW8 8DT
Tel: 020 8566 2510
Collectables and memorabilia,
Art Deco, Art Noureau,
decorative arts, textiles, fabrics,
vintage clothing and accessories,
film memorabilia.

Mallett Antiques
(ref: Mallett)
Nick Wells
141 New Bond Street
London W1S 2BS
Tel. 0207 499 7411
www.mallettantiques.com
nwells@mallettantiques.com
English and Continental antique
furniture, fine art, and decorative
accessories.

Manser's Antiques
Coleham Head
Shrewsbury SY3 7BJ
Tel: 01743 351120
Fax: 01743 271047
www.theantiquedealers.com
mansers@theantiquedealers.
com
Antique furniture, silver, glass,
rugs and carpets and lighting.

The Map House
(ref: Map House)
54 Beauchamp Place
London SW3 1NY
Tel: 020 7584 8559
Fax: 020 7589 1041
www.themaphouse.com
maps@themaphouse.com
Antique maps from fifteenth to
nineteenth century, decorative
engravings from sixteenth to
nineteenth century.

Francesca Martire
F131/137
Alfies Antique Market
13–25 Church Street
London NW8 8DT
Tel: 020 7723 6066
www.alfies.com
Open Tues–Sat 10–6.
Twentieth century lighting, glass,
furniture and jewellery.

Mazar Antiques
(ref: Mazar)
Mr. Dadajan
Unit A29
The Mews at Grays
1–7 Davies Mews
Mayfair, London W1Y 2LP
Tel: 020 7491 3001
Mob: 07930 240692
Antiquities.

Pete McAskie Toys
Stand A12–13, Basement
The Mews at Grays
1–7 Davies Mews
Mayfair, London W1Y 2LP
Tel: 020 7629 2813
Fax: 020 7493 9344
Tin toys from 1895–1980, die-cast toys, robots, battery operated toys and lead figures.

Joachim & Betty Mendes
(ref; J & B Mendes)
Tel: 01273 203317
Tel: 07813 014065
www.mendes.co.uk
antiques@mendes.co.uk
Antique lace and textiles.

Metro Retro
1 White Conduit Street
London N1 9EL
Tel: 020 7278 4884
www.metroretro.co.uk
sales@metroretro.co.uk
Industrial-style and stripped steel furniture, lighting and home accessories.

Michael's Boxes
L15, The Mews at Grays
1–7 Davies Mews
Mayfair, London W1Y 2LP
London W1K 5AB
Tel: 020 7629 5716
Fax: 020 8930 8318
info@michaelboxes.com
www.michaelsboxes.com
Antique boxes.

Millers Antiques Ltd
(ref: Millers Antiques)
Netherbrook House
86 Christchurch
Ringwood
Hampshire, BH24 1DR
Tel: 01425 472062
www.millers-antiques.co.uk
mail@millers-antiques.co.uk
English and Continental Nineteenth century mahogany, walnut, fruitwood and pine furniture, treen, majolica, quimper, brass and copper and decorative accessories.

Nicholas Mitchell
The Swan Antique Centre
Tetsworth
Thame
Oxfordshire
OX9 7AB
Tel: 01844 281777
Fax: 01844 281770
www.theswan.co.uk
English and continental furniture.

Brian Moore Ceramics
(ref: Brian Moore)
Unit C12
South Moulton Lane
London W1K 5AB
Tel: 020 7491 7208
Mob: 07720 430288
Decorative, handpainted, and twentieth century pottery from Honiton, Poole, and Rye.

Walter Moores & Son Antriques
(ref: Walter Moores)
PO Box 5338 Market
Harborough LE16 7WG
Tel.:07071 226202
www.waltermoores.com
peter@waltermoores.com
Eighteenth and nineteenth cenury antique furniture.

Mora & Upham Antiques
(ref: Mora & Upham)
584 Kingís Road
London SW6 2DX
Tel: 020 7331 4444
Fax: 020 7736 0440
mora.upham@talk21.com
Fine English and continental furniture, mirrors and lighting.

Robert Morley and Company Limited
(ref: Robert Morley)
34 Engate Street, Lewisham
London SE13 7HA
Tel: 020 8318 5838
Fax: 020 8297 0720
www.morleypianos.com
Pianoforte and harpsichord workshop.

Maureen Morris
Tel: 01799 521338
Fax: 01799 522802
www.antiqueembroidery.com
mm@antiqueembroidery.com
Samplers and English embroidery from the early sixteenth century to the nineteenth century.

Mousa Antiques
(ref: Mousa)
B20
The Mews at Grays
1–7 Davies Mews
Mayfair, London W1Y 2LP
Tel: 020 7499 8273
Fax: 020 7629 2526
Bohemian glass specialists.

Tony Murland & Mike Hancock
(ref: T. Murland)
78 High St., Needham Market
Suffolk IP6 8AW
Tel. 01449 722992
www.antiquetools.co.uk
tony@antiquetools.co.uk
Antique tools.

**Music & Video Exchange
(ref: Music & Video)**
38 Notting Hill Gate
London W11 3HX
Tel: 020 7243 8574
www.mveshops.co.uk
*CDs, memorabilia, vinyl –
deletions and rarities.*

Music Room Antiques
School House
Bucks Green, Horsham
West Sussex RH12 3JP
Tel: 01403 822189
Fax: 01403 823089
enquiries@musicroomantiques.
com
*Antique musical instruments and
restoration.*

**Myriad Antiques
(ref: Myriad)**
131 Portland Road
London W11 4LW
Tel: 020 7229 1709
Fax: 020 7221 3882
*French painted furniture, garden
furniture, bamboo, Victorian and
Edwardian upholstered chairs,
mirrors and objets d'art.*

**Michael Norman Antiques
(ref: M. Norman)**
4 Frederick Place
Brighton, E. Sussex BN1 4EA
Tel: 01273 326712
www.michaelnorman.com
antiques@michaelnorman.com
*Eighteenth century and nineteenth
century furniture.*

**North West Eight
(ref: North West 8)**
36 Church Street
London NW8 8EP
Tel: 020 7723 9337
Decorative antiques.

Old Advertising
Keith Gretton
26 Honeywell Road
London SW11 6EG
Tel: 020 7228 0741
Advertising items.

**The Old Cinema
(ref: Old Cinema)**
160 Chiswick High Road
London W4 1PR
Tel: 020 8995 4166
Fax: 020 8995 4167
www.antiques-
uk.co.uk/theoldcinema/
theoldcinema@antiques-
uk.co.uk
*Antique furniture from the
eighteenth and nineteenth
century.*

**Old Cities Esstate Jwellery &
Antiques
(ref: Old Cities)**
Tel: 001 509 962 4653
www.oldcities.com
anchor@oldcities.com
Antique jewellery

Old School
130c Junction Road
Tufnell Park
London N19
Tel: 020 7272 5603
Gardens and interiors.

**Jacqueline Oosthuizen
Antiques
(ref: J. Oosthuizen)**
Georgian Village
Camden Passage
London N1 8DU
Tel: 020 7226 5393
*Staffordshire pottery and
jewellery.*

Pieter Oosthuizen
Georgian Village
Camden Passage
London N1 8DU
Tel: 01713 593322
*Dutch and European Art
Nouveau pottery and Boer War
memorabilia.*

Orient Expressions
Studio 3M1, Cooper House
2 Michael Road, London
Tel: 020 7610 9311
www.orientexpressions.com
enquiries@orientexpressions.
com
*Chinese and antique furniture
and accessories.*

**Oriental Rug Gallery Ltd
(ref: Oriental)**
Eton Group Office
115–116 High Street
Eton, Berkshire SL4 6AN
Tel: 01753 623000
www.orientalruggallery.com
rugs@orientalruggallery.com
*Antique carpets, rugs and
cushions.*

**Ormonde Gallery
(ref: Ormonde)**
156 Portobello Road
London W11 2EB
Tel: 020 7229 9800
*Oriental ceramics, furniture,
sculpture and works of art.*

**Anthony Outred Antiques
Ltd
(ref: Anthony Outred)**
46 Pimlico Road
London SW1 8LP
Tel: 020 7730 4782
Fax: 020 7730 5643 fax
www.outred.co.uk
antiques@outred.co.uk
English and continental antiques.

Pars Antiques
(ref: Pars)
A14–15 Grays in the Mews
1–7 Davies Mews
Mayfair, London W1Y 2LP
Tel: 020 7491 9889
Fax: 020 7493 9344
pars1000@aol.com
Antiquities.

Partridge Fine Arts Plc
(ref: Partridge)
144–146 New Bond St.
London W1S 2PF
Tel: 020 7629 0834
Fax: 020 7495 6266
www.partridgefinearts.com
enquiries@partridgefinearts.
com
English, French and continental
furniture and works of art,
pictures, silver, clocks,
barometers, lighting, porcelain
and textiles.

Pavlos S.Pavlou
(ref: Pavlos Pavlour)
Stand DL17
The Mews at Grays
1–7 Davies Mews
Mayfair, London W1Y 2LP
Tel: 020 7629 9449
Mob: 07986 558925
papavlou@hotmail.com
Ancient, medieval and modern
coins.

Pendulum of Mayfair
King House, 51 Maddox Street
London W1R 9LA
Tel: 020 7629 6606
Fax: 020 7629 6616
www.pendulumofmayfair.com
pedulumclocks@aol.com
Clocks: including longcase,
bracket and wall, and
Georgian period furniture.

Percy's Ltd
(ref: Percy's)
Vault 16
The London Silver Vaults
Chancery Lane
London WC2A 1QS
Tel: 020 7242 3618
Fax: 020 7831 6541
www.percysilver.com
sales@percys-silver.com
Eighteenth and nineteenth century
decorative silver and plate.

Period Pieces
Susan Shaw
Saffron Walden, Essex
Tel: 01799 599217
Fax: 01799 599802
susanshaw50@hotmail.com
Antique boxes.

Trevor Philip & Son Ltd
(ref: Trevor Philip)
75a Jermyn Street
London SW1Y 6NP
Tel: 020 7930 2954
Fax: 020 7321 0212
www.trevorphilip.com
globe@trevorphilip.com
Early scientific instruments, and
seventeenth to nineteenth century
globes.

Phoenix Oriental Art
(ref: Phoenix)
359 Upper Street
Islington, London N1 0PD
Tel: 020 7226 4474
Fax: 020 8521 8846
Tel: 07802 763518
www.trocadero.com/okinasan
info@phoenixorientalart.com
Japanese bronzes, Chinese
bronzes, works of art.

Pieces of Time
J. Wachsmann
26 South Molton Lane
London W1Y 2LP
Tel: 020 7629 2422/3272
www.antique-watch.com
info@antique-watch.com
Antique watches.

A. Piotrowski
Bourbon-Hanby Antiques
Centre
151 Sydney Street
London SW3 6NT
Tel: 020 7352 2106
Fax: 020 7565 0003
www.antiques-uk.co.uk/
bourbon-hanby
English ceramics.

Marko Pollo Antiques Limited
(ref: Marko Pollo)
The Mews at Grays
1–7 Davies Mews
Mayfair, London W1Y 2LP
Tel 020 7629 3788
Antiquities.

Poppets Antiques
(ref: Poppets)
Bourbon Hanby Antiques
Centre
151 Sydney Street
London SW3 6NT
Tel: 020 7352 2108
Nineteenth century furniture.

Christopher Preston Ltd
(ref: C. Preston)
The Furniture Cave
533 Kings Road
London SW10 0TZ
Tel: 020 7352 8587
Fax: 020 7376 3627
Antique furniture and decorative
objects.

Hilary Proctor
The Mews at Grays
1–7 Davies Mews
Mayfair, London W1Y 2LP
Tel: 020 7629 7034
Handbags, accessories, and
luggage from 1860–1960.

R. & S. Antiques
Bourbon Hanby Antiques
Centre
151 Sydney Street, Chelsea
London SW3 6NT
Tel: 020 73522106
Fax: 020 7565 0003

Iren Rakosa
Shop 8
Bourbon Hanby Antiques
Centre
151 Sydney Street
London SW3 6NT
Tel: 020 7795 2658
Fax: 020 7565 0003
Mob: 07803 701778
www.eastern-interiors.co.uk
antiques@eastern-
interiors.co.uk
Oriental boxes and furniture.

Rankin & Conn
608 Kings Rd
London SW6 2DX
Tel: 020 7384 1847
www.rankin-conn-
chinatrade.com
daphnerankin@aol.com
Chinese and Japanese export
porcelain wares from the
seventeenth to nineteenth century.

Rasoul Gallery
South Asian Antiques
K34/35
The Mews at Grays
1–7 Davies Mews
Mayfair, London W1Y 2LP
Tel: 020 7495 7422
Mob: 07956 809760
rasoulgallerya@hotmail.com
Islamic ceramics and antiquities.

Rayment Antiques
(ref: Rayment)
Derek & Tina
Orchard House
Barton, Nr. Farndon
Cheshire SY14 7HT
Tel. 01829 270529
www.antique-barometers.com
raymentantiques@aol.com
Antique barometers.

Red Roses
Sallie Ead and Sheryl
Perechocky
Admiral Vernon Antiques
Markets
141–149 Portobello Road
Shops 57&58
London W11
Tel: 01793 790607
Fax: 01793 790607
Sheryl Tel: 001 781 431 0147
High quality wearable vintage
fashion and accessories from the
nineteenth and twentieth
centuries.

Gordon Reece Gallery
(ref: Gordon Reece)
16 Clifford Street
London W1S 3RG
Tel: 020 7439 0007
Fax: 020 7437 5715
www.gordonreecegalleries.com
info@gordonreecegalleries.com
Flat woven rugs and nomadic
carpets, tribal sculpture,
jewellery, furniture, decorative
and non-European folk art
especially ethnic and oriental
ceramics.

The Reel Poster Gallery
(ref: Reel Poster)
72 Westbourne Grove
London W2 5SH
Tel: 020 7727 4488
Fax: 020 7727 4499
www.reelposter.com
info@reelposter.com
Original vintage film posters.

Revenance
David and Vincent
Stand S002
Alfies Antique Market,
12 Church Street
London NW8 8DT
Tel: 07971 410563
Mob: 07949 485316
Revenance@aol.com
Retro, kitsch, and twentieth
century design.

John Riordan
Griffin Fine Art and Antiques
20 Brdige Stret
Hungerford
Berkshire RH17 OEP
Tel: 07808 741823
www.bronzegriffin.com
johnriordan@griffinfineart.co.
uk
Bronzes and antique furniture.

Rookery Farm Antiques and Sara Lemkow
(ref: Rookery Farm)
Stands 20 and 43
Waterside Antqiues Centre
Ely, Cambridgeshire
Tel: 01325 661100
Mob: 07798 405635
www.antique-kitchenalia.co.uk
rachel.lemko@btinternet.com
Kitchenalia and pine furniture.

Ian Roper
L10/11
The Mews at Grays
1–7 Davies Mews
Mayfair, London W1Y 2LP
Tel: 020 7491 4009
ropewine@aol.com
Arms and armour,coins and reference books.

Rowan & Rowan
Shop 360
Grays Antique Market
58 Davies Street
Mayfair, London W1K 5LP
Tel. 020 7629 7234
www.rowanandrowan.com
rowanandrowan@aol.com
Eighteenth and nineteenth century English antique jewellery.

Michele Rowan
V38 Antiquarias Antiques Market
135 Kings Road
London SW3 4PW
Tel: 020 7352 8744
Fax: 020 7352 8744
Antique jewellery.

Samina Inc.
174 New Bond Street
London W1S 4RG
Tel. 020 7495 7482
Fax: 020 7495 7487
saminainc@hotmail.com
Fine antique jewellery.

Salem Antiques
Chacewater, Truo
Cornwall TR4 8NA
Tel: 01872 560347
Fax: 01872 561524
Mob: 07785 798260
www.salem-antiques.co.uk
sales@salem-antiques.co.uk
Furniture from the eighteenth century.

Christopher F. Seidler
(ref: C. Seidler)
G13
The Mews at Grays
1–7 Davies Mews
Mayfair, London W1Y 2LP
Tel: 020 7491 4009
Tel: 020 7629 2851
Medals, arms and militaria.

Serendipity
Rosemary Ford
The Tythings
Preston Court
nr Ledbury
Herefordshire HR8 2LL
Tel: 01531 6045
Fax: 01531 660421
Mob: 07711 245004
www.serendipity-antiques.co.uk
sales@serendipity-antiques.co.uk
Traditional antiques, fine English and continental furniture from the eighteenth and nineteenth century.

Bernard J. Shapero Rare Books
(ref: Bernard Shapero)
32 George Street
London W1S 2EA
Tel: 020 7493 0876
Fax: 020 7229 7860
www.shapero.com
rarebooks@shapero.com
Guide books from the sixteenth to the twentieth century, antiquarian and rare books, English and continental literature, specialising in travel, natural history and colour plate.

Sharif
27 Chepstow Corner
London W2 4XE
Tel: 020 7792 1861
Fax: 020 7792 1861
Oriental rugs, kilims, textiles and furniture.

Anthony Sharpe
F046/7
Alfies Antique Market
13 Church Street
London NW8 8DT
Tel: 020 7706 2118
Faz: 020 7706 2118
Mob: 07977 536806
as@vientos.demon.co.uk
Nineteenth century lighting, bronzes, screens and toile lighting.

Sheryl's Art Deco Emporium
(ref: Sheryl's)
Warlingham, Surrey
Tel: 01883 620767
Mob: 07970 493464
www.sheryls-artdeco.com
www.sheryls-artdeco.co.uk
info@sheryls-artdeco.com
Art Deco figurines, clocks, bronzes and jewellery

B. Silverman
4 Campden Street off
Kensington Chruch Street
London W8 7EP
Tel: 020 7985 0555
Fax: 020 7985 0056
www.silverman-london.com
silver@silverman-london.com
Seventeenth to nineteenth century
fine English silverware and silver
flatware.

Sinai Antiques
(ref: Sinai)
219–221 Kensington Church
Street
London W8 7LX
Tel: 020 7229 6190
Antiques and works of art.

Gloria Sinclair
Stand F023
Alfies Antique Market
13–25 Church Street
London NW8 8DT
Tel: 020 7724 7118
Fax: 020 7224 0999
sinclair@alfires.clara.net
European ceramics.

Sleeping Beauty
212 Church Road
Hove, West Sussex BN3 2DJ
Tel: 01273 205115
www.antiquebeds.com
george@antiquebeds.com
Antique beds.

Julian Smith Antiques
(ref: Julian Smith)
The Lodge
Wheelwrights Close
Sixpenny Handley
Dorset SP5 5SA
Tel: 01725 552820
Mob: 07879 624734
Luggage and gentlemen's
accessories.

Ruth Macklin Smith
(ref: R. Macklin Smith)
Great Grooms Antique Centre
Riverside House
Charnham Street
Hungerford
Berkshire RH17 OEP
Tel: 01685 430350
Fax: 07889 282004
Antique furniture.By
appointment only.

Somervale Antiques
(ref: Somervale)
6 Radstock Road
Midsomer Norton
Bath BA3 2AJ
Tel: 01761 4122686
Mob: 07885 088022
www.somervaleantiquesglass.
co.uk
ronthomas@somervaleantiques
glass.co.uk
Specialist in eighteenth and early
nineteenth century English,
Bristol and Nailsea glass. Shop
open by appt. only, 24-hour
telephone service.

Sporting Times
Unit C 2A
Fitzaarland Road, Arundel
West Sussex BN18 9JS
Tel: 01903 885656
Mob: 07976 9422059
MartinQ.Sportingtimes.
isnet.co.uk
Antique sporting items.

Alan & Kathy Stacey
(ref: A. & K. Stacey)
Tel.(UK): 01963 441333
Tel (USA): 905 529 3613
www.antiqueboxes.uk.com
info@antiqueboxes.uk.com
Tea caddies and fine boxes.

Steinway & Sons
(ref: Steinway)
44 Marylebone Lane
London W1M 6EN
Tel: 020 7487 3391
Fax: 020 7935 0466
www.steinway.com
New and refurbished pianos.

Jane Stewart
L25 Grays in Davies Mews
London W1K 5AB
Tel/Fax: 020 7355 3333
Early seventeenth to nineteenth
century pewter, oak and writing
slopes.

Stockspring Antiques
(ref: Stockspring)
114 Kensington Church Street
London W8 4BH
Tel: 020 7727 7995
Fax: 020 7727 7995
www.antique-porcelain.co.uk
stockspring@antique-
porcelain.co.uk
Antique English and continental
porcelain.

June & Tony Stone
(ref: J. & T. Stone)
5 Burlington Arcade
Bond Street
London W1J 0PD
Tel. 020 7493 9495
www.boxes.co.uk
ba@boxes.co.uk
Fine antique boxes.

Sultani Antiques Ltd
(ref: Sultani)
Unit K28/9
The Mews at Grays
1–7 Davies Mews
Mayfair, London W1Y 2LP
Tel: 020 7491 3842
Mob: 07956 814541
sultani@grays.clara.net
Islamic ceramics and antiquities.

The Swan at Tetsworth
(ref: The Swan)
High Street, Tetsworth Thame
Oxfordshire OX9 7AB
Tel: 01844 281777
Fax: 01844 281770
www.theswan.co.uk
Seventy dealers in historic
Elizabethan coaching inn.

Swans of Oakham
(ref: Swans)
17 Mill Street,Oakham
Rutland LE15 6EA
Tel: 01572 724364
Mob: 0860 304084
www.swansofoakham.co.uk
swans@swansofoakham.co.uk
Fine antque beds.

Themes & Variations
(ref: Themes)
231 Westbourne Grove
London W11 2SE
Tel: 020 7727 5531
Fax: 020 7221 6378
www.themesandvariations.com
go@themesandvariations.com
Post-war and contemporary
design.

Through the Looking Glass
(ref: Looking Glass)
563 Kings Road
London SW6 2EB
Tel: 020 7736 7799
Fax: 020 7602 3678
Nineteenth century mirrors.

Through the Looking Glass
(ref: Looking Glass)
137 Kensington Church Street
London W8 7LP
Tel: 020 7221 4026
Fax: 020 7602 3678
Nineteenth century mirrors.

Toycellars
Colin Willmington
Tel: 01303 252430
Mob: 07712 277605
www.toycellars.com
toycellars@waitrose.com
Meccano, dinky, corgi, railway,
tinplate, and other toys.

Teresa Clayton
(ref: Trio)
L14 Grays Mews Market
Moulton Lane
London W1K 5AB
Tel: 020 7493 2736
Fax: 020 7493 9344
trio@grays.clara.net
Perfume bottles and Bohemian
glass.

Turn on Lighting
116–118 Islington High Street
Camden Passage
London N1 8EG
Tel: 020 7359 7616
Fax: 020 7359 7616
Antique lighting specialists.

Vale Antiques
Great Grooms Antique Centre
Riverside House
Charnham Street
Hungerford
Berkshire RH17 OEP
Tel: 01488 682314
Antique furniture.

Valeri
G10-11
Grays in the Mews
1–7 Davies Mews
London W1Y 2LP
Mob. 07919594622
Antiquities.

Vanbrugh West Antiques Ltd.
(ref: Vanbrugh)
73 Portobello Road
London W11
Tel: 020 7243 6677
Mob: 08801 650780
fergusdowney@aol.com
Nineteenth century ceramics and
decorative items.

James Vanstone
Unit 66 Admiral Vernan
Arcade
147 Portobello Road
London W11 2QB
Tel: 020 8541 4707
Mob: 07050 153018
Specialist in coins and medals.

Ventesimo
Paolo Bonino
Unit G121-2
Alfies Antique Market
13–25 Church Street
London NW8 8DT
Tel: 020 7723 1513
Mob: 07767 498766
Twentieth century ceramics, glass
and lighting.

June Victor
Alfies Antique Market
13–25 Church Street
London NW8 8DT
Tel: 020 7723 6105
Fax: 020 7724 0999
Mob: 07740 704723
Textiles, fabrics, and vintage
clothing and accessories, scent
bottles and embroidery.

Vintage and Rare Guitars
68 Kenway Rd
Tel: 020 7370 7834/6828
Fax: 020 7240 7500
Vintage and rare guitars.

Michael Wakelin & Helen Linfield
(ref: Wakelin & Linfield)
PO Box 48, Billingshurst
West Sussex RH14 0YZ
Tel: 01403 700004
Fax: 01403 701173
wakelin_linfields@lineone.net
Metalware, pottery, treen, lighting, textiles and mirrors.

Westland & Company
(ref: Westland & Co.)
St. Michael's Church
The Clergy House
Mark Street
London EC2A 4ER
Tel: 020 7739 8094
Fax: 020 7729 3620
www.westland.co.uk
westland@westland.co.uk
Period fireplaces, architectural elements and panelling.

Jessie Western
(ref: J. Western)
82B Portobello Road
London W112QD
Tel: 020 7229 2944
www.jessiewestern.com
Native American jewellery and accessories.

Wilde Ones
283 Kings Road, Chelsea
London SW3 5EW
Tel: 020 7352 9531
Fax: 020 7349 0828
www.wildeones.com
info@wildeones.com
Jewellery.

Margaret Williamson
(ref: M. Williamson)
Grays in the Mews
58 Davies St.
London W1Y 2LP
Tel 020 7629 7034
Vintage modes.

O. F. Wilson Ltd
(ref: O. F. Wilson)
3–6 Queen's Elm Parade
Old Church Street
London SW3 6EJ
Tel: 020 7352 9554
Fax: 020 7351 0765
ofw@email.msn.com
Continental furniture, French chimney pieces, English painted decorative furniture and mirrors.

Wimpole Antiques
Lynn Lindsay
Stand 349
Grays Antique Market
58 Davies Street
Mayfair, London W1K 5LP
Tel: 020 7499 2889
wimpoleantiques@compuserve.com
Antique jewellery.

John Wiseman Antiques
(ref: Wiseman)
312 Lillie Road
Fulham, London 3W6 7PS
Tel. 020 7385 3519
Fax 020 7385 1989
Architectural and garden antiques.

Yacobs Gallery
(ref: Yacobs)
Grays Mews Antiques Market
1–7 Davies Mews
London W1Y 2LP
Tel: 020 7629 7034
Fax: 020 7493 9344
yacob@dbk2.fsnet.co.uk
Islamic art.

Younger Antiques
(ref: Younger)
Bourbon Hanby Antiques Centre
151 Sydney Street
SW3 6NT
Tel: 020 7352 2106
Antique furniture.

There follows our selection of the best antiques centres and markets in the country. These present the best of both worlds, with several dealers showing their particular specialities at the fair prices we expect from the reputable retailer.

BEDFORDSHIRE, BUCKINGHAMSHIRE, HERTFORDSHIRE

Ampthill Antiques Emporium
3Bedford Street,Ampthill MK45 2NB
Tel: 01525 402131   Fax: 01582 737527
Dealers:: 40

Antiques at Wendover Antiques Centre
The Old Post Office, 25 High Street,
Wendover HP22 6DU
Tel: 01296 625335   Fax: 01296 620401
Dealers: 30

Barkham Antiques Centre
Barkham Street, Wokingham RG40 4PJ
Tel: 0118 9761 355   Fax: 0118 9764 355

Buck House Antiques Centre
47 Wycombe End, Old Town,
Beaconsfield HP9 1LZ
Tel: 01494 670714   Fax: 01494 670714

Woburn Abbey Antiques Centre
Woburn Abbey, Woburn MK17 9WA
Tel: 01992 504454   Fax: 01992 504454
Dealers: 50

BRISTOL, BATH, SOMERSET

Bartlett Street Antiques Centre
5–10 Bartlett Street, Bath BA1 2QZ
Tel: 01225 469998   Fax: 01225 444146
Dealers: 50–60

Whiteladies Antiques & Collectables
49c Whiteladies Road
Clifton, Bristol BS8 2LS
Tel: 0117 973 5766
Dealers: 25

CAMBRIDGESHIRE

Fitzwilliam Antique Centre
20–22 Fitzwilliam Street, Peterborough PE1 2RX
Tel: 01733 566346
Dealers: 20

Gwydir Street Antiques Centre
Untis 1&2 Dales Brewery, Gwydir Street
Cambridge CB1 2LJ
Tel: 01223 356391
Dealers: 10

The Hive Antiques Market
Unit 3, Dales Brewery, Gwydir Street,
Cambridge CB1 2LG
Tel: 01223 300269
Dealers: 10

Huntingdon Trading Post
1 St Mary's Street, Huntingdon PE29 3PE
Tel: 0140 450998   Fax: 01480 431142
Dealers: 35

CHESHIRE AND STRAFFORDSHIRE

Antique Furniture Warehouse
Unit 3–4 , Royal Oak Buildings, Cooper Street,
Stockport, Cheshire SK1 3QJ
Tel: 0161 429 8590   Fax: 0161 480 5375

Leek Antiques Centre (Barclay House)
4–6 Brook Street, Leek ST13 5JE13
Tel: 01538 398475   Mob: 07721 413095
Dealers: 78

CORNWALL

Chapel Street Arcades
61–62 Chapel Street, Penzance TR18 4AE
Tel: 01736 363267
Dealers: 20–25

Waterfront Antiques Market
4 Quay Street, Falmouth TR11 3HH
Tel: 01326 311491
Dealers: 20

THE COTSWOLDS

TheAntique Centre
51A Long Street, Tetbury GL8 8AA
Tel: 01666 505083
Dealers: 10

CUMBRIA AND LANCASHIRE

Carlisle Antique Centre
Cecil Hall, 40A Cecil Street,
Carlisle CA1 1NT
Tel: 01228 536910   Fax: 01228 536 910
Dealers: 6

Cockermouth Antiques & Crafts Market
The Old Courthouse, Main Street,
Cockermouth CA13 9LUJ
Tel: 01900 824346
Dealers: 4

DERBYSHIRE AND NOTTINGHAMSHIRE

Alfreton Antique Centre
11 King Street, Alfreton DE55 7AF
Tel: 01773 520781   Mob: 07970 786968
Dealers: 35

Castlegate Antique Centre
55 Castle Gate, Newark NG24 1BE
Tel: 01636 700076   Fax: 01636 700144
Dealers: 9

Chappells Antiques Centre, Bakewell
King Street, Bakewell DE45 1DZ
Tel: 01629 812496   Fax: 01629 814 531
Dealers: 30

Memory Lane Antiques Centre
Nottingham Road, Ripley DE5 3AS
Tel: 01773 570184   Mob: 07703 115626
Dealers: 40

Newark Antiques Warehouse Ltd.
Kelham Road, Newark NG24 1BX
Tel: 01636 674869   Fax: 01636 612933
Dealers: 80

Top Hat Antiques Centre
62 Derby Road, Nottingham NG1 5DF
Tel: 0115 9419 143

DEVONSHIRE
Abingdon House
136 High Street, Honiton EX14 1JP
Tel: 01404 42108
Dealers: 20

Barbican Antique Centre
82–84 Vauxhall Street, Plymouth PL4 0EX
Tel: 01752 201752   Fax: 020 8546 1618
Dealers: 60

Exeter's Antiques Centre on the Quay
The Quay, Exeter EX2 4AN
Tel: 01392 493501
Dealers: 21

The Globe Antiques & Art Centre
165 High Street, Honiton EX14 1LQ
Tel: 01404 549372   Fax: 01404 41465
Dealers:25

Honiton Antique Centre
136 High Street, Honiton EX14 8JP
Tel: 01404 42108
Dealers:20

Sidmouth Antiques Centre
Devonshire House
All Saints Road, Sidmouth EX10 8ES
Tel: 01395 512588   Mob 07714 376918
Dealers: 10

DORSET
Bridport Antique Centre
5 West Allington, Bridport DT6 5BJ
Tel: 01308 425885

Colliton Antique Centre
3a Colliton Street, Dorchester DT1 1XH
Tel: 01305 269398   Tel: 01305 260115
Dealers: 6

De Danann Antiques
27 London Road, Dorchester DT1 1NF
Tel: 01305 250066   Fax: 01305 250113
Dealers: 20

Emporium Antiques Centre
908 Christchurch Road, Boscombe BH7 6DL
Tel: 01202 422380   Fax: 01202 433348
Dealers: 10

ESSEX
Baddow Antique Centre
The Bringey, Church Street, Great Baddow
Chelmsford CM2 7JW
Tel: 01245 476159
Dealers: 20

Finchingfield Antiques Centre
The Green, Finchingfield, Braintree CM7 4JX
Tel: 01371 810258   Fax: 01371 810258
Dealers: 45

Harwich International Antique Centre
19 King's Quay St., Harwich, CO12 3ER
Tel: 01255 554719   Fax: 01255 554719
Dealers: 45

Saffron Walden Antiques Centre
1 Market Row, Saffron Walden CB10 1HA
Tel: 01799 524534   Fax: 01799 524703
Dealers: 40

HAMPSHIRE AND ISLE OF WIGHT
The Antique Centre,
Britannia Road, Southampton SO14 0QL
Tel: 0238 0221 022
Dealers: 40

Clocktower Antiques Centre
1 Manor Farm Road, Bitterne Park Triangle
Southampton SO14 0QL
Tel: 0238 055 4303
Dealers: 20

Dolphin Quay Antique Centre
Queen Street, Emsworth PO10 7BU
Tel: 01243 379994   Fax: 01243 379251
Dealers: 30

Eversley Antique Centre Ltd
Church Lane, Eversley, RG27 0PX
Tel: 0118 932 8518
Dealers: 11

Lyndhurst Antique Centre
19–21 High Street, Lyndhurst SO43 7BB
Tel: 0238 0284 000
Dealers: 50

Ventnor Antiques Centre
66 High Street, Ventnor PO38 1LU
Tel: 01983 855302   Fax: 01983 855325
Dealers: 4

GLOUCESTERSHIRE
Circenster Arcade
25 Market Place, Cirenster GL7 2NX
Tel 01285 644214
Dealers: 60

HEREFORD AND WORCESTERSHIRE
The Antique Centre
5–8 Lion Street, Kidderminster DY10 1PT
Tel: 01562 740389 Fax: 01562 740389
Dealers: 12

Antiques & Collectors Market
Public Hall, Bromley Road
Beckenham BR3 5JE
Tel: 020 8660 1369
Dealers: 12

Hereford Antique Centre
128 Widemarsh Street, Hereford HR4 9HN
Tel: 01432 266242
Dealers: 35

Leominster Antique Centre
34 Broad Street, Leominster HR6 8BS
Tel: 01568 615505
Dealers: 35

Leominster Antique Market
14 Broad Street, Leominster HR6 8BS
Tel: 01568 612189
Dealers: 16

Linden House Antiques
1 Drapers Lane, Leominster HR6 8ND
Tel: 01568 620350 Mob: 07790 671722
Dealers: 10

Malvern Link Antiques Centre
154 Worcester Road, MalvernWR14 1AA
Tel: 01684 575750
Dealers: 10

Ross on Wye Antique Gallery
Gloucester Road, Ross-on-Wye,
Herefordshire HR9 5BU
Tel: 01989 762290 Fax: 01989 762291
Dealers: 50

Worcester Antiques Centre
Unit 15 Reindeer Court, Mealcheapen Street
Worcester WR1 4DF
Tel: 01905 610680 Fax: 01905 610681
Dealers: 45

KENT
Antiques at Cranbrook
19 High Street, Cranbrook TN17 3EE
Tel: 01580 712173 Mob: 07885 690913
Dealers: 10

Coach House Antique Centre
2a Duck Lane, Northgate, Canterbury CT1 2AE
Tel: 01227 463117
Dealers: 10

Copperfield Antique & Craft Centre
Unit 4, Copperfield's Walkway, Spital Street,
Dartford, Kent DA1 2DE
Tel: 01322 281445
Dealer: 35

Emporium Antiques, Collectables & Crafts
138–140 Upper Wickham Lane,
Welling DA16 3DP
Tel: 020 8855 8308   Fax: 020 8855 8308
Dealers: 30

Memories
128 High Street, Rochester ME1 1JT
Tel: 01634 811044
Dealers: 12

Village Antique Centre
4 High Street, Brasted, Kent TN16 1RF
Tel: 01959 564545
Dealers: 15

LEICESTERSHIRE, RUTLAND AND NORTHAMPTONESHIRE
Finedon Antiques Ltd.
11–25 Bell Hill, Finedon, Wellingborough
Tel: 01933 681260 Fax: 01933 682210
Dealers: 35

The Village Market Antiques
62 High Street, Weedon NN7 4QD
Tel: 01327 342015
Dealers: 40

LINCOLNSHIRE
Great Expectations
37–43 East Street, Horncastle LN9 6AZ
Tel: 01507 524202 Fax: 01507 524202
Dealers: 60

Guardroom Antiques
RAF Station Henswell,Gainsborough
Tel: 01427 667113
Dealers: 50

Henswell Antiques Centre
Caenby Corner Estate, Henswell Cliff
Gainsborough DN21 5TL
Tel: 01427 668389 Fax: 01427 668935
Dealers:270

Market Deeping Antiquesw & Craft Centre
50–56 High Street, Market Deeping PE6 8EB
Tel: 01778 380238
Dealers: 70

Notions Antiques Centre
1–2a Market Place, Grantham NG31 6LQ
Tel: 01476 563603 Mob: 07974 683120
Dealers: 70

St. Martin's Antique Centre
23a High Street, St Martin's, Stamford PE9 2LF
Tel: 01789 481158 Fax: 01780 481588
Dealers: 58

LONDON
Alfie's Antique Market
13–25 Church Street NW8 8DT
Tel: 020 7723 6066   Fax: 020 7724 0999
Dealers: 200

Antiquarius
131–41 King's Road SW3 4PW
Tel: 020 7351 5353   Fax: 020 7351 5350
Dealers: 100

Bermondsey
corner of Long Lane & Bermondsey Street
Bermondsey Square SE1 3UN
Tel: 020 7969 1500   Fax: 020 7969 1639
Dealers: 400

The Bond Street Antques Centre
124 New Bond Street W1Y 9AE
Tel 020 7493 1854   Fax: 020 7351 5350
Dealers: 35

Bourbon Hanby Antiques Centre
151 Sydney Street SW3 6NT
Tel: 020 7352 2106   Fax: 020 7565 003
Dealers: 30

Camden Passage
12 Camden Passage,N1 8ED
Tel: 020 7359 0190   Fax: 020 7704 2095
Dealers: 300

Charing Cross Markets
1 Embankment Place WC2N 6NN
Tel: 01483 281771   Fax: 01483 281771
Dealers: 35

Grays Antique Markets and Mews
58 Davis Street and 1–7 Davis Mews WIY 2LP
Tel: 020 7629 7034   Fax: 020 7629 3279
Dearlers: 300

Hampstead Antique and Craft Emporium
12 Heath Street NW3 6TE
Tel: 020 7794 3297   Fax: 020 7794 4620
Dealers: 20

Rogers Antiques Gallery
65 Portobello Road W11 2QB
Tel: 020 7969 1500   Fax: 020 7969 1639
Dealers: 65

NORFOLK
Fakenham Antique Centre,
The Old Congregational Church
14 Norwich Road, Fakenham NR21 8AZ
Tel: 01328 862941
Dealers: 20

NORTHUMBERLAND AND DURHAM
The **Village Market Antiques**
62 High Street, Weedon NN7 4QD
Tel: 01327 342015
Dealers: 40

OXFORDSHIRE
Antiques at the George
104 High Street, Burford OX18 4QJ
Tel: 01993 823319
Dealers: 20

Antiques on High Ltd
85 High Street, Oxford OX1 4BG
Tel: 01865 251075   Fax: 0129 665 5580
Dealers: 38

Country Markets Antiques and Collectables
Wyevale Garden Centre, Newbury Road,
Chilton, nr. Didcot OX11 0QN
Tel: 01235 835125   Fax: 01235 833068
Dealers: 35

Station Mill Antique Centre
Station Yard Industrial Estate
Chipping Norton OX7 5HX
Tel: 01608 644563   Fax: 01327 860952
Dealers: 70

The Swan at Tetsworth
High Street, Tetsworth OX9 7AB,
Tel: 01844 281777   Fax: 01844 281770
Dealers:80

SHROPSHIRE
Bridgnorth Antiques Centre
Whitburn Street, Bridgnorth WV16 4QP
Tel: 01746 768055
Dealers: 19

Old Mill Antique Centre
48 Mill Street, Bridgnorth WV15 5AG
Tel: 01746 768778   Fax: 01746 768944
Dealers: 90

Princess Antique Centre
14a The Square, Shrewsbury SY1 1LH
Tel: 01743 343701
Dealers: 100

Shrewsbury Antique Centre
15 Princess House, The Square
Shrewsbury SY1 1J7
Tel: 01743 247704
Dealers: 70

Shrewsbury Antique Market
Frankwell Quay Warehouse, Frankwell
Shrewsbury SY3 8LG
Tel: 01743 350916
Dealers: 45

Stretton Antiques Market
36 Sandford Avenue, Church Stretton SY6 6BH
Tel: 01694 723718   Fax: 01694 723718
Dealers: 60

K.W. Swift
56 Mill Street, Ludlow SY8 1BB
Tel: 01584 878571   Fax: 01746 714407
Dealers: 20

STAFFORDSHIRE
Lion Antique Centre
8 Market Place, Uttoxeter ST14 8HP
Tel: 01889 567717   Fax: 01889 567717
Dealers: 28

Rugeley Antique Centre
161 Main Road
Brereton, Rugeley WS15 1DX
Tel: 01889 577166
Dealers: 35

SUFFOLK
Church Street Centre
6e Church Street, Woodbridge IP12 1DH
Tel: 01394 388887
Dealers: 10

Clare Antique Warehouse
The Mill, Malting Lne, Clare CO10 8NW
Tel: 01787 278449   Fax: 01787 278449
Dealers: 40

Woodbridge Gallery
23 Market Hill, Woodbridge IP12 4OX
Tel: 01394 386500   Fax: 01394 386500
Dealers: 35

SURREY
The Antiques Warehouse
Badshot Farm, St George's Road,
Runfold GU9 9HY
Tel: 01252 317590   Fax: 01252 879751
Dealers: 40

Bourne Mill Antiques
39–43 Guildford Road, Farnham GU9 9PY
Tel: 01252 716663
Dealers: 65–85

The Hampton Court Emporium
52–54 Bridge Road, East Molesey KT8 9HA
Tel: 020 8941 8876
Dealers: 42

Honeypot Antiques
Milford Road, Elstead, Godalming GU8 6HR
Tel: 01252 703614   Fax: 01252 733909
Dealers: 25

The Kingston Antiques Market
29–31 London Road, Kingston-upon-Thames
KT2 6ND
Tel: 020 8549 2004   Fax: 020 8549 3839
Dealers: 80

The Packhouse Antiques Centre
Tongham Road, Runfold, Farnham GU10 1PQ
Tel 01252 781010   Fax: 01252 783876
Dealers: 109

Talbot Walk Antique Centre
Talbot Hotel, High Street, Ripley GU23 6BB
Tel: 01483 211724   Fax: 01483 211724
Dealers: 40

Victoria and Edward Antique Centre
61 West Street, Dorking RH4 1BS
Tel: 01306 889645
Dealers: 26

SUSSEX
Eastbourne Antiques Market
80 Seaside, Eastbourne BN22 7QP
Tel: 01323 642233
Dealers: 25

Great Grooms Antique Centre
Great Grooms, Parbrook, Billinghurst RH14 9EU
Tel: 01403 786202   Fax: 01403 786224

Lewes Antique Centre
20 Cliffe High Street, Lewes BN7 2AH
Tel: 01273 472173   Fax: 01273 476148
Dealers: 60

The Old Town Antiques Centre
52 Ocklynge Road, Eastbourne BN21 1PR
Tel: 01323 416016
Dealers: 16

Olinda House Antiques
South Street, Rotherfield, Crowborough,
East Sussex TN6 3LL,
Tel: 01892 852609

Snooper's Paradise
7–8 Kensington Gardens, Brighton BN1 4AL
Tel: 01273 602558   Fax: 01273 686611
Dealers: 70–80

Spongs Antique Centre
102 High Street, Lindfield RH16 2HS
Tel: 01444 487566
Dealers: 34

Stable Antiques
46 West Street, Storrington RH20 4EE
Tel: 01903 740555   Fax: 01903 740441
Dealers: 35

WARWICKSHIRE
Barn Antique Centre
Station Road, Long Marston
Stratford-upon-Avon CV37 8RP
Tel: 01789 721399   Fax: 01789 721390
Dealers: 40

Bidford Antique Centre
Warwick House, 94–96 High Street
Bidford-on-Avon, Alcester B50 4AF
Tel: 01789 773680
Dealers: 6

Dunchurch Antiques Centre
16a Daventry Road, Dunchurch
Rugby CV22 6NS
Tel: 01788 522450
Dealers: 10

Malthouse Antique Centre
4 Market Place, Alcester B49 5AE
Tel: 01789 764032
Dealers: 15–20

The Stables Antique Centre
Hatton Country World, Dark Lane
Hatton CV35 8XA
Tel: 01926 842405   Fax: 01926 842023
Dealers: 25

Stratford Antiques and Interiors
Dodwell Trading Estate, Evesham Road
Stratford-upon-Avon CV37 9SY
Tel: 01789 297729   Fax: 01789 297710
Dealers: 20

Vintage Antiques Centre
36 Market Place, Warwick CV34 4SH
Tel: 01926 491527
Dealers: 20

Warwick Antiques Centre
22–24 High Street, Warwick CV34 4AP
Tel: 01926 491382   Mob: 07770 897707
Dealers: 30

WILTSHIRE
Brocante Antiques Centre
6 London Road, Marlborough SN8 1PH
Tel: 01672 516512   Fax: 01672 516512
Dealers: 20

The Marlborough Parade Antique Centre
The Parade, Marlborough SN8 1NE
Tel: 01672 515331
Dealers: 70

YORKSHIRE
Arcadia Antiques Centre
10–14 The Arcade, Goole DN14 5QT
Tel: 01405 720549   Fax: 01405 720549
Dealers: 20

Banners Collectables & Antiques Centre
Banners Business Centre, Attercliffe Road
Sheffield S9 3QS
Tel: 0114 244 0742
Dealers: 40

Barmouth Court Antique Centre
Barmouth Court, Barmouth Road
off Abbeydale, Sheffield S7 2DH
Tel: 0114 255 2711   Fax: 0114 258 2672
Dealers: 60

Cavendish Antique & Collectors Centre
44 Stonegate, York YO1 8AS
Tel: 01904 621666   Fax: 01904 644400
Dealers: 60

Halifax Antique Centre
Queens Road, Halifax HX1 4LR
Tel: 01422 366 657   Fax: 01422 369 293
Dealers: 30

Pickering Antique Centre
Southgate, Pickering YO18 8BN
Tel: 01751 477210   Fax: 01751 477210
Dealers: 32

Red House Antique Centre
Duncombe Place, York YO1 2EF
Tel: 01904 637000   Fax: 01904 637000
Dealers: 60

Skipton Antiques & Collectors Centre
The Old Foundry, Cavendish Street
Skipton, BD23 2AB
Tel: 01756 797667
Dealers: 30

Stonegate Antique Centre
41 Stonegate, York YO1 8AW
Tel: 01904 613888   Fax: 01904 644400
Dealers: 120

York Antiques Centre
2a Lendal, York YO1 8AA
Tel: 01904 641445
Dealers: 15

SCOTLAND
Clola Antiques Centre
Shannas School House,Clola
Aberdeenshire, Peterheard AB42 8AE
Tel: 01771 624584   Mob: 07836 537188
Dealers: 6

Scottish Antique & Art Centre
Abernyte, Perthshire PH14 9SJ
Tel: 01828 686401   Fax: 01828 686199
Dealers: 130

WALES
Cardiff Antiques Centre
10–12 Royal Arcade, Cardiff CF10 1AE
Tel: 029 2039 8891
Dealers: 13

Chapel Antiques
Methodist Chapel, Holyhead Road
Froncysyllte, Denbighshire LL20 7RA
Tel: 01691 777624   Fax: 01691 777624
Dealers:8

Jacobs Antique Centre
West Canal Wharf, Cardiff C51 5DB
Tel: 039 2039 0939   Fax: 029 2037 3587
Dealers: 40

The Works Antiques Centre
Station Road, Llandeilo
Carmarthenshire SA19 6NH
Tel: 01558 823964
Dealers: 44

Aarons, Slim 221, 224
Adams, Dudley, of London 152
Adams, George 472
advertising 156–159, 237–241
Aflaco, F G 61
Ainsley 78
Alcock, Samuel 99
Alerius, Olle 540
Alfa Romeo 502
Ali, Muhammad 223
Allcocks 479–482
Alon, Dominique 553
altar 20, 39
Ami Continental 218, 219
Andersen, Hans Christian 60
Anderson, Gerry 504
Angel & Savory 467
Angel, G 449
Angerle, Georges 550
antiquities 11–26, 571–588
Antler 213
archery 63
architectural furniture 27–39
armour 40–46
arms 40–46
Armstrong, Louis 224
Army & Navy 214, 216
art 571–588
Artflex 527
Artifort 527
Asian art 571–577
Asprey 139, 450
Atlas of Hollywood 200
atlases 51–65
Aucoc & Co. 446
Austin Pathfinder 50
Austin Seven 502
autometers 218–220
Automobile Association 4 8
automobilia 47–50

Bacall, Lauren 221
Bactrian art 11–26
Baeau, George 267
Baikie, James 65
Baker, Oliver 455
Ballam, Thomas 469
Ballantine, William 429
Balthazar, Jean Baptiste 55
Bantings of Pall Mall 334
Barbedienne Foundry 262, 266
Bardot, Brigitte 230, 233
Barnard, E E & J W 448
Barnards, The 447, 560
Baron 223
Barratt, William 448
Bassett-Lowke 439
Bateman, Hester 450, 456
Battersby 492

Baxter 540
Beatles, The 223, 234, 239, 240
beds 281–284
Benson, J W 146
Bensons, W A S 555
Bentley 47–50
bergéres 313–334
Bernard & Sons 481
Bernard, Oliver 526
Besson, A P 254
Beswick 517
Betteridge 473
Bettridge, Joseph 450
Beyer, Adam 443
Biedermeier 338, 378
bindings 51–65
Bingeant, Toussaint 462
Blacklin, Isabella 494
Blackstone, Sir William 62
Blackware 81
Blaeu, J W 57
Blister, Vic 421
Bloch, Bernhard 193
Bloor Derby 103
Boer War 174–184
Bogart, Humphrey 221
Bolex 166–171
Bond, James 54, 228, 230, 234
Bonheur, Isidore 266
bonheurs de jour 347–352
Bonneels 311
bookcases 285–288, 300–302
books 51–65
Booths 187
Borderware 72
Boucar of Paris 153
Boucheron of Paris 423
Bourne, Charles 84
Boynton, Charles 565
Breguet 436
Breitling chronograph 145
Bremond 219
Broadwood, John 440, 443, 445
Broderip & Wilkinson 444
Brooklands, speed awards 47–50
Brown, Lucille 224
Brown, William 448
Bru doll 500
Buddha 13, 24, 571–577
Bugatti 47–50
Bulaggi 200
Bullitt 234
Bulova 142–151
Burcham, Phil 223
bureaux 300–302, 525–533
Burleigh Ware 86, 89
Burnett, Frances Hodgson 56
Burrows 511
Busby 41

busts 165, 185–190, 261–280,
    269–272, 564
Byrd, Richard E 65
Byzantine art 11–26

cabinets 303–309, 525–533
Cadestin, Michel 531
Cadillac 47–50, 499
Cain, August 275
Calypso 235
cameras 166–171
campaign furniture 310–311
canterburies 312
Capron, Roger 518
Capucine 221
Carlton Ware 78, 185
carpets 66–71
Carrington, John Bodman 469
Carter II, John 456
Carter, Thomas 266
Carter, Truda 102
Cartier 142–151
Carvin 549
carvings 11–26, 368
Castle Polish 156
Caughley 73
Cenedese 538
ceramics 11–26, 156–159,
    185–190, 223–225, 516–524,
    571–588
Cervantes 64
Chad Valley 502
chairs 313–334, 436, 525–533,
    578–582
Chapman, Ann 494
Charpentiers, A 555
Charteris, Leslie 54
chess sets 172–173, 505
Chesterfield 372–376
chests 369, 525–533
chests of drawers 335–344
chimneypieces 27–39
Chiparus, C D 554
Chiurazzi Foundry 279
Christie, Agatha 54, 56
Christofle, Italy 468
chronographs 142–151
chronometers 436–439
Civil War, English 46, 52
Cliffe, Clarice 89, 516–524
clocks 130–141, 429
Clodion 279
Coalport 72–102
Cobb, John 391
coins 174–184
Colinet, Claire 550
Collings, William 467
commemorative ware 185–190,
    228

Commings, William 474
Comolera, Paul 266
compasses 152–155
Comyn, William 446
Connell, William 449
Constantine & Floyd 450
Conta and Boheme 192
Contax 170
Cooke, W B 65
Coomes Devenport 439
Cooper, Gary 221
Cooper, Susie 89, 94
Copeland Spode 72–102, 186
Cornish Ware 206
Costeau 262
Cosway, Richard 225
Cotton, Charles 61
Creamware 72–102
Crichton, L A 446
Crimean War 85, 174–184
Cross, W, and Son 204
Crossley, Richard 568
Crown Derby 72–102
Crown Devon 78, 189
Crown Ducal 74
Cumberworth, Charles 277
cupboards 303–309, 525–533

Daimler 506
Dali, Salvador 64, 221, 416
Danko, Natalia 586
Dansette 235
Dassin, Jules 232
Daum 538
Dauvergne 557
Davenport ceramics 82
davenports 345–346
Dawson Squire and Lackey 101
De Marco 554, 559
De Morgan, William 521
De Roncourt, Joe 554, 559
Deakin & Francis 450
Decca 235
decorative arts 261–280
Deere 433
Delamarche 152, 153
Delftware 103
Delmester, John 452
Dennis China Works 516–524
Dent chronometer 150
Descomps, Joe 264
desks 347–352, 525–533
Desmond, Dismal 431
Diaz, Laura 540
Dickens, Charles 54, 55, 59
Dickson, James 459
Dinky 499–510
dinosaur egg 574
Disney, Terry 223
Dixon, Tom 546
dolls 18, 499–510

Dolmetsch, Arnold 440
doors 32, 355–357
Doyle, Sir Arthur Conan 55
Drabware 94
Dresden 103–115
dressers 353–354, 525–533
DRGM, Germany 426
Druce & Co 301, 317
Dubois, Paul 262
dumb waiters 355–357
Dyer, Harry 539
Dylan, Bob 64, 239

Eames, Charles 533
EAR 236
Eastwood, Clint 233
Eaton, William 452
Eberlein, J F 110
Ede & Ravenscroft 492
Egyptian art 11–26
Elekthermax 541
Eley & Fearn 464
Elkington, Frederick 452
England, William 222
Engleheart, George 225
Ensign camera 168, 170
Epiphone 442
Erard, S & P 440, 445
Ercol 526
Ericsson 253
escritoires 300–302
Etling, D C 550, 552
Eyre, Jane 64

Fabergé 583–587
Falcon 492
famille rose 116–129
famille verte 116–129
Farnley Co 263
Farrow & Jackson 565
Faucon Frères 273
fauteuils 313–334
Favell, Charles, & Co 462
Fayral 547
Fecuda 400
Fein, Nat 224
Fellini, Federico 221
Fender 440–445
Ferrari 501
film posters 227–234
Finnigans of Bond Street 216
fireplaces 27–39
Fischer, L 249
fishing 61, 479–482
Fleming, Ian 54
Fogelberg & Gilbert 473
Fontaine, G 271
Ford 47–50
Fornasetti 518
Fortuna 211
fountains 27–39

Fox Photos 222
Fox, Charles 469, 472
Foxcroft 213
Fragonard 63
Franke & Heidecke 167, 171
Franklin, John 59
Frechen 103
Fred Flintstone 499
Fremiet, E 266
Fribourg & Treyer 248
Fulham Pottery 74
furniture 281–400, 525–533

Gable, Clark 221
Gachen 586
Gallo, Ignacio 556
Gambone 518
games 172–173, 193, 499–510
Gamma 503
Gannochy 483, 484
Garrard, Robert 564
gates 27–39
Gecophone 254
Generalli, Amadeus 557
gentlemen's accessories 192–194
Getty Images 221–224
Gibbon, Edward 62
Gibson 440–445
Gilda 233
Gillows of Lancaster 348, 349
Girshfeld, Natalya 587
glass 11–26, 160–165, 401–415, 534–540
globes 152–155, 437
Gloster, Joseph 469
Goldscheider 516–524
Goss 187
Goyard 217
Grahame, Kenneth 52
Grammont, Count de 53
Gray of Paris 141
Green Monk 506
Greene, Graham 60, 65
Gretsch 440–445
Grimm Brothers 53
Gruau, Rene 232
Guirande, J D 554
guitars 440–445
Gulf War 174–184
guns 40–46, 483–484
Gunther, Curt 222
Gwenda 433

Hacker 236
Hadfield, Aaron 472
Hall, T, of Newcastle 258
Hamilton & Co 473
Hamilton & Inches 450
Hammersley 78
Hancock, George 467

handbags 195–202
Harcourt, Geoffrey 527
Hardy 479–482
Hardy, Bert 223,
Hardy, Thomas 63
Harispring, W P 521
Harris, Charles Stuart 464
Haskins, Gwen 524
Hasselblad 171
Hayter, Charles 225
headgear 40–46
Heal & Co 303, 528
Heath, Claire 102
Heckel, Augustin 132
Heeley & Sons 565
Heflin, Van 221
Hefner, Hugh 222
Heming, Thomas 464
Hennell III, Robert 452
Hennell, Robert 570
Hepburn, Audrey 233
Hepplewhite 313–334
Herezy, Claire 517
Heubach 501
Heuer chronograph 146
Highland Stoneware 522
Hill Pottery 185
Hille 526
Hilliard & Thomson 469
Hirons, Plante & Co. 469
Hitchcock, Alfred 222, 228, 233
Hoff, Carl Christian 338
Holland & Holland 483–484
Hollar, Wenceslas 57
Holmes, Sherlock 55
Honiton Pottery 100
Hornby 508
Houdon 279
household products 156–159
Hulton Getty 221–226
Hunt & Roskell 456
Hunt, Miriam 494
Huntingdonshire, map of 57
Huntley & Palmers 499
Hutton, Kurt 223, 224
Hutton, William 467

Ikonta 166
Imari ware 116–129
Irish Belleek 104
Isis 235
Islamic art 11–26, 578–582

Jackson, Emily 65
Jackson, Michael 238
Jackson, T G 415
Jacobs, Carl 527
Jacobs, J 408
Jaeger LeCoultre 142–151
Jaguar 47–50, 503

Janle 549
Janowski, Witold 231
Janssonius, J 57, 58
Jarre, Jean–Michel 239
jewellery 11–26, 174–184, 416–435
Johnson, E, & Son Ltd 454
Johnson, Herbert 192–194
Jones, W & S 153
jukeboxes 218–220
Justis, William 456

Kandya 527
Katzhutte 517, 520
Kayserzinn 454
Kennedy, Jacqueline 222
Kestner 502
Khayyam, Omar 63
King, Peter 223
Kirkwood, James 152
kitchenalia, 156–159, 203–212
Knoll 533
Knox, Archibald 447, 449, 468, 471, 554, 585
Knox, E V 61
Kodak 166–171, 548
Kosta 534, 540
Kreher & Bayer Offenbach 171
Kunsai 370
Kustodiev, Boris 586, 587

lacemaking 65
Lakeside Toys 504
Lalique 534, 536
Lambe, Charles 450
Lancôme 161
Lane, Ken 201
Lang, Andrew 53
Lanvin 424
Laurel and Hardy 228
Laurent, George 531
Lawrence, Christopher 459
Lawrence, D H 56
Lawson, Robert 348
Le Bas, James 457
Le Carré, John 63
Le Guayard 553
Le Page Frères à Liege 43
Lee Co. of California 530
Lennon, John 64, 223, 238
Lewis, C S 65
Liberty & Co 313, 446–474, 516–559
Licata, Recardo 535, 538
Liépée 220
lighting 268–274, 541–549
Limoges 103–115
Limousin 559
linen press 369, 399, 400
Lines Bros. 48
Lizars Challenge 169

Lock, J & Co. 192–194
Longines 146
Longman & Broderip 443
Lorenzi, Josef 550, 552
Lorenzl 520, 547
Louys, Pauline 493
Lowestoft ceramics 92
Lubwin 585
Luftwaffe 40–46
luggage 213–217
Lundin, Ingeborg 534
Lypchytz, Samuel 552

Macleay, Kenneth 225
MacNaughton, James 483
Madlestickse of Germany 267
Magistretti, Vico 529
Maiolica 103–115
Mamiya 167
Manhattan 233
Maple and Co 348
maps 51–65
Marcuse 263
Maresch, Johann 192, 193
marine items 436–439
Marlotta 548
Martin guitar 442
Martin, R & Hall, E 462, 464
Marx toys 235
Marx, Groucho 221
masks 12, 513–515
Masson, Clovis 267
Matchbox 506
Matthews, H, of Birmingham 291
Mauetta 587
May, J & J 189
Maynard, John 52
McBindes 560
McCabe, James 131
McClory, Kevin 222
McKay, John 564
McPhedran, R 223
mechanical music 218–220
medals 174–184
Meek, Joe 238
Meissen 103–115
Mellor, Catherine 522
Menneville 556, 559
Meopta 169
Mercator, Gerard 62
Mercie, A 279
Mercury 32
Merian M, the Elder 58
Mermod Frères 219
metalware 275–280, 550–559
MG 47–50, 506
Michael, Edmund 59
Mickey Mouse 157, 501, 503
microscopes 152–155
Midas of Miami 198

militaria 40–46, 174–184
Mills Cabinmakers 356
Milne, A A 62
Minai pottery 109, 116
Ming 116–129
Minton 72–102
Minton Hollins & Co. 528
mirrors 194, 358–365
Mitchell, Margaret 62
Molins–Balleste 549
Moreau, August 267
Morgan & Saunders 313
Morgan Model Co. 47–50
Morris, C S 447
Morson, Richard 564
Mosely 257
Moss, Thos. 139
Moulson, William 457
Movado 143
Muller 555
Murano 534–540, 543
Murini 551
mushrooms 59
music stand 366, 367
musical boxes 218–220, 243
musical instruments 440–445
Myatt & Co. 448

Nailsea glass 408, 409
Nande, Levi 137
Naples 229
Naurio 275
Nereisheimer 472
Newcastle glass 408, 412
Newhalls Walberton 88
Newman & Guardia 166–171
Newman Sinclair 169
Newton Son & Berry 155
Nichetti 535
Nikon 171
Noddy 500
Nudenmiller 104
Nylund, Gunnar 524

O'Connor, Glenda 507
O'Brian, Patrick 52
Odiot 462
Oestergaard, Peter 152
Omega 142–151
Omega Workshop 440
Oriental art 571–577
Orober 504
Orovit 451
Orrefors 540
Osmond, Donny 240
Ovchinnikov 585
Owen, Samuel 65

packaging 156–159
Paillard 218
Paillard Bolex 169

Palla, F 263
Panasonic 235
panels 66–71
Panton, Vernon 531
Paragon ceramics 83, 86, 189
Parker 592
Parsons, John 460
Passenger, Charles 521
Pati, Gaetano, of Rome 493
Patou, Jean 164
Paverley, Ruth 102
Paya 500
Payne & Co, 132
Pedigree 504
PEL 526
Pemberton, Samuel 564
Penry Williams 483
Perdio 236
perfume bottles 160–165
Perkeo 171
Peter, H G 190
Peugeot Frères 207
pewterware 446–474
Philippe, Patek 149
Philippe, Paul 550, 552
photographic equipment
    166–171
photographs 221–226
Pike, Tania 522
Pintel & Godchaux 507
Pittaluga 263
plaques 185–190, 275–280
Plimer, Andrew 225
Plunkett, William 527
Podio, Peter 568
polyphons 218–220
Poole Pottery 519, 524,
    541–549
Pope, Francis 519
Porter, J 325
portrait miniatures 225–226
Posenthal Pottery 519
posters 227–234
Potter, Beatrix 56
Potter, Harry 51, 56
Pratt, Anne 61
Prebenfabricus & Dorgen
    Kastholm 531
Preiss, Ferdinand 264
Premy 320
Presley, Elvis 240
Price, J Johnson 286
Pye 235–236
Pyrex 210

Quiralu 507

Rackham, Arthur 55, 60
radios 235–236
Rajar camera 168
Raleigh, Sir Walter 28

Rams, Dieter 525
Rawlings, Charles & Summers,
    Wm. 570
Read, Alfred 524
Read, Anne 518
records 237–241
Reed, Alfred 100, 102
Regina 219
Renou, Tim 448
Revere 168
Richard, Cliff 237
Richter, Christian 225
Rickenbacker 444
Ridgeway 188
Robb, Charles 452
Roberts 235–236
rock and pop 237–241
Rock–ola 218–220
Rolex 142–151
Rolleiflex 168
Rolling Stones, The 222, 238,
    241
Rolls–Royce 47–50
Roman art 11–26
Romanelli, Raffaello 28
Romer wristwatch 144
Roosevelt, Theodore 59, 63
Roper of Halifax 43
Rorstrand 524
Rosenthal, Leonard 60
Ross, E 310
Rossellini, Roberto 221
Rowling, JK 51, 56
Royal Doulton 72–102,
    185–190, 517
Royal Dux 517
Royal Vienna 103–115
Royal Wintonia 78, 187
Royal Worcester 72–102, 185
rugs 66–71
Russian art 583–587
Rye Pottery 102

Salmon, Nathanael 53
Salter 203, 589
Salvin, Anthony 398
Sanders, Robert 52
Sang, Jacob 411
Savine, Leopold 551
Scalextric 507
Schiaparelli 161
scientific instruments 152–155
Scofield, John 473
Scott, Fred 526
screens 370–371
sculpture 11–26, 571–588
secretaires 285–288, 303–309,
    347–352
Seeburg 218
Segar, Comtesse de 64
Seiun, Kano 556

Semonova 583
Settle, T & J 461
Seuss, Dr 56
Seutter, M 58
Sévres 103–115
sewing items 242–247
sextants 152–155, 436–439
Shakespeare, William 53, 60
Sharman Dermott Neill 448
Sharpe of London 46
Shelley ceramics 80, 516–524
Shelley, P B 60
Shelley, Samuel 225
Sherlock Holmes 228
Shoolbred, J A S 349
shooting 483–484
Sica, Vittorio de 221
silver jewellery 416–435
Silver, S W, & Co 310
silverware 446–474
Siot Foundry 267
Smith, Alan Caiger 522
Smith, Benjamin 562
Smith, G, and Sons 248
Smith, Jean 494
Smith, S, & Son 145
Smith, Stephen 561
smoking equipment 156–159
Solar 200
Soligor 167
Soolmaker 371
Sottsass, Ettore 516, 518, 531
sound equipment 235–236
Sparrow, W H 470
Spencer, Nathaniel 52
Spink, John Marshall 469
Spode 72–102
sporting items 475–484
Staffordshire Pottery 72–102
Standard Cameras of
  Birmingham 167
Starback 482
Staunton 510
Steiff 501
Steinway and Sons 444
Stengelin, Philip 462
Stephenson, Benjamin 564
Stevenson, Robert Louis 55
Stewart James 221
Stilnovo 546
Stodart 443
stools 69, 367, 377–381,
  525–533
Storr, Paul 473
Stowe, Harriet Beecher 62
Stratton 432
Summers, Gerald 529
Susse Frères 264, 277
Swan Hunter & Wigham
  Richardson 439
Swansea Pottery 72–102

Swettenham, Sir Frank
  Athelstane 53

tables 382–397, 525–533,
  578–582
tallboys 335–344
taxidermy 485–486
taylor & Barrett 502
Taylor & Perry 472
Taylor & Son of London 384
Taylor of Bristol 132
Taylor, Elizabeth 223
Tchlenko, Janice 521
teddy bears 62, 499–510
telephones 252–254
telescopes 152–155, 436, 506
televisions 235–236
Tennyson, Lord Alfred 60 57
Tessina 167
textiles 487–498
thermometers 152–155
Thornton, Lawrence 224
Tiffany & Co. 143, 423, 535
Tiffany Studio 268
Timmins 256
tobacco 192–194, 248–251
Tolkien, J R R 64
Tomkinson 445
Tompion 149
tools 194, 255–258
Toso, Stefano 536
Town 195
toys 499–510
Trabert and Hoeffer 419
Traggia, Andre 261
treen 511–513
Tri–ang 50, 499–510
tribal art 513–515
Tunbridge Ware 269, 298, 511
Turner, Samuel 59
Tweedies, W 61
twentieth century design
  516–559
Twinning, E 62

uniforms 40–46
Unwin & Rogers 46
Uriano 552, 557
Urquart & Hart 467
Usher, Frank 491

Vacheron Constantin watch
  144
Valaurido 518
Vander, C J 453
Varenne, H 551, 558
vases 72–102, 401–415,
  446–474, 516–524, 550–559
Velam 507
Vemini 546
Vespa 507

Vesuch, Steffan 462
Veysey 447
Vigliaturo, Silvio 539
Vilde, Rudolf 587
Villanis, E 277
Von Ernodof, Georgina 497
Vuitton, Louis 216

Wahliss, Ernst 520
Wakelin, Edward 462
Waley, Arthur 52
Walford, Edward 65
Walker and Hall 457, 468
walking sticks 259–260
Walton, Isaac 61
wardrobes 398–400
watches 142–151
Webb, Thomas 165
Wedgwood 72–102, 163, 186,
  268, 292
Wegner, Hans 527
Weichert 437
Weir of Dublin 472
Wellsman, John 394
Westerwald ceramics 103–115
Weston Master 169
whatnots 355–357
Whitbread, G 437
White, Samuel 467
Whitefriars 226–228, 539, 540
Whiting & Davis 20
Whitney, Harry 61
Wigful, Alexander 562
Wileman & Co. 73
Wileman, Charles 91, 93
Willmore, Joseph 564
Wilsson, M 350
Wilston, Sir Daniel 53
wine–related items 401–415,
  446–474, 560–570
Wolesley 47–50
Wolfsohn, Helena 108
Wollstonecraft, Mary 62
Wood, Ralph 99
Woolf, Virginia 56, 60
Worcester Ware 204, 553
Wrenn locomotive 509
Wright & Mansfield 348
writing equipment 145, 589–596
Wurlitzer Co. 219

Yates egg cups 84
Yates, James 458
Yenge, Hubert 558

Zaccagnini 518
Zanuso, Marco 527
Zeiss 166–171
Zodiac 219
Zulu War 174–184
Zuni art 416–435, 513–515

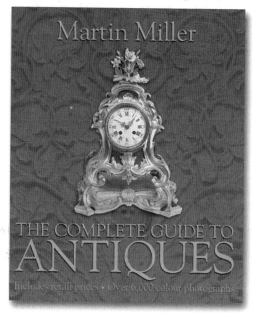

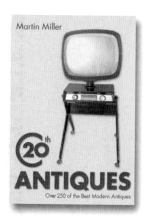